OUR
COMMON
HERITAGE

A WORLD HISTORY

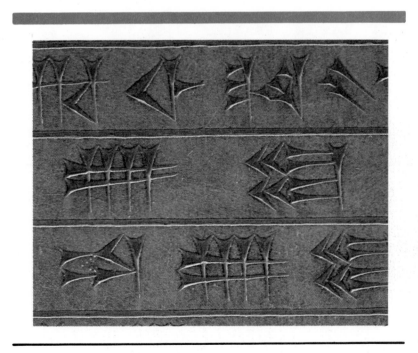

Daniel Roselle

GINN AND COMPANY

OUR
COMMON
HERITAGE
A WORLD HISTORY

About Dr. Roselle

DR. DANIEL ROSELLE, formerly Professor of History at the State University of New York College at Fredonia, is now Editor of *Social Education*, the journal of the National Council for the Social Studies. He received his Bachelor of Social Science degree from the College of the City of New York and was awarded his Master and Doctoral degrees by Columbia University. After teaching in high school, he served for two years as Assistant Professor of History at Fairleigh Dickinson University. He spent a year as a Fulbright Research Professor to France, and was selected as an American scholar to evaluate textbooks for UNESCO. He is the author, co-author, or editor of six books and of numerous articles published in national magazines; and he received the EdPress Association of America Laurence Johnson Award for the best editorial writing in an educational journal.

Dr. Roselle expresses his appreciation to Robert J. Cunningham and James I. Clark for their excellent assistance in the preparation of this text.

Acknowledgments

Grateful acknowledgment is made to the following publishers, authors, and agents for permission to use and adapt copyrighted materials:

Behrman House, Inc., for "Becoming a Rabbi," based on *As a Driven Leaf* by Milton Steinberg. Copyright, 1939, by Milton Steinberg. Used by permission of the publisher.

Basil Davidson, for "Mansa Musa and His Famous Pilgrimage," based on pages 75-79 of his book *The African Past*. Copyright © 1964 by Basil Davidson. Curtis Brown Academic, Ltd. Used by permission of the author.

Little, Brown and Company for "Mansa Musa and His Famous Pilgrimage," based on the report of Al Omari, from *The African Past: Chronicles from Antiquity to Modern Times* by Basil Davidson. Copyright © 1964 by Basil Davidson. By permission of Little, Brown and Company in association with the Atlantic Monthly Press.

University of California Press for a Creation Story on page 223 from the Yakima of the Pacific Northwest. From pages 142-43 of *Indian Legends of the Pacific Northwest* edited by Ella E. Clark, University of California Press, 1953. Reprinted by permission.

Contents

Map List

Prologue

Prehistoric Peoples:
Pioneers, Creators, Inventors

KEYNOTE

"The trees in the streets are old trees used to living with people, family trees that remember your grandfather's name," wrote poet-novelist Stephen Vincent Benét. Other writers have been struck by the relationship between the tree and human life.

On the surface a tree is simply a large plant encased in bark, a trunk with many boughs. Yet that is far from the whole of it. Beneath the soil, in all directions roots fan out. They absorb nourishment to sustain the tree.

Human society today represents what can be observed above the surface. Yet unseen human roots, too, fan out deep into *prehistoric* times, the period before written records. Our society today grows out of roots that spread back hundreds of thousands of years. The discoveries, inventions, and techniques developed by prehistoric peoples form the foundation on which life today is built.

1. Prehistoric Pioneers

Bones lay in abundance below the surface of the cave of Choukoutien near Peking, China. Some of these were the bones of saber-toothed tigers, mammoths, and other huge creatures. This rich store attracted scientists from many countries. They searched there for clues to what life on earth might have been like hundreds of thousands of years ago.

Then, one day in 1926, another kind of bone turned up, one belonging to a creature different from any that the scientists had discovered at Choukoutien. After careful study, a Canadian scientist concluded that the find was a human tooth. Over a ten-year period, diggers at Choukoutien unearthed fourteen human skulls, the same number of lower jaws, more than a hundred teeth, and a few arm and leg bones. They named these remains "Peking Man."

Peking bones were not the first to suggest that humans had been on earth longer than people had realized. On the island of Java in the East Indies a Dutch scientist had discovered ancient remains he named "Java Man." Although named "Peking Man" and "Java Man," it would have been more accurate to refer to "Peking People" and "Java People." Women played as active a role as men in prehistoric times.

Later, anthropologists working in Tanzania, Africa and elsewhere, discovered the remains of creatures who lived much earlier than the "Peking Man" or "Java Man." Their findings are being evaluated.

The Work of Archaeologists

The people of Choukoutien lived some 400,000 years ago. Detective work pieced their story together. Bones of various kinds appeared at different levels, the lowest and oldest beginning 160 feet below the surface. In the oldest and deepest layers, layers of human bones alternated with layers of the bones of the huge animals. This suggested that the people and animals had fought for control of the

Workers above the cave in China where the bones of so-called "Peking Man" were discovered. This cave is about thirty-seven miles from Peking.

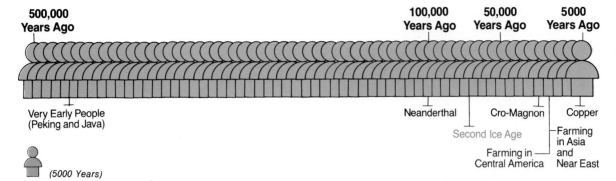

500,000 Years Ago

100,000 Years Ago

50,000 Years Ago

5000 Years Ago

Very Early People (Peking and Java)

(5000 Years)

Neanderthal

Cro-Magnon

Copper

Second Ice Age

Farming in Central America

Farming in Asia and Near East

Choukoutien cave and that the animals often succeeded in driving the people out. In these layers there were no charred bones to indicate that when the people occupied the cave they had fire.

Then at a certain layer, human bones took over permanently, suggesting that the people had at last won out. At this layer charred bones told that these people had discovered fire. They were using fire to keep huge animals out of the cave and to cook the meat of the animals they had killed.

Archaeologists are the chief investigators in such an enterprise. They are concerned with uncovering and studying evidence of life in prehistoric times. This was the period of hundreds of thousands of years before humans learned to write and record their thoughts and deeds.

Artifacts—such human-made objects as a simple hand tool or an arrowhead—tell archaeologists something about a people's skills. Archaeologists also deal with *fossils,* which include not only bones but also traces of bones, footprints, and leaves left in mud that eventually turned to stone. They also study *living sites,* places where humans remained for a time, leaving behind bones, charcoal, and evidence of tools. From bits and pieces of evidence, archaeologists fit together a picture of what a group of people in the distant past might have been like.

Archaeologists are interested in all evidence of a culture. *Culture* means a people's way of life that reflects how they satisfy their needs within a certain environment. Culture includes the kind of shelter a people use, the way they obtain food, their religious ideas and practices, the kinds of tools and weapons they use, and how they communicate and pass on knowledge to children.

Pioneers on Earth

Prehistoric human fossils and artifacts have been found in many parts of the world. The people they represent truly were pioneers. They had to learn to cope with environments that, with respect to climate, vegetation, and animal life, were sometimes unfriendly. They had to develop some means of verbal communication. They had to discover sources of food and how to fashion tools and clothing from materials on hand, at first learning as they went. And, for the group to survive, they had to pass on their knowledge to their children.

Fire was a primary tool, and no one knows how humans first acquired it. Fire offered a means to render meat more tender and tasty. It helped protect humans against wild beasts. Used to ignite a dried grassland, it could frighten animals toward a place where hunters lay in wait. Fire, of course, also conquered the darkness of caves and the night.

Migrations

It is likely that the earliest humans lived in such tropical regions as central Africa and Java, where the climate was warm the year round. They were hunters of animals and gatherers of fruits, nuts, seeds, and roots. It appears that humans gradually spread out from these areas over long periods of time into northern Africa and into Europe and Asia.

There probably were no mass movements of people. Bands of early humans were small, of necessity. A single hunter probably needed ten square miles to find sufficient game to feed one person. A band of thirty people would require three hundred square miles of territory. Early humans probably established more or less permanent base camps. From there hunters ventured out to set up temporary camps some miles away, hunting and returning after a few days with their kills. The population of some bands undoubtedly increased. Then some members of a band would move some miles away from the rest. This, probably, was the style of

Evidence of Very Early People

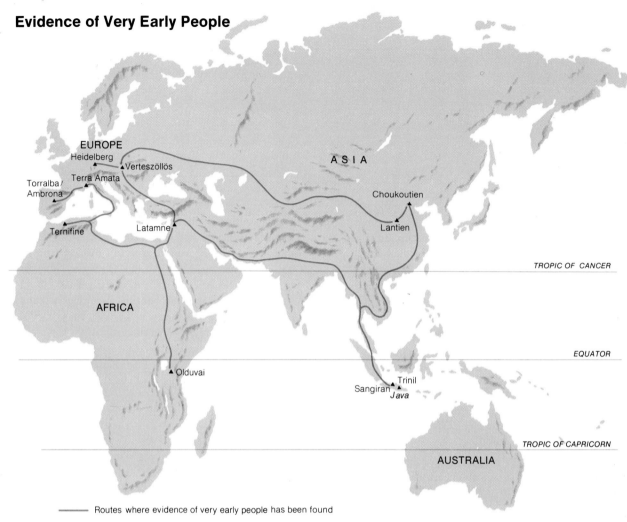

EUROPE
Heidelberg ▲
▲ Verteszöllös
Torralba/ Terra Amata
Ambrona ▲
Ternifine ▲
Latamne ▲

ASIA
Choukoutien ▲
Lantien ▲

TROPIC OF CANCER

AFRICA

▲ Olduvai

EQUATOR

Sangiran ▲ Trinil ▲
Java

TROPIC OF CAPRICORN

AUSTRALIA

—— Routes where evidence of very early people has been found

Evidence seems to indicate that very early humans migrated northward from southern lands.

migration that over hundreds of thousands of years spread early humans through much of Europe and Asia. (See the map above.)

During the later part of this very long period, early humans had to face the challenges of an "Ice Age." Heavy snows fell in the mountains of northern Europe and Asia, as well as in North America. The climate turned so cold that the summer's sun could not melt these snows. Snow gradually filled deep valleys and turned to ice. Slowly these tongues of ice, or glaciers, began to move across the land. Some glaciers were a mile or two thick. Inching their way like gigantic bulldozers, they swept everything in their paths. The cold temperature turned so much water to ice that ocean levels dropped as much as 300 to 500 feet. Glaciers covered northern Europe and Asia, and the climate

immediately to the south became much colder. The very early peoples retreated southward before these tremendous changes and did not return until the Ice Age was over.

Social Organization

Early humans were pioneers in yet another respect. They organized groups based on a division of responsibility and labor between men and women.

Babies and children depended on mothers. Then, as children grew, they depended on adult examples and instruction to learn what they needed to know to survive and to contribute to the group. The group depended on male adults for protection and for meat. Hunting was a cooperative act; each hunter depended on the others. Hunting, however, did not produce enough to eat; so the group also relied on the plant food that women and sometimes children gathered. In northern climates, the plant food supply varied with the seasons. So it became necessary to think ahead, to store up food for a time when it would not be freshly available. As chief gatherers, women assumed this vital task, too.

One can imagine a society in which every member had a place and a role to play, in which a breakdown anywhere along the line could spell disaster for the group. In other words, a social organization.

Mutual dependence among males, females, and young created cooperation. Cooperation meant survival. This interdependence, centered on a man, a woman, and children, formed the basis for the primary social institution—the human family.

Humans and Tools

In most early human living sites, archaeologists have found an abundance of stone tools. This is not surprising. Tools made of stone broke, wore out, or became dull quickly. They were discarded and replaced by new ones.

Undoubtedly, humans made cutting tools out of wood and probably out of bone too. But in most cases, wood and bone tools did not survive decay over the long period of time between their manufacture and discovery. Among the earliest human-made tools were choppers, held in the hand. These were pieces of stone that toolmakers crudely shaped by knocking off chips, or "flakes," to form an edge. With a great deal of effort, a hunter with a chopper could hack through animal sinew and flesh. The flakes served for finer cutting. Archaeologists uncovered tools of these kinds at Choukoutien.

Over a long period of time, better stone tools appeared. They became sharper and more efficient, and they took various shapes. Flint was the ideal stone for tools. It was hard, yet still fairly easily worked by a person who knew where and how to strike with the flaking stone, a hard and durable stone. Sometimes the toolmaker used a sharpened piece of hard wood as a wedge to create flakes.

From a piece of flint one could chip leaflike, flat flakes. Depending on the size and shape of the "core" stone, these flakes could be like long, narrow, and exceedingly sharp knife blades. Such flakes might be used as they fell, or they might be more finely worked with a hard piece of wood or bone.

The toolmaker developed the core itself into a tool. This meant that an early human visualized a tool—perhaps pear-shaped or pointed—and then set out to shape it to match the vision.

Stone tools, along with fire and the ability to make clothing from animal skins, made up early humans' *technology*. When they learned to fasten pointed and cutting tools to handles, their techno-

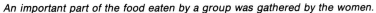

An important part of the food eaten by a group was gathered by the women.

logical efficiency in the hunt and in preparing meat increased. A sharp, knifelike flake tool attached to a pole made a spear. This greatly increased a hunter's capability and safety. With a spear he could place himself at a greater distance from prey and kill with more dispatch. Precisely when this advance occurred no one knows. But the people known today as Neanderthals, who appeared on earth about 100,000 years ago, possessed such tools.

Check on Your Reading

1. With what are archaeologists primarily concerned?
2. Of what does a culture consist?
3. In what ways were early humans pioneers?
4. Why was interdependence among early humans significant?
5. Describe the toolmaking process.

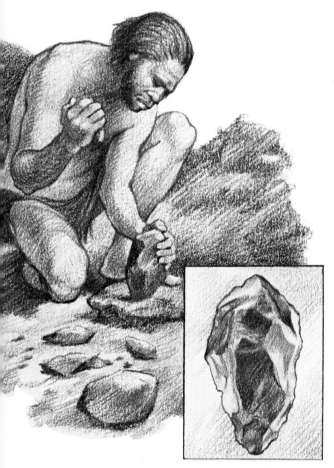

Using a hammerstone to make a hand axe out of a piece of quartzite. The hammerstone is being used to strike off flakes to shape the axe, shown in the inset.

2. The Neanderthals

One summer day in 1856, workmen quarrying limestone in the Neander gorge near Düsseldorf, Germany, blasted open a cave. Exploring and digging into the cave floor, they uncovered bones that appeared to be human. There may have been a complete skeleton there, but only a skullcap, ribs, and a few limb bones survived the digging. Later these remains received the name "Neanderthal."

Neanderthal Culture

Many Neanderthal finds have been in northern Europe. At the time Neanderthals were in northern Europe, about a hundred thousand years ago, that region enjoyed a mild climate. Summers were long, winters short and cool, not cold. Forests and lush grasslands covered much of the land. Neanderthal women and young girls gathered nuts, berries, fruits, and roots in season, and probably preserved and stored a portion of them. Meat was the main food and while there was plenty of game—deer, horses, rabbits, rhinos, mammoths and other animals—it was obviously not neatly slaughtered and packaged for the taking. Hunters had to work for meals, and, on the average, a band of about twenty-five Neanderthals required a quarter ton of meat per week to survive and remain healthy. This meant that men were on the hunt most every day. Hunting was the main Neanderthal male occupation.

Neanderthals possessed fire and serviceable tools and weapons of both the core and the flake variety. With a flake knife fashioned from flint, they could sever an animal tendon and slice a leg at a single stroke. Equally important, Neanderthals apparently discovered how to make a spear by driving a sharp flake point into a shaft made from a tree branch, or by attaching it with a hide thong. This increased their hunting ability considerably.

From an early age a Neanderthal boy learned about animals. By the time he was old enough to take part in the hunt, he was probably thoroughly familiar with their ways and habits. He knew that one approached an animal or a herd from downwind, taking advantage of every scrap of cover and freezing motionless when necessary as he neared the prey. He knew the signs that indicated a weak or slow member of the herd, one to single out for pursuit. And once the animal or herd spooked, he knew he had to be fleet-footed and strong-lunged to run it down. If possible he would chase it toward a bog or cliff. Growing up, Neanderthal boys practiced endlessly with spears.

Girls acquired equally important skills. These included recognizing appropriate food plants, gathering and storing them, and preparing food. Female skills also included scraping smooth the inner sides of animal skins and sewing the hides into clothing. It is likely that in making clothing Neanderthals punched holes along the edges of skins. Then they poked strips of hide through and drew them tight to bring the pieces together.

During the period of mild European climate, Neanderthals probably remained in the open. They probably lived there in shelters constructed from materials around them. At one site in the Soviet Union, for example, archaeologists found circles of stacked mammoth bones. These suggested that the bones, and perhaps long-vanished wood, served as a framework over which Neanderthals stretched skins to make a kind of tent. Circles of hearths—where fires burned—within the bone circles reinforce this conclusion. It is likely that Neanderthals in northern Europe built shelters by using tree boughs as frameworks over which they draped and anchored skins. No evidence of this remains, of course.

Neanderthals Adapt

About 75,000 years ago, the climate of northern Europe and Asia began to change as another Ice Age developed. Glaciers covering northern Europe and Asia drove Neanderthals farther south. But they did not leave the area. Instead, they used intelligence and imagination to adapt to changed conditions.

Although some years were warmer than others, the climate on the whole was too cold for Neanderthals to live the year-round in the open. So they found homes in caves, relying on fire and weapons to drive out whatever animals occupied them. They now needed year-round clothing. It became more necessary than ever to store such gathered food as roots for use in the winter. Neanderthal hunters had to adapt to pursuing game over snowy terrain in below-freezing temperatures. They used the snow to advantage, driving such game as deer into drifts or snow-covered ravines, or trapping them in crusted snow too soft to bear their weight.

South of the glacier line, the land became tundra, similar to that found in Arctic regions today. A

Making clothing from animal skins. The skin was cleaned with a scraper and cured in the smoke from a fire. A stone knife was used to cut the skin into the shape desired. Then holes were punched in the skin and strips of rawhide were used to lace the garment together.

tundra is a treeless area where not far below the surface the soil lies permanently frozen. During a brief but cheerful spring and summer, surface temperatures on a tundra climb as high as 50°F. Then the land becomes a blaze of color as flowers bloom and lichens, mosses, small shrubs, and grasses thrive.

Forage on the tundra attracted game, reindeer in particular. Neanderthal hunters worked in bands to pursue and bring them down. During the short summer, hunters probably lived in temporary shelters on the tundra for days at a time, killing game to be carried back to permanent homes to the south.

During the more difficult winter season, there undoubtedly were days when hunters returned empty-handed. Then roots and dried foods had to do as entire meals. Still, Neanderthals persisted. If they did not overcome their environment, they at least held it at bay.

Communication, Burial, and Religion

Neanderthals undoubtedly had some form of verbal communication. Of course, no one knows what it might have been like, for words flung into the air are lost forever.

There is ample evidence that Neanderthals buried their dead. The remains uncovered near Düs-seldorf in 1856 probably were buried. A find near La Ferrassie in France turned up bones in six graves—those of a man, a woman, two children, and two infants. Flint flakes and animal bones appeared to have been buried with the man.

Archaeologists unearthed another Neanderthal grave site in northern Iraq. Those remains appeared to be about 60,000 years old. Here nine persons had been buried. Not far away from these burials was the grave of a man whose crushed skull seems to indicate that a rockfall had killed him. It appears that flowers had been placed on the man's grave. Archaeologists discovered this through a routine analysis of the soil around the grave. To everyone's surprise, the investigation turned up abundant traces of pollen. Dr. Ralph S. Solecki, who headed the team that made the discoveries, wrote:

The recovery of pollen grains around the Neanderthal burial was in itself unusual and without precedent to our knowledge, but to find flower pollen, and in quantity, was an added extraordinary dividend. The association of flowers with Neanderthals adds a whole new dimension to our knowledge of his humanness, indicating that [the Neanderthal] had "soul."

Such a burial site suggests that Neanderthals felt loss and remorse in the face of death. It might also indicate some idea of life beyond the grave.

Equally interesting, some Neanderthals at least seem to have felt compassion and concern for the handicapped. The skeleton of the man found in northern Iraq apparently had a crippled right arm, useless perhaps since infancy. Yet he had not been abandoned because of his handicap. He had survived until accident took his life in his early forties, in a society that undoubtedly placed a high value on physical strength and skill.

Archaeologists are left guessing as to any formal religion or worship among Neanderthals. Skulls and bones of cave bears have been found at some sites, apparently deliberately arranged in a certain order. To some observers, this suggests the existence of a cult, worship of a single person or object, related to those animals. Some kind of religious impulse, not hunger, may have prompted Neanderthals to kill cave bears and preserve portions of their skeletons. Certainly there were easier meals to bring down than those fearsome creatures, which stood eight or more feet tall when erect and weighed 1500 pounds.

How Did They End?

Much of what we know about Neanderthals represents guesswork, but it is educated guesswork. Also, almost every year additional information turns up. The picture we have of Neanderthals is much different from that of a hundred years ago.

One important puzzle remains, however, and it might never be solved. Neanderthals seem to have disappeared about 35,000 or 40,000 years ago and the reason remains undiscovered. Certainly the Ice Age, which lasted beyond that time, did not do them in; they adapted well to a different climate. Did the Neanderthal line just "sort of die out"? Did some invading group destroy them? No one knows. All that is known about the matter is that another group, known as Cro-Magnon, replaced Neanderthals in northern Europe and elsewhere.

Check on Your Reading

1. Describe the Neanderthal culture.
2. In what ways did Neanderthals adapt to changed conditions in Europe?
3. What evidence suggests altruistic and religious feelings among Neanderthals?

As this map shows, Cro-Magnon peoples spread over the earth. Notice on the map that during the Ice Age some areas once covered by water became land.

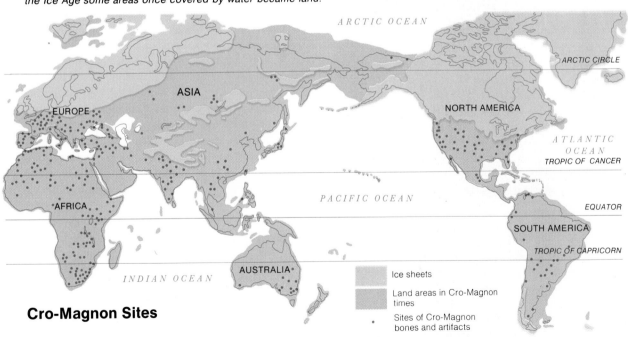

Cro-Magnon Sites

ARCTIC OCEAN
ARCTIC CIRCLE
ASIA
EUROPE
NORTH AMERICA
ATLANTIC OCEAN
TROPIC OF CANCER
PACIFIC OCEAN
AFRICA
EQUATOR
SOUTH AMERICA
TROPIC OF CAPRICORN
INDIAN OCEAN
AUSTRALIA

Ice sheets
Land areas in Cro-Magnon times
Sites of Cro-Magnon bones and artifacts

3. Cro-Magnon

The term Cro-Magnon, like Neanderthal, comes from a place where prehistoric remains were first found. In this case it is a rock shelter called Cro-Magnon, located in southwestern France. Here among the many caves along the Vézère River, archaeologists have uncovered numerous prehistoric sites. At least two of them may have been towns or villages. The first Cro-Magnon remains came to light in 1868, a dozen years after those of Neanderthal in Germany.

Strictly speaking, Cro-Magnon refers to evidence of humans living in southwestern France from about 40,000 to around 10,000 years ago. Of all Cro-Magnon areas, this has been the most thoroughly

Using a burin *to make a needle. The inset shows the tool, the burin, and the needle. With a burin a Cro-Magnon toolmaker chiseled bone and ivory into many kinds of useful tools and objects.*

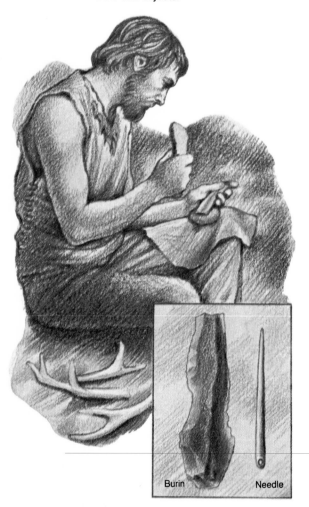

Burin   Needle

explored. The term has, however, been more generally applied to people who lived on earth during Cro-Magnon dates. Human remains fitting that definition have been found in all parts of the earth, including the Arctic regions and southern Australia. (See the map on page 9.) Cro-Magnon peoples lived toward the end of an ice age. During this long age, warmer periods alternated with cold ones. Then about 12,000 years ago, the Ice Age ended. The fact that Cro-Magnons lived in such varied environments speaks for a high order of intelligence and ability to adapt.

On the average, European Cro-Magnons appear to have been much like many Europeans today. Males stood about five feet, eight inches tall. Women were shorter. Cro-Magnons had high foreheads and prominent chins. Their teeth were small and even. Their skulls contained the same brain capacity as the average human today. Cro-Magnons' potential speech ability, too, was probably much the same as that of today's people.

Tools

Cro-Magnons fashioned tools from stone and bone and they developed a wide range of devices. There appear to have been knives for meat-cutting, for cutting wood, and for other purposes. Some were single-edged and others, double-edged. Also, they had chisels, awls, and all kinds of scrapers. It is likely that Cro-Magnons made handles of bones, antlers, or wood for many of their tools.

A most important tool was the *burin,* a tool to make tools. A burin is a type of chisel used by certain engravers today. It could well date from Neanderthal times, but Cro-Magnons made much more extensive use of it. Archaeologists have demonstrated the process by which Cro-Magnons probably made a burin, carefully shaping a chisel point on a length of flint. Cro-Magnon toolmakers then employed a burin to produce, for example, a needle from a piece of antler. They cut three deep grooves in the shape of a long, narrow triangle in the antler. They then lifted the piece out and thinned down the wide end by rubbing it on a piece of sandstone. Next, using a stone awl, they worked an eye into that end. Finally, toolmakers sharpened the needle's point, again on sandstone.

Using tools to make tools is commonplace today. In Cro-Magnon times, that represented a great and significant step forward in technology.

Cro-Magnon peoples also improved hunting tools. For example, they improved the spear by developing the spear-thrower. This device, made of antler or wood, measured from one to two feet long. At one end was a handle. The other end was fashioned into a hook that fit the end of a spear. The hunter balanced the spear on the thrower and rested that on his shoulder. Then he thrust his arm forward and flicked his wrist to hurl the spear with great force as far as one hundred-fifty feet. This marked a great advance in bringing down game.

No conclusive evidence exists that Cro-Magnons used bows and arrows. The earliest indication of these weapons dates from 10,000 to 8,000 years ago. Yet there is a possibility that these people did have bows and arrows. Evidence might be missing simply because wood and other materials used for their construction have long since rotted away.

Probably the same division of labor that existed among Neanderthals persisted among Cro-Magnons too. Women were responsible for the hearth and for caring for young children, two functions essential for the welfare of the group. They also made clothing, and gathered and stored various plant foods. Men were the hunters and protectors, and perhaps concerned with erecting shelters.

Fire, Clothing, and Shelter

Cro-Magnons, of course, possessed that basic tool, fire. Evidence indicates that they could swiftly kindle a blaze at will. One Cro-Magnon site in Belgium revealed a piece of iron pyrite, which, when struck, gives off exceedingly hot sparks. This showed signs of considerable use. At a site in the Soviet Union, archaeologists discovered hearths with grooves dug out along the bottoms. These probably served as vents, suggesting that this group of Cro-Magnons realized that feeding air to a fire makes it hotter. This may have been especially important in the mostly treeless areas where the hearths were found. Possibly those Cro-Magnons used bones as fuel, and these require a higher temperature than wood to ignite. In any case, Cro-Magnons of that site seem to have discovered and used the principle of a blast furnace. This marked another step in prehistoric technology.

Animal skins served as raw material for Cro-Magnon clothing, and how they dressed depended on where they lived. Those in Arctic regions undoubtedly made use of furs, and tunics, trousers, mittens, and boots made from skins. Needles have been discovered in a number of sites, so Cro-Magnon clothing was probably closely fitted and finely sewed.

Cro-Magnons evidently lived in all types of shelters, depending on the environment. In such areas as southwestern France, where caves abound, these were used. A site in Czechoslovakia revealed evidence of huts constructed of wooden posts and poles, covered with skins anchored by rocks at the bottom.

This Czech site, which dates back some 27,000 years, yielded evidence of yet another Cro-Magnon advance. At one hut site, archaeologists found what appeared to be kilns, ovens for baking clay. Around the kilns they discovered many clay figurines representing animals and humans. This did not indicate the dawn of pottery manufacture—that came later. What appear to be among the earliest pieces of pottery date about 12,000 years ago and were uncovered in Japan. But the Czech find does suggest an early date for the beginning of ceramics, another technological step forward.

Cro-Magnon Art

At Altamira, near the Spanish city of Santander, one day in 1868, a hunter's dog trapped itself among some boulders. Removing rocks to free the animal, the hunter uncovered the entrance to a cave. The cave went unexplored for several years. When the owner of the land finally looked into it, he found many bones and stone tools. This was not unusual, but what his twelve-year-old daughter discovered certainly was. She spotted paintings on a ceiling in a portion of the cave. They consisted of figures of animals—bison, wolves, deer, and others—applied in brown, black, yellow, and red colors. In some instances the artist or artists had used rounded stones projecting from the ceiling as an animal's haunch or belly, achieving a three-dimensional effect.

Artists may have applied the colors with brushes. Or, using a hollowed-out piece of bone, they may have blown them onto the surface. They had to work under artificial light, and in the cave were found hollowed-out stones that probably served as lamps. Animal fat rendered into grease was probably the fuel.

Objects showing artistic taste and expression had turned up in prehistoric sites running back through the Neanderthals to Choukoutien in China. Some were simply shiny objects fashioned from quartz crystal or colored rocks. Cro-Magnon artistic finds included ceramic figures, carvings in ivory, and animals made from ivory. But the cave at Altamira yielded the first examples of art that could not be carried around on the person. The ability to mix pigments to obtain shades of various colors repre-sented a tremendous advance. Also, the ability to apply color in artistic shapes signaled a great development of the skill and ability to visualize and use symbols.

Nor was the Altamira find the end of it. A sculptured animal frieze some forty feet long, showing horses, bison, and deer, was found in southwestern

France. In the same area, at Lascaux, another lost dog led to an even greater discovery in a cave. Here were animal paintings showing the subjects in true-to-life action. The cave itself measured 330 feet. A single gallery spread with all kinds of animals stretched for sixty feet.

Then in 1912, still another cave of art came to light at Les Trois-Frères, on the French side of the Pyrenees Mountains. Here were bison modeled in clay and many kinds of animals engraved in rock. One figure was particularly arresting. Antlers topped its head, and its eyes were dark and round. It had the ears of a wolf, the tail of a horse, and the front paws of a bear. The feet appeared to be human. Some observers have concluded that this figure represented a shaman, sometimes called a "medicine man," who had magic powers and often led ceremonies.

The various cave paintings appear to be 20,000 or more years old. Later works of art found in Spain show a shift in emphasis—human figures became prominent. One painting shows a hunter with a bow. Another depicts a hunter about to bring down a huge deer or moose with an arrow. The paintings date from 11,500 to 4,500 years ago.

Some paintings also feature women. One depicts a woman alone. Another shows a woman walking with a child, probably a girl. Still another contains one male figure, several women, and a number of deer and bison or cattle. It suggests some kind of ceremony, placing women in the center of it.

Religion

Ceremonies suggest religion. There is reason to believe that Cro-Magnons expressed religious feelings and perhaps held religious rites, but details are scanty. A number of figurines at the Cro-Magnon sites in Czechoslovakia, Austria, Italy, and in Siberia seem to represent deities. What might have been a representation of a shaman in the cave painting at Les Trois-Frères, as mentioned, hints at magic. Men might have gathered before the various cave paintings for ceremonial chants and perhaps dances in preparation for the hunt.

Cro-Magnon burial rites appear to have been extensive and elaborate. One find, near Moscow, contained two skeletons. One man, about fifty-five years old, had been buried in beaded clothing with many stone ornaments beneath him. A find in

A copy of a painting found in a cave at Les Trois-Frères in the Pyrenees Mountains of France.

1969, again in the Soviet Union, contained the remains of two boys. One had been about nine years old, the other five. They, too, seem to have been clothed in beaded garments, and lay buried along with spears and other weapons. On their wrists and fingers hung ivory bracelets and rings. Similar finds have turned up at other Cro-Magnon sites.

The Presence of Prehistory

Prehistoric humans faced numerous problems and decisions. Their primary concerns were with food, shelter, and clothing. They developed tools to help satisfy these needs. They had to pass on skills and knowledge to the young so that the group would continue. Some, apparently, faced up to the question of what to do with the sick and the handicapped and cared for them. Prehistoric humans seem to have had some idea about a power beyond human, the supernatural, and perhaps in some way adjusted their lives to accommodate that idea.

All these concerns reflect the human condition. They arose among the earliest humans, and they persist today. As Grahame Clark, an archaeologist at Cambridge University in England, has put it: "Prehistory is not something humans lived through long ago. It is with us still."

Check on Your Reading

1. What were some important Cro-Magnon technological advances?
2. What does Cro-Magnon art indicate about these people?
3. What role did women play in Cro-Magnon culture?
4. What might Cro-Magnon religious practices have been like?

4. The Development of Farm Communities

More than 10,000 years ago, humans in some areas entered a transition stage from hunting and gathering to farming. During this period people continued to hunt and gather, but at the same time they began to raise crops as a regular source of food.

The eventual establishment of an agricultural way of life was revolutionary, but not because it happened suddenly. Indeed, the development was slow, extending over centuries. It was revolution-ary in its results. An ability to grow food and preserve some for future months gave humans a degree of control over their environment they had never before enjoyed. Most important, agriculture furnished a base for permanent, settled communities. This led in turn to the creation of new social, political, and economic organizations, and to new technology.

The Beginning of Agriculture

Numerous puzzles nag archaeologists, and one is precisely how farming began. Probably the best hypothesis is that people in certain parts of the world first discovered and harvested such wild grains as wheat and barley. They built communities where these wild grains flourished. In time, these people began to preserve some kernels of wild grain as seeds. They planted them, raised and harvested crops, and produced domesticated seeds.

This, of course, raises a further question: Why did people turn to farming? Preparing soil, planting, and caring for crops as they grow require more labor than do hunting and gathering natural foods. One hypothesis is that necessity forced the change. It may have occurred as a result of an increase in population. This may have been caused at first more by a decline in the death rate than by a rise in

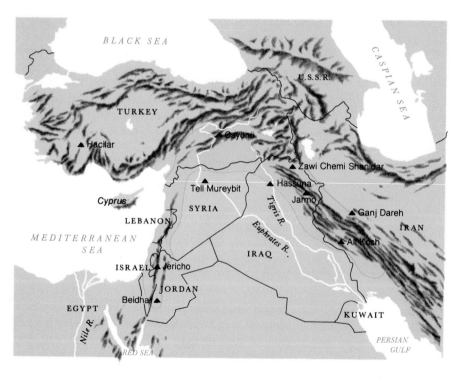

This map shows where evidence of the earliest farming has been found in the Middle East. It also shows that the barley and wheat domesticated by these early farmers still grow in this region.

Early Farming Villages

▲ Sites of villages where early farmers lived

Area where wild barley and wheat still grow

the number of births. On the whole a settled community is safer than a way of life built on hunting and gathering.

For whatever reason, certain groups of settled people apparently found a need for more food than wild grains could furnish. As a result, they began to grow food deliberately, at first in areas nearby where grain did not grow naturally. As a community grew too large for a nearby food supply, "colonists" probably started new villages.

Very likely the domestication of animals proceeded along with agriculture. Residents of transition communities hunted. Some might have depended on hunting and gathering bands for meat, for which they traded grains. At some point, though, hunting and trading for meat as an important means for obtaining food ceased. People in settled communities could rely instead on domesticated goats, pigs, sheep, and cattle.

Two Birthplaces of Farming

Agriculture appears to have developed independently and at different times in several places on earth. In Mexico, for example, archaeologists in the 1950s drilled two hundred and thirty feet into the earth at a site near Mexico City. They brought up traces of the fossil pollen of wild corn. Radiocarbon dating fixed its age at 80,000 years. This was roughly 50,000 years before the people known as Native Americans appeared in North America, probably migrating from Siberia. The pollen's age leaves no doubt that wild corn was there when Native Americans in their migrations reached Mexico. Evidence from caves in northern Mexico indicates that Native Americans of Mexico were cultivating corn, along with squash and other crops, on a regular basis at least 5,000 years ago.

In some other areas, such as China, farming seems to have had an earlier beginning. Archaeologists have unearthed along the Yellow River what appears to have been a village of some six hundred people, dating back at least 6,000 years. At this site they found much evidence of a cultivated grain called millet. Moreover, they uncovered the blades of sickles, used to cut grain, and hoes and spades, all chipped from flint. There seems little doubt that millet at least partly sustained the early Chinese of this community and other communities of northern China.

This handsome storage jar for millet was found in an early farming village in northern China.

Development of Farming in the Middle East

Archaeologists had long considered the Middle East to be a birthplace of agriculture, locating the beginnings of farming in such broad river valleys as the Nile in Egypt and the Tigris and Euphrates in Mesopotamia. But more recent finds have fixed the place of transition from hunting and gathering to farming in the hilly lands of Turkey, Israel, and Iraq, where such grains as wheat and barley grew wild. (See the map on page 14.)

In the 1950s a team headed by University of Chicago archaeologist Robert J. Braidwood uncovered a site known as Jarmo, in the foothills of the Zagros Mountains of northern Iraq. Here lay evidence of sixteen different settlements, all but the lowest resting on the debris of the previous community. Fire might have wiped out a settlement, and people later built a community on the same site. Or invaders may have destroyed a community, building a new one themselves. Or a people might simply have abandoned a site, and later another group moved in to build anew.

The inhabitants of the oldest Jarmo community, dating about 9,000 years ago, lived in houses made of mud-brick walls. Each house contained several rooms. The people used stone bowls and cups and carved figurines from bone and stone.

Bones of ancient donkeys, gazelles, and other animals turned up. So did evidence of snails and nuts. These findings suggested that the people depended on hunting and gathering. But there was also evidence that grain was part of their diet. Braidwood and his party found stone mortars and pestles, special bowls and short rods used for crushing grains. They unearthed flint sickle blades and charred wheat and barley kernels.

Oldest Jarmo seems to have been a transition community. The people there either grew grain or harvested it wild. In addition, they either hunted or obtained meat from hunting and gathering bands in exchange for grain.

In a nearby area, also in the 1950s, a British archaeologist, Kathleen M. Kenyon, found further evidence of the development of agriculture. The Kenyon team dug near Jericho, about twelve miles from Jerusalem, in the foothills of the mountains of Jordan.

At Jericho, as at Jarmo, settlements lay on top of one another. The Kenyon group uncovered at the lowest level, a community dating back about one hundred centuries. Here was evidence of houses built of mud bricks in the shape of cones, like beehives. It appeared that a wall surrounded the community.

Professor Kenyon reasoned that probably as many as 12,000 people had lived in this area of about ten acres. This in itself, plus evidence of grain and the presence of a spring, suggested that the oldest Jericho settlement rested on a system of agriculture. In fact, Professor Kenyon concluded that the community may have developed a system of irrigation to supply fields with water from the spring. It still furnishes irrigation water today.

The settlement that lay just above dated about 8,000 years ago. It featured houses built in the shape of rectangles. They had been constructed of wood and mud bricks, the bricks in the shape of flattened cigars. The floors were covered with red or cream-colored plaster.

Evidence of agriculture among these people included sickle blades, fossil grains, and querns—two stone wheels between which grain is crushed. The Kenyon party also discovered arrowheads and gazelle bones, suggesting that the people hunted. The second oldest Jericho site yielded bones of goats, pigs, and cows, some perhaps wild, others perhaps domesticated.

Concluded Professor Kenyon: "The economy so far revealed is that typical of a community [of the time], consisting of self-sufficient farmers, with some domesticated animals, but still obtaining some of their food supply by hunting." In other words, a transition community.

Women and Farming

The beginning of agriculture was the key to settled life. At the same time, women were probably the key to agriculture.

You have learned that strong evidence indicates that humans proceeded through a transitional stage on the way to depending entirely on agriculture and domesticated animals for food. During this period, people hunted as well as gathered grains. As explained earlier, the division of labor in early societies cast males in the role of hunters. Women were food gatherers. It is reasonable to believe that once grains became an item of gathering, women were the ones to perform the task. We might con-

This quern was found in an ancient farming village in Kurdistan. It is believed to be about 8,000 years old.

clude, then, that while men continued to hunt, women moved from being gatherers to the role of planters, tenders, and harvesters of crops. Perhaps before hunting disappeared as a major means to obtain food, and certainly after, men participated in farming. But it seems likely that women were the original farmers.

Agriculture, Pottery, and Metal

In layers nearer the surface at Jericho, dating back about 5,000 years, the Kenyon team uncovered pottery made of fired clay. The older pottery contained much straw and tended to be crumbly. Later pieces seemed to have been fired at higher temperatures, and had less straw and smoother surfaces. The presence of pottery represents an important advance in technology.

Evidence indicates that by about 5,000 years ago, numerous farming settlements existed in hilly areas of the Near East. Professor Kenyon described one such settlement which lay northeast of the Dead Sea:

The equipment of the houses seems to be almost standardized. Each had well-built storage pits, large jars to hold grain or other food, flat paved spaces which may have been threshing-floors, and querns for grinding grain. Cooking was done both on open hearths and, which represents a considerable advance in the use of fire, in ovens.

Evidence of copperwork in some of these fifty-century-old sites showed yet another advance in the use of fire. Copper is a metal soft enough to work with a stone hammer. Perhaps the first people to use copper worked large pieces they found in this way. But it appears that by around 5,000 years ago some humans had learned to *smelt* ore—that is, apply sufficient heat to cause the pure copper to separate from the rock surrounding it.

Women prepare a meal. The equipment they are using has been found in a number of living sites of farmers.

The older people in a farm community passed important information to the young.

At one site just south of Beersheba, Israel, for example, archaeologists found open fireplaces that were used to begin the process of copper reduction. The ore then went to specially constructed and hotter ovens.

Copper objects found at this site included rings, pins, and other ornaments. This suggests that copper was not yet sufficiently abundant to allow its use for such everyday items as sickle blades. These continued to be made of flint.

The presence of copper objects near Beersheba suggests something more. The nearest source of copper was 60 miles away. The settlement's inhabitants must have had something to trade for the metal, and this may have been agricultural products. Moreover, there must have been sufficient food to support copper smelters and smiths who did not produce food themselves. All this indicates great reliance on agriculture.

Implications of Farming

People now began to alter the environment, rather than simply adapt to it. They encouraged the growth of such grains as corn, millet, wheat, and barley. This discouraged the continuation of other plants, clearing them out as weeds. As more land was needed, people changed forested lands into clearings. They further began to alter the natural balance as they, in effect, warred on animals that threatened their crops or their domesticated animals.

As agriculture became the way of life for more and more people, new skills and tools were developed. Populations grew. Trade and communication increased. By providing a basis for settled community life, farming fostered the development of formal government as well as other institutions that remain with us today.

Check on Your Reading

1. How did farming probably begin?
2. What evidence indicates that farming probably began independently in different places on earth?
3. What might have been the place of women in early agricultural communities?
4. What were some of the results of the development of agriculture?

CHAPTER REVIEW

Key Words

Can you define?

culture	Cro-Magnon
artifact	prehistoric
Neanderthal	archaeologist
technology	social organization
fossil	

Think and Discuss

1. What three achievements of prehistoric peoples do you think were most important? Why?

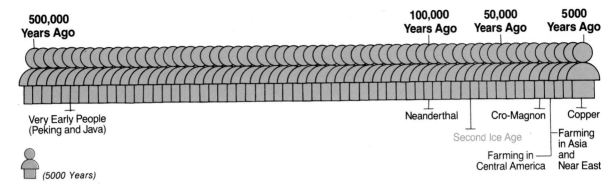

500,000 Years Ago   **100,000 Years Ago**   **50,000 Years Ago**   **5000 Years Ago**

Very Early People
(Peking and Java)

Neanderthal   Cro-Magnon   Copper

Second Ice Age

Farming in
Central America

Farming
in Asia
and
Near East

(5000 Years)

2. How did changes in technology affect prehistoric people? Do changes in technology today affect us also? How?

3. Why do you think it took prehistoric peoples thousands of years to make important discoveries and inventions when today many are made in a short period of time?

4. What is the major idea in the "Keynote" on page 1? Put it in your own words.

5. Do you think the title of this chapter is appropriate? Why or why not?

6. How did the need for survival influence the roles of women and men in prehistoric societies?

Past and Present

1. Name a discovery or invention which occurred within the last 75 years and tell how it has affected your life. Suppose this invention or discovery had not occurred. How would your life be different?

2. How have the inventions of prehistoric peoples helped us today?

3. Flakes, awls, burins, and animal hides are still used today. How are they used and what are their modern equivalents? Can you name other prehistoric tools that are still used today?

Activities

1. Is there any archaeological evidence that prehistoric peoples once lived in your region? Find out and report to the class.

2. Read about an archaeological expedition and summarize what you have read in a brief report.

Two Ways to Measure Time

The length of time covered in this chapter spans thousands and thousands of years. To help us to understand how long the prehistoric period really was, we use a line marked off in years—centuries and even thousand-year periods. This device, which you know as a "time line," shows time measured in distance.

Just how long was the prehistoric period? If you constructed a time line to cover the last ten thousand years, you could draw a line one meter long. Each centimeter (100 centimeters = 1 meter) would represent a century. How long a line would you need to represent one hundred thousand years? How long a line would you have to draw to show one million years?

To find your own place on these time lines you will have to use the millimeter scale (1000 millimeters = 1 meter). At the very end of your line, your time on earth is about 1.5 millimeters long. The airplane was developed less than a centimeter ago. Television arrived just three millimeters ago.

The time lines in this book show a different way to represent the past. The diagram above shows time in human lifetimes. Today you can expect to live about 75 years. Using your lifetime as a measure, you can express how many lifetimes ago an event occurred. For example, an event which took place in the early 1900s was one lifetime ago. Four lifetimes ago (4 × 75 years = 300 years) the Thirteen American Colonies still belonged to England. Columbus reached America between six and seven lifetimes ago.

Using 75 years as a lifetime, calculate your answers to the following questions:

1. The Neanderthals disappeared about 35,000 to 40,000 years ago. About how many lifetimes ago was that?

2. The last Ice Age ended about 12,000 years ago. Express this occurrence in lifetimes.

3. An artifact found in the Jarmo community is thought to be about 9,000 years old. How many lifetimes ago was it made?

1

Civilizations Develop in Four Regions

Some time ago, a torpedo-shaped object was lowered into the ground in New York. It was not to be opened for 5,000 years. The object was a gift to the future, a capsule filled with artifacts that will tell people of the future something about how we lived in the twentieth century.

When archaeologists of the future open the "Time Capsule," they will learn much about our civilization. They will find inside such objects as: A clock, A railroad timetable, A pen, A set of alphabet blocks, A collection of coins, A cosmetic makeup kit, Books on art, music, and science.

Consider what would happen to the contents of the "Time Capsule" if the ancient peoples who built the civilizations of Egypt, the Middle East, India, and China had not existed. If the peoples of these civilizations had not passed on their knowledge to others, how many objects and ideas would we have today to send on to the future?

The clock and the timetable would disappear, for we learned about hours, days, months, and years from ancient peoples. The pen, alphabet blocks, and books would vanish, for writing was a contribution to us from the ancient world. Similarly, we could not include coins and cosmetics, for these can be traced back to the ancient civilizations. The "Time Capsule" for the future would empty rapidly if we took away from it all the materials and ideas that we have absorbed from ancient peoples.

1

Interacting Civilizations in the Middle East

KEYNOTE

An ancient Babylonian fable tells of a quarrel between a proud horse and a wise ox. The horse boasts: "Without me, neither prince nor governor nor rich nor poor could travel." The ox politely agrees, but answers: "Without me, you would not be quite so successful. Remember that humans use an ox's hide to make a horse's harness—and without a harness you could not pull many passengers!"

This fable reminded the Babylonians of the interdependence existing in the animal world, even between those who seemed opposed to each other. In the same way, each human in the ancient world depended on other people, and contacts among them brought an interchange of ways of living and ideas. In the ancient Middle East, many different groups struggled for control of the land. Yet even as their warriors clashed, cultural interaction and exchange occurred.

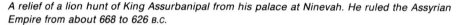

A relief of a lion hunt of King Assurbanipal from his palace at Ninevah. He ruled the Assyrian Empire from about 668 to 626 B.C.

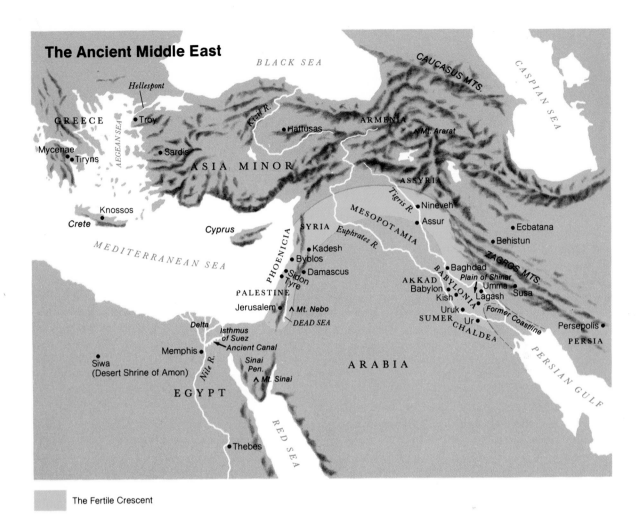

The Ancient Middle East

The Fertile Crescent

Locate Mesopotamia on this map of the ancient Middle East and trace the Tigris and Euphrates rivers from the northern highlands to the Persian Gulf.

1. A Birthplace of Civilization

About 6,000 years ago, probably influenced by the pressure of increased populations, people migrated from farming villages in hilly regions onto the flood plains of the Tigris and Euphrates rivers. The region where they settled later became known as Mesopotamia, "the land between the rivers." In Mesopotamia these settlers established new villages and then developed what appears to have been one of the world's earliest civilizations.

Background to Cities and Civilizations

From mountains in what is now Turkey, the Tigris and Euphrates coursed through hills, grasslands, and desert to the Persian Gulf. Fish abounded in the rivers, and waterfowl lived in the wetlands along them. Reeds grew in marshes, offering material for matting to construct homes and for mixing with mud as a binder in bricks. Date palms grew along the river banks.

The floodplains of the rivers had fertile soil. Rains and melting snow in the northern highlands poured into the rivers in the spring and flooded the lands along the rivers to the south. By annually adding a thin layer of new silt to the land, the floods maintained the soil's fertility.

Moisture from these floods was ample to start crops, but rainfall in the lower valley was slight. Farmers needed a means to provide moisture for plants during all the growing season.

As you have learned, evidence suggests that the settlers on the ancient sites of Jericho developed a

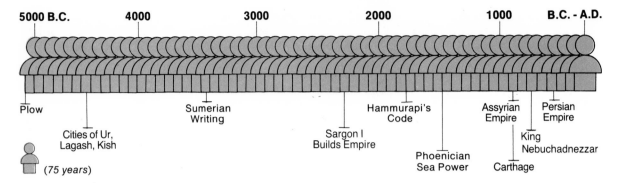

5000 B.C. 4000 3000 2000 1000 B.C. - A.D.

Plow

Cities of Ur,
Lagash, Kish

(75 years)

Sumerian
Writing

Sargon I
Builds Empire

Hammurapi's
Code

Phoenician
Sea Power

Assyrian
Empire

Carthage

Persian
Empire

King
Nebuchadnezzar

system of irrigation. Probably the people who moved into the Tigris-Euphrates valley to start new communities brought the knowledge of irrigation with them.

At first farmers probably irrigated by simply cutting river embankments to release water, when needed, to their fields. Later, as growing populations required more food, farmers developed complex systems of gates, dikes, reservoirs, and canals to expand their fields some distance from the edges of the river.

Technological change springs from need and environment. This level and semiarid environment that spawned the development of extensive irrigation also witnessed another technological advance—the plow. No one knows just when the plow appeared to replace the digging stick as a means to prepare the soil for seeding. It may have been more than 5,000 years ago. It probably did not occur until farmers moved onto more level land.

The first plow was probably a simple curved stick, one end of which the farmer held while the other dug into the earth. Very likely, soon after the plow's invention someone thought of attaching a cow or bullock to it to provide power.

In the past, men as hunters and herders had been associated with animals. They now became associated with domestic animals in the fields. Men took over much of women's work as farmers. Some women probably helped plant wheat, barley, and other seeds. They also helped with the harvest, a task requiring the labor of every able-bodied person. They no doubt remained responsible for vegetable gardens. But generally speaking, with the appearance of the plow, men took over the main jobs of farming.

Communities along river banks were not as isolated from one another as those in hilly regions. Communication among them was fairly easy by

rafts and boats, leading to the development of sailing ships. The relative flatness of the land probably fostered the invention of the wheel and the development of wheeled vehicles pulled by animals.

No one knows the details of the change, but sometime between 5,000 and 6,000 years ago, villages in Mesopotamia began growing into cities. At first a city was merely a village that had grown larger and larger. Then, gradually, the needs and wants of people living in a city led to the development of architecture, writing, institutions of government, and other features of civilization.

The Sumerians Develop Cities

The Sumerians were probably the first to create a civilization in Mesopotamia. Practically nothing is known about Sumerian origins. They probably were already farmers when they moved into the lower Tigris-Euphrates valley. In Mesopotamia they became an urban people, developing such cities as Lagash, Ur, Kish, Uruk, and Umma between 4,000 and 3,000 B.C. These cities were the centers of city-states, each consisting of a city and its surrounding districts.

Irrigation probably existed in Mesopotamia when the Sumerians arrived. They extended it. As a means of organizing agricultural production, they connected land ownership with religion.

Sumerian Religion and the Land

The Sumerians believed in gods and goddesses who controlled the forces of nature, such as the sun, moon, wind, and water. These gods had created the earth and human beings. Since they had created the earth, the gods owned it. They allowed humans to work the land, provided that they set aside a portion of their produce for the gods. In exchange, the gods would see that irrigation works remained intact, that no devastating floods occurred, that the soil produced abundantly, and that no disease or invaders visited the people.

Humans who communicated with the gods were a special group known as priests. As the gods' representatives, the priests assigned farmers land and such tasks as keeping irrigation systems in repair. They decided each year how much of their produce farmers would contribute to the gods. This tribute was stored in dwellings in which the gods resided, temples known as *ziggurats*. At first these were mud-brick structures little different from other buildings in the city. In time, however, they became elaborate buildings several stories high, as shown below.

Ziggurats were centers of worship, too. There, under the leadership of the priests, the people took part in such festivals as those marking planting and the harvest.

The produce brought as tribute to the ziggurats was used by the priests to feed the many people who worked for them. Men and women in the employ of the temples made cloth, products of metal, pottery, jewelry, and articles of wood.

The Beginning of Writing

The priests needed to keep records of the collection of taxes in the form of produce and of the many activities of the temples. As a result, a system of writing was developed. This signaled the beginning of history, which rests on written records. Writing is a key characteristic of a civilized society, but no single people can be credited with "inventing" it at any one time.

Sumerian writing first appeared around 3500 B.C. It consisted of pictograms, representations of objects. For example, a farmer might deposit so many units of barley at the ziggurat. A priest recorded this on a moist clay tablet, impressing a picture of a barley stalk on it with a wedge-shaped reed. He would affix some kind of notation standing for quantity after it, along with a symbol representing the farmer's name. When dry, this clay tablet became a

Sumerian temples, known as Ziggurats, were built on a series of platforms. Over the centuries they developed into complex structures. Reconstructions of two of them are shown above.

permanent record. This system of writing is known as cuneiform, from the Latin *cuneus,* meaning "wedge."

Within three hundred years, Sumerian writing had progressed to ideograms—symbols representing such concepts as night, day, powerful, and weak. They also developed phonograms—symbols standing for the sounds of the spoken language. In our language a phonogram representing the sea would symbolize the sound of "C."

Gradually, writing symbols came to represent mainly the sounds of the spoken language. Their number diminished. The earliest Sumerian writing contained around two thousand symbols. Eventually these symbols were reduced to five or six hundred.

Sumerian priests also developed an institution for teaching language and other important skills to the next generation—the institution of the school. Schools are another feature of civilization. Sumerian schools were designed to convey the knowledge of writing and other mysteries to a select group of boys who showed talent and promise.

Many Specialists

Priests and scribes were not the only specialists supported by the produce supplied by farmers.

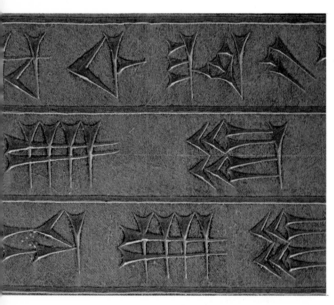

Cuneiform was made up of wedge-shaped characters formed by pressing a wedge-shaped reed against moist clay.

Other specialists were wagon makers, wheelwrights, tool and weapon makers, bakers, potters, weavers, and those who worked with precious stones, leather, and metals.

We do not know when weaving developed, but we do know that Sumerians wore clothing not made from animal skins. This is shown by statues and pictures of human figures on pottery and vases that have been found. Sheep supplied wool. The fields yielded flax, a fiber used to make linen.

Statuettes and carvings reveal yet another thing. Sumerian communities obviously supported those specialists we call artists. Regular artistic endeavor is also an element of civilization.

Sumerian metal workers may have at first worked only with copper, but they soon developed an alloy—bronze. Made of a mixture of copper and tin, bronze is harder and more durable than either copper or tin.

A System of Trade

The Mesopotamian floodplain had no copper, tin, or precious metals, and only a little stone or wood. Since these had to come from elsewhere, the Sumerians developed a network of trade with other peoples.

Sumerians may have obtained some wool from herding peoples living along the fringes of their city-states. Copper, tin, timber, and stones probably came from hill peoples. Gold and silver for ornaments and special objects probably did, too. The Sumerians exchanged grain and such finished products as pottery, tools, and weapons for things they needed. A *system of trade,* which includes transportation, communication, and a class of merchants, also is a feature of civilization.

Social Structure

In the Sumerian city-states a *social structure* developed, another sign of civilization. At first, priests were at the top of this society. Beneath them was a class of artisans, or craftworkers, and probably a class of traders and merchants. Some city dwellers became richer than others, lived in fine houses, and wore finely woven and tailored clothing. Farmers, the majority, who lived in mud-brick huts on the city's outskirts, formed Sumerian society's broad base.

Although they usually had enough food, farmers did not otherwise share in the wealth. They toiled

All the objects on this page were found in the ruins of Sumerian cities. (top right) An eagle made from gold and lapis. (top left) These objects of gold were found in royal tombs at Ur. The bull's head of gold and lapis is on a lyre. (bottom left) This small stone statue is from the Sumerian city of Mari on the Euphrates River. (bottom right) The helmet not only protected the wearer but also was a work of art.

This is either Sargon I or his grandson. Their dynasty united the city-states of Ur and northern Mesopotamia.

to serve the gods and fellow humans, the routine of their lives relieved by occasional religious festivals. Farm families probably made most of their clothing and many of their own tools, relying largely on flint and wood.

Government

During early Sumerian times, priests probably made the laws and saw to their enforcement. Yet before long, the government and the keeping of law and order passed to other hands.

Cities were centers of wealth—such as grain, precious stones, gold and silver obtained in trade, and art objects. This wealth tempted outsiders. Raising and arming followers, a chieftain of a hill or herding people might lead them to attack and plunder a city.

Also, as long as the city-states were relatively small, problems among them were few. But as the city-states increased in size and number and boundaries of one city's fields grew nearer to another's, conflicts arose. There may well have been quarrels

between upriver and downstream cities over rights to irrigation water.

Priests were ill-equipped for war. A skilled warrior who could lead an army became necessary for protection against invaders. So the concept of kingship, and with it formal government—another part of civilization—developed.

At first, cities required military leadership only on occasion. But at some point, rather than disband his army after an emergency, some leader established himself as a city's permanent ruler. Kings later claimed to have been "lowered from heaven," which set them apart from other humans and gave their rule religious sanction. This encouraged subjects to honor and obey them.

Priests probably did not like this much, but most were willing to go along in order to keep their positions and receive armed protection. Some rulers assumed the role of making and administering laws. At the same time, another social class developed— the nobility.

Sumerian tradition tells of "Kings of Kish," the city lying in the northern part of the region, as early as 3000 B.C. There is evidence dating slightly later of a king of Lagash. Also, there was a queen who ruled Ur around 2500 B.C. Excavation of her tomb revealed evidence of royal wealth, including much delicate jewelry, harps, and other beautifully made objects.

Warfare contributed to the development of an additional class besides kings and nobles—slaves. From an early time, debt forced some adults to sell themselves and their children into slavery. The Sumerians, and conquerors who followed them, also enslaved prisoners of war.

Check on Your Reading

1. Why did the Sumerians build complex irrigation systems?
2. What were the functions of priests in early Sumerian cities?
3. How was writing probably developed?
4. Who were some of the specialists who developed in urban society?
5. How did the position of kings probably develop?
6. Describe the Sumerian class structure.

2. Newcomers Build Empires

An early Sumerian king ruled a city and its surrounding fields. One king might conquer another city and exact tribute, but he lacked sufficient forces to hold the city after he returned home.

Lugalzaggisi of Umma broke this pattern around 2375 B.C. Records indicate that for a time he ruled over two or more city-states. The conquest and rule of an empire that included many cities and peoples occurred under Sargon I of Akkad, whose reign began around 2350 B.C.

Sargon I

The land of Akkad lay upriver from Sumer. Its inhabitants spoke a Semitic language. They were nomadic herders who had gradually moved into Mesopotamia and settled down, learning from their civilized neighbors to the south. Led by Sargon, Akkadian troops conquered Lugalzaggisi of Umma and the leaders of other Sumerian city-states. Of the mighty Sargon it was written that

> ...he spread his terror-inspiring glamor over all the countries. He crossed the Sea in the East and he, himself, conquered the country of the West. . . . He marched against the country of Kazilla and turned Kazilla into ruin-hills and heaps of rubble. He even destroyed there every possible perching place for a bird.

Campaigning year after year, Sargon's soldiers became seasoned veterans. There were many more of them than any of Sargon's opponents could muster. To feed them, he periodically moved them from city to city.

From the Sumerians, Akkadians learned refinements in irrigation. They adopted Sumerian writing and record-keeping and the Sumerian language. In turn, Akkadians contributed certain ideas to Sumerian society. One had to do with taxation and religion. Under Akkadian rule in Sumer, military authorities took over much of the task of overseeing agricultural production and collecting taxes in the form of produce. This increased secular power over religion.

Ur III and a Bureaucracy

Akkadian rule came to an end under the grandson of Sargon I. The next to control both Sumer and Akkad was a line of kings known as Ur III. They governed from the Sumerian city of that name between 2150 and 1950 B.C.

These rulers introduced a refinement in government, a bureaucracy. They appointed officials responsible for tax collection and the maintenance of order in the various cities. These officials, in turn, appointed underlings to carry out the details of laws and instructions from the central government.

The bureaucracy functioned as one means to control subject peoples. Especially on the lower levels, it tended to endure and perform its tasks regardless of who ruled at the top. Governments in Mesopotamia from the time of Ur III on relied on a bureaucracy to carry out their functions.

The Coming of the Amorites

The Amorites, a Semitic-speaking people, were the next important invaders of Mesopotamia. Originally, they had been a herding, nomadic people, living in tents made of skins in what is now Syria. Long on the fringe of civilization, they learned from it, and finally achieved sufficient power to make the city of Babylon on the Euphrates River their capital.

In about 1738 B.C. Hammurapi, the sixth Amorite ruler of Babylon, came to the throne. At that time the city's territory extended barely fifty miles around it. At the end of Hammurapi's forty-two-year reign, however, he had conquered an empire that stretched from the Persian Gulf to lands in Turkey. In one of the many statements Hammurapi left behind, he proudly announced:

> I rooted out the enemy above and below;
> I made an end to war;
> I promoted the welfare of the land;
> I made the peoples rest in friendly habitations;
> I did not let them have anyone to terrorize them. . .
> I governed them in peace;
> I have sheltered them in my strength.

Interactions between Civilized Peoples and Barbarians

The interactions between the Sumerians and the Akkadians and Amorites are examples of the relationships between people who enjoyed the benefits of civilization and those who were later known as "barbarians." These were people who did not have such features of civilization as cities, literature, or art.

People of civilized Mesopotamia depended on barbarians for such trade items as stone, timber, metals, and perhaps wool for clothing. Barbarians came to depend on cloth, tools, and other items they received in return. Eventually, having tasted some of the fruits of civilization, the barbarians wanted more. This led to their infiltration and in many cases to conquest. The pattern of civilized-barbarian tension that appeared in Mesopotamia would reappear frequently throughout the history of the world.

Barbarians contributed vitality to the civilized groups they conquered. Also, at first they exerted a leveling influence, for their village or pastoral ways of life did not have great inequalities in wealth and society.

But interchange is a two-way street. Civilization tended to absorb conquerors. The barbarians took on the ways of those they had overcome, just as the Akkadians adopted Sumerian writing. Conquerors and conquered intermarried. Some among the conquerors grew wealthy, others did not. Social and economic inequality soon reappeared.

Barbarians who had become "civilized" in turn spread civilization by conquests. For example, the armies of Hammurapi pushed the boundaries of civilization outward. In any case, conquest, plus ever-expanding trade during times of peace, contributed to the spread of civilization. Civilization gradually moved north from the Persian Gulf region into other parts of the Middle East.

A Code of Laws

Learning from the Ur III kings, Hammurapi used a bureaucracy to run his government. He also spread his army among the various cities he conquered. Farmers had to feed the troops, but the task was not ruinous, as it had been under hordes of Sargon I's soldiers. Garrisons of soldiers in the cities helped Hammurapi control his subjects.

Hammurapi's rule was firm and beneficial. He built temples, reopened old canals, dug new ones, and recorded his achievements:

Lasting water I provided for the land of Sumer and Akkad. Its separated peoples I united. With blessings and abundance I endowed them. In peaceful dwellings I made them live.

He is probably best remembered for the code of laws he established and had engraved on huge stone slabs set up in the cities for all to obey. These laws divided the people of his empire into three groups— nobles, commoners, and slaves. For example:

If a noble has broken another noble's bone, they shall break his bone. If he has destroyed the eye of a commoner or has broken the bone of a commoner, he shall pay one mina of silver. If he has destroyed the eye of a noble's slave or broken the bone of a noble's slave, he shall pay one-half his value.

If a noble has stolen ox, sheep, ass, or pig, whether from a temple, or a house, he shall pay thirtyfold. If he be a commoner he shall return tenfold. If the thief cannot pay, he shall be put to death.

Nearly seventy sections in Hammurapi's code referred to women, marriage, the family, and property. Here are some examples:

If a man slanders a high-priestess or a married lady and cannot prove what he has said, he shall be flogged in the presence of the judges and half his head shall be shaven.

If a man's wife becomes a cripple (with rheumatism, arthritis, etc.) and he decides to marry another woman, he may do so but cannot divorce his first wife, who shall continue to live in the same house and to be cared for the rest of her life.

Besides receiving protection under the law, some women of the Babylonian empire also owned property and engaged in business in their own right. Others became professional scribes, those who earned income from their services as record-keepers and letter-writers. Some, as Hammurapi's code indicates, were connected with temples.

Babylonian Religion

The Babylonians established their god, Marduk, as chief deity in the empire. They adapted the Sumerian story of creation, installing Marduk as the creator.

Under Babylonian rule, priests continued as keepers and transmitters of learning, and they expanded knowledge, especially in astronomy. They probably used ziggurats as towers for observing the heavens and kept accurate records of their observations of the moon, planets, and constellations. Babylonian astronomers learned how to measure the positions of heavenly bodies and express those in terms of degrees, minutes, and seconds. They were able to predict eclipses.

More Conquerors and New Technology

Babylonian rule was destroyed around 1600 B.C. by yet another barbarian invasion. This time it was a people known as Kassites, moving out of what is now Iran. The Kassites arrived in new instruments of war—two-wheeled chariots drawn by horses.

This technological change was the product of cultural interchange. It probably was the result of a mingling of pastoral peoples who had domesticated horses around 4000 B.C. and civilized craftsmen who knew how to make light yet sturdy wheels.

Chariots greatly increased an army's mobility and firepower. They could move quickly against footsoldiers, their drivers unloosing streams of arrows while still guiding their steeds. On level ground the only defense against chariots became other chariots.

Then another technological innovation, iron tools and weapons, appeared on the scene. Iron had been known for some time. But when iron was smelted and shaped, it crystalized as it cooled, becoming not only hard but also brittle. This characteristic made the metal worthless for tools and weapons.

Then the Hittites, who lived in the north on the fringe of Mesopotamian civilization, discovered a way to improve the product. They found that by mixing a small quantity of carbon with iron in the smelting stage they could produce metal that was hard, tough, and flexible. It would also take a good edge.

The Hittites also used chariots, and this combined with iron weapons enabled them to build an empire. They occupied Syria and pushed their frontiers to the Mediterranean Sea along what is now Israel and Lebanon. In 1530 B.C. Hittites staged a raid on Babylon.

The Hittites tried to keep their technology of smelting iron a secret. But when their empire broke up around 1200 B.C., the knowledge of how to make their new kind of iron spread rapidly to other peoples.

Check on Your Reading

1. Who was Sargon I?
2. Characterize Hammurapi's code of laws.
3. Describe some of the cultural interchange among peoples discussed in this section.

The code of Hammurapi was engraved on stone slabs. At the top of this slab, or stela, the ruler is shown receiving the code from a god.

3. Other Peoples, Other Empires

The ebb and flow of war as well as peaceful trade had brought numerous peoples into Mesopotamia. This condition continued after Hittite power disappeared. The next important invaders to conquer the region were the Assyrians, a rugged people who according to the *Bible* "swept down on towns like wolves on the fold."

The Rise of the Assyrians

These people probably originated in hilly lands in what is now Iraq. Like the Akkadians and Amorites, they spoke a Semitic language. On the edge of the Sumerian-Babylonian civilization, the Assyrians borrowed from it. They adapted cuneiform writing to their own language, for example.

As Hittite domination faded, in the 1100s B.C. Assyrians tried to move into the power vacuum that was created. They failed, and for about two hundred years their kingdom consisted of just the land within a short radius of their city of Assur on the middle Tigris River. Then appeared a very forceful leader, Assurnasirpal (884 to 859 B.C.) and Assyrian power began to spread.

The Assyrians first conquered the Aramaeans of northern Syria. Then they moved westward to seize control of sources of metals, stone, timber, and trade routes in the area just east of the Mediterranean Sea. Under successors to Assurnasirpal, the Assyrians pushed into the Tigris-Euphrates valley, and took and destroyed Babylon.

Assyrian armies used iron weapons and armor and they possessed chariots and cavalry units—another new instrument of war. The armies, commanded by members of the Assyrian nobility, were organized into units of tens, hundreds, and thousands. The Assyrians also developed military specialists, such as assault units using battering rams for attacking walled cities. To make troop movements swift and easy, Assyrian engineers built roads throughout the empire. These also served as routes for messengers moving between headquarters and various army units.

Despite an efficient bureaucratic and military network, there were rebellions among subject peoples. The Assyrians developed a reputation for brutality in quelling these uprisings and conquering new peoples. One Assyrian leader boasted: "I destroyed them, tore down the walls and burned the town with fire; I caught the survivors and impaled them on stakes in front of their towns."

Much Assyrian art consisted of relief work carved in stone. (See page 22.) This art often featured war and hunting scenes. Some Assyrian artists and artisans also produced fine ornaments in gold, silver, glass, and ivory. Other works of Assyrian art included beds and chairs inlaid with fine and highly polished wood.

Nineveh, a city on the upper Tigris, became the

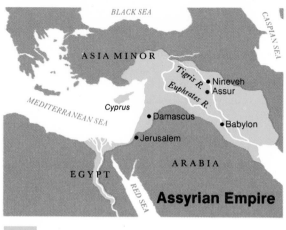

Assyrian Empire 670 B.C.

The Assyrian Empire extended in a curve from the Persian Gulf to the Mediterranean Sea.

Assyrian capital. Here Assurbanipal reigned from 668 to 626 B.C. as the last important Assyrian king. He became learned in astronomy and mathematics and gathered together a great library. Much of what we know about the accumulation of civilization in the Middle East up to his time comes from the more than 20,000 cuneiform clay tablets that archaeologists have excavated at Nineveh.

The Rebirth of Babylon

The Assyrian empire collapsed in 612 B.C. Six years of war between the Assyrians and a combined force of people known as Medes and Chaldeans came to an end when the invaders captured and sacked proud Nineveh.

Over the next century the Chaldeans assumed control of much of Mesopotamia and restored the city of Babylon. Under King Nebuchadnezzar, who reigned from 605 to 562 B.C., Babylon became once more a great center of civilization and trade. The city covered more than 2,000 acres and was surrounded with ten miles of double walls. Artists decorated the main gate, dedicated to the goddess Ishtar, with representations in tile of bulls and monsters. The city held nearly two hundred altars to Ishtar, as well as more than fifty temples to various other deities.

Nebuchadnezzar was also responsible for the construction of a 650-foot high ziggurat to the supreme god, Marduk. On terraces sloping upward from his grand palace, he had built the "hanging gardens of

Babylon." This great work of horticulture and art is often referred to as one of the Seven Wonders of the ancient world.

The Huge Persian Empire

Another conquering people, speaking an Indo-European language, now appeared. They were Persians. The Persians were a group of barbarian tribes living in what is now Iran.

Their power began to develop under King Cyrus, around 550 B.C. His armies defeated the Medes, and then the kingdom of Lydia along the Aegean Sea. From the Lydians, a trading people, the Persians learned to use coins of gold and silver. Turning south from Lydia, King Cyrus in 539 B.C. took the city of Babylon.

Cyrus' son marched his armies west of the Red Sea to conquer the land known as Egypt in 525 B.C. Later, Darius the Great extended Persian power eastward to the Indus River in India. The Persians now controlled the greatest empire the world had ever known. Darius could justly say: "I am Darius, the great king, king of kings, king of this great earth far and wide." The Persians made the magnificent city of Persepolis, located near modern Teheran, their capital.

Persian rulers governed Egypt and Babylonia directly through appointed officials. They divided the remainder of their empire into twenty provinces, called satrapies, each under a local satrap. Subject peoples paid tribute to the satraps. The satraps, in turn, deducted a portion of this tribute to pay for local administration and passed on the remainder to Persepolis.

The provinces were allowed self-government, and the Persians did not disturb local religions. So long as the conquered peoples paid tribute, peace reigned. When trouble arose, Persian armies were quickly dispatched over roads built by the Persians throughout their empire.

A New Religion

Within the empire a new religion developed. It is believed that this religion, *Zoroastrianism,* was created by Zoroaster, whose sayings were recorded in sacred books, the *Avesta.*

According to Zoroaster, two forces struggled for control of the world. One was Ahura Mazda, representing light and goodness. The other was Ahri-

A reconstruction of the gate which guarded the main entrance to the city of Babylon. It was dedicated to the goddess Ishtar.

man, symbolizing evil and darkness. It was believed that after thousands of years of struggle between the two forces, Ahura Mazda would triumph. Humans who cast their lot with Ahura Mazda might know hardship and suffering, but they would also enjoy a pleasant afterlife in paradise when the great fire that Ahura Mazda would send consumed the world.

Unlike numerous gods and goddesses of the times, Ahura Mazda was not a deity of a single person or city. He was universal, offering hope and comfort to all. Separating good from evil, Zoroastrianism held out the promise of reward for good behavior on

Persian Empire 500 B.C.

The Persian Empire was the greatest empire the world had ever seen.

earth, and comfort to the poor and downtrodden of the world. Although Zoroastrianism spread throughout Persia, other peoples did not borrow it. They continued to prefer their local deities.

Check Your Reading

1. For what characteristics were the Assyrians famous?
2. Why is the work of Nebuchadnezzar important?
3. Describe the Persian empire.

4. The Phoenicians: Traders of the Ancient World

Among the many peoples whom the Persians conquered were the Phoenicians. The Phoenicians settled along the eastern Mediterranean coast, mainly in what is now Israel and Lebanon. These Semitic-speaking people lived on narrow plains between mountains to the east and the Mediterranean

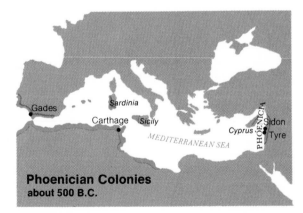

Phoenician Colonies
about 500 B.C.

The Phoenicians built colonies in Spain, North Africa, Sicily, and Cyprus.

to the west. They turned to the sea and trade for a living. Thus, the cities of Tyre, Byblos, Sidon, and Kadesh developed into great seaports and commercial centers.

The Phoenicians became the carriers of goods and ideas throughout the Mediterranean world. Also, they built numerous new cities along the southern and northern edges of the Mediterranean. The Phoenicians connected and expanded civilizations. Probably the most enduring item they transported was an alphabet.

A Salute to Phoenicians

Hailing the great Phoenician city of Tyre, the Old Testament prophet Ezekiel compared it to a ship:

O Tyre, you said,
"I'm perfect in beauty."
Your frontiers are on the high seas,
your builders made your beauty perfect;
    they fashioned all your timbers
      of pine from Senir;
    they took a cedar from Lebanon
    to raise up a mast over you.
They made your oars of oaks from Bashan;
    they made your deck strong with box-wood
      from the coasts of Kittim.
      Your canvas was linen, . . .
      to make your sails; . . .

Ezekiel then went on to list items of Phoenician commerce. They included silver, iron, tin, lead, ivory, ebony, purple garnets, brocade, fine linen, syrup, oil, balsam, wine, and saddle cloth.

Government and Religion

Phoenician beginnings are obscure. As they occupied a crossroads of trade and communication along the eastern Mediterranean, they may well have become a mixture of peoples. The Phoenicians seem to have been seagoing people as early as 3000 B.C. Not until around fifteen hundred years later, though, did they become known as a great sea power.

Kings, who passed on power to descendants, ruled Phoenician city-states. Only occasionally, perhaps to defend themselves against invaders, did the city-states unite for a common purpose.

Like most other peoples of their time, the Phoenicians had numerous goddesses and gods. Each city had its chief deity. Astarte, for example, goddess of love and fertility, reigned supreme at Byblos. Melkarth was the chief god at Tyre.

Manufacturing Accompanied Trade

The Phoenicians engaged in manufacturing as well as trade. The cities of Sidon and Tyre were known for their production of a purple dye. Skilled workers extracted this from murex, shelled sea creatures. Huge piles of murex shells have been uncovered at Phoenician sites.

These people also produced olive oil and wine, and linen and woolen cloth. They traded and worked in silk, which came from the Far East over long sea and caravan routes. Craftsmen turned out items of gold, silver, and ivory, materials obtained in trade with people of Africa. The Phoenicians gathered cedar, fir, and laurel wood from the hilly lands to the east of their cities and they used it for cabinet making. The famous cedars of Lebanon were highly prized export items.

A Phoenician ship possessed a single mast with a sail and banks of oars on both sides so that human power could propel it when wind was slight. Their long and narrow warships had battering rams mounted on the prows. These ships served the Persians as a navy when they sought to expand their conquests westward across the Mediterranean.

Phoenician commercial ships were more round in construction to make space for cargo. These vessels ranged the Mediterranean, carrying on trade with cities in Greece and Egypt, with other parts of Africa, and with various islands in that inland sea. Records tell of three Phoenician voyages around the whole of Africa. Phoenician ships also probably

These Phoenician earrings were probably made in Carthage in the fifth century B.C.

sailed through the Strait of Gibraltar at the western end of the Mediterranean to call at the Azores and perhaps traveled as far north as what is now England to take on cargoes of tin from mines there.

Phoenician sailors had no navigational instruments. They guided their ships by observations of constellations.

New Cities

To further and protect their trade, the Phoenicians founded new cities as colonies along the Mediterranean. One was Carthage, an urban area surrounded by rich agricultural lands in North Africa. Another was Cadiz, now a city on the Spanish Mediterranean coast. Phoenicians also established trading outposts on the island of Sardinia and in Italy.

One famous ruler of Carthage was Queen Dido, the city's legendary founder. As the legend goes, Dido, daughter of the King of Tyre, fled that city with some followers after her brother murdered their father. At the site of Carthage, she was offered as much land as a bull's hide could encompass. The wise queen cut the hide into strips and, stringing them together, surrounded a large area of land. It became the city of Carthage.

The Alphabet

The Phoenicians' greatest contribution was to spread the idea and use of an alphabet. It is not known how this alphabet was created. It probably began, like the Sumerian cuneiform, with pictographs and was improved by people who lived to the north of Phoenicia.

In any case, the alphabet the Phoenicians used consisted of symbols for twenty-two consonant sounds only. It represented an advance over the hundreds of cuneiform symbols. Written words could now be formed by combining symbols that stood purely for sounds of a spoken language.

As the Phoenician alphabet spread along trade routes, people in Greek cities adapted it to their language, adding vowel symbols. From the Greeks it later passed to the Romans in Italy. The Romans made further slight changes, and the basis of the alphabet we use today is derived from Latin, the Roman language.

Over the centuries Phoenician cities enjoyed periods of freedom that alternated with times of control by foreign rulers. At one time or another they were under Assyrian, Babylonian, and then Persian control. Regardless of who ruled, however, trade was vital to the prosperity of empires. As a result, free or dominated, the Phoenicians continued to play an important role in the ancient world.

Check on Your Reading

1. Why were the Phoenicians in a good position to develop as a trading people?
2. Describe Phoenician trade and manufactured products.
3. Describe Phoenician contributions to civilization.

LET'S MEET
THE PEOPLE

A Sumerian Schoolboy

The Sumerian schoolboy awoke in the morning and almost immediately thought: "I must not be late, or the teacher will beat me." Then he hurried to his mother and asked for the lunch that he was to take with him to school. The noonday meal that he received consisted of two rolls!

The schoolboy failed to arrive at school punctually and he later recorded on his clay tablet: "I was afraid and my heart pounded. I entered before my teacher and greeted him most respectfully." In school, his teacher found a section of his tablet missing and beat him. During the day, three assistants of the teacher also beat the Sumerian schoolboy for such infractions of the rules as talking out of turn and standing up without permission. Then another assistant said to him: "Your handwriting is not good"—and beat him again!

The schoolboy later suggested to his father that he invite the unfriendly teacher to their home for dinner and present him with a gift. The father did as his son requested. When he arrived, the teacher was "seated in the seat of honor." Then the father "dressed him in a new garment, gave him a gift, put a ring on his hand."

Pleased by such treatment, the teacher soon changed his attitude toward the schoolboy. Looking with new favor on his young pupil, he said: "Young man, because you did not neglect my work, did not forsake it, may you reach the pinnacle of the scribal art, achieve it completely. Of your brothers may you be their leader, of your companions may you be their chief, may you rank highest of all your classmates." There is no record of whether or not the schoolboy was ever beaten again after that!

The above account is based on information that appears on a clay tablet written by a Sumerian scholar over 4,000 years ago! The words on the tablet can be found in "School Days 4000 Years Ago" by Samuel N. Kramer, *Parents' Magazine,* November 1949.

CHAPTER REVIEW

Think and Discuss

1. What are some of the important features of a civilization?
2. Wars among different peoples in the Middle East caused an intermingling of civilizations. What were some of the important results?
3. Define the word "justice." Do you think the Code of Hammurapi was just? Why? How has the meaning of the word changed?
4. What contributions made by the peoples in this chapter do you think have had the most important influence on us today?
5. It has been said that ideas can outlast buildings or other material things created by humans. How is this true of the peoples in this chapter?
6. What five generalizations can you make about the developments described in this chapter?

Past and Present

1. Phoenician traders helped spread civilization. Does international trade today encourage the spread of ideas and inventions? Explain your answer.
2. A change in technology probably changed women's role as farmers. How have changes in technology in the last one hundred years helped change women's roles in our society?
3. The needs of people living in ancient cities resulted in the development of governmental institutions. In what ways do people living in cities today depend on the services of their government? How does bureaucracy function in our society today?

Activities

1. Find out about the work of one archaeologist in providing information about one of the civilizations of the Middle East. Make a short report to the class on your findings.
2. Obtain two maps of the Middle East. Show the ancient countries of the region on one map and the modern Middle East countries on the other.
3. Find out and report on one of the peoples mentioned but not discussed in this chapter: the Hittites and the Lydians. Report your findings to the class.

A Generation Gap 3500 B.C.: Using a Primary Source

With the development of writing came a means of preserving not only important records but human thoughts and feelings as well. Although archaeologists can tell us much about a society from its artifacts, they can do little but guess at the pain, joy, anger, and other emotions which touched all ancient peoples.

Most of the thousands of clay tablets unearthed from the cities of Sumer record the day-to-day transactions of trade. But some of the tablets found yield poetry, proverbs, and other forms of literature which show how much in common we have with our ancient ancestors.

The following passage, condensed from the original, describes a personal relationship. As you read this father's plea to his son, think about what some modern parents might write to their own children. What generalization could you write based on this passage?

You who wander about in the public square, would you achieve success? Go to school, it will be of benefit to you. Your grumblings have put an end to me, you have brought me to the point of death.

I, never in all my life did I make you carry reeds to the canebrake. The reed rushes that the young and the little carry, you, never in your life did you carry them. I never sent you to work as a laborer. "Go, work and support me," I never in my life said to you. Others like you support their parents by working.

If you spoke to your kin and appreciated them, you would emulate them. They multiplied barley for their father, maintained him in barley, oil and wool. But you, you're a man when it comes to perverseness, but compared to them you're not a man at all. You certainly don't labor like them—they are the sons of fathers who make their sons labor, but me, I didn't make you work like them.

I, night and day am I tortured because of you. Night and day you waste in pleasures. You have expanded far and wide, have become fat and puffed. But your kin waits expectantly for your misfortune and will rejoice at it because you looked not to your humanity.

Egyptian Civilization in the Nile Valley

KEYNOTE

In the midst of a huge desert the Nile flows for hundreds of miles through Egypt to the sea. In Egypt today you can stand with one foot in the light sand of the desert and the other in the dark soil of a lush, green field nourished by water from this river. The Nile has been a silent witness to the hopes, hard work, disappointments, and achievements of men and women for thousands of years.

The monuments of a great civilization that flourished over four thousand years ago still stand along the Nile. Tourists from all over the world come to visit these huge pyramids and magnificent temples. The Nile provided the lifeblood for one of the first civilizations in the world—the Egyptian. Like Mesopotamia, ancient Egypt has been the teacher of many future civilizations.

The three pyramids at Giza are in the desert at the edge of the farmlands along the Nile.

1. The Nile River and Its Gifts

The Nile begins deep in tropical Africa and flows northward over 3,000 miles before it reaches Egypt. Here it continues for another 935 miles before emptying into the Mediterranean Sea. Egypt's climate is warm and very dry. To this land the Nile River has brought its precious gifts.

In recent times the flow of the Nile in Egypt has been regulated by dams like the huge new Aswan Dam. But every summer for thousands of years heavy rains and melting snows in the mountains around the Nile's source washed soil into the upper river. Every year the swollen Nile rose and flooded its banks in Egypt. The flood reached its height in September and spread from five to seven miles on each side. Then slowly the waters drained back, leaving behind a layer of soil.

In time the soil also filled in a large bay at the mouth of the river. This region at the mouth of the Nile is called the "Delta" because it is shaped like the Greek letter Delta Δ.

The Egyptians Use the Nile's Gifts

Sometime after 5000 B.C. groups of farmers settled along the Nile in Egypt. They learned how to plan their work to follow the rise and fall of the river. When the flood waters receded, they planted seed in the muddy soil. In the months that followed, the crops grew and then were harvested. When the river returned to flood the fields, the people worked at other tasks until the land was ready to be planted again. So, using the precious gifts of the Nile—fertile soil and water—the Egyptians prospered and grew in numbers.

They planted wheat, barley, and flax in their fields. Beans, peas, and onions were grown in their gardens. They cultivated fig trees and date palms for their fruit. Cattle, sheep, and goats were fed in the pastures. Fish were caught in the Nile. Grain was threshed by driving oxen over it. Grapes were raised in vineyards.

The Egyptians also found many uses for the tall reed, called papyrus, that grew along the Nile. From the papyrus they made ropes, mats, sandals, boxes, and small boats. Most important of all, they learned how to make an excellent paper from the stalk of the papyrus. From this plant has come our word "paper."

The Nile and the cycle of its rise and fall shaped the religion of the Egyptians. The people were

Egypt and the Nile

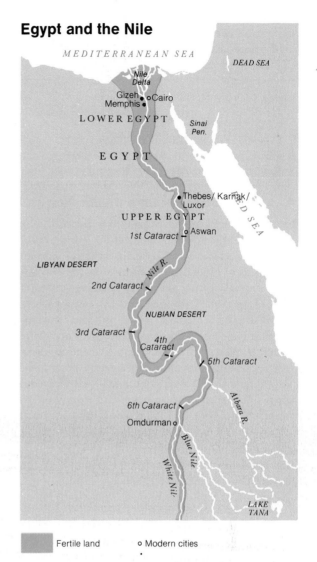

Egyptians built their civilization along the Nile that provided water and soil for growing crops. They called their country the "Black Land" after the dark soil.

deeply grateful to the river for its gifts. Akhnaton, one of their later leaders, wrote a hymn to his god, giving thanks for the gifts of the Nile.

Thou has set a Nile in heaven,
That it may fall for them,
Making floods upon the mountains,
Like the great seas
And watering their fields. . . .

Even today, many Egyptians consider the sounds of the Nile River to be the friendly "music" of their protector, Father Nile. The movement of water has always been the Egyptian rhythm of life, for it made possible the development of an important civilization in this area.

Check on Your Reading
1. How does Egypt have fertile soil and water in the midst of a vast desert?
2. How did the Egyptians use the Nile?
3. What crops did the ancient Egyptians raise?
4. Explain the importance of the Nile in Egyptian life.

2. The Egyptians Build a Civilization

In time, changes and developments in the culture of Egypt led to the creation of one of the world's earliest civilizations. Most civilizations have certain features in common. 1. Their societies are specialized with different people performing different types of jobs. 2. They are ruled by strong governments, usually centered in cities. 3. Their governments provide leadership and direction in achieving specific goals. 4. The society of a civilization uses a system of writing to communicate and record important data. 5. Time is important—calendars and other time-keeping instruments are employed to measure units of work or to provide a basis on which to plan for the future. 6. Civilizations also exhibit varied kinds of creative expression. Literature, art, and music flourish and receive support from the government and the people.

A Unified Government Is Organized

As Egypt's population grew, the Egyptians had to solve several critical problems. The flood waters of the Nile were not evenly distributed. Low places were soaked longer than high ones and thus held more water for growing crops. In some years the flood waters were so low that many fields did not receive enough water to grow crops. Smaller harvests meant less food for Egypt's people.

The Egyptians solved these problems by developing basin irrigation. They built basins, or reservoirs, to hold the flood waters. Dikes were constructed to retain the water in basins. Canals and ditches were dug to carry the water to the fields. The irrigated fields produced a steady surplus of food. The threat of famine was reduced and Egypt's ample food supply freed large numbers of people for other important tasks. Egypt's food surplus supported priests, engineers, architects, artists, and scribes who helped create Egyptian civilization.

By about 3000 B.C. the irrigation system had become very complex. It required strong and intelligent leadership to keep the dikes and canals in repair and to plan a fair use of the precious water. As a result, powerful governments grew up to rule the small city-states which developed along the Nile.

The chiefs of some city-states grew stronger than others. In time these city-states were united into two large states—Lower Egypt in the north and Upper Egypt in the south.

About 3000 B.C. the ruler of Upper Egypt won control of Lower Egypt, and a single large kingdom was created. One of the names given to the first ruler of a united Egypt was Menes. Menes started the first Egyptian *dynasty,* a succession of rulers from the same family line.

Writing Was Developed

By the time of Menes, the Egyptians had created a system of picture writing which we call *hieroglyphics.* Some scholars believe that the idea of picture writing probably came from Mesopotamia. At first each hieroglyph stood for a whole word or idea:

1. ⊞ = lake   2. = man

3. ∿∿∿ = water

The cobra goddess of Lower Egypt (left) and the vulture goddess of Upper Egypt (right) crown a pharaoh who wears the Crown of Lower and Upper Egypt.

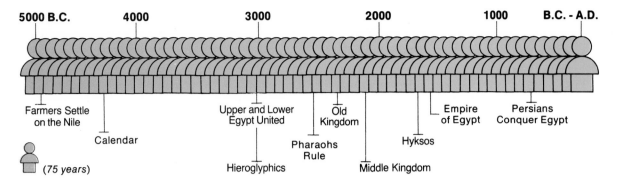

| 5000 B.C. | 4000 | 3000 | 2000 | 1000 | B.C. - A.D. |

Farmers Settle on the Nile

Calendar

(75 years)

Upper and Lower Egypt United

Hieroglyphics

Pharaohs Rule

Old Kingdom

Middle Kingdom

Hyksos

Empire of Egypt

Persians Conquer Egypt

Next, they invented pictures to represent the sounds of words. Finally, they developed twenty-four signs to represent the sounds of letters.

☐ = p

◠ = t

⌡ = b

⌐◷ = d

⌐⌐ = h

The Egyptians had no signs for vowels and they never completely used an alphabet. They mixed pictures of objects, pictures of words, and signs of letters in their writing. Often hieroglyphs were carved on stone in temples, tombs, and monuments. When paper was used, the writing was done by using a pointed reed for a pen. Scribes dipped the reed into an ink made by mixing water, vegetable gum, and soot from blackened pots.

The Egyptians Develop Measures of Time

Egyptian farmers needed to gauge the passage of time between the Nile flood periods in order to plan when to plant their crops. They studied and recorded the paths of the moon, the sun, and the stars in order to plan their farm years. Out of these observations they developed a workable calendar.

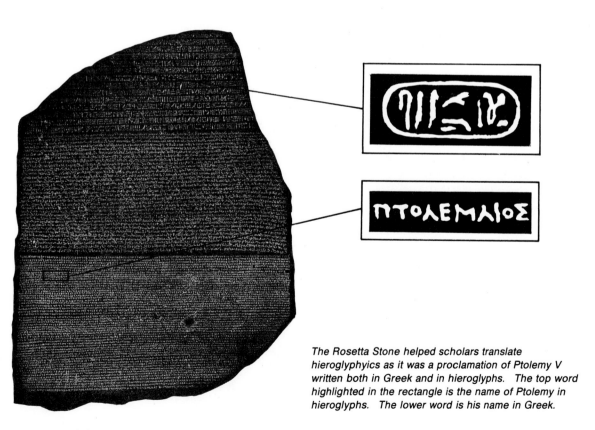

The Rosetta Stone helped scholars translate hieroglyphyics as it was a proclamation of Ptolemy V written both in Greek and in hieroglyphs. The top word highlighted in the rectangle is the name of Ptolemy in hieroglyphs. The lower word is his name in Greek.

41

This calendar had twelve months in it, each of which consisted of thirty days. At the end of each year of 360 days, five days were added for a period of feasting. The Egyptian calendar which was used as early as 4241 B.C. was not completely accurate. It was six hours short of the sun's cycle at the end of each year, and it should have had a "leap year" of 366 days every fourth year. Nonetheless, the Egyptian calendar was an important step toward the exact measurement of time. The calendar we use today developed from it.

The Old Kingdom

The unification of Egypt was followed by a great period that lasted from about 2700 to 2200 B.C. During this time, known as "the Old Kingdom," Egypt was organized under the rule of the *pharaoh*. The pharaoh was believed to be both king and god. He was responsible for the rise of the Nile and the growing of crops. Egyptians hailed him as "a Nile which flows daily giving life to Egypt."

When the pharaoh died it was believed that he would be born again as a god. Just as the pharaoh had a living form on earth, he had a spiritual form in the next life. Because this spiritual form returned at times to live in his corpse, the pharaoh's body had to be preserved and protected. The tomb of the pharaoh was therefore very important. The Egyptians brought gifts and offered prayers to help the pharaoh make his journey to the next world. During the Old Kingdom the great pyramids were built as tombs for the pharaohs. (See the photo on page 38.)

Ancient Egyptian society can be likened to a pyramid. At the top of society stood the pharaoh. Directly below him were the nobles, priests, officials, scribes, architects, and skilled workers. Forming the huge base of the pyramid were the large majority of Egyptians—the farmers and unskilled workers and slaves.

The pharaoh had two kinds of officials to help him rule the land. Local officials in villages and cities collected the taxes and tried law cases. The people paid their taxes in products such as grain, livestock, wine, and linen. These products then were stored in a group of treasury buildings where hundreds of scribes kept the pharaoh's records and accounts.

The officials who helped the pharaoh to govern the whole country lived at the capital. Many of them were nobles or members of the pharaoh's family. The head of all these officials was the *vizier*,

This drawing of three pyramids at Abusir is based on a reconstruction by an archaeologist. Each pyramid had its own temple to the dead ruler. Nearby were the flat-topped tombs of courtiers. In the distance is a sun-temple.

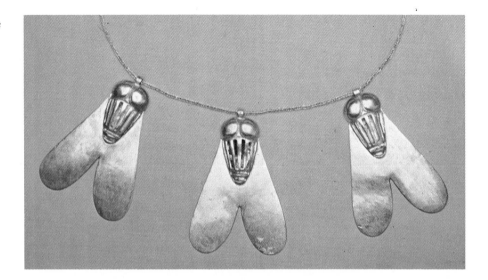

This gold necklace was found in the tomb of Queen Aahotep. It is now in the Cairo Museum.

who could act for the pharaoh in all but religious affairs. The vizier was the minister of war and the police. He supervised all public works and oversaw the collection of taxes.

The Middle Kingdom Followed a Period of Troubles

Gradually much of the pharaoh's power was taken over by nobles who gained more and more of the land. The Old Kingdom ended when nobles seized control of various parts of Egypt. The pharaoh remained in office, but the nobles really ran the country. During this period of about two hundred years, war often broke out among the nobles who were trying to take control of the pharaoh's office.

By about 2050 B.C. the pharaohs had regained their power from the nobles. The period known as the "Middle Kingdom" followed and was a prosperous time for Egypt. Large building projects were undertaken by the pharaohs of this period, and art, architecture, and literature flourished.

A Time of Disorder Was Followed by the Building of an Empire

By 1800 B.C. a series of poor rulers had weakened the power of the pharaoh. Egypt again broke into two parts—Upper Egypt and Lower Egypt. About 1750 B.C. an Asiatic people known as the "Hyksos" conquered Upper Egypt. The Hyksos introduced new weapons from Asia: horse-drawn chariots, body armor, and better daggers and bows than the Egyptians used.

The Hyksos ruled Upper Egypt for about 100 years. Finally a determined family of rulers in Lower Egypt formed a large army equipped with new weapons modeled after those of the Hyksos. They used the army to drive out the Hyksos and unite Egypt again. It is believed that the head of this family, the pharaoh, died in battle and that his wife Aahotep replaced him as leader. She is credited with rallying the soldiers and leading them to victory. Her tomb has been found and her jewelry from the tomb is now in a museum in Cairo, Egypt. Among the jewelry are those awarded to her for her part in the defeat of the Hyksos.

The dynasty of rulers who united Egypt in about 1580 B.C. turned the country into an empire. They were determined to prevent other people from again conquering their country. Amenhotep I extended the boundary of Egypt to the south. Thutmose I pushed Egypt's boundary still farther south and extended his power to the northwest.

His daughter, Hatshepsut, was able to seize power and rule for about twenty years. It was a complete change for a woman to rule as pharaoh, and in some statues Hatshepsut had herself shown in male dress with the false beard worn by the pharaoh. She was not interested in increasing the size of Egypt's empire. Instead, she worked to bring peace and prosperity to her people, increasing trade and planning the building of great temples.

Hatshepsut's nephew became pharaoh as Thutmose III. He strengthened Egypt's control of lands to the south and in fifteen military campaigns expanded Egypt's empire in the northeast. He

Queen Hatshepsut ruled as pharaoh for about twenty years. Above she is shown as a royal sphinx wearing the ritual beard and headdress of a pharaoh. At the left below is her temple built in the "Valley of the Kings" and at the right is an obelisk she had constructed in the great temple at Karnak.

organized this empire so well that it lasted until about 1100 B.C.

Life changed as Egypt became an empire. A large permanent army became important and the number of government officials increased. Wealth poured in from various parts of the empire. Part of the wealth went to build temples and to increase the power of the priests. Contacts with peoples in Asia influenced Egypt's art, architecture, dress, and ways of living and thinking.

Gradually Egypt Weakened and Lost Its Independence

The empire was lost bit by bit, and by 1100 B.C. the first of a series of foreign invaders had conquered Egypt. From the tenth to the middle of the seventh century B.C., Egypt was controlled by foreign rulers. Libyan and Ethiopian dynasties were set up to rule the country.

Then for about sixty years Egyptian rulers regained control of the government. They tried to rebuild Egypt but failed. In 525 B.C. the Persians conquered Egypt and made it a part of the Persian Empire.

Check on Your Reading

1. How did a strong government develop over all of Egypt? How did the pharaohs rule?
2. Describe the Egyptian calendar. How accurate was it?
3. Why can Egyptian society be compared to a pyramid?
4. What did the Egyptians learn from the Hyksos?
5. What was Queen Hatshepsut's attitude toward increasing the size of the empire?
6. What changes took place in Egypt during the Empire period?

3. Some Important Features of Egyptian Civilization

Egypt existed as an independent civilization for over 2,500 years. During this long history there were periods of collapse and of foreign invasion. At times foreign influence brought new forms of dress, ornaments, weapons, and ways of thinking. The role of the pharaoh evolved from that of a remote god in the Old Kingdom to a military leader during much of the Empire. In spite of these developments, life for most of the people did not change greatly.

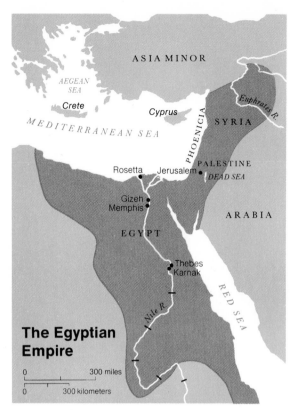

The Egyptian Empire was expanded to its greatest size by Thutmose III. He ruled from about 1481 to 1447 B.C.

Egyptian Society

Society was organized around the central role of the pharaoh. In theory everything belonged to the pharaoh. In reality much of the land was in the hands of the priests and nobles. Stone for buildings and statues was very important in a land of few trees. Throughout Egyptian history the pharaoh had the sole right to quarry stone. Pharaohs often rewarded loyal service by giving grants of stone for tombs.

During the early part of Egyptian history only the pharaoh had the right to send out trading expeditions. Many expeditions searched the lands along the eastern Mediterranean for wood. Ships were sent to the south for gold, ivory, and trees as well as for live animals for the pharaoh's collection. By the time of the Empire, however, trade had greatly increased and a class of independent merchants developed.

The upper class was made up of nobles, priests,

This is a model of a noble's estate. At the left, behind the main entrance, is a shrine. At the lower right are bins for storing grain. At the upper right are stables, servants' quarters, and the kitchen.

government officials, and leaders of the army. These were the people who carried on the complicated work of the pharaoh's central government. Many important government offices were given to able persons who were not members of the pharaoh's family or of the nobility. In time, however, these officials also became part of the noble class, often passing their offices to their children.

A noble's estate centered around an elegant house, workshops, stables, and shrines. An estate needed many servants to work in the kitchens and storerooms and as carpenters, herdsmen, or scribes. Some of these workers were slaves, but slavery was not as important a part of Egyptian society as is generally believed.

Women of the nobility could own, buy, and sell property. They often played an important part in supervising the work of an estate. One father advised his son that "You should not supervise . . . your wife in her house." Some women served as priestesses in temples and held official posts in the food and clothing industries.

Noble families enjoyed fishing, hunting, and entertaining. Wall paintings show that banquets often featured elaborate entertainment by dancers, acrobats, wrestlers, musicians, and storytellers.

The civil service which kept Egyptian society running had many engineers, architects, and other technical experts. Hundreds of scribes were needed to write down government orders and to record tax collections and important events.

The pharaohs, nobles, and priests kept many carpenters, bricklayers, sculptors, and artists busy. The wealthy Egyptians also provided a market for luxury items produced by jewelers, weavers, and cabinetmakers. The army needed the services of skilled metal and leather workers. The demand for these workers and their ability brought them a higher standard of living than that of the farmers.

The vast majority of Egyptians were farmers who lived in villages along the Nile, along canals, and on the estates of the nobles and pharaohs. The work of both women and men lasted from dawn to sunset with a rest from the scorching sun at midday. Women often helped with the farming in addition to their work in the home. At harvest time everyone labored to gather in the crops.

During flood-time, farmers were often enrolled in government projects. They provided the unskilled labor to build temples and tombs and to keep the dikes and irrigation canals in good repair. Archaeologists have uncovered records of several strikes of workers on the royal tombs. These strikes were over delays in the distribution of rations to the workers. The following is a petition of striking workers: "We are hungry, eighteen days of this month have already gone by. . . . We have no clothes, no fish, and no vegetables. Write this to pharaoh, our good Lord. Write to the vizier, our chief, so that we may be given the means to live."

Egyptian Religion

From the very beginning of Egyptian history the people believed that the pharaoh was a god. Since he lived as a god after death, the preservation of his body was extremely important. The body of each pharaoh was mummified, or preserved, by a special treatment. Then it was placed in a large stone coffin in the burial chamber of the pharaoh's tomb. The Egyptians believed that after death the soul of the pharaoh would join the sun god, Re, on his daily trip across the sky from east to west. Some of the pharaohs had ships built to carry their souls to Re.

The Egyptians believed in many gods and goddesses. Osiris was one of the most important. Osiris was the god of the Nile and of the fertile soil in which crops grew. Like the Nile, which rose and fell each year to renew the fertile soil, so Osiris was the god of life. Like the crops which were sown, harvested, and resown, Osiris was the god of the resurrection of life after death. The Egyptians believed that Osiris was the judge of the newly dead. It was necessary for the deceased to prove to Osiris that he or she had not committed any serious crimes. By the time of the Empire it was believed that any good person could have life after death.

A collection of religious writings known as *The Book of the Dead* was buried with the mummified corpse so that the soul would stand before Osiris and express the proper thoughts. Some sayings in the "First Confession" were:

I have not done injury to men.
I have not oppressed those beneath me.
I have not been a doer of mischief.
I have not caused hunger.
I have not murdered.

The Egyptians hoped that *The Book of the Dead* would help them to win immortality.

One pharaoh, Amenhotep IV, turned to a belief in one God. To Amenhotep IV, Aton was the one and only God in the world and the spirit of Aton

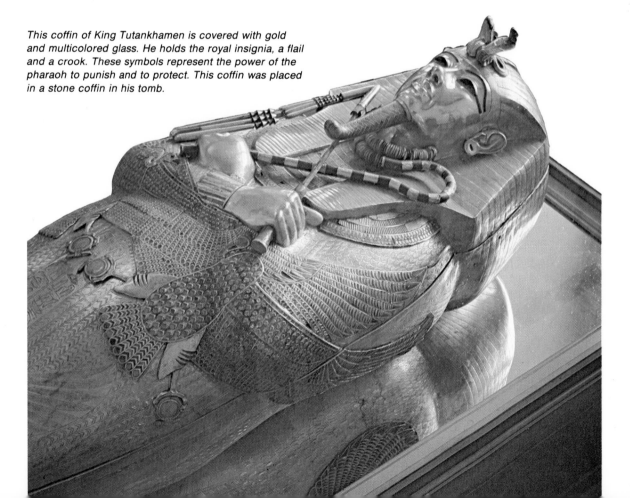

This coffin of King Tutankhamen is covered with gold and multicolored glass. He holds the royal insignia, a flail and a crook. These symbols represent the power of the pharaoh to punish and to protect. This coffin was placed in a stone coffin in his tomb.

was to be found in the sun. About 1375 B.C. Amenhotep IV changed his name to Akhnaton, which means "Profitable to Aton." Soon after Akhnaton died, the belief in Aton died out in most of Egypt.

Literature

The literature of Egypt that has survived includes stories, histories, poetry, songs, and advice concerning moral conduct. Of course, these must be only a small part of what was written.

Some of the literature tells of the life of the farmers. For example, there is the chant that the threshers sang to their oxen:

Thresh for yourselves. Thresh for yourselves.
Straw to eat; corn for your masters.
Let not your heart be weary, your Lord is
    pleased.

Other poems were more sophisticated, such as those that praised a pharaoh. Occasionally there are bits of advice that might well be followed today. The following suggestion concerns eating:

Restrain appetite; gluttony is
    base . . . A cup of water,
it quenches the thirst. A mouth-
    ful of melon, it stayeth
the appetite. . . . It is a base fellow
    who is mastered by his belly.

Some Egyptians also thought deeply about life and death. The following is from a conversation in which a human soul seeks an answer from the god Atum to the problem of death.

Soul: O Atum, what does it
       mean that I must go into
       the wilderness of death?
       It has no water, it has
       no air, it is very deep,
       very dark and boundless.
Atum: I have put blessedness
       in the place of water
       and air . . .; and peace
       of mind in place of
       bread and beer.

Art and Architecture

Brightly colored paintings in tombs tell us much about the daily lives of the Egyptians. The purpose of these paintings was to portray the essentials of a

This painting shows Queen Nefertari playing senet. It is believed that the aim of this game is to move all the pieces through thirty squares and off the board.

scene from the Egyptian point of view. As the pictures above and on page 49 show, artists were not interested in showing perspective, or depth.

The ancient Egyptians are famous for their work in stone construction and their stone and wood sculpture. The photo on page 38 shows the pyramids. They were built of great blocks of granite fitted together precisely, like the pieces of a gigantic jigsaw puzzle. The building of these monumental tombs required the hard labor of thousands of men

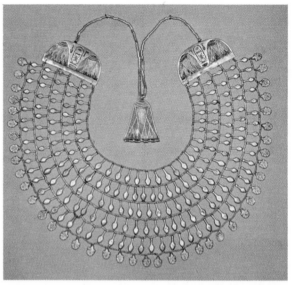

Top left is the head of a life-size statue of Chephren, who built one of the pyramids shown on page 38. At the right above is a gold and enamel necklace found in a royal tomb. The counterpoise at the back prevented the necklace from slipping. The painting above is from a papyrus copy of the so-called Book of the Dead found in the tomb of a scribe. The jackal-headed god Anubis is shown weighing the soul of the scribe in the scale of justice against the feather of truth.

Notice the clerestory at the top of these gigantic columns in the center of the ruins of the temple at Karnak. The twelve columns in the center of the hall of the temple are higher than the columns and roof at the sides of the hall. This allows light and air to come through the clerestory between the two levels of the roof of the hall.

A wooden model of a funerary barge found in a royal tomb. Such barges were believed to bear the dead upon the waters of the next world. Beneath the canopy is the mummy of the owner of the tomb. Beside the mummy is a priest. At its head and feet are two women mourners.

working for long periods of time. The Great Pyramid of Pharaoh Khufu (or Cheops) at Gizeh consists of over two million blocks of stone, each weighing over two tons.

On page 44 is a photo of an obelisk. Notice the crisp beauty of its shape. Obelisks were built as symbols of the sun god.

Statues of the pharaohs are among the world's great art. The aim of the sculptor was to show the god-ruler for eternity. The sculptor did not want to show an exact likeness, but to record for all time the character of the ruler and the majesty of the god.

Egyptian architects did more than hand down to us the tradition of grandeur and size in the building of monuments. They also passed along valuable ideas to later civilizations. Look at the ruins of the temple of Karnak on the opposite page. The center section of the roof is higher than the roof of the sides. In the walls which connect the two roof levels are openings to admit light to the hall. This is called a *clerestory*. The Romans borrowed this idea, and over a thousand years later clerestories were used in the cathedrals of western Europe. Ancient Egypt thus became a reservoir of architectural ideas that were used by later peoples.

Music

Music played a part in the lives of the Egyptians. Music was heard at religious ceremonies and cele-

brations of military victories. Palaces had orchestras, and temples probably had choirs. The harp, flute, lute, and lyre were popular instruments. So was the sistrum, an instrument whose sound was produced by shaking a group of discs on wires.

Even in the matter of death, there were Egyptians who thought of music. Instruments were buried in the vaults of pyramids and other tombs. If death were to carry the pharaohs on a long journey, music would make it more pleasant for them!

Science

Egyptian medicine was a mixture of careful observation and a belief in magic. Often medicine consisted of efforts to drive out the dark demons of sickness which the Egyptians thought had lodged themselves in a sick person's body. On the other hand, Herodotus, a Greek historian, mentioned the great number of Egyptians who practiced medicine, not just magic. *The Edwin Smith Papyrus* lists forty-eight cases of Egyptian surgery. It is one of the earliest known scientific documents.

Egyptian doctors knew of the brain and called the heart the "center" of the human body. They were familiar with anatomy as a result of their study of mummification. In the case of the ordinary "black eye," they agreed with many people today that the best thing to do is to "bind fresh meat upon it."

The Egyptians used mathematics in many of their activities. They made careful measurements in planning their pyramids and temples and in using and controlling the annual flood of the Nile. They had knowledge of the ways to add, subtract, multiply, and divide. They were familiar with fractions, geometry, and a type of decimal system.

The Egyptians knew something about astronomy. They used their study of the heavens to draw up their calendar. They made use of water-clocks to record the hours of the day.

Check on Your Reading

1. How was the government of Egypt organized?
2. Describe the life of the nobles. What was the position of women of the noble class?
3. What kind of life did farmers live?
4. Who was Osiris? What was the purpose of *The Book of the Dead*?
5. What were important features of Egyptian art? Why is Egyptian architecture important to us today?
6. What progress did the Egyptians make in medicine and mathematics?

LET'S MEET THE PEOPLE

An Egyptian Farmer

The Egyptian farmer was of medium height, thin, and muscular. He had dark hair, which he sometimes shaved completely, a clean-shaven face, and skin browned by the sun. In the fields, he wore a cloth around his loins; but he went barefoot. At home, he put on a linen garment. He wore a ring and colorful earrings.

The farmer lived in a cottage with walls of brick. Its flat roof was made of palm branches thrown across beams, over which mats were placed and covered with mud. Most of the year he and his family slept on the roof. The cottage had three small windows and a single door. At night, a seed-oil lamp gave light.

The farmer's main food was bread, vegetables, fish, and barley beer. As a treat, he would catch a bird, salt it, and eat it uncooked. The farm family was self-sufficient. The family milled its own flour and baked its own bread. The women wove flax into linen for the family clothing.

The farmer worked long hours ploughing the earth and planting wheat, barley, sorghum, vegetables, and flax. His tools were a wooden hoe with a stone blade, a wooden sickle that had flint teeth, a copper axe, a bronze saw, and a plough, made mostly of wood, which was drawn by two oxen.

The whole family helped with the grain harvest. As the reapers cut the grain, women with baskets followed to gather what had been cut. Men or donkeys carried the sheaves to the threshing floor. The last step was to store the grain in silos while scribes checked carefully. Most of the grain went to the landlord or to pay taxes. The farm family kept a small portion to pay for the work it had done for its landlord.

On feast days, the farm family joined religious processions to the temple. There priests performed ceremonies in honor of Re, Osiris, and other gods.

Thus the farmer lived. When he died, no stone monuments would be raised in his honor. Such glories were reserved for pharaohs and wealthy people—not for simple farmers.

This sketch of an Egyptian farmer is based on several sources: the writings of Herodotus; V. Gordon Childe, *New Light on the Most Ancient East*, 1953, Praeger; and Sir J. Gardner Wilkinson, *A Popular Account of the Ancient Egyptians*, Harper & Brothers.

CHAPTER REVIEW

Think and Discuss

1. Which features of Egyptian civilization do you think were most important to the Egyptians? to our civilization? Why?
2. Do you agree or disagree with the statement: The story of people is continuous, and yesterday, today, and tomorrow merge together without a break? Why?
3. The historian Arnold Toynbee has written that religion is one of the most inspiring influences in the history of people and their progress in civilization. What part did religion play in the development of Egypt's civilization?
4. What Egyptian invention do you think had the greatest value to them? Why?
5. Egyptians learned from other peoples, but Egyptian civilization did not involve as much intermingling of many peoples as did the civilization that developed in the Middle East. Why do you think there was this difference?
6. Do you think the fact that the Egyptians had paper and stone might have influenced the difference between Egyptian and Sumerian writing? Why?
7. Why do you think that many of Egypt's public buildings have survived, while no Mesopotamian buildings stand today?
8. What do the illustrations on pages 38, 42, 43, 44, 46, 47, 48, 49, and 50 tell you about Egyptian art and architecture?

Past and Present

1. What features of Egyptian government do we still have in modern times? Why did some features disappear and others endure?
2. Social classes emerged in both Mesopotamia and Egypt when civilization developed. How can you explain this development? Will this organization always exist in societies? Explain your answer.

Activities

1. Find out and report on how the Egyptians made paper.
2. Write a report on one of the following topics: the canal that Egyptians built between their land and the Red Sea; Egyptian art and architecture; Egyptian literature; Egyptian religion.
3. Arrange to show a film, filmstrip, or slides on Egypt.
4. Invite a speaker to present a travelogue about her or his trip to Egypt.

Distance and Travel

Distances on maps can be deceiving. When we travel today we may look at a road map to learn the number of miles or kilometers between two places. But what we really want to know is how long the trip will take. Driving ten miles through stop-and-go traffic in a crowded city might take an hour. Covering the same distance on a superhighway would consume ten minutes. While map scales help us to learn distances, there are other factors that affect the answer to our question: How long will it take?

Ancient rulers must have been extremely interested in this same question. Unlike today's messages sent at the speed of light, ancient people could send and receive information only as fast as humans could travel. What this meant can be illustrated by examining the map on page 45. Using the map scale, calculate the distance in miles or kilometers between Memphis and Thebes and Memphis and Jerusalem. Now suppose you were a pharaoh living at Memphis, the capital of ancient Egypt. Your royal messengers can cover 40 miles or 64 kilometers per day. You must send a message to your governors at Thebes and Jerusalem and receive a reply. How long will the round trip take? After you have calculated the time, can you suggest why sometimes pharaohs found it difficult to retain control over their subjects in distant places?

CHAPTER

3

Early Civilizations in India

KEYNOTE

Every time we tell the children's stories of Jack and his magic beanstalk or of Puss and his seven-league boots, we are borrowing tales from ancient India. Such familiar stories are not of Western or European origin; they can be traced back to Indian sources. Every time we write a zero or work with equations, we are drawing on ideas developed in India long ago. India has been called "the world's teacher" in such varied fields as fables, mathematics, grammar, philosophy, and chess.

Yet, of all of India's teachings, none are more interesting than those involving religious ideas. Many of the people of India have searched for the purpose and meaning of life. This fascination with questions of the spirit has been an outstanding feature of Indian life from earliest times to the present.

This Festival of Lights has been celebrated in India for over two thousand years.

Notice how mountains and seas separate the subcontinent of India from the rest of Asia. Passes through the mountains in the northwest were used by invaders such as the Aryans.

Early Civilizations in India

➡ Routes of Aryans

≍ Pass

1. Varied Lands and Climates of a Subcontinent

India is a vast subcontinent occupied today by several countries, the largest of which is known as the Republic of India. India is called a "subcontinent" because its very large land area is separated from the rest of Asia by mountains and seas. (See the map above.)

Varied Lands

India projects southward from the rest of Asia like a huge triangle pointing into the Indian Ocean. It is bounded on the east by the Bay of Bengal and on the west by the Arabian Sea. On the north tower the Himalayas, the highest mountains in the world. Only in the northwest are there openings in the great Himalayan wall.

Two large river systems have played important parts in Indian history—the Indus and the Ganges. Together they form two wide corridors from the northwestern Himalayas, running south to the Arabian Sea and southeast across upper India to the Bay of Bengal.

Desert and barren lands separate most of the plain of the Indus from the rest of India. Hills and low mountains stretch southward from the wide plain of the Ganges to the Deccan Plateau. The Deccan is the huge plateau in the center of the Indian peninsula. On either side of the plateau, hills fall away to coastal plains.

Varied Climates

Most of India lies within the northern tropic zones, but still the climates vary from region to region. They range from the cold and fog of the Himalayan Mountains to the sticky heat of the coastal regions. On the northwestern river plains, summer temperatures of 120°F are followed by cool winds and 50°F in the winter, while in the south it is hot or warm the year-round.

India has some of the wettest lands in the world—along the coasts and in the foothills of the Himalayas—as well as a desert in the northwest. Most of the Deccan Plateau receives from 10 to 30 inches of rain a year, not enough for very productive farming. On the southern coastal plain rainfall

55

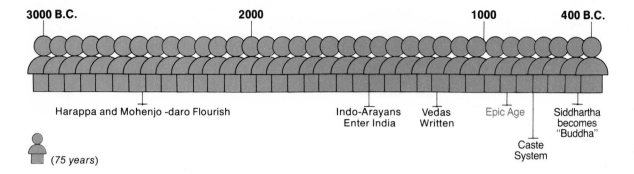

3000 B.C.   2000   1000   400 B.C.

Harappa and Mohenjo -daro Flourish   Indo-Arayans Enter India   Vedas Written   Epic Age   Siddhartha becomes "Buddha"   Caste System

(75 years)

from 80 to 200 inches and a tropical climate make it possible to raise two crops a year.

About 85 percent of India's rain comes during the monsoon season between June and September. The monsoon is a wind that blows from the Indian Ocean in a northeast direction across India during the summer months. This means that most of India's rain falls during a three-month period. For example, in the middle of the Ganges plain, rainfall is about 40 inches a year, and about 37 inches of them fall from June to September. The area around Bombay on the west coast may receive over 40 inches of rain in just a few days of the monsoon season.

Check on Your Reading

1. Why is India called a subcontinent?
2. What two river systems have played important parts in India's history?
3. What is the Deccan? Describe its climate.
4. Why is the word "varied" used to describe India's lands and climates?

---

2. The Ancient Civilization of the Indus River Valley

When the first great pyramid was being constructed in Egypt, a rich civilization flourished on the plain of the Indus River. This exciting chapter of Indian history remained unknown until the 1920s.

What We Know about This Civilization

In 1920 engineers in charge of a railroad project noticed that workmen were finding large quantities of bricks of an unknown type. Archaeologists were notified, and, in the years that followed, their excavations uncovered two major cities, several small cities, and over sixty towns and villages. These sites revealed seals with unknown writing on them, cop-

per weapons and tools, coins, pottery, dice and chess pieces, gold and silver jewelry, and many kinds of pottery toys—some with wheels. The studies of the archaeologists indicated that this civilization probably flourished from about 2500 to 1500 B.C.

The two major cities—Mohenjo-daro and Harappa—were several hundred miles apart. Mohenjo-daro is about 300 miles north of the modern city of Karachi in Pakistan. Both cities measured about 3 miles in circumference. Each contained a citadel on a mound where archaeologists found traces of palaces, halls, granaries, and baths. Beyond the citadel ancient surveyors had laid out a planned city in squares or blocks. The houses were built of fired brick around courtyards. Bathrooms had paved floors, and drains in houses led to sewage systems. Outside the cities, people grew wheat, barley, peas, and cotton; and raised cattle, goats and sheep.

The seals engraved with animal designs and bearing the signs of writing which we still do not understand proved especially interesting. So many seals have been found—over twelve hundred in Mohenjo-daro alone—that archaeologists believe that they were used to identify the owners of certain items of trade. Some of these seals have appeared in the excavations of ancient Mesopotamian cities, suggesting that trade existed between the two civilizations.

The discovery of weights provided further evidence of trade. These weights came in various sizes. Some are so tiny that they could have been used to weigh gold or spices. Others are so big that they could have been used to measure large amounts of grain. Rulers for measurement have been found, based on a foot of 13.2 inches.

Traces of this civilization still exist in Indian life today. For example, boats and carts in modern India exhibit many similarities to those used four

Above, clay figurines of bulls have been found in the ruins of the cities of the Indus River civilization. At the right are the ruins of the great bath in the center of Mohenjo-daro. Made of bricks in perfect alignment it held tons of water. Below is a toy from Mohenjo-daro made from terra-cotta. So many toys have been found in the ruins of the cities of the Indus Valley that some archaeologists believe that they were made for export.

thousand years ago. Many Indian women still continue the custom of wearing anklets and nose ornaments. Also, examples were discovered of the worship of a god similar to Shiva, who is very important in Indian religion today.

A Puzzle

This civilization seems to have ended about 1500 B.C. We are not sure of the causes of its collapse. Some archaeologists believe that changes in the land helped destroy the cities. The salt content of the soil may have increased until it was no longer possible to grow enough food to support the people of the cities. Or great changes in the earth's crust may have lifted the land and changed the course of the Indus River, gradually flooding the cities.

We do know that the Indus cities lay across the route of the Indo-Europeans, or Indo-Aryans who began moving into India from the northwest about 1500 B.C.

Check on Your Reading

1. How would you describe the cities of Harappa and Mohenjo-daro?
2. What do seals and weights suggest about these cities?

3. The Indo-Aryans Build a Civilization

Around 1500 B.C., Indo-Aryan tribes filtered through the northwest passes of the Himalayas onto the Indus Plain. These people spoke an Indo-European language, indicating they may have come from central Europe and the territory near the Caspian Sea. The early literature of these people tells of wars against local people and of the storming of cities. In Harappa, archaeologists have discovered evidence of a great fire.

The Vedic Age

Indo-Aryans called the mighty river they found the "Sindu," or Indus, which was their word for "river." The name "India" is derived from this word.

This seventeenth-century painting illustrates the siege of Lanka from the Ramayana. Prince Rama, with the help of the gods and the king of the monkeys, lays siege to the castle of the demon king Ravana.

Most of what is known about the early period of the Indo-Aryans in India comes from their literature, the *Vedas*. The word *veda* means "knowledge." The Indo-Aryans' hymns and prayers expressed adoration and worship of the gods and goddesses who represented the sun, the rains, the seasons, and other forces of nature. These hymns and prayers were recited and passed on from generation to generation for hundreds of years before they were written down in the four books of the *Vedas*. The *Vedas* form the basis of the Hindu religion.

The first period of Indo-Aryan India, from 1500 to 1000 B.C., is called "the Vedic Age." During this period the Indo-Aryan invaders probably overcame the Indus Valley civilization, learned from the survivors, and settled in villages to tend their animals and to farm. The *Vedas* tell of tribes ruled by chiefs with a council of nobles and a body of freemen. They were a warlike people who also loved dancing, music, and charioteering.

The Epic Age

During the Vedic Age the Indo-Aryans took control of the northwest region. Then in the "Epic Age," from 1000 to 500 B.C., they moved eastward to settle the Ganges plain. They conquered the native people and organized small states ruled by kings, or rajas. The people of India today are mostly descended from the original people, known as the Dravidians, and from the Indo-Aryans.

This period is named for the two great epics, or heroic poems, composed at the time. One epic tells of the wars between two kingdoms along the upper Ganges. A famous part of this epic is the *Bhagavad-Gita*, or *Lord's Song*, which is a dialogue between a warrior leader and the god Khrishna. In this dialogue, Khrishna identifies himself with the Supreme Being. "All things," he says,

> hang on me
> As hangs a row of pearls upon a string.
> I am the fresh taste of the water; I
> The silver of the moon, the gold of the sun. . . .
>   I am the good sweet smell
> of the moistened earth, I am the fire's red light,
> The vital air moving in all which moves,
> The holiness of the hallowed souls, the root
> Undying, whence hath sprung whatever is.

Next to the *Vedas,* the *Bhagavad-Gita* is most re-vered by the Hindus. It is used in the Republic of India today, like the *Bible* in our country, for the swearing of oaths in court.

The other epic, the *Ramayana,* tells of the adventures of Prince Rama and the Princess Sita. When Prince Rama is expelled from a kingdom in northern India, his wife Sita refuses to stay behind. The *Ramayana* tells of their wanderings; Sita's kidnapping by the demon king of Lanka, Ravana; the siege of Lanka; the killing of Ravana; and the triumphant return of the reunited couple to their kingdom. (See the painting on pages 58–59.)

The *Ramayana's* story is celebrated each year in the Republic of India. A ten-day festival recalls the siege of Lanka. On the tenth day great paper images of Ravana and his knights are stuffed with fireworks and burned. The return of Rama and Sita to their kingdom is also remembered in the Festival of Lights. In northern India this festival marks the coming of cool weather. Lights are placed in windows to guide people home, and children receive toys and sweets. (See page 54.)

The Faith of the Hindus

The Hindus gradually made changes and additions to the religion of their Indo-Aryan ancestors. Today the religion of Hinduism has been accepted by over four hundred million people in India. Although there are many differences in individual worship, the faith of the Hindus generally includes the following beliefs:

1. Belief in the unity of all things in the world. Imagine that there is a single string running through all of us. You might say that the part of the string within you belongs to you alone. On the other hand, your part can be considered as only a small piece of the whole string that unites everyone. In this way, the Hindus believe that there is one spirit that runs through all humans, animals, and plants—through everything in the world. Since a part of this spirit is found in each of us, we are all spiritually united. The Hindus call this unifying spirit *Brahman*.

2. Belief in *ahimsa*. Many Hindus believe in *ahimsa*, or the non-injury of any living creature. Since the Hindus feel that we are all united by the same spirit, or *Brahman*, many of them do not injure or kill animals or eat meat. The cow is especially cared for, and to kill one is considered a sin.

3. Belief in many gods and goddesses who are

different forms of one spirit. The Hindus worship Brahma the Creator, Vishnu the Preserver, Siva the Destroyer, and others. Hindus consider each of these to be a special form of the one spirit in the world. This spirit wears many masks and plays many roles but, underneath each, remains unchanged. In the *Bhagavad-Gita* a form of the one God says:

Some [people bow] to the countless gods that are only
My million faces.

4. Belief in transmigration of souls. The Hindus believe that when a person dies, he or she will be reborn as another living creature. This movement, or *transmigration,* of the soul from one body to the next applies to animals as well as to human beings. For example, the soul of a dead animal might transmigrate, or move, to the body of a newborn child. According to the *Bhagavad-Gita,* this cycle or "wheel of death and rebirth" goes on and on. "Just as the dweller in this body passes through childhood, youth, and old age, so at death he merely passes into another kind of body."

5. Belief in *Karma.* Where the soul moves after death depends on *Karma. Karma* is a spiritual law of the universe that has great power, even though we cannot see it or touch it. It records the good and bad deeds that a person does while alive and determines where that person will go in the next life. For example, the soul of an evil person might move to the body of a lowly animal as a punishment. In contrast, a person who performs many good deeds might be rewarded by being reborn a Hindu of the highest caste.

6. Belief in work without worrying about results. Hindus believe that people should do their work in the best way that they can without worrying about success or failure. They accept the idea that:

Work done with anxiety about results is far inferior to work done without such anxiety. . . .
They who work selfishly for results are miserable.

Today in India these six beliefs still form the basis of the Hindu religion and affect ways of living in the Republic of India in many ways.

The Caste System Develops

The Indo-Aryans reserved for themselves what they considered to be the most desirable kinds of work and forced the Dravidians to take the jobs which were left over. The Indo-Aryans became the rulers, religious leaders, traders, and farm owners. The Dravidians had to become farm workers, craftsmen, servants, and animal herders. Sons were expected to follow the occupations of their fathers. In this way, each community would have a continuity of skills which were essential for survival.

The Hindu religion supported this system by teaching that people were not equal and that a person's position was a result of his or her actions in a former life.

Generally, each occupation or group of occupations was considered as a specific *caste*—a hereditary place in society. By 500 B.C., four principal castes had developed. From the highest to the lowest these castes were: *Brahmans*—priests and teachers of religion; *Kshatriyas*—warriors and rulers; *Vaisyas*—craftsmen, merchants, and free farmers; and *Sudras*—servants and serfs. (Serfs are bound to work the soil under the rule of their masters.) Caste regulations forbade members from one caste to marry or even eat meals with someone from another caste.

Besides these four castes, there were prisoners of war, slaves, and others who had been forced from their castes for violation of their customs or rules. These people were considered to be so low in the social system that they were called *outcastes.* They were required to do only the dirtiest jobs and to live in the worst conditions.

Out of the four general groups of castes and the outcastes there evolved perhaps as many as 2,000 castes and subcastes. Each caste had its own code of expected behavior which affected the marriage, customs, and social rank of its members. The caste system continued for over 2,000 years with minor changes into the twentieth century.

The Position of Women in Society

Women had some freedom in the Vedic Age. They often had some choice as to whom they would marry, and they could remarry if they became widows. A woman could study and become a scholar. She took part in religious ceremonies and in feasts.

Women seem to have lost most of these freedoms in the Epic Age. The remarriage of widows became unusual. Society began to exclude women from public activities, and the seclusion of women to one part of the home developed. The Hindu family was ruled by the father, who was master of his

Buddhist monks at a temple in Thailand. Buddhism spread from India to many countries in Asia.

the first to use it. One fact is certain: The zero appeared in early Indian civilization.

It is believed that the Arabs took the idea of zero from the Indians and carried it to Europe in the eighth century A.D. The spread of its use was of great importance to future civilizations. Using a zero, a person could write a complicated term such as ten thousand, one hundred, six with only five numbers—10,106! Without the zero, we would need many additional symbols to set down large numbers.

Check on Your Reading

1. Who were the Dravidians?
2. What was probably the reason for the development of the caste system?
3. Identify: the *Vedas*, the Epic (Heroic) Age, the *Bhagavad-Gita*, and the *Ramayana.*
4. Explain the six beliefs that are basic to the Hindu religion.
5. What freedoms did women probably lose in the Epic Age?

---

4. Gautama and the Religion of Buddhism

By the sixth century B.C., many Brahmans, or priests, had come to stress the importance of religious ceremonies more than they did good behavior. Emphasis was placed on priestly ritual. As a result, some Hindus looked for understandings and guidance beyond the ritual; they looked for spiritual truth. One such seeker for truth was Siddhartha Gautama, who lived from about 563 to 483 B.C.

Prince Gautama and Buddhism

Prince Siddhartha Gautama was the son of a rich king who ruled a small state of northern India in what is now Nepal. He had everything that he wanted, but was disturbed by the sorrow and suffering of some of the people in the kingdom. Therefore, at the age of twenty-nine he left the palace and his wife and infant son, to search for the cause and solution for suffering.

For almost seven years Gautama wandered over the countryside in search of knowledge, trying to find the reason for unhappiness in the world. According to legend, he sometimes lived on a single grain of rice for a day and tested his courage by lying on thorns. Finally, after many years, he sat down under the shade of a tree and resolved not to

wife and children. Only a few women of the noble class were given an education.

It was reported of a somewhat later period that "the Brahmans keep their wives . . . ignorant of all philosophy; for if women learned to look upon pleasure and pain, life and death, philosophically, they would . . . no longer remain in subjection."

Indian Knowledge of Mathematics

Many of our ideas of decimals, minus signs, and our "Arabic" numerals (1, 2, 3, 4, 5, 6, 7, 8, 9) can be traced back to India. So can our place-value system of numbers, in which we say 1,865 is one thousand, eight hundred, sixty-five because of each number's *place* in the figure.

The zero plays a vital part in the place-value system. Some believe that the zero was of Babylonian origin, while others think that the Hindus were move on until he had become enlightened about the meaning of life.

Legend tells us that he meditated for forty-nine days when suddenly he received knowledge *(buddhi)*. He became the *Buddha,* or "the enlightened one." For many years Gautama Buddha traveled through northern India preaching his message.

Buddhism, the religion that developed from the teachings of Gautama Buddha, includes the belief in "Four Noble Truths." 1. There is suffering in the world. 2. Suffering is caused by selfish desire. 3. Suffering can be removed if we will do away with our selfish desire. 4. We can do away with our selfish desire by following the "Eightfold Way." This means following eight principles of proper conduct. These principles include right views, right intentions, right speech, right action, right livelihood, right effort, right mindfulness, and right concentration.

The Buddhists believed that if they accepted the "Four Noble Truths," suffering would be conquered, and they would find *Nirvana,* a state of happiness and peace. Buddhists of ancient times stressed the importance of a person's conduct, rather than emphasizing the performance of ceremonies. How a person acted was more important than how often he or she recited prayers.

Buddha accepted many teachings of Hinduism, such as the idea of *Karma* and the opposition to violence. However, he did not support the worship of many gods and goddesses, and he opposed the caste system. He told his followers:

> Go into all lands and preach this [truth].
> Tell them that the poor and lowly, the rich and the high are all one, and that all castes unite in this religion as do the rivers in the sea.

Buddhism Becomes an Organized Religion

Buddha attracted many followers. Some hoped to win *Nirvana,* or release from the wheel of life. Many of these disciples were organized into an order containing both men and women. They gave up the world, put on orange-colored robes, lived in communities of monks and nuns, and accepted gifts of food from others.

Within a few centuries after Buddha's death, his followers had made Buddhism into an organized religion with rites, scriptures, and a belief in supernatural guidance. As the number of followers in-

The wheel of the Buddha is carved on a temple in India. It is one of the key symbols of the Buddhist religion.

creased, disagreements over interpretation of his teachings led to the development of different sects.

For hundreds of years the Buddha was never represented in human form. His symbol was the wheel. When the Buddha was turned into a god and savior by some sects, his symbol became that of the Buddha sitting in meditation. At the same time, sculpture and painting began to show events from his life.

Buddhism eventually lost most of its followers in India. Meanwhile, however, it had spread to many countries in Asia.

Check on Your Reading

1. How did Gautama Buddha develop his teachings?
2. Explain the basic teachings of Buddhism. What are the "Four Noble Truths"? What is the "Eightfold Way"?

LET'S MEET
THE PEOPLE

An Indo-Aryan Bride and Groom

The Indo-Aryan bride and groom of the Vedic Age knew that the purpose of marriage was to bind them together as harmoniously as the sun and moon.

Contrary to the low position that women later held in Indian society, the Indo-Aryan bride was considered to be on an equal footing with her husband. Although he had purchased his bride, the groom had made sure to gain her consent to marriage. She had already placed a wreath of flowers and leaves on his shoulders to show that she approved of him.

The bride and groom were now brought before a sacred fire where the priest blessed them as they joined hands. The bridegroom next took the bride's right hand and led her seven steps around the fire. As he did so, he recited the following:

"I take thy hand as a pledge of our happiness. I wish thee to become my wife and to grow old with me. The gods gave thee to me to rule over our house together. . . . May there be happiness in our home for both humans and animals. . . . Come, O desired one, beautiful one with the tender heart, with the charming look, good toward thine husband, kind toward animals, destined to bring forth heroes."

After the bride and groom were thus formally united, the priest turned to those who had attended the ceremony and said: "Approach her [the bride], look at her, wish her well, and return to your own home."

When the bride arrived at her husband's house, there were additional ceremonies. As she crossed the threshold, she was told:

"Here may delight be thine through wealth and children. . . . Live with thine husband and in old age mayest thou still rule thy household. Remain here now, never to depart; enjoy the full measure of thy years playing with sons and grandsons. Be glad of heart within thy home."

Finally, the priest accepted a gift of a cow from the bride's parents and pronounced the benediction on the newlyweds:

"Remain here . . . pass your lives together, happy in your home. . . . O generous Indra [a great Indo-Aryan god] make her [the bride] fortunate! May she have a beautiful family. May she give her husband ten children! May he himself [the husband] be like the eleventh!"

The husband now rubbed vermilion, a red coloring matter, in his wife's hair parting and on her forehead. This was the sign that they were at last one.

This description of a wedding ceremony in the "Vedic Age" is based on primary source materials in:

Margaret Cormack, *The Hindu Woman,* 1953, Bureau of Publications, Teachers College, Columbia University; and Zénaide A. Ragozin, *Vedic India,* G. P. Putnam's Sons, 1902.

CHAPTER REVIEW

Think and Discuss

1. What differences or similarities can you find between the Indus Valley civilization and the civilizations of the peoples in Chapters 1 and 2?
2. You learned in Chapter 1 about the interaction between barbarian and civilized peoples. Turn back to pages 29 to 30 and read again the material under "Interactions between Civilized Peoples and Barbarians." How does this apply to the story of ancient India?
3. Do you think the Indian caste system might discourage personal ambition? Why or why not? What might be the result?
4. Give evidence to support the statement: "The Western world does well to look eastward beyond Europe to find some of its heritage."
5. How are Hinduism and Buddhism alike? How are they different?

Past and Present

1. The people of the subcontinent of India have often faced serious problems caused by climate. Watch for articles in newspapers and magazines about such problems today.
2. In the *Reader's Guide to Periodical Literature* find some articles about the efforts that are being made today to do away with the caste system in the Republic of India. Read some of these articles and report your findings to the class.

Learning from Artifacts

The cylinder seals found at Mohenjo-daro and Harappa are helpful for archaeologists, even though the writing on these seals has not been deciphered. Similar seals have been found in ancient Sumer and Babylonia. From this fact, archaeologists reason that the seals were widely used items. The seals are quite small. They exhibit many different styles. These facts suggest that the seals were personal items used as a means of identifying belongings.

As a means of personal identification, cylinder seals have their modern counterparts. Most adult Americans carry a version of these seals with them everyday. Our seals are not round and made of hard clay. They are flat and made of plastic. Yet both versions, ancient and modern, operate on the very same principle. Can you guess what they are?

The fact that we use an item whose basic idea is thousands and thousands of years old should not surprise us. There are many modern tools and other objects which were developed in ancient times. If you identified the credit card as a modern version of an ancient cyclinder seal, give yourself a pat on the back. While we cannot say that seals were used to provide some form of credit to ancient peoples, they appear to have been used to identify ownership of goods. This is what we do when we buy an object—we transfer ownership from the seller to the buyer. The credit card helps to record this transaction and serves as a way to show what we own.

Both ancient seals and modern credit cards make images in the same basic manner. The round seals were rolled across a flat piece of wet clay to produce an image. Today a round roller moves across a flat credit card. Carbon paper has replaced the wet clay to create the image.

Suppose you were an archaeologist in the far distant future. Due to a great worldwide catastrophe which occurred long ago, there is very little knowledge about the so-called "twentieth century." Your excavations have produced hundreds of "strange" plastic cards. They have survived because plastic does not rot or rust. The symbols on the cards are unknown to you. As an archaeologist, knowing nothing else about the 1900s, what would you guess was the purpose of these cards? Write one or two paragraphs explaining your hypothesis. Show your reasoning, just as today's archaeologists have shown their reasons to explain the ancient cylinder seals.

Activities

1. Draw a chart showing the principal ideas of a Hindu and a Buddhist. Point out similarities and differences.
2. Debate the statement: Resolved, that suffering can be removed if we do away with our selfish desires.
3. Excavations and study of the Indus Valley civilization continues. Look for recent information on this work and report your findings to the class. A useful reference is the *Larousse Encyclopedia of Archaeology.* See the section on India and Pakistan.

CHAPTER

4

Civilization Spreads from the Yellow River in China

In a book believed to be by Confucius the following is written: "The ancients who wished to illustrate the highest virtue throughout the empire first ordered well their own states. Wishing to order well their states, they first regulated their families. Wishing to regulate their families, they first cultivated their own selves. Wishing to cultivate their own selves, they first rectified their hearts."

The family had a special significance for the Chinese; it was the model on which the structure of the state came to be based. As the father was the unquestioned head of the family, so the king was the head of the state. The family was also the focus of the most important aspects of religious life. As the Chinese built their civilization, they developed many distinctive characteristics. This Chinese culture shows continuity from the earliest times to the present.

This portrait of a family was painted about five hundred years ago.

66

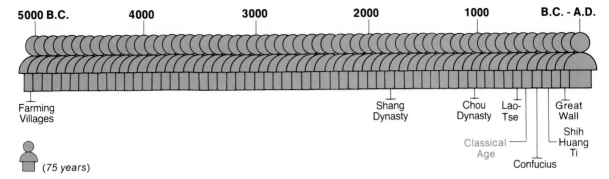

5000 B.C.	4000	3000	2000	1000	B.C. - A.D.

Farming Villages

(75 years)

Shang Dynasty

Chou Dynasty

Lao-Tse

Great Wall

Classical Age

Confucius

Shih Huang Ti

1. The Lands of the Middle Kingdom

The boundaries of "China" have changed greatly through the centuries. Today the People's Republic of China is the third largest country in the world. China's civilization began along the Yellow River in northern China. (See the map on page 68.)

Three Great Rivers

Until modern times, the northern boundary of China was the mountain range which forms the southern boundary of Mongolia, the range along which the Chinese built the Great Wall. (See page 68.) The southern frontier shifted gradually southward with the slow expansion of Chinese civilization out of the Yellow River region.

China has three main geographic divisions, each centered around a great river system. Each of these rivers flows eastward from western mountains to the sea. They descend through rocky gorges in the mountain region to the eastern lowlands.

North China is the region of the Yellow River. Central China is drained by the Yangtze River. To the south is the West River. These river systems flow through areas of different climates. The lowlands of the Yellow River and the mountain region to the north have a dry climate with some rain in the summer and a very cold winter. The Yangtze area has a warmer and wetter climate. The summers are hot and humid and the winters rather cold and wet. The valley of the West River is very hot and damp in the summer and warm and sunny in the winter.

The Middle Kingdom

The Chinese believed their land to be specially located. To the east, there was a vast Pacific Ocean. To the south and west, natural boundaries were formed by jungles, high mountains, or deserts. Only to the north and northwest was China open to attack by foreigners. It was here that the Great Wall was built.

Within this protected homeland, the Chinese felt relatively secure. They were proud of their accomplishments. The very name which they gave to their country shows their pride. In Chinese it is called "Chung kuo," which means "Middle Kingdom," or "The Land at the Center of All Things."

It was not just geography which suggested this particular view of the world. There has also been the persistent belief of the Chinese that their civilization had much from which others could learn. This belief was reinforced when neighboring peoples borrowed and adopted Chinese ideas and inventions.

Check on Your Reading

1. What are the three main river systems of China? On which one did Chinese civilization develop?
2. How does north China differ from the other two main regions?
3. Why did the Chinese call their land "The Middle Kingdom"?

---

2. China Has Had a Civilization for Several Thousand Years

In recent years Chinese archaeologists have found and studied the sites of a number of very early villages. Their work has proved that about 8,000 years ago people in different parts of China were farming and making pottery.

Archaeologists have carefully studied a village that existed around 5000 B.C. on a branch of the Yellow River in north China. It had more than two hundred houses surrounded by a ditch. Beyond the ditch was the village cemetery and kilns where pottery was made. The villagers farmed, fished, and hunted. Millet, a kind of grain, was

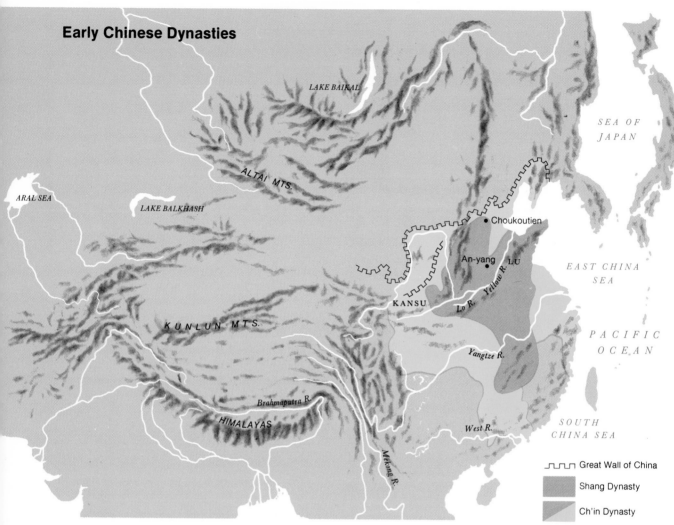

Early Chinese Dynasties

LAKE BAIKAL

SEA OF
JAPAN

ALTAI MTS.

ARAL SEA

LAKE BALKHASH

Choukoutien

An-yang   LU

EAST CHINA
SEA

KANSU

Lo R. Yellow R.

KUNLUN MTS.

PACIFIC
OCEAN

Yangtze R.

Brahmaputra R.

HIMALAYAS

West R.

SOUTH
CHINA SEA

Mekong R.

⌐⌐⌐⌐ Great Wall of China

Shang Dynasty

Ch'in Dynasty

Locate the Yellow, Yangtze, and West rivers. The Great Wall, shown on the map, was completed during the Ch'in dynasty.

their main crop, and they also raised pigs and dogs. Silkworms and hemp were grown for fabrics. Moreover, they used a set of numbers and other symbols that became part of later Chinese writing.

Other larger villages that date from around 2500 to 1850 B.C. have been discovered in this same region. In them archaeologists have found thin, beautifully made pottery and specialized carpenter's tools. Some villages appear to have been attacked by raiders and were protected by earthworks. From such farming settlements there developed the first known civilization of China, the civilization of the Shang dynasty.

The Shang Dynasty

In the early 1900s, scholars became interested in pieces of "oracle bones" that were being sold in antique shops in China. Words scratched on these bones in a very early form of Chinese writing seemed to mention the names of kings of the Shang dynasty (about 1770-1120 B.C.). These kings had been described in early histories of China, but there had been no proof that they had ever existed.

"Oracle bones" were used by priests to answer questions about the future. The questions were addressed to the spirits of the king's ancestors. If a king came to the priest with a question, the priest scratched the date, the king's name, and the question on an animal bone. Then he heated the bone until it cracked. The question was answered by interpreting the position of the cracks.

Archaeologists traced the source of most of these bones to a site near the modern town of An-yang. Excavation proved that this was the site of one of the capitals of the Shang dynasty. In nearby royal tombs were found horse-drawn chariots, magnificent bronze vessels, carved jade, lacquerware, and carved animal sculpture. Soon other sites were excavated in north China, and more then 10,000 pieces of oracle bones were discovered. Dr. Charles O. Hucker has described these oracle bones.

A common formula is: "Date. The diviner X asks on behalf of the king, . . ." Typical questions are: "Will the king's child be a son?" "Will it rain?" "Will tomorrow be good for hunting?" "The king has a headache. Has he offended ancestor X?" "Will the king have a comfortable night?" "Is the long drought caused by ancestor X?" "If we raise an army of 3,000 men to drive X away from X, will we succeed?" "Were the rituals and sacrifices acceptable?"

The Shang Civilization

Most of the people were farmers. At first they had farmed the lands between the wet floodplain of the Yellow River and the dry lands to the north and west. The fertile floodplain was too wet to farm. It took much work and planning to dike and drain the water of the Yellow River so that the rich soil of the floodplain could be farmed. Probably this task was gradually carried out under the direction of kings and their officials.

The Shang state was ruled by a king who also served as chief priest in state religious ceremonies. Officials with many different titles helped the ruler govern his kingdom. Each city-state within the kingdom was ruled by a local chief who often was appointed by the king from among his relatives. The chief was responsible for sending tribute to the king in the form of food and useful and precious goods. He also had to provide the king with fighting men when the king went to war. Skilled workers provided the warriors with bronze chariot fittings and many kinds of weapons, including spears, daggers, and bows and arrows.

A Shang vessel in the shape of an elephant. It probably held water or wine used in religious ceremonies.

In the center of the capital city, the king's palace and the large public buildings and altars were surrounded by the homes of the nobles. Nearby were the shops of workers in bronze and lacquer, potters, stonecutters, and carpenters.

The Shang period has become famous today for the magnificent bronze objects that have been found at sites in north China. Skilled workers created cups, jars, and caldrons. Some of the bronze vessels were evidently used in religious ceremonies. Others were discovered buried in the tombs of kings and nobles and undoubtedly were used to hold wine and food to nourish the spirits of the dead. In the Shang period scholars used an early form of Chinese writing. They used *pictograms,* signs representing objects— such as ⚥ for person. They also wrote with *ideograms,* signs representing ideas in picture form. The calendar they developed used a ten-day week.

In time, the power of the Shang kings weakened, and some of the city-states within the kingdom became more independent. It is believed that one of these city-states was ruled by the Duke of Chou. The lands of the Duke of Chou lay west of the Shang capital. In the eleventh century B.C. he led an army eastward, defeated the Shang king, and sacked his capital city. The Duke of Chou became the founder of the next dynasty.

Check on Your Reading

1. How have scholars learned about the Shang dynasty?
2. What do the oracle bones tell about the Shang period?
3. How was the Shang state ruled?
4. What were some of the accomplishments of the Shang people?

3. The Chou Dynasty

The Chou kings ruled over much the same territory that was controlled by the Shang kings. Their kingdom reached from the southern part of Manchuria to the Yangtze Valley in the south, and from the seacoast all the way to eastern Kansu. (See the map on page 68.)

This illustration shows dikes being strengthened. Large irrigation projects made it possible to grow more crops and to support more people.

The Government

To control this large kingdom, Chou rulers developed a system which has been called Chinese *feudalism.* All land still belonged to the Chou rulers, but they permitted important individual lords to govern parcels of it. These parcels are called *fiefs.* Most of the fiefs were given to the king's relatives. If a fief holder were not related to the king, a family relationship was created. In exchange for the right to control a fief, the lord was expected to be loyal to the Chou ruler and pay him taxes in grain or cattle. The lord would collect most of the taxes from the farmers, who also were called upon to serve as foot soldiers in the army.

The success of feudalism depended on the loyalty of the lords to the ruler. Sometimes, however, powerful lords refused to take orders from the Chou king. By the ninth century B.C. some of these lords were fighting among themselves. As the power of the Chou kings weakened, outside tribes began attacking the northwestern frontiers of the kingdom. In 771 B.C. nomads from the northwest attacked the capital and killed the king.

The remaining members of the Chou dynasty fled eastward and set up a new capital in the Lo River Valley. From that time until their downfall in 256 B.C. the Chou rulers had little governing power. China split into a number of rival states under independent rulers.

The Chinese "Classical Age"

The period from 771 to 256 B.C. was both a time of violence and of progress in technology and ways of living. Most important, it was the time when systems of philosophy and ideas about the world that have had a lasting influence on the culture of China and East Asia were developed. Therefore, this period is sometimes called China's "Classical Age."

Advances in technology improved ways of living. Iron mining and smelting developed. Iron farm implements made it easier to clear new ground for farming. Farmlands were expanded and farming methods were improved. Animal-drawn plows came into use. Large irrigation projects were developed. Crop rotation was used to allow some fields to rebuild the fertility of the soil. Population increased.

In spite of the warfare, trade increased. Metal coins were made both by merchants and the rulers of states. Skilled workers produced fine bronze vessels and jade carvings. Lacquer was used as a finish for furniture, and handsome wood carvings were created.

Some Chinese writers composed lovely poetry during this period. Scholars recorded the histories of the various rulers or wandered from city to city offering their advice and wisdom to rulers and their officials.

Literary leaders of the fourth century B.C. expanded the vocabulary of the Chinese language and refined the writing. The Chinese language has gone through many changes since then, but the structure of the Chinese pictogram and ideogram has remained basically the same. Today, a symbol continues to represent an object (pictogram) or an idea (ideogram).

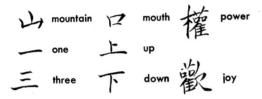

山	mountain	口	mouth	權	power
一	one	上	up		
三	three	下	down	歡	joy

The Chinese written language is beautiful but very difficult to learn. There is a different symbol for every word. The language can be mastered only by memorizing as many of the 40,000 symbols as possible. Today the Chinese Communists are determined to change the structure of the language.

Confucius: A Great Teacher

Of all the Chinese accomplishments of the Chou period, none was more important than the work in philosophy. Chinese philosophy has been deeply influenced by Confucius, or K'ung-fu-tze, which means K'ung the Master. Confucius was born in 551 B.C. in Lu, one of the independent kingdoms during the later years of the Chou dynasty. As a child, he was not very attractive physically. Yet, as Confucius himself later said, fine physical appearance no more makes a great person than a lovely rice blossom guarantees good grain.

When he was twenty-two, Confucius established a school in his home. He was a great teacher and soon attracted a group of devoted followers. Later in life he travelled from kingdom to kingdom instructing rulers and nobles in the philosophy of good government.

Fragments of Chou bronze and iron weapons. During the Chou dynasty the Chinese developed iron mining and smelting.

When he died in Lu at the age of 72, he left behind a heritage of wisdom. Confucius was fortunate to have students who listened carefully and wrote down his sayings. This collection, the *Analects,* and some volumes which Confucius himself compiled form the basis of what is called "Confucianism." For over 2,000 years, his observations on all aspects of life have had a deep influence on the Chinese.

Confucius Seeks Order and Harmony

Confucius lived at a time when the Chou dynasty could no longer control the country. Independent kingdoms fought each other to gain more power, and confusion spread throughout the land. The advice that Confucius gave was concerned with the best ways of keeping order and harmony in a troubled world. This great scholar tried to answer the question: How can people live together in peace and happiness?

Confucius' answer can be found in six of his important principles.

1. The importance of a person's life on this earth. Confucius believed that a person's main purpose was to lead a happy and useful life on this earth. We, he said, should not concern ourselves with questions about the nature of heaven and an afterlife. Rather, we should live out our lives here in accordance with our own nature.

As Confucius said, "We don't know yet about life, how can we know about death?" Therefore, "the superior man discusses all questions of conduct on the basis of himself as the standard" — and not by thinking of punishment and reward in afterlife.

2. The Golden Rule. Confucius said, "Do not do unto others what you do not want others to do unto you." This "Golden Rule," it is important to remember, is a part of every major religion.

3. The middle way. Confucius believed that it is not wise to go to extremes in anything that we do. It is better to take the "middle way" and be moderate in our acts. For example, he felt that we should be neither cowardly nor foolishly bold—rather, we should be courageous, which is the "middle way." As Confucius said: "To go a little too far is as bad as not going far enough."

4. The five relationships. Confucius believed that the five most important relationships in life are

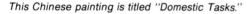

This Chinese painting is titled "Domestic Tasks."

The Great Wall of China was over one thousand eight hundred miles long. About 214 B.C. Shih Huang Ti had various walls that had been built earlier linked to form the Great Wall.

between ruler and subject, father and son, husband and wife, elder brother and younger brother, and friend and friend. According to Confucius, if each of these five relationships were happy, there would be order and harmony in the world.

5. Respect for ancestors. Confucius believed that we should respect our ancestors and heed their words of wisdom.

6. Good government depends on good people. Confucius believed that when the character of the ruler is good, the government will be good.

Lao-Tse Searches for Peace

Another Chinese scholar, Lao-Tse (604–531 B.C.), also sought the answer to the question: How can people live in peace? His answer was quite different from that of Confucius. Lao-Tse believed in the following principles: 1. We should stop striving for success or to "get ahead." We should relax completely and let nature take its course. 2. We should cease to worry about worldly affairs. Nothing should disturb us. We should sit back and say to ourselves: "Nothing matters to a person who says nothing matters." 3. If we can forget completely about worldly problems and personal ambi-

tions, we may be able to lose ourselves in that wonderful peace and calm that runs through the universe.

These principles formed the basis of a philosophy called *Taoism*. "Tao" means "way" or "road." Sometimes this means the "way of nature"; sometimes it is the Taoist way of wise living. In time some Chinese followed Taoism as a religion. Many Chinese valued the wisdom of Confucianism and also tried to follow the principles of Taoism.

The Position of Women

Confucius described the position of women in Chinese society when discussing the importance of obedience. Society, he believed, rests upon the obedience of children to their parents, and of the wife to her husband. Girls were married around the age of sixteen. A girl was trained to obey others gracefully. As a child, she was expected to obey her father and eldest brother; as a wife, she was expected to obey her husband and his mother. She could be divorced if she had no children or was often sick or neglected her duties. During a period of famine, poor families could sell their daughters or place them in the home of a wealthy family.

In practice the senior female family member of the family usually ran the household. She hired, dismissed, and punished the servants, and supervised household accounts. She took part in the arrangement of all family marriages. In rich and official families women often were given some education. They played a crucial role in passing on Chinese culture to the next generation.

Check on Your Reading

1. Describe feudalism in China during the Chou dynasty.
2. Give several reasons why the Chou period is known as China's "Classical Age."
3. What are the principal teachings of Confucius?
4. Describe the position of women in early China.

4. The First Chinese Empire Is Established

During the Classical Age, rulers of the northwest state of Ch'in strengthened their country and government. In the third century B.C., the ruler of Ch'in conquered the other states of the old Chou kingdom and united them under his command. He then took the title of First Emperor, or Shih Huang Ti (246-210 B.C.). The Ch'in dynasty lasted only about thirty years, but the accomplish-ments of the emperor were so impressive that the country over which he ruled came to be known to foreigners as "China."

Shih Huang Ti Rules China

To protect his empire, Shih Huang Ti ordered that the various walls to the north be joined together in what is called the "Great Wall." This great wall stretches from Kansu eastward for 1,400 miles to the Pacific Ocean. Then he increased his empire by conquering land as far south as what is present-day Vietnam. (See the map on page 68.)

Shih Huang Ti Sets the Pattern for Future Dynasties

The old feudal states were abolished, and all the lands of "China" were consolidated into one state ruled by the central government of the emperor. The unified empire was divided into districts called "commanderies." The commanderies were divided into counties, which became the units of local government. Counties were responsible to commanderies. Commanderies were responsible to the central government at the Ch'in capital under the direct supervision of the emperor.

This central government was served by officials who did not inherit their office. All members of the government staff, or bureaucracy, were considered

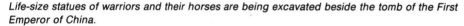

Life-size statues of warriors and their horses are being excavated beside the tomb of the First Emperor of China.

appointees of the emperor. They held their offices as long as he was satisfied with them.

The Ch'in government set up standard weights, measures, and coinage throughout the empire. A network of roads was built to connect the capital with every part of the empire. Waterways were improved, and canals were built to connect important rivers. Great irrigation systems were constructed to increase the amount of farmland.

After the death of Shih Huang Ti, the next ruler was not strong enough to prevent revolt. His government was overthrown, and about 202 B.C. a new dynasty, the Han, took control of the country.

Although the Ch'in dynasty lasted just a short time, it was a turning point in Chinese civilization.

The government that developed under the emperor became the model for the future Chinese political organization.

During the lifetime of Shih Huang Ti, a great tomb was built for the First Emperor. The tomb was covered with a huge mound that was made to resemble a natural hill. This tomb is now being excavated and studied by Chinese archaeologists.

Check on Your Reading

1. What is believed concerning how China got its name?
2. How did Shih Huang Ti unify China? Describe the government he set up.

LET'S MEET THE PEOPLE

A Chinese Son

The Chinese son knew that one of the main purposes in life was to serve his parents. As a child, he soon found that there was much work for children to do. At the first crowing of the cock each morning, he rose, gathered up his sleeping mat, washed his hands and mouth, and dressed. Next he hurried to his parents and asked them if they were well. Then he brought them water with which to wash, and food.

When the Chinese son married, he brought his wife home to live with him and his parents. The wife was respected by her husband. Each morning the wife went to the area where her mother-in-law and father-in-law slept and asked them if their dress was "too warm or too cold." If they had a pain or an itch, the wife "respectfully" rubbed the affected part with her fingers. If her husband's parents were disagreeable, the wife would not complain. She knew her husband was forbidden to offend his father and mother—even when they were wrong—for he had been taught:

When the parents are in error, the son with a humble spirit, pleasing [face], and gentle tone, must point it out to them . . . and if the parents, irritated and displeased [by his criticism], then [punish] their son till the blood flows from him, even then he must not harbor the least resentment; but, on the contrary, should treat them with increased respect and dutifulness.

The Chinese son knew that when his parents died, he would be expected to show them as much honor as when they were alive. He had learned: "Although your father and mother are dead, if you propose to yourself any good work, only [think] how it will make their names illustrious, and your purpose will be fixed."

The Chinese son respected and honored his parents at all times. Soon his own small children would learn to respect him in the same way!

The preceding account is based largely on material appearing in the *Li ki,* an ancient book of rites that Confucius valued.

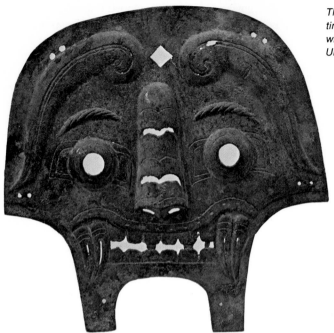

The purpose of this bronze mask from the time of the Chou dynasty was unknown when it was purchased by a museum in the United States.

CHAPTER REVIEW

Think and Discuss

1. Is loyalty an essential feature of other governments as it is of feudalism? Why?
2. Is Confucian philosophy also a religion? What are the differences between a philosophy and a religion?
3. Do you think it is wise to take the "middle way" and never to go to extremes? Why?
4. How might a belief in Taoism affect a country's civilization?
5. Do you agree or disagree with the statement: "Increasing trade among countries is a good way to keep the peace"? Why?
6. How did the Chinese attitude toward a family ruled by the father affect the position of women in Chinese society?
7. The rulers of the first Chinese dynasties strengthened their government by improving irrigation systems. Compare this with the significance of irrigation in Mesopotamia and Egypt.

Past and Present

1. Read articles about the People's Republic of China today. Do you find any ancient Chinese influences that make Chinese communism different from Russian communism? What are they?
2. Emperor Shih Huang Ti banned and had burned all books of Confucianism because he believed that they were hostile to the strong government he wanted to develop. Yet later dynasties reinstated Confucianism and it became a key feature in Chinese civilization. In 1974 the communist government of the People's Republic of China condemned Confucius and his ideas. Four years later, it restored Confucius to a position of importance and declared that he had been wrongly condemned. How can you explain this change?

Activities

1. For many years little archaeological work was done in China. In recent years Chinese archaeologists have been at work all over China. Read articles and books on their work and report your findings to the class. For example, there is an interesting article in the April 1978 *National Geographic* on the excavation of the tomb of the first emperor.
2. On an outline map of the world, shade in the four centers of ancient civilization that you have learned about in this unit.

3. Make a chart of the ancient civilizations you have studied in this unit. Under each civilization list its major achievements.

Analyzing a Hypothesis

Archaeology means "the study of everything ancient." Almost all of our knowledge of ancient peoples is the product of archaeological work. While computers and other sophisticated instruments have joined hand shovels and dust brushes in the archaeologist's tool kit, the same set of questions guides all archaeological investigation:

What is the object? What was its use? When, where, and by whom was it made? How was it made? What does it tell us about the people who made and used it?

Answers to these questions help us understand how people lived many thousands of years ago.

But often archaeologists discover artifacts they cannot explain. When bronze masks like the one shown on the opposite page were found, experts disagreed on what they were. Because some masks had been found in burial pits which contained chariots, it was thought they were attached to the chariots to frighten the enemy. Some experts argued that the masks were used with ceremonial puppets. Still others thought they might be used by shamans, or priests, during the burial ceremony. The masks were hammered out of a thin sheet of bronze, and measured just less than a foot square. Can you suggest how the masks were used?

Finally, the answer was discovered in a new excavation which contained the remains of a chariot and of the horses that pulled it. The mask was found just as shown in the picture below. What was it used for?

Archaeology is not limited to professionals. Many amateur groups have formed to investigate their own local areas. Find out if there is an archaeological association in your state or region. You can also do an archaeological excavation right in your own school. At the end of the day find a classroom wastebasket in a room that you do not use. Pick out the contents, a layer at a time. Note down each item that you find. Can you reconstruct some of the things that happened in the room during the day? Can you tell who was in the room? Are there any artifacts you cannot explain? How certain can you be about your answers?

In the 1950s, masks like the one on this page were found in tombs in China. These masks were attached to the heads of horses, as shown in the photo. Perhaps such masks were to frighten enemies.

2

Early Builders of
the Western Heritage

What do the Greeks, the Romans, the Israelites, and the creators of Christianity have in common? They were all builders of Western civilization. Most of these people built on the foundations laid by the ancient civilizations of the Middle East and Egypt. On these foundations they developed ways of living, thinking, and making tools and products. They created ideas about the individual, art, government, philosophy, morality, and religion that are essential parts of civilization in the United States today. In learning about these people, we are learning about our beginnings and, therefore, about ourselves.

5

The Greeks Build a Western Civilization

KEYNOTE

People from all over ancient Greece came to Delphi to seek advice at the shrine of the god Apollo. There they saw the words "Know Thyself" over the entrance of one of the temples. It demonstrated that to the Greeks the individual was very important.

Most of Greece was made up of small, independent city-states. Together the citizens of these city-states formed a civilization that was quite different from the civilizations that were discussed in Unit 1. The people of the city-state of Athens were probably the first to aim at the idea of democracy. In fact, "democracy" comes from a Greek word meaning "the rule of the people." Many of the world's first great dramatists, philosophers, and historians were Greek. The Greeks were also among the first to study botany, medicine, zoology—the world around them—from a scientific basis. This civilization created by the Greeks forms a basis of what we call "Western" civilization.

An airview of the southern part of the Greek peninsula.

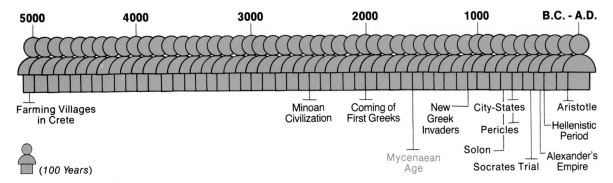

5000	4000	3000	2000	1000	B.C. - A.D.

Farming Villages
in Crete

Minoan
Civilization

Coming of
First Greeks

New
Greek
Invaders

City-States

Pericles

Aristotle

Hellenistic
Period

Mycenaean
Age

Solon

Socrates Trial

Alexander's
Empire

(100 Years)

1. The Land and the People

Ancient Greece included an area of about 300 square miles. In the center of this area was the island-dotted Aegean Sea. Most of Greece was made up of small city-states on the peninsula of Greece, the islands of the Aegean, and the coast of Asia Minor. (See the map on page 82.)

Geography and Culture

The Aegean and its islands link the peninsula of Greece and the coast of Asia Minor. The Greek peninsula in southeastern Europe is rimmed by the Ionian Sea to the west, the Mediterranean Sea to the south, and the Aegean Sea to the east. The Gulf of Corinth drives a wedge between the southern part of the peninsula and the land to the north. The southern part is called the *Peloponnesus*. Nowhere are the people of the southern and central parts of the Greek peninsula more than forty miles from the sea. It is easy to understand why the sea played an important part in Greek culture and history. "Like frogs around a pond, we have settled around the shores of the sea," wrote a famous Greek philosopher, Plato.

Greece developed on the frontier of the great civilizations of Egypt and the Middle East. People with goods and ideas from the civilizations of the Middle East could make their way to the coast of Asia Minor and then across the Aegean Sea. The Mediterranean Sea provided a waterway between Egypt and Greece. At the same time the sea provided a partial barrier against invaders. The people of Greece could borrow ideas and knowledge from others, but they could still protect and build their own civilization.

Mountains and inlets of the sea divided the Greek peninsula into small plains and valleys, helping to separate the people of ancient Greece into small city-states. Mountains also limited the amount of land available for farming. Individual farmers worked the land and lived in small communities. Farming in Greece was different from farming in Mesopotamia, Egypt, China, and India. In these areas farmers worked together using great irrigation systems. In Greece the individual farmer depended on winter rains to water the crops.

Early Peoples

Archaeologists have studied many sites on the peninsula of Greece and the large island of Crete to the south. They have learned that about 6000 B.C. farming villages began to appear. Somewhat later pottery was made in these villages. Then, by about 3000 B.C. objects made of bronze, gold, and silver began to be used. Most archaeologists believe that the knowledge of farming and of the use of bronze and precious metals spread to Greece and to Crete from the East.

The Minoan Civilization

It is believed that civilization began to develop on Crete about 2700 B.C. when people from Asia Minor settled on the island. Cities were built at Knossos and other sites. In time the ruler at Knossos won control over the other cities. A network of roads linked Knossos with these other cities. The kings of Crete were given the title of "Minos," so archaeologists called the civilization "Minoan."

Most Cretans were farmers; but the wealth of Minoan civilization came from trade. Cretan artists fashioned pottery, jewelry, and objects of ivory and bronze for export. Traders started settlements on some of the islands of the Aegean and on the coast of Asia Minor. The Minoan kings collected tribute from these settlements and from some of the people on the peninsula of Greece.

The kings and wealthy families lived in handsome and comfortable palaces and homes. Living

81

Ancient Greece

The Aegean Sea and its islands linked the lands of the ancient Greeks on the peninsula of Greece and on the coast of Asia Minor. The small map shows the relation of the lands of the Greeks to the ancient world around the Mediterranean Sea.

quarters surrounded central courtyards and were equipped with plumbing, drains, and bathrooms. Delightful wall paintings of plants, animals, and people decorated many of the rooms. Games and other entertainments were held in palace court-yards. Palace storerooms contained large clay vessels for storing wine, grain, and olive oil. Scribes used clay tablets to keep records of trade and the king's goods.

The Coming of the First Greeks

Around 2000 B.C. tribes of herders and warriors moved into the peninsula of Greece from the north. Led by chieftains, these nomads conquered the people already living in Greece and set up small kingdoms. They learned much from the people they conquered, and many settled down as farmers in villages.

In time the conquerors built fortified palaces. The king of Mycenae, for example, ruled from his walled palace on a hilltop. Here artisans applied the techniques learned from the Cretans to make pottery, bronze swords, and handsome jewelry.

Around the walled palace most of the people lived in small farming villages. The king of Mycenae became the most powerful ruler in Greece; so this first period of Greek development is called the "Mycenaean Age."

The Mycenaean kings and their warriors gained much of their wealth from trade and from raiding expeditions. Their ships sailed all over the Aegean and to other parts of the Mediterranean Sea. About 1400 B.C. they conquered Crete and adapted the Minoan writing to their own Greek language.

A Troubled Period

About 1100 B.C. a new wave of Greek-speaking nomads and warriors moved into Greece from the north. These newcomers had learned how to forge weapons from iron and were able to conquer the Mycenaeans. Mycenae was burned and pillaged. All over Greece royal palaces and villages were destroyed.

Greece entered what some historians call a "Dark Age." When they uncover more information about this period they may discard the word "dark."

Tales of Heroes, Goddesses, and Gods

Settled life had been disrupted all over the Greek world. Writing had disappeared when the palaces and their record-keeping officials were destroyed. Gradually different chieftains set up their rule over small kingdoms. These kings enjoyed hearing poets recite stories about the great days of the Mycenaean leaders. Many of the stories told of a long war fought by Mycenaean leaders against the city of Troy on the coast of Asia Minor. These tales were recited over and over again for hundreds of years.

A great poet called Homer, or perhaps several poets to whose work Homer's name has been attached, brought some of these stories together in a long poem of heroic adventure, an epic, called the *Iliad*. The *Iliad* tells of the adventures of heroes in the war against Troy. Experts believe that the *Iliad* is a mixture of fact and fiction. It is also a mixture of life during the Mycenaean Age and during the so-called "Dark Age."

Homer or perhaps another poet also combined other stories into the *Odyssey*, an epic that tells of the wanderings of the hero Odysseus after the war. The *Iliad* and the *Odyssey* are part of our Western heritage from the Greeks.

According to the *Iliad* and the *Odyssey*, the Greeks of this period were farmers, herders, and traders. When they exchanged goods, they often used cattle as a standard of value. The fact that a slave might be bought for as little as four head of cattle, while a suit of armor cost nine, indicates that the needs of war sometimes were more important than people.

These epics reveal much about the religion of the Greeks of that time. They believed in gods and goddesses who had many human traits and often took part in the lives of human beings. These gods and goddesses, who often laughed, boasted, and argued with each other, were said to live above the clouds of Mount Olympus in northern Greece. Each goddess or god had some power over the world of nature and of human beings. For example, Athena was the goddess of wisdom, and Apollo was the god of the sun, health, and music. Demeter was the goddess of crops. Zeus ruled over all of the gods and goddesses.

The *Iliad* and the *Odyssey* also reveal the individualistic values of the early Greeks. These epics glorify the individual's valor against all odds. They emphasize that the most serious weakness is cowardice or the failure to seek heroic deeds. A hero's

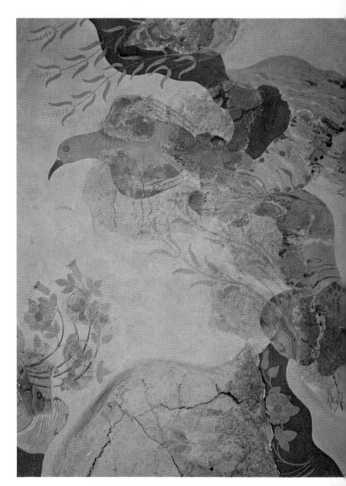

This painting was discovered on the wall of a house in the ruins of ancient Knossos.

main duty is to find the honor that will bring glory. In the *Iliad* the Trojan leader Hector joyfully faces death in battle because he will be remembered for his bravery. He says: "Then men will say in . . . generations to come as they sail along this shore, 'There is the grave of a man dead long ago, a champion whom famous Hector slew.' So my fame will never be forgotten."

These great epic poems have survived because they were set down in writing. This was possible because about the time they were composed the Greeks developed an alphabet and writing. They borrowed most of this alphabet from Phoenician traders.

The Greeks Built Colonies

By 800 B.C. city-states had been set up in the Greek peninsula, on the islands of the Aegean, and on the coast of Asia Minor. The Greeks had learned how to build and sail ships and were trading with people around the Mediterranean and Black seas. Many Greek states also minted their own coins, an idea borrowed from Asia Minor.

At the same time, many Greek families faced increasing problems. Nobles controlled much of the farmland. The small farmers barely supported themselves. Population was increasing and often there was not enough food for everyone. Some said that the god Zeus "in the wrath of his heart" had hidden the good things of life.

Through trade the Greeks had learned much about the world around them. Now the Greek city-states used their knowledge to solve some of their problems. From about 800 to 600 B.C. many Greek states sent some of their people out to build colonies. During this period the Greeks built colonies along the Black Sea, the coast of North Africa, Sicily, southern Italy, and southern France.

These Greek colonies soon grew so strong that they often acted independently of their home states. Still they kept some ties with their homelands and

This Greek vase of the fourth century B.C. shows a scene from the Odyssey. Odysseus, in the center, is visiting the Under World.

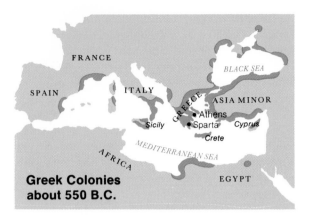

Greek Colonies about 550 B.C.

The Greeks established colonies from the Black Sea to what is now Spain. They all became part of the world of Greater Greece.

became a part of the world of Greater Greece shown on the map above.

Greek colonization had several important results. It led to increased trade. It helped bring about the system of exchange by money.

Check on Your Reading

1. How did geography affect Greek culture?
2. Why can we say that the Cretans had a civilization?
3. What kind of civilization did the early Greeks build in Greece?
4. What do the *Iliad* and the *Odyssey* describe?
5. Why did the Greeks build colonies after 800 B.C.?

2. The City-State: A Greek's "Country"

By 600 B.C. there were many city-states on the Greek peninsula, on the islands in the Aegean, and on the coast of Asia Minor. The city-state had two main parts. The city was the center of government. Around it were farms and villages.

Most cities were built around a fortified hill called an *acropolis*. At first the acropolis was largely occupied by the king's palace. Later, the main temples of the city were built on the acropolis. Below it were the marketplace, theater, government meeting-places, and homes of the people.

These city-states were quite small by our standards today. They ranged from about fifty to five hundred square miles. Some city-states held about five thousand people each, while the city-state of Athens had about a third of a million.

Each city-state was separate and independent from the others. A Greek who was a citizen of a city-state owed all loyalty to that city-state. The city-state was a person's country; each citizen was expected to die to defend it if necessary.

The Government of the City-State

By about 750 B.C. kings had been overthrown or deprived of their power in many Greek city-states. Their power was taken over by wealthy nobles, or aristocrats, who owned large amounts of land. This change was an important step from government by a single ruler to government by a group of people.

In the period from the eighth century to the fifth century the city-states experimented with many types of government. Although not all of the city-states developed in the same way, some of them moved through five forms of government. Starting with a monarchy, they changed to an aristocracy. Then some changed to plutocracy, tyranny, and democracy, as the chart below shows.

It is important to remember that not all the city-states turned to democracy. However, the creation of democracy by 500 B.C. in some city-states was one of the greatest developments in the growth of civilization. The Greeks would become known in history as the first people to discard the idea that one person or a few persons had the right to rule over all the people. This was a step on the way to the ideal of political equality.

Solon Reforms Athens

The story of the development of Greek democracy is in large part the story of Athens. By 600 B.C. Athenians were trading all over the Mediterranean, exporting metal products, cloth, pottery, and olive oil. Owners of shops enlarged their business to take part in this growing trade. Many shop owners bought slaves to do much of the work. These newly wealthy merchants wanted a share in the government of nobles.

At the same time the small farmers found life increasingly difficult. They could not compete with the large farms of the nobles. They sank deeper and deeper into debt. Many had to sell their land. Others were sold into slavery to pay their debts.

In 594 B.C. Solon, a wealthy noble, received

Five forms of government of the city-state

APPROXIMATE TIME	FORM OF GOVERNMENT	FEATURE OF GOVERNMENT	PRIMARY CAUSE OF CHANGE TO NEXT FORM OF GOVERNMENT
8th century B.C.	Monarchy	Rule by a king who gained his power by inheriting it and passed it on to his son.	Powerful landholding nobles desired to run the government.
7th century B.C.	Aristocracy	Rule by a small number of men belonging to important families. (In the Greek city-states, these men usually owned large areas of land.)	Wealthy merchants felt that they were more important than their aristocratic rulers.
7th century B.C.	Plutocracy	Rule by a small number of men of wealth. (In the Greek city-states, many of these men acquired their riches through commerce.)	The new rulers were often more concerned with personal gains than with the good of the city-state.
6th century B.C.	Tyranny	Rule by one man, the tyrant, who usually seized power by force. He did not rule by inheritance (as a king) or by social position (as an aristocrat) or by wealth (as a plutocrat), but by personal strength.	Several tyrants worked hard, introduced needed reforms, and gained the support of the people. However, some of them deprived men of liberty and justice.
5th century B.C.	Democracy	Rule by the citizens.	Lack of unity.

A model of the Acropolis of Athens as it was rebuilt under the direction of Pericles. At the top right is the Parthenon, the temple of Athena, guardian of Athens. Notice the people walking up to the entrance.

special powers to improve life and government in Athens. He repealed most of the harsh laws of Athens that had been passed several centuries earlier. He also freed men forced into slavery because of debt and cancelled the debts of farmers.

Most important were his reforms of the government. He set up a new constitution that gave all citizens the right to vote in a great general assembly. All free men were given equal rights in the courts. Anyone who lost a lawsuit could appeal to a jury of citizens who were chosen by *lot;* that is, by an impartial drawing. These reforms were major steps toward the ideal of democracy, or direct "rule by the people."

Pericles Guides Athenian Democracy

The reforms of Solon were followed by those of other leaders. From 460 B.C. to 429 B.C. the government was directed by a great statesman, Pericles. Under Pericles the Athenian government gave con-

siderable power to its citizens. This democracy, however, was limited. Out of a population of about 315,000 people there were only 43,000 full citizens. These were native-born males over the age of twenty-one. Athenian women, 115,000 slaves, 29,000 Greeks from other city-states, and non-Greeks could not vote.

All citizens were expected to take an active part in the government. Pericles pointed out: "We . . . regard a man who takes no interest in public affairs not as a harmless, but as a useless, character." When meetings of the assembly were held all citizens were expected to attend. Sometimes officials went to the marketplace to find citizens who had not gone to such meetings. These officials carried a rope dipped in wet red dye. They threatened to place the rope around the offenders and pull them from the marketplace to the assembly. Since a red spot on a man's clothing meant a fine, citizens hurried to their duties.

The "Voice of the Citizen" Is Heard

Athenian citizens did not rule through representatives but took part directly in the government. Except for farmers who could not reach the center of Athens easily, the citizens served on the following organs of government:

1. GENERAL ASSEMBLY: LEGISLATURE. The *General Assembly* was the organ that gave citizens the best chance to express their opinions. All Athenian citizens were members of this body, which met anywhere from ten to fifty times a year. The General Assembly's principal duty was to vote on laws—that is, it was a legislature.

2. COUNCIL OF FIVE HUNDRED: EXECUTIVE. A second organ, the *Council of Five Hundred,* served as the executive body—that is, it executed, or carried out, the laws. It also proposed legislation for the General Assembly to vote on, and it controlled financial affairs. Each region of the city-state was represented on the Council by citizens chosen by lot.

3. TEN GENERALS: CHIEF EXECUTIVES. In addition, the General Assembly elected ten generals each year to help the Council of Five Hundred make day-to-day decisions. These men were more than military leaders in war. They were also directors of the government, or chief executives, in peace. Pericles, for example, was reelected a general for thirty years because he was an excellent leader in peace and in war.

4. JURY SYSTEM: JUDICIARY. Citizens took turns serving on juries, and they were paid, so the poor as well as the rich could be jurors. The juries usually numbered from 201 to 501 or more members. Citizens were really judge and jury. They gave their verdict and also determined the punishment that the accused was to receive. Since there were no professional public prosecutors or defense attorneys, each citizen did his own accusing and made his own defense.

Daily Life of the Athenian

A citizen would greet his neighbor in the morning with "Chaire!", meaning "Hail!" or "Rejoice." Most Athenian citizens were farmers. They raised grain, olives, and grapes. Some citizens were wealthy landowners or rich merchants who stayed in Athens and let others work for them. Others were potters, carpenters, craftsmen, and shopkeepers. Slaves did the heavy labor.

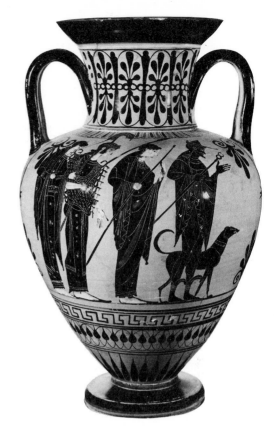

The painting on this Greek vase shows three goddesses and a god. Note the Greek dress.

Athenians, young and old, were active during the day. Children played with dolls, clay soldiers, kites, and tops. There were no public schools. Boys studied music, reading, and writing at the home of some citizen. Girls received no formal education.

Young men sharpened their military skills at the garrison at Piraeus, the busy port of Athens. Citizens often strolled in the *agora,* the noisy marketplace, meeting friends and discussing the latest news. Women usually stayed at home.

The Athenian citizen dressed in a knee-length woolen tunic that was pinned at each shoulder. The tunic for a woman fell below her knees. A white woolen cloak was worn over the tunic. Most men and women wore sandals or boots.

The citizen usually was careful about his appearance. He oiled his hair to shield it from the sun, and he visited a barber to have his beard trimmed. Women used mirrors, hairpins, tweezers, creams, and rouge. They also rubbed lampblack under their eyes. To increase their height, they placed high cork soles on the bottoms of their shoes.

A citizen's home was made of sunbaked brick. It usually had no windows. Small sleeping rooms, a dining room, a living room, and a kitchen surrounded an open central court. The court let sunlight in during the day. At night, olive oil lamps provided light.

The furniture consisted of a few attactively designed couches, benches, stools, and chests. There was no running water or plumbing. Garbage disposal was handled by opening the door, shouting a warning, and throwing it into the street.

There were many fine painted pots and bronze vessels in the home, but eating utensils were as scanty as furniture. The Greeks did not use knives or forks. They ate with their fingers. Knives and forks were not developed until over a thousand years later.

Sparta Was a Different Kind of City-State

In the southern part of the Peloponnesus peninsula was another important city-state whose center was at Sparta. The people of Sparta believed that the main purpose of government was to train good soldiers, not democratic citizens.

The citizens of Sparta stressed the importance of military strength because they were few in number. By the sixth century B.C., most of the population were *helots*. Helots had been defeated in war and forced to farm the land under the orders of their Spartan masters. In addition to the helots, there were many free Greeks from other city-states who handled trade and craft work. Since there was always a danger that the helots might revolt against their masters, the Spartan citizens needed to be trained as soldiers.

The education of a future Spartan citizen was therefore a military one. It began almost at birth. If a baby were "stout and well made," it was permitted to live. If it were "puny and ill-shaped," it was left on a hillside to die. Newborn children were bathed in wine, instead of water, to help them "acquire firmness . . . like steel."

At the age of seven, a Spartan boy was placed in a community training center along with about sixty other boys. Here his leaders toughened his body by making him walk barefoot, sleep on a bed of reeds, and wear a single garment in even the coldest weather. He was taught little reading and writing,

for such knowledge was thought to be unnecessary for a future soldier. Instead, he learned to run, wrestle, swim, sing military songs, and fight. To build up his courage, he was beaten until he bled. To develop his cunning, he was encouraged to steal. If he were caught stealing, the boy was "whipped without mercy" for not being a successful thief!

At eighteen he joined a secret police force whose job it was to kill any helot inclined to rebel. This he did quietly and secretly. Then, for the greater part of his adult life, he served as a hardened soldier of his city-state.

Women in Greek Life

Women's position in Greek life changed at different times through the history of the ancient Greeks. Women were probably never as free as they were in the Minoan society of Crete. Women of the working class ran their homes and also shared in the work of farming and making pottery. Aristocratic women attended the theater and games and took an active part in all social affairs. Women were often in charge of religious ceremonies, and in the Minoan religion, goddesses were more important than gods.

With the coming of the first Greeks, woman's role began to change. Mycenaean Greece was a world of warriors, traders, pirates, and sailors. The family was made up of the husband and wife, all the unmarried children, and the married sons and their wives and children. A married woman lived with the family of her husband. Women worked at home; they ground grain, spun thread, wove cloth, and managed the household. Cooking was usually done by men. Still, women moved about in society, and in the epics and legends women played leading roles in important events.

In the last part of the "Dark Age" women must have reacted strongly to the fact that they were not allowed to take part in or watch the games held every four years at Olympia. There is evidence that women started games of their own that were held every four years. These games were named after the goddess Hera and were called "The Heraea."

By 450 B.C. women had lost most of their rights. Only in Sparta could they inherit property and will it to others. In Athens and other city-states, women were expected to stay in seclusion. A girl was usually only fourteen or fifteen years old when

This tombstone was commissioned by an Athenian husband for his deceased wife. It shows him sorrowfully parting from her.

she married; and she rarely saw her future husband before the marriage. Women did not go with their husbands to dinners at the homes of friends. Even when a man entertained at home, the wife was expected to keep out of sight. Women could not make contracts or incur debts. They could not bring action in the courts. A woman's education was confined to learning how to run a home.

Some women did not accept this subordinate role. One of them was Aspasia. Aspasia came to Athens about 450 B.C. and started a school of philosophy and rhetoric (the art of speaking and writing well). She encouraged women to become educated and to take a more active part in society. Many girls of well-to-do families came to her classes. Men also attended her lectures. Among them was Pericles.

Pericles brought Aspasia home as his wife, though he could not legally marry her as she was a foreigner from the city-state of Miletus on the coast of Asia Minor. She made his home a center where leaders in art, science, literature, philosophy, and government came to exchange ideas and talk about current events.

In the centuries that followed, the position of some women improved. They took a more active role in society. Some became scientists, artists, or writers. Some philosophers admitted women to their schools. Aristodama of Smyrna in Asia Minor gave recitals of her poetry throughout Greece and received many honors.

Check on Your Reading

1. Describe a Greek city-state.
2. What were five forms of government with which some Greek city-states experimented?
3. What were the reforms of Solon?
4. What were the four organs of government in Athens under Pericles?
5. Describe the education that a Spartan received.
6. Describe a woman's position in Athens in 450 B.C.

3. Common Ties Bind the City-States

There were sharp differences between Athens and Sparta. There were also differences among the other city-states. At the same time, common ties bound nearly all Greeks together.

Ancestry and Language

The Greeks were united by their pride in being Greek. They were also united by the fact that they all spoke the same language, with various dialects.

Religion

Religion also bound the people together. In the fifth century B.C., many Greeks still believed in the ancient gods and goddesses described by Homer. Zeus, Apollo, Athena, Demeter, and other gods and goddesses said to live on Mount Olympus were honored as of old.

Oracles

Nearly all Greeks believed in *oracles;* that is, the sacred places and sacred words through which the gods and goddesses were supposed to tell about the

A Greek statue of one of the events in the Olympic Games, the discus throw.

future. One of the most famous oracles was located at Delphi, near the center of the Greek peninsula. Apollo's shrine at Delphi became a religious center for the whole Greek world.

A Greek who brought presents to the priests of this Oracle of Apollo at Delphi could ask a question in writing. A priestess would then sit on a stool over an opening in the rocks, chew laurel leaves, and inhale a vapor which came from the earth. In time, she would become semiconscious or delirious and mumble words in a strange voice. A priest would make a record of her words, usually write them in verse, and then give them to the person who asked the question.

The Olympic Games

The Olympic Games also played an important part in keeping the Greeks together. Every four years Greek citizens from many city-states would gather at Olympia. Since there were no permanent houses at Olympia, they set up tents. Then, for five days, outstanding Greek athletes would compete against each other in such events as the broad jump, discus and javelin throwing, wrestling, boxing, and the two-hundred-yard dash. Winners at the games received wreaths of laurel leaves.

Check on Your Reading

1. What ties helped to unite the Greeks?
2. How did religion help unite the Greeks?
3. What were some events of the Olympic Games?

---

4. The Persian Wars

In the beginning of the fifth century B.C., the Greek city-states were threatened by King Darius of the Persian Empire. Darius and earlier rulers had forced Greek cities in Asia Minor to submit to their rule. In 500 B.C. these cities revolted, aided by a fleet from Athens. Darius crushed the revolt and determined to punish Athens for its interference. His first attempt ended in disaster when storms wrecked the Persian fleet.

Act 1—Battle of Marathon

In 490 B.C. Darius organized a second army to conquer Athens, Sparta, and the rest of Greece. Ships carried this army to the plain of Marathon, only twenty-five miles from the walls of Athens. All of Greece was in danger.

Miltiades, a great Athenian general, took command in this crisis. His army was outnumbered at least four to one. In the battle of Marathon that followed, the Persians fought with bows and arrows, the Greeks with spears. Miltiades cleverly let the Persians charge through the center of his line. Then he attacked them on both sides with groups of his finest spearmen. Bows and arrows were useless at close quarters, and the Persians fled, leaving behind six thousand dead. The Greeks had won the battle at Marathon!

Act 2—Thermopylae and Salamis

Ten years later, King Xerxes, the son of Darius, determined to avenge the defeat of his father. In 480 B.C. he led a tremendous Persian army across the Hellespont, the strait separating Asia and Europe. Then he marched around the coast of the Aegean to Greece. (See the map on page 91.)

Greece During the Persian Wars

In the fifth century B.C. Persian kings ruled the greatest empire in the world. This map shows the main campaigns in the wars between the mighty Persian army and navy and the little city-states of Greece.

When the Persian troops reached the mountain pass at Thermopylae, 85 miles northwest of Athens, they met serious Greek resistance. Here Leonidas, king of Sparta, and about five thousand Greeks made a heroic attempt to stop the Persians. For three days they held back the invaders. Then they were betrayed by a traitor who led the Persians behind their lines. Leonidas sent the main body of the Greek army back to safety. To gain time for them to get away, Leonidas and three hundred picked warriors stood their ground in the pass until almost all were killed.

Spartan heroism at Thermopylae merely delayed the Persians. The way to Athens was open and the Athenians fled in ships to nearby islands. When the Persians reached Athens, they burned the city. Only the Greek fleet of about four hundred warships, most of them Athenian, remained between the Persians and total victory.

Over eight hundred Persian warships attacked this Greek fleet near the island of Salamis. King Xerxes had his throne set up where he could watch the battle. The strategy of the Athenian, Themistocles, and the superior ability of the Greek seamen resulted in defeat of the Persian fleet.

The Greek historian Herodotus wrote that as Xerxes watched the battle he had kind words for only one person, a queen. Queen Artemisia of a city-state of Asia Minor had come with her five warships to fight the Greeks, and she and her forces had done some of the best fighting.

His fleet defeated and his sea routes blocked, Xerxes and most of his troops returned wearily to Persia. The army that they left behind to attack the Greeks was completely routed in 479 B.C. The Persian Wars were over.

Check on Your Reading

1. What started the Persian Wars?
2. Name the chief victories for each side.

5. The Art of Greece: A Riddle Solved

Very few Greeks were wealthy. A Greek city-state was small. Yet the Greeks created some of the loveliest art in the history of the world! Here is a riddle to solve: How did this people produce so many beautiful works of art?

One possible answer is that the Greeks had contact with the Middle East and the Egyptians and learned some of their techniques of art. Another answer is that the Greek city-state stimulated the pride of its people. It encouraged them to surpass other city-states in art and architecture.

In addition, Greek artists were able to study the movements of the human body at public gymnasiums, athletic contests, and the Olympic Games. The muscular bodies of Greek athletes furnished artists with fine living models of the human form.

Finally, Greece was fortunate in having a number of outstanding individual artists and artisans. The solution to the riddle lies in a combination of all of these points.

Greek Art Was Public Art

It was also important that Greek art was public art. Most fine statues were not created for the private collections of wealthy individuals. They were ordered for the people and were placed in the open for all to see.

Beautiful buildings were built as temples and for meeting places. Athenian citizens used their houses merely as places to eat and to sleep. Since the climate of Greece was mild, they spent most of their time outdoors. There they could walk about and enjoy works of art that have rarely been equaled.

Many of the Greek city-states had beautiful art and handsome public buildings. It was Athens, however, that became most famous for its wonderful art. Art treasures were within walking distance of an Athenian's home. Many of them could be seen clearly on the Acropolis. There the Athenians erected beautiful statues and temples to Athena and other gods and goddesses.

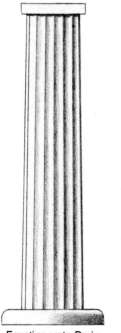 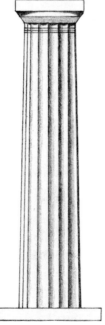 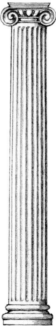 

The three styles of Greek columns probably developed from the Egyptian column.

Egyptian proto-Doric   Doric   Ionic   Corinthian

The Parthenon: Queen of the Acropolis

The loveliest temple on the Athenian acropolis was the temple to Athena, the *Parthenon.* The architects Ictinus and Callicrates planned its design. The great sculptor Phidias supervised its construction and designed the many beautiful reliefs that decorated it.

The Parthenon was rectangular in shape and surrounded by forty-six Doric columns. Greek architects knew that perfectly straight columns often give the appearance of sagging in the middle. The columns of the Parthenon, therefore, were gently curved so that they would appear straight from a distance.

Inside the columns, at the top of the outside wall, was a band, or *frieze,* of sculptures. Here Phidias and his pupils carved scenes of Athens on a great festival day. Brilliant colors were used to make the scenes even more lifelike.

Inside the Parthenon was a large statue of Athena, carved by Phidias from ivory and gold. Behind the temple was another statue of the goddess by Phidias. This bronze statue was seventy feet high and showed Athena as protectress of Athens carrying a shield and spear.

The Appeal of Greek Art Remains Strong

The remains of the Parthenon and other temples throughout Greece have continued to inspire people all over the world. Today Greek influence is seen in our homes and public buildings.

Why has Greek art fascinated people? The answer can be found by noting the appealing features of Greek art. Greek art is balanced and harmonious. Each part of a statue or building seems to fit perfectly into the next, and all blend together naturally. Greek art avoids unnecessary decorations that hide the basic beauty of objects. Greek art has an air of calmness about it. Even an athlete in the process of throwing a discus seems poised and calm. Greek art usually chooses for its subject matter figures and events in which people can take pride, avoiding unimportant or ugly subjects. Many statues show the heroism, beauty, and strength of the Greek gods and goddesses—but few point out their weaknesses. Greek sculpture shows how perfect nature could be. Sculptors eliminated the physical weaknesses of human beings and created figures of the finest physical forms possible.

These features combined to make the work of Greek artists appealing to people all over the world in every century.

Check on Your Reading

1. How did Greek art belong to all the people?
2. Why has Greek art fascinated people?
3. What is meant by *public art?*

This cutaway drawing shows the structure of the Parthenon. Notice that there is a frieze over the pediment and over the inside columns.

6. Philosophers Search for Wisdom

The word *philosophy* means "love of wisdom." Greek philosophers sought the wisdom that would help people to lead happy and worthwhile lives.

The Sophists

Some of the earliest teachers of philosophy were called *Sophists,* or "wisdom-mongers." They taught courses in mathematics, grammar, astronomy, and speech. Many Sophists were good teachers, honestly seeking to impart wisdom. Other Sophists taught tricks for winning arguments in law courts and elsewhere, rather than how to search for truth. For example, here is a conversation to illustrate how a Sophist almost tricked a man into admitting that puppies were his brothers:

You say that you have a dog? [a Sophist]
Yes . . . [the man].
And he has puppies?
Yes . . .
And the dog is the father of them?
Yes . . .
And is he not yours?
To be sure he is.
Then he is a father, and he is yours: therefore, he is your father, and the puppies are your brothers.

Some Sophists taught more than tricks. One of them, Protagoras, made clear that what appears beautiful and good to one person may not seem so to another. No individual should be forced to accept the ideas of others. Sophists also helped to develop grammar, logic, and speech techniques.

Socrates

More important than the Sophists was an Athenian philosopher known as Socrates (469-399 B.C.). Socrates was a stout, baldheaded man with a snub nose. He spent much of his time teaching and asking questions of the people he met. He asked: "What is the purpose of life? What is good? What is justice?" Such questions stimulated people to examine the conduct of their lives. Socrates believed that "a life without inquiry is not worth living."

Socrates wrote nothing himself, but from the writings of his student Plato we know the important ideas he taught. He taught that people should examine their lives carefully to see whether or not their conduct is desirable. Each person should think for himself or herself. Each person should seek knowledge, for knowledge helps a person to be virtuous. Each person should learn to understand himself or herself. "Know Thyself" was the motto of Socrates.

Some leaders of Athens were afraid of these ideas. They accused Socrates of teaching young people dangerous ideas, and they brought him to trial. If Socrates had agreed to stop teaching, he probably would have been freed. He told his accusers:

If you say to me: Socrates, this time you shall be let off, but upon one condition, that you are not to inquire . . . in this way any more . . . I should reply: Men of Athens . . . while I have life . . . I shall never cease from the practice and teaching of philosophy. . . .

Since he refused to change his ways, Socrates was sentenced to die. At the age of seventy, he was executed in the Greek way by being given a cup of the poison hemlock.

Plato

The death of Socrates did not stop other Greeks from continuing the search for wisdom. Plato (about 428-347 B.C.), a student of Socrates, became the leading philosopher. Plato attracted so many followers that he set up a school of philosophy in a grove of trees on the outskirts of Athens. This was known as the Academy.

Plato wrote many *dialogues,* books describing real and imaginary philosophical conversations among his friends. In such dialogues as the *Republic* Plato explained his ideas: People should be guided in their lives by eternal principles, such as justice, honor, goodness, and love. They should stop thinking only of wealth, fine clothing, and rich food; for all material things disappear with time. People should do the jobs for which they are best fitted. Good laborers should work; strong warriors should fight; and people of wisdom should rule. Only the wisest men and women should rule the people. There should be no rule by vote of the majority. Women should have equal rights with men.

Aristotle

One of the students who studied under Plato at the Academy was Aristotle. Aristotle (384-322 B.C.) was born in Macedonia, about two hundred miles north of Athens. He soon became so famous that he was chosen to tutor Alexander, the son and heir of King Philip of Macedon. Then at the age of fifty, Aristotle returned to Athens to set up a school there.

Aristotle was interested in many fields: astronomy, physics, mathematics, anatomy, politics, speech, art, and philosophy. He collected information on over five hundred kinds of living organisms.

From his writings, we know much about the ideas of Aristotle. He believed that people should examine, describe, and classify as many forms of life as possible, since it is important to have scientific knowledge of the world. People should use their ability at reasoning—that is, at thinking out problems—to help them lead happy lives. People should not go to extremes; they should always take the mean. By the word *mean,* Aristotle meant a middle position—"that which is neither too much nor too little for the particular individual." For example, a person should be neither rash nor cowardly. Instead, a person should go between these extremes and be sensibly courageous. People should learn to live with each other. "A person who is unable to live in society or who has no need to do so must be either a beast or a god."

The books, methods, and ideas of Aristotle strongly influenced European scholars for over fifteen hundred years. Even today many students in universities study his writings. One of his wise sayings, which has a very modern ring, is that we "learn by doing."

Check on Your Reading

1. What did the Sophists contribute?
2. What were the principal ideas of Socrates?
3. What do you think of the ideas of Plato?
4. Explain some of the ideas of Aristotle.

---

7. The Greeks Support "People's Theaters"

The Greeks loved to go to the theater, and they had strong opinions on the merits of their playwrights.

The Theater of Dionysus

In the fifth century B.C., the Theater of Dionysus was the most famous in Greece. This was an open-air theater on the southern hillside of the Acropolis of Athens. During the March Festival in honor of the Wine God, over seventeen thousand Athenians sat jammed together on hard wooden seats to watch a series of plays. Tragedies were given in the afternoon. The theater belonged to the public. Admission prices were low, and poor citizens were given the money needed to buy a ticket.

At the foot of the sloping semicircle, where the people sat, was the *orchestra.* The orchestra was a circular area of beaten earth where the actors and chorus performed. Usually only three actors, always men, appeared at the same time. All actors wore huge masks over their heads, so the players could change masks and take many different roles. A chorus of men chanted, gestured, and danced during each play to explain the characters' actions or to help set the mood.

The audience expressed their opinions in a Greek theater. A good play or good acting brought cheers of "Authis! Authis!" (Again! Again!) A poor play or poor acting made the audience hiss and groan.

At the end of the three-day March Festival, five judges, selected from the audience, awarded prizes to the best playwrights and actors. The judges naturally were influenced by the comments and opinions of the audience. Greek theaters were "people's theaters." The people not only owned them but helped select the best plays.

Playwrights Examine Life

Aeschylus (525-456 B.C.) and Sophocles (496-406 B.C.) won fame for the excellence of their tragedies. Their plays stressed two points: Individuals must struggle courageously against fate, or the will of the gods, even if they cannot change the plans that the gods have for them. Individuals can gain wisdom through suffering.

Euripides (about 480-406 B.C.), a third major writer of Greek tragedy, felt that events were the result of natural causes. They were not an expression of the will of the gods and goddesses. Euripides doubted that the Greek gods and goddesses existed. He also condemned war in his play *The Trojan Women.* He was not popular with state and military officials.

Euripides' attacks on the Greek religion did not go unanswered. Aristophanes (about 448-380 B.C.) ridiculed some ideas of Euripides in such comedies as *The Frogs.* Aristophanes was a clever playwright whose puns and coarse humor delighted Greek audiences. He defended religion, opposed war, and

A rehearsal of a play in the partly reconstructed theater in Athens below the Acropolis.

tried to prevent the people from getting too much power.

Aristophanes warned the Athenians against men who were frauds and rascals. Be careful, he said, of the tricky fellows who "tickle your vanity" or praise the richness of Athens.

Check on Your Reading

1. How did the acting and the performance in the Greek theater differ from ours today?
2. What were major ideas of Aeschylus, Sophocles, Euripides, and Aristophanes?

8. Greek Historians, Poets, and Scientists

Greek historians and poets helped people understand themselves and the world around them. Greek scientists and mathematicians made important contributions too.

Greek Historians and Poets

Herodotus (about 484-425 B.C.) wrote a colorful and entertaining history of the Persian Wars. Herodotus is often called the "father of history" because he was among the first to write an organized narrative of past occurrences which can be called "history."

Thucydides (about 460-400 B.C.) is called the first scientific historian. In his *History of the Peloponnesian War,* he tried to check his facts carefully and to present events in an accurate chronological order. He believed that "exact knowledge of the past" was "an aid to the interpretation of the future."

While the Greek historians set down their knowledge of the past, Greek poets described their feelings about the past and present. Pindar (about 518-438 B.C.) authored *lyric poetry,* short poems designed to be sung. He wrote many pieces honoring the victors in athletic games.

Sappho (sixth century B.C.) was the first woman poet whose writings we have. Although only a few of her poems remain, they show that she was a sensitive writer. Sappho was right in predicting:

I think there will be memory
of us yet in after days.

Contributions to Science and Mathematics

The Greeks drew on the scientific knowledge of the Egyptians and Babylonians, added their own ideas, and passed on the information to others. In general there were two features of Greek science. The Greeks reasoned about scientific matters but did few experiments to test their beliefs. That is why their best work was in geometry, and their poorest in physics and chemistry. The Greeks studied the structure and function of the physical world, but usually they did not put their knowledge to practical use. They would be similar to a modern scholar who works out principles of speed but does not apply them to build faster planes or rockets.

Thales (about 640?-546 B.C.) was one of the first persons to see the importance of establishing principles in geometry. Thales also was interested in astronomy. He predicted an eclipse of the sun and probably studied the effects of magnetism.

Pythagoras (about 580-500 B.C.) did important work with numbers and helped to develop several principles of geometry. Greek mathematics certainly is not dead—your high school geometry textbook teaches you many of these same principles!

Other Greeks suggested that the world was not a fixed and rigid place. Heraclitus (540-475 B.C.) believed that everything in life changed except change. Democritus (about 460-370 B.C.) advanced the idea that the universe was composed of invisible atoms that moved about continuously.

Extremely important, too, were the contributions of Hippocrates (about 460-377 B.C.). Hippocrates is known as the "father of medical science" because he taught that diseases were the results of natural causes.

Hippocrates urged his students to observe carefully and classify diseases. Tradition says that he drew up a pledge that new doctors were to take. Modern doctors are familiar with the words of this so-called Hippocratic Oath, which includes the lines:

> I will use treatment to help the sick according to my ability and judgment . . . I will keep pure and holy both my life and my art.

Check on Your Reading

1. Why is Thucydides considered a "scientific historian"?
2. Who were Pindar and Sappho?
3. What contributions did the Greeks make to science and mathematics?
4. Why is Hippocrates called the "father of medical science"?

9. The Peloponnesian War and the Conquest of Greece

Many of the splendid achievements in art, science, and literature took place during the time of Pericles. Pericles was the leader of Athens from about 460 to 429 B.C. He encouraged the Greeks in art, philosophy, and literature. The period of thirty years covered by his administration in Athens is often called the "Golden Age of Athens."

At the same time, however, Greek leaders could not solve the problems caused by the jealous rivalry of the Greek city-states. In 477 B.C., under the leadership of Athens, several Greek city-states did form the Delian League. Members of the League were to continue to be independent, but they were to give money or ships for a common defensive fleet.

In time, Athens changed the original purpose of the League. Athens used federation funds to beautify its city. Athens forced the other city-states to obey it in matters of trade and foreign affairs. Athens soon had so much control over the others that the Delian League became an Athenian empire.

Wars Weaken Athens, Sparta, and Thebes

Angered by the growing power of Athens, Sparta and other city-states fought a long war against Athens and its allies. This Peloponnesian War lasted from 431 to 404 B.C. and ended in the defeat of the Athenians. During the war a great plague killed about a fourth of the Athenians, including Pericles.

Athens was forced to surrender its empire. Then the protective Long Walls built from the city to its port at Piraeus were destroyed. The once proud Athenians had to obey the orders of Sparta.

Sparta proved to be an oppressive leader of the Greeks. As a result, troops from the city-state of Thebes overthrew Spartan rule in 371 B.C. Thebes now tried to lead the Greeks, but within ten years it too lost control.

Athens, Sparta, and Thebes had each failed to bring the Greeks together. The individual ambitions and jealousies of the city-states kept them apart. The disorganized Greeks were a perfect target for the army of a foreign invader.

Philip of Macedonia Conquers the Greeks

The invader came from Macedonia, north of Greece. The Macedonians were a rough Greek-speaking people who lived as shepherds, hunters, and farmers. About the middle of the fourth century B.C., Philip, a Macedonian king, united many of the tribes. Then he molded them into an effective fighting force. He was determined to bring all the Greek city-states under his control by arms or by bribery.

There were some Greeks who saw the danger and warned the people. The great orator Demosthenes, for example, denounced the Athenians for caring more about amusements than defense. He urged them to unite with other Greeks and prepare to meet the Macedonian attack.

In 338 B.C. troops from Athens and Thebes finally united long enough to fight Philip's forces at Chaeronea. The Greeks fought courageously, but the Macedonian cavalry drove them back until they fled from the battle. The independence of the city-states was at an end. The Macedonians controlled the future of Greek civilization.

Alexander the Great Builds a Great Empire

Philip did not long enjoy his conquests. He was killed in 336 B.C. by one of his own officers. His son Alexander became the king of Macedonia and its Greek subjects.

Alexander was twenty years old. He was a handsome, energetic young man who loved sports. Alexander was a fine runner and an excellent horseman and hunter. Military action always pleased him and he looked forward eagerly to the tests of battle. His greatest fear had been that his father would conquer so many towns that there would be none left for him to take when he became king!

Educated by the philosopher Aristotle, Alexander had learned to admire Greek civilization. It is said that he kept Homer's *Iliad* under his pillow at night and enjoyed reading the plays of Aeschylus, Sophocles, and Euripides. Alexander wrote to Aristotle:

> . . . I had rather excel others in the knowledge of what is excellent, than in the extent of my power and dominion.

These words must have been pleasant for Aristotle to read, but Alexander was a man of great ambition. He wanted "opportunities of performing great and illustrious actions."

Conquest provided the best opportunities for "glory." Alexander spent the rest of his life trying to conquer other lands and peoples. He crushed a

Alexander's empire extended from Greece and Egypt to India.

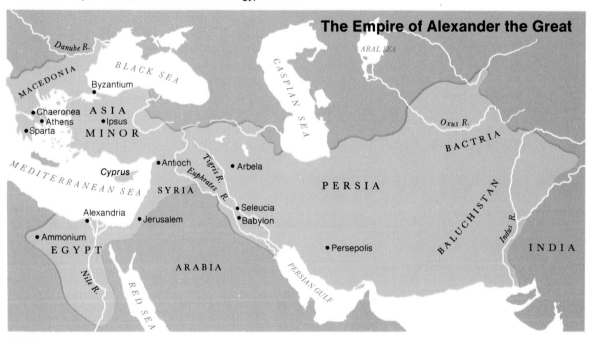

Alexander's Empire and allied states

A mosaic of the great battle in which Alexander defeated Darius III, ruler of the Persian Empire.

Greek revolt and kept all of Greece under Macedonian control. Then he took Asia Minor, Syria, and Egypt. Eventually, the whole Persian Empire and lands as far east as the Indus River fell to his forces.

By 327 B.C. Alexander's empire extended east and west from India to Greece, and north and south from the Black Sea to Egypt, as the map on page 98 shows. Alexander insisted that all the peoples in this empire—both his Macedonians and those whom they had conquered—should feel a sense of unity with each other. "I count all of you as my kinsmen," he told them, and prayed for "fellowship in the realm."

The Accomplishments of Alexander

Alexander the Great died before his ability as an administrator of his empire could be tested. In 323 B.C. he became ill with a fever, and within two weeks he died. At the time of his death, Alexander was not quite thirty-three.

Alexander's empire eventually was divided into three major parts, each ruled by a dynasty founded by one of his generals. Macedonia and Greece were controlled by the Antigonus Gonatas group. Egypt was ruled by the Ptolemy group. Syria and Persia were controlled by the Seleucid group.

Alexander's military empire had split apart;

however, many of his ideas and achievements remained. Alexander had helped to found cities—such as Alexandria in Egypt—as part of his policy to spread Greek ideas. Alexandria developed into a great center of learning.

He had stimulated trade among various parts of his empire. Alexandria and Antioch became the most important trading centers.

Alexander had encouraged scientific investigations. The specimens of plants and animals collected by the specialists who accompanied his army proved valuable to biologists of the period.

He had advanced the idea that people—whether they were Macedonians, Greeks, or Persians—should feel a sense of kinship with each other. As Plutarch, a Greek biographer, wrote:

> [Alexander] believed that he had a mission
> . . . to harmonize men generally, and to be the
> reconciler of the world. . . . Mixing, as in a
> loving-cup, their ways of life and their customs
> . . . he bade them all consider the whole of the
> inhabited world as their country.

Alexander's soldiers and traders brought Greek ideas to the areas they invaded and received many new ideas in exchange. Cultures spread and interacted. Greek art, for example, had considerable influence on Buddhist sculpture in India. Greek civilization came in contact with non-Greek civilizations, including those in the East. This mingling produced a new cultural era known as the *Hellenistic* period.

Check on Your Reading

1. Why did the Delian League fail to unite the Greeks permanently?
2. How did the Peloponnesian War end?
3. Why was Philip of Macedonia able to conquer Greece?
4. Describe Alexander's character and achievements. What happened to his empire?

---

10. The Hellenistic Period

The Hellenistic period lasted from the death of Alexander to about the first century B.C. (from about 322-90 B.C.). During this period there were important changes in art, literature, and philosophy. However, the greatest achievements occurred in the sciences, where Greek and non-Greek scientific ideas mingled to produce remarkable results.

The Sciences Make Important Gains

Euclid gathered and organized Greek knowledge of geometry. Eratosthenes calculated the circumference of the earth, and his figures came close to being right. Aristarchus of Samos suggested the theory that the earth moves around the sun. At this time people believed in the theory that the sun moved around the earth.

Hipparchus developed the technique of finding position by latitude and longitude. He was also one of the first to use trigonometry for the study of astronomy.

No one of the period was more devoted to science than Archimedes (about 287-212 B.C.). It was said that he loved his studies so well that he even drew diagrams when he bathed! Archimedes did outstanding work in physics. He developed principles for floating bodies and demonstrated the many uses of levers, pulleys, and cranes. When his city of Syracuse was attacked, he used his various engines to destroy the enemy's ships.

The work of Archimedes was concerned with both the principles and the practice of science. He showed a basic difference between a Hellenistic and a Greek scientist. Both were interested in developing scientific theories and principles, but the Hellenistic scientist also wished to put them to practical use. The practical inventions of Hellenistic scientists included a steam engine and methods for supplying water and carrying off sewage from cities.

A reconstruction of a Hellenistic city in Asia Minor. The cities built during this period were planned for the comfort of the citizens. In the foreground are the gymnasium and stadium.

Greek and Hellenistic Art Compared

There were also differences between Greek and Hellenistic art. These differences are shown in the chart below.

In general, Greek art has been considered by most critics to be superior to Hellenistic art. On the other hand, some sculpture of the Hellenistic period, such as the Laocoön group, was very fine. The famous *Nike* (or *Victory*) of Samothrace also was striking because it combined several of the best features of Greek and Hellenistic styles.

Hellenistic Writers and Philosophers

Polybius recorded history with considerable accuracy and wisdom. Theocritus created the *pastoral* poem, a short lyric poem dealing with life and beauty in the countryside. Menander wrote clever comedies that pointed out the faults and weaknesses of his time.

Philosophers continued to ask the question: "What is the best way for people to live?" The answers of Epicurus and Zeno were particularly important.

Epicurus (about 342–270 B.C.) and his followers, the *Epicureans,* believed that happiness depended on finding pleasure. Pleasure came from having a healthy body and a calm mind—not from continuous merrymaking. Epicurus wrote that people should use their intelligence to choose between trivial and truly enjoyable things in life:

> By pleasure we mean the absence of pain in
> the body and trouble in the soul. It is not an
> unbroken succession of . . . revelry . . . that
> makes life pleasant; it is sober reasoning which
> searches out the ground for every choice. . . .

Zeno (336–264 B.C.) and later philosophers developed another approach to life known as *stoicism.* Stoics believed that an event became good or bad

This statue of Victory was erected on the island of Samothrace. It is believed that it was to commemorate a Greek naval victory. It is in the Hellenistic style and was designed to appear as if it stood on the prow of a ship.

Greek Sculpture and Architecture	**Hellenistic Sculpture and Architecture**
1. Simple.	1. Elaborate. Stressed large size and ornamentation.
2. Balanced and harmonious.	2. Often lacked balance and harmony.
3. Calm and restrained in appearance.	3. Emotional and active in appearance.
4. Interested in showing various types of gods and heroes. Not concerned with representing the faces and bodies of specific individuals.	4. In many cases, interested in representing the faces and bodies of individual men and women.
5. Considerable use of the Doric column in architecture.	5. Considerable use of the Corinthian column in architecture.

depending on how a person viewed it. For example, a fire was called "bad" by a man whose house had burned down. Yet it was called "good" by his wife who had long wanted a new house and would have one. Actually then, the Stoics said, the fire was neither good nor bad—it was an event. It was a person's attitude that made it good or bad.

The Stoics, therefore, advised people to view all events with calmness and self-control and to accept success and failure without emotion. They believed that if people would use their intelligence to control their passions, they would find peace of mind.

The Stoics also expressed belief in a universal spirit and in the basic kinship of all human beings. They urged that people should live like "one flock on a common pasture feeding together under a common law." This idea later helped to pave the way for the acceptance of Christian teachings.

Check on Your Reading

1. What were the important gains made in science in Hellenistic times?
2. Compare Hellenistic and Greek art.
3. What is Stoicism?

LET'S MEET
THE PEOPLE

An Athenian Juror

The Athenian juror walked to the courtrooms near the marketplace. He entered and sat down on a hard wooden bench covered with a mat. Surrounding him were two hundred other jurors.

The juror listened carefully to the case before him. First he heard the plaintiff, the accuser. Then he paid attention to the defendant, the accused. The statements of the witnesses had been written down at an earlier hearing. Witnesses had little to do at the trial; they could not be cross-examined.

Both plaintiff and defendant had finished speaking. It was time to vote. The juror had two metal discs. The one that was solid was the "not guilty" disc. The one with a hole in it was the "guilty" disc. The juror took the disc with the hole and dropped it into an urn. He was voting: "Guilty." Most of the other jurors agreed.

The juror then watched the defendant rise before him and ask for a light sentence. Standing at their father's side, little children of the accused wept and begged the jury to show mercy. The plaintiff then insisted that the accused had forced his children to weep. The result: the juror and the jury ordered the accused to pay a heavy fine.

His day's work over, the Athenian juror collected his pay and tossed it into his mouth between the cheeks and the gums. He did not want to have to turn this money over to his wife or daughter when he got home.

This sketch of an Athenian juror includes material from a play by Aristophanes (c. 448–388 B.C.); a speech by Demosthenes (4th century B.C.); *A Day in Old Athens* by William Stearns Davis, 1914, Allyn and Bacon, Inc.; and *The Wasps*, trans. by Roger, G. Bell and Sons, Ltd.

CHAPTER REVIEW

Think and Discuss

1. Attack or defend these statements: a) Sparta did not achieve as great a civilization as Athens did because Spartan life and thought were too regimented. b) People who differ to a large degree in their beliefs and practices can unite when they are faced by a common enemy.
2. Why did the colonialism of ancient Greece seem a good practice while today it is regarded as bad policy by most people?
3. Define democracy as the Greeks practiced it. Define democracy as it exists in the United States today. Explain the differences.
4. Can governments prevent ideas they consider

unacceptable from spreading by killing persons who teach these ideas? Explain your answer.

5. Plato believed that only the wise should rule. Do you think this idea is a good or bad one? Why?

6. Why do you think the Greeks were more interested in the principles and theories of science than in their practical application?

7. Do you agree or disagree with these statements? Why? a) When two civilizations come into contact with each other, a stronger civilization will result. b) The person who spreads ideas is as important to the world as the person who first had the idea.

Past and Present

1. Can we avoid the mistakes of past history? If so, how? Give examples.

2. Find examples of Doric, Ionic, and Corinthian columns in your area.

3. Plato's idea on equal rights for women is still being debated in the United States. Prepare for a discussion of this topic by reading Plato's dialogue on "Equal Rights and Duties for Women."

Activities

1. Write a report on archaeologist Heinrich Schliemann's discoveries of ancient Troy. Or report on the work of Arthur Evans in Crete.

2. The Greeks left a wealth of literature. Read a selection from Greek history, the *Iliad*, or the *Odyssey*. What do you learn about the early Greeks from these sources?

3. Reenact an Athenian Assembly in your class. Some members of the class may act as famous Greeks while others take the parts of artisans. Debate this statement: Resolved, that in a democracy citizens should be required to vote.

4. Write a report on the trial and death of Socrates.

5. Read a Greek play. What ideas did the author express in the play?

Learning from Primary Sources

Unlike the artifacts of prehistoric cultures, the recorded writings of civilized societies speak directly to us across the centuries. Greek literature forms a rich body of primary sources from which historians can reconstruct not only daily activities but attitudes and values which guided Greek society.

In 431 B.C., the Athenian leader Pericles honored the soldiers who had died in battle to defend Athens. His oration is important because it sheds light on how Athenians felt about their society. Read the excerpt below, and then answer each of the questions as carefully as you can.

We are called a democracy because the power to make laws is given to many rather than a few. But while the law gives equal justice to everyone, it has not failed to reward excellence. While every citizen has an equal opportunity to serve the public, we reward our most distinguished citizens by asking them to make our political decisions. Nor do we discriminate against the poor. A man may serve his country no matter how low his position on the social scale. . . . Our city is thrown open to the world. We have never expelled a foreigner nor prevented him from seeing or learning anything that might help him defeat us if he became our enemy. We do not rely upon controlling cities to assure victory. Instead, we depend on the patriotism of our hearts and the skills of our hands. . . . Therefore, our city is an excellent place to live when we are at peace as well as when we are at war. For we are lovers of the beautiful, yet we have simple tastes. We cultivate the mind without losing our manliness. We use our wealth for our real needs, not for luxuries which will give us false prestige. To be poor is no disgrace; the true disgrace is doing nothing to avoid poverty. . . . An Athenian citizen does not put his private affairs before affairs of the state; even our merchants and businessmen know something about politics. We alone believe that a man who takes no interest in public affairs is more than harmless—he is useless.

1. According to Pericles, what are important characteristics of Athenian society?

2. What value is placed on the individual in Athens? What is not important in the society of Athens?

3. To be a successful citizen of Athens, what should a person do?

4. To what extent can you believe Pericles? Would he have any reason not to tell the truth? What knowledge would you need to have in order to find out?

6

The Romans Build an Empire

KEYNOTE

In 500 B.C. Rome was just one of a number of towns in central Italy. The Romans were threatened by enemies abroad and by difficult problems of government at home. Yet in the centuries that followed Rome developed into the capital of the greatest empire in the world!

Today our lives are strongly affected by the achievements of the Romans. The hands of clocks on churches and public buildings often circle around Roman numbers—I, III, VI, IX, XII. The months of July and August are named after two Roman statesmen, Julius and Augustus Caesar. January is named for Janus, the Roman god of gates and doors and therefore of all beginnings. Indeed, the names of nearly all our months come from Roman words. The tradition of baking a wedding cake can be traced back to an old Roman custom. The cold cream that many people use today was probably developed by a physician in Rome.

The Romans adopted and passed on to us the leading achievements of Greek and Hellenistic civilization. Particularly important to us are the original Roman contributions in the fields of government and law, engineering, architecture, and language. Roman achievements in these areas form a fundamental part of the modern world.

This Roman aqueduct carried water to the city of Nîmes in what is now southern France.

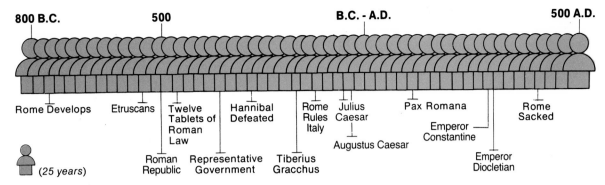

| 800 B.C. | 500 | | | B.C. - A.D. | | | 500 A.D. |

Rome Develops   Etruscans   Twelve Tablets of Roman Law   Hannibal Defeated   Rome Rules Italy   Julius Caesar   Pax Romana   Rome Sacked

Augustus Caesar   Emperor Constantine

Roman Republic   Representative Government   Tiberius Gracchus   Emperor Diocletian

(25 years)

1. The Land and the People

From south central Europe the boot-shaped peninsula of Italy extends over seven hundred miles into the Mediterranean Sea. At its toe is the large island of Sicily. (See the map on page 106.)

Italy has a central position in the Mediterranean area. (See the map on page 113.) The seas to the west, east, and south have provided highways for trade, expansion, and the exchange of ideas with other peoples.

The Land

On the north the Alps stand guard over the wide fertile valley of the Po River. Passes through these mountains connect Italy with the rest of Europe. The Apennine Mountains stretch like a gigantic spine from the Po Valley to the toe of the peninsula. Ranges of hills and low mountains slope down from the Apennines to the sea, dividing the peninsula into many compartments.

Eastern Italy has few harbors and is handicapped by the slopes of the Apennines. The western side of the peninsula has most of the plains and harbors, so civilization developed first in western Italy.

Much of Italy is pleasantly warmed by the sun and gentle winds the year-round. Virgil, a Roman poet, described the contrasts of this land:

stubborn lands and churlish hill-sides . . .
fields strewn wide with woodland berries . . .
soil that is rich, in moisture sweet exulting,
and the plain that teams with grasses.

"Here," he wrote, "is eternal spring, and summer even in months not her own. Twice in the year the cattle breed, twice the trees serve us with fruit."

The Latins Settle Rome

Starting around 2000 B.C.—while the earliest Greeks were migrating into the Aegean area—other people began moving southward into the Italian peninsula. These newcomers came from central Europe and spoke Indo-European languages. Some of them, the Latins, settled on a western plain south of the Tiber River.

One group of Latins built homes on low hills near the river about fifteen miles inland from the sea. They had picked a good location, for they built their settlement of Rome near the spot where major trade routes crossed the main river of western Italy. Around 750 B.C. Rome was a growing town.

The Etruscans Conquer the Latins

Meanwhile two other peoples also moved into Italy. Rome and other Latin towns found themselves sandwiched in between the Greeks to the

This painting of a musician playing a lyre was found in an Etruscan tomb. The Etruscans helped bring civilization to the Romans.

Peninsula of Italy in 700 B.C.

Etruscans   Greek colonies

Northwest of Greece is the peninsula of Italy. Two important influences on the early Romans were the Greeks and the Etruscans.

south and the Etruscans to the north. The Greeks started colonies in southern Italy and Sicily. The Etruscans probably came from Asia Minor and settled north of the Tiber River by about 900 B.C. They were a civilized people who developed small city-states.

The Etruscans expanded southward and, during most of the sixth century B.C., Etruscan kings ruled Rome and other Latin towns. While they occupied Rome, the Etruscans built walls and sewers. They drained the swampy Forum area and paved it. The Forum soon became the center of the government and business activity of Rome. A bridge was built across the Tiber and trade grew. Temples were constructed, and it is believed that the Etruscans taught the Romans how to build arches and vaults. The Etruscans probably had learned these architectural principles from people in the Middle East.

Etruscan work in metals is famous. They mined copper, iron, tin, lead, and silver. They made handsome jewelry and fashioned bronze into beau-

tiful sculptures of people, gods and goddesses, and animals. Etruscan wall paintings discovered in underground tombs show everyday scenes of boating and fishing as well as banquet scenes.

The foundation for the alphabet we use today was borrowed by the Romans from the Etruscans who had taken it from the Greeks. In later times, Roman historians pointed out that many Roman customs, ceremonies, and religious beliefs had come from the Etruscans.

Check on Your Reading

1. How did the geography of Italy affect its early history?
2. Explain why Rome was in a good location.
3. What were the chief contributions of the Etruscans to Rome?

2. The Roman Republic Develops

Under the Etruscan kings of Rome was an advisory body of Romans known as the *Senate*. The Senate was made up of *patricians,* the heads of families who had won the best lands and had become the leaders of society. By the end of the sixth century B.C. the power of the Etruscans in central Italy was weakening. The Roman Senate was therefore able to expel the Etruscan king in 509 B.C.

Rome and other Latin towns then joined to defeat the Etruscans in battle. A few years later, the Greeks destroyed the Etruscan navy in a battle off the coast of southern Italy.

The Romans Set up a Republic

According to Roman tradition, the Senate called a meeting of all citizen soldiers. The meeting elected two *Consuls* who were to rule for a year. This marked the beginning of the *Roman Republic.*

For hundreds of years two Consuls headed the Roman government, sharing the executive powers. Each Consul could "veto," or prohibit, the action of the other. Their jobs were to interpret and carry out the laws, to control the military forces, and to draw up bills for the Assembly to vote on.

The *Assembly* consisted of all citizens who served in the army. This included both the patricians and the *plebians.* The plebians owned little or no land and were the main body of citizens who served as soldiers in the army. Some plebians were artisans or traders; most were small farmers. The job of the Assembly was to choose the two Consuls and other government officials every year and to vote on bills presented to it by the Consuls and the Senate.

The *Senate* directed foreign affairs and controlled taxes and finances. It could reject or accept any bills passed by the Assembly. Only patricians could be Senators and they became members of the Senate for life. Former Consuls became Senators, and if a Senator died, the Consuls could appoint a new Senator.

The Plebians Win the Struggle for a True Republic

The government of the early Republic actually was in the hands of the patricians. The Consuls and their officials, as well as the members of the Senate, were always patricians. The patricians even controlled the Assembly. The plebians were deeply angry at their inferior position and began a two-hundred-year struggle to win equal rights.

The plebians had three advantages in their struggle. Rome needed them for its many wars. The plebians made it clear that they would not fight unless they received the rights they wanted. Also the plebians had strong leaders. Some came from among the group of traders and businessmen who were becoming wealthy. Other leaders were wealthy farmers from areas in Italy that Rome had conquered. Important, too, was the wisdom and patriotism of many patricians. These leaders knew that Rome could become strong only if the plebians were given the rights they wanted. The struggle often seemed to threaten to tear Rome apart, but in every crisis the Romans managed to compromise and work together.

First, the plebians received the right to meet in their own assembly and to elect their own officials, called *Tribunes*. The Tribunes had the right to veto any decision by an official or by the Senate that injured the well-being of the plebians.

The plebians also protested that Roman laws were vague and unwritten. Often the plebians were punished for breaking ancient customs and rules that they did not know even existed. The plebians demanded that a written record be made of their duties and privileges.

As a result, the *Twelve Tables* were drawn up (about 451-450 B.C.). This was probably the first written code of Roman law. It did not provide

A statue of a Roman orator. The art of public speaking was important in influencing the people of Rome.

equal punishment to all offenders for the same type of offense. Some of the provisions of the Twelve Tables included the following:

> If one has broken the bone of a freeman . . .
> let him pay a penalty of three hundred coins.
> If he has broken the bones of a slave, let him
> pay one hundred and fifty coins.

You will recall that exactly the same distinctions were used in the Code of Hammurapi (page 30). Equality before the law was still in the future. But in spite of inequalities, the Twelve Tables helped to establish for future generations one of the first principles of law: *Laws are to be written.*

The plebians did not stop their struggle when the Twelve Tables were written. They next won the right to marry patricians. Intermarriage helped to break down distinctions between the two groups.

In the fourth century B.C. (400 B.C. to 300 B.C.) the plebians gained the right to be elected to any office, including that of Consul. Finally, in 287 B.C., a new law made the decisions of a plebian Assembly binding on all citizens.

So by the middle of the third century B.C., the Romans had developed a working system of *representative government*. This is a government in which people choose those who are to represent them and run the country. As in Greece, women and slaves had no official share in the government.

Roman Power Spreads through Italy

While the plebians were slowly winning their rights, Rome was conquering Italy. At first, the Romans did not deliberately plan to expand. They were threatened by dangerous rivals to the north and to the south and decided that expansion was their best defense. At times other peoples asked the Romans to help them defend themselves, and Rome moved in. Later, the Romans became more ambitious; they wanted to dominate all of Italy.

The Romans first joined neighboring Latin peoples in a league for mutual defense. When the other league members challenged Rome's leadership, the Romans defeated them.

Next, Roman armies pushed back hostile tribes in the Apennines and kept them under Roman rule. Then Roman leaders used diplomacy and force to check the Gauls who had come over the Alps and plundered Rome.

Finally, the Romans conquered the Greeks who blocked their expansion southward. By 265 B.C. the one-time village of Rome controlled nearly all of the peninsula of Italy. (See the map on page 113.)

How did the Romans achieve and then keep such conquests? There are at least two answers to this question.

Rome's citizen armies were always kept in readiness. Both their fighting methods and their organization were effective. Also Roman soldiers believed that they were fighting for a just cause. They fought hard because they felt that they were defending their homes and the honor of their country.

At the same time discipline was strict. A Roman soldier who fled in combat could expect the death penalty if caught. A deserter in peacetime would have a hand cut off.

The Romans also succeeded because they treated conquered peoples in Italy fairly well. These peoples often were given some self-government and some were given certain privileges of Roman citizenship. In addition, conquered peoples were permitted to keep their own customs. By such liberal policies, the Romans were able to prevent dangerous uprisings.

Check on Your Reading

1. How did Rome win its independence from the Etruscans?
2. How did the plebians turn the government of Rome into a representative government?
3. Why were the Twelve Tables important?
4. Why was the Roman army so successful in battle?
5. How did the Romans expand their power?

---

3. Roman Rule Spreads around the Mediterranean

The Roman conquest of Italy brought them in contact with Carthage, a powerful city on the coast of North Africa. Carthage had been founded by the Phoenicians about one hundred years before the village of Rome was established. By the third century B.C. it had become the center of a rich and powerful commercial empire which included parts of Spain.

Carthage angered the Romans by refusing to permit them to trade in the western Mediterranean area. Then Carthage tried to occupy northeastern Sicily—dangerously close to the coast of Italy. The Romans turned to war in an effort to crush this new threat. The three wars fought between Rome and Carthage are called the Punic Wars. "Punic" meant Phoenician in Latin.

Rome Wins the First Punic War

In the First Punic War (264-241 B.C.) the Romans built ships, learned how to maneuver them, and finally defeated Carthage on the sea. As a result, Rome gained control of a major part of Sicily and freedom to travel on the Mediterranean Sea. The First Punic War did not settle the basic issues between Rome and Carthage. Both sides knew that the struggle would continue. Each used the period of peace to prepare for further war.

A scene from the relief of Roman victories on Trajan's Column in Rome. In this scene Roman soldiers are defending a fort against attackers.

Hannibal Crosses the Alps in the Second Punic War

The Second Punic War (218–201 B.C.) was marked by the extraordinary exploits of Hannibal, a great Carthaginian general. He decided to march an army over the Alps to make a surprise attack on the Romans. In 218 B.C., Hannibal led 40,000 foot soldiers, 37 African elephants, and 8,000 horsemen through what is now Spain and France to the Alps. Then, in November, he started the dangerous 10,000-foot climb over the mountains.

It was a disastrous journey, but Hannibal refused to give up. "No part of the [Alps] reaches the sky," he shouted to his men and promised them that they would cross the Alps. And cross them they did—although only one-half of them made it safely to the plain in northern Italy. Here Hannibal rested his men and prepared to fight.

The Romans sent an army to meet the Carthaginians. Hannibal's troops crushed the Roman forces and moved forward. Hannibal lacked the equipment to batter down the walls of Rome, so he could not take the Roman capital. Instead, he remained in Italy over fifteen years and caused much destruction.

Finally, in an effort to draw Hannibal from Italy, the Romans ordered an army under Scipio to attack Carthage directly. The Carthaginians sent a hurried call to Hannibal to return home at once to defend his people. He did, and at the Battle of Zama (202 B.C.), south of the city of Carthage, the great Carthaginian general at last was defeated. The defeat of Hannibal ended the Second Punic War. Carthage was forced to disarm and to give up to Rome most of its lands, including those in Spain.

The Third Punic War Destroys Carthage

Some Romans were not satisfied with the punishment given to Carthage. Cato, a Roman official, warned that Carthage was still "full of riches and all sorts of arms and ammunition." He urged that the city be completely crushed. "Delenda est Carthago!" ("Carthage must be destroyed!") cried Cato, and soon many Romans agreed.

The Romans were again victorious in the Third Punic War. This time they killed most of the Carthaginians, sold the rest into slavery, and burned every building in Carthage.

Provinces Are Organized

Between the Second and Third Punic Wars, the Romans also had conquered Macedonia, parts of Asia Minor, and Greece. A Roman empire was growing. By 133 B.C. the Romans controlled large areas around the Mediterranean Sea. (See the map on page 113.)

They allowed several kingdoms to govern themselves under Roman protection. These kingdoms were independent except for foreign affairs. Most of the empire, however, was organized into *provinces*. There were eight provinces by 133 B.C. Each province was administered by a governor sent by Rome. The governor ruled the province and collected taxes, while the Roman Senate made general laws for the provinces.

A governor was appointed for just one year without salary. Unfortunately, therefore, many governors considered the provinces as private treasure chests to be raided for their own profit. They taxed the people heavily, pocketed part of the money for themselves, and ignored protests. It was clear that Rome had not yet solved the problems of governing an empire.

Check on Your Reading

1. What caused the Punic Wars?
2. Describe Hannibal's campaign.
3. How large was the Roman Empire by 133 B.C.? How was it organized?

4. Problems within the Empire

The problems that the Romans faced at home were as serious as those that they encountered in foreign lands.

Populares Oppose Optimates

The changes in Italy after the Punic Wars had split the people into two clashing groups. The *Populares* were the majority group of city workers and small farmers. The *Optimates* were the Senators and wealthy merchants and businessmen.

The Populares included many farmers who had served as soldiers. During the wars they had been

Portrait statues of a husband and wife. The family was the basic unit of Roman society.

unable to work their lands or pay taxes because they had been busy fighting. When they returned, their farms had been sold for nonpayment of debt!

Other returning farmer-veterans found that their homes and farms had been destroyed by Hannibal's men. Many also faced ruin because of the importation of cheap grain from Africa. Some of them sought jobs as hired workers on the great estates that were being developed by wealthy people to raise olives and fruit. They were refused even this labor because slaves were working for nothing.

Bewildered and hungry, the farmers drifted to the city, where slaves were doing most of the work. They joined the unemployed in Rome, ready to support men like Tiberius Gracchus who said:

> The wild beasts that roam over Italy. . . have their dens and lairs to shelter them. . . . But the men who fight and die for Italy enjoy nothing but air and light. Homeless and footless, they wander. . . . They are called masters of the world, [yet] they have no clod of earth to call their own.

Chief targets for the anger of these men were the Optimates, who included those who had bought up the farmers' lands and combined them into large farms worked by slaves. Many traders who had become rich during the wars and most of the Senators also were Optimates. The Roman Senate itself had turned into a stronghold for the upper groups. Filled with selfish aristocrats and men who had gained office by wealth, it opposed the interests of the people as a whole.

Many of the Optimates built elegant homes while the slums of Rome grew rapidly. The Optimates proudly displayed their wealth and expected special privileges such as their own sections at the theater. Roman society had been a community of free farmers. Now in Italy many people moved to Rome where they saw exciting games and often sold their votes to the highest bidder.

The Gracchi Fight and Die for Reforms

The struggle between the Populares and the Optimates continued from about 140 to 31 B.C., and each side had its heroes. One of the first attempts to improve the conditions of the Populares was made by two Tribunes, the brothers Tiberius and Gaius Gracchus, the Gracchi.

The Gracchi were members of the Optimates. Their father had been Consul twice. Their mother, Cornelia, was the daughter of the general who had defeated Hannibal. When their father died, Cornelia took over their education. She taught them the ideals and the discipline of early Roman leaders.

Tiberius was elected Tribune. He tried to limit the size of farms so that no one person could own great amounts of land. He hoped this would prevent the small farmers from losing their property. Tiberius angered the Senate when he used unconstitutional means to pass laws and remain in office as Tribune. In 133 B.C. some Senators killed him.

Gaius became Tribune ten years after his brother Tiberius. Gaius suggested that the state sell grain to the poor at very low prices. He also proposed that colonies be used as places of settlement for unemployed Romans. Gaius offended the Senate by giving special powers to certain businessmen to win their support against the Senators. One day he was trapped by his enemies, and he ordered his servant to kill him.

Civil War: Sulla Triumphs over Marius

In this time of confusion the people turned to a strong military hero for direction. Marius (157-86 B.C.), a general who had been elected a Consul in 108 B.C., became the leader of the Populares.

Marius lacked skill as an administrator and brought about no reforms in government. He did make some very important changes in the organization of the Roman army. Formerly, it had been made up of citizen-soldiers who were drafted to serve in a particular campaign. Now it was to be filled with volunteers. Since many of these volunteers enlisted for terms as long as twenty years, there developed an army of permanent "professional" soldiers. To them, their general was more important than the government officials.

The Senators and the other Optimates did not approve of General Marius. They, therefore, threw their support behind Sulla, another military leader. Sulla's troops clashed with the followers of Marius, and eventually Sulla's forces won. Sulla returned political power to the Senate.

The struggle between Marius and Sulla was the beginning of a new period in Roman history. In the future, military strength would play a large part in deciding who would rule Italy and the Empire.

Another important change took place at about

this time. Many of Rome's allies in Italy wanted Roman citizenship. Some of them revolted and set up a confederacy called "Italia." In this time of crisis the Senate made a wise decision. Roman citizenship was given to all the free peoples of the Italian peninsula. Now Italy shared in ruling the Roman Empire.

Check on Your Reading

1. How was the Roman Empire governed?
2. Describe the causes for the rivalry between the Populares and the Optimates.
3. What did the Gracchi accomplish?
4. In what way was the struggle between Marius and Sulla a turning point in Roman history?

5. Julius Caesar Becomes Ruler

From 60 to 50 B.C. Rome was dominated by a partnership of three men, known as the *First Triumvirate*, from the Latin words for *three* and *men*. The partners were Pompey, Caesar, and Crassus.

While Pompey strengthened his position at home, Julius Caesar sought fame abroad. In 58 B.C. he became governor of Gaul—roughly, modern France. In the next eight years Caesar's troops brought Gaul under Roman control. Caesar even successfully invaded Britain, but soon withdrew to Gaul.

Caesar Becomes Ruler

Caesar wanted the people in Rome to know of his exploits in Gaul. He therefore wrote his *Commentaries,* a history of his military accomplishments in Gaul.

Back in Rome, Pompey had become disturbed at Caesar's ambitions. Since the death of Crassus, Pompey had been the only Consul. Leaning more and more to the side of the Optimates, he had won the support of the Senate. Pompey and the Senators warned Caesar that he was to return to Italy without his troops!

In 49 B.C. Caesar led his army to the Rubicon, a small river that separated Gaul from Italy. Here a decision would have to be made. Should he cross the river with his soldiers and risk a war with Pompey? Should he return to Rome alone and give up all his political ambitions? Caesar made his decision, shouted, "The die is cast!"—and marched his troops across the Rubicon into Italy.

This bust of Julius Caesar was created six years after he was killed.

Pompey, fearing Caesar's popularity with the people, fled to Greece. Here Pompey's army was defeated by Caesar's soldiers. Pompey escaped, but was finally killed in Egypt. By 45 B.C. Caesar was the undisputed Roman ruler.

Julius Caesar was granted many of the important powers of government. Soon the Senate and the other governmental bodies lost most of their authority and Caesar was made *dictator* for life. That is, he was given great power over the government and the people for as long as he lived.

Caesar—like all human beings—was a mixture of many traits. If we judge him by his wild conduct as a young man, he was a selfish and self-centered person. If we judge him by the large sum of money that he paid each of his soldiers after a great victory, he was very generous. Or, if we judge him by his plans to build canals, he was concerned with helping others. If we judge him by the comments of the men who later killed him, Caesar was hungry for personal power.

Which was the true Caesar? Obviously, none of the four judgments by themselves can do him justice. Caesar was a complex Roman with a passion "to do great things."

Caesar's Program Brings Reform

Julius Caesar was an outstanding leader whose program greatly helped many people. As leader of the Roman Empire, he was responsible for many policies that benefited the people and the Empire.

In his short time as ruler Caesar accomplished a great deal. He extended citizenship privileges to many people in the provinces. He also reformed the administration of the provinces; corrupt governors were removed from office.

Julius Caesar set up colonies throughout the Empire that could serve as farming settlements for the unemployed. He introduced a fairer system of taxation for the colonies. He started a program of public works so that there would be additional jobs for the unemployed. He tried to limit the number of slaves who could work on estates, in order to provide jobs for free farmers. He distributed land to the poor. He established a law of bankruptcy; that is, a law to help people who could not pay their debts.

Caesar Is Struck Down!

Caesar's accomplishments, his excellent administration, and his fairness to his enemies were hailed by many Romans. However, there were others who hated him for acting like an absolute monarch. Some Senators were afraid that Caesar would abolish the Republic completely and make himself king.

The Roman Empire was expanded until it included all the lands around the Mediterranean Sea. About 50,000 miles of roads were built to help bring the scattered parts of the Empire together.

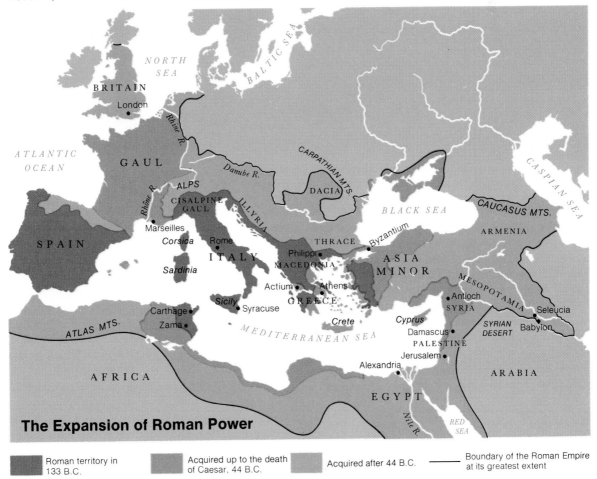

The Expansion of Roman Power

Roman territory in 133 B.C.

Acquired up to the death of Caesar, 44 B.C.

Acquired after 44 B.C.

Boundary of the Roman Empire at its greatest extent

Augustus and the emperors who followed him made Rome into a city of magnificent public buildings. The circular building at the top right is the Colosseum.

These opponents of Caesar decided to destroy him. On March 15, 44 B.C. (called the Ides of March), a group of conspirators surrounded Caesar in the Senate. At a sign, they pulled his robe from his neck, and stabbed him to death.

Thus Caesar was murdered before he had a chance to develop fully his program of reforms. He had said: "I have lived enough . . . for fame." Time has proven that he was correct.

Check on Your Reading

1. How did Julius Caesar gain power?
2. How did Caesar change the government?
3. What reforms did Caesar bring?
4. Why was Caesar assassinated?

6. Octavian Becomes Emperor Augustus

Two men challenged each other for Caesar's power—Antony and Octavian. Antony, a close friend of Caesar, was a military man. Octavian was Caesar's eighteen-year-old nephew and adopted son.

At first Antony and Octavian cooperated in running the Empire, with Antony directing the eastern part. Then Antony went to Egypt, where he came under the influence of the queen, Cleopatra. Queen Cleopatra was a clever ruler with a charming manner and a voice as pleasant as "an instrument of many strings." One account reported that she used a "thousand" kinds of flattery to win Antony to her side. It was rumored that she and Antony planned to cut off the eastern part of the

Roman Empire and rule it together. Octavian decided to stop them.

In 31 B.C. Octavian's fleet met and defeated the forces of Antony and Cleopatra in a great sea battle at Actium. Antony and Cleopatra later committed suicide, and Octavian ruled the Roman world.

The Roman Republic Ends

During Octavian's rule, the Roman Republic came to an end. The governing bodies of the Republic gradually lost their powers to Octavian. Yet, even after they had given up their duties, the Senate and the other organs of government continued to meet.

Octavian was known as *imperator,* or commander of military forces. He was chief priest for the state, and first among the Senators. He was called *Augustus,* revered ruler. Many features of the Republic seemed to exist, but actually Augustus Caesar had become the first emperor. He was the first to hold complete authority over the Roman Empire.

This change in government from a republic to rule by an emperor did not greatly disturb the people. They were tired of constant civil war and confusion, and grateful for a leader who could bring order and peace.

Augustus Brings Peace and Prosperity

Early in his reign Augustus conquered parts of Spain. Then he stopped his fighting and kept peace, although he still sent armies out to stabilize his northern boundary at the Rhine and Danube rivers. (See the map on page 113.) This *Pax Romana,* or Roman peace, was to last from 27 B.C. to 180 A.D. During this time the Empire was free of any major wars.

Augustus brought more than peace to the people of the huge Empire. He carried out a program that contributed to the well-being of millions of people. He created an empire that lasted for hundreds of years.

Augustus established an honest administration system for the provinces and built an effective military organization for guarding the frontiers. He protected people by well-administered laws. Roads and highways were constructed throughout the Empire. Sea routes were protected and trade encouraged. Public buildings such as temples, theaters, baths, and libraries were built, not only in Italy but in the provinces.

Toward the end of his life, Augustus claimed that he "had found Rome a city of brick and left it a city of marble." While this was an exaggeration, much had been accomplished. A new Forum was built where the business of finance and the courts was carried on. Over eighty temples, a new Senate house, a theater, and colonnades to shade the Romans from the sun had been constructed.

As a result of his accomplishments, Augustus helped the Empire to prosper. Literature and architecture flourished during this time. The period of Augustus is known as a "Golden Age."

Check on Your Reading

1. How did Octavian become ruler of the Roman world?
2. What was the Pax Romana?
3. Evaluate the accomplishments of Augustus, the first Roman emperor.

7. The Lives of the Romans

By the side of a dusty highway in Italy, an ancient Roman tombstone still calls to passersby:

> This mute stone begs thee to stop, stranger,
> until it has . . . told thee whose shade it covers.
> Here lie the bones of a [Roman]. ' . . . It
> wanted thee not to be unaware of this.

This appeal should help us remember that the lives of people are the materials on which history is based.

The Roman Family

The family was the center of Roman society under the Republic. The training children received within the family was the basis of Roman discipline,

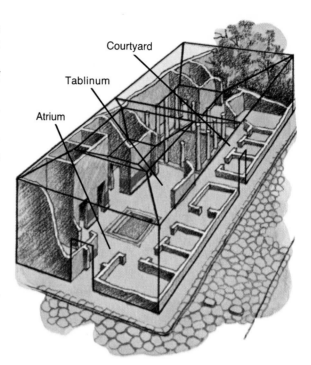

This house of a well-to-do Roman consisted of an atrium, a tablinum, and a courtyard, or peristylum, off which were several rooms.

courage, and loyalty to the state. The Roman family usually consisted of the father, the mother, the unmarried daughters, and the married sons with their wives and children. The father held great power over the others, but was often influenced by the mother. He made major decisions, directed the education of his sons, and served as priest by conducting services before the family altar.

The Roman mother also was treated with honor and respect. She ate her meals with her husband, helped to bring up the children, and sometimes advised her family on personal matters. In time, the power of women grew. The orator Cato once felt that Roman women influenced their men so greatly that he cried: "We Romans, who rule all men, are ruled by our women."

During the period of the Roman Empire, family ties loosened and relationships between husbands and wives lost their closeness. Nevertheless, in the early days of the Republic the Romans demonstrated that a good family can make for a stable life.

Roman Homes

In the early days of the Republic, houses were simple. They consisted of a single large room, called the *atrium*. This room had no windows, but a hole in the roof permitted some light to enter. Rain coming through this hole was caught in a hollow in the ground and used for household purposes. It was in the atrium that the Romans cooked, slept, and prayed.

In time, a narrow extension was built to one side of the main room. This was called the *tablinum*. Then the Romans borrowed architectural ideas from the Greeks. They added a courtyard surrounded by several rooms. In time, three features developed in the home. The atrium became the reception room. The tablinum served as the combination dining room and hallway. The rooms around the courtyard were used as bedrooms, living room, and kitchen.

A wealthy Roman often constructed a country home, or *villa*, that was far more complicated and expensive than the average house. At the same time, poor people had few of the comforts of the rich. In Rome they lived in crowded brick or wooden tenements six stories high. Fires frequently broke out in such tenements. Indeed, there were so many fires in Rome that one sharp businessman used them to make a fortune. He organized squads of fire fighters, who hurried to the flames. Then he charged the people large fees to put out the flames.

Roman Education

Roman citizens were educated to learn their relationships to the family, slaves, and other members of society. In the early days of the Republic a boy received his education from his father, while a girl was trained by her mother. Later, regular schools were set up for those boys whose parents could afford to pay the small fee. Girls continued to be taught at home to sew, spin, and cook.

Discipline at school was very strict. Thrashing was permitted, and more than one teacher was called "a man of blows." The teacher usually was a slave or a former slave who had been freed. Many were Greek.

In a Roman elementary school of the first century B.C., the child learned reading, writing, and arithmetic. The pupil also was instructed in proper conduct. He was taught to recite such maxims as:

A scar on the conscience is the same as a wound.—Valour grows by daring, fear by holding back.—A man dies as often as he loses his friends.—Man has been lent, not given, life.

After elementary school, the student could go on to a grammar school. Here he would study Greek and Latin literature. Then he might continue his training at a still higher school, where he would learn the art of public speaking. Between the ages of fourteen and seventeen the boy put on the adult's white toga, and was fully accepted as a man.

Some wealthy Romans hired or bought Greek scholars to teach their children privately. Later they gave their sons enough money to meet all living expenses and sent them abroad to study at higher centers of learning. One Roman student in Athens was not satisfied with this generous treatment. He demanded still another favor and wrote home:

I beg you to send me a secretary at the first opportunity, if possible a Greek; for he will save me much trouble in copying out notes.

NAME OF GREEK GOD	NAME OF ROMAN GOD	DUTIES
Zeus	Jupiter	King of all the gods.
Ares	Mars	God of war.
Aphrodite	Venus	Goddess of beauty and of love.
Hermes	Mercury	Messenger of the gods.
Athena	Minerva	Goddess of wisdom.

Roman Religion

An important part of Roman education was the training received from parents in the field of religion. The practices of the Roman religion did not always remain the same. When the Romans came in contact with the Greeks and other people, their religious ideas changed.

In the early days of the Republic, the Romans believed that there were spirits everywhere. There were a fire spirit, a water spirit, a spirit that supervised the planting of seeds, and many others. These spirits did not have any shape or form, but they were active all the time.

To protect his home and family, the Roman father performed certain ceremonies believed to be pleasing to the spirits of the household. The spirits included Janus, the spirit of the doorway; and Vesta, spirit of the hearth. There were also public ceremonies to worship the gods and goddesses of the whole Roman state. There was a national hearth, or temple, for Vesta. Jupiter was the favorite god, representing the powers of the sky—the sun, moon, and rain.

When the Romans came in contact with the Greeks, they accepted many Greek goddesses and gods, and gave them Roman names. (See the chart on page 117.) The Romans also accepted the Etruscan and Greek idea that the deities had human forms. As a result, many similarities appeared between the powers of the Greek and the Roman gods and goddesses.

Roman Slaves

In time, the Romans came to depend on the labor, skills, and knowledge of slaves. These were men and women seized in war or captured by slave hunters. Slaves held many jobs in Rome and throughout Italy. They were cleaners of public buildings, miners, servants, stevedores, artists, musicians, businessmen, farmers, teachers, and doctors. Most of the workers on the large farms were slaves. In the approximately one million population of Rome in the second century A.D. there were so many slaves that citizens rarely did any manual work.

Some slaves were treated well, but others—particularly farm workers—were made to labor long and hard at heavy work. One Roman liked to "break in" his slaves "like young dogs and colts." Another treated his slaves like his sons. One master beat his slaves; another shared his food with them. As in other periods of history, the fate of the slave depended completely on the character of his or her owner.

Roman Dress and Appearance

A Roman citizen wore a *tunica* and *toga*. A tunica was a short-sleeved woolen garment that usually extended below the knees. A toga was a woolen robe that was close to eighteen feet in length. The Roman draped the toga around his body, over the tunica, so that only his right arm was uncovered. Only a Roman citizen could wear a toga. In a sense, it was his cloak of membership in Roman society.

This relief on the Altar of Peace in Rome shows members of the imperial family. Notice their dress.

Women dressed in a *stola,* an undergarment that reached to the ground, and a *palla,* a loose wrap that was worn over the stola. Footwear for both women and men consisted of sandals or high leather shoes bound with straps at the top.

Many people in ancient Rome were quite as vain as people today. Men covered their bald spots with false hair. Women placed a mask of rice and bean flour on their faces at night to remove their wrinkles. Wealthy women decorated themselves with jewels, including brooches, rings, earrings, bracelets, pearl necklaces, and hairpins of ivory. There were no glass mirrors in those days. Instead mirrors of polished metal showed the Romans the success or failure of their efforts to make themselves attractive.

Recreation Provided by the State

In the early Roman Republic, religion was closely connected with recreation. The great public games that amused the people were presented as special tributes to the gods and goddesses. Later, these spectacles lost most of their religious meaning. State officials and some private individuals arranged for free public entertainments.

The Romans were particularly fond of chariot racing and gladiatorial fights. The big chariot races in Rome were held in the *Circus Maximus.* It was an elliptical structure that was enlarged several times until it held about 175,000 people. Light chariots drawn by four horses were raced seven dangerous laps around the course to the finish line.

Gladiatorial contests were held in amphitheaters such as the *Colosseum,* which seated about 50,000 people. *Gladiators,* who were war captives, criminals, or slaves, were forced to fight each other in man-to-man combat. Their weapons were usually daggers, spears, nets, and/or swords. These gladiators were at the mercy of the crowd. If the spectators waved white cloths or handkerchiefs, a defeated gladiator who had fought bravely might be permitted to live. If the crowd and the emperor turned their "thumbs down," the winner would kill the loser.

Check on Your Reading

1. What was the significance of the toga?
2. What role did the family play in the Roman state?
3. Describe Roman education and religion.

---

8. Roman Contributions in Law, Engineering, and Architecture

The Romans are linked to us by the contributions that they made to modern civilizations. We are particularly indebted to the Romans for their achievements in government and law, engineering, and architecture.

Roman Law

Romans learned to administer their Empire wisely. For example, their policy of granting citizenship to people of newly acquired provinces helped gain their loyalty. As the Roman Empire grew, the structure of its government gradually changed. Side by side with changes in government went the development of Roman law.

The Romans drew up laws explaining the rights and duties of the Roman citizen and of the various peoples in the Empire. In doing this, they passed on to future generations important legal principles. 1. Laws are to be written wherever possible. This was not new with the Romans, but they fully accepted it. 2. Citizens are to be protected by law against damage to their property. 3. Laws are to consider the rights of women. 4. An accused person is to be considered innocent until proven guilty. 5. Legal marriages can take place between citizens of different economic and social positions. 6. All persons are to be considered equal before the law. No person is to receive special treatment over any other person in cases of law.

Between 528 and 534 A.D., Emperor Justinian directed that the various Roman laws should be gathered together into one complete code. This *Justinian Code* made clear the legal rules involved in cases of adoption, guardianship, wills, and contracts. Most important of all, the Justinian Code tried to introduce the principle of the equality of all persons before the law. Although the Romans sometimes violated this ideal, other peoples later built on the Roman foundation to establish a true legal equality of all persons.

Today, Roman law is still a part of our modern world. It is the basis for the legal systems of many countries in Europe and Latin America. Equality before the law is one of our basic legal principles.

Roman Engineering

Roman engineering was as impressive as Roman law. The Romans built many excellent bridges, public parks, and aqueducts. Roman aqueducts and other construction works were extremely useful. Even today there is an ancient aqueduct that still brings water to Rome.

Above all, the Romans excelled in the construction of roads. Roman roads served three purposes. They made it easier to move troops. They helped the government in Rome to keep in touch with the peoples of the Empire. They increased trade.

In addition, Roman roads brought improved commmuncations that helped the spread of ideas. Rome was flooded with ideas from the East, especially philosophical and religious ideas. In time, one Eastern idea, Christianity, created vast changes in Roman life and in later history.

Roman Architecture

The Romans were superb architects of public buildings. They constructed temples, basilicas (halls originally used as banking centers and law courts), government buildings, and huge public baths.

These structures showed the outstanding features of Roman architecture. 1. They used arches capable of bearing great weight. The Romans may have gained their knowledge of the arch from the Etruscans, Persians, or Babylonians. 2. They used the vault, an arched roof or ceiling. 3. They used the dome, a rounded vault that often served as the roof of a building. 4. They used concrete. The use of concrete was one of the Romans' most important contributions to architecture. With it they could build huge structures using materials that could be found almost anywhere. 5. The Romans frequently used Grecian columns for ornamentation, rather than for support. The Romans borrowed many architectural forms from the Greeks. 6. They placed importance on making the interiors of buildings attractive, rather than concentrating on the outside. The Pantheon, in Rome, contained most of the features of Roman architecture.

This drawing shows the construction of a Roman highway in 312 B.C.

From the barrel vault the Romans developed the groin vault and then the dome. Perhaps their most famous use of the dome was in the Pantheon, shown above.

These principles of Roman architecture are still important, for they were handed down and used by later generations. For example, the Capitol in Washington, D.C., shows Roman influence.

Check on Your Reading

1. Why are the legal principles passed on by the Romans so important?
2. What practical engineering contributions were made by the Romans?
3. What were the achievements of Roman architecture?

9. Roman Literature, Language, and Science

It has been written that Rome conquered Greece and then Greece conquered Rome. Roman art, philosophy, and literature used Greek ideas as a base. The Roman political writer and essayist, Cicero, wrote, "It was no little brook that flowed from Greece into our city, but a mighty river of culture and learning." The Romans were not just imitators, however. On the base of Greek literature they created Roman literature.

Some of the more interesting Roman authors were: Cicero, essayist; Lucretius, Virgil, and Horace, poets; Livy and Tacitus, historians; Juvenal, satirist; and Martial, writer of epigrams. Only a few of them will be discussed below.

Virgil

Virgil (70-19 B.C.) was the Roman poet who wrote the *Aeneid*. The *Aeneid* was written to stir up the pride and patriotism of the people of Rome. Also Virgil wanted to encourage Romans to keep

A portrait bust of Livia, the wife of the Emperor Augustus.

at the foolishness and evils in society. The Romans are said to have been the first people to develop the satire as a literary form. Note how well Juvenal satirized the Roman practice of throwing things out of the window:

> How often cracked and chipped earthenware falls from the windows! . . . You may well be accounted [careless in not protecting yourself] against unforeseen accident, if you go out to supper without having made your will. It is clear that there are just so many chances of death, as there are open windows. . . .

Martial

Martial (40-104 A.D.) was born in Spain and lived in Rome for many years. He is important because he helped to make popular the *epigram*. A Roman epigram is a short poem that usually ends with a humorous or satirical twist. Martial wrote this poem:

Silence is Golden

> You're pretty, I know it; and
>   young, that is true;
> And wealthy—there's none but
>   confesses that too;
> But you trumpet your praises
>   with so loud a tongue
> That you cease to be wealthy
>   or pretty or young!

The Latin Language

The Roman language, *Latin,* is a part of our heritage. Latin spread to many peoples throughout the Empire. Eventually it became the basis for the *Romance* languages of French, Spanish, Italian, Portuguese, and Rumanian. Even the English language, which developed from other sources, was influenced by Latin.

Contributions to Science

The Roman contributions to science were in the practical application of knowledge. The Romans set up one of the earliest systems of medical service for the public. Government doctors gave free treatments to the poor. The Romans also established a number of hospitals, the first in Europe. They organized medical groups to accompany Roman troops into battle. They improved the methods of public sanitation.

the peace throughout the Empire. He believed that the Romans had a double mission in the world: "To rule the nations as their master [and] . . . to establish firmly the law of peace."

Horace

Horace (65-8 B.C.) wrote a number of excellent *odes.* An ode is a poem designed to be sung, or to be read with a musical rhythm. In his poetry, Horace urged people to enjoy living in the present. "Mistrust tomorrow," he said, "catch the blossom of today." Horace also told the Romans to follow "the golden mean"; that is, not to go to extremes.

Juvenal

Juvenal (about 65-140 A.D.) is known for his *satires.* A satire is literature that ridicules or pokes fun

Ruins of the Roman theater at Arles, France. Roman cities were built throughout the Empire.

One physician who increased medical knowledge was Galen. Galen (130–200 A.D.) was born in Asia Minor and practiced medicine in Rome. He made valuable studies of the spinal cord and the nervous system. He also compiled an encyclopedia of medical knowledge.

Under the direction of Julius Caesar, a more accurate calendar, the *Julian Calendar,* was drawn up. It remained unchanged until the sixteenth century A.D. Today, the number of days in each of our months can be traced back to the Julian Calendar.

Check on Your Reading

1. Why did Virgil write the *Aeneid*?
2. What is an ode? a satire? an epigram?
3. How does the study of Latin help with the study of other languages?
4. What did the Romans achieve in medicine and public health?

10. The Roman Peace Was Followed by Gradual Decline

The powers of the government of the Roman Empire had been gathered into the hands of the emperor. This meant that there was a very serious problem. How was the emperor to be chosen? The men who followed the reign of Augustus varied in their characters and abilities.

The Roman Peace

The four emperors who followed Augustus were men of various temperaments. Together they reigned for fifty-four years. Two were satisfactory emperors; but the other two were brutal tyrants who died violently. After the death of the last, the hated Emperor Nero, a series of emperors followed who were largely supported by the army.

Then in 96 A.D. a distinguished Senator, Nerva, became emperor. He used the principle of adoption to choose the successful general Trajan as his successor. This principle was followed by Trajan and the next three emperors. Nerva and the four emperors who followed him were known as the "good emperors." The last of the "good emperors" was Marcus Aurelius (ruled from 161–180 A.D.). Emperor Marcus Aurelius was a famous Stoic philosopher, whose *Meditations* are still read.

During the period from the death of Augustus to 180 A.D., the troubles at Rome with the poor emperors did not greatly affect the Roman Empire as a whole. This may have been one of the most peaceful and secure periods that the ancient Mediterranean world had ever had.

The Roman peace, or *Pax Romana*, was due in part to the wise arrangements Augustus had made for the Empire. During this period trade flourished, and towns and cities throughout the Empire

were centers of Roman civilization. Latin became the language of government officials and the well-to-do throughout the Empire.

Two Strong Emperors Reorganize the Government

From 180 to 284 A.D., the conditions of the Roman government became increasingly confused. Roman armies often used the threat of force to place their favorites at the head of the Empire. The office of emperor soon became a prize to be awarded to the highest bidder. At the same time the Roman Empire was being forced to give up some of its territories to Germanic tribes pressing over its borders. The Empire also suffered a plague lasting fifteen years in the middle of the third century. This reduced the population tremendously.

The Roman Empire was reorganized under Diocletian. He divided the Empire into two parts, the West Roman Empire and the East Roman Empire.

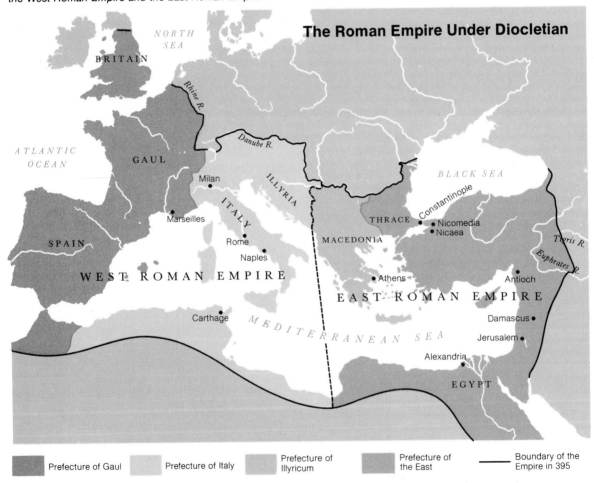

The Roman Empire Under Diocletian

Prefecture of Gaul	Prefecture of Italy	Prefecture of Illyricum	Prefecture of the East	Boundary of the Empire in 395

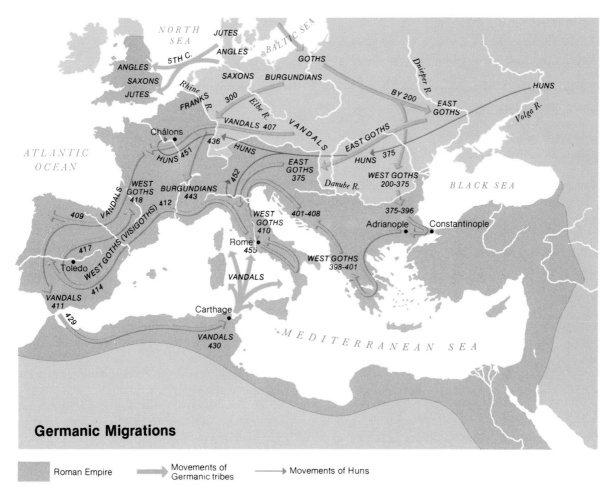

Germanic Migrations

▬ Roman Empire	➡ Movements of Germanic tribes	→ Movements of Huns

Germanic tribes began to move into the Roman Empire in the fourth century A.D.

Diocletian became emperor in 284 A.D. He was a strong leader who brought order to the Roman Empire by making the government a powerful director of the people's affairs. Diocletian took several extreme actions in his attempt to stabilize economic and political conditions. For example, he issued an edict fixing maximum prices for goods, so that high prices would no longer cause unrest. Unfortunately, the edict could not keep prices from rising.

Diocletian did succeed in his reorganization of the government. He divided the Empire into two administrative parts. He supervised the eastern half from Asia Minor, and he chose a co-emperor to run the western half of the Empire from Italy. Each half was subdivided into prefectures, dioceses, and provinces. This reorganization permitted the central government to control many distant areas. Diocletian also reorganized the army and strengthened border defenses. By such changes, Diocletian brought order.

Under Emperor Constantine, in the early part of the fourth century A.D., the two parts of Diocletian's empire were governed from a single headquarters in the east. Constantine built a new capital in a strategically located city along the Bosporus. (See the map on page 124.) This city, called Byzantium by the Greeks, was renamed Constantinople for the emperor.

The efforts of Diocletian and Constantine to restore order checked temporarily the deterioration of the Roman Empire. However, after the death of Constantine, the decline continued.

What caused this giant Empire to decay? Most historians feel that no one answer can be given. They point out that there were a number of factors that interacted on each other to produce the gradual decline of the Roman Empire.

Reasons for the Decline

The Empire was not always governed efficiently. There were many rulers who weakened the Empire by their dishonesty, corruption, or stupidity.

The people lost their rights to participate in the government. Lacking these rights, many of them soon ceased to take any serious interest in the welfare of the state.

Roman armies lost their patriotic spirit and discipline. Their ranks were now filled with professional soldiers from the provinces. Often these men were more interested in loot than in victory for the Empire.

Economic conditions became worse. Farms were not well run, as people moved to the cities and left the slaves to work the land. Trade decreased throughout the Empire. Many city workers lived in poverty. Population declined, partially as a result of epidemics and wars.

Moral standards fell. As the Romans saw scoundrels profit by dishonest acts and go unpunished, some of them lost their confidence in the value of truth and honesty.

Germanic Tribes Move into the Empire

This process of decline might have gone on for a long time had not Germanic tribes begun to pour across the frontiers of the Empire. Individual Germanic families had moved into the Roman Empire near the end of the second century A.D. Many of the men became soldiers in the Roman armies. Mass migrations of the Germans began about two hundred years later. The origin of these German tribes is not clear. They may have come from an area near the Baltic Sea and then moved to the east and southwest.

In battle, the Germans were brave and bold. A German faced disgrace for life if he surrendered. Romans called the Germans "barbarians," a term which originally meant "foreigners" but which later was interpreted to mean "uncivilized people." The early Germans had none of the Roman skills in literature, art, philosophy, or government. On the other hand, they had developed tribal law, had organized family and community life, and were familiar with some methods of agriculture.

The Germans first entered the Roman Empire in a mass to protect themselves from the attacks of warring peoples from Asia. Then they fought to increase their possessions and killed to destroy their enemies. They were more than invaders intent on destruction for its own sake.

Visigoths Defeat the Romans

The Germanic tribe known as the *Visigoths* (Western Goths) provides a good example of the way some Germans entered the Roman Empire for protection from attack—and then in turn became the attackers.

In the fourth century A.D. the Visigoths were in danger of being destroyed by the Huns, fierce warriors from Asia. The Visigoths, therefore, moved west until they reached the Danube River, a boundary of the Roman Empire. (See the map on page 125.) Here they asked the Romans for permission to cross to safety.

The Romans permitted many thousands of Visigoths to enter the Empire. However, Roman officials cheated them and did little to help them obtain food. The Romans further angered the Visigoths by refusing to permit the rest of their tribe to enter the Empire. In anger the Visigoths rose in rebellion and defeated the Roman emperor and his army near Adrianople (378 A.D.).

When the western Roman Emperor refused the Visigoth king, Alaric, lands in what is now Austria, Alaric marched on Rome. Alaric's troops entered and sacked Rome in 410 A.D. Then the Visigoths moved on and finally settled in southern Gaul and Spain.

Other Germanic groups now pushed into the Empire. (See the map on page 125.) As in the case of the Visigoths, most of the Germanic tribes in the east were probably pushed westward by the pressure of the Huns.

A number of chieftains of these Germanic groups, such as Theodoric the Ostrogoth, admired Roman achievements and tried to imitate the ways of the Romans. Roman civilization was thus increasingly absorbed by the Germans.

The Huns Spread Terror

The Huns had occupied the area of modern Hungary and Rumania in the fourth century A.D. In the fifth century, hard-riding Hun horsemen erupted from the Hungarian plain into the Roman Empire.

The leader of the Huns was Attila, a short, broad-chested man of whom it was said: "He was the scourge of all countries and reports concerning

In the center of the Baptistry of the Orthodox in Ravenna is a baptismal font. The Baptistry is probably the best preserved of all early Christian buildings. Built in the 500s, much of its decoration was derived from late Roman art which was used to carry the message of Christianity. The influence of Rome continued after the fall of the Empire.

him terrified all mankind." At the Battle of Châlons in 451 A.D., Attila and his men were temporarily checked by the combined forces of the Romans and Goths. A few years later, Attila died, and the Huns withdrew.

The Western Roman Empire Deteriorates

Although the Huns had been stopped, the power of the Germanic tribes increased. In 476 A.D., a German chieftain, Odoacer, forced the emperor of Rome to abdicate "of his own accord." Odoacer made himself king of Italy, and other German leaders seized control of lands throughout the Empire.

The rise of this German to the position of ruler of Italy is taken as the symbol of the final deterioration of the Roman Empire in the West. Although the Eastern Roman Empire continued, the Western Roman Empire ceased to exist. Roman achievements were not completely lost, however. They had a strong influence on the new rulers of Europe.

Check on Your Reading

1. Why did the Roman Empire decline?
2. Why did Germanic tribes move into the Empire? What were the results?

A Roman Bather

Shortly after 2 P.M., the Roman bather paid a small admission fee and entered the public baths. He strolled about and enjoyed the handsome building. There were expensive mirrors on the walls and the vaulted ceilings were "buried in glass." The swimming pool was marble-lined, and silver spigots poured filtered water.

The bather changed clothes in the dressing room. A well-built man, he was not embarrassed about bathing with others. He and his companions laughed at the humor in these lines by the poet Martial:

> Your legs, so like the moon at crescent,
>> A bathing-tub will scarce look neat in;
>> So here I send you, for a present,
>> A drinking-horn to wash your feet in.

The bather now went to the exercise room. He grunted as he raised each weight and "whenever he released his imprisoned breath, [other bathers] could hear him panting in wheezy and high-pitched tones." He then moved to the massage room, where a slave rubbed his body. A sudden commotion occurred. A pickpocket had been caught, and angry men called an attendant to arrest the scoundrel!

After the excitement, the bather walked to a "hot-air room," where artificial heat made his body perspire. He took a warm bath, washed with soap, and finished with a cold bath. This was followed by a swim in the pool. Then an attendant rubbed perfumed ointment over his body.

Clean and comfortable, he gossiped with friends, bought a snack, and tried his luck at dice. After this relaxation, he went home. He felt that he deserved a good supper after his busy day.

This sketch of a Roman bather in the first century A.D. is based on information in two letters written by the philosopher Seneca. Seneca, Lucius A., *Ad Lucilium Epistulae Morales,* with English translation by Richard M. Gummere, 1917, G. P. Putman's Sons.

CHAPTER REVIEW

Think and Discuss

1. How did the Athenian democracy and the Roman Republic differ?
2. Caesar felt that it was necessary to become a dictator to accomplish his goals. Do you think a representative government would have accomplished the same things he did? Why?
3. How important is the character of a government official, especially the ruler?
4. In your opinion, does a close-knit family life result in a stable society? What examples can you give?

5. Many Roman amusements were brutal. How do you explain this?
6. Some scholars believe that the Romans' failure to respond to all of the rising challenges contributed to the decline of Rome. What were the challenges or problems that the Romans never solved?

Past and Present

1. Make a list of features in the United States government which have come from a) Greece, and b) Rome. Is the United States a republic, a democracy, or both?
2. It was said during the Depression of the 1930s

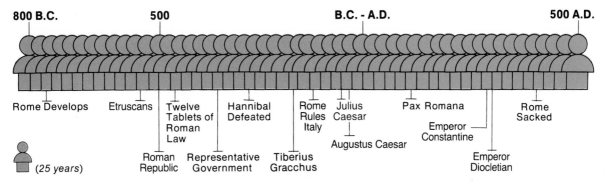

| 800 B.C. | | 500 | | | B.C. - A.D. | | | | 500 A.D. |

Rome Develops   Etruscans   Twelve Tablets of Roman Law   Hannibal Defeated   Rome Rules Italy   Julius Caesar   Pax Romana   Emperor Constantine   Rome Sacked

(25 years)

Roman Republic   Representative Government   Tiberius Gracchus   Augustus Caesar   Emperor Diocletian

that the United States tried to aid recovery by using methods similar to those proposed by the Gracchi brothers and Caesar. Find points of similarities and differences.

3. Compare the six legal principles of Roman law with the first ten amendments to our Constitution. What is missing in Roman law that we value highly?

Our System of Measuring Time

Imagine what it would be like if we referred to the years as some ancient peoples did. If someone asked for the year of your birth, you might answer: "I was born in the third year of the first full term of President Johnson." That would mean the year 1966. Of course such a system would require everyone to know the order of the Presidents and how long their terms were.

As you know, the system of counting years is no longer so cumbersome. Today many people use the terms B.C. and A.D. to keep years in order. In this system, the years before Christ start with 1 B.C. and move backwards: 2 B.C., 3 B.C., . . . 100 B.C., and so on. Years after Jesus start with A.D. 1. Calculating a span of time which crosses over the B.C./A.D. line is like using a ruler whose end is in the middle. First you count the B.C. years and then add them to the A.D. years.

1. If a person were born in the year 30 B.C. and died in A.D. 25, how many years did the person live?

2. If a comet were observed in 250 B.C. and then again in A.D. 400, how many years passed between the two sightings?

3. If a king were born in 150 B.C., in what year would he celebrate his fiftieth birthday?

4. If someone were 30 years old in A.D. 10, in what year was that person born?

Correct answers are: 55 years, 650 years, 100 B.C., and 20 B.C.

Activities

1. Make a collection of pictures of beautiful buildings in our country and the world. Which show the influence of Greek or Roman architecture?

2. A knowledge of mythology is essential to the understanding of classical literature. Read and then report on several myths.

3. Read and report on a selection from Roman literature.

4. Write a biography of Julius Caesar.

5. Write a report on archaeological discoveries at Pompeii.

6. Debate the statement: Resolved, that the Golden Age of Augustus Caesar was superior to the Golden Age of Pericles.

CHAPTER

7

Two Great Religions Develop in the Middle East

KEYNOTE

A religion based on the belief in one God is so much a part of Western culture that most of us take such a religion for granted. We often forget that this part of the Western heritage came from the Middle East.

One of the prophets of the *Old Testament,* Micah, summarized an important part of this heritage:

What doth the Lord require of thee
But to do justly, to love mercy,
And to walk humbly with thy God?

Mount Sinai where, according to the Bible, *Moses received the "Ten Commandments."*

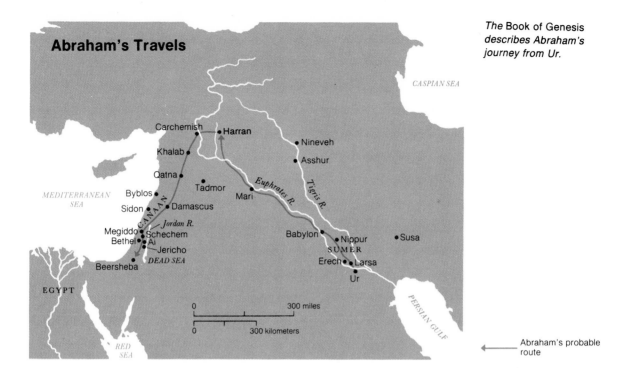

Abraham's Travels

The Book of Genesis *describes Abraham's journey from Ur.*

CASPIAN SEA

Carchemish • • Harran

Khalab •

Qatna •

Byblos • Tadmor

MEDITERRANEAN SEA

Sidon • • Damascus

Megiddo • Schechem

Bethel • • Ai

• Jericho

Beersheba • DEAD SEA

EGYPT

RED SEA

Mari

Euphrates R.

Tigris R.

Jordan R.

Nineveh •

Asshur •

Babylon • • Nippur

SUMER

Erech • • Larsa

Ur

• Susa

PERSIAN GULF

0 — 300 miles

0 — 300 kilometers

Abraham's probable route

1. The Hebrews and Monotheism

Amenhotep IV, who reigned as pharaoh of Egypt from about 1370 to 1353 B.C., attempted to set up Aton, a sun god, as the only Egyptian deity. However, soon after he died, the belief in one God died out in most of Egypt.

It was the people known first as Hebrews, then as Israelites, and finally as Jews who gave to the world the idea of *monotheism*, the belief in one God. At no time did these people occupy a large expanse of land in the Middle East; nor were they very numerous during ancient times. Yet their influence on history has been immense.

Mesopotamia seems to have been the first home of the Hebrews who were nomadic herders. Gradually they migrated southwestward to a crossroads of the Middle East today known as Israel. This migration probably took place around the twentieth century B.C., and, according to the *Bible,* was led by Abraham.

Abraham and His Descendants

The *Book of Genesis* tells Abraham's story.

> Terah took his son Abraham, his grandson Lot, and his daughter-in-law Sarai, Abraham's wife, and they set out from Ur of the Chaldees for the land of Canaan. But when they reached Harran, they settled there.

That city lay along a branch of the Euphrates River. Later, again according to the *Bible:*

> The Lord said to Abraham, "Leave your own country, your kinsmen, and your father's house, and go to a country that I will show you. I will make you into a great nation. I will bless you and make your name so great that it shall be used in blessings."

And so, under Abraham's leadership, his people set out south and west to what to them would become the land promised by God.

There the Hebrews found a dry land of barren hills and mountains, dotted with lush green oases nourished by lifegiving springs. Between two ranges of mountains the Jordan River wound through a fertile plain on its way southward to the Dead Sea.

Canaanites then occupied the area. Such communities as Jerusalem and Jericho had been long established, dating from 3000 B.C. or before.

Much of *Genesis* concerns Abraham and his immediate descendants and their families. We learn, for example, about Rebecca. Abraham's emissary discovered her in Mesopotamia when he was seeking a wife for Abraham's son, Isaac. Rebecca journeyed to Canaan to marry Isaac. Rebecca bore Isaac twin sons, Jacob and Esau.

131

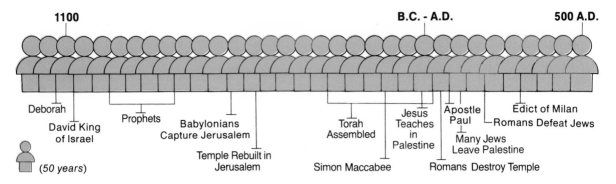

Deborah

David King of Israel

Prophets

Babylonians Capture Jerusalem

Temple Rebuilt in Jerusalem

Simon Maccabee

Torah Assembled

Jesus Teaches in Palestine

Apostle Paul

Many Jews Leave Palestine

Romans Destroy Temple

Edict of Milan

Romans Defeat Jews

(50 years)

Egypt and the Exodus

Jacob, who was given the name Israel, had twelve sons. They and their descendants are called the children of Israel, or Israelites. Circumstances compelled one of Israel's sons, Joseph, to move with numerous Israelites to Egypt, apparently during a period of poor crops and famine. There Joseph became a trusted adviser to the pharaoh, and the Israelites lived comfortably and well.

But then, the *Bible* says, "A pharaoh arose who knew not Joseph." The Israelites in Egypt became a persecuted people, forced to work on building projects for the pharaoh. The accounts of Egyptian oppression handed down through generations instilled in the Israelites an intense hatred of tyranny. "Remember your bondage in Egypt" became a reminder among them.

A leader, Moses, finally arose to rally the Israelites and lead them from Egypt back to the land that they believed the Lord had promised them. This probably occurred sometime during the thirteenth century B.C.

The *Bible* relates how Moses led the Israelites during forty years of wandering through the Sinai peninsula. It tells how Moses received "Ten Commandments" from the Lord on Mount Sinai, located perhaps in the southern part of the peninsula. These became the cornerstone of Hebrew belief, Law, and society. The Commandments read:

You shall have no other god to set against me.

You shall not make a carved image for yourselves, nor the likeness of anything in the heavens above, or on the earth below, or in the water under the earth. . . .

You shall not make wrong use of the name of the Lord your god. . . .

Remember to keep the sabbath day holy. . . .

Honor your father and your mother. . . .

You shall not commit murder.

You shall not commit adultery.

You shall not steal.

You shall not give false evidence against your neighbor.

You shall not covet your neighbor's house; . . . or anything that belongs to him.

Moses did not live to enter the Promised Land. Large numbers of Israelites living among the Canaanites joined the Israelites coming from Sinai. Together under Joshua, Moses' successor, and other commanders they fought a long series of battles to slowly win the land from the Canaanites.

The Israelites at the time were divided into twelve tribes. Each was assigned a territory in Canaan, which became known as Israel. Soon after the conquest, the leaders of the twelve tribes met to make a solemn covenant, or agreement, that they were the people of the Lord and would worship only the Lord.

Check on Your Reading

1. Who was Abraham and what did he accomplish?
2. Describe the Israelite experience in Egypt.
3. Why are the Ten Commandments important? What items do they cover?

2. Triumph and Tragedy

During this period most of the Israelites became farmers and settled in villages. Gradually they learned the skills of civilization from the people they conquered and those around them.

Time of the Judges

They had only partly won control of the land. Security remained a precious commodity. On frequent occasions the Israelites had to fight off attacks from the Canaanites, the Moabites, and others. During such a time of crisis, a leader often arose to rally the people against the enemy. Such a leader was known as a *Judge,* a person upon whom "the Spirit of the Lord rushed."

In the 1100s B.C., for example, the Israelites joined together to fight the Canaanites under the inspiration of Deborah, one of the Judges. Deborah persuaded Barak to lead his troops against the forces of the Canaanite general, which included nine hundred chariots of iron. Deborah promised General Barak that the Lord would aid him. According to the account, rain, hail, and sleet poured down on the battlefield bogging down the Canaanite chariots in mud. Victory went to the Israelite foot soldiers.

The "Song of Deborah" in the *Book of Judges* in the *Bible* celebrates the Israelite triumph. Its verses begin:

For the leaders, the leaders in Israel,
for the people who answered the call,
bless ye the Lord.

Hear me, you kings; princes, give ear;
I will sing, I will sing to the Lord.
I will raise a psalm to the Lord the God of
    Israel.

And at the conclusion of the war, "The land was at peace for forty years."

Kings of Israel

Kings came relatively late to the Israelites, and a united kingdom lasted for only about seventy years. Kingship developed as a result of wars with the Philistines, who had migrated to the area to settle along the Mediterranean soon after the Israelites arrived.

The Philistines were ruled by a military aristocracy and were formidable warriors. They were organized into a disciplined army whose weapons of iron were superior to those of the Israelites. In a series of battles the Philistines succeeded in occupying part of the land of the tribes of Israel. It was in this crisis that Saul, a young farmer, rose to lead the tribe of Benjamin and others to victory against the Philistines. According to the *Bible,* the Lord chose Saul for leadership. His success as a military leader

The people around the Israelites worshipped many gods and goddesses. At the left, a tomb painting of the Egyptian god Osiris. At the right, a winged god of the Assyrians.

elevated him to the Israelite kingship around 1025 B.C. Saul spent most of his reign in battle.

Upon Saul's death, the Israelites, about 1000 B.C., turned to David, who had become an outstanding leader in battles with the Philistines. Through a series of wars King David enlarged Israel. The Phoenicians now controlled only a narrow strip of coastline. The Philistines were squeezed into a small area that included their chief city, Gaza.

Symbols of Faith and Unity

David conquered the centrally located town of Jerusalem and made it his capital. He made it the center of the Israelite nation and a lasting symbol of Israelite religious unity. There he had brought the Holy Ark of the Lord, known as the *Ark of the Covenant,* and enshrined it. The *Bible* tells that the Lord had instructed Moses to make this chest during those years of wandering in the Sinai peninsula. It held the *Tables of the Law,* and was to the Israelites the holiest of holies.

During David's reign, trade, argiculture, and industry flourished. Government became more complicated and officials were chosen to help run the country and keep it together. David himself was not only a king and a warrior, but a poet as well. Many of the *Psalms* in the *Bible* have been attributed to him.

The crown passed from David to his son Solomon. Solomon became known for his wisdom and as the builder of the great Temple in Jerusalem. Stone for the temple was quarried nearby. The king of the little Phoenician state of Tyre sent wood from the cedars of Lebanon and skilled architects. In return Solomon sent corn, oil, and other supplies to Tyre. In addition, Solomon had built a magnificent palace and many forts throughout the land, and he enlarged and beautified several towns.

Solomon's death in about 922 B.C. brought Israelite unity to an end. The kingdom split in two. The tribes of Judah and Benjamin in the south made up *Judah.* The other ten tribes formed Israel in the north.

Israel and Judah Are Conquered

In the meantime, the Assyrian power was growing in the east. In the eighth century B.C. the Assyrians attacked and conquered Israel, taking its major city and capital, Samaria. The Assyrians dispersed the population, and the northern state of Israel disappeared. Little Judah now stood alone as the seas of empire swirled around it. It was under constant threat from Egyptians, Assyrians, and others.

In 597 B.C. the Babylonians under Nebuchadnezzar besieged and captured Jerusalem. He then transported thousands of artisans, soldiers, and others from Judah to Babylon.

The people remaining in Judah were rebellious under Babylonian rule. Revolt brought Nebuchadnezzar back in 586 B.C. to besiege and conquer Jerusalem once more. This time he threw the city open to his soldiers to plunder, and the Babylonians destroyed the Temple.

Nebuchadnezzar deported many of the Israelites to his homeland. What is known as the "Babylonian Captivity" began.

In Exile

After such devastation, one would expect the Israelite civilization to come to an end. But it survived because of the Israelites' religious faith. Now they came to be known as *Jews,* after Judah, and their religion was called *Judaism.*

Many Jews were assimilated into the Babylonian culture. Many others, however, were not. One reason for this was the *prophets* who kept alive the people's history, traditions, and faith.

Prophets arose in the ninth and eighth centuries B.C. in times of trouble, danger, and distress, to provide guidance to a deeply troubled people. Prophets warned of dire consequences if a danger were not met or if the people did not follow the ways of the Lord. At this period, also, the traditions and experiences of the Israelites were being written down for what was probably the first time. Dr. Abram Sacher describes the prophets and their magnificent leadership. "They labored to substitute plain, moral requirements for elaborate ceremonial and formal creed. They were the stern guardians of individual and national conduct, the living Hebrew conscience. . . . They were completely fearless in their mission, bearing abuse with sublime patience."

The development of the *synagogue,* at first a community meeting place, also helped hold Jews in Babylon to their beliefs. Here the people met on the Sabbath to hear prayers and sermons and to take part in ceremonies. The synagogue became the center of Judaism.

The Torah

The fortunes of war eventually brought help. The Persians under Cyrus conquered Babylon. Jews who wished to do so were allowed to return to their homeland. In Jerusalem in 516 B.C., they rebuilt that symbol of unity and faith, the Temple.

Over the next two hundred years or so, Jewish priests and scholars devoted much attention to bringing together and writing down the books that are the foundation of Judaism. The Law and historical traditions of the Jews had been passed on from generation to generation. Now they were organized and written down. Later, scholars brought together the first five books of the *Bible* and added the accounts and the words of the prophets and the *Psalms* and *Proverbs*. These became the sacred scriptures of the Jews.

The general principles stated in the *Torah,* the first five books of the *Bible,* needed interpretation. This task was carried out by *scribes,* who became leaders in the synagogues. Scribes devoted themselves to the study of the *Torah,* developed the oral law, and passed on their knowledge and experience to their disciples.

The Jews and the Empire of Alexander the Great

When Alexander the Great conquered the Persians, Palestine, as the Jewish homeland was called, became part of a new empire. During Hellenistic times, following the death of Alexander in 323 B.C., the Jews faced a severe challenge from Greek ideas that placed human beings at the center of the universe. Jewish thinkers disagreed over how they should respond, as Judaism struggled against being swallowed up in a sea of ideas alien to it.

In 198 B.C. the dynasty that ruled Asia Minor established control over Palestine. Antiochus IV, who became king in 175 B.C., attempted to force Hellenistic ideas on the Jews. The Jews resisted, which led to persecution. Five brothers, the Maccabees, led a rebellion against Antiochus. In 142 B.C., Simon Maccabee won independence for Judah, or Juda. Successors to Simon extended Juda's power until the kingdom encompassed about as much land as it had under Solomon.

The Roman Empire

But soon the Jews faced yet another power—that of the Roman Empire. The Romans joined Palestine to Syria as a province of the Roman Empire.

The Jews rebelled, unsuccessfully, against their Roman rulers. Over the years of Roman control, disagreement developed in Jewish society over whether to submit peacefully to the Romans or attempt to regain freedom. In 68 A.D. those wishing to throw off the Roman yoke won control.

The Romans reacted by sending Vespasian at the head of an army to conquer the Jews once more.

The Arch of Titus shows Roman soldiers carrying spoils from the destruction of Jerusalem.

After many months, in 70 A.D., Vespasian's army captured Jerusalem, destroyed the Temple, and regained control of Palestine. Hundreds of thousands of Jews were killed, sold into slavery, or shipped off to become gladiators before audiences in Roman cities.

In 132 A.D. the Jews again rebelled. Once more the Romans reacted swiftly and brutally. Following this uprising, the Romans forbade Jews to enter Jerusalem on pain of death. Many had left Palestine after the Temple's destruction in 70 A.D. Now more departed, dispersing throughout the world.

The Jews' political power was broken, but their determination to preserve their religion survived. They carried their faith with them wherever they went.

Check on Your Reading

1. What did Deborah, Saul, David, and Solomon accomplish?
2. What was the role of the prophets in the development of Judaism?
3. How did the Jews meet the threat of Hellenism?
4. Describe Jewish relations with the Romans.

3. The Beginnings of Christianity

Josephus, a Jewish historian who wrote in the first century A.D., had this to say in his *Antiquities of the Jews:*

> At that time lived Jesus, a holy man, . . . for he performed wonderful works, and taught men, and joyfully received the truth. And he was followed by many Jews and many Greeks. He was the Messiah.

The idea of a Messiah, a leader who would restore the Jewish state to what it was under David and Solomon, was a part of Jewish tradition. It became especially important when the Jews were ruled by Rome in the first century B.C.

Jesus, whom some Jews considered a Messiah, did appear; but Jesus did not come, as it turned out, to restore past splendor. Rather, Jesus became the founder of a new religion.

The Background

We rely on the *New Testament* of the *Bible* for information concerning Jesus and his works. According to the *Gospels* of *Matthew* and *Luke*, Jesus was born to Mary in Bethlehem, a little town five miles south of Jerusalem. He grew up in the town of Nazareth. Little is known about his childhood. Joseph, the husband of Mary, was a carpenter, and Jesus may have learned this trade.

According to *Luke,* at the age of twelve Jesus accompanied his parents to Jerusalem to celebrate the religious festival of Passover. When the festival ended and Mary and Joseph started for home, they discovered that Jesus was not among their group. Returning to the city, Joseph and Mary found Jesus in the Temple, talking learnedly with priests and scholars.

The Teachings of Jesus

At about the age of thirty, Jesus began to teach. He taught in synagogues and to crowds gathered in the open along the Sea of Galilee and elsewhere in Palestine. His message was one of love of God and of fellow humans. He spoke often of compassion and forgiveness for wrongdoing. Much of Jesus' message was directed toward the poor and disreputable, and placed spiritual needs above material rewards.

"Do not store up for yourselves treasure on earth, where it grows rusty and moth-eaten, and thieves break in to steal it," Jesus said. "Store up treasure in heaven, where there is no moth and no rust to spoil it, no thieves to break in and steal. For where your treasure is, there will your heart be also." In the "Sermon on the Mount" Jesus said: "How blest are you that you now go hungry; your hunger will be satisfied."

Frequently Jesus spoke in *parables,* brief tales concerning everyday problems designed to make a point or teach a lesson.

Much of what Jesus preached lay within the Jewish tradition. "I came not to destroy the Law of Moses but to fulfill it," Jesus said. Jesus emphasized a heavenly, not a temporal, reward for all humans who placed their faith in God.

According to the *Gospels,* Jesus attracted much attention by working miracles. Jesus also gathered twelve disciples, or *apostles.* He gave these men from humble backgrounds the responsibility of spreading the gospel, the "good news."

At about the age of thirty-three, Jesus encountered the serious opposition of religious leaders in Jerusalem. They rejected the idea of some of his followers that Jesus was the Messiah. He was denounced for blasphemy and charged with wanting to become king of the Jews. He was turned over to the Roman governor, Pontius Pilate.

Jesus was accused by the Romans of causing unrest and of challenging Roman authority. Condemned to death, Jesus was crucified. According to the beliefs of his disciples, Jesus rose from the dead soon after and later ascended to heaven.

The *Bible* relates that Jesus later appeared before his disciples. The *Gospel according to John* states that

The Italian artist Masaccio (1401–1428) painted this scene of Jesus and some of his disciples.

Jesus promised to send the Holy Spirit, or Holy Ghost, to aid and comfort them. He also promised to return on the day of final judgment, when all believers would be gathered into heaven. After that, the *Gospels* say, Jesus ascended into heaven to take his place as the Son at the right hand of God the Father. Father, Son, and Holy Spirit make up the Trinity, the three-in-one godhead of the Christian religion.

Check on Your Reading

1. Relate incidents of Jesus' life.
2. What were the principal teachings of Jesus?
3. What was the Roman attitude toward Jesus?

4. The Early Christian Church

A new religion had been born—Christianity, taken from *Christ*, a Greek word meaning "the Anointed," or "the Chosen One." It would, in time, spread throughout the world.

The Principles of Christianity

Today, about one out of every three persons in the world is a Christian. Although there are many different Christian churches, most of them are still based on four principles of early Christianity. 1. There is one God, creator of all things. 2. Jesus Christ is the Divine Son of God and to most Christians a member of the Trinity. 3. The teachings of Jesus are to be followed. Specifically, people are to love God, treat all human beings justly, and live in peace. 4. Each person is judged by God for his or her conduct on earth. A faithful Christian can look forward to an eternal life after death, a sinner to punishment.

The heart of Christianity is found in two great commandments:

Thou shalt love the Lord thy God with all thy heart, and with all thy soul and with all thy mind.
This is the first and great commandment.
And the second is like unto it, Thou shalt love thy neighbor as thyself.
On these two commandments hang all the law. . . .

To the *Old Testament* the Christians later added the *New Testament,* which includes accounts of the life and teachings of Jesus, and the writings of early Christians.

The Spread of Christianity

After recovering from the initial shock and despondency of their leader's death, the Apostles set out to establish churches and make converts, at first only among Jews. They eventually covered much of the Roman world, working even in Rome itself.

The Apostle Peter was particularly important. He traveled and preached as far as Rome where, it is believed, he was crucified about 65 A.D.

Beginning about 50 A.D. one man, Paul, gave Christianity particular impetus. He was tireless in his travel and missionary activity.

Paul was born in about the year 10 A.D. in the city of Tarsus near the Mediterranean coast in the southern part of what now is Turkey. He was given the name Saul, and received a sound education in Jewish tradition and Law and in the Hebrew language. He also learned Greek. Tarsus was in the Roman Empire and Saul's father was a Roman citizen. He passed on that heritage to his son. By trade, Saul was a tentmaker. He was also active in trying to prevent the spread of the Christian faith.

Then, one day on the road from Jerusalem to the Syrian city of Damascus, Saul experienced an overwhelming vision. It is described in the *Acts of the Apostles:*

While he was still on the road and nearing Damascus, suddenly a light flashed from the sky all around him. He fell to the ground and heard a voice saying, "Saul, Saul, why do you persecute me?" "Tell me, Lord," he said, "who you are." The voice answered, "I am Jesus, whom you are persecuting. But get up and go into the city, and you will be told what you have to do." Meanwhile the men who were traveling with him stood speechless. They heard the voice, but could see no one. Saul got up from the ground, but when he opened his eyes he could not see; so they led him by the hand and brought him into Damascus. He was blind for three days, and took no food or drink.

This experience marked Saul's conversion to Christianity, changing his life and his name. He became Paul the Apostle, devoting himself now to preaching the message of Christ and bringing converts to the new faith.

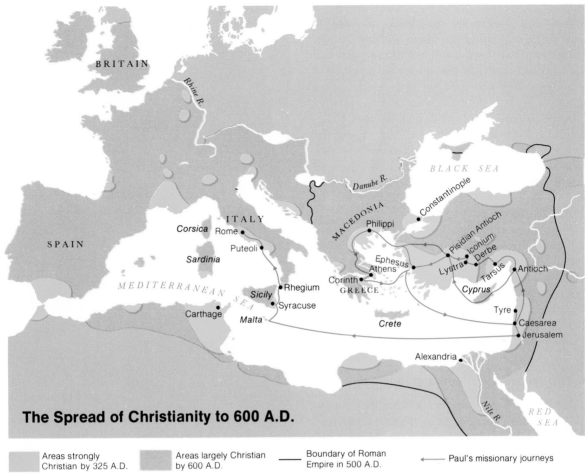

The Spread of Christianity to 600 A.D.

| Areas strongly Christian by 325 A.D. | Areas largely Christian by 600 A.D. | —— Boundary of Roman Empire in 500 A.D. | ◄— Paul's missionary journeys |

The efforts of countless women and men resulted in the spread of Christianity to many peoples.

Paul's Travels

Paul lived in the period of the *Pax Romana*. (See page 124.) Roman roads linked all parts of the Empire. Sea lanes were busy with ships carrying people and freight. As a Roman citizen, Paul could travel anywhere in the Empire. An average day's journey on foot probably took him about 16 miles, traveling during the cooler morning hours.

Paul traveled thousands of miles, starting Christian churches across Asia Minor and Greece. (See the map above.) He suffered persecution, imprisonment, and shipwreck. Yet his missionary zeal never flagged, and his teachings laid the groundwork for Christian theology.

As an example of his activity, a chronicler of the *Acts of the Apostles* recorded this:

So we sailed from Troas [on the Aegean Sea] and made a straight run to Samothrace [an island in that sea], the next day to Neapolis [on the Macedonian coast] and from there to Philippi, a city of the first rank in that district of Macedonia, and a Roman colony. Here we stayed for some days, and on the Sabbath day we went outside the city gate by the riverside, where we thought there would be a place of prayer, and sat down and talked to the women who had gathered there. One of them named Lydia, a dealer in purple fabric from the city of Thyatira, who was a worshipper of God, was listening, and the Lord opened her heart to respond to what Paul said. She was baptized, and her household with her, and then she said to us, "If you have judged me to be a believer in the Lord, I beg you to come and stay in my house." And she insisted on our going.

Lydia was a businesswoman; she was a dealer in the purple dyes for which the Phoenicians had been famous, as well as in various fabrics. She apparently had a number of employees working for her. She seems to have been involved in the organization of a Christian church in Philippi, to the members of which Paul later addressed one of his *epistles,* or his letters.

In the eastern half of the Roman Empire, Hellenistic Greek was the common language. It was the language in which Paul wrote his letters of guidance to churches he had founded, and to Christian friends. His epistles and those of disciples who traveled with him form a large part of the *New Testament* of the Christian *Bible.*

Paul's missionary activity—and his life—ended in Rome. Seized by Roman authorities in about 65 A.D. and accused of what amounted to treason, he was beheaded, becoming an early martyr to Christianity. This occurred during the reign of the emperor Nero (54–68 A.D.). It was also during Nero's time that Peter, the first disciple chosen by Jesus, was executed in Rome.

The Christian Religion and Worship

Early Christians assembled on what they considered the Lord's day, Sunday. Their leaders read from the *Scriptures,* and led congregations in prayers. They then preached sermons exhorting their listeners to be firm in the faith and to lead moral lives.

Gradually Sunday worship evolved into what came to be known as the *mass.* This centered on a re-enactment of the "Last Supper" that Jesus and his disciples had shared in Jerusalem before his death.

The early Christians had to contend with opposing points of view concerning whether Jesus was a divine figure, or a human teacher. They also had to make decisions about other beliefs and ceremonies within the churches. There was, at times, intense discussion and argument within the growing church.

It became the practice to turn for guidance and leadership to churches that had been founded by the Apostles. Of these, the Church at Rome was considered most important, as it had been founded by two martyred Apostles—Peter and Paul.

Most of what was later assembled as the *New Testament* of the Christian *Bible* was written during the first century A.D. By about the middle of the third century, the books that make up the *New Testament*

This mosaic from Ravenna, Italy portrays an early Christian martyr, St. Stephen.

were commonly recognized as the Holy Scriptures on which the Christian Church was founded.

Early Christians Die for Their Faith

Christianity was not easily established in the Roman Empire. Peter, Paul, and other religious leaders have been remembered for their heroism. Yet there were thousands of other people whose names have been forgotten. These people were early Christian *martyrs,* men and women who gave up their lives rather than renounce their religion.

For example, when Nero was emperor (54–68 A.D.), persecutions of the Christians were so extreme that on one occasion:

The victims [Christians] . . . were covered with the skins of wild beasts and torn to pieces by dogs; while others were fixed to crosses and burnt to light the night when daylight had failed.

In this room of the Catacomb of Priscilla near Rome religious services were probably held.

The emperors of Rome were not opposed to Christianity as a religion. They permitted different religions to exist in the Empire, provided that the members of those religions accepted the Roman emperor as a god. A number of religions from Egypt and Persia existed peacefully side by side with the Roman religion. Their members accepted the Roman emperor as a god.

The Christians, however, refused to offer up the customary sacrifices to the emperors or to recognize them as gods. Their religion permitted them to recognize but one God. The emperors, therefore, considered them to be a threat against Roman authority and a challenge to their political power.

For almost two centuries after the death of Nero (68 A.D.) there was no concerted effort to wipe out

Christianity. Then in the third century A.D. several rulers determined to check the spread of Christianity. Thousands of devout Christians were thrown into arenas to be killed by wild animals. Others were beaten to death by Roman soldiers.

Under the pressure of such persecution, some Christians changed their beliefs and again worshipped the emperor's image. Most of them, however, continued to cling to their faith.

Between 100 and 320 A.D. these Christians buried their dead in catacombs—long, twisting underground passages. The catacombs probably were used also as safe hiding places for Christians during periods of persecution. They remain as silent reminders of the days when persecuted women and men clung to their religion.

The Church of S. Apolinare was built in the fifth century in northern Italy. It was constructed in the form of a Roman basilica, as were many early Christian churches.

Church Organization Develops

As the number of churches increased, their officials came to be known as the *clergy*. Finally, there evolved an organization which became known as the *Roman Catholic Church*. The *Church* was an organization through which Christians could practice their religion under a common authority. Although there were several religious groups that refused to accept its supervision, the Church extended its control over many Christians.

By the fourth century, the Church had developed certain basic features. Men known as *bishops* supervised Christian worhip in various cities and territories throughout the old Roman Empire. The area administered by a bishop was called a *diocese.*

Later, *archbishops* acted as overall directors of areas in the West where there were several bishops. (In the eastern part of the Roman Empire, chief bishops were known as *metropolitans* instead of archbishops. Leading metropolitans were called *patriarchs.*) *Priests* helped the bishops by administering local church areas, or *parishes.* Priests were appointed to their duties by the bishops.

The term *Pope,* which came from a Greek word

meaning "father," at first referred to any bishop or even priest. It started to be used more particularly as the title of the bishop of Rome as early as the sixth century. The bishop of Rome eventually became the most influential leader of the Church in the West.

Christianity Wins Official Acceptance

During the early part of the fourth century A.D., Emperor Constantine was the ruler of the Roman Empire. Legend tells that just before an important battle, he saw a lighted cross in the sky and the words "By this sign thou shalt conquer." Constantine did win the battle, and there were many who said that the victory had come through the aid of the cross of Christ.

Constantine now decided to help the Christians. He may have reached this decision because he was deeply moved by his victory. Or he may have realized that Christianity was spreading so widely that it would be a wise political move to recognize it. Whatever his motive, Constantine issued the *Edict of Milan* (313 A.D.), which gave full toleration to all religions, including Christianity. Toleration meant that Christians could now practice their religion "freely and absolutely . . . and were not to be disturbed in any ways or molested."

When there were disagreements over Christian beliefs among Christian leaders, Constantine called them together into a great meeting, or council, in Nicaea, Asia Minor. The Council of Nicaea (325 A.D.) attempted to put an end to arguments about Christian beliefs by preparing the *Nicene Creed.* This statement forms the foundation of most Christian theology today.

Later, Emperor Theodosius (379-395 A.D.) made Christianity the *state religion;* that is, the official religion of the Roman Empire. He began persecuting pagans and closed the Olympic Games because they had pagan religious significance.

Check on Your Reading

1. Describe the activities and influence of Paul.
2. What was the Romans' objection to Christianity and what actions did they take against that religion?
3. Describe the development of the organization of the Roman Catholic Church.
4. Under what circumstances did Christianity finally triumph under the Romans?

The altar of a basilica church in northern Italy. Early Christian art was strongly influenced by Graeco-Roman art.

Becoming a Rabbi

In the door of a hut, isolated among the hills, stood Rabbi Joshua, a wrinkled old man in a threadbare robe. Elisha's heart sank. This was where he would be living and this was his teacher!

Elisha had been brought by his uncle to Rabbi Joshua because it had been decided that Elisha would learn the Law, and, after many years of study, become a rabbi himself. That distant goal was a fine one, but the present was disheartening.

Rabbi Joshua was one of a number of teachers who trained young men not only to become experts in the Jewish Law, but also to become wise judges in the Sanhedrin (the highest court and council). Elisha had learned much about the Scriptures and the Tradition from his uncle. Now he would master much more knowledge as he lived with Joshua. Elisha would also learn blacksmithing, for that was how the rabbi earned his living.

As they worked at the forge, prayed and meditated, examined Jewish history and the Law, and walked in the hills, Elisha's apprehension and loneliness disappeared. He found his master a wise and kindly man, sympathetic to the concerns of youth, and delighted with his apprentice's sharp and probing questions. Elisha forgot time as his zest for learning grew, kindled and fed by Joshua's teaching.

One day, after many months, Elisha accompanied his teacher to a meeting of the Sanhedrin. There Elisha sat, squeezed into a crowded room, watching and listening with wonder as Joshua and other rabbis discussed questions sent to them and dictated answers to the scribes. "Might the restrictions on labor on the Sabbath be waived in tending a sick person?" "Did the obligation to love one's fellows extend to all persons, even persecutors?"

Elisha had no doubts now, even though he knew he had years of study ahead. Someday he hoped to become learned and wise enough to be a rabbi like his teacher.

Years later, that great day finally arrived. Standing before the Sanhedrin, feeling the Rabbi Gamliel's hand upon his bowed head, Elisha heard the treasured words: "In accordance with the will of God and with the authority invested in me by the Sanhedrin, I endow Elisha, the son of Abuyah, with the title of Elder and with membership in this body. I declare him a Rabbi in Israel."

Elisha had achieved his goal. Later, after he had given his first lecture before the Sanhedrin, young men crowded around him. "Master," they said, "thou hast expounded well. May thy strength increase."

The above account is based upon *As a Driven Leaf,* by Milton Steinberg. Used by permission of Berman House, Inc., Publisher.

CHAPTER REVIEW

Think and Discuss

1. Compare the early account of the Hebrews as a nomadic people with the accounts of other nomadic peoples in the Middle East whom you learned about in Chapter 1. How were they alike? How different?

2. Compare the reasons for the development of kings in Israel with the reasons given in Chapter 1 for the development of kings in Sumeria.

3. What part did the rise and fall of empires play in the history of the Jews? Give examples.

4. How did the *Pax Romana* help the spread of Christianity?

5. Why do you think that so many people became Christians within the Roman Empire?
6. Does persecution make one's faith stronger or weaker? Why?

Past and Present

1. Both the Jews and the early Christians were persecuted because of their religion. Does religious persecution take place in modern times? If so, give examples.
2. On page 134 the heading and the material under it discuss symbols. Why are symbols important? What symbols are important in our culture?

Activities

1. Read a selection from a primary source, such as the *Book of Ruth* or the *Book of Judges* in the *Old Testament*. What does the selection tell about living conditions and ways of thinking?

2. Write an account of a secret meeting of Christians in Rome during the persecution. Consult references.

Making a Timeline

Since the time of Columbus, flags from many different nations have flown over various parts of the United States. Each flag has symbolized control by a different government. Texans, for example, can count six flags that have flown over their soil. But perhaps no other land in recorded history has been claimed or ruled by so many rulers as has the land of Palestine.

Starting with the Canaanites, construct a timeline that shows the major ruling groups whose flags might have waved over Palestine. Use information in the Text and in reference books to show the approximate length of time each of these groups had control of Palestine. End your timeline with the Romans.

3

Great Civilizations in Asia

Most of us look at the world from the point of view of the place, culture, and time in which we live. Thus, in the past, different peoples of European and other Western cultures have assumed that their ways of living were superior to those of peoples of the East.

Yet, as anthrolopogist Ralph Linton has pointed out, Americans who rise in the morning and remove their pajamas (a garment which originated in India), put on clothing (some items of which were derived from the nomads of Asia), eat waffles (from wheat domesticated in Asia Minor), and read the newspapers (printed on material invented in China) should know that no Western country has a monopoly on influencing the lives of human beings. Certainly, Asia's influence has been felt throughout the world.

Proof of this point can be found in the following unit, which focuses on Asia. In the period covered by this unit, the peoples of Asia, building on past achievements, created some of the world's greatest civilizations.

8

Islam Comes out of the Middle East

KEYNOTE

Like the religions of the Jews and the Christians, Islam is a monotheistic religion. *The Koran,* the sacred book of Islam, begins:

> In the name of Allah,
> The Merciful, the Compassionate
> Praise be to Allah, the Lord of mankind,
> The Merciful, the Compassionate
> Master of the Day of Judgment.
> Thee do we worship, and to Thee do we turn for help.
> Guide us in the straightest path.
> The path of those to whom Thou hast been gracious.
> Not of those with whom thou art angered,
> nor of those who go astray.

Today, one out of every seven people in the world is a member of the Islamic religion. Followers of Islam have played an important part in the civilization of many lands.

Reading the Koran.

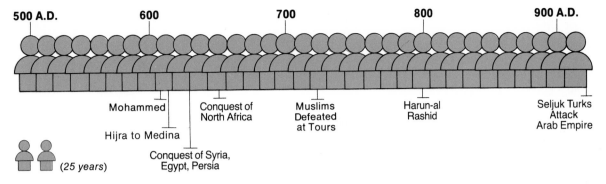

Mohammed

Conquest of North Africa

Muslims Defeated at Tours

Harun-al Rashid

Seljuk Turks Attack Arab Empire

Hijra to Medina

Conquest of Syria, Egypt, Persia

(25 years)

1. Backgrounds

There lived in the Middle East yet another Semitic people who would place an indelible stamp on history. These were Arabs. Most of their homeland, the Arabian peninsula, is now occupied by Saudi Arabia.

The Setting

Arabia is a huge peninsula on the southwestern edge of the continent of Asia; and it is connected to Africa by the Isthmus of Suez. It is bounded on the west by the Red Sea, on the south by the Arabian Sea, and on the east by the Persian Gulf. Much of the Arabian peninsula is barren and forbidding. Mountains form a huge L along the western and southern edges. Desert covers most of the interior. Within the desert are oases, green patches fed by springs. Fifteen hundred years ago, the oases offered life support to nomads and their herds and flocks. Some towns had developed around oases on trade routes, and others served as farming and trading centers along the coasts.

Bedouin Customs and Leadership

Most of the Arabs were nomads, known as *Bedouins*. The word came from *badw*, meaning desert.

Bedouins had molded themselves to the desert ecology, using its resources while being prepared to meet its dangers. They adjusted their ways of living to the relentless sun of day, and to the chill of night, to winds driving stinging sand, and to a land of almost no rainfall. They moved from place to place, following regular routes to oases, where they found nourishment for themselves and their camels, horses, sheep, and goats. Families owned their tents, some animals, and a few personal possessions. But those items essential to survival—water and pasture—Bedouins held in common.

The desert had no mercy for the individual. No person *alone* could survive there long. Loyalty to the group, on which every individual depended, was vital if human life were to endure.

Among Bedouins, each person leaned first on the family. Families, in turn, made up clans, and a cluster of clans composed a tribe. Loyalty flowed to the family, then to the clan and tribe.

Within the family, the father ruled supreme. Each clan had its chieftain. Tribal leaders, called *sheiks*, were elected by family elders. Sheiks frequently came from the same families, but this was not always the case.

The main qualifications for sheikdom were wisdom, generosity, and courage, not family background. The ideal sheik, it was said, was a man who would "keep open house; be gentle of speech; make no demands on anyone; show the same cordiality to rich and poor alike—in short, treat all men as equals." Sheiks did not rule alone. A council of elected elders assisted them.

Sheiks commanded during war, but at other times their authority was mainly limited to settling disputes. A sheik could impose no duties or penalties on tribal members. Rights and obligations rested on the family and the clan. The family especially bore responsibility for individual behavior. It settled such serious matters as murder and theft.

Bedouins bred fine horses, in which they took great pride. But their most important animal was the camel, which like the Bedouins was well adapted to the desert. This animal furnished transportation and served as a beast of burden. It also provided hides for tents, clothing, and waterbags; milk and meat; and dung for fuel. Life on the desert would have been impossible without the camel.

Bedouins worshipped numerous gods and goddesses. As a rule, each clan and tribe had its own deity; but there was a chief god. He was *Allah*,

149

A camel caravan crosses the desert.

which came from the word *al-ilah,* meaning "the God."

Bedouins and Towns

Bedouins were fiercely independent. Customarily they honored no authority save that which they had granted and could withdraw. To them the desert represented freedom.

Bedouins, nonetheless, used the towns. They came to them to exchange camels, horses, goat and camel hair, and wool for such items as knives, swords, saddles, and sometimes cloth. At times, some Bedouins raided towns and plundered them. On occasion, they also captured and looted caravans carrying trade goods.

By the end of the sixth century A.D. one town, Mecca, had achieved special importance. Mecca was on the western side of the Arabian peninsula about fifty miles from the Red Sea. It was on caravan routes going north and south near the Red Sea and east and west from the Red Sea to the Persian Gulf. Trade brought wealth. It also brought contacts with ideas from the outside world, including those of such religions as Judaism and Christianity.

The city of Mecca represented the change that was taking place in Arab society. The Bedouin clan and tribal solidarity necessary in the desert was out of place in Mecca. There the pursuit of wealth and personal advantage fostered individualism. Social and economic classes had developed in contrast to the essentially democratic way of life of the desert. In the towns the older ideals of family, stern justice, and independence were under attack by the newer ideas of personal gain.

In this changing society, in about the year 570 A.D., an Arab was born who would establish a monotheistic religion to give the Arabs a basis for unity, whether they were nomads or town dwellers. He was Mohammed.

Proclaiming Allah as the only God and himself his Prophet, he was responsible for the founding of Islam. Mohammed gave Arabs not only a new religion, but a new identity as well.

Check on Your Reading

1. Describe Bedouin values and indicate how they reflected the Bedouin environment.
2. In what ways did the city of Mecca symbolize change in Arab society?

150

2. Mohammed and the Birth of Islam

Mohammed, a name that means "highly praised," was born into the Quraysh tribe in Mecca. Misfortune befell him early in life. Before Mohammed was born, his father died while on a caravan journey to Syria. His mother died when he was six. A grandfather took in the orphan, but two years later he, too, died. Then an uncle raised the orphan.

When Mohammed was twelve, he went with his uncle on a caravan northbound from Mecca. On the journey he met a Christian monk, which may have been one of his first exposures to the concept of monotheism. During his days in trade, Mohammed undoubtedly met other Christians, and Jews as well, thus becoming more familiar with those two religions.

Mohammed probably continued to be active in trade for the next several years, accompanying caravans and conducting business in Mecca itself. When he was twenty-five, he married Khadija, a wealthy, strong-minded, and wise widow who had employed him in the caravan trade she conducted.

Revelations

Marriage brought Mohammed security, as well as leisure to consider the social and economic changes going on about him and the religious ideas he had encountered. He spent much of his time in seclusion, particularly in a cave on a hillside on Mecca's outskirts. There, according to his followers, one day when he was forty, Mohammed experienced a vision.

Wrapped in his thoughts, Mohammed, it is said,

The first monumental building erected by the Muslims that has survived is the "Dome of the Rock" in Jerusalem. The plan of this mosque follows a pre-Muslim style of building.

suddenly heard a voice commanding, "Read, in the name of the Lord!" Mohammed had had no formal schooling but possibly had learned to read as part of his business dealings. In a startled voice he responded: "How can I?" The voice replied:

Read, for your Lord is the most bounteous,
Who teaches by the pen,
Teaching man what he did not know.

Rushing home, Mohammed related the experience to Khadija. He later decided that the archangel Gabriel, speaking for Allah, had addressed him. In the years that followed, Mohammed is said to have received more revelations concerning Allah's greatness and the need to recognize Allah as the only and all-powerful deity.

Mohammed became the Messenger of Allah, determined to spread God's word. Khadija became the first convert to *Islam,* which means submission to the will of Allah.

Hardship

The Prophet took his message to the people of Mecca. He preached belief in Allah as the only true God. He emphasized the right of the poor to a share of wealth and a decent living. He stressed brotherhood centered on a religious faith that cut across clan and tribal lines.

Mohammed gained some followers among Mecca's lower classes. His followers were called *Muslims,* or "those who surrender to Allah." Mohammed earned the hatred of many of the merchants and the leaders of the Quraysh tribe who controlled the city. These wealthy people did not care to have the poor stirred up. Also, there were shrines to various gods in Mecca. The most important was a Black Stone housed in a building called the *Kaaba.* These shrines attracted Arab pilgrims to the city. Pilgrims, of course, spent money in Mecca. If the idea of one God prevailed, the merchants might lose considerable business. Furthermore, Mohammed's insistence on religious brotherhood disturbed a number of tribal leaders because it threatened the concept of loyalty based on kinship.

Mohammed was ridiculed by those with a stake in things as they were. They accused him of being possessed by devilish forces. They called him a bogus magician. For five years Mohammed made little headway.

Still Mohammed persisted, and tribal leaders at last tried to isolate him. They restricted all members of his clan to a certain section of Mecca and refused to have any dealings with them. Nor would they allow any individuals of their clans to marry one of Mohammed's group.

The Hijra

Finally, Mohammed looked about for more fertile fields. He met people from Yathrib, a town about 250 miles north of Mecca. They said that he and his few hundred followers might be welcomed there.

So, in the year 622 A.D., Mohammed and some of his followers set out northward from Mecca. This in Islamic tradition was the *hijra*—the "flight," although it could as well be called a migration. The move from Mecca marked the real beginning of Islam. Yathrib later was given the name Medina, "the city of the Prophet."

Medina was a more varied community than Mecca. It had no ruling tribe. Within it were members of three tribes that followed Judaism. Mohammed found many converts in Medina. Now the Prophet became a political as well as a religious leader.

Medina, in contrast to Mecca, was relatively poor. It had few resources. Mohammed proposed increasing them by raiding a caravan. He chose a caravan belonging to a clan of the Quraysh tribe. It was bound from Syria to Mecca and was due to stop at a watering place southwest of Medina. There Mohammed lay in wait with a force of about 300 Muslims to attack nearly three times as many guardians of the caravan.

Inspired by their new faith as well as by their need for goods, Mohammed's followers won a victory in March 624. They set aside one-fifth of the goods they snatched from the caravan for Allah. Mohammed's prestige increased considerably.

The next year, Meccan forces retaliated and won a victory over Mohammed. In 627 a Meccan army lay siege to Medina, but the defenders beat it off.

In 628 Mohammed made peace with the Quraysh in Mecca. He and his followers would no longer be persecuted there. Two years later Mohammed led a thousand of his people back to Mecca to enter the city in triumph. He smashed idols and made the Kaaba and its Black Stone an Islamic shrine. Later he addressed the people:

Harken, O ye men, unto my words and take ye them to heart. Know ye that every Muslim is a brother unto every other Muslim, and that ye are now one brotherhood. It is, therefore, not legitimate for any one of you to appropriate unto himself anything that belongs to his brother unless it is willingly given by that brother.

On June 8, 632, Mohammed died.

The Koran

The revelations Mohammed had experienced were written down after his death as the *Koran*, the Islamic holy book. The *Koran* and the *hadith*—"sayings" of Mohammed—formed the core of the *shari'a*, the Islamic holy law. Like the Jewish Law, it covered much more than religion. The *shari'a* touched upon, among other things, marriage, family life, divorce, and inheritance. It concerned military operations and the treatment of booty and prisoners of war; punishment for wrongdoing; and food and drink.

Muslims, for example, were not to eat pork. They were to avoid alcoholic beverages. They were forbidden to gamble. They could not make images representing Allah. They were freely to give alms to the poor, not charge interest when lending money, and be lenient toward debtors who had difficulty repaying loans.

Arabs placed women in a position subordinate to men. Many also practiced polygamy, the custom of taking more than one wife. The *Koran*, however, prohibited a man from having more than four wives. It upheld virtue in women and cautioned all men to protect a woman's good name.

Mohammed honored Abraham, Jesus, and numerous other biblical figures as prophets. He considered himself the final prophet whom God had sent and established a faith resting on the "Five Pillars of Islam."

The Five Pillars

The first pillar is an expression of faith: "There is no god but Allah and Mohammed is his Prophet." This is the basic testimony of faith in Islam.

Prayer, of which two kinds developed, became the second pillar. One kind of prayer is personal, following no ritual or rule. The other is ritual

The Kaaba at Mecca, now in Saudi Arabia.

prayer to be offered regularly five times a day—at sunrise, midday, afternoon, sunset, and evening. At these times, each person bows low, forehead to ground, facing the direction of Mecca, and recites prayers. There are also ritual prayers each Friday, the Muslim day of worship. Then the people gather in the *mosque*, the place of worship. Usually a person is chosen to call the people to prayer. This *muezzen* often sends out the call to prayer from a tall slender tower which rises beside the mosque. This tower is known as a *minaret*.

The third pillar is the giving of alms, or charity. This has been interpreted as giving to the poor or as a form of tax paid to the community or the state. As the latter, it represents acceptance of the authority of Islam and allegiance to it.

Fasting forms the fourth pillar. Fasting is required during the month of *Ramadan*, the ninth month of the Islamic calendar. During Ramadan, all but the sick and aged are to go without food and drink between sunrise and sunset. All are to recite special prayers at night. Then, as the new moon appears and Ramadan ends, a three-day festival begins.

A pilgrimage to Mecca is the fifth pillar of Islam. Mohammed's return to Mecca in 630 became known as the *hajj*, or pilgrimage. Each Muslim, if possible, at least once in a lifetime, was to make a pilgrimage to that holy city.

Check on Your Reading

1. Describe Mohammed's early attempts to spread his message.
2. What contributed to his final success?
3. Describe the *shari'a* and some of the items it contained.
4. Explain the Five Pillars of Islam.

---

3. The Spread of Islam

Mohammed was not only the Prophet. He had also been lawmaker, ruler, judge, and military commander. His death posed a vital question of succession. Abu-Bakr, who had been associated with the Prophet for many years, was chosen the *caliph*—the successor.

Mohammed had molded together many of the Arabs under the banner of Islam. He had infused them with a desire to spread the new religion.

There were at the time two great empires in the Middle East. Persia, which included modern Iraq as well as Iran, had Zoroastrianism as the state religion. The other empire, the Byzantine, included Syria, Egypt, and Palestine. The Byzantine religion was Greek Orthodox Christianity.

The Byzantine and Persian empires had fought numerous wars, and one that ended in 628 left both powers weak. This would work to the advantage of the Arabs.

Early Conquests

Under Abu-Bakr, Muslim armies subdued several Arab tribes that refused to recognize Islam. These conquests provided the encouragement needed to carry Islam outside the boundaries of the Arabian peninsula.

Abu-Bakr in 633 sent several small expeditions into Syria and Palestine. In the spring of the following year his top general, Khalid, conquered Damascus, the capital of Syria, sacked it, and then departed.

In August 634 Abu-Bakr died and Omar became caliph. The wars of conquest continued with another attack on Damascus and its fall after a six-month siege in September 635.

Syria was Christian, and the terms of Muslim conquest there set a pattern for dealing with people of different religious faiths outside Arabia:

> In the name of Allah, the compassionate, the merciful. This is what Khalid would grant the people of Damascus if he enters it: he promises to give them security for their lives, property and churches. Their city walls shall not be demolished and no Muslims shall be quartered in their dwellings. There unto we give them the pact of Allah and the protection of his Prophet, the caliphs, and the believers. So long as they pay poll-tax, nothing but good shall befall them.

In 636 Arab armies dealt Byzantine forces a crushing blow in another battle in Syria. Most of the Syrians felt no loyalty to the harsh rule of the Byzantine emperor and welcomed the Muslim conquerors. Syria was quickly occupied. Muslim armies then moved south to capture Jerusalem and add Palestine to the Islamic Empire.

Arabs were new to the task of conquest and at governing an empire. Like numerous conquerors before them, they learned from those they subdued.

Omar kept the framework of government that the Romans and then the Byzantines had established in Syria. He left the bureaucracy intact, allowing Syrians to operate it. The major difference was that tax money now flowed into Muslim, not Byzantine, hands.

Omar followed the same procedure after his armies had conquered Egypt in 640. Egypt would serve as a base for further operations in North Africa. It also became an important source of food supply, mainly grain, as it had been when part of the Roman Empire.

The Conquest of the Persian Empire

Meanwhile, in the east, Muslim armies were moving into Iraq, one of the richest regions of the Persian Empire. In 637 they captured the Persian capital of Iraq, sending the emperor and his court fleeing for their lives. The Arab occupation of this royal city brought them into contact with the luxuries and comforts of a great civilization. The people of Iraq had no love for their Persian rulers, and the Arab armies easily took over the rest of Iraq.

The conquest of Persia itself was much more difficult. It took Muslim armies about 10 years to win control of the country. In time, Arabic became the official language of Persia. At the same time, however, a considerable part of Persian civilization conquered the Arabs. Persian science, art, literature, and philosophy became the common heritage of the Arab world.

Umayyad Beginnings

In 644 a Persian assassinated Caliph Omar as he entered a mosque in Medina on a Friday to pray. Then in 656 the next caliph was also murdered; the

By 750 A.D. Arab armies had conquered a huge empire.

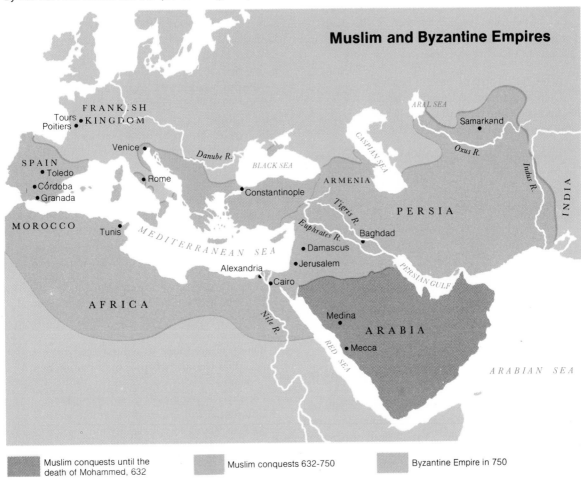

Muslim and Byzantine Empires

Muslim conquests until the death of Mohammed, 632

Muslim conquests 632-750

Byzantine Empire in 750

assassins in this case were Muslims. This murder touched off a struggle for the caliphate that led to civil war.

Ali, a cousin to Mohammed and husband of one of the Prophet's daughters, won the caliphate. But he had to fight to hold it, and in 661 he was assassinated. Mu'awiyah, who had been governor of Syria and a rival of Ali, now became caliph. Reigning for twenty years, he began the Umayyad dynasty.

Mu'awiyah established his capital at Damascus. He was a brilliant administrator who used every device possible to knit the lands that Muslim armies had conquered into a strong empire. For example, he set up a well-organized postal system throughout the Empire.

Arabs had a deep love for poetry and Mu'awiyah rewarded poets for works that promoted unity and patriotism among his people. He probably was not pleased, however, with the poetic efforts of one of his wives, Maysun. She was a Christian who had grown up in the Syrian desert with her nomadic tribe. She preferred the freedom of the desert to settled life in Damascus. It is believed that she expressed her love for the desert in these verses:

A tent with rustling breezes cool
Delight me more than palace high,
And more the cloak of simple wool
Than robes in which I learned to sigh. . . .

Mu'awiyah accommodated Maysun by sending her back to her desert tribe.

Further Conquests

As caliph, Mu'awiyah continued the war against the Byzantine Empire. He began the building of a Muslim navy as a military force in this war. Mu'awiyah used the former Byzantine shipyard of a Syrian port to build his ships, and manned them with Greek and Syrian sailors. At one point his navy and army laid unsuccessful siege to Constantinople itself. In northern Africa his armies spread as far west as the site of ancient Carthage. In the east, Mu'awiyah extended the Islamic Empire beyond Persia.

Although he sent Maysun away, Mu'awiyah did select Yazid, the son she had borne him, to succeed him as caliph. Under Yazid and succeeding Umayyads, the Empire continued to grow, especially in the west.

All North Africa from Egypt to Morocco was taken by Muslim armies. Arab forces then crossed over into Spain early in the 700s. Within a few years Muslim armies had conquered most of Spain. They then crossed the Pyrenees Mountains into southern France. There a group of Muslim raiders met defeat at the hands of the Franks at the so-called Battle of Tours in 732. Muslims then retired to Spain.

The third generation of Arabs after Mohammed's death controlled an empire that stretched from southwestern Europe across North Africa to include the Middle East and into the valley of the Indus River in India. It was an empire to rival that of Rome at its height. Throughout the Empire, Arabic was the official language.

Abbassid Beginnings and Spain

After ninety years, the Umayyad dynasty came to an end in 750. It was overthrown by members of a branch of Mohammed's family known as Abbassids. The victorious Abbassids declared death to all Umayyads. One member of the family, the youthful Abd-al-Rahman, escaped. After five years of wandering he reached Morocco.

Muslim Spain at the time was seething with unrest and civil war following the change in dynasties. Abd-al-Rahman crossed the Mediterranean from Morocco to land in Spain, where he was welcomed as the survivor of the royal Umayyad family. He then raised an army and marched on Córdoba, the capital. He defeated an opposing army, and eventually made himself caliph of Spain.

Abd-al-Rahman proved to be an able and successful ruler. Yet he always remembered the land from which he had come, expressing his nostalgia at one time in a poem addressed to a date palm tree:

O Palm, thou art a stranger in the West,
Far from the Orient home, like me unblest.
Weep! But thou canst not, dumb, dejected
    tree,
Thou are not made to sympathize with me.
Ah, thou wouldst weep, if thou had tears to
    pour,
For thy companions on Euphrates' shore;
But yonder tall groves thou rememberest not,
As I, in hating foes, have my old friends forgot.

Having split Spain off from the Islamic Empire, Umayyads would rule that land until 1031.

The Shah Mosque in Isfahan, Iran. The Arabs were deeply influenced by the civilization of the Persians whom they conquered. Notice the two minarets.

4. Islamic Civilization

The scholar Philip K. Hitti in his *History of the Arabs* writes:

> It was not only an empire that the Arabs built, but a culture as well. Heirs of the ancient civilization that flourished on the banks of the Tigris and the Euphrates, in the land of the Nile and on the eastern shore of the Mediterranean, they likewise absorbed and assimilated the main features of the Graeco-Roman cultures. Subsequently they acted as a medium for transmitting to medieval Europe many of the intellectual influences which ultimately resulted in the awakening of the Western world and in setting it on the road towards its modern renaissance.

One center of Islamic civilization was the court of the caliph.

Baghdad

The Abbassid caliph moved the capital of the Islamic Empire from Damascus to a new community, Baghdad. Baghdad was built on the banks of the Tigris, near the ruins of the Persian capital. Baghdad became a magnificent city. It was the city of "The Thousand and One Nights," tales told during the splendid reign of Caliph Harun al-Rashid, who held power between 786 and 809.

In Baghdad, the caliph lived in a great palace of many rooms. Here his court had dinner served on dishes made of gold and silver. Such ceremonies as marriage were celebrated with pomp and extravagance. In 825, for example, Caliph al-Mamun married the daughter of his chief adviser. At the wedding a thousand large-sized pearls were showered on the couple as they sat on a mat made of golden threads and decorated with pearls and sapphires.

Another caliph, Muqtadir, in 917 assembled 160,000 cavalry and footmen and more than 7,000 other attendants to greet envoys from Constantinople. A hundred lions were paraded before the guests. The Byzantine representatives were especially impressed with the Hall of Trees, which housed an artificial gold and silver tree in whose branches rested birds also made of those precious metals.

Trade and Crafts

Ships from many countries moved up the Tigris to dock at Baghdad wharves, and overland trade by caravan flourished. In the city's open markets—the *bazaars*—one could find silk and porcelain from China; spices and dyes from India; cloth from central Asia; honey, furs, and wax from Russia and Scandinavia; and ivory from Africa. Arab merchants, in turn, exported to many distant places

This manuscript shows Muslim astronomers at work.

such items as cloth, jewelry, mirrors made of metal, glass beads, and spices.

In Baghdad artisans produced all kinds of jewelry; fabrics of cotton, wool, goat and camel hair, and silk; carpets and glassware and pottery. Arabs learned about papermaking from the Chinese, and the first paper mill in Baghdad began operating near the end of the eighth century. Furniture and kitchenware were other items made in Baghdad.

Intellectual Life

Islamic scholars drew knowledge and inspiration from many civilizations, particularly the Graeco-Roman and the Persian. They translated and preserved works of the Greek philosopher Aristotle and the physicians Hippocrates and Galen.

From India, Arab scholars derived Arabic numerals, a decimal system, and the concept of zero as a placeholder. Al-Fazari translated Indian works on astronomy and became the first great Arab astronomer.

Arab physicians made contributions to the study of leprosy and diseases of the eye. Al-Razi, also known as Rhases (865-925), has been called the most original of all Muslim physicians. He was chief doctor at the hospital in Baghdad, established under Caliph Harun al-Rashid. Al-Razi produced over a hundred works on medicine and on alchemy—in a sense, the forerunner of modern chemistry. One treatise dealt with measles, and Al-Razi's work on smallpox was the first known clinical study of that disease.

Al-Razi was Persian, and so were Ibn Sina, known also as Avicenna (980-1037) and Al-Biruni (973-1048). Avicenna was both a physician and a philosopher who wrote many books on science and philosophy. Al-Biruni was another scholar in many fields: an astronomer, mathematician, physicist, alchemist, geographer, and historian.

Intellectual life in Córdoba, Spain, was equally stimulating and varied. In Córdoba Arab translators kept alive Greek works in philosophy, medicine, mathematics, and other subjects. It was from these Arab translations that some western Europeans during the Middle Ages learned the knowledge and ideas of ancient Greece.

Every year, it was said, some 60,000 books were produced in Córdoba, a city of 500,000 people. About 170 women earned a living copying manuscripts there. Caliph Al-Haquem established a library in the city that had about 500,000 volumes.

The Mosque

At the center of Islamic life stood the mosque. Here the people gathered for religious services on Friday when the prayer-leader offered prayers and read from the *Koran*.

During the rest of the week, people gathered in the mosque for other reasons. In the early days of Islam, the mosque was part of a complex of buildings housing government offices. Officials wishing to announce news of war or government policy did so from the pulpit of the mosque. The mosque also served as a court of justice.

In addition, the mosque was a center for education. Education centered on the *Koran* and other parts of the holy law. It also included grammar, poetry and other literature, arithmetic, stories about the Prophet, and reading and writing. Those wishing to enter a profession such as law or medicine apprenticed themselves to established professionals.

The first mosques were simple buildings, constructed of palm boughs and mud. Then as Islamic civilization developed, the Muslims drew architectural ideas from themselves and from different peoples to create large and handsome buildings. Often mosques were beautifully decorated with tiles and Arabic writing.

The Decline of Arab Power

As in the case of the Roman Empire, weakness within made it possible for nomad warriors to invade and eventually conquer the Islamic Empire. Overtaxation angered many people and weakened the economy. Power and luxurious living some-

The Arabs' language and writing spread throughout their empire. A page of an illustrated album probably created in Persia.

times corrupted the caliph's court and many of the ruling families. Also there was no overall sense of a common ancestry to hold the various peoples of the Empire together. For example, Persia with its proud heritage never completely accepted the idea of Arab control.

Near the end of the 900s, the nomadic Seljuk Turks began migrating out of Central Asia into the Islamic Empire. They accepted Islam and by 1055 had conquered most of Persia and taken Baghdad. With the fall of Baghdad, the Arab control of the Islamic Empire was lost forever. The Seljuks also extended their power into Syria and Palestine.

The Islamic Empire had been conquered, but its rich civilization was not lost. The vitality of the religion of Islam has continued through the centuries.

Check on Your Reading

1. Describe Baghdad at the height of the Islamic Empire.
2. Describe Islamic intellectual life and accomplishments.
3. How was the mosque used?

LET'S MEET THE PEOPLE

A Student in Baghdad

When al-Amin was about six years old, his father, al-Rashid, took him for the first time to the mosque school in Baghdad. As he left the school, al-Rashid said to al-Amin's teacher: "Do not be so strict with him as to turn him against learning. But do not be so easy that he learns to enjoy idleness."

Al-Amin had been taught from the *Koran* at home. By the time he entered the school, he was able to recite important prayers without error. He found his teacher kind and gentle, though iron-willed on the subject of reciting the *Koran* correctly. Islamic education centered on the holy book, and the student who could recite accurately the most passages won the highest marks. Such a student sometimes was given a day's holiday as a reward.

Al-Amin also studied arithmetic, Arabic grammar, and writing. After what seemed endless practice, he mastered the flowing script of the written Arabic language. The words and phrases he and his fellow students copied were never from the *Koran*. In practicing he might need to erase, and to erase the words of the Prophet was forbidden.

The curriculum included learning about famous figures in Islamic history, such as Abu-Bakr and Omar. Students also read poetry and were required to write poems of their own.

Al-Amin tried to write verses, but was not a good poet. However, he did excel in arithmetic and wrote with a good hand. Al-Amin also memorized much of the *Koran* and recited well. Among his fond memories was the day he and some other top students were honored by being paraded through the streets of Baghdad on camels as people along the way tossed almonds at them in recognition of their achievements.

Al-Amin's schooling ended when he was about thirteen. He then had to make a very important decision. Would he become a merchant like his father, or seek further education and become a scholar in medicine, Islamic law, or history? He was not sure what to do, but he was very grateful for the schooling he had had. He could say with Ali, Mohammed's son-in-law: "I am the slave of him who hath taught me even one letter."

The sketch above is based primarily on information in *History of the Arabs,* by Phillip Hitti, St. Martin's Press, 1967, pages 408–409.

CHAPTER REVIEW

Past and Present

1. Islam played a large part in the government of the Arabic Empire. Do some research on the part Islam plays in the government of Saudi Arabia today and make a comparison. Also find out if Bedouin society still plays an important part in the life of this country.
2. Islam became the official religion of Persia. Read magazine articles and newspapers to learn what part Islam plays in Iran today.

Activities

1. The Arabs who lived in a desert land had a great love of water and gardens. A famous garden from Muslim Spain is still in existence at the Generalife in Granada. Do some research on this garden and report to the class.
2. Do research and report on the modern Muslim's pilgrimage to Mecca.
3. Look through pictures of famous mosques in books on Islamic art and architecture. Make a list of features of the architecture of mosques. Include the mosque that is still standing in Córdoba, Spain, as well as those in Cairo, Egypt.

Think and Discuss

1. You have learned of different groups of nomads who conquered civilizations and then learned from them. Give two examples from this chapter. In what ways did the civilization of ancient Mesopotamia pass on to later peoples?
2. "Geography plays an important part in history." Do you agree or disagree with this statement? Why? Do you think this is true today? Why?
3. Arabic was the official language of the huge Islamic Empire. How do you think this helped the spread of civilization?
4. Why do you think women had a subordinate role in Arab society?
5. Read again on page 154 the statement of General Khalid that set the Arabs' policy for dealing with the people they conquered. Do you think that this policy helped the Arabs build an empire? Why?

9

Two Civilizations Build India

KEYNOTE

The history of India—like the history of several other ancient areas—is marked by periods of special brightness. These periods seem to shine with the achievements of leaders in the fields of religion, literature, art, architecture, and government. Under the Maurya and Gupta dynasties, and later under the Mogul dynasty, India enjoyed creative "golden years." The last of these dynasties, the Mogul, represents a blending of two civilizations—Hindu and Muslim.

It is important to remember that these achievements depended on the hard work of the overwhelming majority of women and men in India who were farmers and lived in thousands of villages throughout the land. Dynasties rose and fell, but it was the daily work of these people who made the golden periods of Indian civilization possible.

Planting a field in India.

1. The First Great Indian Empire

In 322 B.C. Chandragupta Maurya seized the throne of a kingdom in the eastern part of the Ganges plain. In the years that followed he conquered most of northeastern India. Chandragupta was the first of a line of rulers known as the *Maurya dynasty*.

The Maurya Dynasty

Under Chandragupta, the people of India developed an impressive civilization. Irrigation systems were expanded and roads were built and kept in good repair. A royal highway extended twelve hundred miles from the capital to the northwestern frontier. Chandragupta's capital on the Ganges River was described by a Greek visitor. He wrote that the city was more than nine miles long and almost two miles wide. It was an attractive city with fine theaters, marketplaces, and a magnificent royal palace.

The Greek visitor wrote that Chandragupta had a professional army of 600,000 men. He described the farmers as cultivating the soil in peace and security. Farmers and Brahmans were exempted from military service.

The government was centered in the capital under the control of the emperor. It was organized into departments that supervised nearly every important political, economic, and social activity throughout the Empire. The provinces and towns were governed by officials who were appointed from the capital.

Scholars and artists were paid by the government. Students from all over Asia came to study at the medical school of the university at Taxila. This was one of several Indian universities where professors taught the arts and sciences.

Asoka Spreads the Buddhist Principles of Peace

Chandragupta's son conquered part of southern India. He was followed by one of the most famous rulers in history, Asoka (c. 273–232 B.C.). Asoka conquered the east coast of India. Then, repelled by the horrors of war, he decided to follow the principles of the religion of Buddhism. He wanted to spread the Buddhist spirit of peace to his people.

Asoka wanted his people to know the rules that would help them to lead good lives. He therefore ordered that special edicts, or proclamations, be in-

India Under the Maurya Dynasty

The Maurya Empire reached its height under Asoka.

Maurya Dynasty under Asoka in 232 B.C.

Ancient ruins

scribed on rocks and pillars. These "rock edicts" taught the people to be peaceful, honest, and kind. Some said:

> [Do] many benefits to others; [believe] in compassion; liberality; truth; purity.
>
> . . . .
>
> Not to injure living beings is good.
>
> . . . .
>
> Let a man watch over himself, saying: "Such . . . acts lead to corruption, such as brutality, cruelty, anger, and pride. I will [avoid them]."

The Rock Edicts have been found in many parts of India, and ten of the pillars are still standing.

While Asoka remained faithful to Buddhism, he insisted that all religions should be treated with equal respect. In one edict he proclaimed:

> All sects deserve reverence for one reason or another. By thus acting a man exalts his own sect and at the same time does service to the sects of other people.

Asoka also spread the principles of Buddhism to other lands. His missionaries carried the Buddhist

163

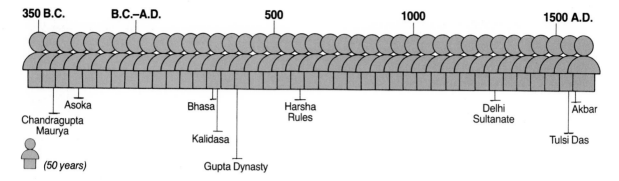

| 350 B.C. | B.C.–A.D. | | 500 | | 1000 | | 1500 A.D. |

Asoka
Chandragupta
Maurya

Bhasa

Harsha
Rules

Delhi
Sultanate

Akbar

Kalidasa

Tulsi Das

(50 years)

Gupta Dynasty

doctrines to southern India, Ceylon, Burma, Macedonia, Egypt, and Syria.

Charities were organized throughout the Empire and many monasteries were built. Asoka's sister Sanghamitra started nunneries. Stone *stupas* were constructed throughout the land. Stupas were originally Buddhist burial mounds. Then they became shrines in which were buried the relics of Buddhist saints.

This lion capital from a pillar at Sarnath shows the high quality of sculpture during the reign of Asoka.

When Asoka died about 232 B.C., the great Maurya Empire fell apart. (See the map on page 163.) For the next 600 years, the subcontinent of India was made up of separate kingdoms.

A Rich Civilization

During this long period Indian civilization continued to develop. Handsome buildings and beautiful statues of Buddha were created. Medicine, science, and the arts were studied in universities. The Sanskrit languages continued to develop.

The famous poet Bhasa (about 300 A.D.) turned to Sanskrit to write lines that are known today by many students in modern-day India:

> When [the moon's] rays fall on its cheeks the
>   cat licks them, thinking them milk;
> When they are caught in the cleft of a tree
>   the elephant deems them a lotus;
> . . . .
> The moon in truth, proud of its brilliance, doth
>   lead astray all this world.

Check on Your Reading

1. What were the achievements of Chandragupta?
2. What were some of the ideas of Asoka and what were some of his accomplishments?

2. The Guptas Rule over a Great Civilization

In the fourth century A.D., rulers known as the Guptas united nearly all of northern India. (See the map on page 166.) This was a time when India had contact and trade with the Roman Empire, the Near East, Persia, China, and Indonesia. During this time a Chinese Buddhist pilgrim spent six years in India, moving from monastery to monastery. He wrote a book about his experiences. He admired the hospitals and charitable organizations he found

This Buddhist stupa at Sanchi was built of brick and stone during the reign of Asoka.

throughout the Empire. He was astonished at the great cities, the splendor of the emperor's palace, and at the many students in the universities of the Empire.

The most famous Gupta leader was Chandragupta II. He gathered together and supported at his capital artists, poets, philosophers, and scientists. One of the most famous of these was Kalidasa.

Literature

Kalidasa, the greatest poet-dramatist of the time, is still enjoyed in India today. Kalidasa loved nature deeply. His descriptions of the seasons of India are sensitive and charming. One can almost "feel" the heat in this selection from his poem *Summer:*

Beneath the garland of the rays
    That leave no corner cool,
The water vanishes in haze
    And leaves a muddy pool;
The cobra does not hunt for food
    Nor heed the frog at all
Who finds beneath the serpent's hood
    A sheltering parasol.

About one hundred years later, the witty and imaginative poet Bhartrihari pleased many readers. Bhartrihari reflected with humor upon the strange ways of Fate. In the poem *Dilemma*, he lamented his habit of being in the wrong place at the wrong time:

I see a dog—no stone to [throw] at him;
    Yonder a stone—no dog is in view:
There is your dog, here stones to [throw]
        at him—
The king's dog! What's a man to do?

On page 60 you learned about the *Ramayana* and the other great epic of the Epic Age. It was during this period that these poems were written down in their present form.

Art

The Gupta Empire excelled in religious art, as well as in literature. Beautiful sculptures were created to adorn both Hindu and Buddhist temples. These figures have a grace and a dignity that has been admired through the ages.

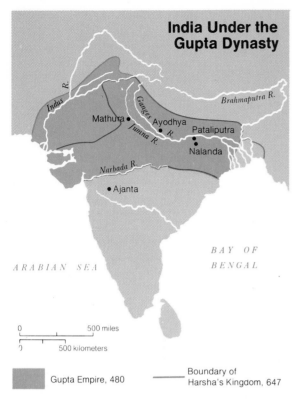

India Under the Gupta Dynasty

BAY OF BENGAL

ARABIAN SEA

0 — 500 miles
0 — 500 kilometers

Gupta Empire, 480

Boundary of Harsha's Kingdom, 647

The Gupta Empire in India lasted from 320 to 480 A.D. It was destroyed by Huns from central Asia.

In painting, the Ajanta Caves are treasuries of Indian art. These caves are rock temples that were cut into a mountainside near modern Bombay between 100 A.D. and 700 A.D. On the walls and ceilings are magnificent frescoes. Here are pictures of wild flowers alive with rhythm, forest animals in graceful motion, and legendary scenes from the life of Buddha. The art of the Ajanta Caves tells us about the feelings of the people of this period. These caves are like picture books whose paintings are far more important than words.

Science

Impressive gains also were made in science in the period from 300 A.D. to 700 A.D. It has been mentioned that the so-called "Arabic numerals" came from ancient India. Indians also developed a decimal system, and their work in algebra has had an important influence on modern mathematics.

In astronomy, Brahmagupta (7th century A.D.) came close to formulating correct ideas on gravitation long before Newton (17th century A.D.). Brahmagupta wrote:

All things fall to the earth by a law of nature, for it is the nature of the earth to attract. . . .

In medicine, free hospitals were established for the poor three hundred years before the first hospitals were built in Europe. Although Europeans pride themselves on discovering the vaccination technique in the eighteenth century, inoculation may have been known in India as early as the sixth century.

Also some scientists of India were skilled in chemistry and in the application of chemical knowledge to industrial needs. The artisans of India excelled in tempering steel, dyeing cloth, making soap, and preparing glass.

Check on Your Reading

1. What impressed the Chinese Buddhist pilgrim about India in this period?
2. Identify one outstanding writer of the Gupta Empire.
3. Describe the Ajanta Cave paintings. Why are they important?
4. In what areas of science and mathematics did Indian scholars make progress in this period?

A scene from Shakuntala, *by Kalidasa, is performed by the Hindustani Theater at New Delhi.*

3. Harsha Restores Orderly Government to North India

The Gupta dynasty was destroyed by 480 A.D. by Huns, warrior nomads who swept out of central Asia, overrunning lands to the west and to the east. It was a similar invasion of the Huns that helped destroy the Roman Empire. (See the Text and map on pages 125 and 126.)

In the first half of the seventh century, an Indian leader named Harsha restored peace and order in the north. Harsha, one of the great kings of Indian history, permitted religious freedom, and established systems of justice and education. He also supported the arts and wrote poetry and plays that are still enjoyed in India today.

Reports from a Chinese Pilgrim

During the rule of Harsha another Chinese Buddhist pilgrim came to India. He stayed for almost ten years, spending three of those years in a Buddhist university.

He described the emperor as "indefatigable; the day was too short for him; he forgot sleep in his devotion to the good deeds." This pilgrim also watched a great festival of charity that the emperor held every five years. This festival was attended by officials of all religions as well as the poor from all over the Empire. During the two or three months of the festival Harsha gave away much of the wealth that had accumulated in his treasury over the past five years.

Education

Harsha encouraged education and learning. While he ruled, higher education continued to flourish in India. Particularly impressive were the activities of the great Buddhist University of Nalanda. Here scholars from many regions in the East studied grammar, logic, medicine, and religious philosophy. There were said to be one hundred lecture rooms, several fine libraries, ten swimming pools, and observatories where "the upper rooms seemed to tower above the clouds."

Check on Your Reading

1. What were some of Harsha's accomplishments?
2. What did the Chinese pilgrim tell about the emperor?
3. What were some of the features of Nalanda University?

This statue of Buddha was carved in the fifth century A.D.

4. The Muslims Take Control

The death of Harsha in 647 A.D. was followed by the disintegration of his empire. During the centuries that followed, independent kingdoms fought each other for control of northern India.

A Time of Change

In northern India kingdoms rose and fell and new peoples moved in from the northwest. It was a time of important changes. The new peoples settled in northern India. Buddhism declined and Hinduism developed into its modern form. The caste system evolved and new subcastes developed.

During this period there was greater prosperity and peace in the south than in the north. In the south the people developed a civilization strongly influenced by the civilization of the north. Trade flourished with other lands. Separate kingdoms minted coins and supported art and literature. Great Hindu temples were built, some of which are still standing.

The Coming of the Muslims

Starting in the eighth century, Muslims from central Asia invaded northwest India. From the end of the tenth through the twelfth century, waves of Muslims continued to force back the Hindus who opposed them.

Finally, in 1206, a group of Muslims was powerful enough to establish an empire with a capital at Delhi. This empire is known as the "Delhi Sultanate." The Indian rulers and their officials were not often replaced, but instead became dependents of the Turkish rulers, or sultans, at Delhi. The sultans brought in architects and artists from Muslim Persia, but they also supported Hindu artists and craft workers. A new Indo-Muslim style of art and architecture developed, and impressive public buildings were built throughout the Sultanate.

At the same time, India was divided into two cultures. These invaders of India were Muslims.

The Mogul Empire was established by Babar in 1524. Under his grandson, Akbar, Indian civilization enjoyed another "Golden Age."

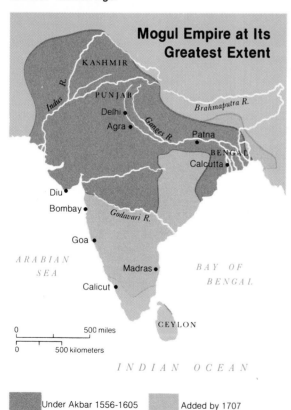

Mogul Empire at Its Greatest Extent

KASHMIR

Indus R.

PUNJAB

Delhi

Agra

Brahmaputra R.

Ganges R.

Patna

BENGAL

Calcutta

Diu

Bombay

Godavari R.

Goa

ARABIAN SEA

Madras

BAY OF BENGAL

Calicut

CEYLON

0   500 miles

0   500 kilometers

INDIAN OCEAN

Under Akbar 1556-1605   Added by 1707

The Muslim culture did not blend into India as had the culture of past invaders. The two religions were different. Religious statues were forbidden to the Muslims but not to the Hindus. The sacred cow of the Hindu was meat for the Muslim. Muslims believed in equality for men; while the Hindus had the graded inequality of the caste system.

The Mogul Dynasty Rises to Power

In the fourteenth century the Delhi Sultanate weakened and parts of it broke away into separate kingdoms. At the same time, Timur the Lame, or Tamerlane, built an empire that stretched from the Middle East to the northwest borders of India. In 1398 Tamerlane invaded northern India. He sacked the city of Delhi before returning to his Empire north of the Himalayas.

Then in 1524 Babar, a Muslim ruler from Turkestan, deposed the last leader of the "Delhi Sultanate." Babar, who could trace his ancestry back to Tamerlane, set up what is known as the *Mogul dynasty.*

Babar conquered northern India. His grandson, Akbar, extended Mogul conquests to the south.

Check on Your Reading

1. What was the Delhi Sultanate? What were some of its accomplishments?
2. What part did Babar play in Indian history?

5. Akbar the Great

Under the leadership of Akbar (1556-1605) and other Mogul rulers, the government was organized into fifteen provinces. Taxes were levied more fairly. An effective system of justice was developed. More schools were established and universities became known as "the lights and ornaments of the Empire." Indian civilization prospered.

Religious Toleration

Akbar urged people to respect every religion, for "if men walk in the way of God's will, interference with them would be unfair." He pointed out:

Miracles occur in the temples of every creed. . . .

Each person according to his condition gives the [same] Supreme Being a name. . . .

At a time when people were slaughtering each other because of their religions, Akbar stood out for his attempt to show the oneness of God and the humanity of all people.

Literature

Akbar was a leader who was interested in all kinds of knowledge. He collected a large library and supported historians, poets, and other writers. The outstanding writer of this period was Tulsi Das (c. 1532-1624).

The *Ramayana of Tulsi Das,* written in the Hindi language, has been called "the Bible of the Hindi-speaking people of India." Mahatma Gandhi, Indian leader of the twentieth century, hailed it as "the greatest book" in all the literature of devotion. Tulsi Das voiced the feelings of Akbar the Great when he wrote: "There is one God . . . creator of heaven and earth, and redeemer of mankind. . . ."

Art and Architecture

Art flourished under Akbar, who believed that artistic expression was linked with the love of God. He wrote:

> It appears to me [that] a painter has quite a peculiar means of recognizing God; a painter, in sketching anything that has life . . . must come to feel that he cannot bestow personality upon his work, and is thus forced to think of God, the giver of life. . . .

The architects of Akbar and of the Mogul rulers who followed him combined Indian and Muslim architecture from Persia into a new and graceful style. Their buildings had domes shaped like bulbs, the slender towers of minarets, graceful gateways, and interlacing designs on windows.

Akbar's grandson, Shah Jahan, directed the building of the Taj Mahal, a great tomb for his beloved wife. The Taj Mahal is one of the most famous structures in the world. Millions of visitors have marveled at its fine marble, lovely minarets, and beautiful dome.

Akbar and the rulers who followed him supported many painters who created small, delicate, and bright paintings of people and of the world of

A page from a Mogul manuscript shows a ruler holding court.

nature. Calligraphy, or ornamental writing, also developed as a rich decorative art.

Check on Your Reading

1. Describe the government of Akbar.
2. Who was Tulsi Das?
3. What were some of the features of Mogul architecture?

A Farm Family of the Mogul Period

This Indian farmer and his wife lived in the northeast province of Bengal. Their life was spent close to the blessed Ganges River and the soil. Their hands were calloused from labor.

They felt a bond with this land and with the creatures that shared it with them: the wild elephants in the woods; the black, racket-tailed Drongo birds, the restless geese that flew in darting patterns above the trees; the shaggy goats that strayed leisurely down the paths. They loved their land and could understand why foreigners wanted to live in this region. It was said that "Bengal has a hundred gates for entrance, but not one for departure!" For who, indeed, would want to leave this fascinating land?

The Indian farmers worked carefully in their rice fields. When the marshes were fairly dry, they sowed the seeds. When the rains fell, they watched the plants gradually grow by the miracle of life.

The water rose; the rice stalks grew. The farmers sowed and reaped "three times a year on the same piece of land with little injury to the crop." The harvests were usually good, and the farmers paid their rent to the government promptly in *mohurs* and *rupees* (coins).

Their home was made of bamboo, and they rarely moved away from it. When they traveled they used their small riverboat or walked.

Once, on the first day of the new moon, the farmer and his family journeyed to the seashore. It was a tragic trip. At three P.M. the following afternoon:

. . . a terrible [flood] occurred . . . which swept over the whole district. The Rajah [local ruler] at once embarked on board a boat while his son . . . with some others climbed to the top of the temple. . . . For four hours and a half the sea raged amid thunder and a hurricane of wind. Houses and boats were engulfed but no damage occurred to the temple.
. . . Nearly two hundred thousand living creatures perished in this flood.

There no longer seemed to be truth to the saying:

"Bengal has a hundred gates for entrance, but not one for departure!" One terrible exit gate had been thrown wide open, the exit of the sea. The sea had taken away the lives of thousands of helpless people—and the Indian farmer and his family were among them.

The sketch above is based primarily on information in the *Aín i Akbari,* a history written by Abul Fazl. Abul Fazl was an important historian and statesman during the reign of the great Emperor Akbar.

CHAPTER REVIEW

Think and Discuss

1. How does Asoka's attitude toward other religions compare with attitudes today?
2. During periods of great achievements in the arts in India, there were also powerful rulers. Is one fact necessarily related to the other? Why or why not?
3. The common humanity of all people is a belief that is accepted by several religions. Why has it not eliminated wars?
4. Do you think that this line of Rudyard Kipling's poetry is true: "Oh, East is East, and West is

West, and never the twain shall meet"? Give reasons for your answer.
5. What contributions do you think Buddhism has made to other peoples?
6. On page 166 the author writes that the pictures of the Ajanta Caves are far more important than words. What do you think he means? How does the art of a civilization tell about that civilization?

Past and Present

1. Two different cultures developed in the subcontinent of India during the time covered by this chapter. Do research about the history of this subcontinent in the last forty years. How has the development of these two cultures affected the history of modern India?
2. Study India's history through the eyes of a statesman, Jawaharlal Nehru, in his book, *The Discovery of India*. You will gain some insight into the thinking of a person who was one of modern India's important leaders.

Activities

1. Visit an art museum and examine Hindu, Buddhist, and Muslim art.
2. Study at least four great rulers, such as Akbar the Great, about whom you have read. Note their characters and achievements. Write your conclusions about the reasons for their accomplishments as rulers.
3. Collect pictures of the Taj Mahal and write a report about it.

Messages from the Government

As the ruler of a mighty nation, Asoka tried to ensure that his people would live in peace and harmony. Asoka's major problem was how to communicate his message to the people. His solution was to proclaim his message on rocks and pillars scattered throughout his Empire.

All modern governments, including our own, also try to communicate their messages to the citizens of their nations. Today, radio, television, and newspapers have replaced the rocks and pillars; but the need for communication remains the same.

Think about the messages you receive from the United States government. What are these messages about? What kinds of concerns does our government relay to us in its "commercials"? Make a list of these messages. Then write one paragraph in which you compare the messages of Asoka with those you receive from your government. Try to note as many similarities and differences as you can.

Chinese Civilization Reaches New Peaks

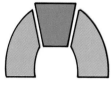

KEYNOTE

This chapter begins with the rise of the Han dynasty in 202 B.C. and ends with the Mongol dynasty 1,500 years later. In terms of our life spans, this represents 60 generations. As times of disorder and famine were followed by periods of order and prosperity, Chinese civilization was enriched by inventors, artists, scholars, writers, philosophers, and rulers.

During Han times a national university was started to train government officials. An efficient collar-harness was developed to make it possible for horses to pull heavy loads. The stern-post rudder for steering ships, and the wheelbarrow were invented a thousand years before these devices were used in Europe.

In the seventh century another great period of Chinese civilization developed under the Tang dynasty. At a time when Europeans of the early Middle Ages were struggling with the problems of survival, the capital of the Tang dynasty had about two million people. Ch'ang-an was probably the largest, most cosmopolitan, and most brilliant city in the world.

About five hundred years later, a Venetian traveler, Marco Polo, visited the empire of the Mongols. When he returned to Italy, he astonished many Europeans with his stories of China's rich cities, great palaces and temples, busy highways and canals, and efficient postal system. Europeans had much to learn from the Chinese.

A relief of riders and carriages from a Han tomb.

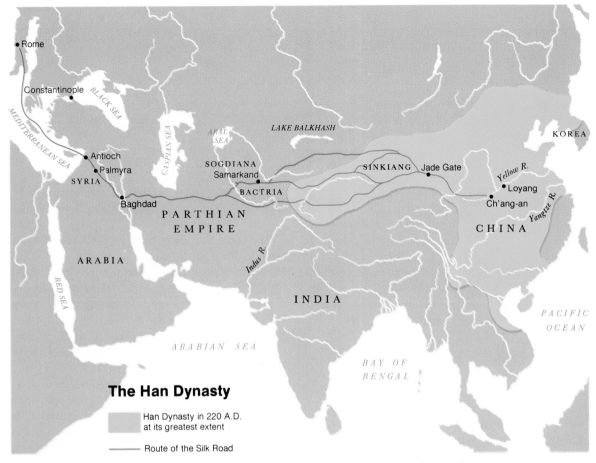

The Han emperors expanded their empire deep into central Asia. *During this period trade with Rome developed along the so-called "Silk Road."*

1. The Achievements of the Han Dynasty

The uprisings against the Ch'in dynasty (see page 75) developed into a struggle for control between two military leaders. Kao Tsu, who had been a poor farmer, won, and was proclaimed emperor of Han. He was the first commoner in Chinese history to fight his way to the throne.

The Han Dynasty

Kao Tsu won support because of his fair treatment of both his friends and his enemies. He and the Han emperors who followed him made permanent the system of government set up by the Ch'in dynasty. That is, they organized a centralized government controlled by the emperor.

The Han dynasty ruled from 202 B.C. to about 220 A.D. The most famous Han ruler was Wu Ti.

Wu Ti became emperor when he was sixteen and ruled for about fifty years. His armies conquered South China, northern Vietnam, most of Korea, southern Manchuria, and Inner Mongolia. (See the map above.)

In Central Asia, Wu Ti set up a *tributary system.* The local rulers of Central Asia had to send gifts to the emperor and come to his court to show respect. Also their sons were sent to the Chinese court to be educated and to serve as hostages so their fathers would not rebel against the emperor.

This was the beginning of a period of contact with western Asia along what has been called the "Silk Road." The Chinese exported silk and in return obtained horses and other trade goods. By the second century A.D. Chinese silks and furs were being exchanged by traders for the products of India, western Asia, and even the Roman Empire.

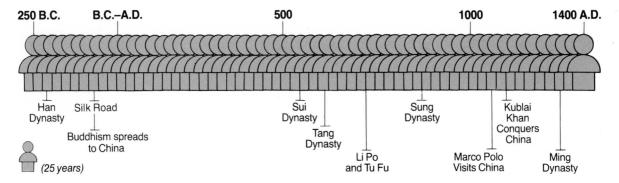

250 B.C.   B.C.–A.D.   500   1000   1400 A.D.

Han   Silk Road   Sui   Sung   Kublai
Dynasty   Dynasty   Dynasty   Khan
                                                               Conquers
           Buddhism spreads   Tang   China
           to China   Dynasty

(25 years)   Li Po   Marco Polo   Ming
                                        and Tu Fu   Visits China Dynasty

Wu Ti centralized all aspects of Chinese life under the bureaucracy of the emperor. All coins were issued in the emperor's mints. The production of iron, salt, and liquor were made state monopolies. He set up an "ever-normal granary" system by which the state stored surplus grain to be used in times of famine. Written examinations began to be used to find officials for his government, and a national university was set up to train officials.

China under the Hans

The first Han emperor, Kao Tsu, accepted the Confucian theory that government must be for the benefit of the governed. He and his successors restored Confucianism to the prestige it had before the Ch'in dynasty. There is an interesting story about Kao Tsu and one of his ministers who was a Confucian scholar. Kao Tsu became very tired of hearing his minister quote Confucius and exclaimed:

"I conquered the Empire on horseback. What is the good of the *Odes* and *Histories*?" His minister replied, "That is correct, but you won't be able to govern it on horseback. . . . If Chin, having made itself the master of the Empire, had governed it in humanity and righteousness . . . then Han would not have got it." The emperor . . . said, "Explain to me the reasons for the collapse of Chin and the rise of Han, as well as what it was that won and lost kingdoms of old." In obedience to the emperor's wish, the minister wrote about state craft, in twelve chapters. When Emperor Kao Tsu listened to the minister reading aloud his book, he praised his ideas strongly.

During Han times, Buddhism spread in China. By 166 B.C. Buddhist religious altars had been set up in the palace of the emperor. At the same time, Buddhist communities were started throughout China.

One of the first major histories of China appeared early in the Han dynasty. In English it is called *Historical Memoirs* and was written by Ssŭ-ma Ch'ien. He was an important official at court and could use the court records. Ssŭ-ma Ch'ien wrote history with a respect for facts and a spirit of fairness. He wove many quotations from primary sources into his history. The organization of his history set the pattern for later writers.

Scholars studied and commented on the ancient writers. They gathered together in the emperor's library over 2,700 volumes of philosophy and 1,300 volumes of poetry. Some scholars produced dictionaries. They also created new works. Perhaps the most important of these was a short book called *Classic of Filial Piety,* which praises respect and honor for parents as the root of all other virtues. This book became the introduction to learning for all young men training to become scholars and government officials.

Writing poetry became a skill expected of every educated person. Court ladies and gentlemen amused themselves with poetry games and contests.

For tax purposes, local officials had to submit regular reports on the population and ownership of land in their districts. In 1 A.D., an official census recorded a population of about sixty million in China. Most of these people were farmers, and between six and ten million were urban dwellers.

The most serious problem of the countryside was the proper use and regulation of water. All the working members of a village shared in the care and repair of irrigation ditches. Large-scale improvements were organized by the officials of the central government. New equipment helped workers on large farms. Such equipment included improved plows, water-raising machinery, and tilt-hammers and circular grinding-stones powered by animals or water to mill grain.

The state-controlled salt industry developed improved technology to collect saltwater, or brine, from underground pools. Iron and steel bits were used to drill to depths of 2,000 feet. Bamboo tubes with valves raised the brine to the surface. Then it was evaporated in large iron pans.

In this period the Chinese improved their calendar and recorded the observation of sunspots—spots on the sun that appeared darker than the sun's regular surface. Officials in the workshops of the emperor made paper. A seismograph was used to record earthquakes.

Check on Your Reading

1. What lands did Wu Ti conquer? What was the tributary system?
2. What changes did Wu Ti make in the government?
3. What influence did Confucianism have during the Han dynasty? What religion spread in China in this period?
4. What were some of the advances in science and technology?
5. Name and describe two important books written during the Han dynasty.

2. The Brilliant Civilization of the Tang Dynasty

Gradually the central government of the Han dynasty grew weaker. After 220 A.D. China split into rival kingdoms. Then, in the 300s, nomadic warriors from Central Asia began invading North China. These people were related to the Huns who were invading the Roman Empire at the same time.

Chinese Civilization Persists

For over three hundred years there was almost constant warfare among rival kingdoms; but this was also a period of achievement. The nomad invasions forced the migration of millions of Chinese from the north to the south. During this period, southern China became a center of Chinese civilization. From the south came the Chinese custom of drinking tea; and, far more important, art and literature flourished there.

Gradually in the north the non-Chinese conquerors adopted Chinese civilization. Many of the

This bronze horse from the Han period was found in a tomb in 1969.

northern rulers and powerful families supported Chinese learning, art, and literature. At the same time the Buddhist faith continued to spread rapidly throughout China.

Then near the close of the sixth century, the country was united again under the Sui dynasty. The Sui were followed by the Tang dynasty (618-907 A.D.). The Sui and Tang dynasties inherited the civilization of the Han dynasty that had persisted and grown through all the hundreds of years of upheaval.

The Government of the Tangs

T'ai Tsung (627-650 A.D.), the son of the first Tang emperor, strengthened China's government and expanded its rule into Afghanistan, Tibet, and Mongolia. He organized his government on the principles of Confucianism, but he was interested in many ideas and religions. T'ai Tsung encouraged both the Buddhists and the Taoists, and built a church for a Christian missionary from Central Asia. During his rule, China's famous Buddhist pilgrim, Hsuan Tsang, made a 16-year journey to India and back. Then, supported by the emperor, he spent the rest of his life translating the Buddhist texts he had brought back with him.

Emperor T'ai Tsung created a system of recruiting civil servants by public examination. The examinations were difficult. The men who passed

This pagoda was built in the seventh century A.D. in honor of the monk Hsuan Tsang. It has been restored several times.

them were not usually members of the aristocratic military class. Thus the power of the aristocracy was broken and a new world of power, influence, and wealth was opened to scholars. Under later emperors, public examinations had to be passed in order to enter the civil service.

The next emperor was weak, and his wife, Empress Wu, became the real ruler of China. When the emperor died, she pushed his sons aside and became the only woman in Chinese history to hold the official title of ruler. Empress Wu ruled China well and strengthened its prestige in foreign affairs. During her rule, Korea paid tribute to China.

The grandson of Empress Wu is known as Ming Huang, the "Brilliant Emperor" (712-756). He was a strong and wise ruler who governed through a competent civil service. He is best known, however, as a patron of the arts. At his court lived many artists, scholars, writers, and poets, including Li Po and Tu Fu.

Literature

The Tang period can be called "the brightest age of Chinese poetry." In those years the Chinese honored their poets highly. Nearly fifty thousand poems were composed.

The finest poets were Li Po and Tu Fu. Li Po was a particularly sensitive and lyrical writer. He wrote many poems about the beauty of nature. In these graceful lines, he expresses his envy of a friend who can live close to nature:

My friend is lodging high in the Eastern Range.
. . .
A pine-tree wind dusts his sleeves and coat;
A pebbly stream cleans his heart and ears.
I envy you, who far from strife and talk
Are high-propped on a pillow of a blue cloud.

Terra-cotta figures from the seventh century A.D. show women playing polo. Tang dynasty women sometimes took part in vigorous outdoor games.

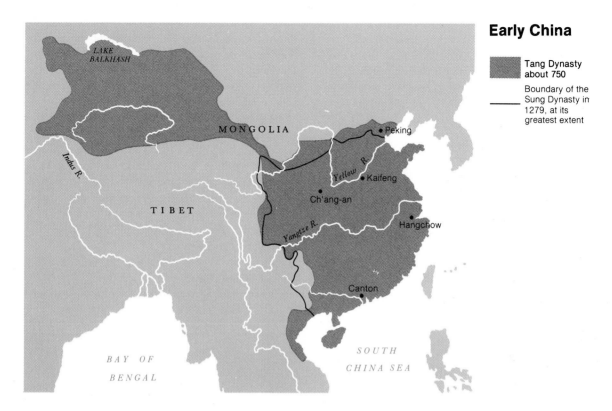

Early China

■ Tang Dynasty
about 750

▬▬ Boundary of the
Sung Dynasty in
1279, at its
greatest extent

Po Chü-i was the most popular Tang writer. In his famous poem, *The Red Cockatoo,* he protests against loss of freedom:

Sent as a present from Annam—
A red cockatoo.
Colored like the peach-tree blossom,
Speaking with the speech of men.
And they did to it what is always done
To the learned and eloquent.
They took a cage with stout bars
And shut it up inside.

The influence that literature has on society often depends on how widely it is read. It was, therefore, fortunate that block printing was invented in the general region of Korea and China about the end of the sixth century. A page of writing was cut out on a woodblock, which was then inked. When paper was pressed on the block, the writing was stamped on the paper. One of the oldest printed notices was a small sign reading:

Beware of the Dog!

From such beginnings, Chinese printing developed to a point where Confucian classics were cut on woodblocks, printed, and distributed throughout the country.

Art

Tang art has been praised as highly as Tang literature. Tang pottery and porcelain were exquisite, and some cups were so delicately formed that they could produce musical sounds. Above all, the Chinese excelled at painting.

Artists specialized in painting landscapes, religious scenes, and animals. Wu Tao-tzu was the most famous painter of the period. Legend has it that Wu Tao-tzu once painted such a beautiful picture of paradise that he was able to walk into it and disappear! It is regrettable that none of his paintings remain so that we might enjoy their beauty.

Chinese painting was done in ink on silk or fine paper. Color was used sparingly. A painting was the artist's attempt to capture the inner spirit of the scene. The artist did not fill every blank space with an object because space was considered to be as beautiful as lines or figures. Paintings often gave the impression of being done from a mountaintop. The observer had the feeling of "looking down" on the scene. Landscapes, rather than human forms, were represented.

Art was a major activity of the scholar class. Artists were among the educated leaders of the Tang period and often held high government offices. In order to be a painter, it was necessary to be able to write, as the strokes used by artists in painting were based on the strokes used in writing.

The Largest City in the World

The Tang period was an outstanding time in China. Much of the creative activity centered in the capital of China, Ch'ang-an. Ch'ang-an was not only the government center of China, but also the center of literature, art, and scholarship.

Within the walls of the city lived about a million people. The walls enclosed about thirty square miles. At the center was the huge palace complex which was almost a city in a city. Nearby was the administrative quarter where much of the government business was carried on and many government officials lived. There was also an area for the artisans who worked for the emperor and the wealthy officials of the capital.

The outer city had over one hundred wards and nine market areas. Each ward was surrounded by a wall controlled by a single gate that was closed at night. Each household was also surrounded by a wall with a gate. A house centered on a courtyard, referred to as the "Well of Heaven." No matter how small the house, the courtyard was made into a garden with trees and potted plants. A wealthy family had two courtyards.

Goods from all over Asia as well as from every region of China were sold in the markets. Great fairs were held at which musical troops, jugglers,

This painting shows candidates for high office composing essays demonstrating their knowledge of Confucian texts. In the pavilion at the rear the Emperor watches.

This Sung landscape is titled "An Inn in the Country."

and acrobats entertained. Within the city were over 100 temples, including a Muslim mosque.

The city was always crowded with visitors from abroad. There were diplomats from all over Asia, Arab traders from the Persian Gulf, Buddhist monks and students from Korea and Japan, and religious leaders from India. Horsemen from Mongolia stayed in the inns of the city, and camel caravans arrived from Central Asia.

Check on Your Reading

1. What were the achievements of Emperor T'ai Tsung?
2. What happened to religion under the Tang dynasty?
3. Why might the Tang period be called "the brightest age of Chinese poetry"?
4. What were the major characteristics of Chinese painting in the Tang period?

3. Civilization Flourished under the Sung Dynasty

By 750 the Tang government had begun to weaken and become inefficient. Rebellions broke out, and, although these uprisings were put down, the Tang emperors ruled in name only. Weak and corrupt government and the anger of large numbers of unhappy farmers finally brought about the collapse of the Tang dynasty in 907.

Fifty years of confusion followed. Then order was established over part of China by a new dynasty, the Sung (960–1279 A.D.).

The Sung Government

The Sung emperors expanded the system of recruiting officials for the civil service through government examinations. The power of the emperor was centralized in the civil service that ran the country. Thus the scholar-officials became the governing class of China.

The Sung rulers controlled only a part of China. Mongols in the north and other invaders in the south were a constant threat. In 1127 the Mongols successfully invaded North China and the Sung family moved its capital to South China, where it ruled for about one hundred years.

The Sung Period Excels in Art

In the regions controlled by the Sung government, civilization flourished. New cities were built, rivers were controlled, and public and private schools were organized. Students from all over China came to study at the medical school established in the Sung capital.

In the field of invention, the idea of the firecracker was used to develop war explosives. The magnetic compass helped captains sail their large cargo ships across open seas. Water-powered machinery was used to spin silk thread.

The Sung period is most famous for its art. The Emperor Hui-tsung introduced painting as one of the examinations for entry to the civil service. He set up a Painting Academy in his capital and supported many artists at his court. He had printed a catalogue of his art collection that listed over 6,000 paintings. Hui-tsung was himself a fine painter of birds and flowers.

Sung artists are best known, however, for their landscape paintings. They produced some of the finest landscapes in the history of art. In these landscapes, artists expressed a deep love of nature.

Many Sung painters were poetic and imaginative in their approach to art. They did not try to represent an object exactly as it was, but sought the spirit of the scene. Lin Yu-t'ang, a modern philosopher, points out how the quality of imagination was treasured in Sung art:

. . . once the subject for a painting contest was a line:
Bamboos cover a wine-shop by a bridge.

Many competitors tried to concentrate on the wine-shop as the center of the picture. There was one man, however, who painted only a bridge, a bamboo grove by its side, and hidden

The Mongols ruled China from 1279 to 1368. As the map shows, they controlled a huge empire. During this period Marco Polo traveled to China from Venice.

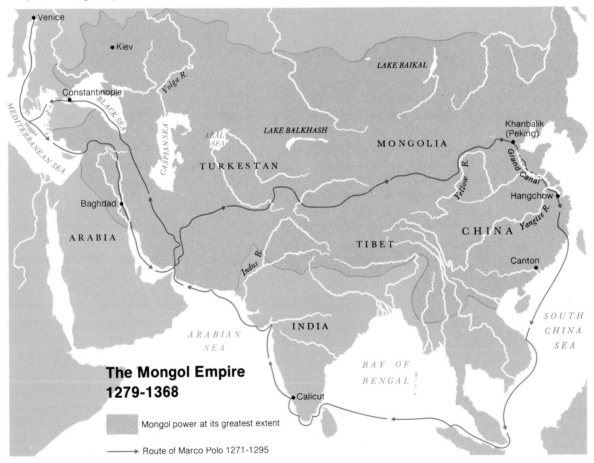

The Mongol Empire 1279-1368

Mongol power at its greatest extent

→ Route of Marco Polo 1271-1295

in that grove, only a shop-sign bearing the character 'wine,' but no wine-shop at all. This picture won because the wine-shop was hidden in the imagination.

In addition, Sung artists did excellent work with metal and jade. Porcelain-making reached a high level of excellence. For example, delicate teapots and lovely flower vases were made.

Check on Your Reading

1. How did the Sung emperors rule China? What happened to North China in 1127 A.D.?
2. How did Hui-tsung encourage painting?
3. What qualities distinguished Sung art?

4. The Mongols Conquer China

While nomads ruled several kingdoms in northern China, other nomads in Mongolia were being organized by a Mongol chieftain. He became known as Genghis Khan (leader from 1206-1227). Mongol horsemen lived in small kinship groups that spent much of their time fighting each other over pasturelands for their horses. Genghis Khan was a magnificent leader who was able to organize these fierce warriors into a mighty army.

Led by Genghis Khan, Mongol forces conquered the divided nomad states of northern China. It was reported that Mongol warriors could march for ten days without lighting a fire or taking a full meal. The sight of Mongol troops, dressed in tough buffalo hides and armed with bows and iron maces, was terrifying.

The Sung dynasty to the south did its best to defend itself against Genghis Khan and his successors. It was finally defeated in 1279 by Kublai Khan, grandson of Genghis. All of China now was ruled by Mongol emperors (1279-1368).

China Becomes Part of a Huge Empire

The Mongol rulers used their armies to build a great empire that included China, Turkestan, Persia, and lands in Russia and eastern Europe. (See the map on page 180.) The Mongol invasions destroyed cities and ruined large areas of the countryside, sending many thousands of farmers fleeing to the mountains. Kublai Khan at first suppressed the Chinese system of government and did away with the civil service system. However, Kublai Khan was a wise leader who wanted to enjoy the

It is believed that the last emperor of the Northern Sung dynasty, Hui-tsung, created this painting of two chickens and their young.

wealth and the civilization of China. So he restored land to the farmers and set up an efficient government.

Improved roads and waterways stimulated trade. Trade increased between East and West and between China and India. A postal service kept centers of government informed of important news. Ideas as well as goods were exchanged. The Chinese learned from foreigners the valuable uses of cotton and sorghum. Europeans received the idea of gunpowder from the Chinese. Europeans also may have gained their knowledge of printing from the Chinese; and Chinese artistic techniques were exchanged with those of Persia.

Marco Polo Has Amazing Adventures

China under the great Mongol ruler Kublai Khan was a fascinating country. A young Venetian named Marco Polo traveled to China with his father and uncle in 1275. Kublai Khan took the Polos into his service. Marco was about twenty-one

This painting is part of a twelfth-century scroll showing the city of K'ai-feng during the celebration of a spring festival. In the right center of the picture on this page a crowd is listening to a storyteller. Also urbanites enjoy themselves on the upper two stories of a restaurant. On the far right of the part of the painting on page 183 Bactrian camels pass through one of the city's main gates.

when he entered the service of the emperor, and worked for him for seventeen years.

When the Polos returned to Venice, they told such amazing tales that they were not believed. Later, when Marco Polo was imprisoned during a war, he related his tales to a fellow prisoner who wrote them down. These adventures make up the *Book of the Travels of Marco Polo,* a world-famous travel book about the marvels Marco Polo had seen.

What marvels they were! Marco described the forest of Kublai Khan where:

Frequently, when [the Khan] rides about this enclosed forest, he has one or more small

leopards carried on horseback, behind his keepers; and when he pleases to give direction for their being released, they instantly [run and catch] a stag, goat, or fallow deer, which he gives to his hawks, and in this manner he amuses himself.

Marco went on to tell of the remarkable Grand Canal that linked distant cities together. He described the Khan's private tree collection where "whenever his Majesty receives information of a handsome tree growing any place, he causes it to be dug up . . . and transported by means of elephants [to be replanted with his collection]." He told of a

city where "no fewer than a thousand carriages and packhorses, loaded with raw silk, make their daily entry" and many other wonders.

Marco was so impressed by the things that he had seen that he hailed Kublai Khan as the greatest ruler of the world. There can be little doubt that Marco Polo was overly charmed by Kublai Khan. Certainly, many Chinese were unhappy under the Khan's rule. Nevertheless, the *Book of the Travels of Marco Polo* was a valuable record of life in China under the Mongol dynasty.

The Mongol Dynasty Did Not Last Long

The Mongol rulers kept themselves apart from their Chinese subjects. They rejected the Confucian system of government and adopted a different form of Buddhism than that of the Chinese. The Mongols were, therefore, always regarded as foreigners by the Chinese.

The Mongol rulers who followed Kublai Khan were weak, and they could not handle the difficult problems caused by floods and famines. In 1368, after a series of rebellions, the Mongol dynasty was overthrown. The Ming dynasty, whose leaders were of Chinese ancestry, took control.

Check on Your Reading

1. Who were the Mongols?
2. Describe the achievements of Genghis Khan and Kublai Khan.
3. What impressed Marco Polo?
4. Why did the Mongol dynasty last a relatively short time?

LET'S MEET THE PEOPLE

A Mongolian Postman

The Mongolian postman ran out of the *yamb,* or post-house, and leaped to his horse. The clothes he wore were designed to aid him in his fight against time. A white cloth was wrapped about his head to protect him from the sun, and a wide belt was strapped around his waist. Several shining bells were attached to the belt so that he could be seen and heard by the villagers. His jacket fitted tightly against his skin to permit his body to cut the air sharply.

In a pouch, the postman carried a message from the Great Khan and a falcon-shaped tablet that meant that this message was URGENT. The postman's destination was a post-house two hundred miles away.

As the postman urged his horse forward, a government clerk made a careful note of "the day and time at which the courier [departed]." The postman knew that his time of arrival also would be recorded. If he were slow, he might lose his excellent job and his right to be exempt from government taxes. Postal regulations were quite clear on this matter:

. . . officers are directed to pay monthly visits to every station, in order to examine into the management of them, and to punish those couriers [whose records of speed and efficiency show that they] have neglected to use proper diligence.

Faster and faster the postman rode, for he knew that time was slipping away. Finally, when he had covered twenty-five miles, he arrived at a second post-house. Here:

[he] found another horse, fresh and in a state for work; [he] sprang upon it without taking any repose, and changing in the same manner at every stage, [he rode] until the day closed. . . .

Night came. Five miles from his goal it was so dark that the postman could not find the road. Suddenly, he saw a torch waving just ahead. Then he heard a voice calling to him: "Over here! Over here!" It was a runner from the post-house who had come to show the postman his way.

The runner held his torch high and ran as fast as he could in front of the horse. The rider followed him closely, the light from the torch brightening his way. At last they reached the post-house.

The Mongolian postman jumped off his horse, ran into postal headquarters, and delivered his dispatch. Then he rested quietly on the ground until strength began to return to his exhausted body.

That night the postman would have a good sleep. When dawn came, he would be ready to ride again!

This sketch is based on information that appears in "The Travels of Marco Polo," Edited by Manuel Komroff, by permission of Liveright Publishing Corporation. Copyright 1930 by Horace Liveright, Inc. Copyright renewed 1953 by Manual Komroff.

CHAPTER REVIEW

Think and Discuss

1. Compare the disintegration of the Han Empire with that of the Roman Empire.
2. "No area of the world has a monopoly on greatness." Why?
3. "No society has cultivated more graciously than China the art of civilized living." Explain this statement. Do you agree or disagree? Why?
4. It is said that China often absorbed the people who conquered it. How do you explain this statement?
5. It is said that Confucius would have felt at home in any century down to the present one. Do you think that this is true? Justify your answer.
6. Empress Wu was not popular with Chinese historians, who severely criticized her. Why do you think they did this?
7. Why was the development of printing in China important?

Past and Present

1. Find examples of Chinese influence in your community.
2. The emperors of China developed a system of civil service examinations to obtain civil servants. Find out about the system of civil service examinations in our country. When did it start? Compare it with the Chinese system.
3. Large irrigation projects were carried out by the Chinese central government. How are such projects handled in our country?

Activities

1. Write a report on Genghis Khan or Kublai Khan. What do you conclude from your study?
2. Read part of Marco Polo's book. Prepare a report in the form of a book review.
3. Arrange for a display of Chinese art in your classroom.

The Japanese Build a Civilization

KEYNOTE

The Japanese are islanders. The islands of Japan lie off the eastern edge of the huge land mass of Asia. More than a hundred miles of ocean separate the main Japanese islands from the tip of Korea. Over five hundred miles of water stretch between the coast of China and Japan.

Throughout most of Japan's history, these watery distances served either as barriers or as highways for ideas. Much of Japanese civilization was built on a Chinese base, but at the same time the Japanese developed a unique civilization of their own. As Edwin Reischauer points out: "What distinguishes them is . . . their distinctiveness and their skill at learning and adapting while not losing their own cultural identity. Others have tried to do the same but with less success."

A Shinto shrine and Torii gate along the Inland Sea of Japan.

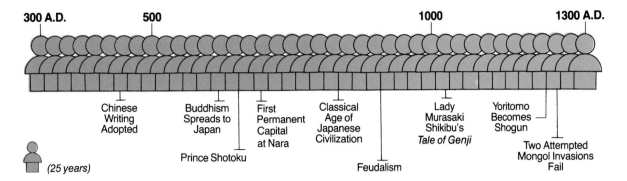

300 A.D.   500   1000   1300 A.D.

Chinese Writing Adopted

Buddhism Spreads to Japan

Prince Shotoku

First Permanent Capital at Nara

Classical Age of Japanese Civilization

Feudalism

Lady Murasaki Shikibu's *Tale of Genji*

Yoritomo Becomes Shogun

Two Attempted Mongol Invasions Fail

(25 years)

1. Japan: A Country in Harmony with Nature

There is an old Japanese poem about a man who went to his well for water. As he was about to draw up the bucket, he noticed the tendrils of a lovely plant twined around the rope. "Nature is showing her face to me again," he thought. Rather than disturb the plant, he drew his water from a neighbor's well!

The close relationship between the Japanese and Nature is an important feature of their culture. This is a land marked by the many moods of Nature, and the people are respectful of those moods.

One can sense the presence of Nature everywhere: in the park at Nara, where deer roam freely among centuries-old cedar trees; or in the special beauty of a small Japanese garden. On a boat in the Inland Sea, fishermen may thank the waters for their tasty catch of fish. In the month of April, thousands of Japanese families visit the flowering cherry trees and celebrate the coming of spring. In every generation, the Japanese have deeply appreciated the wonder and the power of Nature.

The Geography of Japan Is Distinctive

Nature is especially important to the Japanese people because of the distinctive geographic features of their country. Japan consists of a string of islands in the north Pacific. These islands are of volcanic origin and extend in an arc for about 1300 miles off the northeastern coast of the Asian mainland. (See the map on page 188.) This distance compares in length with the coastal stretch between Portland, Maine, and Daytona Beach, Florida. The four principal islands are Hokkaido, Honshu, Shikoku, and Kyushu; but there are hundreds of Japanese islets scattered among them. There are excellent harbors on many islands, and no point in

Japan is farther than seventy-two miles from the sea.

The whole country is so mountainous that about three-fourths of the land cannot be used for farming. The only relatively large plain is around Tokyo, and this plain is just one hundred and twenty miles at its longest. Elsewhere, people live on small coastal plains, in narrow river valleys, and in basins in the mountains. Japan is heavily dependent on the sea for food.

The climate varies from north to south. In many areas, the winters are fairly cold and the summers are hot and damp. There is considerable rain during June and the early part of July. Autumn and spring are the loveliest seasons of the year.

Earthquakes, typhoons, and floods are fairly common disasters. In spite of these problems, the people of Japan continue to love their country for its beauty and charm.

The Japanese Are a Mixture of Peoples

The Japanese, evidence indicates, are the product of a mixture of peoples. Among the earliest that we know of were the *Ainus.* The Ainus probably came from the Asian mainland and lived in Japan hundreds of years before the birth of Jesus.

People from northern Asia moved down through Korea, crossed the sea to Japan, and gradually took over most of the lands of the Ainus. Other groups from either southeast China or islands in the southwest Pacific also migrated to Japan.

The Culture of the Early Japanese

By the third century A.D., the culture of the Japanese was based on farming and fishing. The Japanese were using irrigation to raise rice, and making tools and weapons from bronze and iron. Much of this farming and metal technology had spread to Japan from China. Chinese records of the

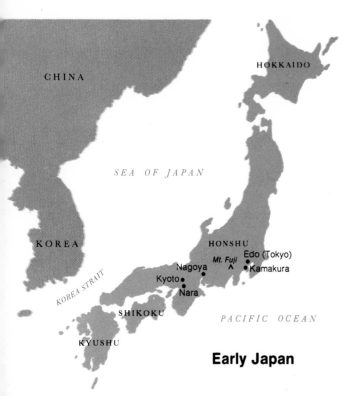

Early Japan

Locate the four main islands of Japan.

importance of cleanliness when taking part in religious ceremonies.

Check on Your Reading

1. How do many Japanese feel about Nature?
2. What has been the effect of Japan's island position on its history?
3. What is known about Japanese ways of living in the third century A.D.? From where did much of the Japanese technology of this period probably come?
4. What are the chief features of the Shinto religion?

---

2. Buddhism and Chinese Civilization Change Japanese Life

Japan had long had some contact with China, as you learned. Chinese writing was being used in Japan in the fifth century A.D. Later, the flow of Chinese civilization quickened with the arrival of Buddhist priests in Japan. This was the time when a golden age of Chinese civilization was developing under the Tang dynasty. In the centuries that followed, China was probably the most powerful and advanced civilization in the world.

These clay figures were found in a tomb. They are over sixteen hundred years old.

third century provide the first written information about Japan. They tell of people living in tribes ruled by female and male chieftains.

Delightful pottery figurines of horses and armored warriors have been found in the mound tombs of nobles and rulers of this period. They suggest a society ruled by an aristocracy of important warriors. By 500 A.D. the priest-chiefs of Yamato had won control of much of Japan. These rulers developed into the line of emperors from which the present emperor of Japan is descended.

The religion of the early Japanese is known as *Shinto,* which means the "Way of the Gods" or the "Way of the Good Spirits." Shinto is built around respect for and worship of spirits, gods, and goddesses of Nature. Some of these spirits are found in trees, rocks, mountains, waterfalls, certain animals, and special persons. Shinto also includes the worship of ancestors whose guidance is needed if the living are to have good lives.

Shrines were built at holy places where prayers were said and ceremonies were held. Shinto had no holy books or extensive rules of behavior except reverence for Nature and ancestors and stress on the

The Horyuji Buddhist temple was built originally in the seventh century. It has been restored several times.

The Japanese Turn to Mahayana Buddhism

Shinto did not meet all of the religious needs of the Japanese. Thus, when Buddhism was introduced, it quickly won acceptance. However, Shinto was not discarded, but merged with Buddhism in many ways.

You learned that Gautama Buddha taught that suffering is caused by our selfish desires and that we can remove suffering by doing away with these desires. *Mahayana Buddhism,* the Buddhist religion in Japan, China, and Tibet, accepted this basic teaching. To this idea, it added other important beliefs.

1. Faith is as important as monastic life. You need not try to subdue your desires by living in a monastery or avoiding the activities of daily life. If you have faith in the Buddhist religion, you can gain peace.

2. The *Amitabha Buddha* will help people. The *Amitabha Buddha* is a great god. Buddhists pray to him for help.

3. There are many Buddhas to guide people. Gautama was a Buddha. There will be other Buddhas after him. All of them will guide sincere Buddhists in their lives.

4. *Bodhisattvas* will answer prayers. *Bodhisattvas* are supernatural beings who are so worthy that they could gain peace in paradise forever. However, they love people so well that they continue to remain in contact with this world. If a Buddhist prays honestly to them, they will give aid.

The Buddhism that reached Japan had turned into a religion in which various supernatural beings aided and protected humans. Buddhism originally had taught that people must cast off their desires by themselves. Mahayana Buddhism taught that people could turn for help to powers greater than themselves.

189

This Buddhist temple and monastery about one hundred miles from the present city of Tokyo was founded in the seventh century A.D.

Chinese Civilization Moves to Japan

Buddhism had a tremendous effect on Japanese life. It was a powerful current that carried Chinese civilization and deposited it on the shores of Japan.

Prince Shotoku of the ruling family of Japan was a champion of Buddhism and Chinese civilization. The prince wrote commentaries on Buddhist scriptures and built Buddhist monasteries. One of them near Nara is still standing and has the oldest wooden buildings in the world. (See the photo on page 189.) It shows the balanced beauty of the architecture of the Tang dynasty of China.

From the sixth through the eighth centuries A.D., the great knowledge and skills of China came through Korea into Japan. It was on a foundation of Chinese civilization that the Japanese built a good part of their civilization.

The Japanese were much more than borrowers, however. Like fine artisans, they took Chinese materials and ideas and shaped them to produce a civilization of their own.

Check on Your Reading

1. Describe Mahayana Buddhism.
2. How did China influence Japan?

3. Japan's "Classical Age"

The Chinese had a centralized form of government under the emperor. The Japanese adopted this idea, so the Yamato ruler became the emperor of Japan. Prince Shotoku even wrote a letter to the Chinese emperor as coming from the Emperor of the Rising Sun to the Emperor of the Setting Sun.

At the same time, the custom of having women rulers was dropped. Japanese women who seemed to have had a powerful position in society began to lose their rights. For a while they had important positions at the emperor's court, but gradually they sank to a position of subservience.

A Rich Civilization Centers around the Capital

A centralized system of government needed a capital city. Now the Japanese built a capital around a huge palace and government buildings. This first permanent capital was at Nara. From about 710 to 794 A.D., the emperor made his headquarters at this city, although powerful Japanese families actually ruled many parts of the country. Then the capital was moved to the site of present-day Kyoto, where it remained until 1867.

From about the end of the eighth to the twelfth century, Japan had its so-called "Classical Age." During this period, the Japanese were very creative in literature, art, and architecture. Activities in these and other fields centered around the emperors and the aristocrats who lived in the capital.

Literature

Several histories were written at court during this period, two of which have survived. Poetry, however, was the most important literary form during the first half of the "Classical Age." Japanese poetry was usually brief. In a few lines the beauty of a scene was suggested or an emotion or sudden insight was described.

In the eleventh century, the writing of prose reached a peak. Many of the writers were court ladies. It was at this time that the most famous of all Japanese novels, *The Tale of Genji,* was written by Lady Murasaki Shikibu. Edwin Reischauer describes it as "not only the world's first great novel but one of the literary masterpieces of all time."

A second major book was *The Pillow Book* (about 1002 A.D.). Written by Lady Shōnagon, it has a light and graceful quality. If you are an active letter writer, you should enjoy her description of a returned letter:

> One writes a letter, taking particular trouble to get it up as prettily as possible; then waits for the answer, making sure every moment that it cannot be much longer before something comes. At last, frightfully late, is brought in—one's own note, still folded or tied exactly as one sent it, but so fingermarked and smudged that even the address is barely legible. "The family is not in residence," the messenger says, giving one back the note. . . . Such experiences are dismally depressing.

Although their language was not similar to Chinese, the Japanese made use of Chinese characters in their writing. They used the written symbols of

In the twelfth century a scroll was painted illustrating Lady Murasaki Shikibu's The Tale of Genji.

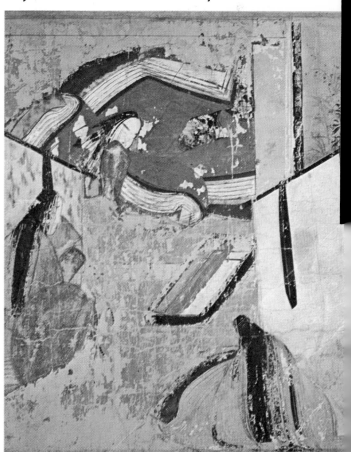

the Chinese language to write down their own speech. By the tenth century, the Japanese had modified many Chinese characters, and a distinctive Japanese form of writing gradually developed.

Art and Architecture

Japanese art during this period was greatly influenced by ideas coming from China. Early Japanese architecture, sculpture, and painting were inspired by the religion of Buddhism.

Many Buddhist temples and monasteries were built. Statues of the Buddha in bronze, wood, and lacquer were made for the temples. Also, temples housed exquisite religious paintings.

The Japanese made much use of wood in their buildings. In their wooden homes, they showed their feeling for Nature by arranging lovely gardens that were united with the house itself. Inside their homes they used little furniture and few ornaments.

Instead, they found beauty in the artistic arrangement of a few delicate objects.

When the Tang dynasty of China fell at the beginning of the tenth century, Japan's official contacts with China lessened. Japanese artists had to depend more on themselves for ideas, and they soon began to add their own touches.

A style of Japanese painting developed. It portrayed everyday scenes, such as the life at the emperor's court. Also landscape paintings became popular.

Check on Your Reading

1. What were the achievements of the Japanese during the "Classical Age"?
2. Describe some Japanese literature of this period.
3. In art, what did Japan borrow from China? What original contributions did the Japanese make?

This scroll portrays a samurai in armor. He is cutting a flying arrow with his sword.

4. Feudalism Emerges in Japan

At the same time, an important political change was taking place. Between the end of the eighth and the twelfth centuries, *feudalism* developed.

Feudalism usually had three features. Lords held the land and protected the peasants who worked it. People promised to be loyal to their superiors. Local governments took the place of a central government.

All three features appeared in Japan. Gradually more and more of the land came under the control of great families at court or of important temples and shrines. At the same time small farmers who could not pay high taxes to the emperor turned over their lands to great lords. In return for protection, the farmers agreed to work the soil, pay rent to their lords, and be loyal to them.

By the twelfth century, much of the farmland of Japan had become divided up into tax-free private estates. Also the right to appoint provincial governors and control local taxes became a privilege of certain great families. As a result, the power of the emperors grew weaker while they grew poorer. This meant that the emperor was no longer able to protect the people. In theory, the emperor continued to govern the country. In fact, Japanese life was dominated by powerful Japanese families at court and by strong feudal lords throughout the country.

The Samurai Serve as Feudal Warriors

The heads of leading families, or clans, gathered warriors to protect their lands. These military men were called *Samurai*.

The Samurai were supposed to live by a code of conduct known as *Bushido,* or "the warrior-knight-way." Bushido was an unwritten code, and many warriors did not follow all of its rules. Nevertheless, it served as a guide for a military man's behavior.

According to Bushido, a Samurai warrior must be brave, a man of honor, loyal to his emperor and lord, and must not show emotion. To redeem his honor, a Samurai did not hesitate to commit *seppuku (hara-kiri)*—that is, to kill himself by "ripping the belly" with a short sword.

The Shogunate Is Established

As the feudal system grew, ambitious clans struggled to gain control of Japan. The Fujiwara were the strongest for several centuries. Then they were

A portrait of Yoritomo, leader of the Minamoto clan, who became the first Shogun.

succeeded by the Taira clan. In turn the Taira were defeated by the Minamoto clan.

In 1192 A.D., the emperor appointed Yoritomo, leader of the Minamoto clan, to be *Shogun.* Shogun meant "great general" or "barbarian-subduing general." As Shogun, Yoritomo ruled Japan with a military government whose capital was at Kamakura. The emperor remained at his court in Kyoto, but he had little power.

Yoritomo is extremely important in the history of Japan. When his military government took the place of civil rule, he started a system which was to last until 1868. This system was called the *Shogunate.* It meant that the emperor was merely a ceremonial head. A military chief called a *Shogun* ruled Japan in the name of the emperor.

The Shogunate under Yoritomo provided Japan with an effective government. Yoritomo reorganized the administration of the provinces, strengthened the legal system, and forced some feudal lords to pay land taxes. When Yoritomo died, the actual powers of government passed to another family.

During this period, civilization that largely had been limited to the capital area spread through most of Japan. Stirring tales were written of the exploits of feudal heroes. Wonderful scroll paintings portrayed the lives of particularly holy Buddhists. Fine statues were created. Probably the most famous is the great Buddha at Kamakura, which is one of the largest bronze figures in the world.

"Kami-Kaze" Helps Destroy Mongol Invaders

In the thirteenth century, the Mongols conquered vast lands, including China and Korea. Then they sent envoys to Japan demanding the surrender of the island kingdom. The Shogun's court at Kamakura refused and even beheaded some of the envoys. Such an insult could not go unpunished. The Mongols attempted two sea invasions of Japan. Both times Nature came to the aid of the Japanese. Storms hindered the movements of the enemy's first fleet. A typhoon saved Japan again in 1281.

During this famous typhoon, "the wind blew fiercely the . . . billows surged up to heaven, the thunder rolled and the lightning dashed against the ground so that it seemed as if mountains were crumbling down and high heaven falling to the earth." The storm destroyed the Mongol fleet. This typhoon is known as "kami-kaze" or "divine wind."

The Shogun had supported many warriors to defend the country and had built a large defense wall around a bay where he thought the Mongols would land. The defense of Japan was successful, but it weakened the government by draining the treasury of funds. Ambitious men tried to seize power, and civil war broke out. A new Shogunate family, the *Ashikaga,* finally won control.

Check on Your Reading

1. How did Japanese feudalism develop?
2. How did the Shogunate govern Japan?
3. What was the code of the Samurai?
4. What happened to civilization during the feudal period?

LET'S MEET
THE PEOPLE

The Flower Feast

On the twentieth day of the second month the Emperor gave a Chinese banquet under the great cherry tree in the Southern Court. Before the feast the Emperor handed each guest a word which he had drawn by lot. Royal princes, guests, and professional poets all set to work to compose their poems, using the words given them by the Emperor.

Many of the professional poets were nervous because much was expected of them, and the Emperor's special interest in Chinese poetry had spread throughout his court. A Chinese verse was not too much to ask of a professional poet; but many of them wore expressions of deepest gloom.

Toward dusk the delightful dance known as "the Warbling of Spring Nightingales" was performed. Then Genji danced a fragment of the "Wave" Dance and Chujo performed the "Park of Willow Flowers." After this, other young noblemen also danced.

Then the poems were opened and read aloud. The reading of Genji's verses was often interrupted by applause. Even the professional poets were deeply impressed.

It was now very late and the Emperor and Empress returned to the palace. All the guests except Genji left. He stayed to watch the bright beauty of the rising moon.

The above is based on an episode in Lady Murasaki Shikibu's *The Tale of Genji,* translated from the Japanese by Arthur Waley. (Houghton Mifflin.)

CHAPTER REVIEW

Think and Discuss

1. Why has the sea been so important to the Japanese?
2. "History never begins a new chapter. Only historians do." What might this statement mean?
3. The Japanese learned from China skills and knowledge on which a considerable part of their civilization was based. What other peoples have you learned about who developed civilizations in this way? From whom did they draw knowledge and skills?
4. How would you describe the Japanese paintings shown on pages 191, 192, and 193?
5. Japanese society of the feudal age was a military society. How do you think this might have affected the position of women?
6. Why do you think that Yoritomo allowed the position of Emperor to continue?

Past and Present

1. Read again the quotation from Edwin Reischauer in the second paragraph of the "Keynote." Do you think that this quotation applies to the modernization of Japan in the last one hundred years? Explain.
2. Do many Japanese today appreciate Nature as much as their ancestors did in the past? Do research to determine a possible answer to this question.

Activities

1. Do research and report on the position of the emperor in Japanese society today.
2. Obtain books on Japanese art and try to create a Japanese painting.
3. Translations of Japanese poetry, especially *haikus,* have been made. Read some of them and try to compose a *haiku.*

4

The Many Worlds of Africa and the Americas

Today we are making vast changes in our environments with the aid of modern technology and science. Before the coming of the scientific and industrial "revolutions" of the 1700s and 1800s, human beings had relatively few tools with which to respond to the challenges of the various environments in which they lived. In responding to these challenges, the peoples of Africa and the Americas created rich and varied cultures and civilizations.

12

Unity and Diversity:
Peoples and Civilizations of Africa

KEYNOTE

In the 1850s, David Livingstone, a Scot, "discovered" a magnificent waterfall on the Zambesi River in south central Africa. He named it "Victoria Falls" after the British queen; but this waterfall, which the Africans called "Smoke that Thunders," had been there for thousands of years. Livingstone was merely the first European who saw it.

So it is with the histories of the diverse peoples of Africa. In this century, inhabitants of Western societies have begun to "discover" that the peoples of Africa created over the centuries rich and varied cultures. Westerners may have just begun to learn this; but Africans have long known and been proud of the achievements of their ancestors.

African textiles and gold ring.

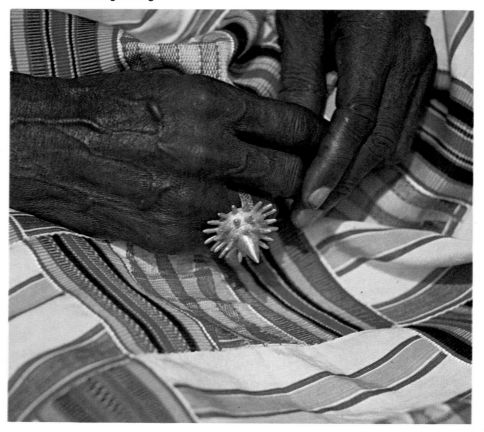

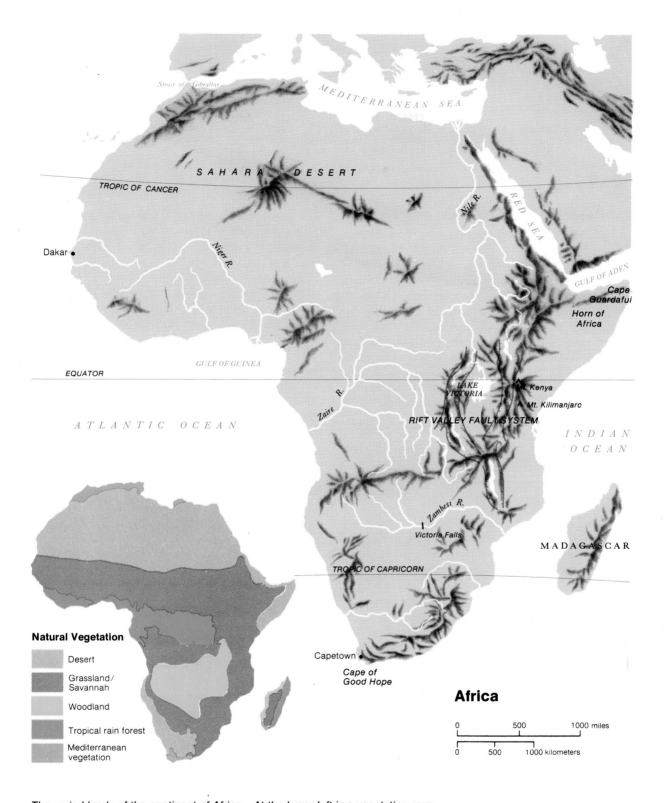

Strait of Gibraltar

MEDITERRANEAN SEA

SAHARA DESERT

TROPIC OF CANCER

Nile R.

RED SEA

Dakar

Niger R.

GULF OF ADEN

Cape
Guardafui

Horn of
Africa

GULF OF GUINEA

EQUATOR

ATLANTIC OCEAN

Zaire R.

LAKE
VICTORIA

Mt. Kenya

Mt. Kilimanjaro

RIFT VALLEY FAULT SYSTEM

INDIAN
OCEAN

Zambesi R.

Victoria Falls

MADAGASCAR

TROPIC OF CAPRICORN

Natural Vegetation

Desert

Grassland/
Savannah

Woodland

Tropical rain forest

Mediterranean
vegetation

Capetown

Cape of
Good Hope

Africa

0   500   1000 miles

0   500   1000 kilometers

The varied lands of the continent of Africa. At the lower left is a vegetation map.

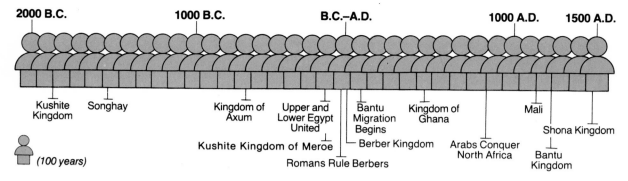

2000 B.C.   1000 B.C.   B.C.–A.D.   1000 A.D.   1500 A.D.

Kushite Kingdom — Songhay — Kingdom of Axum — Upper and Lower Egypt United — Bantu Migration Begins — Kingdom of Ghana — Mali — Shona Kingdom

Kushite Kingdom of Meroë — Berber Kingdom — Arabs Conquer North Africa — Bantu Kingdom

Romans Rule Berbers

(100 years)

1. Geography and Peoples

Africa is the second largest continent. The distance between the city of Tangier, on the Mediterranean Sea, and Capetown, on Africa's southern tip, is about 5,000 miles, or 8,045 kilometers. About 4,600 miles, or 7,400 kilometers, separate Dakar, on the west coast, and Cape Guardafui, the easternmost point on the Horn of Africa.

By 1500, when this chapter ends, Africa had many different cultures, ranging from hunting-gathering societies to farming villages, city states, and empires. These various cultures were the result of the creative use of the various environments of Africa and of the migrations and interaction of peoples over thousands of years. This interaction provided a certain unity under the diversity of the many cultures of the large continent.

Lands and Climates

Most of Africa is a series of plateaus tilting upward to the south and east, and occasionally broken by highlands. The plateaus are bordered by narrow lowlands along the coasts. Only along some sections of the Mediterranean do the lowlands sweep back many miles from the coast.

The rolling plateau lands are interrupted in the east by a great fracture in the earth's crust, known as the *Rift Valley fault system*. This system of depressions and mountains begins near the head of the Red Sea and continues southward for about 4,000 miles to the coast of the modern nation of Mozambique. Volcanic activity along the Rift long ago produced such high peaks as Mount Kenya and Mount Kilimanjaro.

From the highlands of the plateaus, mighty rivers, such as the Zaire (Congo), Niger, Nile, and Zambesi, flow to the coast, occasionally spreading out into broad shallow basins and swamps. Near the coast they spill over the edge of the plateau lands in a series of rapids or waterfalls. Therefore, these rivers are not navigable for any great distance from the coast.

The equator runs across the center of the continent. As a result, about four-fifths of Africa is in the tropics. Where the rainfall is heavy, a belt of rain forests stretches over 1,200 miles from the west coast to the headwaters of the Zaire River. East of these headwaters, the rainfall diminishes and grasslands mixed with trees take over.

North and south of the rain forests, the rainfall gradually decreases; and the rain forest, ever green the year round, gives way to the grasslands, called *savannas*. More than two-fifths of Africa is covered by these grasslands interspersed with stands of trees that lose their leaves in the dry season. The farther away from the equator, the longer is the tropical dry season or winter.

North and south of the savanna lands are deserts. The Sahara in the north is one of the world's largest deserts. Only along the western Mediterranean coast do winds bring enough rainfall to grow crops without irrigation. This pleasant "Mediterranean climate" also occurs along the southern tip of the continent.

Early Peoples of Africa

The oldest bones of human beings so far studied have been discovered in Africa. Also, as noted in the Prologue, evidence indicates that both Neanderthal and Cro-Magnon peoples occupied parts of Africa. These peoples were hunters, gatherers, and fishers.

By about 5,000 years ago the ancestors of modern Africans were living in different parts of the continent. In the north, the Sahara was not the dry land it is today. Sufficient rains fell there to support a variety of vegetation and animal life. Into this region, in what are now the countries of Libya, Tunisia, Algeria, and Morocco, moved light-skinned peoples known as *Berbers*. From the south, Negroid peoples moved into the southern part of this region.

Evidence indicates that Negroid peoples had long occupied the West African forests and parts of Central and East Africa. In the rain forests lived a small people now called Pygmies.

In the southern part of Africa were the "Bushmen." Today many of these people still lead a hunting and gathering life on the Kalahari desert.

By about 5000 B.C. peoples in what is now Egypt began to turn from hunting and gathering to farming and raising cattle, sheep, and goats. Then in the centuries that followed, the peoples we now call Egyptians developed the great civilization described in Chapter 2.

Archaeologists and other scientists do not agree as to when farming developed in other parts of Africa, as the evidence so far discovered is skimpy. Some scientists believe that by about 3500 B.C., the peoples of what is now the Sahara were beginning to experiment with agriculture and to raise cattle. Then by about 2500 B.C., the Sahara region began to lose its rains, rivers, grasslands, and forests. As a result, the Saharan peoples began to move to more favorable lands nearby. Those that moved southward no doubt took with them their cattle and their farming skills.

Check on Your Reading

1. Describe the lands, climates, and vegetations of Africa today.
2. Why are the rivers of Africa not navigable near the coasts?
3. What peoples lived in North Africa about 5,000 years ago? In West, Central, and East Africa? In South Africa?
4. In what areas and about when is it believed that agriculture first developed in Africa? How did the Sahara region change in the centuries following 2500 B.C.? What civilization in Africa has already been discussed in this book?

2. Ancient Glories

Although the Egyptian was the oldest and best known civilization in Africa, it was not the only one of ancient times. Another such civilization developed in the Nile region south of Egypt.

The Land of Kush

The land of Kush lay south of Egypt, within what is now the nation of Sudan. A great kingdom flourished there hundreds of years before the birth of Christ.

The Kushites were a mixture of peoples from the north, south, and east. They raised cattle, made handsome pottery, and carved ivory figures of birds and animals. Egyptians traded and raided in Kush as early as 2300 B.C. After 2000 B.C. several pharaohs of Egypt sent armies south to take control of more and more land.

The pharaohs of the New Kingdom brought Kush under their direct control and it became a part of Egypt. Many Kushites served in the Egyptian army and government. Then after 1000 B.C. Egypt grew weaker, and the Kushites set up an independent kingdom with its capital at Napata. Kashta, the first "great king" of Kush, embarked on a conquest of Egypt itself. His son completed this conquest in about 725 B.C.

Archaeologists discovered this frieze of Kushite gods at Naga in Sudan.

During the next century, Assyrians invaded Egypt. Their iron weapons overwhelmed Kushite forces equipped with arms of bronze and stone, and the Kushites retired southward. They later moved their capital southward from Napata on the Nile to Meroe, at the fork of the Nile and another river. The tombs of Kushite queens found around Meroe date from about 520 B.C. and after.

The City of Meroe

Meroe was a good river port on caravan routes leading southward into what is now Ethiopia, and from there to ports on the Red Sea. It became an important center for iron smelting and the manufacture of tools and weapons made of that metal. Smelters used the plentiful nearby resources of iron ore and of wood for charcoal. In addition, Meroe was surrounded by good grazing land. This was important to these people who raised cattle, goats, and sheep.

Archaeologists have been excavating Meroe. The archaeological evidence and the descriptions of Meroe in ancient texts indicate that it was the center of a rich civilization.

Meroe's walled palace and great temples were well known. Many of its kings and queens were buried in pyramids. King Netekamani and Queen Amantari were great builders in the second century B.C. They built the Lion Temple, dedicated to a god of war, which featured a lion with three heads and four forelegs. Another temple they erected shows the influence of both Roman architecture and Egyptian art.

Like the Egyptians, Kushites seem to have considered their rulers divine. There appears to have been a belief in an afterlife, because there have

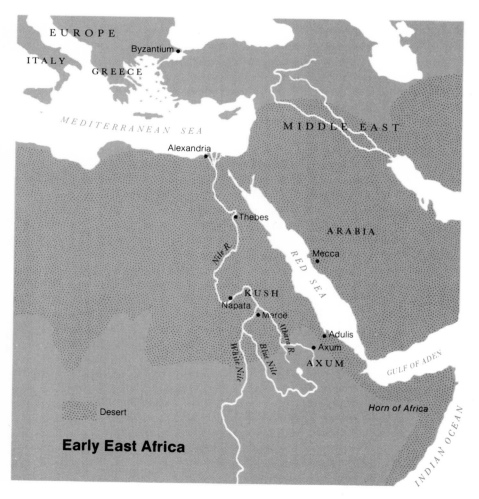

Civilizations developed in ancient times in East Africa.

Early East Africa

This Church of St. George in Ethiopia was built in the 1200s for King Lalibela of the Zagwe dynasty. King Lalibela had several churches cut out of rock during his reign. He was later venerated as a saint by Christian Ethiopians.

been found in the tombs of kings and queens gold and enameled jewelry; beads; vessels of glass, silver, and bronze; pottery; weapons; and many other objects. There is some evidence that succession to the throne may have been through the female line, a practice also found in other parts of Africa.

Kushite potters turned out beautifully decorated vases and jars. Craftsmen also worked in bronze.

There is some evidence that the Kushites might have had some trade contact with the ancient Far East. Chinese documents of the time suggest that ships from China might have reached East African ports as early as the first century A.D.

Educated residents of Meroe wrote in Egyptian hieroglyphics, although by Roman times they had developed a writing system apparently using an alphabet. Archaeologists have not yet been able to learn how to read this writing, however.

Kushite trade eventually fell off. The kingdom of Kush gradually became isolated, and its civilization declined. As this occurred, a power was developing to the southeast around the city of Axum in the highlands of what is now Ethiopia. In about 350 A.D., a king of Axum conquered Kush. This king boasted about the conquest of Kush as follows:

> I burnt their towns, both those built of bricks and those built of reeds, and my army carried off their food and copper and iron . . . and destroyed the statues in their temples, their granaries, and cotton trees and cast them into the [Nile].

The Kingdom of Axum

By about 3000 B.C. farming had spread to the Ethiopian highlands. The rise of Axum seems to have begun around 700 B.C., when peoples of the southern Arabian peninsula began to cross the Red Sea into the Ethiopian highlands. These people spoke a Semitic language. They were farmers who used terracing, irrigation, and plows. One group of them established a kingdom centered on the city of Axum in the second or third century B.C.

Many Greek and Jewish merchants settled in the kingdom of Axum in the first century A.D., establishing themselves principally in the Red Sea port of Adulis. This became a center of Mediterranean-Red Sea commerce. Traders shipped northward elephants, tortoise shells, rhinoceros horns, and various spices, perfumes, and incense.

Greeks probably brought Christianity to the Axumite kingdom, perhaps in the fourth century A.D. By the next century, Christianity had become the official religion, and many Ethiopians today are Christians.

Axumite architects created buildings with columns and stepped walls. They also built stelae, tall upright stones or slabs with inscribed or sculptured surfaces that served as monuments. Many of these were as tall as sixty feet.

Axumite power gradually declined as its trade was increasingly disrupted, first by the destruction of the Roman Empire and then by the Arabs' conquests of Mediterranean lands. However, much of its culture survived to become a part of the Ethiopian civilization that lived in comparative isolation in the centuries that followed. This civilization created some remarkable architecture, as the photo on page 203 shows.

Developments in Northern Coastal Lands

By about 1000 B.C., iron and the horse had been introduced into this region. Gradually Berber chieftains conquered neighboring peoples and set up several kingdoms.

By the third century B.C. three large Berber kingdoms dominated the lands of what are now Morocco, Algeria, and Tunisia. Most of the wealth of these kingdoms came from the products of the farming population. A main function of the king was to protect farmers against the raids of nomadic peoples and to protect town dwellers against attacks by foreign invaders.

The first foreign settlements were made by the Phoenicians, who developed Carthage into a city-state. The Berber kings used their armies to fight first against Carthage, and later against Rome. They were not able to defeat the armies of Rome. By 100 A.D. the Berber kingdoms, as well as Egypt, had become parts of the Roman Empire.

The Phoenicians and the Romans brought new crops and farming techniques into the region. The raising of olive trees, grapevines, and wheat gradually spread throughout the region. The Romans built cities and set up Roman government, granting citizenship to many of the local peoples. Berbers joined Roman armies, and became contributors to Roman civilization. Later, they shared in the development of Christian churches and theology.

In the second century A.D. the Romans imported

A number of kingdoms developed in West Africa after 500 A.D. Trade played an important part in the life of these kingdoms.

West Africa from 500 A.D. to 1600 A.D.

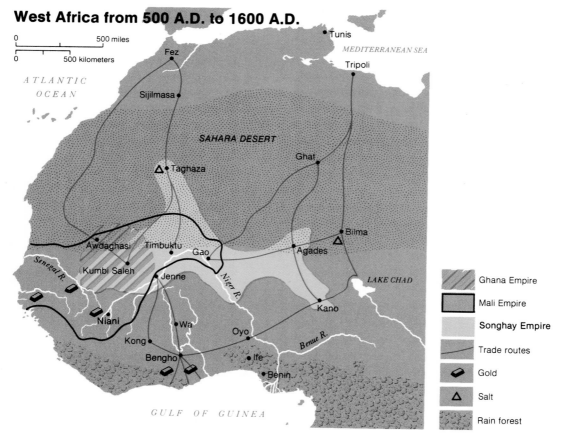

These Ashanti weights were used in weighing gold.

as soldiers camel-riding Syrian nomads. With the coming of the camels, trade routes were developed by the Berbers across the Sahara.

Then in the fifth century A.D. Germanic invaders destroyed Roman control of this region. As a result, independent Berber kingdoms again developed. By 750 all of the lands north of the Sahara, as well as Egypt, had become a part of the Arabic Empire.

Check on Your Reading

1. What were some features of the Kushite civilization?
2. What speculations can be made about Kushite religious beliefs?
3. What helped to cause the rise of the kingdom of Axum? What caused its decline?
4. What were some features of the Berber kingdoms? What changes were brought by the Romans?

3. Peoples and Kingdoms of West Africa

In West Africa a number of large kingdoms developed after 500 A.D. The earliest of these grew up in the savanna lands south of the Sahara.

After 1000 B.C. the population of this region steadily increased. This was due in part to the development of farming and herding. Also peoples migrated into the region from the expanding desert known as the Sahara.

Between 300 and 100 B.C. the use of iron was introduced into the region. Iron tools no doubt enabled farmers to raise more crops. Iron weapons helped chieftains to extend their rule over neighboring peoples.

Probably by the first century A.D. the savanna region was occupied by large populations living in villages bound together by kinship ties and in small kingdoms ruled by "divine" kings. Something must have encouraged some of these people to develop larger kingdoms. This stimulus was probably the growth of trade.

Trade and the Camel

Evidence indicates that by 1000 B.C. two main caravan routes had been established by Berber traders across the Sahara to the Niger River. Later, both Carthaginians and Romans bought goods traded along these routes. Through the centuries these goods were carried over the desert routes by horses and bullocks, but these animals were not well adapted to the desert.

Then the camel was introduced in the first century A.D. Trade increased and a complicated network of caravan routes was developed across the Sahara.

As trade expanded, more people became wealthy, and urban centers grew both in size and influence. Wealth and the desire to control trade routes in turn led to the creation of large kingdoms by ambitious leaders.

The Kingdom of Ghana

Ghana, located along the Niger and Senegal rivers, seems to have been the first large West African kingdom. Ghanian tradition dates the foundation of the kingdom to about 300 A.D., and Ghana had probably developed into a powerful state by the fifth century. By the late 700s, Arab traders knew it as the "Land of Gold."

Ghana's wealth came from trade in salt from mines in the Sahara and gold from mines to the south which the kingdom controlled. Ibn Hawqal, the Arab explorer, described the sovereign of Ghana in his tenth-century book as "the wealthiest of all kings on the face of the earth on account of . . . the hoards of gold acquired by him and inherited from his predecessors since ancient times."

The Arab writer al-Bakri described how the Ghanian court benefited from trade:

. . . for every donkey loaded with salt that enters the country, the king takes a duty of one gold dinar, and two dinars from every one that leaves. From a load of copper the king's due is five mithqals and from a load of other goods ten mithqals.

Other trade goods that moved through Ghana included ivory, kola nuts, horses, swords, books and writing paper, leather, and textiles.

Two towns made up the Ghanian capital of Kumbi Saleh, which probably had about 30,000 people. Muslim traders dominated one. In 1067 observers reported that this town had a dozen mosques. The king and court and other Ghanians resided in the other town, the court occupying a walled palace.

It is probable that the king of Ghana was considered divine by most of his subjects. Al-Bakri described the court ceremonies as follows:

The court of Appeal is held in a domed pavilion around which stand ten horses covered with gold-embroidered materials. Behind the king stand ten pages holding shields and swords decorated with gold and on his right are the sons of the vassal kings of his country wearing splendid garments and their hair plaited with

An engraving made in 1855 of a camel caravan approaching Timbuktu.

gold. The governor of the city sits on the ground before the king and around are ministers seated likewise. . . . The audience is announced by the beating of a drum. . . . When the people who profess the same religion as the king approach him, they fall on their knees and sprinkle dust on their heads.

Almoravids and Sossos

Ghana declined in the eleventh century, and was conquered by Almoravids, a Muslim sect made up of Berbers from the Sahara. Almoravid control was short. Their rule ended in 1235 when the Sossos people conquered Ghana.

A Sossos king also conquered the Mandingo kingdom of Mali, to the south. He taxed the Mandingo without mercy, extracting gold, food, and slaves. Eventually a member of the royal family of Mandingo, Sundiata, rallied Malian forces against the Sossos. After Sundiata became king of Mali in 1230, he won a great battle against the Sossos. Sundiata's victory marked the beginning of the Empire of Mali.

Mali

Niani, on the Niger River, became Mali's capital. From that center Mandingo rulers, who had become Muslims, developed a great Islamic empire.

The Arab Ibn Battuta was deeply impressed by their devotion to Islam. "They are careful to observe the hours of prayer," he wrote, "and assiduous in attending them in congregations, and in bringing up their children to them."

African Religions

In Ghana, as in other West African kingdoms, Islam was mainly a religion of city dwellers. Most people followed their traditional beliefs. Like many African peoples south of the Sahara, those of West Africa worshipped ancestors and spirits.

Throughout most of Africa there was a common belief in a supreme deity who created all things. Most cultures had a story of creation, even though different groups had different versions of the story. In addition, there was a common idea about a happy and peaceful time between humans and God, and then a break, resulting from human misdeed or error. It was believed that humans were restored to God's favor through the deeds and teachings of great heroes of the past—"founding heroes" or "founding ancestors"—who led their people to the particular land they occupied. People believed that the founders established rules which, if observed, would keep people worthy in the eyes of God. These heroes linked peoples to their dead ancestors, whom they venerated. One scholar says:

It has been suggested that African religion can roughly be depicted as a triangle. At the top, head of all powers, is God. On the two sides of the triangle are the next greatest powers, gods and ancestors. At the base are lower forces, with which magic and medicine are concerned. Man is in the middle, and must live in harmony with all the powers that affect his life, family, and world. The powers extend into the animal world, for animals have great forces which need to be watched and harnessed if possible. Even . . . inorganic nature is not dead, but may be a vehicle of power. . . . Body and soul are closely interwoven . . . , though it is known that at death the spirit leaves the body. . . . Medicine is given to heal disease, but a spiritual remedy is also needed.

A Famous City

In Niani, Malian merchants traded in salt, ivory, gold, and other items with traders from Egypt, Morocco, and elsewhere. This trade stimulated the growth of several cities besides the capital. One was Gao, down the Niger from Niani. Another was Timbuktu, a city on the great bend of the Niger River. Caravans of thousands of camels moved to and from Timbuktu carrying gold, copper, shells, fine swords, silks, and countless other goods.

Timbuktu was for centuries an Islamic center of commerce and learning. Many scholars studied and taught in that city of mosques, and also moved out from there to set up schools in other parts of West Africa. Timbuktu had a university, Sakore, and as many as 150 Koranic schools. One visitor to the city spoke of

the great store of doctors, judges, priests, and other learned men that are bountifully maintained at the king's cost and charges. And hither are brought diverse manuscripts or written books out of Barbarie [along the Mediterranean] which are sold for more money than any other merchandise.

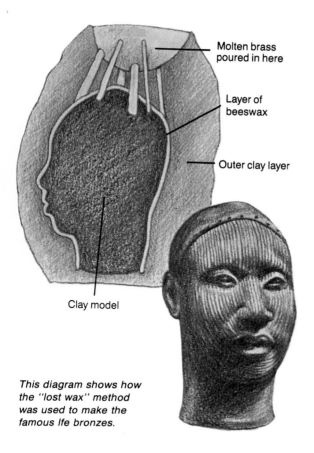

Molten brass poured in here

Layer of beeswax

Outer clay layer

Clay model

This diagram shows how the "lost wax" method was used to make the famous Ife bronzes.

Peace and Order

The capital, Niani, and other Malian cities depended on the products raised by farmers as well as on trade. The farmers produced rich crops of grain, peanuts, and other foods, and also cotton.

Visitors to Mali were impressed by the peace and orderliness of the people. Ibn Battuta wrote in the 1350s:

> They are seldom unjust and have a greater abhorrence of injustice than any other people. Their Sultan shows no mercy to anyone guilty of the least act of it. There is complete security in their country. Neither traveler nor inhabitant in it has anything to fear from robbers or men of violence.

Ibn Battuta also wrote that the women of Mali "were shown more respect than the men." The succession to the throne was through the women of the royal family. It was the son of the sister of the king who became the next ruler.

Mansa Musa

The greatest emperor of Mali was Mansa Kankan Musa ("mansa" meaning sultan, or emperor), the grandson of one of Sundiata's sisters. He came to the throne in 1312 and reigned until 1337.

It was said that Mansa Musa had an army of a hundred thousand men, ten thousand of them mounted on camels or horses. He expanded the empire until it covered an area equal in size to present-day Germany, France, and Spain combined.

On a pilgrimage to Mecca in 1324, Mansa Musa met the Muslim poet, scholar, and architect Abu Saheli. He persuaded Abu Saheli to return with him to Mali. There Abu Saheli introduced brick as the main building material for palaces and mosques. He built several mosques in Timbuktu for Mansa Musa.

Mansa Musa's reign ended after twenty-five years. The rulers who came after him were weak. Gradually Mali lost many of its lands to other peoples, including those of Songhay.

Songhay

By 1475 Songhay controlled nearly all the land that had once been part of Mali.

The origins of the people of Songhay are obscure. They were farmers and fishers who had settled along the Niger River. The King Kossi was said to have accepted Islam in 1009. Songhay became the most powerful state in West Africa under Sunni Ali, who began his reign in 1464. He conquered many lands and then set up a system of government for his empire. He divided the empire into provinces governed by officials whom he appointed. His successor, Muhammad Toure, became emperor in 1493 and added even more land to the empire.

The Famous Sculpture of Ife

Other states also developed in West Africa, including some in the forests south of the savanna lands. (See the map on page 204.) The people of these forests had a tradition that their ancestors came from the north and east. They may have been part of the migration of Negroid peoples who left the Sahara as it grew drier and drier.

The development of these states was no doubt stimulated by the growth of trade. Trade routes from the north were extended into the forest lands. At the same time, coastal peoples developed a trade in salt and fish with the peoples in the interior.

Probably the oldest of the states that developed in the western forest lands was Ife, in what is now Nigeria. Ife was a city-state ruled by a divine king. The knowledge of metal working in both bronze and iron had spread to this region some time before 800 A.D. It was in Ife that the world-famous West African bronze sculpture was first developed. (See the photo on page 196.)

The great artists of Ife taught their skills to other artists in West Africa, including those of the kingdom of Benin that became a powerful state in the fifteenth century.

Check on Your Reading

1. What were some of the probable reasons that kingdoms developed in West Africa?
2. What was the significance of the coming of the camel to Africa?
3. Describe the government of the ruler of Ghana. How did he get his wealth?
4. What are some features of traditional African religion?
5. Why was the small city-state of Ife especially important?

4. Great Migrations

The story of Africa south and east of what is now central Nigeria is in large part the story of the migrations of Bantu-speaking peoples. These migrations peopled much of the African continent. As a result, hundreds of different Bantu languages developed, all related to each other, as are the Romance languages or the Germanic languages.

The Migrations Begin

The original Bantu-speaking people probably lived south of the Benue River on the fringes of savanna and forest lands. They were a fishing people who also hunted wild animals and grew yams, sorghum, and millet. They raised cattle, wove bark fiber into cloth, and made pottery from clay. Goods and the power to govern were inherited through the female line. Villages may have been governed by a council of elders. Evidently some chieftains ruled over several villages. The Bantu worshipped spirits and their ancestors.

The migrations of Bantu-speaking peoples from central Nigeria began in the first century A.D. They were probably triggered by a great increase in

The bronze lions were created in the kingdom of Benin in the fifteenth or sixteenth century.

population. One cause of this increase must have been the arrival of people from the north as the Sahara turned into arid land.

The Bantu-speaking peoples traveled in canoes along rivers and coasts. The migration occurred gradually with small groups moving on when neighbors seemed too close or when quarrels broke out within villages or with their neighbors. The whole process took many centuries.

Knowledge of iron had reached Nigeria before these migrations began. The emigrants, therefore, were iron-using farmers. This gave them an important advantage over the Pygmies, the Bushmen, and most other people they encountered in the new environments in which they settled.

New Environments

Originally the Bantu-speaking peoples had adapted their lives to their environment. When they migrated, some settled in regions where savanna and forest combined, and others moved into tropical rain forests. The rain forest was a completely new environment. Grain did not grow well, and trees and underbrush had to be cleared before crops could be planted. The Bantu speakers also lost the cattle they had brought with them to disease carried by the tsetse fly. They, therefore, gave up their cattle and learned to adapt their agriculture to the ecology of the rain forest. They also found many animals to hunt and rivers that teemed with fish.

One migration route lay along the Zaire River and its tributaries. This led migrants to the headwaters of the Zambesi and down that river to the Indian Ocean. Another route led east to the Great Rift Valley. As the migrants moved into East Africa they encountered the banana and the taro (a starchy edible root) that had been introduced from Southeast Asia. These important new crops were well adapted to the tropical rain forest. It is very possible that it was Bantu-speaking peoples who spread the cultivation of these crops as they migrated from one region to the other.

When the Bantu-speaking peoples moved from the rain forest into East Africa, they encountered another environment—grasslands and grassland interspersed with forests. They met with cattle-herding peoples and again learned the skills of raising cattle.

Cattle took on particular significance to some Bantu-speaking groups. This was true of the Malawi, of the area of what is now Malawi; the Shona, of present-day Rhodesia-Zimbabwe; and the Sotho of South Africa. Cattle furnished meat, milk, skins, and horns. They also represented wealth. People paid taxes in the form of cattle. Cattle were the subject of poetry, and, among some peoples, cattle found a place in religious ceremonies.

Then the migration began again. Between the first and the fifth century A.D., the cattle-herding, Bantu-speaking peoples moved southward from the Zambesi Valley to the northern part of what is now the Republic of South Africa.

Varied Systems of Government

Archaeological evidence indicates that by 1200 A.D. different but related Bantu cultures had developed in different regions. These Bantu cultures evolved varied systems of government.

Tribal chieftains and village councils governed in some areas. The Karimojong of northern Uganda developed another system. They were herders who lived in an area of sparse vegetation. They had to move their herds frequently in order to provide them with sufficient grass. This meant that the men had to spend much time in cattle camps, away from their villages. To maintain order in the cattle camps, the Karimojong developed "age sets." At ten, a boy became a member of the youngest age set, and then moved from set to set at about five-year intervals. He was taught the behavior and responsibilities expected of the members of each age set. This ensured order in the camp and that each group carried out the responsibilities suited to its age level. At sixty, a male Karimojong retired from herding to become an elder in his village, helping to govern there.

Other people developed kingdoms, and, in some cases, empires. Two of these Bantu kingdoms were established in the copper-rich region of what is now Zaire. By the twelfth century A.D. population had increased in this region and a long-distance trade in copper had developed. The Luba kingdom was established by Kalala Ilunga, who introduced the idea of sacred kingship. Descendants of his line were believed to possess blood that could protect the people from harm and ensure success in hunting and abundant crops. The Luba kings ruled through local chieftains and a bureaucracy made up mainly of members of the royal family.

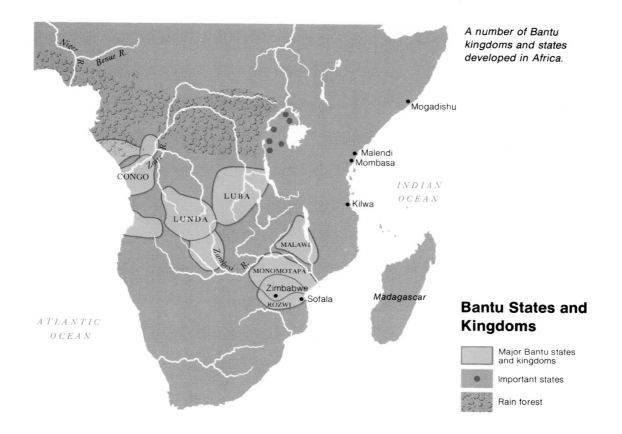

A number of Bantu kingdoms and states developed in Africa.

Niger R.
Benue R.
CONGO
Zaire R.
LUBA
LUNDA
Zambezi R.
MALAWI
MONOMOTAPA
Zimbabwe
ROZWI • Sofala

Mogadishu
Malendi
Mombasa
Kilwa

INDIAN OCEAN

Madagascar

ATLANTIC OCEAN

Bantu States and Kingdoms

- Major Bantu states and kingdoms
- ● Important states
- Rain forest

The Lunda, a people living to the west of the Luba, also established a kingdom headed by a divine ruler. In addition, they created an empire containing at least a million people.

Congo was another empire, dating probably to the twelfth century. It controlled territory along the Zaire River and part of what is now northern Angola. Congo culture was famous for its pottery, weaving, ironworking, and for its stone sculpture. A strong central government set up state-controlled currency based on a small seashell.

Writing about the Bantu-speaking peoples of Africa's interior, one student of the continent, Jan Vansina, has said:

As these civilizations emerged, they left a unique legacy for all mankind. Inner Africa has been less affected by the world outside than most of the other civilizations elsewhere on the earth. At the same time the complexity of these ways of life takes them out of the range of the simple societies; there is nothing primitive about them. As Leo Frobenius, the German

ethnologist and explorer, said: "They are civilized to the marrow of their bones." Because they grew in relative isolation, the flowering of human ingenuity and creativity that these civilizations and their history represents is a unique thread in the cloth that is the achievement of mankind.

Check on Your Reading

1. Where was the original home of the Bantu peoples? What were the probable reasons for their migration?
2. What technology and foods did the original Bantu have? What were some of the ways in which they adapted to new environments?
3. What forms of government did they develop?

5. The Commercial World of East Africa

When Europeans in the fifteenth century sailed along the Indian Ocean coastal lands of Africa, they saw busy trading cities and met peoples speaking Swahili, a Bantu-Arabic language. They had, from their point of view, "discovered" the cosmopolitan world of east-coast Africa.

A reconstruction of the royal palace at Kilwa on the coast of East Africa. Find this city on the map on page 211.

Trade and City-States

Little is known about the early history of the region. Soon after the death of Mohammed, settlements along the coast of what is now known as Somalia became involved in the rapidly developing ocean trade of the Arabs. Arab and Persian traders carried African ivory to India and China. Muslim merchants settled in towns such as Zeila and Berbera and married local women. Gradually, a mixed Somali-Arabic culture developed.

Later, trading towns developed to the south along the Indian Ocean from Mogadishu to Sofala. Trade and the variety of goods traded increased. A widely-traveled Muslim writer reported in the twelfth century that East Africa was famous for its iron exports. He described how traders from the eastern Indian Ocean visited the ports of East Africa to buy African iron which they "carried to all the lands of India." Gold also became an important East African export.

It is not clear how these trading settlements developed into African-Arabic city-states. Perhaps Muslim merchants built trading posts at or near African towns, converting many of the local people to Islam. Or perhaps African trading centers may have developed in response to the growth of trade, with African rulers gradually becoming converts to Islam under the influence of Arab merchants living in these settlements.

Each of the city-states kept its independence, although some became more powerful than others. In any event, as more and more Arab settlers arrived and became absorbed into the Bantu majority, a Swahili culture developed.

Swahili Culture

The basic language of the east coast came to be "Swahili," which wove Arabic words into a Bantu base. The word "Swahili" derived from the Arabic for "coastal plain." The Swahili speakers took much from the Arabic culture but transformed it to become a part of their own culture. For example, the Swahili were influenced by the poetic literature of the Arabs, but they evolved their own form of verse and style of storytelling. The poet and story-teller was much admired and could always gather an audience to enjoy stories of adventure at sea or romances of daring deeds and love.

Swahili towns were built near the beach or on small islands and were sometimes surrounded by a wall. Tall stone houses lined narrow streets that led to a square along the waterfront. Mosques were built in the Arabic style. Basil Davidson, a scholar of African history, describes the houses:

> Many of the larger houses enclosed a pillared courtyard, usually shaped as a rectangle, off which there opened a series of small rooms kept dark and cool against the brilliant light and fierce heat of the glittering coastland. Skilled craftsmen decorated these houses with painted pottery and plates from Persia and China, arranging them in decorative niches carved in the coral walls. Much attention was given to the supply of fresh water for washing and sanitary purposes.

Zimbabwe

In the nineteenth century a British explorer "discovered" the ruins of great stone walls and a large tower at a place called "Zimbabwe" in what is now the country of Zimbabwe. Later explorers found other ruins nearby and various manufactured objects such as fine plates from the East and bracelets of gold. Who were the people who built Zimbabwe? At first, most Europeans believed that the people must have come from outside Africa.

The study of Africa's past has revealed a very different story, however. The walls of Zimbabwe were first started about a thousand years ago by the Shona people who spoke a Bantu language. They had migrated into Zimbabwe bringing knowledge of iron-making and mining. In time they began to mine the gold ore found in the region and were drawn into the long-distance trade across the Indian Ocean. They sold gold and copper to Swahili merchants.

One group of Shona people, led by priest-chieftains, embarked on a series of conquests. Probably they were motivated by the need for more land for a growing population and by the desire to have a greater share of the long-distance trade. By 1480, a number of Shona and other peoples had been organized into an empire. Zimbabwe was an important religious center of the empire.

When the empire broke in two, the ruler of the most powerful kingdom established his capital at Zimbabwe. He and his successors completed the building of the high walls. The walls surrounded

This type of ship was used in trade along the coast of East Africa. It is believed that the sails of these ships influenced the development of the ships that were used by Western explorers to cross the Atlantic in the 1500s and 1600s.

the quarters of the divine king and the dwellings of his family and ministers. The tower was probably where the king held religious ceremonies.

At Zimbabwe the ruler, his family, and his ministers enjoyed the wealth brought by the trade in gold and copper. They wore handsome gold bracelets made by Shona craftsmen and used fine plates and glassware from China and Persia. So, as with other Africans, the Shona people of Zimbabwe interacted with their neighbors and were part of a great trade network.

Check on Your Reading

1. What is "Swahili"?
2. What led to the development of city-states along the coast of East Africa? What was the religion of the rulers of these city-states?
3. What were the main African products traded across the Indian Ocean?
4. Who built Zimbabwe? What knowledge and skills did they have that helped them build a wealthy kingdom?

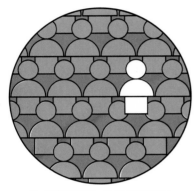

LET'S MEET THE PEOPLE

Mansa Musa and His Famous Pilgrimage

Like all Muslims, Mansa Musa of Mali had long waited to make the pilgrimage to Mecca. When he did so, his pilgrimage was probably the grandest that had been made to the holy city, establishing him in the eyes of the Muslim world as a powerful and wealthy ruler.

A historian of Timbuktu wrote that Mansa Musa took with him some 8,000 courtiers and servants. Each of these servants was said to carry a staff of solid gold. There were eighty camel-loads of gold, each weighing about three hundred pounds. Also strapped on camels' backs were bundles of articles made of copper, precious stones, and finely-woven cotton cloth to serve as gifts for rulers whom Mansa Musa might encounter on the journey.

Moving out of the city of Niani, the capital, and crossing savanna and desert northeastward, the huge caravan reached Cairo, Egypt, in July 1324. There it remained three days. Mansa Musa turned sightseer, visiting the great pyramids and Cairo's bazaars, spending an ample portion of his wealth on goods to take home with him.

The sultan of Egypt proved less impressed with the tall and powerfully built emperor of Mali than were most residents of Cairo. When Mansa Musa visited him, the sultan insisted that the emperor kiss his hand or bow low. Mansa Musa refused to perform either act of obeisance. The two rulers finally reached a compromise. Mansa Musa consented to bow, but only in honor of Allah, not the sultan.

Although he spent a great deal of his wealth in Cairo, Mansa Musa still had much gold remaining to bestow as gifts upon the cities of Medina and Mecca in Arabia. The return passage, however, left him without funds. He had to borrow from Cairo bankers, who gave him a loan at 133 percent interest, to finance the remainder of his homeward journey. This did not concern him. There was much gold still in Mali.

Mansa Musa had wished to impress people with the power and glory of the Malian empire. He succeeded. As a result of his great pilgrimage, trade with Egypt in particular increased. And the wealth and fame of Mali grew.

Based on the report of Al Omari from *The African Past* by Basil Davidson. Grosset & Dunlap, 1964.

CHAPTER REVIEW

Think and Discuss

1. Throughout history, the cultures of various peoples were in large part shaped by their environment. How does the geography of an area encourage people to develop knowledge and skills? What examples can you give from African history?
2. How do you think the knowledge of iron-working helped the Bantu settle in different environments?
3. Some experts believe that peoples in West Africa independently discovered how to raise food. Do you think that this could have happened? Why or why not?
4. Does the development of trade encourage the development of states with strong central governments? Why do you think so? Give examples to support your position.
5. Do you think the title of this chapter is a good one? Why or why not?

Past and Present

1. When the desert called the Sahara developed after 2500 B.C. it changed the lives of many peoples and influenced the course of history. What is happening today along the edges of the Sahara? Do some research and report your findings to the class.
2. Do some research to find out how African music strongly influenced the development of American jazz.

Activities

1. The opera *Aida* by Verdi tells a story based on events in ancient African history. Do some research to learn on what events in African history this story is based.
2. Prepare an exhibit of pictures of various kinds of African art.
3. Read some folktales from various regions in Africa. Then compare them with folktales from other parts of the world.

13

Cultures and Civilizations of the Americas

KEYNOTE

In 1492 Christopher Columbus, sailing west across the Atlantic Ocean from Spain, came upon the "New World." The land was new, however, only to Europeans.

Humans had lived in what came to be known as the Americas for thousands of years. By the time Europeans chanced upon the continents, more than 20 million people inhabited them. Through an accident of history these varied peoples became known as "Indians."

These early American peoples responded creatively to the varied environments of the Americas. They developed many different cultures, and some created civilizations.

A reconstruction of "Temple II" in the Maya city of Tikal in what is now Guatemala.

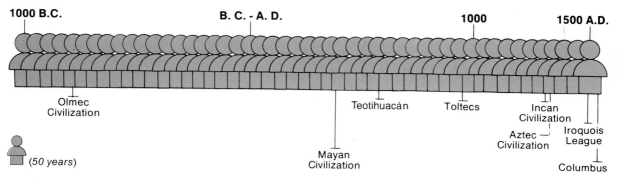

1000 B.C.   **B. C. - A. D.**   **1000**   **1500 A.D.**

Olmec Civilization

Teotihuacán   Toltecs   Incan Civilization

Aztec Civilization   Iroquois League

Mayan Civilization

Columbus

(50 years)

1. People Spread Out over the Americas

As noted in the Prologue, Cro-Magnon peoples lived in numerous parts of the world, including Siberia. It was apparently from Siberia that hunting and gathering Cro-Magnon bands migrated eastward to populate the Americas. Before their arrival, there were probably no humans on the two continents. Such animals as the big-horned bison, the woolly mammoth, and the camel had migrated earlier. These, as well as some other species, eventually became extinct in the Americas.

The Immigrants

Human migration from Siberia to the Americas may have begun some 25,000 years ago, perhaps even earlier. It was not a mass movement of people. Small bands filtered into North America over a long period of time, probably on the trail of game.

They crossed what is now the Bering Strait that separates Siberia from Alaska. Some fifty thousand years ago, during an Ice Age, that area became land. It remained so for thousands of years until climatic change melted the ice and covered the strait with water once again.

Population gradually built up in Alaska. This caused competition for food, and some hunting and gathering bands moved south. Little by little, over thousands of years, people spread out over North, Central, and South America.

The Beginning of Farming

Few of these peoples at first led settled existences. They migrated from time to time, following game animals, and living also off wild plants. Then, about seven thousand years ago, farming appeared in the Americas. Archaeologists have found the earliest evidence of agriculture so far in the Teohuacán valley south of Mexico City, Mexico.

As in the "Old World," farming developed in the Americas as a result of domesticating wild plants. The first plants the people of the Teohuacán valley grew were avocados, squash, and chili peppers. Then, about 5,000 years ago, they learned to grow maize, or corn, which grew as a wild plant. Corn cultivation spread north and south from Mexico and corn became the most important grain of the Americas. It changed ways of living, for corn provided the basis for settled communities.

At about the same time, root crops, like the potato, were grown in parts of South America. Evidence also indicates that five thousand years ago, cotton was being grown along the west coast of South America.

Almost every Native American group that grew corn had a legend about how corn originated. Here is one told by the Iroquois:

Long and earnestly a young man wooed a beautiful maiden. Fearing that she might be stolen by one of her many admirers, or that danger might come to her, the young man slept at night in the forest that he might be near to protect her. One night he was awakened by a light footstep and saw his loved one stealing out of her lodge as a sleepwalker. He followed her, but, as if fleeing in her dreams from a danger that threatened her life, she ran from him. On and on he followed, and finally drew so near that he could hear her quick breath. With all his remaining strength he sprang forward and clasped the maiden in his arms. What was his grief and astonishment to find that his arms clasped, not the maiden, but a strange plant which he had never seen before. The maiden had awakened and had been so frightened at her surroundings that she was transformed. When she raised her arms to her head her uplifted hands were changed into ears of corn.

217

Where her fingers caught her hair the corn
bears beautiful silken threads.

Some Were Not Farmers

Not all early American peoples adopted farming.
Agriculture was impossible in Arctic regions, for example. People there—now known as Eskimos—
lived mainly off walrus, seal, and certain kinds of
fish. As was the case with other early Americans,
their ways of living reflected their environment.
They dressed in sealskin clothing, made tools of
bone, and learned to make bone frameworks over
which they stretched sealskins to fashion boats.
They used blocks of snow and ice, an abundant resource, to construct shelters known as igloos.

Other non-farming peoples lived in the Pacific
Northwest. It was easier for them to live off the
abundant fish than to plant crops. Such tribes as
the Bella Coola of British Columbia and the Chi-
nook of Washington gathered halibut, salmon, cod,
and other fish from rivers and the Pacific Ocean.

The Pacific Northwest region had a thick forest of
firs, redwoods, cedars, and other trees. Cedar was
especially useful. This durable wood is fairly easy
to work with stone tools, the only kind most early
Native Americans had. Pacific Northwest people
felled cedars with stone hatchets and fire, and built
large boats, some sixty or more feet long. In these
boats they fished in the Pacific and also hunted for
whales, subduing those huge creatures with stone-
tipped harpoons.

Cedar was also a valuable resource for building.
People of the Pacific Northwest made posts and
planks from cedar logs for building houses. Such
logs also furnished raw material for totems, logs
carved into human and animal shapes and placed
upright in the ground.

Check on Your Reading

1. From where did the First Americans, or Native
   Americans, probably come? About how many
   Native Americans were living in the Americas at the
   time of Columbus?
2. In what areas was farming probably first developed?
   What crops were grown?
3. Who were some Native Americans who did not
   adopt farming? On what did they depend for food?
   How did they make use of the resources of their
   environments?

---

2. Some Varied Cultures of North America

Alvin M. Josephy, Jr. reminds us that

> To a large extent, Indian cultures reflected
> the environments in which they were shaped.
> As the various peoples . . . spread through the
> Americas and occupied different portions of
> both continents, they adopted the traits and
> techniques necessary for their survival. There
> were local and regional adjustments to extremes
> in temperature and climate, to mountain,
> desert, jungle, woodland, grassland, and coastal
> topography and to the availability of various
> kinds of food resources.

The Dry Southwest

Ancestors of the peoples now known as Pima,
Zuñi, Hopi, and others settled in the southwestern
part of what is now the United States. Here they
faced a dry environment where hardly more than a
dozen inches of rain fell each year, an environment
to which they adapted their technology.

For thousands of years they were gatherers of
nuts, seeds, fruits, and plants, as well as hunters of
small animals. Then about two thousand years ago
they began to raise the crops that had gradually
spread northward from Mexico. They learned how
to use the limited amount of water of their environment to raise enough food to support quite large
numbers of people.

Some raised crops on land that held water from
previous rains. Others developed irrigation systems, using water from such rivers as the Salt, the
Gila, and the Rio Grande. One network of irrigation canals has been discovered that covered one
hundred and fifty miles.

These Native Americans became known as Pueblos, a Spanish word for "towns." This was because they used sun-dried bricks to construct dwellings that looked something like apartment
buildings. Some were four stories high. Hundreds
of people lived in a pueblo.

This aspect of their environment also influenced
their culture. Living so close together, the people
of a pueblo had to get along peacefully. They
brought up their children to value cooperation and
nonaggression. Pueblo groups seldom engaged in
warfare. The word Hopi, referring to one of these
groups, itself means "peaceful people."

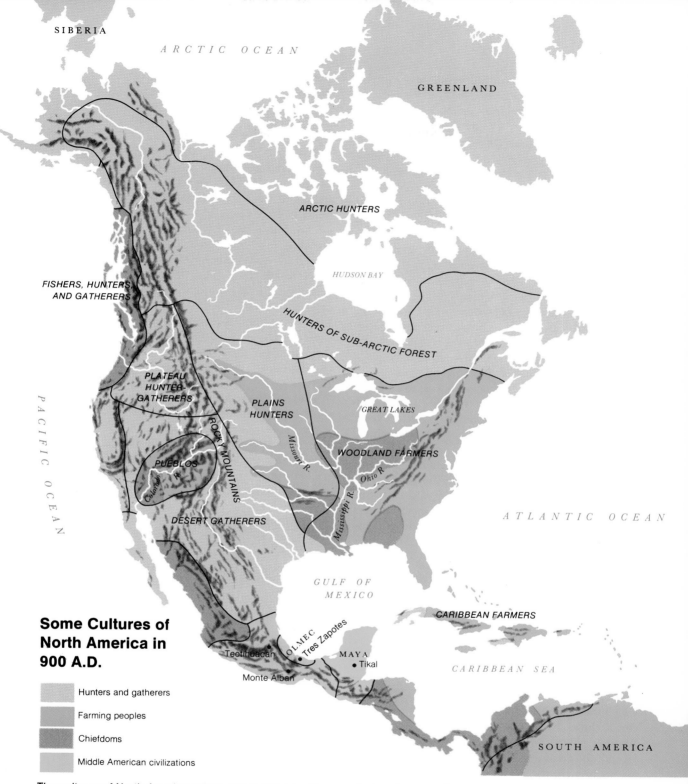

SIBERIA

ARCTIC OCEAN

GREENLAND

ARCTIC HUNTERS

HUDSON BAY

FISHERS, HUNTERS,
AND GATHERERS

HUNTERS OF SUB-ARCTIC FOREST

*PACIFIC
OCEAN*

PLATEAU
HUNTER-
GATHERERS

PLAINS
HUNTERS

GREAT LAKES

ROCKY MOUNTAINS

Missouri R.

WOODLAND FARMERS

PUEBLOS

Colorado R.

Ohio R.

Mississippi R.

ATLANTIC OCEAN

DESERT GATHERERS

Some Cultures of
North America in
900 A.D.

*GULF OF
MEXICO*

CARIBBEAN FARMERS

OLMEC
Tres Zapotes

Teotihuacán

MAYA
Tikal

CARIBBEAN SEA

Monte Albán

	Hunters and gatherers
	Farming peoples
	Chiefdoms
	Middle American civilizations

SOUTH AMERICA

*The cultures of North Americans from 300 to 900 A.D. These early American peoples
responded creatively to the varied environments of North America.*

Woodlands Regions

Native Americans who lived in the area east of the Mississippi River adapted to a very different environment. Much of that region was wooded, and in it lived such groups as the Sauk and Ojibwa of the Great Lakes area; the Petun, Ottawa, and Huron of eastern Canada; the Iroquois and Delaware of New York and Pennsylvania; and the Chickasaw, Choctaw, and Creek of the southeastern United States.

Woodlands peoples fashioned shelters from frameworks of small tree limbs which they covered with bark. They felled trees with fire and stone hatchets to clear patches of forest to plant corn and other crops. They also hunted and fished and gathered the fruits of wild plants. These Native Americans made boats of wooden frameworks covered with bark from elm or birch trees.

Some peoples of the Great Lakes region took advantage of a resource found there in abundance—copper, which they mined and smelted. They also found a way to anneal copper—that is, to cool the smelted metal slowly after it had been extracted from rock at high heat. This process made the tools and weapons they made tougher and less brittle.

Although Woodlands peoples lived in settled communities, these were not permanent. The soil of forested regions is not especially fertile. Many Woodlands peoples fertilized the soil with fish, but even so it eventually became nonproductive. At that point, whole villages moved to another location, where people once again hacked out clearings in the forest.

The Iroquois

The Iroquois were one large group of Woodlands peoples. The Iroquois lived in bark and sapling dwellings called longhouses, each of which held several families. Log palisades surrounded longhouse villages.

Men hunted and fished, women gathered and farmed. They raised corn, beans, and squash, which they called the "Three Sisters." A council of chiefs, chosen by the leading women, governed each Iroquois village and tribe. According to Iroquois legend, the great hero Dekanawidah, aided by Hiawatha, brought the five tribes of Onondaga, Seneca, Oneida, Mohawk, and Cayuga together into the great League of the Iroquois.

This legend tells that, in the land north of Lake Ontario, a woman one day brought forth a child. Later, in a dream, a messenger appeared. "Your son will be a great man," he said. "You will name him Dekanawidah, and he will go south among the People of the Flint and there raise up the Tree of Peace."

As a man, Dekanawidah did journey south to try to bring peace to constantly warring peoples. He said to them: "The longhouse will stand for peace among the people. In it will burn many fires. There will live many families, all living under law."

The Flint People—the Mohawk of the Iroquois—refused to listen to Dekanawidah until he proved his immortality. He agreed to allow them to try to kill him. They failed because in reality Dekanawidah was a god, so the Mohawk agreed to peace.

Dekanawidah then met Hiawatha, an Onondaga warrior. Together they visited the tribes, urging them to plant the Tree of Peace. At last the five tribes stopped their wars, and formed the Great League.

Evidence indicates that the Iroquois established the League sometime in the 1500s A.D., although it is not known how it developed. The League operated through a council of fifty chiefs, ten from each tribe, chosen by women. The council settled intertribal disputes and decided such questions as war or peace with non-Iroquois groups.

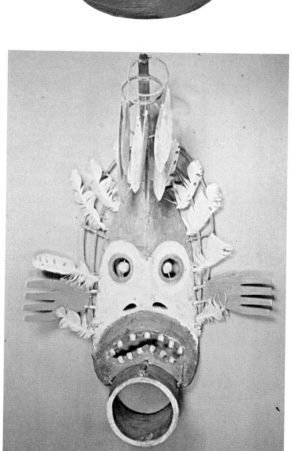

The varied peoples of North America created many forms of art. On the opposite page, a bag for carrying a pipe made by a Native American of the Great Plains. Above, a wooden raven mask from the Pacific Northwest. At the left, an Eskimo mask of the cold weather spirit. At the top right is a figurine of a mother and child found in excavating a site of the Mound Builders. At the top left is a pot from the Pueblo cultures of the Southwest.

An airview of a huge mound in the shape of an eagle built in what is now the state of Georgia.

Mound Builders

Some peoples of the Mississippi and Ohio river valleys are known as Mound Builders. These peoples buried in huge mounds important deceased members of their groups, along with their weapons and other possessions. Although most mounds were round, some were representations of living creatures. One, discovered in Ohio, is called the Great Serpent Mound. It measures 1,254 feet from tail to nose and averages 20 feet in width. Another found in Ohio is an earthen enclosure about a thousand feet in diameter and 8 to 14 feet high. In the center is a mound in the shape of an eagle.

Archaeologists have learned much from the items found in these mounds. These people were farmers whose main crop was corn. They made tools and weapons from stone and copper. They undoubtedly obtained metal in trade with peoples of the Great Lakes region. Through trade, they also obtained shells from peoples living along the ocean, and grizzly bear teeth for ornaments from peoples of the Rocky Mountain region. They wove cloth from the soft inner fibers of bark, and engraved stone, bone, and shell ornaments.

It is not known how these cultures developed, or why they disappeared. One of them seems to have reached its peak between the years 500 and 700 A.D. Then it gradually faded, leaving only the mounds behind.

Another mound-building group seems to have flourished around 400 A.D. It left behind huge flat-topped earth pyramids that probably had temples of wood on their tops. These temple mounds are similar in shape to pyramids built by some groups in Mexico and Central America. However, no definite connection between the peoples of those regions and the people of the temple mound area has been established.

One temple mound site is near Ocmulgee, Georgia, where people may have begun to live 5,000 years ago. Here they began making pottery about 3,500 years ago, and the first temple mounds date from around 900 A.D.

Aztalan, Wisconsin, holds another temple mound site. Here, during the twelfth and thirteenth centuries, there existed a village with a stockade enclosing about 10,000 square yards surrounding two pyramids. The people of Aztalan used stone, bone, antlers, and copper to make tools and weapons. They fashioned hoes from clamshells for use in cornfields. They also made pottery, ranging from simple, unadorned pieces to highly decorated bowls, jars, and bottles.

The Great Plains

Peoples from the fringes of the Woodlands region moved onto the Great Plains of what is now the United States. In areas where rainfall was sufficient, some Plains groups continued to farm. Others pushed into areas of scanty rainfall and left farming to depend on the short-horned bison, or buffalo, as their main food. Those animals also furnished hides for robes and clothing and for covering over poles for their tipis. The tipis were easy to take down and move as they followed the herds of bison.

There were no horses in the Americas at that time, those animals having long since become extinct. Consequently, Plains peoples had to hunt the buffalo on foot. Bands of hunters sometimes drove herds over a cliff. At other times, hunters moved stealthily upon a herd of buffalo to within shooting distance. They then brought down their prey with bows and arrows.

Things in Common

Early Americans developed many different cultures and languages. Yet they also shared certain ideas and beliefs.

All believed in an all-powerful creator. They treasured stories about how the world was created, the old passing them on to the young. Here is a creation story from the Yakima of the Pacific Northwest:

In the beginning of the world, all was water. Whee-me-me-ow-ah, the Great Chief Above, lived in the sky, above the water, all alone. When he decided to make the world, he went down to the shallow places and began to throw up great handfuls of mud. Thus he made the land.

He piled some of the mud up so high that it froze hard and made the mountains. The rain, when it came, was turned into ice and snow on top of the high mountains. Some of the mud was made hard, into rocks. Since that time the rocks have not changed, except that they have become harder. . . .

The Great Chief Above made trees grow on the earth, and also roots and berries. He made a man out of a ball of mud and told him what he should do. He should get fish from the waters, and deer and other game in the forests. When the man became lonely the Great Chief Above made a woman, to be a companion to him, and told her what she should do. He taught her how to dress skins, and how to make baskets out of bark and roots which he showed her how to find. He taught her which berries to gather for food and how to pick them and dry them. He showed her how to cook the salmon and the game which the man brought.

One time when she was asleep, she had a dream. In her dream the Great Chief Above blew his breath on her, giving her something which she could not see or hear, smell or touch. This invisible something was preserved in a basket. Through it, the first woman taught her daughters and granddaughters the designs and skills which had been taught her.

But in spite of all the things the Great Chief Above did for them, the new people quarreled. They quarreled so much that Mother Earth was angry. In her anger, she shook the mountains so hard that those hanging over the narrow part of Big River fell down. The rocks, falling into the water, dammed the stream and also made the rapids and waterfalls there. Many people and animals were killed and buried under the rocks and mountains.

Some day the Great Chief Above will overturn those mountains and rocks. Then the spirits that once lived in the bones buried there will go back into them. Now, those spirits live in the tops of the mountains, watching their children on the earth and waiting for the great change which is to come.

No one knows when the Great Chief Above will overturn the mountains. But we do know this: the spirits will return only to the bones of people who in life kept the beliefs of their grandfathers.

The Native Americans' great respect for nature formed the basis of their religious beliefs. Their creator had given them land and animals to sustain them, and they believed that they must use those resources wisely and with respect.

Ruth M. Underhill describes this attitude toward the natural resources of their environment:

"Hunting is a holy occupation," said the Naskapi. So was the gathering of plants, the cutting of trees, even the digging of clay. For these Nature Persons had long ago offered their "flesh" for . . . use—but on certain conditions. Every step in obtaining the flesh must be taken with care and ceremony, or the gift would be withdrawn. The Papago woman of southern Arizona, in digging materials for pots, told the clay: "I take only what I need. It is to cook for my children." If possible, she left a small gift. . . . [A member of the Fox people] in the wooded country of the Mississippi Valley said:

"We do not like to harm the trees. Whenever we can, we always make an offering of tobacco to the trees before we cut them down. We never waste the wood, but use all that we cut down. If we did not think of their feelings, and did not offer them tobacco before cutting them down, all the trees in the forest would weep, and that would make our hearts sad, too!"

Check on Your Reading

1. What were some of the achievements of the Iroquois?
2. What have archaeologists discovered about the Mound Builders?
3. What was characteristic about the life of the peoples of the Great Plains?
4. What were some of the beliefs that various Native American peoples held in common? What was their attitude toward the environment?

3. Civilizations of Middle America

Alvin M. Josephy, Jr. writes: "The culture history of Middle America is one of nomadic hunters and gathers who . . . became farmers and villagers. In time, as population increased, societies became more complex and sophisticated; arts, skills, and crafts flourished; and gradually true civilizations arose."

The Olmecs

The oldest civilization in Middle America seems to have been developed by the people now called *Olmecs*. The Olmec civilization developed in what is now the Mexican state of Vera Cruz.

An Olmec artist created this head of a woman. It is carved from jadeite.

By 1200 B.C. the Olmecs were building great religious centers that were supported by surrounding farm villages. These centers were at their height around 800 B.C. and had largely fallen into ruins by 400 B.C. They seem to have been mainly places of worship and residence for officials and priests who governed the surrounding farming population. A center included temple-pyramids, altars and *stelae*—vertical stone slabs. On the stelae were sculptured images of priests, chieftains, animals, and important dates in their history.

Other Olmec art included huge stone heads, decorated pottery, figurines, jade statuettes, and carved masks. The Olmecs may have developed a form of hieroglyphic writing as hieroglyphs appear on some small Olmec jades that have been discovered. Archaeologists have found that the Olmec civilization had a great influence on other peoples of Middle America. The Olmec has been called the "mother culture of all Middle America."

The Maya

The Maya developed a civilization that flourished between 250 A.D. and 900. There were three Maya centers — the highlands of Guatemala and part of El Salvador, the Yucatán peninsula, and the lowlands of Guatemala and Honduras.

Evidence indicates that this civilization developed in the rain forest environment of the lowlands. Rainfall amounted to more than 120 inches a year, and stretches of dense underbrush and trees had to be cleared with stone tools and fire before anyone could farm. The region contained few rivers, and the Maya stored rainwater in large reservoirs.

Religious centers, the main features of Maya civilization, may have been an inheritance from the Olmec culture. These were composed of buildings surrounding flat-topped pyramids, some as high as sixty feet. The pyramids were constructed of earth and stone and finished with white stucco. On one side, steps led to a temple at the top.

Priests, who were the learned men among the Maya, probably ruled the main centers. The centers also housed skilled workers, merchants, and those who attended the priests. In one, Tikal, perhaps as many as 10,000 people lived permanently, and the population swelled during religious ceremonies when farm families from surrounding villages came to worship.

The Maya worshipped numerous gods and goddesses. One was corn itself, on which they so heavily depended. The sun was another. Maya people also believed in a god of death and in a place called Mitnal, where people who had not lived proper lives suffered endlessly after death.

A pyramid temple at Chichen Itza, a Maya city that was invaded by warriors from central Mexico.

A jade mask created by a Maya artist.

Maya Accomplishments

Maya civilization was in many ways the equal to any found in Europe at the time. The Maya did not work out an alphabet, but priests wrote in hieroglyphics. The Maya writing system expressed words, ideas, concepts, and numbers. The Maya number system was based on 20, and the Maya developed a symbol to represent zero.

Priests observed and recorded movements of the stars. They learned to predict eclipses and developed calendars based on the sun and the moon.

The Maya learned to tap rubber trees, drawing milky white latex from them. They used rubber to make balls for games and as soles for sandals. Weavers produced cotton cloth and used numerous dyes for coloring and decorating it. Paper was made from bark.

The Maya carried on extensive trade with other peoples. From highlands regions of Middle America they obtained obsidian, an unusually hard, glass-like volcanic rock for tools and weapons. They used shells that came from the shores of the Pacific Ocean, copper from Central Mexico, and salt from the northern part of the Yucatán peninsula. The Maya conducted much of their trade along the Gulf of Mexico, traveling great distances in boats capable of holding forty to fifty people each.

Nobody knows why, but in about 900 A.D. the Maya civilization began to decline. Perhaps the soil no longer produced enough to maintain the population. Other people may have conquered the Maya. In any event, the jungle eventually covered the religious centers. Grasses and vines of the rain forest gradually covered pyramids and temples.

The City of Teotihuacán

One Maya trading partner was the city of Teotihuacán, located about thirty miles north of Mexico City. At the height of its power, around the year 500 A.D., Teotihuacán rivaled ancient Rome in size.

It covered eight square miles and had at least 50,000 people.

Teotihuacán, with its many temples, served a religious function, but it was also a true city. Teotihuacán was a bustling center of industry and trade.

The land surrounding Teotihuacán was fertile with lakes and springs nearby. An irrigation system was built to bring water to the city and its surrounding farms. Large deposits of obsidian were found in nearby hillsides, and that rock was an important item of the trade with other peoples.

The people laid out their city in squares. The major north-south avenue ran for two miles to end at the so-called Pyramid of the Moon.

The Temple of Quetzalcoatl lay along the southern end of this avenue. Quetzalcoatl was a major god who was often represented in the form of a plumed serpent. He was the bringer of civilization and the good ways of life. Across the street from this temple, buildings surrounded what was probably the city's principal marketplace. About halfway between the Temple of the Moon and that of Quetzalcoatl stood the huge pyramid-temple of the Sun.

Priests, bureaucrats, and military leaders lived in palaces decorated with paintings. These paintings portrayed priests taking part in religious ceremonies and gods and goddesses.

Part of the excavations of the city of Teotihuacán. This photo looks down the main avenue of the center of the city. The city was at the height of its power about 500 A.D.

Some farmers lived in Teotihuacán, and so did many people who worked with cotton cloth, jade, feathered decorations, clay, and obsidian. Pottery making and the fashioning of obsidian tools were highly specialized crafts.

It appears that each neighborhood of Teotihuacán was made up of people following a certain trade. Archaeologists have uncovered many of the city's residences, which were one-story dwellings resting on foundations of concrete. The walls were made of stone and sunbaked brick, and the roofs were constructed of material similar to that used for the foundations. Inside, wall and floor surfaces were finished with highly polished plaster. The rooms of each house were arranged around an open patio, or courtyard. No windows faced the streets.

After about 500 A.D., Teotihuacán went into decline, although no one knows just why. Soil erosion, destroying cropland and helping to reduce food production, may have contributed. In any event, evidence suggests that around 750 A.D. Teotihuacán was looted and burned.

Check on Your Reading

1. In what ways did the Olmecs seem to influence other cultures of Middle America?
2. What were some of the accomplishments of the Maya?
3. Describe what is known about the city of Teotihuacán.

4. The Aztec Empire

New people, probably from the north, learned from the civilization of Teotihuacán. Among them were the Toltecs whose capital city was Tula.

By the year 1000 A.D., the Toltecs had spread their power over much of central Mexico and into Guatemala. They also occupied some Maya religious centers. Shortly after 1000 A.D., Toltec power went into decline. Then several hundred years later, another people made their appearance. They were the Aztecs.

The Aztec Capital, Tenochtitlán

The Aztecs settled along Lake Texcoco, now a part of Mexico City. On an island in the lake, they built one of the great cities of the world, Tenochtitlán. Archaeologists estimate that at its height it had a population of about three hundred thousand people. A complex irrigation system made it possible for farmers to grow enough food for Tenochtitlán and other cities.

By about 1400 A.D., the Aztecs had conquered much of central Mexico and established an empire containing at least five million subject peoples. Conquered peoples supplied the Aztecs with many products. They also mined gold and silver, which were made into ornaments, cups, dishes, and other objects for the wealthy.

Temple-pyramids dominated the central part of Tenochtitlán. The largest stood one hundred feet high, with two temples resting at the top. One belonged to the sun god and the other to the rain god.

Tenochtitlán's central marketplace held a large variety of goods, and thousands of people crowded into it to buy and sell. Merchants offered sandals, silver and gold objects, dressed small game, live hawks and falcons, corn, honey, cacao beans, tools of obsidian and copper, furniture, dyes, pottery, and many other items.

The magnificent city astonished visitors, including a Spanish soldier, writing in the 1590s:

> Some of the soldiers among us who have been in many parts of the world . . . said that so large a marketplace and so full of people, and so well regulated and arranged, they had never seen before.

Aztec Society and Government

The people of Tenochtitlán were organized into twenty clans. Each clan had its own area in the city and its own government officials, temples, priests, and schools. Children in the schools studied farming, arts and crafts, religion, warfare, and Aztec history. Gifted youth were sent on to train for the priesthood.

Residents of each clan area sent representatives to a council of state. Council members selected four from among them as executive officers. The council also chose the empire's ruler, who was chief priest as well.

The ruler lived in a palace of a hundred rooms and ate from dishes made of gold. Below him was the nobility that included priests, war chieftains, government officials, and wealthy merchants. Aztec priests, among their other duties, kept government records, writing in a form of hieroglyphics. Priests also conducted astronomical observations and developed a calendar.

All able-bodied males over fifteen years of age, except government officials and priests, served in the Aztec army. Each soldier wore a wooden helmet on which was carved the figure of an animal representing the military order to which he belonged. Aztec soldiers were armed with obsidian swords, maces, dart throwers, clubs, and bows and arrows. They carried shields of quilted cotton and wore armor made of the same material.

Among their other accomplishments, the Aztecs created songs and poetry. Much of their poetry concerned religion and the hereafter, but some celebrated the joys of the world, including friendship.

Let us have friends here!
It is the time to know our faces. . . .
We will have gone to His house,
but our word

shall live here on earth.
We will go, leaving behind
our grief, our song.
For this will be known,
The song shall remain real.
We will have gone to His house,
but our word
shall live here on earth.

Check on Your Reading

1. What were some features of Aztec civilization?
2. Describe Aztec society and government.

5. The Inca Empire of Peru

The Incas of the high Andes Mountains of Peru also established an empire. According to Inca legend, which seems to have some basis in fact, they first

Find the lands ruled by the Aztecs and the Incas.

Two Native American Empires in the 1400s

Aztec Empire

Inca Empire

lived on the shores of Lake Titicaca. This lake lies on the border between Bolivia and Peru. Under their leader, Manco Capac, they migrated to settle in a high mountain valley of Peru.

Building an Empire

The Inca migration occurred around 1200 A.D. For a time they remained only one of a number of Native American peoples along the coast and in the western mountains. In about 1400 A.D., the Incas began to conquer neighboring peoples. Within about fifty years they established a vast empire that stretched more than two thousand miles from north to south.

Many of the skills and much of the knowledge that enabled the Incas to build their empire were learned from other peoples. The rich cultures of these peoples had been inherited from states that had developed many hundreds of years before. Skilled workers of these states had learned to weave fine cloth, build large stone buildings, and create fine objects from copper, gold, and silver.

The people of some states had built complex irrigation systems, terraced farms, and systems of roads. They had organized central governments that planned and controlled these construction projects, directing large numbers of people.

Inca Cities, Roads, and Bridges

The Incas built temples, government buildings, and palaces in their capital of Cuzco. With bronze tools, builders shaped huge blocks of stone that fitted together perfectly without mortar. They covered some buildings with gold and the inside walls with silver.

The Incas also built the cities of Quito in the north and Tumbez on the coast. They connected these communities to Cuzco with roads averaging about 20 feet in width. In some places roads were cut from rock along the sides of cliffs. At very steep places, the roads became steps carved out from rock.

Streams and gorges lay along the route of some of the roads. To span them, builders erected bridges. They used fiber from the maguey plant. They twisted the fibers into thick cables that were used both to support the bridge and as railings.

This communication system greatly aided the Incas in their control of their empire. Government messengers, running in relays between rest stations, could carry information six hundred miles in just

five days. Inca armies could quickly move along the roads to put down rebellion in any part of the empire.

Conquered Peoples

Most people of the empire were farmers living in small houses of mud bricks thatched with straw. They grew corn, beans, potatoes, and other food, as well as cotton. The government required them to contribute a portion of their crops to support the Inca people and the army. This tribute was stored in government granaries after every harvest.

Subject peoples also labored in gold and silver mines and served in the Inca army. They were required to work on roads and other construction projects when needed.

The Empire's Ruler and Religion

"Inca" had two meanings. It referred to the ruler. It also meant the Inca people themselves.

The ruler had advisers, but he was all-powerful. He was believed to be the son of the sun and a direct descendant of the first Inca, Manco Capac. The Inca's clothing was made from the soft, fine wool of the vicuña. He ate from dishes of gold and silver, and the throne on which he sat to hold court was of solid gold.

As chief priest, the Inca presided over important religious ceremonies. For example, he planted the first corn at the beginning of a planting season. After calling on Inca gods for bountiful crops, he made a hole in the soil with a digging stick and dropped in a few seeds of corn.

The most important religious ceremonies took place at the Temple of the Sun in Cuzco. Sheets of gold covered the outside of that huge stone building, and five fountains graced its courtyard. Here priests washed offerings of animals and food before presenting them to the Sun. The interior of the temple has been called

a mine of gold. On the western wall was emblazoned a representation of the deity, consisting of a human face looking forth from amidst many rays of light. . . . The figure was engraved on a massive plate of gold . . . thickly powdered with emeralds and precious stones. It was so situated in front of the great eastern doorway that the rays of the morning sun fell directly upon it at its rising, lighting up the

This bronze bird was probably on the top of a staff carried by an official of the Inca Empire.

whole room. . . . [The brilliance] was reflected back from the golden ornaments with which the walls and ceiling were everywhere encrusted.

Cuzco's other main temple belonged to the Moon, the bride of the Sun. Silver adorned outside and inside walls of the temple. In one room hung a silver likeness of the Moon, showing the face of a woman.

A System of Communication

Although they did not develop a system of writing, the Incas did have a means of communicating words, ideas, and numbers called the *quipu*. It has been described in this way:

The quipu was a cord about two feet long, composed of different colored threads tightly twisted together, from which a quantity of smaller threads were suspended in the manner of a fringe. The threads were of different colors and were tied into knots. The word quipu, indeed, signifies a knot. The colors denoted certain things . . . white represented silver, and yellow, gold. They sometimes also stood for abstract ideas. Thus, white signified peace, and red, war. But the quipus were chiefly used for arithmetical purposes. The knots served instead of ciphers, and could be combined in such a manner as to represent numbers to any amount they required.

Check on Your Reading

1. Name some Inca accomplishments.
2. In what ways were the Incas like the Aztecs, and in what ways were they different?

231

Marriage among the Maya

Ah Pitz Nic, twenty years old, found Ix Bacal attractive. Nic wanted her to be his wife.

He first saw her while on his way down the trail with friends to bathe one day. Ix Bacal was returning from a well with a pottery jar of water on her head. Nic frequented that trail often after that. He saw Ix Bacal often, but only gazed on her. Neither of them spoke. Then one day Nic killed a deer, skinned it, and stuffed the skin with ashes. He delivered it to Ix Bacal's house as a symbol that he could be a good provider.

Nic's parents agreed that it was time for him to marry, and they accepted his choice of a wife. They contacted a marriage broker, with whom they discussed the terms of marriage. The broker then went to Ix Bacal's parents. After much discussion, her parents agreed to the marriage if Nic would help Ix Bacal's father farm for four years. Also his parents would have to pay certain quantities of cacao beans, beads, and cotton to them. The bargain was sealed.

Next a priest consulted heavenly signs. He decided that they were favorable to the marriage and that the couple's birthdates made them suitable to each other. A wedding day was set.

In the meantime, friends gathered to build a house for the couple on Ix Bacal's father's land. When the house was finished, there was a feast of beans, squash, venison, sweet potatoes, and tortillas.

On her wedding day, Ix Bacal dressed in a new skirt and brocaded blouse. Nic donned the pair of new sandals his father had made for him, a necklace of beetle wings, and a pair of wooden ear ornaments his uncle had given him. Before the evening ceremony, relatives from both sides gathered in the Bacal house for a huge feast. Following this, the priest pronounced the appropriate words, and the party moved on to the newlyweds' house. There the priest burned copal, an aromatic resin obtained from trees.

The morning after the wedding Ix Bacal was up early preparing tortillas for her husband. He, in turn, prepared to go with his father-in-law to the fields, to begin fulfilling his promise of four years' work.

Based on J. Eric S. Thompson, *The Rise and Fall of Maya Civilization.* University of Oklahoma Press, pp. 245-52.

CHAPTER REVIEW

Think and Discuss

1. What can we learn from many Native Americans' attitude toward their environment?
2. Compare the migrations of the Bantu-speaking peoples in Africa with migrations of Native American peoples in the Americas.
3. How is the term "Native American" similar to the term "European" or "Asian"?
4. In what ways is the creation account of the Yakima similar to the creation accounts of the Africans?

5. Why do you think that it usually was priests who developed calendars?
6. Some archaeologists believe that the first cities (not religious centers) in the Americas developed when Native Americans built irrigation systems in order to grow more food. Compare this with the development of cities in Mesopotamia and in Egypt.
7. Several times the Aztecs were chased away by stronger people when they first tried to settle in the Valley of Mexico. Do you think that these experiences had any influence on their creation of an empire? If so, how?

Past and Present

1. Native Americans raised corn, potatoes, squash, and pumpkins, and used other foods such as cacao that were unique to the Americas. Find out about the use of one of these foods throughout the world today.
2. In the distant past, people usually responded to the pressures of a growing population by migrating. How do peoples respond to such pressures today?

Activities

1. Pick one of the Native American peoples mentioned in this chapter and do some research to learn more about their ways of living.
2. A number of Native American peoples are working hard to adjust to modern western technology while retaining the richness, strength, and integrity of their own cultures. Do some research on the efforts of such people as the Tlinget of the Pacific Northwest and the Navajo, Zuñi, and Hopi of the Southwest.
3. Set up a display of ancient and modern Native American art. Do some research for the exhibit on the work of Native Americans who have revived ancient arts while adding their own ideas to their creations. Examples are Maria Martinez of San Ildefonso Pueblo and the Nampeyo family of Arizona.
4. In the recent celebration of the bicentennial of the United States, many Native American contributions were largely ignored. Do some research and draw up a plan for a celebration of Native American cultures and contributions. Such a celebration is now being discussed by Native Americans.

5

Europe in Transition:
From Feudalism to Nations

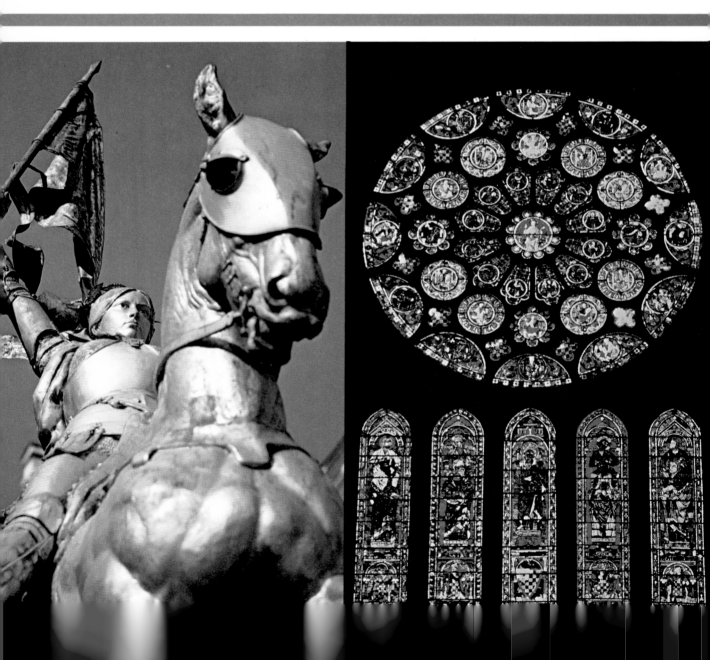

What a difference the years make! In the early seventh century A.D. the Chinese were creating the brilliant civilization of the Tang dynasty and the Arabs were building a great empire. At the same time the Western Roman Empire was in shambles. The system of Roman law and order that brought stability and Graeco-Roman civilization to much of Europe had been disrupted. Settled Europeans were threatened by armies of warriors and by raids of robbers and pirates. Trade was limited, and cities were rapidly dwindling in size and number. The future looked bleak.

Less than a thousand years later, however, trade, business, and cities were flourishing and growing in Europe. Europeans were making important discoveries in science and creating great art, literature, music, and architecture. Daring leaders from strong European nations were setting up trading posts overseas and building colonies all over the world.

The story of this transition in Europe is a fascinating one that will be discussed in this unit. We will focus on both change and continuity, however. As the Greek philosopher Heraclitus said, "There is nothing permanent except change," but every change has its roots in the past and reaches out into the future.

Christianity and Feudalism in Europe

Eugene Fitch Ware once wrote the following lines:

"Human hopes and human creeds
Have their roots in human needs."

Many of the events in the period which followed the breakup of the Roman Empire in Europe prove the accuracy of this view.

During this troubled time, people felt the need of spiritual direction to guide their lives. What was the result? The Church became increasingly powerful. During these years, too, people had a need for protection against invaders. What was the result? They organized themselves into a protective system known as feudalism.

Needs were thus key factors in this period. Needs stimulated both the growth of Christianity and the development of *feudalism.*

Knights attack a walled town.

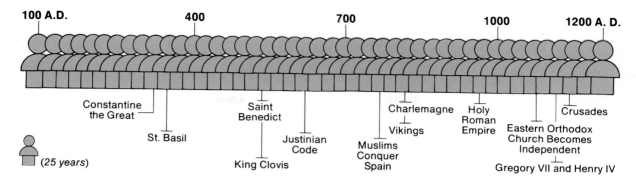

100 A.D.   400   700   1000   1200 A.D.

Constantine the Great

St. Basil

Saint Benedict

King Clovis

Justinian Code

Muslims Conquer Spain

Vikings

Charlemagne

Holy Roman Empire

Eastern Orthodox Church Becomes Independent

Gregory VII and Henry IV

Crusades

(25 years)

1. The Church Provides Strength and Guidance in Troubled Times

Europe in 500 A.D. was no longer the well-organized society it had been a hundred years earlier. To a large extent the old system of Roman law and order had broken down. Trade was almost at a halt because of dangers from pirates by sea and robbers by land. Many Romans had lost their lives during the invasions of the Germanic tribes. Cities had become smaller, and most people in western Europe now lived as farmers in rural areas. Life had become more hazardous. A number of Germanic kingdoms had replaced the Roman government in Britain, Gaul, Italy, Spain, and North Africa.

The period from about 500 to 1450 A.D. is known as the *Middle Ages*. This term was first used by some Italian writers of the late 1400s who greatly admired the civilizations of the Greeks and Romans, and wanted to revive them in Europe. These writers considered the Middle Ages as an unexciting time between the end of the Roman Empire and the middle 1400s. As we shall see, however, the people of the Middle Ages, or *medieval period*, made many wonderful advances in religion and the arts, and in political and economic life.

Although the spread of the Germanic tribes and other factors brought about the disintegration of the Roman Empire in the West, many Roman customs and the Latin language survived. Most of the new rulers admired Roman civilization, and they used Roman officials to help them govern their new kingdoms. In much of western Europe, there was a slow mingling of the Germanic conquerors and their Roman subjects.

The Angles and the Saxons in Britain

In Britain, Roman civilization was overwhelmed, except in the far western region of the island. The Angles and Saxons invaded from northern Europe and attacked with such fury that the Celts—the inhabitants of Britain before the coming of the Romans—and the Romans took refuge in Wales and Cornwall. Others fled overseas to Brittany, a peninsula of Gaul.

According to legend, a Christian leader named King Arthur tried to rally forces in Britain and to drive back the invaders. Stories about King Arthur and his Knights of the Round Table recall this famous legend. No resistance was successful for long, however. Soon the once prosperous cities of Britain lay in ruins, and with them Roman civilization declined. The English language, which grew out of the Anglo-Saxon speech of the conquerors, is basically a Germanic tongue with additions from other languages. Later Britain was called the "land of the Angles" or England.

Leadership of the Popes

The Roman Catholic Church and its leaders played an important role in keeping alive the traditions of the Greeks and Romans. Christianity gave spiritual comfort to the Romans in their sufferings. It also had a message for the invaders, many of whom gave up their tribal gods and goddesses to become Christians.

The Church's organization in many ways continued the organization of the Roman Empire. In rural areas, where most people lived, the person in charge of the local church was the *parish priest*. The priest said Mass and administered the other sacraments of the Church. He also tried to teach the people how to live according to Christ's teachings. The *bishop*, who was often a better educated man, was in charge of a larger unit of territory—the *diocese*. An *archbishop* was in charge of several dioceses. As the Roman style of order and justice declined, the bishops and archbishops took over much of the responsibility of supervising the people.

Even during the invasions, some Germanic chieftains showed respect for the Church and its leaders. Special honor was given to the bishop of Rome, who was known as the Pope. The word *Pope* comes from the Latin *papa* meaning "father." The Popes claimed supreme power over the Christian Church throughout the world. They based their claim on the belief that St. Peter, the leader of Christ's apostles, was the first bishop of Rome.

Under a strong Pope like Leo I (440-461 A.D.), the Church had considerable influence. Pope Leo went outside Rome to meet Attila, chief of the Huns, and persuaded him not to destroy the city. In time, the Popes became rulers of Rome and its surrounding area. Pope Leo and his successors tried to put an end to religious challenges known as "heresies" that broke out from time to time among Christians.

Orders of Monks and Nuns Are Founded

Starting in the fourth century, religious communities were founded. Many men and women decided to settle in rural areas in order to serve God. Some wanted to escape the evils of life in the cities. Others were disturbed by the invasions and the general breakdown of order. The men were known as *monks,* and the places where they lived were *monasteries.* The women were called *nuns,* and their residences were known as *convents.*

A leader of religious communities in the East was St. Basil (329-379 A.D.). Basil wanted his monks to live together as a peaceful community. They were to devote themselves to intellectual work, such as the study of the *Bible,* or to manual work for the community. *St. Basil's Rule,* or set of regulations, is still in use today by monasteries of the Eastern Orthodox Church.

In Italy in the sixth century, St. Benedict founded a monastery at Monte Cassino. The *Rule* that Benedict gave his monks became a model for many monasteries and convents in western Europe. It is still important today in Benedictine communities around the world, including the United States. Benedict's sister, St. Scholastica, founded a community of nuns.

The monks or nuns made three vows, or promises. By the vow of poverty they put aside all worldly goods. By the vow of chastity they gave up the right to marry. By the vow of obedience they showed their willingness to obey their leader, the abbot or abbess, without question. Benedict's *Rule* is a balanced statement on how monks should live.

It contained the following instruction:

> Idleness is the enemy of the soul. And therefore, at fixed times, the brothers ought to be occupied in manual labor; and again, at fixed times, in sacred reading.

The Work of the Monks and Nuns

Each of the Benedictine communities tried to be self-sufficient. The monks raised crops on the lands they received as gifts from devout Christians. Later they taught their successful methods of agriculture to farmers living in the surrounding areas.

At a time when important documents and records were being destroyed through neglect and abuse, monks made beautiful copies of old manuscripts. Thus they preserved important writings of the Greeks and Romans for future generations. They also recorded some of the events of their times in *chronicles*. In this way they passed on to us valuable historical information about the Middle Ages.

Monks and nuns established schools in which they taught young people. They helped the poor, provided safe resting places for travelers, and kept hospitals for the sick. The gardens of religious communities grew herbs that were used as medicines.

Monks and nuns helped spread the Christian religion among the Germanic invaders. Late in the sixth century Pope Gregory the Great sent St. Augustine of Canterbury, a Benedictine monk from Italy, to England. Soon he converted the king of Kent, and in time many of the Angles and Saxons became Christians.

About a century later the Angles and Saxons themselves became missionaries for the Church. A Benedictine monk named St. Boniface brought Christianity to people in Germany. He persuaded some Benedictine nuns to join him as missionaries among the Germans. Their leader was St. Lioba. Boniface and Lioba founded many religious communities and made many converts to Christianity.

Check on Your Reading

1. Why did Roman civilization almost die out in Britain?
2. How did the Church affect the Germanic invaders?
3. How was the Roman Catholic Church organized?
4. Describe some functions of the Benedictine Rule.
5. What were some of the activities of the Benedictine monks and nuns?

Many medieval manuscripts were beautifully illustrated. This painting from a manuscript shows a friar preaching to the people. Friars were members of religious orders who worked among the people.

2. The Franks Become Leaders of the West

When the Roman Empire in western Europe broke up, a Germanic people called the Franks moved across the Rhine River into Gaul. Their leaders were members of the Merovingian family that ruled the Franks for almost three hundred years.

King Clovis

The greatest of the Merovingians, King Clovis (481-511), defeated a Roman-German army in 486. He then kept another Germanic tribe, the Alemanni, from entering Gaul, part of which we know today as France. Perhaps the most significant act of Clovis was his acceptance of Christianity.

The Rise of the Mayors of the Palace

After Clovis, the Merovingian kings became weaker. Clovis' kingdom split into several parts, and the kings and their nobles plotted against each other. Gradually the kings handed over real power to officials called "mayors of the palace."

A mayor of the palace named Charles (714-741) was a vigorous leader who defended the Frankish borders against new invaders. He earned the nickname "Martel" meaning the "Hammer." At the

The coronation of Charlemagne by Pope Leo III in the Church of St. Peter is shown in a miniature painting from *The Great Chronicles of France.*

Battle of Tours (732), Charles Martel and Frankish warriors on horseback defeated a group of Muslim raiders from North Africa and Spain and checked their advance into western Europe.

Charles Martel's son, Pepin the Short (741–768), was also a strong leader. He demanded of the Pope that the man who was actually defending the land should be king, rather than the weak king who was doing little. The Pope agreed, and Pepin was made king of the Franks. He and his descendants are known as *Carolingian* rulers.

In return for the Pope's support, Pepin helped to defend the Church. He drove back the Lombards, a Germanic people in northern Italy who were threatening Rome. He then greatly extended the territories in central Italy ruled by the Pope.

The Empire of Charlemagne

Pepin's son was Charles the Great, or Charlemagne (768–814). Charlemagne's secretary, Einhard, described him as a tall, majestic ruler, a mighty hunter, and a tireless swimmer. Charlemagne kept writing tablets beneath his bed and of-

ten tried to use them. His writing skill was limited, however, because he had taken up writing late in life.

Charlemagne was a great warrior-king. He crossed the Pyrenees with an army to fight the Muslims, and formed a defense area in northern Spain called the *Spanish March.* He also drove back the Saxons, a Germanic people who lived east of the Rhine, and set up military outposts among them. The Saxons were forced to become Christians; and bishops, monks, and nuns were sent to build churches in the newly conquered region.

When the Lombard king again threatened the Pope, Charlemagne led an army into Italy. He defeated the Lombards, and occupied northern Italy. (See the map on page 241.)

Charlemagne's Coronation as Emperor

Some subjects of Pope Leo III accused him of misconduct, and led a revolt against him. The Pope appealed to Charlemagne, who came to Rome, examined the charges, and cleared the Pope of any guilt.

On Christmas Day, 800 A.D., as Charlemagne prayed in the Church of St. Peter, Pope Leo set a crown upon his head. At once the people shouted: "Long life and victory to the mighty Charles, the great and peaceful Emperor of the Romans, crowned of God!"

It is not clear whether Charlemagne knew that he was going to be crowned by the Pope. Nevertheless, the coronation showed that Charlemagne was considered the successor of the old Roman emperors. It also seemed to indicate that the Pope was claiming to be superior to all temporal rulers. For this reason there is some question whether Charlemagne was altogether pleased with the Pope's action.

Life under Charlemagne

From his capital at Aix-la-Chapelle (Aachen in German), Charlemagne ruled an impressive empire. He brought together the cultures of the Roman and the Germanic peoples. He tried to give order and justice by sending out *missi dominici,* persons who checked to see whether officials of the empire and the Church were doing their jobs properly.

Charlemagne built churches and monasteries, and supported education. One of the finest schools he founded was in his own palace, where he and his

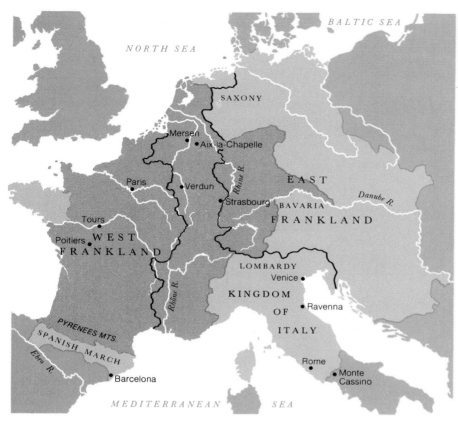

Charlemagne extended his control over much of western Europe by 800 A.D. Note the division of his empire into three parts by the Treaty of Verdun in 843 A.D.

NORTH SEA

BALTIC SEA

SAXONY

Mersen

Aix-la-Chapelle

Paris

Verdun

Rhine R.

EAST

Danube R.

Strasbourg

BAVARIA

FRANKLAND

Tours

Poitiers

WEST

FRANKLAND

Rhone R.

LOMBARDY

Venice

KINGDOM

OF

Ravenna

ITALY

PYRENEES MTS.

SPANISH MARCH

Ebro R.

Barcelona

Rome

Monte
Cassino

MEDITERRANEAN   SEA

Carolingian Empire

Charlemagne's original possessions

Charlemagne's conquests and tributary peoples

——— Division of his empire in 843 by the Treaty of Verdun

officials studied under Alcuin, a famous scholar from Britain.

The Treaty of Verdun

Charlemagne's empire brought some peace to the people of a large part of Europe. After Charlemagne's death, three of his grandsons—Lothair, Louis the German, and Charles the Bald—quarreled over who should rule the empire. In 842 Louis and Charles took the Oath of Strasbourg, in which they promised that they would help each other against the third brother, Lothair. The oaths were spoken in early German and early French, which was a sign that the empire was dividing into two language areas.

In the Treaty of Verdun in 843 A.D., the three brothers agreed to divide the empire. Louis received East Frankland, which years later became the basis for Germany. Charles received West Frankland, which years later became the basis for France. Lothair had the area between the lands of his two brothers plus northern Italy. (See the map above.)

Check on Your Reading

1. Who were the mayors of the palace?
2. Why was the coronation of Charlemagne by Pope Leo III important?
3. What were some of the achievements of Charlemagne?
4. How was Charlemagne's empire divided by the Treaty of Verdun? What effect did this have on the future of Europe?

3. The People of Europe Seek Safety from New Invaders

During the ninth and tenth centuries the heirs of Charlemagne showed themselves to be weak rulers. The Frankish kingdoms broke up as a result of poor government and fresh attacks from new invaders.

Magyar horsemen invaded parts of Italy and France. Muslims in North Africa and Spain seized control of the Mediterranean Sea and interfered with trade between western Europe and Constantinople. They also swept into Sicily and sent raiding parties into southern Italy.

Most feared were the Viking invaders from the

north of Europe, who were the greatest sailors and warriors of their time. The sight of the long Viking ships with figures of dragons and animals carved into the prows would cause some Europeans to pray:

> From the fury of the Northmen [Vikings], O Lord deliver us.

The range of the Vikings' voyages was impressive. Some sailed far to the west to the coast of North America. Others went down the rivers of Russia to the Black and Caspian seas. They attacked the towns, villages, and monasteries of the British Isles, France, and Spain.

Some Vikings eventually settled in lands across the seas. They set up colonies in Iceland and Greenland, and in a section of eastern England known as "the Danelaw."

An Anglo-Saxon king, Alfred the Great (871–899), fought many battles to keep the Vikings from taking over all England. He finally forced them to stay within the Danelaw. Later the Vikings were given a large peninsula in what is now France, known as Normandy. The Vikings' descendants eventually became Christians.

Development of Feudalism

As the power of the Frankish kings declined, the common people of Europe sought protection from the attacks of the invaders. More and more of them handed over their lands to local nobles in return for protection. This encouraged the development of a political and economic system known as *feudalism.*

Some features of feudalism also can be traced back to developments in the late Roman Empire. Great nobles built up large estates. People living on the estates were expected to work as farmers in the fields and to serve in the landlord's private army in time of danger. The feudal system also owed something to the military customs of the Germanic peoples. Tribal chieftains would pick young men as their followers in the wars. These young men were expected to be loyal to their leaders.

The Frankish kings after Charlemagne began to reward important men who could bring together bands of armed horsemen, or knights, to defend the kingdom. Such men were given titles of nobility. In theory, all the land within the kingdom belonged to the king. In return for the services of the great nobles, however, the king let them make use of large pieces of land known as *estates.* The king also kept sizable tracts of land for himself.

Gradually, the nobles' lands, or *fiefs,* became hereditary. That is, the fiefs could be passed on to heirs. Nobles with huge land holdings were allowed to distribute parts of their estates as smaller fiefs to lesser nobles.

The Feudal Contract

Although feudalism varied from place to place, it usually had the following features. First, there was a personal bond between the lord and "his man," who was known as a *vassal.* Second, the lord made a contract (generally oral) with his vassal, who was allowed to hold a tract of land in return for agreeing to perform certain services for the lord. Third, the nobles could set up a system of local government in their fiefs.

The personal relationship between the lord and his vassal was shown in a ceremony called the act of *homage.* The vassal-to-be knelt before his lord and promised to be faithful to him against all other persons. The lord helped the man up and kissed him as a sign that he was accepting him as a vassal. The vassal then swore an *oath of fealty,* by which he vowed to carry out all his duties to the lord.

A feudal contract was binding on both lord and vassal. The lord had to provide his vassal with the authority to manage the fief. He also had to protect the vassal and his family from enemies who might attack the fief. In return, the vassal was expected to give military help to his lord. This included not more than forty days and nights of military service each year by the vassal and his knights. Second, the vassal was obligated to help ransom the lord if he became a captive. Third, the vassal had to provide money payments when the lord's eldest daughter married and when the lord's eldest son became a knight. Fourth, the vassal had to give food, lodging, and entertainment to the lord and his followers whenever they visited the vassal's fief.

If a vassal failed in his duties, the lord had the right to take away the fief from the vassal. In practice, the vassal usually was fined. If a lord did not fulfill his obligations, the vassal's duties toward him came to an end—in theory. In practice, events and actions varied from place to place.

Fiefs did not have to be land. They could consist of the right to hold a castle, the right to collect

bridge tolls, the right to hear court cases, and other similar rights.

Advantages and Disadvantages of Feudalism

In a time of almost constant warfare, the feudal system provided a crude system of order and justice. Society was divided into three classes: nobles, peasants, and clergy. The nobles were the landholders, and they were responsible for managing the fiefs, administering justice, and fighting in the wars. The peasants were the great majority of the people. They tilled the soil and performed all kinds of services for the lords.

The clergy were the people of the Church—the parish priests, monks and nuns, abbots and abbesses, bishops and archbishops. The people of the Church might come from either noble or peasant families. In fact, some of the greatest Church leaders, including Popes, were children of poor parents. During the early Middle Ages, members of the clergy were often the only educated people in western Europe.

Living conditions for the peasants were hard. Men and women had an endless round of farm labor, except for Sundays and the holy days of the Church. Peasants were often badly treated during the frequent wars of the feudal lords. When a lord made war on another nobleman, it was standard practice to burn the enemy's villages and set fire to the fields of his peasants.

Women in the early Middle Ages had a few legal rights. They could inherit land, but a widow with an estate or a young heiress might be forced by her guardian to marry. For a long time no woman was allowed to appear in court. A woman involved in a lawsuit was represented by a guardian—her father, husband, or some other male relative. A few girls

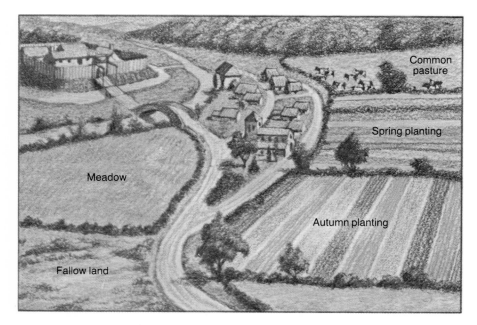

This plan shows a manor of about the tenth or eleventh century. It shows the manor house, the village, fields, pasture, and woodland. Great variations occurred throughout Europe in the size and arrangement of manors. In this period manor houses or castles were usually built of wood. Compare this one with the castles illustrated on page 247.

Common pasture

Spring planting

Meadow

Autumn planting

Fallow land

of the upper class attended convent schools, where they were taught good manners and how to do fine sewing. Some also learned to read the *Bible* and stories about the saints.

Children of noble families could be married at a very early age. Their parents were often more concerned about adding to the family estate than about the young people's future happiness. Women were under the strict control of their fathers or husbands. Husbands had the right to beat their wives. As a rule, noblewomen were treated with respect, however. In time of war many took over from their husbands the task of managing the fief. Many ladies learned how to defend the family castle during their husbands' absences.

Nuns were generally honored because they were under the protection of the Church. Abbesses in charge of large convents managed the convent lands, directed the nuns, and gave orders to peasants on convent property. One of the most remarkable women of the medieval period was St. Hildegard of Bingen (1098-1179), the abbess of a Benedictine convent in the Rhineland region of Germany. A student of medicine and natural history, she never hesitated to speak her mind, even to the emperor or her archbishop.

The Church in the Feudal Period

Because the Church owned a great deal of land, many bishops and abbots became rich and power-

ful. Some churchmen became the vassals of kings and great nobles. Their loyalty to their lord in the temporal world brought them into conflict with their duties toward the Pope as their spiritual lord.

Churchmen were not forced to perform military service since members of the clergy were forbidden to kill. The Church used its influence to limit the feudal wars, and it expected knights to respect women, children, and unarmed persons as well as holy places. *The Truce of God* forbade fighting on certain days of the week and at certain times of the year.

Check on Your Reading

1. What new invaders attacked Europe in the ninth and tenth centuries?
2. How did feudalism develop?
3. Describe the feudal contract.
4. Describe the position of women in the early Middle Ages.

4. Life on a Manor

During the Middle Ages most fiefs were in the form of a manor, an agricultural settlement. A manor consisted of an estate with a castle or a manor house, and a village or several villages in which peasants lived. The total area of a manor might vary from five hundred to seven thousand acres. Part of the land was set aside for the use of the lord of the manor. The lord's farmland, which was usually the best on the manor, was cultivated for the lord by peasants under the direction of the lord's officials. All other farmland was held by the peasants. There were also woods, meadows, and open land on the manor that were used by both the lord and his peasants.

The manor was self-sufficient. Each manor supplied all or almost all the needs of the people who lived on it. Most villagers did not travel, and the average peasant probably did not see more than a few hundred people in his or her lifetime.

The Peasant Village

A small village might contain fifty inhabitants, while a larger one might have several hundred persons. The center of village life was the church, and the parish priest was the spiritual leader of the people of the village.

Scattered about the village were the peasants' houses, which were usually one-room cottages. The walls of a typical cottage were of intertwining sticks with twigs and branches plastered over with mud. Its floor was of pounded earth. The roof was thatched and was attractive to rats. The chimney was often a hole in the roof. The cottage was furnished with a bench, a rough wooden table, stools, and a bed of straw. Usually the whole family slept in the same bed.

Farm animals—perhaps a horse, mule, or ox— were housed in a small stable. Nearby were a vegetable garden, a pig sty, and a chicken coop.

The peasants wore coarse woolen tunics and stockings. In cold weather they added a heavy cloak. In the summer, usually they went barefoot in the fields, but on Sundays they might put on wooden clogs or leather shoes. Clothing was made by the women and the girls. The peasants had a limited diet, and often there was not enough food. Rarely was there any fresh meat, but pork could be salted and kept for a long time. Heavy soups with bread and cheese were the usual fare. Drink might consist of beer or cider.

The Position of the Peasants

There were several kinds of peasants on a manor. The position of the women and children was determined by the status of the men. *Freemen* had the right to move from one manor to another under certain conditions. They also came under the king's courts, not under the local court of the lord of the manor.

Some peasants who were not free were *slaves*. They could be bought or sold at their lord's wish. Slaves were not very numerous, however, and by the eleventh century slavery was dying out in northwestern Europe.

Most of the peasants were *serfs* who lived under definite rules and restrictions. Serfdom, or the condition of being a serf, was hereditary, which means that a serf's children became serfs at birth. They could not leave the manor or marry without the consent of the lord.

Serfs had to pay taxes to the lord, usually in animals or grain. They had to work on the lord's land two or three days each week. They could grind their own corn only in the lord's mill and could bake their bread only in the lord's oven. For the use of the mill and the oven, special payments were made to the lord.

The peasants had some rights, however. They elected a village headman to deal with the lord's officials. They could not easily be turned off the land assigned to them. Their cattle could use the common pastures, and their pigs could look for food in the common woods.

Farming Methods

Farming technology was gradually improved in the Middle Ages. To protect the fertility of the soil, the three-field system was introduced about the eleventh century. Under this arrangement, farmland was divided into three fields, and crops were rotated on a regular basis. Each field remained fallow for one year in each three-year cycle. The fallow field was plowed but not seeded, so that the soil might recover its richness by resting. Each peasant had a number of strips of land, each of which was approximately an acre in size. These strips were scattered throughout the fields in such a way that no peasant had all the best or all the poorest soil.

All the peasants in a village—men, women, and children— cooperated in the plowing, sowing, and harvesting. During the Middle Ages several technical improvements were made in tools and equipment. One was the development of a plow that made it possible to turn over the heavy soil of northern Europe. About 1000 A.D. a new kind of horseshoe was invented, and an improved horse collar

A manuscript of the Middle Ages showing peasants harvesting grain.

stone. The key building within a castle was the *donjon,* a stone tower that was the lord's home and fortress. It was surrounded by a courtyard in which the chapel and storerooms were located. The courtyard was protected by a high wall. Soldiers could stand on it in times of danger, and aim arrows, stones, or boiling oil at attackers. Outside the wall was a *moat,* or a ditch usually full of water. Entrance to the castle was by a drawbridge over the moat.

Most castles had a great hall in the donjon that served as a dining room, court of justice, and sleeping area. There were other buildings: granary, bakery, stables, and sheds for the cattle and the chickens.

The rooms of most castles and manor houses had few comforts. The floors were of stone, covered by rushes or straw. The walls were bare, and there was not much furniture. The great hall might be decorated with hangings known as tapestries, which provided a note of color in a gloomy room and helped keep out the dampness. Here the lord and lady ate, surrounded by the men and women of the castle. Fresh meat was usually plentiful since the lord and his knights were tireless hunters. Most cooking was done on a spit in the open fireplace.

Wandering minstrels (singers) might entertain the people of the castle with tales of military heroes. Such poems kept alive the spirit of *chivalry,* an expression that refers to the manners, customs, and ceremonies of knighthood.

Training of a Knight

Because the Middle Ages was a warlike period, the training of knights was very important. Until the age of seven the son of a nobleman remained at home under his mother's supervision. He was then sent to the castle or manor house of another noble— perhaps his father's lord or close friend. There he served as a *page,* or young attendant. A page was taught good manners, how to serve at table, and how to play such games as backgammon or chess. He also was expected to protect ladies of the castle when they went out in the fields to hunt with hawks.

At fifteen the page became a *squire.* Under the supervision of the knights he was trained in a nobleman's skills. He learned to ride and hunt, and to fight with a lance and a sword. He might also be trained to sing or play a musical instrument.

greatly increased the pulling power of horses. Slowly more and more land was brought under cultivation as peasants drained swamps and cleared forests all over western Europe.

The Manor House or Castle

Close to the peasants' village was the home of the lord. It might be a manor house, which was usually a building of timber and clay. Better suited for defense was a castle, which was often located on a hilltop. In the ninth century castles were built of wood, but in the thirteenth century many were of

These drawings illustrate two types of castles of the later Middle Ages. The donjon is shown clearly in the castle at the top. The sizes and styles of castles varied throughout Europe.

If war broke out, he accompanied his lord into battle. Many squires were "knighted" during the feudal wars. If not, at the age of twenty-one a young man was thought ready for knighthood. At this point the Church played an important part. The future knight would wash away his sins by taking a ceremonial bath and confessing his faults to a priest. He then spent the night watching his weapons before the altar of the castle chapel. After praying earnestly to become a worthy knight, he attended Mass the next day. He then knelt before his lord, who struck him on the back of the neck or shoulders with his fist or the flat of a sword. This action was known as *dubbing* a man a knight.

The new knight was thoroughly instructed in his duties. He was to fear God and defend the Church. In battle he was to be brave and loyal to his lord. He was to respect women, protect widows and orphans, and defend the weak. All his life he was to be honorable and speak the truth. Not all knights were able—or tried—to fulfill their duties to others. The noble ideals of chivalry, however, became desirable goals. They still are honored by many people in the modern view of what makes a gentleman.

Check on Your Reading

1. Describe the life of the peasants on a manor.
2. What was serfdom?
3. Describe the position of women.
4. How did a young man become a knight?

5. Feudal Lords and the Church Clash

As you learned (page 241), in 843 Louis the German became ruler of the part of the Frankish Empire that was eventually to become Germany. During the tenth century, Otto the Great took over this kingdom. Then he brought other German dukes under his control.

Otto was a powerful warrior-king. His armies defeated the Magyar tribes who were invading Europe from Asia. He conquered the Slavs, people who spoke a Slavic language and lived east of the Elbe River and in present-day Czechoslovakia. His armies pushed back some of the Slavic tribes to the East. Otto also occupied northern Italy.

The Holy Roman Empire

In 962 A.D. Otto the Great traveled to Rome to be crowned Emperor by the Pope. Historians later called the territories ruled by Otto and his successors the *Holy Roman Empire.* The Empire included much German and Italian land. It extended from the North Sea to south of Rome. (See the map at right.) The Holy Roman Empire claimed to be the successor of the Roman Empire and Charlemagne's empire, but it never was centralized or strong.

Within the Holy Roman Empire, German nobles and peasants began to settle the lands of central Europe formerly held by Slavs. The Church also sent bishops and abbots there to build churches and monasteries. Many Slavs were converted to the Christian religion. The Magyars were forced back into present-day Hungary, where they settled down in farming villages. Disputes over land in central and eastern Europe between Germans and Slavs have continued to the present.

The Holy Roman Empire was not a centralized state. The people of Germany were ruled by many local nobles. Italy, too, was divided into a number of states.

The Holy Roman Empire needed well-educated officials to run its vast lands. The emperor persuaded many bishops and abbots to help him in the government. This led to abuses, as many churchmen no longer represented the poor people. It was said that the Church and its leaders had become tied to the power and wealth of the Empire.

The Dispute between the Emperors and the Popes

The Holy Roman emperors became involved in a bitter quarrel with the Popes. Because the Church owned much land under the feudal system, the emperors claimed the right to appoint bishops and abbots who would be their loyal vassals.

Meanwhile, a Pope was elected who was determined to reform the Church. He was Gregory VII (1073-1085), who was influenced by the monks of Cluny in France. The monks of Cluny tried to improve the Church by removing abuses. First, they wanted to put an end to *lay investiture,* which means that a ruler might appoint his men to positions of power in the Church. Second, they were opposed to *simony,* or the selling of positions in the Church. Third, they wanted all members of the clergy to remain unmarried. Finally, they did not want rulers to influence the election of Popes.

Pope Gregory believed that he alone as Pope had

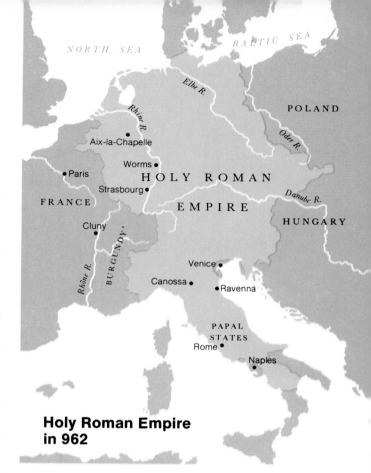

Holy Roman Empire in 962

Otto I became the first Holy Roman Emperor in 962. His territory included lands in what are now Germany and Italy.

the power to appoint and remove bishops. Going further, he wrote:

> If the Pope is supreme judge in spiritual ways, why not also in secular worldly ways?

Thus he claimed the right to remove rulers from power if they were enemies of the Church or did things against the welfare of their people.

The new Holy Roman Emperor, Henry IV (1056-1106 A.D.), would not go along with the wishes of the Pope. Henry appointed a number of bishops and abbots. When Pope Gregory opposed him, Henry answered with anger that the Pope had brought the Church "not honor but disgrace, not a blessing but a curse."

The Pope then *excommunicated* the Emperor. That is, he cut him off from membership in the Church and forbade him to take the sacraments of the Church. He also announced that Henry's Christian subjects should no longer regard him as

A woodcut of Pope Gregory VII. He claimed the right to remove rulers from power.

their ruler. A number of lords in Germany then threatened to overthrow the Emperor and elect a successor unless the Pope removed the decree of excommunication.

Afraid of losing his crown, Henry came before the Pope, who was in a castle in Italy. Waiting in the snow in early 1077:

> [The Emperor] stood in wretchedness, barefooted and clad in woolen, for three days before the gate of the castle, and implored with profuse weeping . . . until he had moved all who saw or heard it to . . . pity.

Pope Gregory then removed the excommunication and allowed Henry back into the Church.

We might think that Gregory had won the dispute. However, the Emperor and the Pope continued to disagree. In 1081 Henry led an army into Italy, seized Rome in 1084, and forced Gregory to flee. In fact, the struggle between Church and the Empire did not end for many years.

The Concordat of Worms: a Compromise

The dispute over lay investiture was finally settled in 1122 by the Concordat (or formal agreement) of Worms, a city in Germany. It was agreed that in Germany the Church could hold elections for bishops and abbots. These elections were to be held by the Church in the presence of the Emperor or his representatives. Only the Pope could give

bishops and abbots their religious or spiritual powers. However, the Emperor had authority to give the new bishops and abbots their political powers before they were placed in office by the Church.

The Concordat of Worms was a fairly satisfactory solution to a long dispute. However, much distrust still remained between the Church and temporal rulers.

Check on Your Reading

1. Who was Otto the Great, and what were his main accomplishments?
2. Why did the Church and the Holy Roman Empire clash?
3. Describe the quarrel between Gregory VII and Henry IV.
4. What was the Concordat of Worms?

---

6. Byzantine Civilization Flourishes for Many Centuries

Constantine the Great set up Constantinople as the eastern capital of the Roman Empire in 330 A.D. After the Roman Empire in the West disintegrated in the fifth century, the Eastern Roman Empire continued for almost a thousand years. Its capital remained Constantinople, a Greek city originally known as Byzantium. For this reason the Eastern Roman Empire was also called the Byzantine Empire. Byzantine civilization made important contributions to Europe in law, art, architecture, literature, and religion.

Constantinople: City of Contrasts

The capital of the Byzantine Empire was strategically located between the Black Sea and the Sea of Marmara, where Europe and Asia come together. It was a vital point on the trade route that extended between the Black and Mediterranean seas. (See the map on page 252.)

During the Middle Ages Constantinople with its million inhabitants was one of the most important cities of the world. It had huge palaces where rulers lived a life of ceremony. The Palace of the Emperor was famous for its marble halls and fountains and its golden birds and lions. There were many monasteries and convents where monks and nuns sang the praises of God. Everywhere were busy markets. There was also a great Circus, where horse races were run before cheering spectators.

A small part of the great Church of Hagia Sophia (Divine Wisdom) in Constantinople. Built under the direction of Emperor Justinian, it opened its huge bronze doors in 537 A.D. Both of the main architects were Greeks from Asia Minor and fused the architecture of imperial Rome with the ideas of the Byzantine church. A historian of the period recorded that Justinian gathered "all the artisans from the whole world" to build the church.

Devout ladies of the upper classes walked modestly to church, and there were women acrobats and actresses entertaining in theaters. This was a city bustling with people who had many different ways of life.

The Achievements of the Byzantine Empire

The Byzantine Empire was defended by a fine army and navy. The Empire expanded and contracted in size at various times. It reached its largest size under Justinian (527–565), when Byzantine armies won back lands in the West from Germanic kings. Under Justinian the Empire included Spain, Egypt, and North Africa.

Justinian had Roman laws gathered together into one complete code called the *Justinian Code*.

Through it the great principles of Roman law were passed on to western Europe.

Byzantine civilization was highly creative. Its works of art were deeply influenced by the Christian religion. Mingling the styles of Greece, Rome, and the East, artists made *mosaics,* pictures or designs produced by cementing together small pieces of colored glass or other objects. They also created *frescoes,* wall paintings done on wet plaster or mortar that is not completely dry. Their architecture was splendid. One of the most impressive buildings of the world was the Church of Hagia Sophia (Divine Wisdom), which still stands in Constantinople.

The people of the Byzantine Empire kept the Greek language alive. They preserved writings of ancient Greece for later generations. Writers also produced histories, encyclopedias, religious poems, and other church literature.

The Split between the Eastern and Western Churches

Throughout western Europe the Popes of Rome were recognized as the spiritual leaders of the Christian Church. The Popes' claim to supremacy was not recognized, however, in the Byzantine Empire. The emperors at Constantinople felt that Constantinople, which was called the "second Rome," was superior to the first Rome in Italy. They wanted to control the Church in their Empire. So they insisted that the bishop of Constantinople, the *Patriarch*, should not follow the orders of the Pope.

For many centuries there were disputes between the Popes and the leaders of the Byzantine Empire. Finally, in 1054 A.D., the Eastern and Western churches separated.

The *Eastern Orthodox Church*, as the Church in the Byzantine Empire was called, developed its own ceremonies. It brought Christianity to the Slavs and other peoples in lands under Byzantine influence. Most people in the Balkan Peninsula and Russia became Eastern Orthodox Christians.

Trade

Byzantine merchants set up trade routes between Constantinople and central Europe, Italy, southern Russia, Africa, and Asia. They imported wheat, honey, spices, salt, and fish. They also imported ivory from Africa and rare fabrics from India and China. They exported embroidered silks, elaborate jewelry, and carved ivory.

The Weakening of the Empire

The Byzantine Empire gradually lost more and more of its lands to Muslim armies. Struggles broke out among rival leaders at Constantinople who wished to become the emperor. Taxes grew too heavy for the people to pay. New Muslim invaders called Turks began to take over the Byzantine lands in Asia Minor.

The Empire was then greatly weakened early in the 1200s when the Crusaders arrived. These were warriors and pilgrims from the West trying to win back the Holy Land for Christianity. Their actions helped destroy the Byzantine Empire.

Check on Your Reading

1. Why was Constantinople's location advantageous? Describe life in the city.
2. What were some of the Byzantine contributions to law, art, and architecture?
3. What caused the difference between the Eastern Orthodox and the Roman Catholic churches?
4. What factors weakened the Byzantine Empire?

This mosaic from the Church of San Vitale in Ravenna shows Theodora, the wife of Emperor Justinian, and her attendants. She had a great influence on the political and religious life of the Byzantine Empire.

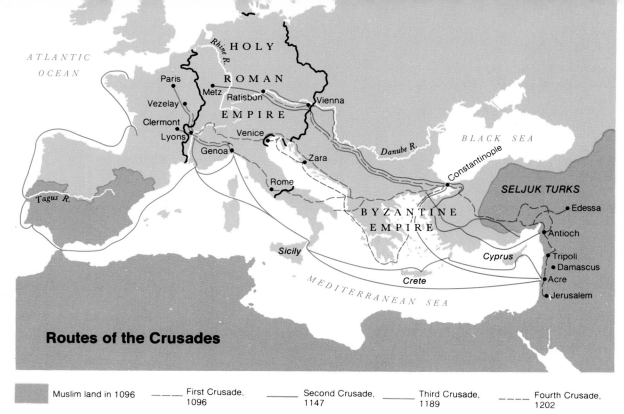

Routes of the Crusades

▨ Muslim land in 1096	----- First Crusade, 1096	—— Second Crusade, 1147	—— Third Crusade, 1189
		---- Fourth Crusade, 1202	

The Crusades were military campaigns and pilgrimages by European Christians to win back the Holy Land from the Muslims. Between 1096 and 1204 four Crusades were organized.

7. The Crusaders Attack Islam

The Crusades (1096-1291) were military campaigns and pilgrimages by European Christians to conquer Palestine and take it from the Muslims. Judea in Palestine was called the "Holy Land" because Jesus had lived there. Christians longed to see the places where he had been born and died.

In the eleventh century the Seljuk Turks, who had become Muslims, took over much of Syria. In 1071 they captured Jerusalem from other Muslims. They were less tolerant of Christians than the earlier Muslims had been. Soon the Turkish masters of the Holy Land began to persecute Christian pilgrims. The Turks also threatened to take over more territory from the Byzantine Empire. So the Emperor appealed to Pope Urban II for help.

Pope Urban answered this appeal at the Council of Clermont in France in 1095. He called upon Christians to start a great Crusade to occupy the Holy Land. He promised that God would bless the Crusade.

> When an armed attack is made upon the enemy, let this one cry be raised by all the soldiers of God: "God wills it!"

Motives of the Crusaders

The Crusades were fought for many reasons. Many religious people went on the Crusades because they felt that it was their duty to free the Holy Land from the Muslims. Some nobles joined because they saw a chance to win land for themselves. Restless knights went for the love of adventure. Criminals became Crusaders to escape punishment at home. Debtors went along to escape their creditors.

The Pope preached that Christians who were killed in a Crusade would be certain of salvation. This was an important reason for going on a Crusade. Medieval people were greatly concerned about life after death and dreaded the horrors of punishment for their sins in hell.

Wearing a cross as the symbol of their faith, Crusaders set out from all over Europe. Among them were kings and noblemen, poor people and children. Most of the Crusaders' wives stayed behind in Europe to look after the fiefs or farms. Some of them had run such estates before when their husbands went off to war. A few queens and noblewomen, however, accompanied their husbands.

Crusaders in the Holy Land

Between 1096 and 1204 there were four major Crusades as well as a number of smaller ones. (See map on the opposite page.) The First Crusade, which was begun in 1096 by French, Italian, and German nobles, was the most successful.

The army of the Crusaders occupied a strip of land along the Mediterranean Sea, and took Jerusalem. An eyewitness described the bloody battle for the city:

> Then certain Saracens [Muslims] sought refuge in the citadel of David. . . . At the temple of Solomon to which they had climbed in their flight, many were shot down fatally by arrows. From its roof they tumbled to their doom. And in that temple at least ten thousand fell.

The kingdom that the Crusaders set up in the Holy Land was soon threatened by the Muslims. The Second Crusade of 1147 was organized by King Louis VII of France, and King Conrad III of Germany. It ended in failure when the Christians failed to capture Damascus.

A leader of the Turks, Saladin, then united most of the Muslims and recaptured Jerusalem in 1187. Saladin was inspired by noble ideals similar to the principles of Christian chivalry. He told his son:

> If I have become great, it is because I have won the hearts [of people] by kindness and gentleness.

During the Third Crusade Emperor Frederick Barbarossa (Redbeard) of Germany met death by drowning. Richard I of England and Philip II of France quarreled, and Philip went home. After much fighting, Richard and Saladin agreed on a three-year truce in 1192. Unarmed pilgrims were allowed to visit Jerusalem, and the Christians controlled a strip of land along the coast.

In the Fourth Crusade the Crusaders fell into debt to the merchants of the Italian port city of Venice. To pay their bills they agreed to attack Zara, a Christian town that had rebelled against the Venetians. Thus the Fourth Crusade involved a battle between Christians.

The leaders of the Fourth Crusade next attacked Constantinople. A French leader described the impressions of the Crusaders as they approached the city in their ships:

> They [the Crusaders] never imagined that such a rich city could exist in the whole world until they saw those high walls and splendid towers that enclosed it, and those rich palaces and tall churches of which there were so many that no one could believe it.

After looting the capital, the Crusaders set up the Latin Empire of Constantinople; it lasted until 1261. The people of Constantinople eventually put a Byzantine Emperor back on the throne, but the Empire never recovered its full strength. A new group of Muslims—the Ottoman Turks—occupied the city in 1453. This brought to an end the power and rule of the Byzantine Empire.

There were also two other Crusades that ended in failure. Slowly, Christians lost all their lands in the Middle East until their last stronghold, Acre, fell in 1291. The Crusades were over, as the Christian armies were forced out of the Holy Land.

Results of the Crusades

The Crusades had a considerable effect on European life. They introduced or made popular in Europe new foods and goods: sugar and lemons, rice and melons, muslin and damask cloth, glass mirrors and fine steel swords. Trade fairs all over Europe stimulated demand for these products.

New ideas were brought back by the Crusaders. From the Muslims they learned the principle of the windmill, and gained new knowledge about medicine, mathematics, and astronomy.

Several Italian cities grew larger and richer. Venice and Genoa became prosperous by selling ships and supplies to the Crusaders. Italian bankers helped finance the expensive military campaigns. Sea power in the Mediterranean shifted westward. Italian, French, and Spanish ports on the Mediterranean Sea began to rival Constantinople and Muslim trading centers.

The Crusades helped break down feudalism. Many feudal lords sold their lands to obtain money and supplies so that they could go on a Crusade. Other nobles who were Crusaders neglected their fiefs in Europe. Many peasants left their villages to travel to the East and never returned. New opportunities and new ideas drew them into the growing towns. In some regions local government by feudal lords was replaced by the central government of a king.

Considerable money and supplies were needed for the armies of the Crusaders, which numbered from ten thousand to twenty-five thousand men. Kings therefore began to tax their people to support the Crusades. Increased trade put more money in circulation and helped make such taxation possible. By 1300 national taxes were levied in England and France.

The early Crusades probably added to the power of the Popes. The Church had taken the lead in calling for the wars against the Muslims, and it was respected for doing so. Later, the Church often was blamed for the selfish acts of some of the Crusaders.

Check on Your Reading

1. What were the reasons for the Crusades?
2. What places were taken by the Crusaders?
3. Give examples of how one Crusade was misused.
4. Evaluate the results of the Crusades.

LET'S MEET THE PEOPLE

A Benedictine Nun

Twenty nuns were asleep in the convent sleeping room. A single candle gave a dim light. Each nun was resting on a separate bed under a plain woolen blanket. She was fully clothed.

At 2 A.M. a bell awakened the nun. She and her companions went downstairs in the cold to the chapel. There they recited and sang *matins* (early morning prayers). This was the first of several services at which the nun prayed each day. She then went back to the sleeping quarters to rest for three hours. In all she had about eight hours' sleep broken by the prayers in the middle of the night. During the rest of the morning the nun was busy with the care of the convent and with prayers.

From noon until 5 P.M. in winter and from 1 P.M. to 6 P.M. in summer the nun worked. She might spin or embroider vestments, the articles of clothing worn by priests to say Mass. In summer she might work in the convent garden or go haymaking in the fields. Often her work was of an intellectual nature. She might read the *Bible,* or teach reading, music, and good manners to schoolgirls living in the convent. When the nun worked outdoors, she put on a simple work costume. At other times she was clothed in a long robe with flowing sleeves. On her head was a veil, and a long string of prayer beads hung from a cord around her waist.

The nun took three meals each day in the convent dining hall. Breakfast consisted of a light serving of bread and ale. In the middle of the day dinner consisted of meat or fish, vegetables, bread, and butter. During dinner a nun read to the community from a book on the lives of the saints. After *vespers* (evening prayers) came a light supper.

In the early evening the nun enjoyed a time of relaxation with her companions before going to bed. At all other times in the day a rule of strict silence was observed. If the nun needed to give a message to a companion she used a kind of sign language. For example, if she wanted some milk during dinner, she would take hold of her left little finger and imitate the action of milking a cow.

At 7 P.M. in winter and 8 P.M. in summer, the last religious service was sung. Then the nun went straight to bed. As she lay down, she thanked God for the events of the day and asked protection through the night.

The above sketch of a day in the life of a nun in the Middle Ages is based on information in *Medieval People* by Eileen Power, 1963, Barnes & Noble, New York.

CHAPTER REVIEW

Think and Discuss

1. Feudalism was based upon a set of *political* conditions. Explain.
2. The manorial system was based upon a set of *economic* conditions. Explain.
3. Read the "Keynote" on page 236 again. How did human needs influence the development of feudalism and of both the Roman Catholic Church and Eastern Orthodox Church?
4. In medieval society every person probably knew his or her position in society. Explain.
5. A peasant rarely met more than three hundred persons during a lifetime. How might the number of people a person knows affect that person?
6. How did the Crusades help to end feudalism? With what results?
7. Do you think from your study of the Crusades that it is a good thing on the whole for people to travel and see how other people live? Why?

Past and Present

1. What did the Middle Ages contribute to present-day society?
2. On what kind of economy was feudalism based? What kind of economy is there in the United States today? What effects did each system have on social, economic, and political life?

Activities

1. Draw a picture diagram of a feudal manor. The diagram on page 244 should give you ideas.
2. Draw a diagram showing the organization or class structure of medieval society.
3. There is a theory that only the Roman Empire in its political form ceased to exist, but that its social, economic, and religious life continued in the Middle Ages. Can you find any evidence to support this theory? Consult several references.
4. Draw a picture diagram of a castle and identify its parts.

15

The Rise of Trade, Towns, and Nations

KEYNOTE

The pattern of society in Europe changed in the years after 1000. Beginning in the eleventh century, a relative peace was established. Trade revived, new towns were built, and some towns grew into cities. An urban middle class, or *bourgeoisie*, developed, whose loyalty was to cities and to kings rather than to feudal lords.

The new bourgeoisie were pleased that they had wrested freedoms from the feudal lords, proud of their cities, and eager to show their loyalty to the Church. From 1050 to 1350, in France alone eighty cathedrals and five hundred large churches were built. The creative building of these magnificent structures reflected the revival of trade and free cities, advances in technology, and the birth of an urban middle class.

The Cathedral rises in the midst of the town of Chartres, France.

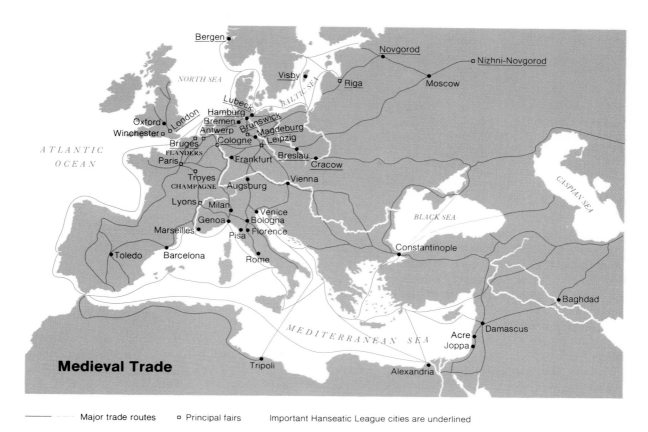

Trade increased rapidly after 1000 A.D. Trade routes crisscrossed Europe and the surrounding oceans and seas and were connected with trade routes from the East.

1. Trade Expands and Towns Grow

By the late tenth century the Magyars and Vikings were no longer a threat to Europe. More peaceful conditions made it safer to travel. Population increased as Europeans raised more crops, ate better food, and lived longer. Many peasants left the manors to settle in towns where they found opportunities "to get ahead." The growing numbers of people needed more goods and wanted new products. To meet these demands, merchants developed trade networks across Europe, to the Middle East, and to northern Africa.

The expansion of trade and the growth of towns had begun even before the Crusades. These developments were greatly stimulated by the military expeditions of the Crusaders to the Middle East.

The Rebirth of Large-Scale Trade

Europe was crisscrossed by a network of water and land trade routes. Many old Roman roads and bridges were repaired, although tolls had to be paid to local lords at intervals along the highways. Fords and ferries were put into operation. Travelers could rest at inns in the towns. Inns were not comfortable by present-day standards. Five or more merchants might have to share a large bed; but they could find food and drink for themselves and fodder for their horses. For protection against robbers, merchants traveled in large groups.

From the time of the First Crusade, the Italian ports of Venice, Genoa, and Pisa traded with the ports of Acre, Joppa, and Alexandria in the Middle East. European merchants exchanged their wines, tin, and money for spices, ivory, incense, and cloth of gold. Silks and porcelain from China as well as pearls and rubies from India were also available in Middle Eastern ports. Some Far Eastern products reached the Middle East along the Silk Road. Arab ships also carried goods from India and the Spice Islands to ports on the Red Sea and Persian Gulf.

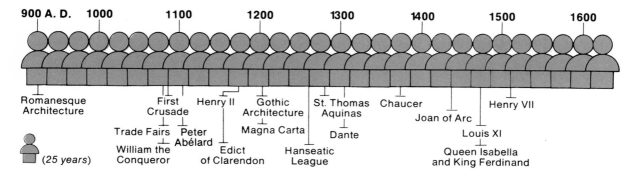

900 A.D.	**1000**	**1100**	**1200**	**1300**	**1400**	**1500**	**1600**

Romanesque Architecture

(25 years)

First Crusade

Henry II

Gothic Architecture

St. Thomas Aquinas

Chaucer

Henry VII

Trade Fairs Peter Abélard

Magna Carta

Joan of Arc

Louis XI

Dante

William the Conqueror

Edict of Clarendon

Hanseatic League

Queen Isabella and King Ferdinand

The introduction of the *mariner's compass* about the twelfth century made navigation safer. This invention, which was originally developed in China, made it possible to travel across open seas by observing the stars. It was no longer necessary to hug the coastline or travel from one island to another. A little later an improved kind of rudder and sails allowed sea captains to steer closer to the wind. They no longer had to wait for winds from their ship's stern, but could use winds from all directions. European merchants were able to send large fleets across the Mediterranean. In the fourteenth century, Italian galleys opened a new sea route by sailing through the Straits of Gibraltar to England and ports on the North and Baltic seas.

This trade also developed links with the trans-Saharan trade of Africa, discussed in Chapter 12. Muslim merchants crossed the desert to trade for gold in the African states south of the Sahara. These states, in turn, imported the gold from lands farther south. By the thirteenth century, most of the gold used in Europe for coins, jewelry, and other purposes came from Africa south of the Sahara.

The Growth of Towns and Cities

The goods of the Middle East and Far East were transferred by merchants from Italian coastal towns to rapidly growing cities of the interior, such as Florence and Milan. Milanese merchants, in turn, organized trading expeditions to towns in Germany.

The old Roman cities in southern France—Marseilles, Nîmes, and Arles—began to trade via the Rhone Valley with the northern cities of Lyons and Paris. Flanders (in present-day Belgium) was transformed in the thirteenth century by the use of such devices as the spinning wheel, probably an Indian invention. The town of Ghent grew rapidly as it became a center of the textile industry. Bruges

and Antwerp became important market towns, second only in wealth to the Italian cities. Cambrai was famous for its cambric, and Lille for its lisle cloth. Because of the great demand for Flemish textiles, the clothmakers had to import wool from England. Later, English merchants decided to produce their own cloth, which brought high prices in other regions.

Different parts of Europe specialized in different products. French wines from the Bordeaux region found a ready market in England. Grains from England and northern France were sold to heavily populated Flanders and to Scandinavia. Mining also became important. Tin from Cornwall, iron ore from Austria, and coal from Newcastle in England and from Belgium were used to make metal products in many parts of Europe.

Not only did old Roman towns revive, but also new settlements were founded. Some grew up around monasteries. For instance, Munich in southern Germany means the "place of the monks." Many towns were originally small settlements under the protection of feudal castles. Their growth was often stimulated by a favorable location along a major trade route. The English university centers of Oxford and Cambridge, for example, were on strategic river crossings.

Later, feudal lords encouraged peasants and townspeople from settled areas to move to new lands where swamps had been drained or forests cut down. Such a place was a so-called New Town. It might be known in French as *Villeneuve;* in German as *Neudorf* or *Neustadt;* or in English as *Newton, Newport,* or *Newcastle.*

Fairs as Centers of Trade and Ideas

During the twelfth and thirteenth centuries important fairs were held in many major European towns. Originally they were connected with religious feasts, such as the great fair that took place each year at the monastery of St. Denis outside Paris. Fairs were held for a certain number of days and were run according to carefully stated rules. In 1173 the Holy Roman Emperor Frederick Barbarossa authorized a fair twice a year at Aix-la-Chapelle (Aachen) in these words:

> We have given . . . this liberty to all
> merchants—that they may be quit and free of
> all tolls throughout the year at these fairs . . .
> and that they may buy and sell goods freely.
> . . . No merchant . . . may take a merchant to
> court for the payment of any debt during these
> fairs.

Merchants came from far and wide to great fairs in the Champagne region southeast of Paris. Stalls were set up where local wines, grains, and cattle were exchanged for hides and furs from Scandinavia, Flemish textiles, and the products of Italy and the Middle East. Other fairs took place at towns in Flanders, England, Spain, and Germany. Men, women, and children went for entertainment and information as well as to buy and sell. Jugglers, acrobats, and storytellers drew large audiences.

Coins from many parts of Europe circulated at the fairs. This greatly increased the supply of money. Italian bankers at this time developed international *letters of credit*. Such letters made it possible for merchants who had money in a bank in Milan, for example, to transfer it to a bank in London. Because people did not have to run the risk of carrying large sums from one region to another, they were able to expand trade more easily.

Business leaders from cities in northern Italy opened banks in London and other north European towns. The Medici family of Florence, Italy, and the Fugger family of Augsburg, in southern Germany, acted as bankers for Popes and kings.

Check on Your Reading

1. Why did the population increase in the tenth and eleventh centuries?
2. Why did trade increase in Europe after 1000?
3. What two inventions made navigation safer?
4. Why did Flanders become a rich industrial center?
5. Why did people go to fairs? How were the merchants helped by letters of credit?

This painting from a medieval manuscript pictures the marketplace of a town. Shopkeepers usually lived above their shops.

2. Townspeople Develop New Ways of Living

Towns in the Middle Ages were protected by sturdy walls. Soldiers kept watch at heavily fortified gates and from towers built at intervals along the walls. Within the security of the towns a new social class developed: the townspeople. They were also called *burghers* or *bourgeoisie* from words which meant "fortified place" in German and French. The bourgeoisie did not rank as high as the upper clergy and the nobility, but they had a much higher standard of living than the peasants.

There was a general rule in some areas that a serf who lived a year and a day in a town could become free. This caused many peasants to run away from their manors to seek opportunities in the towns. Gradually the bourgeoisie developed a new way of

A guild master judges the work of a carpenter and a stonemason.

of its membership in order to prevent an oversupply of skilled workers of the same trade from gathering in a town. Members also helped each other in time of trouble.

Craft guilds were controlled by the *masters*. They were skilled workers who directed assistants known as *apprentices* and *journeymen*. An apprentice agreed to work in a master's shop generally for seven years while learning the trade. An apprentice received no pay but was given food, clothing, and shelter in the master's house. When training was completed, the apprentice became a journeyman. A journeyman was entitled to receive fair pay for each day's work. After working a few years for one or several masters, a journeyman would ask the guild to admit him as a master. He had to show his skill by presenting a masterpiece; for example, a well-executed table. Then the guild might authorize him to become a master and to open his own shop.

Merchant guilds were associations of a town's merchants to protect the interests of their members. 1. Guild members agreed on the quality and the quantity of their goods. 2. They set down rules for competing with each other. 3. They protected goods that their members sent to foreign countries. 4. Visiting merchants from other towns were carefully controlled; they had to pay tolls on any business they did within the town. 5. The guilds built warehouses for storing the goods of members. 6. They assisted guild members and their families. Members who fell into debt were helped. If necessary, a guild paid its members' burial costs and looked after their widows and children.

Members of guilds enjoyed marching in processions to local churches on their patron saint's day. After a religious service they might have a feast in their guildhall. They gave money to local churches, monasteries, and convents to help the sick and poor.

living that helped put an end to feudalism and gave rise to the modern economic system of *capitalism*.

Craft and Merchant Guilds

The economic life of the towns was dominated by two kinds of guilds. *Craft guilds* were associations of skilled workers who carried on the same trade in a town, such as shoemakers, carpenters, and tailors. A craft guild was responsible for the quality and price of its members' products. It regulated the size

Town Governments and Leagues

Because of their wealth and power, the merchant guilds often dominated town governments. As town officials, the leading merchants sought to encourage the trade on which the prosperity of the town depended. For this reason they tried to get rid of feudal restrictions imposed by the lord or king who owned the land on which the town had been built. Sometimes town leaders obtained a *charter* from their ruler. This was a written contract that allowed the town certain rights. For example, the townspeople might be granted self-government in return for a lump sum of money and a promise to pay taxes each year.

Italian towns took the lead in shaking off feudal controls. Florence, Siena, Pisa, and Venice became small but powerful republics. Milan and other northern cities formed the *Lombard League.* By defeating the army of Emperor Frederick Barbarossa in 1176 at Legnano, they kept their political and economic independence.

During the thirteenth and fourteenth centuries a number of north German towns agreed to cooperate to increase their trade and to establish a monopoly of trade and fishing in the Baltic Sea. They formed an association known as the *Hanseatic League.* The Holy Roman Empire was too weak at the time to prevent this development. The cities of Lübeck and Hamburg were the leaders of this league, which became an international association that dominated trade in the North and Baltic seas. Its activities extended from London in the west to Novgorod, Russia, in the east. The League guarded and encouraged shipping expeditions of member towns. It promoted a system of uniform weights and measures as well as a uniform currency. It also tried to settle disputes among its members by peaceful means. The League had immense political and economic power until the fifteenth century when it began to decline.

Life in the Towns

Medieval towns might have between ten and forty thousand inhabitants. Paris with its 300,000 people was the largest city of Europe in 1450. Streets in most towns were dark, narrow, and noisy. There was a clatter of pedestrians and riders, of workers in the shops, and of delivery carts drawn by horses or oxen. Entertainers sometimes performed in the town squares. Church bells tolled the hours and called people to their prayers. Dogs, horses, and even pigs roamed the streets. Some townspeople kept chickens and cows in their private gardens.

Although the interior of a rich merchant's home was dark, it could be attractive. The rooms had wooden ceilings and walls paneled in wood. The doors were often beautifully carved. The floors might be of stone, wood, or tiles. There were tables and chairs with bright cushions. Cupboards and painted chests provided storage space. Beds were provided with cloth canopies for warmth and privacy. Quilts, blankets, and pillows added comfort. A large hearth in the kitchen supplied heat. Bedrooms usually had an open fireplace.

Sundays and holidays were times of celebration for the townspeople. As an observer of London in the twelfth century reported:

On feast days throughout the summer the young men indulge in the sports of archery, running, jumping, wrestling, hurling the javelin beyond a mark and fighting with sword and buckler. . . . In winter . . . swarms of young men issue forth to play games on the ice. . . . Others, more skilled at winter sports, put on their feet the shin-bones of animals, binding them firmly round their ankles, and, holding poles shod with iron in their hands, which they strike from time to time against the ice, they are propelled swift as a bird in flight or a bolt shot from an engine of war.

Women and Courtly Love

As you learned earlier, women had few legal rights in the early Middle Ages. The attitude of society was largely formed by the men of the Church and the nobility. On the one hand, women were looked upon with scorn by some people who believed that Eve, the first woman, had brought sin and death into the world. On the other hand, women were respected by others because of Mary, the mother of Christ.

Love for Mary was proclaimed by saints like Bernard of Clairvaux, by kings and nobles, by rich and poor townspeople, and by peasants in the fields. Churches and chapels were built in her name. Under the code of chivalry, knights performed brave deeds in her honor.

About the twelfth century, respect for Mary helped to form the basis for a new and romantic kind of love that a knight was supposed to feel for a noble lady. This involved the theory of *courtly love.*

Under the influence of Eleanor, Duchess of Aquitaine (1122?–1204), the nobility of Europe established a new form of social conduct. Eleanor had a long and influential life, negotiating on equal terms with kings, Popes, and emperors. As heiress to a great territory in southwestern France, she first married the man who would become King Louis VII of France. She went with him on the Second Crusade. Later she had her marriage annulled, and soon after married Louis' enemy, Henry II, who became king of England.

Eleanor's court at Poitiers, as well as the court of her daughter Marie of Champagne at Troyes, were important cultural centers. Great nobles became accustomed to a life of elaborate ceremonies in which noble ladies played an important part. Unlike the crude warriors of the early Middle Ages, the knights of this period took an interest in music and poetry. Knights and ladies conversed about the code of courtly love, which told how a nobleman might even fall in love with a married lady. There were complex rules for such relationships, which included treating the lady with honor and respect.

Women in the Towns

Courtly love was restricted to the nobility. In theory, women in towns were strictly controlled by their husbands. In fact, many wives were more or less equal to their husbands. They were busy from morning to night, looking after their children, supervising servants, preparing butter and cheese, and brewing beer and ale. They made wax candles, and often spun cloth for the family's clothing and linens. They shopped in local markets or at fairs.

When a husband was away, his wife often ran the business, kept the accounts, and informed him by letter of what was going on. Widows often carried on their husband's trade. They trained apprentices. A number of women owned shops and supervised trading operations on a large scale.

Single women were successful as owners of textile firms and as clothing merchants. Almost all women knew how to spin, and in the textile regions of Italy, England, and Flanders women were valued as skilled workers. Most craft guilds restricted membership to men only. On the whole, however, women were treated with respect in the towns both as housewives and as workers.

Check on Your Reading

1. What was the importance of the craft guilds? Of merchant guilds? Of town charters?
2. Describe the work and organization of the Hanseatic League.
3. In what ways did the position of women of the noble class change in this period?
4. What were the responsibilities of many women in towns?

3. Great Architecture and Art Are Created

After the year 1000, architects began to design buildings to meet the needs of an expanding society. Drawing on the achievements of Rome, Constantinople, and the Middle East, they developed new methods of constructing churches and castles, convents and hospitals, and city halls and private homes. They left works of great beauty that still express the creativity of the Middle Ages.

Romanesque Beginnings

In Italy and southern France, regions still full of monuments of the past, an interesting style of architecture developed. Because it owed a great deal to the buildings and sculpture of the Romans, it is called *Romanesque.* It dominated church architecture in the West from about 450 to 1150 A.D. Its features included thick walls, rounded arches, small windows, and handsome decorations.

San Miniato's Church at Florence (eleventh century) is a good example (see page 263). Its construction is basically simple: classical pillars, rounded arches, and walls of different colored marbles. The *apse,* or rounded section at the altar end of the church, is richly decorated with Byzantine mosaics.

In southern France, St. Trophime's Church at Arles (11th and 12th centuries) has an elaborate doorway that looks like a Roman triumphal arch. It is decorated with a sculpture of Christ in glory as well as statues of the apostles. (See page 263.)

The Romanesque style spread quickly to northern France, England, and Germany. At Vézelay in northern France, a new form of sculpture developed that was quite different from works in the classical tradition. A monumental statue of Christ over the church doorway at Vézelay is filled with vigor and religious enthusiasm. Rays of stone emerge from Christ's hands as symbols of the power given to Peter and the other apostles to preach the Gospel to the world. Below, on a smaller scale, moves a procession of the people of the earth. Their strangely agitated forms indicate the joy and excitement with which they are receiving the Christian message.

Gothic Splendor

About 1150, architects in northern France began to work out the principles of a different type of architecture. Writers in the eighteenth century,

The interior of the Romanesque church known as the Basilica of San Miniato in Florence, Italy.

them with *flying buttresses,* stone or wood structures against walls. In this way the stone roof could be supported without thick, massive walls. When the walls were no longer needed to support the roof, they could be made thinner and higher and the wall spaces filled with windows.

The Gothic style is characterized by pointed arches. This feature originally came from the Middle East by way of the Arabs. The pointed arch first appeared in some Romanesque buildings in areas where there was a strong Arabic influence, as in Spain and southern Italy. Gothic architects used the pointed arch for the crossed ribs that carried the weight of the roof to the pillars.

The change from the Romanesque to the Gothic style can be traced in a number of churches in northern France. In a burst of religious and civic enthusiasm, the great cathedrals of Paris, Chartres, Reims, Rouen, Amiens, and Bourges were begun.

These Gothic cathedrals reflected the Christian faith of the towns. Kings and queens, nobles, and townspeople contributed their money and efforts to

The Church of St. Trophime is another example of a Romanesque church. It was built in about 1150 in Arles, France.

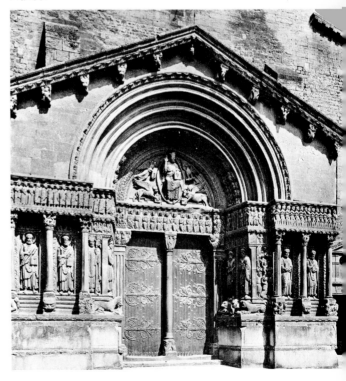

who admired only the Graeco-Roman style, called this building style "Gothic." To them it reflected the influence of the Goths, who had helped to destroy Roman civilization. Today we recognize the Gothic architects as brilliantly creative engineers and artists.

The architects of the second half of the eleventh century had several goals. They needed to build bigger churches for the increasing population. They also wanted to do away with the thick walls of the Romanesque churches, which had only narrow slits for windows. They sought a way to construct walls which would admit floods of light and yet support the weight of the roof.

To achieve their goals they invented new ways to support the weight of the roof. They gathered this weight at certain points by using arches and by supporting the arches by pillars. The vaults of the roof were supported by four crossed ribs, or arches, that carried the weight of the roof to the pillars of the aisles and to pillars built into the outside walls. To help the pillars in the outside walls bear the burden that was transferred to them, architects braced

the cathedrals. At Chartres, townspeople of all classes helped the workers drag heavy blocks of stone from the quarries for the church, whose construction reflected a tremendous civic pride.

Local Church leaders worked out an elaborate plan of religious symbols to be used in creating statues and stained glass windows. These were handed over as guides to the chief architect, assistant architects, and artists. Stonemasons, sculptors, and glass workers were hired to carry out the architect's detailed designs.

The Gothic style spread across Europe and even to the lands held by the Crusaders in Palestine. Massive castles were erected for defense. Beautiful halls and guildhalls were built. An outstanding example of a Gothic private home is Jacques Coeur's house at Bourges, France. Coeur, the son of a humble craftsman, became the richest merchant and banker in fifteenth-century France. He even lent large sums of money to the king of France. The comfortable rooms of Coeur's mansion are furnished with many personal touches, such as stone carvings of one of his ships and a portrait of him and his wife playing chess.

Check on Your Reading

1. What are the main differences between Romanesque and Gothic architecture?
2. Medieval churches have been called "storybooks in stone and glass." What kinds of stories did they tell to the people? Why was this important?

Various aspects of the splendor of Gothic architecture and art are shown on these pages. At the left on page 264, Amiens Cathedral is shown. It took several hundred years to build. At the right on page 264, notice the sculpture around an entrance to the Cathedral of Rouen. At the left, the house of a wealthy merchant and banker of Bourges, Jacques Coeur, competed in grandeur with the castles of nobles. At the left below, sculpture beside an entrance to Chartres Cathedral. At the right below, the center aisle of Cologne Cathedral that was built in a late Gothic style.

4. Universities and Learning

After the 1000s, the Church and the governments of towns and kings needed educated persons. So did the businesses of the growing numbers of bourgeoisie. At the same time a rebirth of classical learning was taking place in Europe, and many people were becoming interested in studying this field. To meet these needs, teachers and students developed organizations called "universities." The Latin word, "universitas," means "the corporation."

About seventy-five universities were established. Among the most important were the universities of Bologna (Italy), Paris (France), Oxford (England), and Toledo (Spain).

The Founding of Universities

Universities developed in two ways. At Bologna a great teacher taught law with such success that students from far and wide were drawn to the city. Soon the students organized a guild that regulated just what books had to be taught, and how much teaching the professors had to do in return for the students' fees. The students were also able to fix prices for their books and rents for their rooms. The professors organized their own guild, which regulated the qualifications students had to meet to obtain a doctorate degree in law. The pattern set at Bologna was followed at the universities of Naples and Padua in Italy, at Montpellier in France, and at Salamanca in Spain.

At Paris the university grew out of the cathedral school of Notre Dame and two other church schools within the city. The focus was on philosophy and theology. Soon crowds of students came from many regions to hear brilliant professors like Abélard. The Left Bank of Paris became known as the *Latin Quarter*, since this was the language of the professors and students.

The chancellor (head) of the university refused to let guilds of students or professors have control in Paris. The chancellor and his assistants decided which students were entitled to the master's and doctor's degrees. In time the university was recognized by the Pope and the king of France as a self-governing association of professors and scholars. Student life was not always peaceful. There were frequent riots between "town and gown"; that is, between townspeople and students.

Universities were organized according to the system of the University of Paris in England, Germany, and Flanders. Oxford was founded about 1167 by a group of English students returning from Paris. After a students' riot, a band of Oxford students and professors left to start a new university at Cambridge. In many university towns the students lived in rented rooms, more or less on their own. Later rich benefactors of certain universities founded "colleges," or residence halls. Some of these colleges are still in existence at Oxford and Cambridge.

The Influence of Muslim and Jewish Scholars

After the Muslim conquest of areas in the Middle East and North Africa in the seventh century, the works of Greek scholars were translated into Arabic. The Arabs not only studied the books of the Greeks and the Romans, but also made their own valuable advances in arithmetic, algebra, and trigonometry. They were particularly gifted in medicine.

During the twelfth century the achievements of learned Muslims and Jews were transmitted to western Europeans in a number of places. The first place was the Middle East during the Crusades. The next was the island of Sicily, which Christian forces reconquered from the Muslims in the tenth century. Of special importance was Spain, large parts of which were under Muslim rule in the Middle Ages.

Many of the writings of the Greeks had been translated long ago into Arabic or Hebrew. They were now retranslated into Spanish, often by Jewish scholars. From Spanish they were then translated into Latin. Although there were some inaccuracies in these translations, the end result was a greatly increased supply of information about philosophy and the natural sciences for the Christian world.

Thanks to such writings, people in western Europe rediscovered the teachings of important physicians of ancient times, Hippocrates and Galen. They began to dissect in order to learn about human anatomy. Surgical methods improved, and some gains were made in treating diseases.

Science

We have already learned about a number of practical inventions of the Middle Ages—the horse collar, compass, and sternpost rudder. Mechanical clocks were developed also at this time. By making it possible to count the hours more accurately, clocks had a lasting effect on the lives of people everywhere, especially of workers.

After the First Crusade, windmills were introduced into Europe. Their power was used to cast iron, saw wood, and full (stretch and moisten) heavy woolen cloth. Since most village blacksmiths were unable to repair complex windmills, a guild of millwrights grew up. They may have been the first mechanics on an organized basis. Traveling from region to region, they repaired and constructed gears not only for mills but also for dams and sluices used in canals and irrigation works.

Despite these technical advances, medieval people made little progress in scientific theory. Most scholars were churchmen who were reluctant to explore ideas opposed by the Church. Acceptance of the teachings of Greek scholars hindered independent scientific research to some degree. Although Aristotle had not done much practical research, many of his statements were accepted without question. The geographer Ptolemy had taught that the earth was the center of the universe. This incorrect idea was held by most Europeans for centuries.

The Rise of the Schoolmen

Great thinkers began to reexamine Christian teachings in the light of the writings of the Greek philosophers and other scholars. They were known as the *schoolmen*, or *scholastics*. Their system of thought is called *scholasticism.*

A brilliant young teacher at the school of Paris, Peter Abélard (1079-1142) became impatient with the discussions of the schoolmen. He wrote a book called *Sic et Non* (Yes and No) in which he opposed the idea of accepting the authority of the Church without question. Many churchmen objected to Abélard's approach, and his book was condemned by the Church. After much turmoil Abélard found peace in a monastery.

The greatest of the schoolmen was St. Thomas Aquinas (1225?-1274). He was an Italian Dominican friar who studied at Monte Cassino, Naples, and Paris. The aim of his great book, *Summa Theologica,* was to reconcile the beliefs of the Church with the philosophy of Aristotle. He was convinced that there did not need to be conflict between reason and faith. As he put it:

> Therefore some intelligent being exists by whom all natural things are directed to their end; and this being we call God.

After some hesitation the Church enthusiastically endorsed St. Thomas Aquinas' philosophy as a correct statement of Christian teaching.

Check on Your Reading

1. How did Muslim and Jewish scholars help the growth of learning in western Europe? Give some examples.
2. Name some technical inventions of the Middle Ages. Why was little progress made in scientific theory?
3. Describe the differences between the organization of the universities at Paris and Bologna.
4. What was St. Thomas Aquinas' position on faith and reason?

5. Nations Develop

Between 1300 and 1500 the feudal system declined in western Europe. The great landowners were not able to give a satisfactory system of law and order to the people. The nobles waged too many wars among themselves. They had too many private law courts. They issued too many private currencies. Often they hindered trade by taxing merchants crossing their lands. As the towns and trade expanded, people in the towns turned to kings for a stable form of government. The kings organized nations, or national states, in England, France, Spain, and other parts of Europe.

The term *nation* refers to a people who feel united in a common loyalty to a country that occupies a definite territory and has its own independent existence. Many factors helped unite people into a nation. Geographic barriers, such as mountains and large bodies of water, sometimes separated and protected one group from another. A common government played an important role in the development of national states. As feudalism disintegrated, kings were able to set up a strong central administration, including the beginnings of a bureaucracy.

Finally, a common language and common traditions are also factors in forming a nation. People who speak the same language develop their own forms of literature and songs. They feel close to other groups who speak as they do and who follow the same way of life.

The Norman Conquest of England

Celts, Romans, Angles, Saxons, and Vikings—all had left their mark on England. The last group of conquerors were the Normans.

This scene from the Bayeux tapestry shows part of the Norman fleet under Duke William sailing for England in 1066.

In 1066 William the Conqueror, Duke of Normandy, led a strong army of his Norman followers in an attack on England. William claimed the right to the English throne. At the Battle of Hastings the Normans killed the last Anglo-Saxon king and took control of the country. William was proclaimed king, and proceeded to organize a strong central government. He rewarded his followers by granting them fiefs. He then forced them and all landowners of the kingdom to swear an oath of allegiance to him. Because of William's possessions in Normandy, England was deeply involved in French affairs until 1453.

At first the Norman conquerors felt superior to the rest of the population. Gradually, however, the French-speaking Normans intermarried with the Anglo-Saxons. Today the people of England are the descendants of all the different groups that settled in the country.

A System of Law Unites the Nation

About the middle of the twelfth century Henry II (king from 1154–1189) became king of England and Duke of Normandy. By his marriage to Eleanor of Aquitaine, he added so many lands to his French possessions that he was more powerful than the king of France. Henry tried to replace the chaotic system of feudal justice that varied from place to place with the "king's justice."

In 1166 Henry issued the Edict of Clarendon. It stated:

. . . twelve of the more legal men of [each district] . . . [should investigate] whether there is . . . any man who has been accused or publicly suspected of himself being a robber, or murderer, or thief. . . .

Such an individual was to be brought to trial before one or more of the judges King Henry sent throughout the country.

Henry's edict contributed to the development of the jury system. A *grand jury* came to mean a group of people who decide whether or not an accused person should be brought to trial. Later a system was organized that involved a *petit jury*. This was a trial jury that might take over some duties of judges. A petit jury was a group of people who decided the guilt or innocence of an accused person at a trial. Today both grand and petit juries are found in our own country.

King Henry's purpose in setting up his judicial system was to tighten his control over the country by enforcing justice. However, by calling some people to participate in the legal system, the king also helped the development of a democratic institution. His jurors had to investigate facts and swear that such facts were true. In this way they gained experience in governing themselves.

Trial by jury in an early English law court. The Edict of Clarendon issued by Henry II was important in the development of the jury system.

sions. Centuries later, common law was introduced into the English colonies in North America. It became the basis of the United States legal system.

The Growth of Representative Government in England

John (king from 1199-1216), a son of Henry II, became king of England at the end of the twelfth century. He lost land and prestige as a result of quarrels with the king of France and the Pope. In addition, he annoyed members of the Great Council of England by trying to collect illegal taxes from them. The Great Council was an association of the most important members of the kingdom—nobles, religious leaders, and rich landowners. It met to advise the king on matters of policy and taxation. It also served as a court of justice. In 1215, a group of barons threatened to attack the king if he did not assure them of certain rights. The king gave in and affixed his royal seal on a famous document known as the *Magna Carta*, or Great Charter. It limited the king's powers in a number of ways. Among the conditions he agreed to were the following:

No freeman [most freemen were nobles or religious leaders] shall be taken, or imprisoned, or . . . outlawed, or exiled, or in any way harmed . . . save by the lawful judgment of his peers or by the law of the land.

No taxes except the customary feudal ones shall be levied without the consent of the Great Council.

[The nobles] shall elect twenty-five barons of the kingdom . . . who ought with all their power [see that the king does not violate the Magna Carta].

At this time the Magna Carta represented only an agreement between the king and his great landowners. Nevertheless it became a landmark in the growth of democracy. It helped establish the principle that the king's actions had to conform to the customs and laws of England. After most people in England won freedom from serfdom in the fifteenth century, the Magna Carta was referred to as a guarantee of basic human rights for even the poorest members of society.

During the thirteenth century, King Edward I (king from 1272-1307) needed funds to carry on a war. He summoned his Grand Council, to which he also invited two knights from every shire and two

The early judges whom Henry sent around England discovered that some customs differed from region to region, while others were more or less the same. Wisely these judges tried to base their decisions on the "common customs of the realm." As a result, *common law*—a uniform system of laws for all England based on common custom—gradually replaced the many laws based on local custom. If no uniform custom could be found, the judges sometimes drew up new rules, which then became a part of common law. A distinctive feature of English common law was the development of the *case system*. This means that cases decided by judges were considered sources of law and *precedents* for future deci-

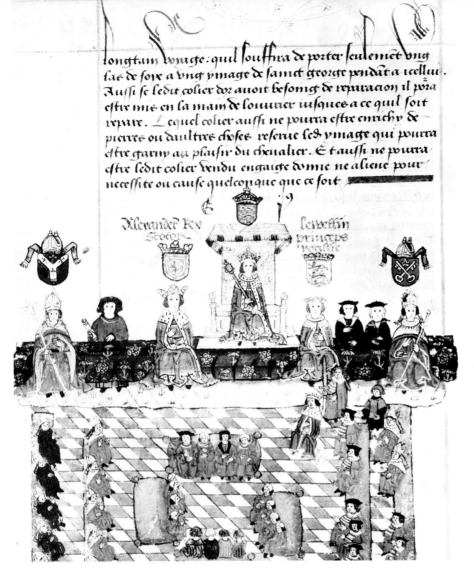

longtam ymage: qui souffra de porter seulemet ung
sae de soye a ung ymage de sainct george pendat a icellui.
Auffi se ledit colier doz auoit besoing de reparacion il pora
estre mis en la main de soruuier iusques a ce quil soit
repair. Lequel colier auffi ne pourra estre enrichy de
picrres ou daultres chofes referue les ymage qui pourra
estre garny au plaifir du chenalier. Et tauffi ne pourra
estre ledit colier vendu engaigte dorme ne aliene pour
neceffite ou caufe quelconque que ce foit

Alexander Rex Scotor.

Leowllin princeps wallie

A meeting of Parliament with King Edward I at the end of the thirteenth century.

townsmen from every borough. (The *shires* and *boroughs* were administrative divisions of the kingdom.) Some historians have called this gathering the "model Parliament." The term *Parliament* comes from the French word *parler,* meaning "to speak."

At first, members of Parliament met in three separate groups or *estates.* The first estate included members of the clergy. The second estate was made up of earls, barons, and knights. The third estate consisted of representatives of the towns. Gradually the nobles and higher clergy were organized in the *House of Lords.* The knights and townsmen eventually became the *House of Commons.*

Parliament was not representative by modern standards, since few people had the right to vote.

At first, its members' main task was to approve taxes. This was an important power since Parliament could sometimes force the king to accept reforms by refusing to grant taxes unless he put through changes requested by Parliament. After 1400 Parliament won the right to help make the laws.

Henry VII Strengthens the Central Government

During the thirteenth and fourteenth centuries England became involved in a war with the French. The English kings wanted to increase their already large holdings in France. This led to what is known as the *Hundred Years' War,* which lasted from 1337 to 1453. The fighting was not continuous;

periods of truce were followed by periods of war. We shall learn more about the war when we consider French history (see page 272). In the end, the English were driven out of France. Of their vast holdings in France only the port of Calais remained to them.

Afterward, England was split by a savage civil war between two families who wanted the crown. One group—the House of Lancaster—took a red rose as its symbol. The House of York was represented by a white rose. Their struggle is known as the *War of the Roses* (1455-1485). In the end the House of Lancaster won, and Henry Tudor became Henry VII (king from 1485-1509). He founded the House of Tudor, which ruled England until 1603.

Henry VII developed a strong central government. The king weakened the power of the nobles. He collected taxes efficiently. He won the support of traders and other business leaders by encouraging and supporting their activities. England had several of the features of a strong nation by 1500. It had a Parliament and a king who was in firm control of his land and his subjects. Its people spoke a common language and shared common customs.

The Early Kings of France

In the tenth century some feudal lords in northern France elected a noble named Hugh Capet as king of a small region, with his capital at Paris. Hugh Capet (king from 987-996) and his successors slowly increased their holdings. From this beginning the kingdom of France grew. People in the towns sought the protection of the king against local nobles. During the Crusades many nobles left their lands and homes to fight in the East. This weakened feudalism and strengthened the monarchy.

Philip Augustus (king from 1180-1223) had a long and successful reign. He increased the royal land holdings and power in many ways. A military victory against King John of England in 1214 enabled Philip Augustus to take over some of the territory once ruled by the king of England. He appointed men to public office who were loyal to him, not to feudal nobles. He improved the administration of finances, and made Paris the permanent capital of the whole kingdom.

Joan of Arc: Symbol of a People

The developing French national unity was put to a severe test during the Hundred Years' War.

This painting from a fifteenth century manuscript depicts the Battle of Agincourt. The English foot soldiers armed with longbows and arrows defeated the French knights in their heavy armor.

Joan of Arc leads the French troops in battle against the English.

King Edward III of England (king from 1327-1377) claimed to be the rightful king of France and led an army of invasion in 1346. The heavily armed knights of France were no match for English footsoldiers with their powerful longbows. Many French knights were either killed outright or taken prisoner and held for ransom.

In addition to military defeat, the people of France were overwhelmed by peasant uprisings and a terrible plague—the Black Death—that killed almost a third of the population of Europe. During periods of truce in the war with England, bands of soldiers under the orders of lawless captains went about the countryside killing and looting innocent people.

In the 1420s English armies held Paris and much of France. They were allied with the powerful Duke of Burgundy, who ruled a vast territory in eastern France. The French kingdom was rapidly falling apart.

In this crisis a young Frenchwoman rallied her country's forces. She was Joan of Arc (1412-1431), a deeply religious peasant who claimed to have heard the "voices" of saints. These voices, she believed, instructed her to restore the French ruler to power and to thrust the English armies out of France. Although many mocked her almost hopeless cause, Joan finally received the support of a few high officials.

With difficulty Joan convinced Charles, the weak French heir to the throne, to believe in her mission. A French army was placed under her command. Joan boldly issued a warning to the enemy:

> You, men of England, have no right to be in this kingdom of France, the King of Heaven commands you through me . . . to go back where you belong; which if you fail to do, I will make such a *ha-hai* [commotion] as will be eternally remembered.

When the English refused to leave French soil, Joan and her forces attacked. What a *ha-hai* it was! She and her forces won a resounding victory over the English at Orleans.

Joan then led Charles across France to Reims, where he was crowned in the cathedral as Charles VII, king of France. Not long afterward Joan was captured before Paris and sold to the English. She was tried for heresy and burnt alive at the age of nineteen. Joan became a national symbol that inspired the French with pride in their country.

France Becomes a Unified Nation

After the death of Joan of Arc, Charles VII made peace with the Burgundians. He reorganized his forces, and won support from the townspeople. French artillery units outfought the English and their longbows. All these developments helped the French drive the English out of France. When the Hundred Years' War ended, the French regained almost all their national territory.

An important long-range result of the Hundred Years' War was that it helped to strengthen the position of the French king and his government. During the war the wealthy townsmen and traders had become financial supporters of the king because their business activities depended on having a stable and unified government. Many nobles were killed; others lost control of much of their land. The king had used an army paid by the national government, and he did not have to rely on his nobles for military assistance. All three developments aided the growth of the central government and nation.

France recovered rapidly from the war under a forceful and crafty ruler, Louis XI (king from 1461–1481). He encouraged trade, organized a postal system, and added new territories to the kingdom. He also increased the control of the monarchy over the feudal lords and set up an efficient central administration. When the fifteenth century ended, France was well on its way to becoming a stable nation.

The Unification of Spain

Spain occupies most of the Iberian Peninsula. In 711 an army of *Moors* from North Africa had overrun the kingdom of the Visigoths and conquered most of the Iberian Peninsula. They ruled Spain for almost eight hundred years.

As the Moors swept into Spain, defenders of the Christian kingdom of the Visigoths fell back into the mountains of the northwest. From remote strongholds the Christians began the *Reconquista*—a long

crusade to push the Moors out of the Iberian Peninsula. They declared that they fought for "God and St. James." The center of their religious faith was the church of St. James (Santiago de Compostela) in the northwestern corner of the country. Slowly the Christian armies moved southward, capturing first Toledo and later Valencia. One of the Spanish national heroes was a famous warrior, the Cid. After a Christian victory in 1219, Córdoba and Seville fell to the Spaniards. In numerous battles the armies of the Christian states took over more and more Moorish territory.

Queen Isabella and King Ferdinand from their tomb in Granada, Spain.

In 1469 Isabella, the future ruler of Castile and León, married Ferdinand of Aragon. Their marriage helped unify all of the Iberian Peninsula except for the Christian kingdoms of Navarre and Portugal, and Granada, which was the last Muslim stronghold.

In a war that lasted ten years the Christian armies captured Granada, thus ending the *Reconquista*. After Isabella's death King Ferdinand annexed the part of Navarre that lies south of the Pyrenees. Spain was now a unified kingdom, and eventually Madrid in Castile became its capital. The dialect of Castile was becoming the national language.

The victory of the Christian armies was followed by a persecution of the Jews and Muslims. Many were forced to convert to Christianity. Those who refused baptism were expelled from Spain. The *Inquisition,* an institution designed to fight heresy, and government decrees deprived the kingdom of some of its most gifted and productive subjects.

Portugal, which occupies much of the western seacoast of the Iberian Peninsula, became a separate kingdom under King Alfonso in 1143. During the wars of the *Reconquista* all Portugal was liberated from the Moors in the thirteenth century. Lisbon on the Tagus River developed into the capital. Portugal was to lead Europe's drive for expansion overseas.

Check on Your Reading

1. What factors helped unite people into nations?
2. What was the significance of the Magna Carta?
3. Describe how the English Parliament developed from the king's Grand Council.
4. What effect did the Hundred Years' War have on France? On England?
5. What was the *Reconquista?* How was it brought to a close?

---

6. Literature Is Created in Vernacular Languages

Throughout the Middle Ages a number of people throughout western Europe continued to speak and write Latin. Latin was the international language of the Church and of educated people. At the same time, however, the average person no longer understood classical Latin. Slowly *vernacular languages* evolved. They were the languages spoken and understood by the people. Italian, French, Spanish, and Portuguese developed in regions where the influence of Latin remained strong. In other parts of western Europe—Germany, Scandinavia, and England—a number of Germanic languages were spoken. On the fringes of western Europe, Celtic tongues were found in Ireland, Scotland, Wales, Cornwall, and Brittany.

At different times people began to create songs, poems, and prose writings in their own languages. Some of their works are admired and read today.

Literature for Warriors

Knights in their castles enjoyed especially the *chansons de geste.* These were a series of ballads revolving around the same general subject, and focused on the deeds and deaths of heroes. One of the greatest chansons de geste is the French *Song of Roland,* which tells of Count Roland, a nephew of Charlemagne. According to the legend, Roland was the leader of the Frankish army's rear guard in the Pyrenees. Attacked by Moors, he and his companions fought fiercely to the end. The example of Roland is said to have inspired William the Conqueror's followers at the Battle of Hastings.

In Spain an epic about the Cid was much admired. In Iceland the sagas related in prose the adventures of the Vikings.

Stories of Romance

At the courts of Eleanor of Aquitaine and other noble ladies, a new literature developed. It included stories of King Arthur and the Knights of the Round Table. Poets known as *troubadours* in France and as *minnesingers* in Germany composed songs in praise of courtly love. *The Song of the Niebelungen,* an epic about Siegfried and Brunhild, brought together legends from Scandinavia and Germany.

Fabliaux and the Revival of the Theater

All the works described above were intended mainly for an aristocratic audience. After the towns became important, the townspeople enjoyed a new kind of literature. The amusing *fabliaux,* or fables, were down-to-earth stories of everyday life in which animals poked fun at the foolishness of people. Such animal stories were very popular, particularly stories of Reynard the Fox, who always managed to outwit the Lion. Townspeople identified Reynard with themselves and Lion with the feudal overlords.

With the Church's encouragement, plays were created for audiences in towns. Morality plays like *Everyman* were presented in a square in front of the cathedral. Miracle and mystery plays were also written and provided with elaborate stage settings. The miracle plays showed Mary, the Queen of heaven, responding to men and women who asked for her help in their problems. The mystery plays might include serious scenes from the *Old Testament* and *New Testament,* as well as incidents about Noah and the ark.

This frontispiece from a book by Chaucer shows the poet reading to an audience of nobles.

Dante and Chaucer

Two great poets in the fourteenth century wrote in the native languages of their homelands. The Italian poet Dante (1265-1321) took his readers on an imaginary trip through hell, purgatory, and heaven in *The Divine Comedy.* This great poem has been compared to a Gothic cathedral, and it is regarded as a magnificent expression of medieval thought. Dante hoped to explain "the Love [God] that moves the sun and the other stars." Other writers in Italy followed his example of writing in the vernacular, which led eventually to the development of modern Italian.

Geoffrey Chaucer (c. 1340-1400) vividly de-scribed in his *Canterbury Tales* a group of pilgrims gathering at an inn south of London. They are about to go on a pilgrimage to the shrine of St. Thomas à Becket at Canterbury. In the stories they tell to amuse each other on the journey, we catch a glimpse of how people of different social backgrounds lived and what they thought. Chaucer used the East Midland dialect of England.

Two French Writers of the Fifteenth Century

Christine of Pisan (1363-1430?) was the daughter of an Italian astrologer. When her father received a position at the court of the king of France,

Christine went with him to Paris and married a Frenchman. Left a widow with three children, she made a living as a writer. Her writings include a poem in memory of Joan of Arc and a prose essay, *The Book of the Three Virtues,* which is a spirited defense of women's rights and abilities.

François Villon (1431–1463?) was a fine French lyric poet. Although born to a poor family, he was admitted to the University of Paris through the help of his uncle, a priest. Villon took his bachelor's degree at an early age, but was more attracted to students' taverns and to the life of criminals of Paris than to a career as a scholar. He participated in a number of break-ins, riots, and violence.

François Villon was both a representative of the medieval scene and a poet of city life. His verses vividly depict the life of the rapidly growing city of Paris. Some of his poems express his love of his war-torn country. He ridiculed the powerful and the rich, and joyfully described the rowdy life of students, thieves, and tricksters. However, he was also intensely religious, writing beautiful poems to the Virgin Mary.

Check on Your Reading

1. Why did Latin survive as an international language?
2. What were the *chansons de geste?* For what audience were they intended?
3. How did writers encourage the development of vernacular languages?
4. What were the *fabliaux?* For what group in society were they written?
5. Why are the writings of Dante and Chaucer still read today?

LET'S MEET THE PEOPLE

John Brid: A Guild Baker

On June 4, 1327, Sheriff Roger Chauntecler and a group of aldermen gathered at a London Guildhall to hear the charges against John Brid, baker. The accusations were serious. It was charged that John "did skillfully and artfully cause a certain hole to be made upon a [baking] table of his . . . after the manner of a mouse-trap in which mice are caught. . . ." It was said further that when his neighbors brought their dough to be baked into bread, Brid placed it on the table just above the hole. Then:

> . . . John had one of his household, . . . sitting in secret beneath [the hole in the table] and carefully opening it, . . . and bit by bit craftily [withdrawing] some of the dough . . . falsely, wickedly, and maliciously; to the great loss of all his neighbours.

Neighbors now testified that they had been cheated—that the hole in the baking table had robbed them of part of their bread—that the baker was a thief. The men judging the case listened carefully to the evidence. They then handed down their verdict: GUILTY!

The Saturday after John Brid's case was settled, the mayor, aldermen, and sheriffs took steps to prevent any further stealing by a baker. They issued a decree that declared:

> All those of the bakers . . ., beneath whose tables with holes dough had been found, should be put upon the pillory, with a certain quantity of such dough hung from their necks; . . . and they should so remain upon the pillory all day.

John Brid would not cheat in the future. If he did, his guild would take away his right to bake—and the sheriff would hang around his neck the cold white dough that branded him THIEF!

This sketch is based on an account in "Memorials of London," edited by H. T. Riley, in *The Portable Medieval Reader,* David McKay Company, 1955.

CHAPTER REVIEW

Think and Discuss

1. What conditions are necessary for the growth of large-scale trade between different regions and countries?
2. Compare the reasons for the growth of medieval towns and cities with those responsible for the growth of cities today.
3. Is it true that groups first gain economic rights and then political power? Give reasons for your answer.
4. Joan of Arc became a symbol of French unity. Do you think symbols are important in building national pride? Give reasons for your answer.
5. What links were there between the growth of towns and the building of Gothic cathedrals?
6. Why do you think that universities developed after 1100?
7. How do you think that the *Reconquista* helped Spain develop a sense of being a nation?
8. How do you explain the fact that the power of the English kings was gradually restricted while the power of the French kings became more autocratic?

Past and Present

1. Religion stimulated people in the Middle Ages to achieve many things. What stirs people to achieve today?

2. How does a medieval craft guild compare with a modern labor union? A merchant guild with a local Chamber of Commerce?
3. How are modern universities similar to, or different from, medieval ones?
4. Explain how the *petit* and *grand* juries function in your state.
5. The struggle for representative government in England has had an important influence on life in the United States today. What developments in the United States during the last fifty years do you think will have an important influence on life a hundred years from now?

Activities

1. Write a report on one of the early bankers: Jacques Coeur in France, the Fuggers of Germany, or the Medicis of Italy.
2. Read a modern version of the *Canterbury Tales, Beowulf,* or the *Song of Roland.* Give an oral report emphasizing what you have learned about medieval life from your reading.
3. Make a list of the achievements of the people of the Middle Ages. Explain how some of them are important to us today.
4. Write a report on the Black Death. What were its effects on economic and social conditions, feudalism, and the emancipation of serfs?
5. Write a report on the influence of Queen Eleanor of Acquitaine on cultural developments.

16

New Ways of Thinking Change Europe

KEYNOTE

Leonardo da Vinci, the famous Italian painter, was talented in many fields: anatomy, architecture, engineering, geology, mathematics, map-making, music, and optics. He was fascinated by all kinds of natural phenomena, especially by the flight of birds. Leonardo believed that human beings also could learn to fly by imitating the movements of a bird's wings. Although his experiments with gliders and parachutes were unsuccessful, his example inspired later inventors such as the Wright brothers.

Leonardo's interest in many aspects of the world around him was typical of the period in history known as the *Renaissance*. Renaissance means a "rebirth." The artists and scholars of this period sought to revive the spirit and achievements of the ancient Greek and Roman artists, poets, and scientists. They also eagerly explored new ideas and experiences.

The Renaissance began in Italy, and gradually spread to many European countries. It led to great achievements in the arts and to important discoveries in the sciences. This spirit of inquiry also helped cause the Protestant Reformation, in which almost half the people of Europe threw off the authority of the Popes and broke away from the Roman Catholic Church.

This painting from the Medici Palace in Florence shows members of the family.

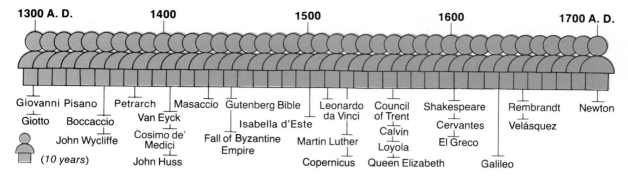

| 1300 A.D. | 1400 | 1500 | 1600 | 1700 A.D. |

Giovanni Pisano | Petrarch | Masaccio | Gutenberg Bible | Leonardo da Vinci | Council of Trent | Shakespeare | Rembrandt | Newton
Giotto | Boccaccio | Van Eyck | Isabella d'Este | | Calvin | Cervantes | Velásquez
John Wycliffe | Cosimo de' Medici | Fall of Byzantine Empire | Martin Luther | Loyola | El Greco
(10 years) | John Huss | | Copernicus | Queen Elizabeth | Galileo

1. The Renaissance Develops

There is no agreement among historians about the year when the Renaissance began. Most people would agree, however, that the changes we associate with the Renaissance began about the fourteenth century. In certain lands on the fringe of the continent—such as Russia—the Renaissance did not appear at all.

Major Changes in European Life

The transition from the Middle Ages to the Renaissance was gradual. Many medieval ways of looking at life persisted into later times. Major political, economic, and social changes during the Middle Ages helped stimulate the new Renaissance way of life. As the power of rulers increased, people were able to travel with greater safety in Europe. Men and women from widely separate regions were able to meet and exchange ideas.

Because of the more settled conditions of life, more and more trading companies were organized. Through these companies an ever-growing number of people were able to invest in business enterprises and to share in the profits. As members of the bourgeoisie extended their trading activities, they grew richer. The Italian banking system expanded to strengthen commercial investments and money transactions in many lands.

Cities and towns grew with the growth of business and trade. Merchants and manufacturers wanted attractive buildings both for personal dwellings and for the civic activities of their cities. Beautiful works of art were also desired as part of an increased enjoyment of life. Artists were paid to create paintings and works of sculpture for well-to-do art lovers.

About this time the use of movable type in Europe greatly stimulated the exchange of ideas. (People in China and Korea had movable type as early as the eleventh century.) In the 1450s some printers of Mainz, Germany, began to produce books from movable metal type. The man generally credited with this important development is Johann Gutenberg, although he probably had a number of helpers. He printed the *Bible* in movable type about 1456. Knowledge of the new printing process spread quickly across Europe, and printing presses were set up in many cities.

In the Middle Ages all books had been copied slowly by hand. Only Church leaders, kings and princes, or wealthy persons could own a library. Now typesetters were able to arrange individual letters of movable type to form words, sentences, and pages. When ink was applied to the type, many impressions of each page were made. Then the type could be disassembled and used over and over. Thus, hundreds of copies of a book could be produced and offered for sale at a reasonable price. Now many people could buy the writings of the classical authors. Later, printing greatly helped to spread new ideas and new books across Europe.

In 1490 Aldus Manutius (1449-1515) set up at Venice, Italy, a press that turned out beautifully printed books by ancient Greek and Latin authors. Manutius was himself a careful scholar and a talented book designer, and he was responsible for the designing of *italic type*. The greatest scholars of the day were his friends, and frequently visited his printing rooms. Manutius' elegant books were eagerly purchased by lovers of literature, and are regarded today as masterpieces of bookmaking.

The Renaissance Begins in Italy

It is not surprising that the Renaissance began in Italy. The memory and respect for Roman greatness had never died out there. Roman ruins were all around the people. The feudal system had not struck deep roots in this land where some city life

A terra-cotta bust of Lorenzo de' Medici is by Andrea Verrocchio.

Florence under the Medici

Florence provides an excellent example of the rise of an Italian city-state. An inland city on the Arno River, it was a center of the wool and silk trades and of banking. Around the city were many farms, rich vineyards, olive groves, and herds of goats and sheep. In 1422 Florence had seventy-two banks. The *florin*—the gold coin of Florence—was accepted all over Italy and Europe. The city was surrounded by a high stone wall with sturdy gates. Tall defensive towers marked the well-built palaces of the leading families.

Florence was also noted for the violence of its political life. Great families engaged in quarrels among themselves for control of the government. In 1378, the cloth makers rioted to demand their democratic rights, burning down the palaces of the rich and looting their possessions. When order was restored, one of the banking families—the Medici—slowly and cautiously took control of the city. Between 1434 and 1471 they paid more than 660,000 gold florins for taxes, charities, and public buildings.

The career of Cosimo de' Medici (1389-1464) illustrates conditions in Florence at that time. As a young man, Cosimo was sent on a tour of the Medici banking interests in Germany, France, Flanders (now split between Belgium and France), and Rome. On his return to Florence, he became involved in a political dispute and had to take refuge in Venice. When political conditions at home changed, Cosimo returned. From 1434 until his death he was master of Florence.

After Cosimo became immensely rich through international trade, he turned his attention to scholarship. He collected works of ancient Greek and Latin writers. He was founder of the Platonic Academy, whose members were eager to reconcile Greek philosophy with Christian teachings. Cosimo was a devout Christian and an art lover. He attended Mass every morning in the private chapel of his palace. On the chapel walls was Benozzo Gozzoli's fresco, *Journey of the Magi*, in which Cosimo himself was shown with four members of his family. (See page 278.)

Cosimo's grandson Lorenzo (1449-1492) was known as "the Magnificent." As a youth he was depicted as one of the Magi in his grandfather's favorite painting. Lorenzo was a practical man of business and politics. He was also a generous patron of the arts and a talented poet. His verses in

survived. Trade went on despite the difficulties of travel. From the time of the Crusades, city living and trade blossomed in ports like Venice, Pisa, and Genoa whose ships carried Crusaders to the Holy Land. Commercial ties with the cities of the Middle East and other parts of Europe first developed in Italy. Italian bankers and traders accumulated great fortunes through international commerce.

In theory, Italy was a part of the Holy Roman Empire, with the exception of Rome and its surroundings, which were ruled by the Pope. In fact, however, the emperors were not able to supervise from Germany their possessions in Italy. Because Italy was not under a strong central government, its many rich city-states developed their own political systems. Florence thrived under the Medici merchant-princes. Milan dominated Lombardy from the great castle of its dukes. The shrewd *doges* or dukes of Venice ruled over the region of Venetia and other territories along the Adriatic Sea.

praise of love and the beauties of nature are filled with a spirit typical of certain aspects of the Italian Renaissance. He wrote:

Let those who wish to be happy be so;
There's nothing sure about tomorrow.

Check on Your Reading

1. About when did the Renaissance begin?
2. What were some of the changes that helped cause the Renaissance?
3. Who was Johann Gutenberg? Who was Aldus Manutius?
4. Why did the Renaissance begin in Italy?
5. What were some of the activities of the Medici?

2. The Renaissance Flowers in Italy

The achievements of the people of Italy in the arts, literature, music, and other forms of creativity changed the ways Europeans thought about themselves, how they lived, and what they wanted out of life. There was a shift from the attitudes of the Middle Ages, when most people were dominated by a fear of the world to come. Many Renaissance men and women eagerly sought fame and glory in the present life. They believed in the value of the individual. This attitude is called *humanism* because, inspired by the civilizations of classical Greece and Rome, it emphasizes the importance of human concerns. Although humanism did not displace Christianity as an explanation of human life, it had great influence on many people.

The Rebirth of Ancient Greek and Roman Culture

During the Middle Ages, Muslim and Jewish scholars in the Middle East and Spain had transmitted to western Europeans many of the long-forgotten writings and scientific ideas of ancient Greece and Rome. Around 1453, as the Byzantine Empire came under siege from the Ottoman Turks, many Greek scholars fled to the West. They were welcomed in cities such as Florence, Rome, and Padua, where they often became teachers of Greek. Their arrival brought about a revival of interest in the ancient Greek language and culture.

Petrarch and the Humanists

A leader in the revival of classical learning was the Italian poet Petrarch (1304-1374), who became famous as an early humanist. Petrarch's father sent him to the University of Bologna to study for a law career. Petrarch, however, was so attracted by the classical writers and their works that he neglected his legal studies. His father then removed all his Latin books except the works of Cicero and St. Augustine, which his son begged to be allowed to keep. From Cicero he learned how to write a pure, classical Latin. From St. Augustine he acquired a combination of Christian idealism and the philosophy of Plato.

As a young man Petrarch fell deeply in love with Laura, a young woman who died in 1348 during the Black Death. Petrarch never forgot her, however, and wrote a series of Italian sonnets and other poems in her honor. These poems strike a note of tenderness and respect that is still fresh and moving after six centuries. Petrarch also wrote a long epic poem, *Africa*, in classical Latin verse. He thought *Africa* was his masterpiece, but modern readers judge it far less interesting than his Italian poems to Laura.

Petrarch had a wide range of interests: politics, music, gardening, and travel. One day he and his brother climbed a mountain in southern France purely for the pleasure of the view. He wrote about this experience in such tones of delight that he has been called "the first alpinist." Although always a good Christian, Petrarch spoke out sharply against the corruption in the Church of his time. His writings made him a celebrity, and the high point of his life was Easter Sunday 1341 when he was solemnly crowned poet laureate in Rome.

Petrarch was an eager collector of previously unknown classical manuscripts, many of which were being discovered at this time in monastery libraries. He disliked the scholastic philosophers of his day, many of whom were repeating in a mechanical way the ideas of St. Thomas Aquinas. The schoolmen of the Middle Ages had stressed the scientific writings of Aristotle and other classical works in medicine, mathematics, and astronomy. Petrarch and his followers shifted the emphasis to the humanities: grammar, history, the philosophy of Plato, and poetry. They touched the hand of the past—and raced on to add their own contributions.

Patrons of the Arts

The enthusiastic support that Cosimo and Lorenzo de' Medici gave to the arts in Florence was

A drawing of Isabella d'Este by Leonardo da Vinci. She collected rare books, antiques, and art and supported artists and scholars.

echoed in other city-states of Italy. At Mantua, the court of the d'Este family was a brilliant cultural center. Its atmosphere of learning and enjoyment of the beauties of the world was encouraged by the wife of the ruler, Marchioness Isabella d'Este (1474-1539).

Isabella had been brought up in splendor among art treasures and books. She studied music and philosophy and learned to sing and dance gracefully at court festivals. According to people who knew her, Isabella spoke Latin better than most scholars. At the age of sixteen Isabella was married to Francesco Gonzaga, heir to the throne of Mantua. Francesco was a professional military leader, first for the Venetians and later for the Milanese. When the Venetians made Francesco a prisoner of war, Isabella helped to rule Mantua with skill and firmness.

Francesco returned safely from captivity, and Isabella continued to help in the government of Mantua. After her husband's death she gave wise advice to her son, who became the new ruler.

Isabella kept in touch by letter or in person with many of the prominent leaders, writers, scholars and artists of Italy. Leonardo da Vinci did a portrait sketch of her, shown at the left. Andrea Mantegna (1431-1506) and other artists were commissioned to do paintings for Mantua's churches and palaces. The decorations of Isabella's private apartments were the talk of Italy because of their elegance and good taste. She purchased from the Venetian printer Aldus Manutius his books by classical authors as well as the works of French and Italian writers of the day.

In a corrupt age Isabella kept the atmosphere of her court on a high moral tone. Baldassare Castiglione, a writer who was an expert on the courts of Italy (see page 298), said of Isabella d'Este: "She is so outstanding in her manners and virtue that no praise can come up to her merits."

Other ruling families were also great collectors of rare manuscripts and books. Isabella d'Este's sister, Beatrice, was married to Lodovico Sforza (1451-1508), the powerful duke of Milan. One of his proudest possessions was his library of ancient Greek and Latin writings. He employed scholars as "scouts" to search remote monasteries for forgotten classical manuscripts, which were then copied for Lodovico's collection. At the court of Urbino the reigning duke had thirty to forty copyists at work turning out beautiful books adorned with gold and other colors.

Literature

In addition to collecting books, the educated people of the Renaissance were fond of writing them. One of Petrarch's closest friends was Giovanni Boccaccio (1313-1375), who is known for his writing of Italian prose. Most of the writing in Italian up to his time had been in poetry. Boccaccio developed a vigorous prose style, using the dialect of Florence. He is best known for his love story, *La Fiammetta*, and for *The Decameron*, an amusing collection of stories that show down-to-earth pictures of Italian life.

Niccolò Machiavelli (1469-1527) was a diplomat in the service of the government of Florence. He traveled widely on official business, observing shrewdly the deadly wars of conquest among various states. As a sincere patriot, he longed to see Italy united under a strong ruler. Machiavelli felt that the important thing for a ruler was to achieve

Brunelleschi's dome of the Cathedral rises above the roofs of Florence.

success no matter what the means used. His book *The Prince* was a kind of textbook for rulers. He recommended:

> A prince therefore must be a fox so as to know the snares, and a lion so as to frighten the wolves. . . . For this reason a ruler cannot and should not keep his word if this would be against his interest. . . . And if human beings were all good, this teaching would not be fitting; but since they are bad, and would not keep faith with you, you do not have to keep it with them.

Architecture, Painting, and Sculpture

The cathedrals of the Middle Ages had been erected by architect-builders, people who were closely connected to the actual work of construction. Often the names of these architect-builders are not even known. By contrast, the great buildings of the Renaissance were designed by well-known architects.

One of the earliest of the new architects was Filippo Brunelleschi (1377-1446), who added the beautiful dome to the Cathedral of our Lady of the Flower in Florence. Brunelleschi started as a sculptor, but changed his career after he failed to win a contest to model the bronze doors of Florence's baptistery. Young Brunelleschi went to Rome, where he studied ancient Roman buildings. Returning to Florence, he built the great dome for the cathedral. It was the first large-scale dome constructed in Italy since the fall of the Roman Empire.

Another architect, Leon Battista Alberti (1404-1472), examined scientifically the principles of Roman architecture. He studied books written by the Roman architect Vitruvius, and applied Vitruvius' rules in designing the Roman arches of a great church at Rimini in eastern Italy. Alberti also worked as an architect in Mantua. Because of his competence in many fields—mathematics, sculpture, poetry, and education as well as architecture—he was known as a "universal" person.

Nicola Pisano (c. 1205-1278) and his son Giovanni Pisano (1240-1320) were among the earliest sculptors in the new classical style. They carved pulpits for the baptistery and cathedral of their native city of Pisa with great success. Their works combined in a new way figures and architectural elements such as columns.

Lorenzo Ghiberti (c. 1378-1455) was the Florentine sculptor whose proposal for the baptistery doors at Florence was accepted over that of Brunelleschi. Ghiberti spent twenty-two years working on a set of bronze doors. His work was so well received that he was asked to produce a second set of doors. His later work introduced such new effects as crowds of figures, trees, clouds, and an impression of depth. The grateful Florentines ever since have called these doors the "Gates of paradise."

Andrea del Verrocchio (1435-1488) cast at Venice the huge bronze statue of the general called Colleoni. This statue is the ancestor of bronze statues in our parks of generals on horseback.

Renaissance painting grew out of medieval painting, which was symbolic and stylized and based on early Christian and Byzantine models. Giotto, the first great Florentine painter (c. 1267-1337), drew on this tradition but created beautiful and harmonious wall paintings that have a three-dimensional reality. His paintings in the Arena Chapel at Padua had a great influence on artists all over Italy. He was an innovator who started a movement toward naturalness in depicting people.

Masaccio (1401-1428), in a very short life, started a revolution in painting. In his painting of the *Expulsion of Adam and Eve* in a chapel in Florence, Masaccio led the way toward realism in art. He defined clearly, by light and shadow, the nude human figures in his work. Also he began the scientific exploration of perspective, another important advance in Renaissance painting. (See page 137.)

Later Florentine artists like Fra Filippo Lippi and Fra Angelico used vivid colors to depict scenes from the life of Christ as well as the Madonna and Child. Sandro Botticelli (c. 1444-1510) painted attractive representations of pagan mythology for the court of Lorenzo de' Medici. Among his masterpieces are *Primavera* (Spring) and *The Birth of Venus.*

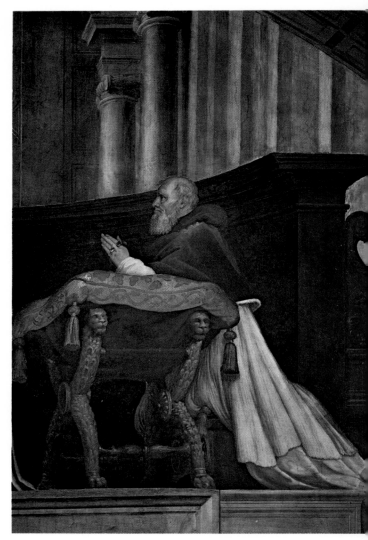

Raphael painted the portrait of Pope Julius II. It is part of a large picture titled "The Mass of Bolsena."

Leonardo da Vinci (1452-1519) was not only a painter, sculptor, architect, and scientist, but also an engineer and inventor. He was a strong athlete who, it was said, had enough strength in his hands to bend a horseshoe. Yet he was also gentle. It is reported that when he saw caged birds in a marketplace, he would often buy them and set them free.

When applying for employment with the duke of Milan, Leonardo described his qualifications in these words:

I have plans for bridges . . . for making cannons . . . for constructing many engines most suitable for attack or defense. . . . I can make cars, safe and unassailable, which will enter among the enemy. . . . I can give you as complete satisfaction as anyone in architecture. . . . I can execute sculpture in marble, bronze, or clay, and also I can do in painting whatever can be done.

No wonder that the duke of Milan was glad to have Leonardo's services! Leonardo built fortifications, designed a dome for the cathedral (which was never built), and proposed to construct a model city of the future. Toward the end of his life Leonardo accepted employment at the French royal court. His famous *Mona Lisa,* the portrait of a Florentine lady, remained in France where the artist died.

The Renaissance at the Papal Court

The Renaissance also flowered after 1500 in Rome. Here a number of cultured Popes established a magnificent court. The library of the Vatican was the finest in the world. Recently discovered statues by Greek and Roman sculptors were on display in the papal art collection. Princes and cardinals from all parts of Europe were frequent visitors, and the city was a colorful and exciting place. On feast days of the Church the streets were crowded with religious processions. Artists and musicians were drawn to Rome in the hope of obtaining commissions. Among them was Raphael (1483-1520), one of the best-loved Italian artists. His paintings of Madonnas are admired for their sweetness and fine composition.

Countless builders and artists were kept busy on the new St. Peter's Basilica, which Pope Julius II decided to erect in 1503. It was to be the largest church in the world. Julius II was succeeded as Pope by Leo X, who reigned from 1513 to 1521. He was a son of Lorenzo de' Medici. Leo X supported artists and scholars with such generosity that his reign was known as a "Golden Age."

Attracted to Rome at this time was Michelangelo (1475-1564). He was trained as a sculptor in a school for talented young artists which the Medici had opened at Florence. In fact, although he was also an unusually gifted painter and architect, Michelangelo always thought of himself primarily as a sculptor. In Florence he produced a gigantic statue of *David* and the impressive tombs of the Medici princes.

Michelangelo was in his early twenties when he carved the Pietà *that is now in St. Peter's Cathedral in Rome.*

At Rome he carved the beautiful *Pietà,* a representation of Mary mourning over the dead Christ. At the request of Julius II, he created the wonderful ceiling paintings of the Sistine Chapel. On one wall of the same building he completed the powerful *The Last Judgment.* Toward the end of his life Michelangelo became head architect of St. Peter's. The mighty dome he designed was to some degree inspired by Brunelleschi's dome at Florence.

Michelangelo's art reflected his deep faith as a Christian, and also re-created idealized human forms with power and grace. Seeking to explain the mystery and wonder of life, the artist exclaimed in a poem:

My soul can find no stair
To mount to heaven, save earth's loveliness.

Music

Music was also much appreciated, especially at the courts of rulers. Most courts had orchestras, and no evening's entertainment was complete without a concert by professional musicians or talented amateurs. The men and women of the courts enjoyed singing and playing for their own pleasure and to please others.

Venice was the main center for popular music. Madrigals were developed at this time. *Madrigals* were generally non-religious songs for several voices usually unaccompanied by instruments. This form of music made use of *polyphony;* that is, several lines of melody harmonize with each other. (The music of the Middle Ages was based on a single musical line.) At the papal court in Rome the leading composer was Giovanni da Palestrina (c. 1524-1594), who wrote masses for the Vatican choir and orchestra.

Education

Very few peasants or poor people in towns knew how to read or write. Workers who were members of a guild were taught enough reading and writing during their time as apprentices to enable them to master their particular skills. Members of the upper classes were educated at home by private tutors. There was an interesting innovation at Mantua, where Vittorino da Feltre (c. 1378-1446) developed a model school with the encouragement of the prince. Feltre introduced the Greek and Roman classics into the school curriculum. He believed it was important to respect individual differences in children. His school made use of sports and gymnastics as well as academic subjects. Rich youths came in numbers to Feltre, who also admitted free of charge some boys from poor families.

Women of the Renaissance

If they were peasants, women during the Renaissance had lives of hard work in the fields. If they lived in a town, they might help their husbands in their trades or help keep the family shop. In addition, they were busy with duties as housewives and mothers.

For women of the upper classes, life was more varied and interesting. Many of them received an excellent education from tutors in their fathers' houses. They learned how to ride a horse and play games, and they were taught to sing and dance.

Marriages were carefully arranged between the families of the bride and groom. An upper-class man expected a substantial dowry, or marriage settlement, from the family of his future wife. Often the personal wishes of the young lady might be overlooked.

Great ladies like Isabella d'Este (see page 282) were able to make many changes in the social life of upper-class Italians. Isabella's sister-in-law, Elizabetta Gonzaga (1471-1526), was married to the learned Duke of Urbino. Elizabetta presided with wit and good taste over a lively group of gentlemen and ladies at the court of Urbino. Baldassare Castiglione (1478-1529), a writer and diplomat, was a frequent visitor at this court. In his book, *The Book of the Courtier,* he described how a gentleman of the Renaissance should conduct himself. Castiglione also told approvingly of the great freedom ladies had in discussing new ideas and new ways of life as the intellectual equals of men.

Renaissance women distinguished themselves as painters and writers. Vittoria Colonna was an excellent poet. Michelangelo admired her greatly, and wrote poems in her honor. Gaspara Stampa was a poet who boldly defended the rights of women.

Check on Your Reading

1. Trace the career of Petrarch. Name some of his accomplishments.
2. Why was Leonardo da Vinci called a universal genius?
3. How did the revival of interest in ancient Greece and Rome affect the Renaissance way of life?
4. Who was Isabella d'Este? How did she influence other people?
5. Compare the achievements of Michelangelo to those of Leonardo da Vinci.

3. The Renaissance Spreads in Europe

The news of Italy's wealth and dazzling civilization spread throughout Europe. Italy was split up into a number of republics or kingdoms, and the Papal States. These states were often at war with one another. Armies of mercenaries—soldiers for hire by the highest bidder—were led by professional generals.

These wars helped to block the national unity which many Italians had hoped to achieve. Italy also was a battlefield for the armies of the kings of

When King Francis I returned from Italy he rebuilt his ancestral home at Blois. In the years that followed he and his nobles built other chateaux in the region of the Loire Valley.

France and Spain and of the Holy Roman Emperor. These wars had one positive effect; they exposed the people of other countries to the civilization of the Renaissance. Italian artists, engineers, musicians, and scholars also carried their new ideas and skills to people in other lands. Here the Italian discoveries were adapted to the local ways of life. Students from northern Europe went to Italy for their training. The spirit of the Renaissance quickly moved to lands north of the Alps and across the Mediterranean to Spain and Portugal.

France

At the invitation of the Duke of Milan, the army of Charles VIII of France invaded Italy in 1494. The French king passed unopposed as far south as Naples, which he claimed for France. Charles VIII, however, was unable to retain his conquests in the face of a growing Italian resistance and retreated to France in 1495.

Later the dashing young Francis I (king from 1515-1547) came to Italy with an army and captured Milan. But in 1525 at the battle of Pavia the French were soundly defeated by soldiers of the Holy Roman Emperor, Charles V (Emperor from 1519 to 1558).

Francis I determined to bring the Italian Renaissance to France. He enthusiastically welcomed Leonardo da Vinci, the sculptor Benvenuto Cellini, and other Italian artists to France. A special institution—the *Collège de France*—was set up to teach Latin, Greek, and Hebrew. Many French architects gave up the Gothic style of the Middle Ages for the Graeco-Roman style of Italian builders. So

El Greco painted this view of the city where he lived, Toledo.

many beautiful castles in this style were put up along the Loire River that this region became known as "the garden of France." At Paris the Palace of the Louvre was also constructed in the new style.

Soon French writers reflected the spirit and style of Greek, Latin, and Italian authors. One of the first to write poetry in the new manner was Louise Labé of Lyons. François Rabelais (1494-1553), a physician with a great joy in living, published comical accounts of the adventures of *Gargantua* and *Pantagruel,* two legendary giants. Michel de Montaigne (1533-1592) became famous for his *Essays,* which were reflections about life and human destiny. He was a great student of the classics and was also a skeptic about the ability of human beings to discover an easy way out of the problems of life. Pierre de Ronsard (c. 1524-1585), one of the greatest poets of the French Renaissance, was an expert in the classical forms. His work greatly influenced other French poets. Queen Marguerite of Navarre (1492-1549), Sister of Francis I, was a learned woman and a supporter of the humanists of the French Renaissance. She was author of the *Heptameron,* a collection of short stories.

Spain

Spain was the most powerful nation of Europe during the sixteenth century. Italian artists received offers to work in Spain after 1500. Soon the Spaniards developed their own school of painting, which owed a great deal to the Italians.

El Greco (1548?-1614), which means "The Greek," was born of Greek parents on the island of Crete. He studied under the great Venetian masters, Titian and Tintoretto. Later he moved to Toledo in Spain, a city noted for its intense Catholic faith. There he turned out his extraordinary canvases, including the *View of Toledo* and *Assumption of the Virgin.* His landscapes show sharp contrasts between light and dark. The figures are elongated in such a way as to accent the emotions portrayed in his paintings. Once seen, the works of El Greco are not easily forgotten.

Diego Velásquez (1599-1660) was the favorite painter of King Philip IV of Spain. Like El Greco, Velásquez studied for a time in Italy. His portraits of members of the royal family are much admired, as is his famous *Surrender of Breda,* a brilliantly composed scene of a Spanish victory in Holland.

Miguel de Cervantes (1547-1616) produced one of the most famous novels ever written: *Don Quixote de la Mancha.* In one sense the work is a satire of medieval ideals of chivalry, which had become old-fashioned by that time. The contrast between the idealistic Don Quixote and his earthy squire, Sancho Panza, is extremely comical. In another sense, however, the sympathy and love that many people feel for the old hero reveal how much human beings long for an impossible world in which such idealism triumphs.

Developments in Northern Europe

Flanders was at that time a small country along the North Sea. Its cities had grown rich through trade. There had long been a flourishing school of Flemish painters. These artists, who were deeply religious, decorated the churches of Ghent, Bruges, and Antwerp with paintings of Christ, Mary, and the saints. They liked to paint the details of ordinary life. Often Mary or the apostles of Christ were shown as Flemish townspeople and peasants. Realistic details, such as pots of flowers, glassware, or silver, were depicted with great care.

About 1400, painters in Flanders began to experiment with oil as a base for colors on wooden panels. They found that it gave a jewel-like quality to their work. From these early experiments, oil painting, as we know it today, was developed. At this time the Italians and other European painters used two methods: colors applied to wet plaster, or *fresco painting;* and *tempera,* that is, mixing colors with an egg base. They soon began to use oil as well.

Two brothers, Hubert van Eyck (c. 1365-1426) and Jan van Eyck (1385-1441), perfected the oil technique. Their joint masterpiece was the

Pieter Breughel painted "The Harvesters" in oil on wood.

Adoration of the Lamb, which was made for a church in Ghent.

Pieter Breughel (c. 1525-1569) painted lively scenes of peasant life. Among the most famous of his works are *Peasant Dance* and *The Hired Shepherd.*

Albrecht Dürer (1471-1528) of Nuremberg, Germany, studied both at Antwerp in Flanders and at Venice. Although he learned much from artists there, Dürer developed his own personal style. He was an excellent painter, engraver, and etcher. His woodcuts in black and white were turned out for a popular market, and large numbers were sold at fairs.

The Netherlands in the early seventeenth century had become very prosperous. The Dutch had freed themselves from Spanish rule through a series of bitter wars. (See Chapter 17.) Dutch merchants made enormous profits from trading posts in Africa, Asia, and the islands off the coast of southeast Asia. Many rich Dutch merchants became art patrons. Unlike the patrons of the past—church leaders, princes, and members of the nobility—the Dutch art lovers wanted down-to-earth paintings. They bought portraits of themselves and paintings of boats on canals, cows, peasant girls dancing, people drinking in taverns, and scenes of comfortable homes.

Franz Hals (c. 1580-1666) had a vigorous and vivid style. Jan Vermeer (1632-1675) specialized in delicate canvases like *Woman Weighing Gold.* Few could render more beautifully the quality of light streaming through a window or the feel and texture of materials.

Rembrandt van Rijn (1606-1669) as a young man enjoyed a huge success in Amsterdam. He earned large commissions from his portraits of fellow citizens, owned a big house, and was extremely happy with his wife, Saskia, and his son, Titus. Many people consider him among the greatest of all artists. Among his masterpieces of oil painting are the so-called *The Night Watch* and *The Anatomy Lesson.* Rembrandt also created wonderful etchings in black and white of religious scenes, such as *The Three Crosses* and *Christ Healing the Sick.* Later Rembrandt lost popularity with his customers. His later years were saddened by many sorrows and disappointments.

One of the greatest of the humanists of the Renaissance, Desiderius Erasmus (1466?-1536), was born in Rotterdam, in the Netherlands. After studies in Italy, he lived in Germany, England, and Switzerland. Respected as the outstanding philosopher of the northern Renaissance, he was in contact with many religious leaders, princes, scientists, and writers. He taught Latin and Greek, and produced a new edition of the Greek New Testament. *The Praise of Folly,* his best-known work, revealed his deep faith in human dignity and freedom.

England

The Renaissance reached England during the time of the Tudor monarchs, who ruled from 1485 to 1603. Already William Caxton had set up the first printing press in the kingdom in 1477. Soon quantities of books by Greek, Roman, English, French, and Italian authors began to pour from the presses at London, Oxford, Cambridge, and other cities.

Under Henry VIII (king from 1509-1547), there was a burst of intellectual activity. Among the best-known humanists was Sir Thomas More (1478-1535), an official in the king's government. More was also a close friend of Erasmus. In a book entitled *Utopia,* More described an ideal state. According to More:

> . . . they [the Utopians] never discuss happiness without combining the rational principles of philosophy with principles taken from religion. They think any inquiry concerning true happiness weak and defective unless it is based on religion.

During the long reign of Henry VIII's daughter, Elizabeth I (queen from 1558 to 1603), she encouraged many fine writers at her brilliant court. This was the period of the Protestant Reformation. (See pp. 293-297.) Queen Elizabeth became involved in a dangerous struggle with the Catholic king of Spain who threatened to invade England. Queen Elizabeth was well prepared to lead and inspire her people. She was ambitious, wise, determined, and brave. She learned to read Greek and Latin and to speak Italian, French, and Spanish with ease.

The leading playwright of Elizabeth's time was William Shakespeare (1564-1616). Many of his plays were inspired by Greek and Roman history and literature, such as *Timon of Athens, A Midsummer Night's Dream,* and *Antony and Cleopatra.* Other plays have Italian characters or are set in Renaissance

This painting shows Queen Elizabeth I being carried by courtiers on a visit to a theater in London.

Italy, such as *Romeo and Juliet*, *The Merchant of Venice*, and *Othello*. Shakespeare's love of England was revealed in words he gave the dying John of Gaunt in *King Richard II*:

> This royal throne of kings, this scepter'd isle
> [England],
> This earth of majesty, this seat of Mars,
> This other Eden, demi-paradise . . .
> This happy breed of men, this little world,
> This precious stone set in the silver sea. . . .

Check on Your Reading

1. How did Francis I encourage the spread of the Renaissance to France? Who were some important writers of his reign?
2. When was oil painting developed in Europe? Who was Rembrandt, and what did he do?
3. The reign of Elizabeth produced many great writers. Why do you think this was so?
4. What were Shakespeare's feelings toward England?

4. Great Progress in the Sciences

In the Middle Ages most people of Europe accepted the ideas of the ancient astronomer Ptolemy. Ptolemy believed that the Earth was the fixed and motionless center of the universe. The moon, sun, and stars were all thought to be spheres circulating around the Earth.

Beginning in the sixteenth century, a series of original thinkers from many parts of Europe overthrew Ptolemy's system of astronomy. They also refuted other false notions about the nature of the physical universe. Their ideas introduced our modern world of science, which is based on physical observations and experiments.

Copernicus Puts the Sun in Its Place

Nicolaus Copernicus (1473-1543) was born in Poland and studied at the University of Cracow. Becoming a priest, he went to Italy where he studied mathematics at the universities of Padua, Bologna, and Ferrara. On his return to Poland, he became dissatisfied with Ptolemy's explanation of the universe, which was in conflict with ideas he had encountered in Italy. He argued:

> . . . for all these reasons it is more probable that the Earth moves than that it is at rest— especially in the case of the daily revolution, as it is the Earth's very own.

In his book *Concerning the Revolutions of the Heavenly Spheres,* published in 1543, Copernicus came to three conclusions. First, the sun, not the Earth, was the center of our universe. Second, the Earth and the other planets moved in orbit around the sun. Third, the Earth also made a daily spin on its axis, thus causing day and night.

Copernicus' ideas did not attract a great deal of attention during his lifetime. Later, however, the detailed astronomical observations of Tycho Brahe (1546-1601), a Danish astronomer, were studied by Johannes Kepler (1571-1630), a German mathematician. Kepler confirmed and refined the original theory of Copernicus. On the basis of Brahe's records, Kepler was able to prove that the paths of the planets around the sun were ellipses, not circles as Copernicus had believed.

Galileo Supports the Theory of Copernicus

Galileo Galilei (1564-1642) was a gifted mathematician at the University of Padua in Italy. He

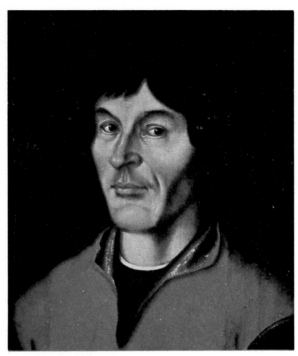

A portrait of Nicolaus Copernicus by Lorman.

learned of a new kind of telescope that had been invented in the Netherlands. Galileo built his own telescope that enabled him to examine spots on the sun, mountains on the moon, and the rings of Saturn. His study convinced him that the Copernican theory was correct. Galileo defended his belief in the accuracy of Copernicus' theory, despite the attacks of opponents, in these words:

> I do not feel obliged to believe that the same God who has given us senses, reason, and intellect has intended us to forego their use and by some other means give us knowledge which we can attain by them.

When he expressed his views, they were condemned by religious leaders. Galileo was even imprisoned for a while.

Discoverers in Medicine

Ambroise Paré (c. 1510-1590) was a surgeon for the French army. He became expert at removing bullets, treating wounds, and amputating limbs. He learned how to use ligatures to stop hemorrhages after amputations.

Andreas Vesalius (1514-1564), a Flemish physician, was born at Brussels. He objected to passing on to medical students the old, and often inaccurate, ideas of anatomy based on what the Greeks had taught. Vesalius insisted that all his students at the University of Padua must dissect human bodies so that they could learn about anatomy for themselves. His textbook *Fabric of the Human Body,* with its masterly drawings of muscles, was a milestone in medicine.

An important advance in internal medicine was made by William Harvey (1578-1657). He was an English physiologist who studied at the University of Padua in Italy. When Harvey returned to England, he carried out painstaking research on the circulation of blood in human beings. Up to that time, people did not know of the central role of the heart in pumping blood through a complex system of arteries, nor that the blood returns to the heart through the veins. Contradicting the traditional views, Harvey wrote:

> The heart is the beginning of life . . . for it is the heart by whose virtue and pulse the blood is moved.

Harvey's findings were important for all aspects of medicine. He also made important discoveries about the embryo. He showed how embryos developed through definite stages of growth from small, simple organisms to large, complex organisms.

Descartes, The Philosopher-Mathematician

The discoveries of Copernicus, Kepler, and others caused many European thinkers to rely on mathematics and the power of human reason to find solutions to problems. René Descartes (1596-1650), a French mathematician and philosopher, argued in favor of using a series of rational steps and logical reasoning until we arrive at truths. Descartes believed that the mathematical method could be applied to all human knowledge.

Descartes began by doubting everything except his own existence. He expressed this idea in his famous phrase: "Cogito, ergo sum—" "I think, therefore I am." From this point he used reasoning to show the necessity for God's existence and the existence of the rest of the world.

Newton and the Law of Gravitation

An English mathematician, Isaac Newton (1642-1727), made three important scientific discoveries before he was thirty years old. Little won-

der, for Newton worked hard on problems, often forgetting to eat, rest, or even put on his stockings properly. He described the law of gravitation, formulated the principles of a form of mathematics called calculus, and explained the nature of light. Newton's law of gravitation states:

> Every particle of matter in the universe is attracted by or gravitates to every other particle of matter. . . .

Newton described the law of gravitation in mathematical terms. He came up with an important concept for modern science: the existence of a basic order within the forces of the universe.

Newton freely admitted the debt he owed to other scientists who had gone before him, and compared himself to one who stood on the "shoulders of giants." He once remarked:

> I seem to have been only a boy playing on the seashore, [amusing] myself in now and then finding a smoother pebble or a prettier shell than ordinary, while the great ocean of truth lay all undiscovered before me.

Check on Your Reading

1. What were the contributions to astronomy of Copernicus and Galileo?
2. What discoveries did Paré, Vesalius, and Harvey make in medicine?
3. Who was Isaac Newton? What did he accomplish?

5. The Protestant Reformation

From its earliest beginnings the Catholic Church had been faced with differences of opinions over *dogma.* Dogma are religious beliefs that church leaders expect all church members to accept. Extreme differences of opinion were condemned by the church as *heresies,* or doctrines or beliefs contrary to the truth. Persons holding heretical ideas were expelled from the Church. In some cases they were handed over by the Church to officials of the State, who put the heretics to death.

The Protestant Reformation began as differences of opinion among Christians. It ended, however, by splitting the unity of the Church.

Causes of the Reformation

During the fourteenth and fifteenth centuries a number of Europeans began to question some of the

Lucas Cranach painted this portrait of his friend Martin Luther.

who attacked the wealth of the clergy. He translated the *Bible* from Latin into English and told his followers that the *Bible,* and not the Pope or the bishops, was the real authority in religious matters.

Many of Wycliffe's ideas were taken up by John Huss (1369?-1415), the head of the University of Prague in Bohemia. Huss preached that lay people shared in the priesthood as followers of Christ. He was excommunicated because of his attacks on Church dogma. Later he was condemned as a heretic and burned at the stake. This made him a martyr in the eyes of his followers in Bohemia, who became rebels against the Catholic Church.

The humanists of the Renaissance stimulated many people to reexamine their religious beliefs. As scholars studied the *Bible* and the early history of the Catholic Church, they became critical of abuses in the Church of their time. Many peasants resented having to pay heavy taxes to the Church. Business leaders felt that the Church's teachings on fair prices and usury—the practice of lending money at high rates of interest—were harmful to the expansion of trade. In addition, the growth of nationalism in countries like England and France caused difficulties for the Church, which was an international institution. Many kings and princes disliked seeing so much money leave their countries each year to support the papal court at Rome.

Luther's Challenge

Europe's religious situation might be compared to a tinderbox. The spark that set off the great explosion was supplied by a bold religious leader in Germany.

Martin Luther (1483-1546) was born to a German peasant family. He became a monk and later a professor of theology at the University of Wittenberg. A man of strong feelings, Luther was disturbed by the practice of *indulgences.* Indulgences were granted by the Church under certain conditions. They were supposed to take away some of the penance a repentant sinner had to do on this earth and some of his or her punishment in *purgatory,* a midway state between heaven and hell. Many people believed that by offering money to the Church for indulgences they could free themselves or their relatives from the results of their sins. About this time Pope Leo X needed money to finish the costly building of St. Peter's Basilica in Rome. He sent a number of preachers to Germany to pro-

actions of the Popes. From 1309 to 1377 the Popes came under the influence of France. They even moved the papal court from Rome to Avignon in southern France. Many people resented the seeming willingness of the Popes to do the will of the kings of France.

After the Popes returned to Rome, a dispute broke out about the way in which a new Pope had been elected. The nations of Europe chose different candidates, and two or three Popes competed for recognition as the real Pope. This was the *Great Schism,* which greatly undermined the prestige of papal authority. Finally a general council was called of Church leaders from all over Europe to elect a new Pope. This put an end to the Great Schism.

Meanwhile, a number of religious leaders began to demand far-reaching reforms. Among them was John Wycliffe (1320?-1384), an English theologian mote indulgences there. Luther objected to the way in which one of these preachers went about extracting money from devout Germans.

In 1517 Luther put up ninety-five *theses,* or propositions, on the door of a church at Wittenberg. Luther stated:

> . . . those who preach indulgences are in error when they say that a man is . . . saved from every penalty by the Pope's indulgences.

Luther's theses were written in Latin, and intended mainly for debate among members of the clergy. Soon, however, they were translated into German and were read widely in Germany.

As time went on, Luther became bolder in attacking the organization of the Church and in proclaiming his support for many ideas of Wycliffe and Huss. Leo X replied by excommunicating him.

In 1521 Luther was told to appear before the imperial Diet at Worms, a city in Germany. The Diet was a group of high officials of Church and State who gave advice to Charles V, the Holy Roman Emperor. Although urged by members of the Diet to withdraw his views, Luther refused to back down:

> Unless I am convinced by the testimony of the Scriptures or by clear reason . . . my conscience is captive to the Word of God. I cannot and will not retract anything. . . . I cannot do otherwise. Here I stand. May God help me.

The Diet then decreed:

> Luther is to be regarded as a convicted heretic. . . . His followers also are to be condemned. His books are to be eradicated from the memory of man.

Luther was declared an outlaw in the Holy Roman Empire as well as being excommuncniated by the Church. He went into hiding for a year at Wartburg Castle, where he translated the *New Testament* into German. Luther's translation became known throughout German-speaking lands.

In 1524 the peasants rose up against their feudal lords, demanding improvements in German social and economic life. To a large degree the peasants may have been inspired by Luther's rebellion against authority. In fact, Luther favored their demands at first. Later, however, he opposed their violent methods because he feared that the rebellion would result in the collapse of all government. The German princes put down the rebellious peasants, with a great loss of life to the peasants.

The Protestant Reformation Spreads

Soon two groups of princes emerged in the Holy Roman Empire. Some princes remained faithful to the Catholic Church to which the Emperor Charles V belonged. Others followed the teachings of Luther. In time, Luther's followers became known as "Protestants." After a bitter civil war among the Germans, a compromise agreement was reached in 1555. It was agreed that the German princes would decide the religion of their own states. Germany was split into Protestant states, mainly in the North, and Catholic states, mainly in the South. The Scandinavian lands also were won for Lutheranism at this time.

The followers of Luther believed that Christians should be guided by the *Bible,* not by the traditions of the Catholic Church. They felt that people must justify themselves through their deep faith in God, not through faith and good works, as the Catholics taught. In Lutheran areas the monasteries and convents were dissolved. Monks and nuns were free to marry. Luther himself gave the example by marrying an ex-nun. The Mass was dropped and a church service was developed that emphasized sermons and the singing of hymns.

The Reformation in Switzerland

Switzerland at this time was a confederation of thirteen separate states. Some of its people spoke German, while others spoke French or Italian. The Swiss had organized in an effort to gain their freedom from the Holy Roman Empire in the thirteenth century. Many Swiss welcomed the new religious ideas of the Reformation. In the German-speaking areas Ulrich Zwingli (1484-1531) introduced the Reformation at Zurich.

Soon a civil war broke out in Switzerland. Zwingli himself was slain in battle. At the peace treaty after this war, the Swiss decided to let each state decide its own religious beliefs.

John Calvin: A Leader of Protestants

One of the most important leaders of the Reformation was John Calvin (1509-1564). He was born in France, and studied law and theology at the

This painting by Peter Paul Rubens shows St. Ignatius Loyola preaching.

University of Paris. Attracted to Protestantism at an early age, he fled to Switzerland to escape persecution in France. He published, first in Latin and later in French, the *Institutes of the Christian Religion.* This work developed the doctrine of *predestination.* This meant that when God created humankind, God chose some people to be saved and others to be doomed. The people predestined to be saved Calvin called *the elect.*

Calvin organized a church-dominated government in the Swiss city of Geneva. He insisted that people must live according to strict rules of morality. He did not believe in religious tolerance. A Spanish physician named Servetus sought refuge at Geneva from Catholic persecution. Calvin disagreed with Servetus's religious views and approved of his being burned as a heretic.

Calvinist ideas were soon introduced into the Netherlands. John Knox (1505?-1572) spread Calvinist teachings in Scotland and organized what became known as the Presbyterian Church. Many English people became Calvinists as well. They were known as Puritans, and some of their descendants founded the Congregational churches of New England.

Henry VIII and the Church of England

Henry VIII of England (king from 1509 to 1547) was an ambitious, head-strong ruler. He introduced the Reformation into his kingdom primarily for political rather than religious reasons. He wanted to seize the fine lands of Church officials and to free the country from the political activities of some churchmen. Henry also wanted a male heir to the throne. When his wife, Catherine of Aragon, did not give him a son, Henry applied to the Pope to dissolve their marriage. The Pope refused to do this, and Henry decided to break with the Catholic Church.

In 1534, Henry VIII split with the Pope and made himself the head of an independent, national church—the Church of England. He dissolved monasteries and convents of England, and distributed their properties to people who agreed with his religious policies. Members of the clergy were declared free to marry. The Mass was celebrated in English rather than Latin.

Check on Your Reading

1. What were the causes of the Protestant Reformation?
2. What changes did Martin Luther bring about?
3. How were disagreements between Catholics and Protestants settled in Germany? in Switzerland?
4. Who was John Calvin? Describe Calvinism.
5. Why did Henry VIII set up the Church of England?

---

6. The Catholic Reformation

Even before the Protestant Reformation there were men and women who worked to eliminate abuses within the Catholic Church. As the Protestants increased in numbers, a reform movement gathered strength within the Catholic Church. Its leaders slowly but surely carried out the *Catholic Reformation,* or Counter Reformation. Their aims were to strengthen Catholicism throughout the world, and to check the spread of Protestantism.

Achievements of the Jesuits

Ignatius Loyola (1491?-1556) was a Spanish nobleman and army officer. Injured in battle, he experienced a religious conversion in 1521. He studied at the University of Paris, where he found his first disciples among fellow students. The religious order he founded—the *Society of Jesus,* which is called the *Jesuits*—was organized along military lines. Loyola became the first Father General of the society. In his *Spiritual Exercises,* which are still used to train Jesuits today, Loyola helped his followers attain strict self-discipline. The Jesuits took the usual vows of poverty, chastity, and obedience. In addition, they took a special vow of loyalty to the Pope.

The Jesuits led Catholic efforts to stop the spread of Protestantism. They went everywhere as preachers and educators, established schools and colleges in many different lands, and acted as advisers to rulers. The Jesuit system of education had many attractive features. Students were well trained in Latin, Greek, and mathematics as well as in philosophy and religion. Public speaking and dramatics were part of the school program. The Jesuits had remarkable success in reconverting many Protestants in France, Flanders, Germany, Hungary, Bohemia, and Poland. Other Jesuits went overseas as missionaries to people in distant lands.

The Catholic Reformation succeeded to a great extent in its attempt to revive Catholic faith and purify the Church. It also encouraged the construction of new churches, and supported the work of many fine painters, sculptors, and composers.

Reform of the Papal Court and the Council of Trent

Paul III, who was Pope from 1534 to 1549, began the task of purifying the court at Rome. He put an end to the sale of indulgences. Corrupt men were no longer appointed as cardinals or bishops, and high offices of the Church were no longer given to very young children of noble families. The administration of the Church was improved. The sound policies of Paul III were continued by his successors.

A council of the leaders of the Catholic Church met at Trent in northern Italy in several sessions between 1545 and 1563. An attempt to persuade Protestant leaders to participate failed. The Council restated the traditional Catholic doctrines. It upheld both the *Bible* and the traditions of the Catholic Church as sources of Christian truth. The Mass was to be celebrated in Latin. The seven sacraments of the Church were upheld. The authority of the Pope as Vicar of Christ on earth was acknowledged. Respect for the Virgin Mary and the saints was continued. The Council did away with many abuses in the Church. It supported the Pope's efforts to improve the administration of the Church, and to ensure better education of priests.

Check on Your Reading

1. Who was Ignatius Loyola? What were some of the achievements of the Society of Jesus?
2. Name some of the steps the Popes took to reform the papal court.
3. What was the Council of Trent? What did it accomplish?

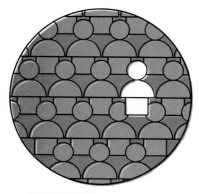

LET'S MEET THE PEOPLE

The Ideal Renaissance Gentleman

The ideal gentleman of the Italian Renaissance served his ruler loyally in war and peace. He was well dressed, but never conspicuous. All his equipment—his weapons, armor, saddle, and garments—were elegant and always in fine condition. At all public gatherings he made a fine impression.

From the time of his earliest youth he had been interested in sports. He was an excellent horseman, a strong wrestler, and a tireless swimmer. He could fight for long periods on foot or from horseback.

This gentleman had studied Latin and Greek, and could understand some French and Spanish. He spoke and wrote Italian well, and was careful to avoid affected expressions.

He was a pleasant companion at the court of the ruler. He could bowl, play chess, sing, and play the viola. When he told a joke, he had respect for the time, the persons, and the circumstances. He sought friends who were respected, noble, and good. Because of his unfailing good manners, he favorably impressed all the people of the court.

When the gentleman fell in love he treated his lady with every respect and consideration. He never boasted about his romance. In fact, he revealed his affection only to the lady in question! He knew that his feelings for his lady should lift him up to a knowledge of divine love; that is, to God.

Of course, not every Renaissance gentleman was a saint. Often he fell short of the noble ideal he was trying to follow, but he was generally a man of honor. In accord with the spirit of his time, he served his Prince and his God to the best of his ability.

Based on *The Book of the Courtier* by Baldassare Castiglione.

CHAPTER REVIEW

Think and Discuss

1. Why did the Renaissance begin in Italy?
2. Machiavelli observed that the end justifies the means. Do you agree or disagree? Give examples to support your position.
3. It is said that the Renaissance affected the rich more than the poor. What do you think?
4. Compare Isabella d'Este with Eleanor of Aquitaine.
5. We know the names of many more artists and architects of the Renaissance than of the Middle Ages. Why do you think this is so?
6. Historical events are caused by many factors. What factors caused the Protestant Reformation?

Past and Present

1. What work do we classify as "creative" today? Do today's creative people have talents similar to those of the Renaissance?
2. What rulers of our own period do you think follow Machiavellian ideas? Explain why you think they are Machiavellian.
3. Is there any evidence that the Renaissance is still going on today? Support your answer.
4. What features of life in our century can be traced back to the sixteenth and seventeenth centuries?

Activities

1. Visit an art museum to view Renaissance art. Also visit galleries in a museum that features Gothic art. Make a list of the differences between the two types of art.
2. Write a short biography of a Renaissance writer, artist, architect, or musician.
3. Stage an exhibit of Renaissance art in your classroom.
4. Consult references to find out why and how a famous work of art was created. Suggestions: Dürer's "The Praying Hands," or da Vinci's "Mona Lisa."
5. Listen to some records of music written during the Renaissance. Identify some characteristics of this music.
6. Write a report on the activities of one religious reformer.

17

European Nations Explore the World and Struggle for Power

KEYNOTE

In the early 1400s, most people of Europe knew little about the rest of the world. Since the Crusades they had traded with the Muslims of the Middle East, but most Europeans had heard only vague rumors and myths about the more remote parts of Asia and Africa. They did not even know that the Americas existed.

Then one of the greatest adventures of all time began—the European voyages of discovery. These voyages started in the middle of the 1400s with the Portuguese expeditions organized by Prince Henry the Navigator. In the following years other European nations also sent out explorers and traders to all parts of the globe. By 1650 a number of European nations had trading posts and colonies in Africa, Asia, and the Americas.

These momentous developments took place while the nations of Europe were fighting among themselves. As European trade and colony-building spread, the power struggle in Europe became part of a worldwide contest for trade and colonies.

Galleons in the harbor of Lisbon about 1600.

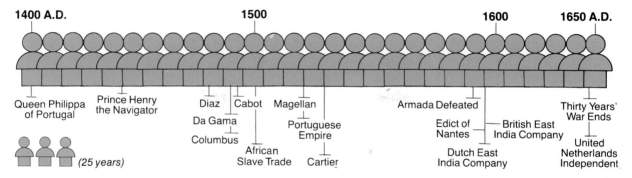

1400 A.D.	1500	1600	1650 A.D.

Queen Philippa of Portugal
Prince Henry the Navigator
Diaz
Da Gama
Columbus
Cabot
African Slave Trade
Magellan
Portuguese Empire
Cartier
Armada Defeated
Edict of Nantes
Dutch East India Company
British East India Company
Thirty Years' War Ends
United Netherlands Independent

(25 years)

1. Europeans Discover Other Parts of the World

A small nation of less than a million people in the southwestern part of the Iberian Peninsula, led the way. By the thirteenth century the Portuguese had freed themselves from the Moors. Portugal's neighbor, the powerful Spanish kingdom of Castile, wanted to annex it. The Portuguese, cut off by Castile from land contacts with the rest of Europe, took to the sea.

Fleets of Caravels and an Important Alliance

The king of Portugal encouraged his nobles to set up shipbuilding yards, and expert shipbuilders from Italy were brought in, to train Portuguese workers. For a while the Portuguese relied on *galleys*—ships with three tiers of rowers. However, they soon discovered that the galleys were impractical for voyages on the stormy Atlantic. During the late 1300s and early 1400s they developed the *caravel*, a sturdy, round-bottomed ship with lateen, or triangular, sails. Lateen rigs, which long had been used by the Arabs, enabled crews of the caravels to tack, or change direction, into the wind. Caravels were about eighty feet in length and twenty feet wide. Compared to modern liners, these small ships were as a mouse is to a lion.

Fleets of caravels sailed each summer to England, carrying casks of port wine, sardines, cork, and dried fruit. They returned about a year later with wool and tin from England as well as other products of northern Europe.

When forces of the king of Castile invaded Portugal in 1385, the Portuguese appealed to England for help. Knights and archers arrived from England on Portuguese ships and drove off Castilian vessels that were blockading Lisbon. Later that year a combined English and Portuguese army defeated a much larger Castilian force. This victory led to an alliance between the English and the Portuguese that has lasted to the present day.

Queen Philippa Provides Leadership

One of the leaders of the English government was John of Gaunt, Duke of Lancaster (1340-1399). To strengthen the alliance with Portugal, John of Gaunt married his daughter, Philippa of Lancaster, to King John I of Portugal. Queen Philippa had received an excellent education. Her teachers probably included the poet Geoffrey Chaucer (see page 275), and the religious reformer John Wycliffe (see page 294).

At first, John was not overjoyed about his marriage. In time, however, Philippa's loyalty, intelligence, good sense, and strength of character won his affection and respect. They had six sons and four daughters. While John was busy defending his country's border with Castile, Philippa played a role in helping to run the government. She worked closely with members of the growing middle class and with Jewish scholars, who contributed to Portugal their special skills in medicine and their knowledge of Greek, Roman, and Arab scientific discoveries. With Philippa's careful administration, the war-torn nation began to revive.

Philippa also tried to persuade King John and their children that Portugal should move into Africa to find a new way to reach the riches of the Indies. She pointed out that, if the attempt succeeded, Portugal would have direct access to the gold of Africa as well as to the silks and pearls of Asia. The Portuguese would become rich by bypassing the Mediterranean trade routes controlled by the Muslims and Venetians.

She convinced King John to begin the exploration of Africa by capturing Ceuta, a Muslim stronghold on the northern shore of the continent. Just as

Queen Philippa of Portugal. Her leadership encouraged Portugal's overseas exploration and colony building.

fourth son of King John and Queen Philippa. Henry wanted to continue the crusade against the Muslims and to find the kingdom of Prester John, a legendary Christian ruler in Africa.

For more than forty years Prince Henry dedicated his fortune and talents to expanding Portugal's commerce and knowledge of the world. At Sagres on Cape St. Vincent he set up a center for geographical and navigational studies. Here Muslim, Jewish, German, and Italian experts on astronomy and geography had long talks with Portuguese sea captains returning from voyages down the coast of Africa. Henry's extensive library contained books on geography and maps produced by a group of Jewish scholars on the Mediterranean island of Majorca.

Under Henry's supervision improved caravels were built. The latest maps and navigation aids were furnished to his sea captains. These aids included the *windrose compass,* an improvement of the mariner's compass, and the *astrolabe,* a device for finding one's bearings at sea by measuring the altitude of the stars. From the Arabs Henry adopted a new method of keeping water fresh on long voyages—watertight casks or *toneis.* Soon the size of a ship was indicated by the number of casks, or tons, it could store. We still describe ships today as having a certain number of tons.

Slowly Henry the Navigator's sea captains moved southward along the African coast. In 1420 one of them sighted the beautiful island of Madeira. Prince Henry settled it with Portuguese colonists. He provided them with grapes from Sicily and seeds of wheat and other grains. Madeira's fertile soil began to produce wine, wheat, and hardwoods for export.

Another captain, whose ship was swept by a storm far out to sea, discovered a group of islands known today as the Azores. Prince Henry asked his sister Isabel, who was married to the duke of Burgundy, to encourage farmers from Flanders to settle there. (At that time the dukes of Burgundy ruled Flanders.) The Flemish colonists brought with them herds of cattle as well as building tools and farm equipment.

As the Portuguese ships moved down the African coast, they brought back exotic plants and animals. One expedition carried away some Africans as prisoners. Later expeditions imported into Portugal and Madeira African slaves. This was the begin-

the expedition was about to set sail, Philippa fell ill with the plague. On her deathbed she had her husband and children swear to her that they would not give up the expedition.

The expedition to Ceuta got under way without delay. It consisted of more than two hundred warships, and was led by King John and his sons. The Portuguese made a successful surprise attack on the Muslim garrison at Ceuta in August of 1415. The victorious army seized a treasure in African gold as well as valuable supplies of spices. They also liberated many Christian prisoners who had been forced into slavery.

News of the capture of Ceuta electrified people in Europe. It was a signal that the Christian forces, which had been losing to the Muslim Turks in the eastern Mediterranean, had gone on the offensive against the Muslims of North Africa.

Prince Henry the Navigator

One of the Portuguese leaders at Ceuta was Prince Henry the Navigator (1394-1460), the ning of Portugal's involvement in the slave trade, although Henry later forbade the kidnaping of blacks.

At the time of Prince Henry's death, his sea captains had sailed two thousand miles along the African coast and explored the mouths of the Senegal and Gambia rivers. The grand nephew of Prince Henry, King John II, continued to sponsor the voyages of discovery.

Vasco da Gama's Expedition to India

In 1488 the Portuguese navigator Bartholomeu Diaz succeeded in reaching the southernmost tip of Africa. Because his crew was threatening to mutiny, he had to turn back at this point. Diaz called the tip of the continent the "Cape of Storms" because of the rough weather frequently found there. King John II optimistically renamed it the "Cape of Good Hope."

Nine years later, in 1497, an expedition of four ships was placed under the command of Vasco da Gama (c. 1469-1524). He led his ships around the Cape of Good Hope, up the east coast of Africa, and across the Indian Ocean to Calicut, a port on the west coast of India. On the way to and from India, da Gama's expedition was attacked by Arab and Persian traders who wished to keep the monopoly of the Indian and Chinese trade for themselves.

Two years after leaving Portugal, da Gama returned home. He had lost two of his ships, and many of his men had died. His cargo of spices, however, brought in a profit equal to sixty times the cost of the whole expedition.

Columbus's Rediscovery of America

No one knows for certain who first "discovered" the Americas. The Asian ancestors of the Native Americans probably first migrated to North America between 50,000 and 25,000 B.C. Almost five hundred years before Columbus's famous voyage, Leif Ericson and a group of Vikings crossed the Atlantic in ships with thirty-two oars and single sails. They set up a camp on Newfoundland that has been found by archaeologists. They made no permanent settlements in North America, however, and knowledge of their discovery was eventually forgotten.

The important point about Columbus's rediscovery of the New World is that it had important results for the people of the whole world. Columbus

(1451?-1506) was an Italian from Genoa who believed that by sailing westward across the Atlantic he could reach Japan and China and other areas in Asia. He had read the book in which Marco Polo described his travel to the Far East. Columbus and many people of his day believed that the Earth was much smaller than it actually is. He confidently claimed that the islands he reached off the North American continent were very close to the east coast of Asia. He did not realize that he had discovered a New World.

Under the sponsorship of Queen Isabella of Spain, the three ships of Columbus landed in October 1492 on an island of the Bahamas, which he called San Salvador. Columbus then explored Cuba and other islands of the West Indies. Returning to Europe, he announced his findings in these words:

> All these islands are very beautiful. . . . [The people] show greater love for all others than for themselves; they give valuable things for trifles . . . however, I forbade that things so small and of no value should be given to them, such as pieces of plate, dishes, and glass, likewise keys and shoestraps; although if they were able to obtain them, it seemed to them like getting the most beautiful jewels in the world. . . .

Because Columbus thought that the people of the Americas were East Indians, or Asians, he called them "Indians." It is ironic that the New World he had found was named after another explorer, Amerigo Vespucci, who later sailed along the northern coast of South America.

Magellan's Expedition: A Voyage around the World

Ferdinand Magellan (1480?-1521) was born in Portugal, but he made his great voyage for the King of Spain. In the fall of 1519 he set out with five ships and a crew of two hundred and forty-three to find a passage to the Far East by traveling to the West.

Magellan crossed the Atlantic to Brazil, which had been discovered for Portugal by Pedro Cabral. He sailed south along the coast of South America and through what is now called the Strait of Magellan to the Pacific. Then he sailed across the Pacific to the Philippine Islands. There Magellan was

This old print shows one of Magellan's ships in the harbor of what became known as Rio de Janeiro.

killed during a quarrel between two tribes. An Italian gentleman who had been at Magellan's side reported:

> They killed . . . our light, and our true guide. . . . He was always the most constant in greatest adversity. He endured hunger better than all the rest, and more accurately than any man of the world he understood dead reckoning and celestial navigation. . . . I hope that . . . the fame of so noble a captain will never die.

One of his ships, the *Victoria*, continued all the way. It crossed the Indian Ocean and sailed by the Cape of Good Hope. Three years after its departure from Spain the *Victoria* with its remaining crew members returned to Spain. The survivors included a cabin boy of about fifteen years of age.

It had been a brutal trip. Many of the crew had died of diseases. Others had been killed by the poisoned arrows of hostile tribes. At one point in the voyage, the crew almost starved to death. A crew member reported that for over three months:

> . . . we only ate old biscuit reduced to powder, and full of [worms] . . . and we drank water that was yellow. . . . We also ate the sawdust of wood, and rats which cost half a crown each. . . .

Despite these misfortunes, Magellan's crew had accomplished a remarkable feat of navigation.

They had circled the Earth. For the first time human beings had an accurate idea of the size and shape of the Earth, and of the location of the Earth's continents.

The Discoveries of Other Explorers

About this time other Europeans were making important explorations of distant lands and waters. For example, the following explorers made voyages of discovery to the New World. (You can trace the routes they followed on the map on this page.)

John Cabot—1497. Cabot was an Italian navigator in the service of England. He reached North America in the region of Cape Breton Island in Canada. He looked in vain for a sea passage across North America to Asia. On the basis of his findings, the English laid claim to parts of Canada and the lands later settled by the American colonists.

Pedro Cabral—1500. While sailing from Portugal to the Indies, this Portuguese captain reached Brazil, which he claimed for his homeland.

Vasco Nuñez de Balboa—1513. Balboa was a Spanish commander who led his men in a march from the east to the west coast of the Isthmus of Panama. He may have been the first European to see the Pacific Ocean.

Jacques Cartier—1534-1536. This Frenchman located the channel that led to the St. Lawrence River in Canada. Then he sailed up the river to the present-day sites of Quebec and Montreal.

Hernando de Soto—1539-1542. De Soto, a Spaniard, led an expedition that landed on the coast of Florida. He explored parts of what is known today as the southern United States, and came to the Mississippi River. He died on the trip, and his men buried him in the great river he had discovered.

In the fifteenth and sixteenth centuries, Portugal, Spain, France, and England supported voyages of exploration. As a result of these voyages, European nations built overseas colonies.

Voyages of Discovery

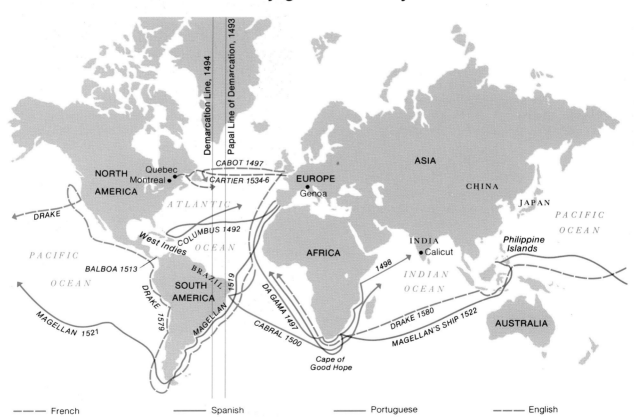

- - - - French ——— Spanish ——— Portuguese - - - - English

1. Describe the Portuguese caravels. What cargoes did they carry between England and Portugal?
2. Who was Philippa of Lancaster? How did she help the Portuguese?
3. Who was Prince Henry the Navigator? How did he launch Portugal on its voyage of discovery?
4. Describe the achievements of Bartholomeu Diaz, Vasco da Gama, Christopher Columbus, and Ferdinand Magellan.
5. What nations besides Portugal sent out explorers to the New World? Name some of these explorers and their findings.

2. Causes and Effects

What were the reasons for European explorations of foreign lands in the latter fifteenth and early sixteenth centuries? There are many answers to this question, some of which you have learned. Economic developments were certainly among the most important factors.

The Influence of Capitalism

Capitalism is an economic system based on the following ideas. 1. The right to own private property must be respected. 2. Most of the production, distribution, and ownership of the goods of a country should be in the hands of private individuals and private companies. 3. The desire to make a profit is one of the principal reasons for undertaking economic activities. 4. People have the right to compete with each other to attain their economic goals.

Some factors of capitalism had existed to some degree in ancient Greece and Rome. They almost disappeared in most of western Europe after the disintegration of the Roman Empire. Toward the end of the Middle Ages, however, the middle class or bourgeoisie increased trade and manufacturing in order to make a profit. The growth of capitalism during the Renaissance made it possible for some people to acquire great wealth. Many early capitalists sought to make further profits by investing in expeditions to the newly discovered lands. In this way, the development of capitalism gave impetus to the explorations of the Europeans.

Italian Cities and National States Compete

After the Crusades, the Italian cities had gained control of handling much of the trade between western Europe and the Far East. Italian banking houses dominated the financing of the new commerce. When the new national states appeared, serious competition arose between them and the Italian cities for trade.

For example, Italian cities bought up most of the products from the Far East that reached ports on the eastern Mediterranean. They dominated the trade in these products in the Mediterranean and Europe. Both Portugal and Spain hoped to share in this trade by finding better sea routes to the Far East.

Competition among National States

Exploration was also stimulated by the competition among the new national states. Portugal, Spain, England, France, and the Netherlands all competed for the rich resources and markets of foreign lands.

The desire of European rulers for foreign gold and silver, and the demand of European peoples for the spices and goods of foreign countries also led to support for voyages of exploration.

Other Reasons for Exploration

There were other motives for the voyages of discovery. Many European rulers and their subjects wanted to bring Christianity to peoples in distant lands. Missionaries accompanied the explorers and preached the Christian message to thousands of people in Asia, the Americas, and Africa.

Others wanted to satisfy their curiosity and their desire for adventure. The thrill of adventure has stirred people from prehistoric times to our present flights into space.

The Portuguese Build an Empire in the Far East

As the Portuguese traveled around Africa to India, they set up forts as posts for trading with the people of the interior. After da Gama's successful voyage, Portuguese fleets entered the Indian Ocean in increasing numbers. In 1507 they occupied Mozambique on the east coast of Africa and other strongholds along the Indian Ocean. In 1509, a Portuguese naval force soundly defeated a large Muslim fleet of the Sultan of Egypt off the west coast of India. Then Alfonso de Albuquerque (1453-1515) took control of Ormuz in Persia, Goa in India, and the port of Malacca on the Strait of Malacca.

This old print shows the English fleet of Sir Francis Drake in the harbor of the Spanish colony of Santo Domingo.

The occupation of Malacca in 1511 enabled the Portuguese to set up trading posts in the Moluccas, or Spice Islands, which produced the finest spices in the world. In 1557 Portugal took over a base at Macao, an area on the coast of China that is still Portuguese. Other Portuguese traders and missionaries appeared in Japan. The aggressive policies of the Portuguese and other Europeans in the Far East caused the Chinese government to restrict severely contacts between Chinese and foreigners. In Japan the government expelled all foreign missionaries and persecuted Japanese Christians.

Spain, the Netherlands, and Britain Enter the Race for Overseas Empires

Shortly after Columbus's rediscovery of the New World, the Spaniards built bases on the islands of Hispaniola (present-day Haiti and the Dominican Republic) and Cuba. From there Spanish explorers and military expeditions spread the rule of Spain to Mexico and Central America, and then from California to the southern tip of South America.

The Portuguese were not left for long as undisputed masters of their commercial empire in the East. The Spaniards started to take over the Philippine Islands around 1565. Soon Spanish officials organized a profitable trade in Chinese goods from the Philippines to Mexico, and then across the Atlantic to Spain.

Meanwhile, the Dutch East India Company began to challenge the Portuguese in the Spice Islands, setting up trading posts on such islands as Java. In this connection a Dutch colony was set up in 1652 at the Cape of Good Hope in southern Africa. It was used as a refueling point on the long voyage between the Netherlands and Dutch possessions on the island of Java. The Japanese government distrusted the Portuguese and Spaniards, but allowed a Dutch trading post to operate in southern Japan.

At about the same time, the French and the British began to dispute Portugal's dominance of India. In 1600 the British East India Company was organized. It acquired in 1639 a permanent footing at

Madras on India's east coast. (You will learn about French colonial activities on pages 358-359.)

A Commercial Revolution

The trade channeled through overseas colonies resulted in such a tremendous commercial expansion that it helped to bring about what is called a *Commercial Revolution*. A significant result of this expansion of trade was that capitalism developed more fully.

Under capitalism some people accumulated enough profits to be able to invest large sums in speculative enterprises. Some of these funds had been used to support exploration, which, in turn, led to the further development of capitalism in the following ways: 1. The increased trade between East and West made certain individuals and companies wealthy. 2. The gold and silver from the colonies provided Europeans with more capital, or wealth that could be used to obtain or produce additional goods. 3. The demand for funds and other economic services helped banking to grow still further. 4. The expansion of commercial activities increased the importance and power of the bourgeoisie. 5. The problems that arose with the expansion of trade and the founding of colonies led to the development of different types of business organizations. For example, *joint-stock companies* were organized mainly to develop overseas trade. In a joint-stock company a number of people placed money in a common fund. In return, each person was given shares in the company. The number of shares a person received depended on the amount of money invested.

The shareholders chose directors to run the company. If the company made a profit, each person received a part in accordance with the number of shares owned. Joint-stock companies had some features of later corporations.

The Slave Trade and the New World

The development by Europeans of plantations and mines in the New World led to the need for many workers. There was an acute labor shortage in the West Indies because the Native American population of the islands was dying off, partly as a result of diseases brought by the Europeans. The solution was to prove inhumane and callous of the rights of human beings—use slaves captured in Af-

A nineteenth century print of a raid for slaves on a village during market day.

rica. The first slaves from West Africa were probably brought to the West Indies in 1503. Shortly afterward, Africans were also brought in to work as slaves on plantations in Venezuela and Brazil. The Dutch employed African slaves in their possessions, as did the English colonists. After the establishment of the Virginia colony, a Dutch ship sold twenty Africans to the English settlers as early as 1619.

The practice of buying and selling Africans had gone on for centuries before the appearance of Europeans on the west coast of Africa. Prisoners of war were regularly sent by African kings to coastal forts. There Arab traders bought these prisoners for the slave markets of East Africa and the Middle East.

With the coming of the Portuguese, however, the slave trade took on new and larger dimensions. Lisbon became a center for the rapidly growing trade in African slaves for the New World. At first the Portuguese had a monopoly on this trade. Gradually, however, Spaniards, Swedes, Danes, French, Germans, Dutch, and British engaged in a profitable three-cornered trade with the New World. Guns and other products from Europe were exchanged with Arab and local chiefs on the west coast of Africa for a shipload of slaves—men, women, and children. The slaves were carried across the Atlantic amid the horrors of the infamous slave ships. Then the sea captains picked up products of the New World—molasses, tobacco, and rum—for the return voyage to Europe. Countless slaves died en route to the New World. Many others survived and were sold in the markets of the West Indies and of North and South America. It is estimated that between 18 million and 24 million Africans were transported to the New World between 1500 and the end of the slave trade in the 1800s.

Check on Your Reading

1. What were three motives for European exploration and building of colonies overseas?
2. How did Portugal build an empire in the Far East? What countries challenged Portugal?
3. In what ways was capitalism affected by the growth of trade and by European empires in the Far East and the Americas?
4. What was one tragic effect of European commercial and colonial expansion in Africa?

3. The Power Struggle Is Stepped Up in Europe

While Europeans were exploring and colonizing distant parts of the world, a struggle for power was raging in Europe itself. This contest reflected political and economic rivalries among the nations of Europe, religious tensions between Catholics and Protestants, and the rising power of the Ottoman Empire.

As a result of these factors, the Europeans became involved in foreign and civil wars, as well as in a complex set of alliances. Often these wars and alliances had serious effects on the lives of people living in the overseas colonies of the European nations.

The Expansion of the Ottoman Empire

In 1453 the Muslim army of the Ottoman Turks captured Constantinople, and brought to an end the power of the Byzantine Empire. (See page 281.) Annexing the lands of the Byzantine Empire, the Ottoman Turks moved steadily into the Balkan Peninsula. Belgrade, the capital of Serbia, fell in 1521. In 1526 the king of Hungary and many of his nobles were killed in a great battle with the Turks. Early in the 1500s the Muslim states of North Africa recognized the sultan, or ruler, of the Ottoman Turks as their overlord. Thus nearly all of Christian Europe—from the Iberian Peninsula to Vienna on the Danube River—was threatened by the ambitions of the Ottoman sultan.

The Ottoman Empire reached its high point under Sultan Suleiman the Magnificent (1520–1566). After occupying Budapest, the Hungarian capital, Suleiman's armies in 1529 and 1532 attacked Vienna, the capital of Austria. They were pushed back, but the Hapsburgs, who ruled in Vienna, were forced to recognize Suleiman as overlord of Hungary. Suleiman had an alliance with King Francis I of France. Francis was eager to help the Turks against the empire of the Hapsburgs.

The Turks usually did not disturb greatly the existing form of government of the lands they annexed. They kept the previous officials, placing over them a representative of the sultan. Christians were expected to follow the orders of the sultan's representative, and to pay their taxes.

The Ottoman Empire was really like a vast army of military occupation. It relied for its strength on slaves. The Christian lands the Turks ruled were required to pay a "boy tax" every five years. A certain number of youth between the ages of twelve and twenty were taken by the Turks as slaves. The boys were converted to Islam and enrolled in the *janissary corps*. Janissaries were elite soldiers trained to be brave in warfare and personally loyal to the sultan. They were given a privileged position within the empire. The most intelligent members of the janissary corps might command armies or rule over conquered provinces. Thanks to the Muslim cavalry and the janissary corps, the Turkish army was perhaps the best in the world in the 1500s.

Charles V and the Rise of the Hapsburgs

In order to understand why the King of France allied himself with the enemy of Christian Europe, we need to trace the rise to power of the Hapsburgs. During the 1200s the Hapsburgs became dukes of Austria, and in time gained such power that a Hapsburg was usually elected as Holy Roman Emperor. The Austrian rulers made so many powerful

Europe at the Time of Charles V

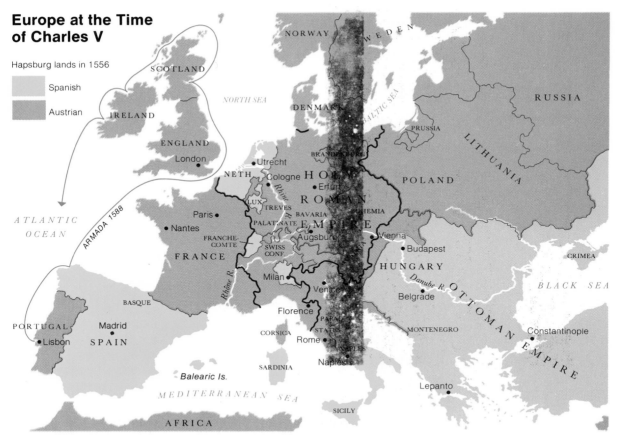

Hapsburg lands in 1556

Spanish

Austrian

Charles V as Holy Roman Emperor and King of Spain ruled a great empire. In 1556 he turned over the Holy Roman Empire to Ferdinand and his other holdings to Philip II.

connections through marriage that people often quoted the following saying about them:

> Let other nations wage war [to gain power],
> but you, happy Austria, marry!

Charles V (1500–1558) was the grandson of Queen Isabella and King Ferdinand of Spain and of Emperor Maximilian I and Mary of Burgundy. He inherited Austria, the Netherlands (Flanders and Holland), Spain, southern Italy, and the Spanish possessions in the New World. In 1519 he was elected Holy Roman Emperor. Thus Charles was the richest and most powerful ruler in Europe before the age of twenty. (See the map on this page.)

Remember that Charles V presided over the Diet of Worms at which Martin Luther appeared to answer for his challenge to the authority of the Church. (See page 295.) For the rest of his life Charles tried in vain to crush the Protestant Reformation. Although he did not want to increase the

power of the Pope, he was committed to making Catholicism the only religion in Europe.

In the religious wars that broke out in Germany between Catholics and Protestants, Charles tried to help the Catholic princes. However, he was also engaged at the time in a series of wars with King Francis I of France over Milan in Italy and Burgundy in eastern France. In 1527 Charles's army captured and sacked Rome because the Pope was allied to France. King Henry VIII of England was allied first with Charles V and later with King Francis I of France. Eventually Charles V had to give up the duchy of Burgundy to France, but he kept Milan and the Netherlands.

At about the same time, the Turkish invasion of Hungary and Austria distracted Charles from his attempts to defeat the French and put down the Protestant princes of Germany. At the Peace of Augsburg (1555), Charles recognized the right of the Protestant princes to hold the areas they con-

A portrait of Philip II of Spain by Alonso Sanchez.

trolled at the time. The princes of Germany were to choose their own religion, whether Lutheran or Catholic, as the official religion of their states.

Worn out by the long struggle, Charles gradually gave up his power in 1554-1556. He turned over the Holy Roman Empire to his younger brother, Ferdinand I. He gave all his other land holdings to his son, Philip II of Spain. He then spent the rest of his life in a monastery in Spain.

Although Charles had failed in his major goals, his reign was very important. First, it revealed the growth of a new idea—the *balance of power* in Europe. England, for example, changed its alliances chiefly to keep either France or the Holy Roman Empire from dominating the rest of Europe. Second, it showed that rulers like Francis I of France were willing to ally themselves with the Turks to serve their own national interests. As Machiavelli had predicted in *The Prince*, each nation was prepared to use whatever methods were necessary to defend its own interests.

Philip II of Spain and the Dutch Rebellion

Philip II (King of Spain and other areas from 1556 to 1598) did all he could to increase the power

of Spain and to promote the cause of Catholicism. During his reign Spanish and other Catholic naval forces achieved a victory against the Turks in the Mediterranean at the Battle of Lepanto (1571). In governing his immense empire, Philip was a hard-working but an autocratic monarch. He denied political rights to many of his subjects, restricted their economic activities, and did all he could to prevent freedom of religious belief.

When the Portuguese royal family died out in 1580, Philip claimed and seized the throne of Portugal. For sixty years (1580-1640), the Portuguese people were ruled by the Spanish Hapsburgs. During this period Portugal's empire in the Far East was seriously weakened.

Philip II was particularly severe in his conduct toward the Spanish Netherlands, which are today divided between the Netherlands and Belgium. He was determined to wipe out the Protestant heresies there. His methods of repression, however, were so severe that the people of the North Netherlands—the Dutch—revolted in 1568.

Prince William of Orange accepted the leadership of the rebels. Philip II hated William and promised to pay to the person "delivering him to us, alive or dead, or taking his life . . . the sum of twenty-five thousand crowns in gold." William was assassinated in 1584, but not before Dutch Independence had been achieved. He is regarded as a national hero.

In 1581 the people of the northern provinces declared themselves an independent nation, the United Netherlands. The preamble to their statement of independence reminds us of the Declaration of Independence of the United States. The Dutch Declaration stated:

> All mankind know that a prince is appointed by God to cherish his subjects even as a shepherd to guard his sheep. When, therefore, the prince does not fulfill his duty as a protector; when he oppresses his subjects, destroys their ancient liberties, and treats them as slaves . . . the [representatives] of the land may lawfully and reasonably depose him and elect another.

The Duke of Alva, Philip II's governor in the Netherlands, attempted to crush the rebels by executions and confiscating private property. The Dutch navy attacked the Spaniards on the sea, and

Dutch citizens at times opened the dikes and flooded the land in front of the advancing Spanish soldiers. The Dutch were also helped by other Protestant nations, especially by England.

In 1648 Spain finally acknowledged the independence of the United Netherlands. The southern provinces, which were mainly Catholic in religion, remained under the rule of the Hapsburgs. Early in the 1800s the southern provinces were added to the Dutch nation. In 1830, however, the Belgians established their own independent kingdom.

Queen Elizabeth I Leads a Strong England

After the death of Henry VIII in 1547, there was much confusion over religion in England. Henry was succeeded, in turn, by three of his children, each of whom changed the religion of the kingdom. The boy king Edward VI, who ruled until 1553, was a Protestant. His sister, Mary, was a Catholic. Queen Mary (ruled from 1553 to 1558) wanted to restore the Catholic Church as the official religion. She married Philip (later Philip II of Spain) and, acting in part on his advice, began a severe persecution of the Protestants.

When Mary died, her sister Elizabeth came to the throne at the age of twenty-five. Elizabeth had great intelligence and had received an excellent education. She wanted her subjects to take pride in their country. "I am the most English woman of the Kingdom," she proclaimed. Then she worked diligently to make the people proud that they were English, too.

Elizabeth was committed to the Protestant cause, and quickly restored a Church of England that was Protestant. In 1563 Parliament enacted the Thirty-Nine Articles that outline the doctrines of the Anglican Church. In 1570 the Pope excommunicated Elizabeth and invited her subjects to depose her.

Tensions among the various religious groups continued in England. The Roman Catholics wanted to make England Catholic again. The Anglicans favored the Church of the Thirty-Nine Articles. The Puritans and other dissenters wanted to erase many features of the Anglican Church that still showed the influence of Catholicism.

Until the kingdom was united under her rule, Elizabeth was careful to avoid an open quarrel with

The Religions of Europe in 1560

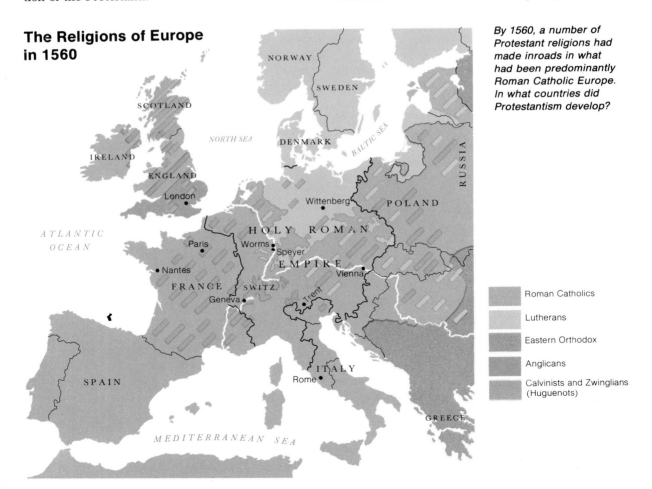

By 1560, a number of Protestant religions had made inroads in what had been predominantly Roman Catholic Europe. In what countries did Protestantism develop?

Roman Catholics

Lutherans

Eastern Orthodox

Anglicans

Calvinists and Zwinglians (Huguenots)

This painting shows the English and Spanish ships off the southern coast of England in the Battle of the Spanish Armada.

Philip II of Spain. She let him think that perhaps one day she might marry him or a man of his choice. All along, however, Elizabeth aimed at strengthening England's position in the world. She strengthened the military power of her nation and encouraged foreign trade and exploration. She chartered the British East India Company to trade with lands in the Indian and Pacific oceans.

England and Spain Are Bitter Rivals

The Queen encouraged two English sea captains—Sir John Hawkins and Sir Francis Drake—in their bold attacks on Spanish colonies in the New World. On one voyage Drake robbed Spanish ships and towns along the western coast of Central America. Afterward, he took his ship, *The Golden Hind,* around the world. Passing through the Strait of Magellan, he looted Spanish cities along the west coast of South America. Then he sailed to San Francisco harbor and returned to England by sailing across the Pacific and Indian oceans. Upon his return Elizabeth received a share of Drake's loot from the Spanish colonies. She complimented him for "singeing the Spanish king's beard," and knighted him for his bravery.

Soon relations between Elizabeth and Philip reached the breaking point. The Spaniards strongly objected to the attacks of English sea captains on their colonies and treasure ships. They also objected to the military and other assistance the English were giving to the Dutch rebels. Matters came to a crisis when Mary Stuart, queen of Scotland, was accused by her subjects of murdering her husband, and was forced to flee to England. Mary was a Catholic and, as Elizabeth's cousin, she was considered by a number of people to be next in line to the throne of England. While being held as a prisoner in England, Mary was accused of being involved in a series of plots against Elizabeth's life, and Elizabeth consented to her beheading in 1587.

England Defeats the Spanish Armada

The year after Mary Stuart's execution, King Philip sent a fleet of 130 ships—the so-called *Invincible Armada*—to invade England and depose Queen Elizabeth. The English fleet of 187 vessels, directed by Admiral Howard, met the enemy fleet off the southern coast of England. The lightness and speed of the English ships gave them an advantage over the unwieldly Spanish ships. The weather proved to be stormy, and a number of Spanish ships were damaged. Then a great North Sea storm sank many more. Only half the Armada returned to its home port.

The Spaniards never recovered from this blow to their military power and pride. In the seventeenth century the Dutch and later the English became masters of the seas.

The Religious Wars in France

The teachings of Luther and Calvin quickly spread throughout France. By 1560 the Protestant Huguenots were a strong minority of the French population. Their supporters included some noble families, such as the powerful Bourbon family.

A bitter struggle soon broke out between the Huguenots and the Roman Catholics. The fighting, which lasted almost eight years, was ended by a truce in 1570. However, peace was not permanently restored. On August 24, 1572—St. Bartholomew's Day—the Queen Mother, Catherine de' Medici, according to some accounts, waved a white handkerchief from a window of the Louvre Palace in Paris. This was the signal for a general massacre of the Huguenots, beginning with their leader in Paris, Admiral de Coligny.

The massacre in Paris and clashes elsewhere in France reopened the war between Catholics and Protestants. Philip II of Spain supported the Roman Catholics in France. The most convinced Catholics were led by the powerful Guise family. The weak king of France, Charles IX, died in 1574 at the age of twenty-four.

For the next nineteen years France was the scene of a bloody civil war between Catholics and Protestants. There was a real danger that the pro-Spanish Guise family might take over the government. Finally, Henri de Bourbon, a Protestant and heir to the throne, made a great decision. It is alleged that he said, "Paris is well worth a Mass," and he became a Catholic in 1593. In this way he satisfied the wishes of the Roman Catholic majority of the French people. He also put an end to the plans of the Guise family and Philip II to make France a puppet of Spain. With joy, France accepted Henri de Bourbon as its king under the name of Henry IV.

One of the most important acts of Henry IV was the proclamation, in 1598, of the *Edict of Nantes*. This gave the following rights to French Protestants: 1. freedom of religious belief; 2. the right of private worship wherever they lived; 3. the right to conduct public worship in a number of specific towns and castles; 4. the right to hold public

A contemporary artist depicted the horrors of the Thirty Years' War. This engraving shows civilian hostages being hung by the army that has captured them.

office; and 5. the right to control a number of walled towns and castles for their protection.

The Edict of Nantes marked a new era of tolerance. Slowly the French nation recovered from the civil war. Henry IV promoted trade and industry. He is reputed to have promised to every French family "a chicken in the pot every Sunday." Unfortunately, not all the hatreds left over from the civil war were forgotten. In 1610, while the king was seated in his carriage in Paris, he was stabbed to death by a religious fanatic. Henry IV was sincerely mourned by the people. Even today the French people remember him with affection as one of the best of their kings.

The Thirty Years' War (1618–1648)

In 1618 one of the most terrible wars in European history broke out. This conflict, known as the *Thirty Years' War,* was a complicated political-religious struggle that involved several countries and religious groups.

On one side were: 1. Protestants, who wished to gain the right to worship as they pleased; 2. the princes of Germany, who wanted greater independence from the Holy Roman Emperor; 3. the Catholic Bourbon dynasty of France, which feared the expansion of the Hapsburg rulers; and 4. the Protestant rulers of Denmark and Sweden, who desired to defend Protestantism and weaken the power of the Holy Roman Emperor.

On the other side were: 1. Catholics, who wished to defend their faith and prevent Protestantism from spreading; 2. the Holy Roman Emperor, who wanted to keep control over the German princes and preserve Catholicism; and 3. the Hapsburg dynasties of Austria and Spain, which were determined to check the ambitions of the Bourbon dynasty of France.

The war spread all across Germany and central Europe and even into France and Italy. Germany and its people were exhausted by the bloody struggle. Now this part and now that part of the Holy Roman Empire was devastated by troops of the different armies. Bands of mercenary soldiers began to kill and rob the defenseless civilian population. Here is how one eyewitness described the activities of the soldiers:

Nothing but hurting and harming and being in their turn hurt and harmed: this was their

whole purpose and existence. From this nothing could divert them—not winter or summer, snow or ice, heat or cold, wind or rain, mountain or valley . . . or the very fear of eternal damnation itself. At this task they labored until at last, in battles, sieges, assaults, campaigns, or even in their winter quarters, which is the soldiers' paradise, one by one they died, perished, or rotted.

When peace finally was declared, many people could not believe it. They had lived so long among the horrors of war that they did not know any other way of life.

The Treaty of Westphalia (1648) ended the Thirty Years' War. By this treaty Calvinism received the same status as Catholicism and Lutherism within the Holy Roman Empire. Each German prince could still decide the religion of his state, but people who belonged to none of these three religions could emigrate.

The efforts of the Hapsburg rulers to restore the authority of the Holy Roman Emperor within Germany were defeated by this treaty. More than

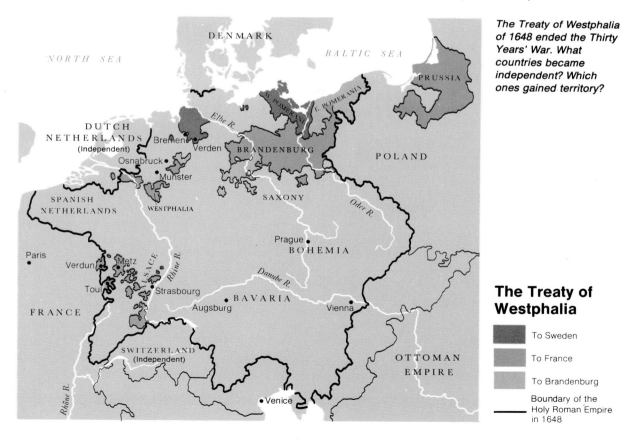

The Treaty of Westphalia of 1648 ended the Thirty Years' War. What countries became independent? Which ones gained territory?

The Treaty of Westphalia

- To Sweden
- To France
- To Brandenburg
- Boundary of the Holy Roman Empire in 1648

three hundred German states were recognized as independent governments. Also Switzerland was recognized as independent of the Holy Roman Empire. The Dutch Netherlands received their independence of Spain. France obtained most of Alsace, and Sweden took possession of western Pomerania and Bremen. Some of the German princes gained in territory.

The Thirty Years' War greatly weakened the power of the Holy Roman Empire. Henceforth the Hapsburgs concentrated on building their holdings in Austria, Bohemia, and Hungary. Brandenburg-Prussia was becoming one of the strong powers of central Europe. The position of Spain began to decline. Because the French and Spaniards could not settle their differences at the Treaty of West-

phalia, the war between them went on for another eleven years until 1659.

Check on Your Reading

1. How did the Ottoman Turks govern the Christian lands they occupied in Europe? What were some of the reasons for the military success of the Turks?
2. Why was Charles V unable to keep Protestantism from spreading in the Holy Roman Empire?
3. How did the Dutch manage to liberate themselves from Spanish control?
4. Why did Spain send its Armada against England in 1588?
5. What were the causes of the Thirty Years' War? What were the main provisions of the Treaty of Westphalia?

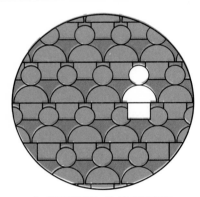

LET'S MEET THE PEOPLE

A Sailor of the Sixteenth Century

It was daybreak, and the seaman joined the crew on the narrow deck of the ship. He wore a shirt with wide sleeves, loose-fitting breeches, and a wool cap. Inside his belt, he carried a knife.

The seaman listened quietly now as a page recited aloud the Lord's Prayer. When prayers for the safety of the ship were finished, the pages placed three platters of food in the middle part of the upper deck and called out: "Who does not come will not eat!"

The hungry seaman sat down quickly and ate his food with his hands and knife. His meal consisted of a portion of dwarf peas, a strip of dried mutton, and a biscuit that was "black, wormy, and gnawed by mice." His ration of water was very small.

All that morning the seaman worked hard. He climbed to the rigging and checked the sails. He helped to pump out the water that had seeped into the bottom of the ship. He hauled ropes to the rhythmic chant of old songs called *salomas*.

That afternoon the seaman amused himself by searching for bugs that crawled about his clothing. Then he listened with terror to the rumor that a sea serpent had been sighted. He hoped that the darkness of night would protect the ship.

In the evening, the stern lantern and the compass lamp were lighted. An altar was set up and candles were lit.

The master of the ship now stepped forward.

"Are we all here?" the master asked.

"God be with us!" answered the seaman and the crew.

The master and crew prayed to God. They ended their religious service with the words: "Amen, and God give us a good night."

That night was good to the voyagers. A brisk wind came up and drove their ship on toward the unknown land that lay ahead.

Based on information in "Sailing by Caravel," an article by Fernando Romero in *Américas* magazine, a monthly publication of the Pan American Union.

CHAPTER REVIEW

Think and Discuss

1. Do you think that the Renaissance education of Queen Philippa helped her develop into a strong and wise leader? Give reasons for your answer.
2. The success of Prince Henry's exploring voyages was due in part to the knowledge and abilities of Italians, Arabs, Jews, and Germans. Explain this statement.
3. Columbus's discovery of the New World set up a series of chain reactions. Explain this statement.
4. Are the "expeditions" exploring space today impelled by the same motives as those of the early explorers? Why or why not?
5. The building of overseas European colonies is usually written about in our country from the point of view of the Europeans. What do you think the people of the lands being conquered and colonized would have said about the actions of Europeans?
6. Religion played a part in the wars of the sixteenth and seventeenth centuries. What were other reasons for the wars? Which reasons do you think were most important? Defend your answer.
7. Do you think the Edict of Nantes was a sensible compromise? Why?
8. How did the Thirty Years' War affect Europe?

Past and Present

1. The Europeans' knowledge and ideas about the rest of the world changed greatly in the sixteenth century. What rapid changes in knowledge about the world have taken place in the twentieth century?
2. Capital was used to finance voyages of exploration and the building of colonies in the sixteenth and seventeenth centuries. How is capital used in our country today?
3. The balance-of-power system developed in Europe in the sixteenth century. Is it still a part of international relations today? Give examples to support your answer.

Activities

1. Use reference books to make a report on the improvements in ocean-going ships and methods of navigation in the fifteenth and sixteenth centuries.
2. Write a sea log such as an explorer might have kept on his voyage. Read excerpts from Columbus's log as an example.
3. Write a report on the development of capitalism in Europe. Consult several references.
4. Three women played an important role in encouraging the voyages of exploration: Queen Philippa of Portugal, Queen Isabella of Spain, and Queen Elizabeth of England. Do research on the activities of one of these leaders and report your findings.
5. Do reading on the history of slavery before 1400 and report your findings.
6. Both the Dutch and the Swiss had a long struggle to win their independence. Draw a chart showing similarities and differences in their steps toward independence.

18

Autocratic Rulers Contrast with Cultural Achievements

KEYNOTE

Persons who have great power are often given special titles. Sometimes they are called *Caesar, Emperor* or *Empress, Mikado,* or *Mogul.* Even in the world of sports we often use a title to describe a powerful performer. For example, Babe Ruth, one of the greatest hitters in baseball, was known as the "Sultan of Swat."

Men and women holding absolute power have played an important role in shaping the course of history. Such rulers are known as *autocrats.* The governments they dominate are known as *autocracies.* An autocracy is a form of government in which one person usually holds all the power of the state. He or she may allow others to share some of the power, but it still belongs to the ruler. Such rulers do not believe that their power comes to them by consent of the people. Their actions, therefore, are not governed by a sense of responsibility to their subjects.

Between 1650 and 1780 many changes took place in Europe. The Holy Roman Empire and the Ottoman Empire declined. The kingdoms of Spain, Portugal, Sweden, and Poland also lost power. Meanwhile, France, Austria, Prussia, and Russia achieved prominence under autocratic rulers.

At the same time that autocratic rulers competed and clashed with each other in Europe, there were remarkable accomplishments in architecture, art, music, and literature. Today the wars of these autocrats are little remembered, but the cultural achievements of the period are an important part of our lives.

Louis XIV giving the order of the Holy Spirit to one of his courtiers.

Factors such as location, mountains, rivers, plains, and fertile soils have influenced the development of France. The inset map shows the territories added to France by Louis XIV.

France

Present political boundary of France

Added during the reign of Louis XIV

1. French Rulers Expand Their Power

France was one of the first nations of Europe to become a strong and unified state. During the reign of Henry IV (king from 1589 to 1610) the country recovered from the disorders of the wars of religion. In the seventeenth century France became the dominant power in Europe. French was the language of diplomacy and of educated people all over Europe. French styles in literature and architecture were widely imitated.

The Geography of France

France is a country of western Europe about twice the size of Colorado. On the north it is separated from Britain by the Strait of Dover and the English Channel. To the west lie the Bay of Biscay and the Atlantic Ocean. On the east France borders on Belgium, Luxembourg, Germany, Switzerland, and Italy. To the south lie the Mediterranean and Spain. The fact that France borders on many other nations has helped to involve the French in many European developments.

The Vosges Mountains lie between France and Germany. The Jura Mountains are between France and Switzerland. The Alps lie between France and Italy. The Pyrenees extend between France and Spain. In the past these mountains have provided some protection for France against attack.

France is also a land of many rivers, including such important waterways as the Loire, Rhine, Garonne, and Seine. The Rhine is in certain areas a border between France and Germany. France's rivers provide a valuable means of inland transportation that has helped unite the country.

The soil of France is rich in many areas, particularly in the northern plains. Here wheat, cereals, sugar beets, and grapes for wine are grown. The plateaus are good grazing lands. Mineral deposits, including coal and iron in northern and eastern France, provide a basis for industry.

Richelieu Strengthens the Royal Power

After Henry IV's death his widow, Marie de' Medici, ruled in place of her young son, Louis XIII.

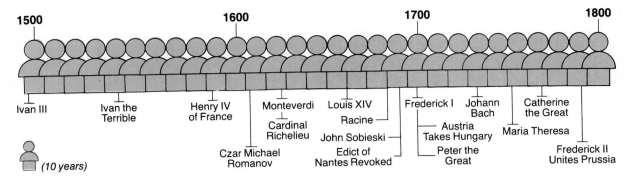

| 1500 | | | | 1600 | | | | 1700 | | | | 1800 |

Ivan III

Ivan the
Terrible

Henry IV
of France

Monteverdi
Cardinal
Richelieu

Czar Michael
Romanov

Louis XIV
Racine
John Sobieski

Edict of
Nantes Revoked

Frederick I

Austria
Takes Hungary

Peter the
Great

Johann
Bach

Catherine
the Great

Maria Theresa

Frederick II
Unites Prussia

(10 years)

There was a period of disorder, which continued even after King Louis came of age. Things went from bad to worse until the king appointed as his chief adviser Cardinal de Richelieu.

Armand Jean du Plessis, Cardinal de Richelieu (1585–1642) firmly directed the French government from 1624 until his death. In his *Political Will and Testament,* he recalled for the benefit of Louis XIII the difficult conditions in which he had found France:

> When Your Majesty was first pleased to admit me into your councils and to repose a great confidence in me for the direction of your affairs, I may state with truth that the Huguenots shared the state with you, that the great nobles behaved as if they were not your subjects, and that the most powerful governors of provinces behaved as if they were rulers in their own right.

Richelieu devoted himself principally to one cause. His goal was to strengthen the power of the monarchy and central government at home and abroad. He once said, "My first goal was the majesty of the king; the second was the greatness of the realm."

Richelieu first attacked the problem of the Huguenots, who had become a state within the state. He broke their power by capturing in 1628 their last great stronghold at La Rochelle on the Atlantic coast. However, he was wise enough to guarantee to the Huguenots their religious freedoms.

Next, Richelieu crushed those great nobles who were involved in countless plots against the royal authority. He executed some of the ringleaders as a warning that the French monarchy would no longer put up with feudal disorders.

Richelieu also chose high officials from the middle class to help unify the kingdom and put down the abuses of the provincial governors. He increased the power of officials who were known as *intendants.* Intendants were directly responsible to the king. They traveled about the country and had broad powers in matters of public order, justice, and finance.

Richelieu extended French commercial interests in the West Indies and Africa, and encouraged the colonization of Canada. He sent French armies of occupation into Alsace on the east, Roussillon on the south, and Artois on the north. Under his administration the handsome Royal Palace was built in Paris. The French Academy was founded to encourage French writers and improve the French language.

Richelieu was disliked by the people of France for his harshness, but he made France a great force in European affairs. He created a strong professional army, and defended French interests against the power of the Hapsburgs in Germany and Spain. He allied France with the Protestant powers against the Hapsburgs during the Thirty Years' War.

Mazarin Continues Richelieu's Policies

Richelieu died in 1642, and Louis XIII died the following year. The heir to the throne was Louis XIV (1638–1715). He had one of the longest reigns in history, from 1643 until his death. Since the new king was only a child, his mother, Anne of Austria, was named regent. The queen turned over control of the state to Cardinal Jules Mazarin, who played a key role in the French government until his death in 1661. Many French nobles resented Mazarin's rise to power because he was originally an Italian of humble origin.

Mazarin continued many of Richelieu's policies. In foreign affairs the high point of this period was the signing of the Treaties of Westphalia (1648), which ended the Thirty Years' War (see pages

This painting of Cardinal de Richelieu now hangs in the Louvre in Paris.

315-316). This was a triumph for France, which increased its power and territory at the expense of the Austrian Hapsburgs.

Neither France nor Spain was willing to end the warfare, which went on for another eleven years. Western France and other areas suffered as a result of invasions. Mazarin then made an alliance with Oliver Cromwell, the Puritan virtual dictator of England. English and French armies defeated the Spaniards, who were forced to ask for peace. The Treaty of the Pyrenees (1659) was a humiliation for the Spanish Hapsburgs. To the French they had to turn over Artois in the north and territory in the

south that extended the French boundaries to the Pyrenees. It was also agreed that Marie Thérèse, the daughter of the Spanish monarch, would marry Louis XIV of France. France had become the strongest nation of Europe.

Within France, Mazarin continued Richelieu's policy of making the crown absolute. Mazarin's restrictions on the privileges of the nobles and the rising price of food in Paris led to two uprisings against the regent and her hated "foreign" adviser. These rebellions were known as *Frondes* from the French word for "the sling."

The Frondes were preceded by a popular disturbance in the streets of Paris during August 1648. The following year high officials of the Paris law courts staged the first Fronde. It was put down by royal troops. In February 1651 a second Fronde, led by dissatisfied nobles, took place. When the people of Paris failed to support the leaders of the Fronde, it collapsed. Louis XIV and his mother, who had fled from Paris, came back in triumph. Mazarin returned a few months later.

When young Louis XIV took over the reins of power at the death of Mazarin, he found himself the absolute ruler of France.

Louis XIV, the "Sun King"

Louis XIV (1643-1715) was a handsome young monarch. A solidly built man of medium height, he added to his stature by wearing high heels. His nose was long and curved like the beak of an eagle. His hair was abundant and fell in curls about his shoulders. And his blue eyes took on whatever expression he felt was necessary for the role he played in what he called the "profession of king." He was a fine horseman, an enthusiastic hunter, a graceful dancer, a charming companion of the ladies, and a polite host.

Louis XIV was not a man of brilliant intellect. Neither was he especially well educated. Nevertheless, he was dignified, energetic, hard-working, and wise enough to use common sense to counteract the flattery that surrounded him and his court. The king's motto was *Nec Pluribus Impar*—"None His Equal." His emblem was the sun, for he saw himself as the Sun King whose rays touched every aspect of French life. Although he probably did not make the statement often attributed to him, "L'état, c'est moi!" ("I am the State!"), he acted as if he believed it. Little wonder that the wigged and perfumed lords and ladies of his court hurried to do his slightest wish.

The "Divine Right of Kings"

Louis XIV's absolutism was based on the idea of the *divine right of kings*. This is the idea that rulers derive their powers from God and are responsible only to God. This idea was best expressed in *Politics Drawn from the Words of the Holy Scriptures,* written by Bishop Jacques Bossuet (1627-1704). He stated:

> The royal throne is not the throne of a man, but the throne of God himself. . . . It appears from . . . this that the person of the king is sacred, and that to attack him in any way is sacrilege. . . . Therefore, the royal power is absolute.

Bossuet added, however, that kings were subject to the judgment of God for their actions.

Colbert as Finance Minister

In economics Louis XIV turned for advice to a remarkable financier, Jean Baptiste Colbert (1619-1683). Working sixteen hours a day, Colbert made important contributions to France by developing its economy. He stimulated trade and supported the establishment of trading companies and colonies in India and North America. He encouraged the growth of industries and subsidized factories for producing wool and silk. Industrial crops, such as flax and hemp, were developed. An effective merchant marine and navy were formed to protect France's interests. In addition, the quality and quantity of goods were regulated.

Colbert followed the economic philosophy of *mercantilism*. He believed that France should export more in value than it imported; and that it should establish and use its colonies to increase the wealth of the home country. This meant that France should keep a strong navy to protect its national interests, and that French industries should be helped by placing high tariffs on the goods of other countries. The basic aim was to attract and keep as much gold and silver as possible within the country. Colbert stated his policy in these words:

> I believe . . . that it is only the abundance of money in a state which makes the difference in its greatness and power.

Colbert did his best to balance the budget of the government. He urged the king to save even pennies and declared that an expensive state dinner brought him "unbelievable pain." Louis XIV was not inclined to accept any advice to economize. Colbert's hard work could not eliminate the evils that came as a result of the king's extravagance and costly wars.

Nevertheless, many European countries followed Colbert's economic policies during the late seventeenth and a considerable part of the eighteenth century. Extreme mercantilism has been termed aptly "the economic phase of royal absolutism."

Revocation of the Edict of Nantes

An event that had important repercussions in religious and economic matters in France took place in 1685. In that year Louis XIV revoked the Edict of Nantes. The Huguenots, or French Protestants, made up less than 10 percent of the population of France. As a group, they were active and successful in industry. Many were merchants, traders, and skilled artisans who had frequently demonstrated their loyalty to France. Since the Edict of Nantes (1598) they had been permitted freedom of religious belief.

Louis XIV decided to unite his subjects through religious conformity. With the support of ardent Catholic advisers, he first excluded the Huguenots from many privileges. Then he tried to convert them by force. Finally, he revoked the Edict of Nantes and ordered all Protestant churches closed. Protestant religious leaders were told to leave France within two weeks under threat of being sent to the galleys, or prison ships, if they resisted. The children of Huguenots were to be brought up as Catholics.

Louis XIV's actions against the Huguenots proved economically disastrous to France. Although not permitted by law to leave France, thousands of Huguenots fled. Eventually more than 300,000 went to Prussia, Switzerland, the Dutch Netherlands, Britain, South Africa, and the English colonies of North America. As a result of the exodus of the Huguenots, the silk industry of Tours crumbled, the province of Normandy was almost depopulated, and trade declined alarmingly. Other countries gained by France's loss. Huguenots contributed to the economic welfare of the lands where they found refuge—often lands that were bitter rivals of France.

The Palace of Versailles

Nowhere did Louis XIV express more clearly his taste for magnificence than in the palace of Versailles. He had Versailles built on a marshland by such architects as Jules Hardouin Mansart. The marsh was transformed by Le Nôtre, a famous gardener, into a magnificent park adorned with formal gardens, a canal, and hundreds of marble and bronze statues. Louis XIV and his court moved into Versailles in 1682.

Several thousand persons could be assembled in the palace. There were beautiful arched windows and mirrors in the "Hall of Mirrors." There were graceful fountains with fourteen hundred jets. Versailles was the architectural reflection of the "Sun King." Other rulers tried to imitate its splendor in palaces built all over Europe.

At Versailles, King Louis XIV was cut off from contact with his people. The nobles of the court went hunting with the king in the surrounding park, or strolled among the gardens and fountains. In the evenings there were balls, concerts, and other entertainments. The noblemen wore embroidered coats and covered their heads with powdered wigs. The ladies dressed in jewelled robes and supported

The large photo shows the Hall of Mirrors of the Palace of Versailles. The painting shows the Palace and its grounds in the 1660s. Versailles influenced the style of small and large palaces built throughout Europe in the years that followed.

high and elaborate headdresses. Living in this tinselled world, far from their neglected estates, the nobles lost their sense of independence and became human puppets.

Four Wars of Expansion

France had become the strongest power in Europe, and its rivalry with the Austrian Hapsburgs continued. Overseas, France had an empire in India and North America, which brought the French into conflict with the English. Louis XIV's foreign policy had four main objectives: 1. He wanted to make France supreme in Europe. 2. He planned to extend the country's boundaries to the Alps, and to the Rhine and Scheldt rivers. 3. He wished to increase French trade and the French empire. 4. He wanted to win glory for himself.

To achieve these objectives Louis XIV prepared for war with the help of his military advisers. Marquis de Louvois, the French Minister of War, created the first standing army in Europe. Vauban, a talented engineer, built strong fortresses on the French frontiers, and developed the use of shells to destroy enemy defensive works. Brilliant generals like Turenne and Condé led French armies into battle.

The *War of Devolution* (1667-1668) arose over Louis XIV's claim that he was entitled to Spanish territory through his wife, Marie Thérèse, a Spanish princess. France gained Lille and eleven other towns in the Spanish Netherlands. Plans to expand these conquests were checked by the opposition of the Triple Alliance of the Netherlands, England, and Sweden.

A few years later, angered over the Dutch opposition, Louis attacked the Netherlands. In the *War against the Dutch* (1672-1678), the opponents were France and England against the Netherlands, the Holy Roman Empire, Spain, Sweden, and Denmark. At the end of the war, France gained Franche-Comté as well as several fortresses from the Hapsburgs, which extended the French boundaries toward the Alps.

In 1686, the Palatinate, a rich country west of the Rhine, joined the Holy Roman Empire, Sweden, Spain, Bavaria, and Saxony in the League of Augsburg. One of its leaders was William of Orange, the Dutch general who became king of England in 1688. Later England became a member of the League. In the *War of the Palatinate* (1689-1697)

France opposed all the powers of the League. At the end of the war France lost territory on the right bank of the Rhine, but kept Strasbourg and part of Alsace. Louis XIV granted commercial concessions to the Dutch and allowed them to station troops in forts in the Spanish Netherlands. France recognized William of Orange as King of England.

The War of the Palatinate was also fought in lands overseas, where the English struggled with the French for colonial empire. When the conflict ended, France regained Nova Scotia in North America and gave Fort Albany on Hudson Bay to England.

The last war into which Louis XIV led France—the *War of the Spanish Succession* (1701-1713)—proved a disaster for the French. This conflict began when Charles II, King of Spain, died, leaving his realm to Philip of Anjou, the grandson of Louis XIV. England and Austria were determined not to allow the crowns of Spain and France to be united.

In this war the English general John Churchill, Duke of Marlborough, crushed the French and Bavarians at the Battle of Blenheim in Germany. After other French defeats, France was invaded. Economic conditions in France became desperate; and in rapid succession Louis XIV's son, two grandsons, and a great grandson suddenly died. The king did not sink under these heavy losses but stubbornly rallied his people to defend their country. Eventually he was able to negotiate the Treaties of Utrecht (1713) that ended the war. Under the terms, Philip V, the grandson of Louis XIV, was recognized as King of Spain on condition that the crowns of France and Spain were never to be united. Austria received the Spanish Netherlands (modern Belgium) and a solid foothold in the Italian Peninsula. England received Minorca and Gibraltar from Spain. France gave Nova Scotia to England and recognized England's claims to Newfoundland and the Hudson Bay region in North America. (The war in North America was called *Queen Anne's War.*) As a result of the War of the Spanish Succession, the French royal treasury was drained.

On his deathbed Louis XIV gave this advice to his great-grandson, who was to become Louis XV:

> My child, you are going to be a great king.
> Do not imitate me in my fondness for buildings
> nor in my fondness for war. Try, on the

contrary, to have peace with your neighbors . . . Try to comfort your subjects, which I am very unhappy not to have done.

According to an observer at the court, when the French people learned that the king was dead, they "trembled with joy" . . . and "thanked God . . . for their deliverance."

Check on Your Reading

1. Name three important achievements of Cardinal Richelieu.
2. What did Cardinal Mazarin gain for France in the Treaty of the Pyrenees? What were the Frondes?
3. Explain the meaning of the expressions "I am the State" and the "divine right of kings."
4. How did Colbert strengthen France?
5. What were the results of the revocation of the Edict of Nantes?
6. What were the four main objectives of Louis XIV's foreign policy? To what extent did he attain them?

2. The Growth of the Austrian Empire

The history of Austria is closely linked to its geographical position in the center of Europe. (See the map below.) Austria is located at crossroads between north and south and east and west. As a result, Austria was overrun by invaders from other parts of Europe and from Asia during ancient and medieval times. Its population at the end of the Middle Ages was basically German-speaking.

The Alps cut across Austria so that only one-half of the land could be used for agriculture. Wheat, rye, oats, and grapes for wine were raised in the fertile valley of the Danube River. Vienna, the capital, became an important center of trade during the late Middle Ages and Renaissance.

Chapter 17 described how Charles V, the Holy Roman Emperor, divided his empire in 1555 between his son Philip II of Spain, and his brother, Ferdinand I of Austria. Under the Hapsburg rulers at Vienna, Austria was the most powerful state of the Holy Roman Empire. It had acquired through marriage and war other parts of the Holy Roman Empire, including Silesia, Bohemia, Moravia, and the Tyrol. (See the map on page 327.) The Hapsburgs were also beginning to expand their land holdings beyond the Holy Roman Empire into the Balkans, the rugged, mountainous peninsula in

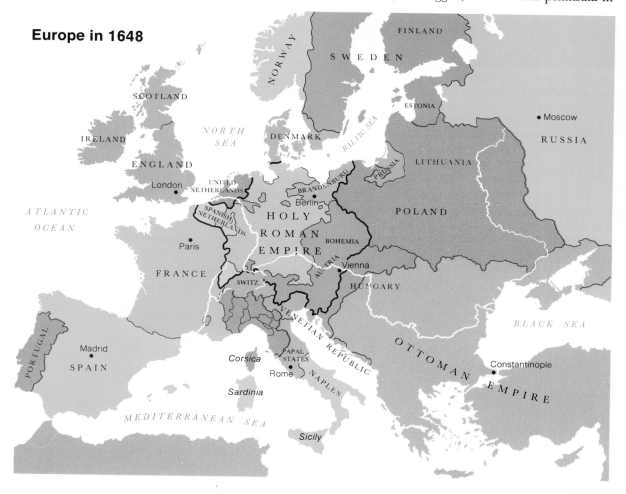

Europe in 1648

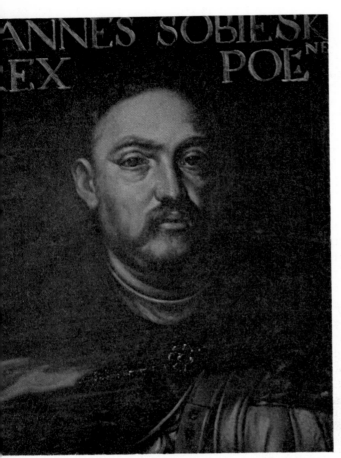

In 1683 King John Sobieski of Poland led the army that defeated the Turks who were marching on Vienna.

southeast Europe. Here they came into conflict with the Turks.

Resistance to the Turks

As described in Chapter 17 (page 309), Austria came under serious attack from the Turks after the Battle of Mohacs (1526) and had to accept the annexation of Hungary by the Ottoman Empire. The garrison at Vienna repelled sieges by the Turks in 1529 and 1532.

The Turkish armies returned again to Vienna in 1683. The hard-pressed Austrians received help just in time from John Sobieski, King of Poland. Assembling his troops on a hill outside Vienna, Sobieski led a cavalry charge against the Turks that saved the city. The Polish king claimed that the Turkish general had "barely escaped, on horseback, with nothing but the coat on his back."

Austria Expands

As a result of continued pressure from Austria, Poland, and Russia, the Turks were forced to give up some of their land holdings in the Balkans. Also, by the end of the seventeenth century, Hungary was under Austrian control.

By the Treaties of Utrecht (1713), which ended the War of the Spanish Succession, Austria received the Spanish Netherlands (modern Belgium) as well as Naples, Milan, and Sardinia, which were formerly held by Spain.

Maria Theresa Becomes Ruler of Austria

The next big conflict in Europe broke out when Maria Theresa inherited the throne from her father, Charles VI, in 1740. Before his death Charles VI had tried to protect his daughter by having the rulers of Europe accept the *Pragmatic Sanction*. This was an agreement of the European monarchs not to seize Maria Theresa's possessions. Although Charles VI had given them territories in exchange for this promise, several rulers broke the Pragmatic Sanction.

Frederick II of Prussia occupied the rich province of Silesia. Soon France, Spain, Bavaria, and Saxony entered the war, trying to profit at Austria's expense. In 1742 Britain, the Netherlands, and Hanover joined the conflict on Austria's side (known as the War of the Austrian Succession). Under Maria Theresa's determined leadership, Austria fought back successfully against its enemies. However, the Treaty of Aix-la-Chapelle awarded Silesia to Prussia.

Eager to obtain revenge against Prussia, Maria Theresa soon proposed an alliance to Austria's old enemy, France. In the Seven Years' War (1756-1763) Austria and France fought against Britain and Prussia. Russia, Spain, and a number of German states joined Austria and France in the exhausting struggle. There were no changes of territories in Europe as a result of this conflict. However, many changes took place in India and North America, where the French and British were locked in a long struggle. (See Chapter 20.)

After the Seven Years' War, Maria Theresa concentrated on internal reforms for the people of her vast empire. She proved to be one of the strongest of the Austrian Hapsburg rulers. In time of trouble she pawned her personal jewels to aid her country. She was happily married to the Duke of Lorraine,

The Austrian Empire in 1740

When Maria Theresa became Empress of Austria, the Austrian Empire included lands in Italy, Germany, Hungary, and the Netherlands.

NORTH SEA

HOLY ROMAN EMPIRE

POLAND

AUSTRIAN NETHERLANDS

SILESIA

BOHEMIA

MORAVIA

AUSTRIA

Vienna

TRANSYLVANIA

HUNGARY

FRANCE

SWITZ.

TYROL

Milan

Mohacs

WALLACHIA AND SERBIA (Austrian until 1739)

TUSCANY

Constantinople

CORSICA

Rome

OTTOMAN EMPIRE

Naples

SARDINIA (Austrian until 1720)

KINGDOM OF THE TWO SICILIES (Austrian until 1735)

MEDITERRANEAN SEA

who became Emperor of the Holy Roman Empire in 1745. They had sixteen children and a happy domestic life. Among her children were Joseph II, Emperor of Austria, and Maria Antoinette, who became Queen of France.

Maria Theresa and the Enlightenment

During the reign of Maria Theresa an intellectual movement known as the *Enlightenment* swept across most of Europe. The Enlightenment stressed the idea that people should gain as much knowledge as possible and solve their problems by reason and intelligence. As the eighteenth-century German philosher Immanuel Kant (1724–1804) pointed out: "Dare to use your own understanding [was] the motto of the Enlightenment."

Maria Theresa was influenced to some extent by the Enlightenment. She carried out many reforms in her realm: 1. She centralized the government and weakened the power of the nobles. 2. She reorganized and centralized the financial system. 3. She improved living conditions for the peasants. 4. She strengthened education. 5. She introduced a new penal code. In religious matters, however, she was less progressive. A staunch Roman Catholic, she persecuted her Protestant and Jewish subjects.

The reforms introduced by Maria Theresa never departed from the principle that the empress was Austria's absolute ruler. Once she wrote:

I flatter myself that I shall be able to prevent the ruin of the State.

It was her deep conviction that she—and not the people—should run the Empire.

Maria Theresa's son, Joseph II, ruled jointly with her from 1765 to 1780, and alone from 1780 to 1790. Under Joseph II's supervision many other important reforms in Austria were carried out. He completed the freeing of the serfs, and took away

Maria Theresa, her husband, and some of their children are shown on the terrace of her magnificent palace in Vienna.

from the nobles the right to administer justice to the peasants. He established greater equality for his subjects before the law, abolishing capital punishment and limiting the use of torture in most cases. Under Joseph II the school system was improved by providing good elementary-school texts and well-trained teachers. Religious toleration was granted to Calvinist, Lutherans, and Orthodox Christians, as well as better treatment to the Jews.

Maria Theresa and Joseph II faced the problem of ruling a widespread empire of many different nationalities. Both tried to "Germanize" their subjects; that is, to make them Germanic in language and culture. However, this attempt failed. Not even such strong leaders could solve all the problems facing the Hapsburgs. How could they when their possessions were scattered over Germany, Italy, Bohemia, the Netherlands, and Hungary!

Check on Your Reading

1. How did Austria resist the Turks?
2. What caused the War of the Austrian Succession?
3. What was the Enlightenment?
4. Evaluate Maria Theresa and Joseph II as rulers.

3. The Rise of Prussia

During the eighteenth century Prussia, a North German state, emerged as a strong rival to Austria. At that time Prussia was chiefly an agricultural land. Its central plain was divided into many large estates owned by *Junkers,* or great nobles. The estates of the Junkers were worked by serfs while many of the estate owners served as officers in the Prussian army. The Junkers were a powerful class that had great influence in the Prussian state.

Prussia also had important mineral resources— deposits of coal, lead, zinc, copper, and potash. Such resources are essential to the development of industry and manufacturing.

The Rise of the Hohenzollerns

During the Middle Ages the *Teutonic Knights,* a German religious order organized along military lines, conquered the Slavs in the area now known as Prussia. Gradually the Teutonic Knights carved out an empire for themselves and their descendants along the Baltic Sea, including East Prussia.

In the fifteenth century a member of the House of Hohenzollern, which originally came from southern Germany, was chosen by the Holy Roman Emperor to be the Elector (ruler) of Brandenburg. Brandenburg was a border area of the Holy Roman Empire east of the Elbe River. (See the map on page 329.) At the time of the Reformation, the Hohenzollerns turned Lutheran. In 1614 they obtained territory in western Germany. Four years later the Elector of Brandenburg greatly increased his territory by inheriting the duchy of Prussia (East Prussia). Brandenburg-Prussia was a widely scattered state.

Frederick William (1640-1688), who was known as the Great Elector, provided his subjects with forceful leadership. He helped unify the government, centralized the system of finances, and stimulated business activities. He also built a small but well-trained army.

The Great Elector was succeeded by his son, Frederick I. In exchange for Frederick I's aid in the War of the Spanish Succession, the Holy Roman Emperor permitted him in 1701 to take the title of "King in Prussia." Prussia had thus officially emerged from what was once a small German province. It lay outside the Holy Roman Empire, and for this reason the Elector of Brandenburg was called "King in Prussia." His entire domain was at first known as "Brandenburg-Prussia" and later just "Prussia." Its capital was the small town of Berlin.

Prussia's Drillmaster King

Frederick William I (king from 1713 to 1740) was a short, stout man with a metallic voice and an ambition to make Prussia a great power. He was an eccentric individual who would order market women selling apples to knit while they sat at their stalls. When he caught men lounging about the town with nothing to do, he would hit them with his cane and order them to take up an honest trade. He also collected tall soldiers for his army. Once he paid out twice the annual salary of a Prussian general to recruit a giant Irish soldier for one of his favorite regiments.

Frederick William I was a hard-working and efficient king. He worked long hours to improve education, increase trade, establish centers for manufacturing, introduce new methods of farming, and run the government economically. His main concern was to build a strong army. By 1740 Prussia had 80,000 men under arms, a force just behind the armies of France, Russia, and Austria. In France there was one soldier for every one hundred and fifty inhabitants, while Prussia had one soldier for every twenty-five inhabitants. Commenting on this

Find the small state of Brandenburg-Prussia on this map. Then use the key to trace its growth into a large and powerful state in central and eastern Europe.

The Growth of Prussia

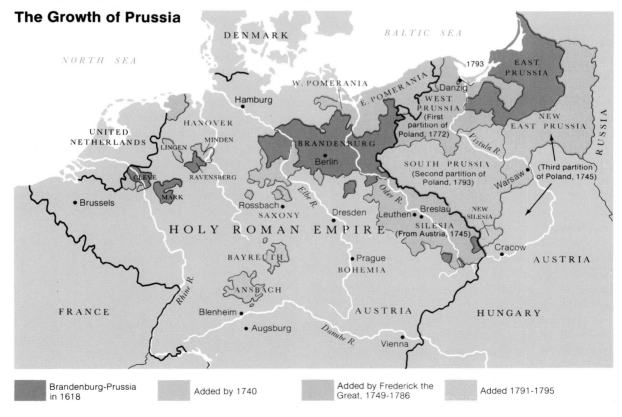

Brandenburg-Prussia in 1618		Added by 1740		Added by Frederick the Great, 1749–1786		Added 1791–1795

This print shows Frederick II of Prussia in his old age reviewing some of his troops. He was both a skilled general and a crafty diplomat.

development, Scottish historian Thomas Carlyle said:

> In a military, and also in a much deeper sense, [Frederick William I] may be defined as the great Drill-sergeant of the Prussian Nation . . . Prussia is all a drilled phalanx, ready to the word of command.

The Achievements of Frederick the Great

Frederick II (ruled Prussia from 1740–1786) became ruler of Prussia in 1740. As a young man Frederick II was in frequent conflict with his domineering father, Frederick William I. On one occasion the young prince was threatened with death for trying to run away to Paris. However, partly as a result of his father's rigorous training, Frederick II became a strong monarch. He is known as Frederick the Great because during his reign Prussia secured recognition as a major power in Europe.

Frederick II was one of the most skilled generals of his day as well as a crafty diplomat. Extremely fond of French culture, he enjoyed exchanging ideas with the French philosopher Voltaire. In accord with the principles of the Enlightenment, Frederick was tolerant of all religions.

Frederick the Great was determined to expand his kingdom. For this reason he invaded Silesia, thus starting the War of the Austrian Succession. By the war he gained Silesia, a rich land south and east of Prussia.

During the Seven Years' War, Prussia faced a formidable group of enemies. Under Frederick the Great's leadership Prussia was able to win important battles; but Prussian armies were greatly outnumbered. Just when it appeared that Prussia could no longer withstand the forces of its enemies, Peter III ascended the Russian throne. This new Russian ruler was favorable to Frederick. He helped prevent Prussia's military collapse by taking Russia out of the fighting. Frederick the Great was allowed to keep Silesia by the treaty which ended the war in 1763.

Frederick the Great had lost many soldiers as well as considerable money and property during the war. The king set to work to help rebuild the Prussian economy as soon as peace returned.

The Unification of Prussia

Frederick the Great was concerned because his kingdom was not territorially united. The region of East Prussia was separated from the rest of Prussia by a province belonging to Poland. Poland had emerged from the late Middle Ages as a large kingdom with a weak government and hard-to-defend frontiers. Its monarch was elected, and its nobles were intent only on preserving all their rights and privileges. Frederick the Great saw the opportunity to unify his own lands at the expense of the Poles. He joined with Austria and Russia to take part in the First Partition of Poland (1772). (See map on page 329.)

In many ways, Frederick was an "enlightened despot" like Maria Theresa and Joseph II of Austria. He once wrote:

> . . . the sovereign represents the state. . . . The prince is to the nation he governs what the head is to the man; it is his duty to see, think, and act for the whole community.

The rise of Prussia as a united power would lead in the nineteenth century to the formation of the German nation.

Changes in Methods of Warfare

Great changes in the methods of warfare made it possible for military leaders like Frederick the Great to change the course of history. Gunpowder was probably discovered in the Far East, where the Chinese used it for centuries in fireworks and rockets. This invention was passed on to the Arabs and Byzantine people of the Middle Ages. The Byzantine fighters used gunpowder in wooden tubes—the ancestors of modern cannons. The Turkish armies that captured Constantinople in 1453 attacked the walls of the city with thirteen great "bombards," large cannons, and over sixty smaller cannons.

In 1492 Queen Isabella of Castile found that the old feudal-type armies, consisting of regiments of knights and their vassals, were not effective against the Moors of Granada. She hired professional soldiers—mercenary troops from Switzerland—and also trained her police force to become a professional army. Isabella's armies contained artillery units furnished with metal cannons. Well-trained engineers built roads for the artillery pieces. There was a large supply train of about eighty thousand mules. Isabella organized a field hospital as well as a corps of field messengers.

Between 1450 and the end of the 1500s the Spaniards developed firearms for the infantry: explosive shells, pistols, fragmentation shells (that burst apart upon impact), and rifling (grooving the barrel of a cannon or firearm so as to improve its accuracy, speed, and range).

All these technical improvements had immense consequences in warfare. A skilled common soldier could bring down with artillery shell or with a pistol shot a nobleman on horseback. Mercenary troops were used frequently in the Italian wars during the Renaissance. Gustavus Adolphus of Sweden introduced new tactics into the Thirty Years' War. Swedish cavalrymen were trained to gallop toward the enemy lines, firing their pistols as they rode. They could also use swords and axes. For this reason they were described by military historians as "mounted infantry."

Like Gustavus Adolphus, Frederick the Great of Prussia was a skillful military leader. He used horse-drawn artillery units to support the cavalry. By skillful use of flanking attacks, Frederick proved that an army of thirty thousand men could defeat one of seventy thousand in rapid time. His victo-

ries at Rossbach and Leuthen are military achievements. Until the French Revolution, warfare remained a matter for professional officers and their well-drilled soldiers.

Check on Your Reading

1. How did the Hohenzollerns build their power and acquire territory up to 1701?
2. Evaluate Frederick William I as king.
3. Summarize the achievements of Frederick the Great.
4. What were some important changes in warfare between 1450 and 1750?

4. Russia Becomes a Nation

Most of Russia consists of a huge plain extending from Poland into Siberia. This great plain has served as a passageway for many invaders. Its openness has made it difficult to defend.

Russia has many great rivers. Among them are the Volga, which flows into the Caspian Sea; the Dnieper, which flows into the Black Sea; and the Don, which flows into the Sea of Azov. These rivers help tie the country together.

Early Slavs and the State at Kiev

The original homeland of the Slavic peoples is thought to be an area near the present city of Kiev. (See the map on page 333.) As the Germanic tribes moved west into the Roman Empire, the Slavs also migrated. They split into three main groups. 1. The western Slavs settled in Poland and Bohemia and became Roman Catholics. 2. The southern Slavs moved into the Balkans. 3. The eastern Slavs were the ancestors of the Russians although the Ukrainians are distinctive from the Russians. Most of the southern and eastern Slavs, with the exception of the Catholic Croats and Slovenes, adopted the Orthodox faith of Constantinople.

People of Scandinavian origin traveled down the rivers of Russia to Constantinople in search of trade and plunder. They were known to the Slavs as *Varangians.* They set up trading posts at Kiev and Novgorod. Eventually, Kiev became the center of a Varangian-Slavic State dominated by the Slavic culture. The people and the state of Kiev gradually became known as *Russian.* About 988 Prince Vladimir of Kiev became an Orthodox Christian, and ordered all his subjects to be baptized in the Dnieper.

This portrait of Czar Ivan IV shows the influence of Byzantine art on Russian artists.

In the thirteenth century, Mongol warriors of the "Golden Horde" swept across the plains and conquered Kiev. In time, small Russian states arose that were forced to pay tribute to the Mongols, or Tatars.

The Rise of Muscovy

During the Tatar period, the Russian state of Muscovy rose to prominence. It was strategically located near water routes. Under Ivan III (prince from 1462-1505), who was known as Ivan the Great, Moscow developed into an autocratic state. Ivan III extended his state to include Novgorod and other northern territories. (Within another hundred years the Muscovite state had taken over most of the other Russian states.) Ivan III encouraged expansion to the west, the east, and toward the Baltic Sea. He also put an end to Tatar control.

At the same time Ivan the Great deprived Novgorod of the right to call assemblies. He weakened the power of the *boyars,* or nobles. He brought the Russian Orthodox Church under his close control, and used it to increase his autocratic rule. Muscovy became the center from which there gradually emerged a new major nation. That nation was Russia.

Ivan the Great married a Byzantine princess, the niece of the last emperor of Byzantium. He imported Italian architects to build imposing churches and an elaborate palace for his capital at Moscow. He also claimed that Moscow, as the Third Rome, was the successor of ancient Rome and Constantinople, the Second Rome. This meant that Moscow was to be responsible in the future for maintaining the purity of the Christian faith.

The Despotic Rule of "Ivan the Terrible"

The grandson of Ivan the Great was Ivan IV (Czar from 1547 to 1584), who has gone down in history as "Ivan the Terrible." Ivan IV was the first ruler to take the title of "Czar." Some believe that the word may have come from the term *Caesar,* which was a title of great authority in Roman times. This ruler did everything possible to concentrate all power in his hands. A Czar, he declared, was "born into [power] by the will of God"—and was responsible only to God for his acts. Czar Ivan IV crushed the power of the boyars, depriving many of them of their lands. He then helped to organize a new group of nobles who would be faithful to him in exchange for the lands and positions he gave them.

To all who opposed him Ivan showed a cruelty that has rarely been surpassed. He tortured rebellious boyars, set bears on unarmed peasants, and in a fit of rage killed his own son. He destroyed a considerable part of the city of Novgorod, but it was later rebuilt. Ivan sent out special officials who had the task of destroying his enemies. Dressed in black and riding black horses, these officials spread terror and death to many Russians.

While using fear to build his despotic power, Ivan IV also built the power of Russia. He fought with Poland and Sweden in an effort to extend Russia's borders to the Baltic Sea.

Under his reign the Tatars had to give up their control over eastern Russia. Settlers were sent across the Ural Mountains. Just as Americans "went west," the Russians, drawn by the fur trade and the lure of new lands, "went east." Russian expansion into frontier lands, however, was more thoroughly planned and controlled by the government. Also, Ivan IV allowed English traders to set up a commercial center at Archangel, close to the White Sea in the far North.

"A Time of Troubles" and the Rise of the Romanovs

A "time of troubles" followed the death of Ivan the Terrible. Between 1604 and 1613 the country was torn apart by the struggles of rival leaders seeking the throne, peasant uprisings, famines, and foreign invasions. Swedish forces occupied Novgorod, and the Poles seized Moscow. During this difficult time Russians began to develop a national feeling.

A National Assembly, or *Zemsky Sobor*, which could give advice to the Czar but could not pass laws or force a ruler to take action, was first called in 1550. Other Zemsky Sobors followed. Then, in 1613, a particularly important one met. Its members consisted of government and church officials, nobles, and important merchants. A few free peasants may also have been included, although as a rule the majority of the people were ignored. This assembly unanimously elected Michael Romanov, the grandnephew of Ivan the Terrible, as Czar of all the Russians. Michael (ruled from 1613 to 1645) was the first of the Romanov dynasty, which ruled Russia until 1917.

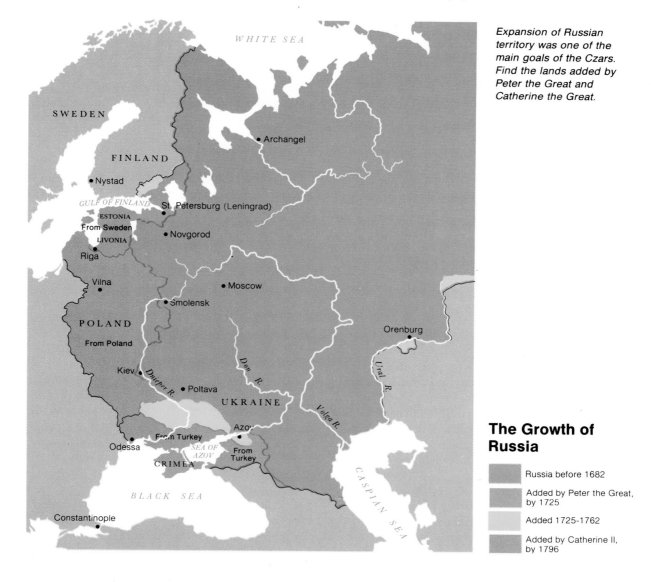

Expansion of Russian territory was one of the main goals of the Czars. Find the lands added by Peter the Great and Catherine the Great.

The Growth of Russia

- Russia before 1682
- Added by Peter the Great, by 1725
- Added 1725-1762
- Added by Catherine II, by 1796

Serfdom Grows More Oppressive

Serfdom, which died out in most of western Europe at the end of the Middle Ages, slowly developed into an oppressive system in Russia during the 1400s, 1500s, and early 1600s. In 1649 the Romanov dynasty gave it legal recognition. After that time the peasants were legally bound to the estates of their landlords. The serfs had few personal freedoms, and were trained to till the soil and serve their masters.

The *Cossacks,* a bold and sturdy group established along the Don and Dnieper rivers and in other regions, kept alive a tradition of freedom in Russia. Yet the Cossacks were a tiny minority. Most Russians, by the middle of the seventeenth century, lived under the heavy yoke of serfdom.

Check on Your Reading

1. Who founded the state at Kiev? What important decision was taken by Prince Vladimir of Kiev?
2. How did Ivan the Great change Russia? What did he mean by his claim that Moscow was the "Third Rome"?
3. How did Ivan IV contribute to the expansion of the Russian nation?
4. How did the Romanovs come to power? What effects did serfdom have on life in Russia?

5. Peter the Great and Catherine the Great

The Zemsky Sobor (national assembly) did not develop into a permanent or democratic institution. It declined and came to an end in 1682. Autocracy continued to grow strong under the Romanovs.

The Beginnings of Westernization in Russia

The reign of Peter the Great (Czar from 1682 to 1725) was particularly important in Russia's development. Peter was very tall—about 6 feet 7 inches in height. Dynamic, energetic, and filled with restless curiosity, he was determined to make Russia one of the great nations of the world. To achieve this goal, he believed that Russia had to sweep away many of its old ways.

The young Czar organized a group of about two hundred Russians who were sent to western Europe to study Western methods and techniques. Traveling with them as a private citizen, the Czar worked for a while as a carpenter in Holland in order to learn how the Dutch built ships. Peter and his companions visited Germany, Holland, England, and other countries. The Russians soon discovered that they had much to learn about Western life. A noblewoman in Germany reported:

> . . . in dancing, [the Russians mistook] the whalebones of our corsets for our bones, and the Czar showed his astonishment by saying that the German ladies had . . . hard bones.

Despite such mistakes, the Russians returned home with many valuable ideas. Peter the Great now decided to use drastic measures to make his people give up their old ways. He ordered the nobles to shave off their old-fashioned beards. He told the Russians to cut off the long sleeves of their robes and to copy the clothing of people in the West. He even arranged for the publication of a book of etiquette.

Some of the changes introduced by Peter were superficial. Nevertheless, he must be given considerable recognition for his serious efforts to westernize Russia.

Peter the Great: Reformer and Autocrat

Peter was active in many fields. He fought against the Swedes and others and obtained territory along the Baltic Sea. This gave Russia a "window to the West" through which the Russians could have trade and cultural contacts with the nations of western Europe.

Peter reformed the Russian army and helped build a Russian navy. He put down savagely a revolt among the troops guarding his palace, executing many of the leaders with his own sword. Russia was recognized as a major military power when its troops defeated the forces of Charles XII of Sweden at the Battle of Poltava (1709).

During his reign, exploration, trade, and industry were stimulated. Peter made use of architects from the West to build at enormous cost a new city, St. Petersburg (now Leningrad) on the Gulf of Finland. It became the Russian capital in place of Moscow. Peter also revised the structure of government, but was unable to develop a really honest or efficient system of government.

Education of the upper classes was encouraged. Peter approved the founding of the first Russian newspaper, and he supported plans to establish a Russian Academy of Sciences. He had the alphabet of Church Slavonic simplified, making it easier to use for secular literature.

Despite these accomplishments, Peter ruled as all Czars were expected to rule—as an autocrat. He was very severe with people of the lower classes and the clergy. The serfs were treated harshly, and their young men were forced to serve in his army as soldiers. The Russian Orthodox Church was brought more completely under state control. Peter hoped to raise Russia to a point where it would rival the nations of western Europe.

Catherine the Great: An "Enlightened" Despot

The reign of Catherine II, or Catherine the Great (from 1762 to 1796), was another important period in Russian history. Catherine was a German princess who had come to Russia to marry the heir to the throne. She quickly learned Russian, and converted from Protestantism to the Russian Orthodox faith. She impressed the Russians with her alert mind and determination to bring "glory" to Russia and herself. When her husband, who was erratic and emotionally unstable, became Czar in 1762, people looked to her for leadership. After her husband was murdered, she became Empress in her own right.

Catherine was greatly affected by the ideas of the Enlightenment. Like Joseph II of Austria, Frederick the Great of Prussia, and other monarchs of the time, Catherine was an "enlightened" despot. She exchanged brilliant letters with many leading intellects of Europe, including the French philosopher Voltaire. She wrote plays, satires, and fairy tales; compiled books of proverbs; and wrote one of the first Russian textbooks for children.

For a time she was influenced by the liberal ideas of Voltaire and other philosophers of the Enlightenment. Her reputation as an "enlightened" ruler was partially deserved because she performed many useful acts. For example, she encouraged the education of the children of the nobility and supported the study of science and medicine. She stimulated the writing of literature, the creation of works of art, and the construction of new buildings. Catherine also extended freedom of worship to several religious groups.

Catherine Extended Serfdom

In other ways, however, Catherine the Great was not truly enlightened. She extended serfdom in

Catherine II, a German princess who married the heir to the Russian throne, became known as Catherine the Great.

many parts of Russia, and took away most of the remaining rights of the serfs. She treated the serfs brutally, ignoring their basic needs and making their lives wretched.

Of the 34 million peasants in Russia about 20 million were serfs on private estates. The rest were serfs of the state or monarchy, or "free peasants." They were not much better off than the privately owned serfs. This meant that out of 36 million Russians the great majority were in some condition of forced service.

In 1773 a major revolt broke out among the oppressed peasants. It was led by a Cossack named Pugachev, whose followers consisted of runaway serfs, religious dissenters, Cossacks, Tatars, and others. Sweeping through the Ural region, the rebels threatened Moscow before they were put down.

Poland Is Partitioned

By the eighteenth century Poland, which was once a powerful kingdom, had become a weak country with a feudal society. Russia, Austria, and the new kingdom of Prussia were eager to share Polish territory. Despite the efforts of Polish heroes like Thaddeus Kosciuszko, Poland was partitioned, or divided, among Russia, Austria, and Prussia three times—in 1772, 1793, and 1795. (See the map on page 336.) Russia received a large share.

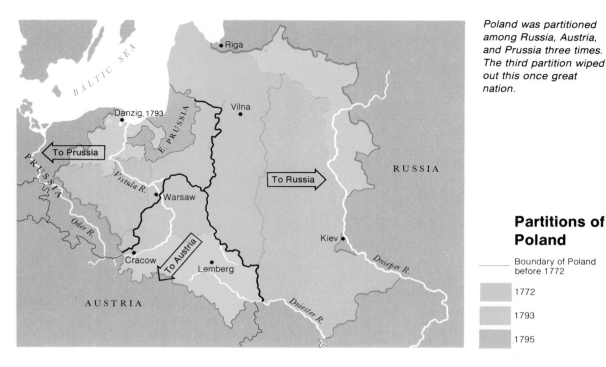

Poland was partitioned among Russia, Austria, and Prussia three times. The third partition wiped out this once great nation.

Partitions of Poland

——— Boundary of Poland before 1772

1772

1793

1795

By the end of the third partition, Poland as a nation had ceased to exist. It did not reappear on the map until 1919.

Russia and the Ottoman Empire

During the reign of Catherine the Great, the Russians fought against the Ottoman Empire, conquering the Crimea. This gave Russia a stronghold on the northern shore of the Black Sea. It increased Russia's desire to control Constantinople and the straits that linked the Black Sea to the Mediterranean.

In the east, Russians continued to settle the vast spaces of Siberia. By 1800 Russia was the largest country of Europe. Like a giant stretching out its arms, it embraced many lands and peoples.

Check on Your Reading

1. How did Peter the Great attempt to westernize Russia? What success did he have?
2. List five of Peter the Great's achievements. Evaluate him as Czar.
3. Why was Catherine the Great called an "enlightened despot"? How would you describe her character?
4. What happened to the serfs during the reign of Catherine the Great?
5. How did Catherine act toward Poland and the Ottoman Empire?

6. A Flowering of the Arts

While autocratic rulers were dominating Europe, there was a remarkable flowering of the arts. France led the way and set an example of creativity that was followed by other nations. However, the arts were cultivated primarily by and for the aristocrats. Society was ruled by a carefully contrived code of elegance; people greeted each other with formal manners and delighted in witty conversations. Many of the customs of social gatherings were set by a number of ladies in Paris who received friends once or twice each week. In these salons, men and women of the aristocracy exchanged ideas with leading artists, writers, and philosophers.

The Baroque Style

Italian architects, weary of the strict "classic" style of the Renaissance, developed a new style of building—the baroque. One of the best known examples of this architecture is the church of Santa Maria della Salute at Venice. With its attractive mixture of arches, columns, cornices, statues, and a great dome, the church seems to float on the waters of the Grand Canal!

Italian architects soon carried the new style of building to other parts of Europe. French architects tended to be more restrained or "classical" in their use of the baroque, as shown by the east front

At the right, the baroque Church of Johann Von Nepomuk in Austria. Below, the rococo Church of Our Lady in Germany.

of the Louvre and by the great palace at Versailles. Versailles perfectly reflected Louis XIV's sense of artistic order and regularity as well as his desire to impress people with the dignity of his court.

The most famous baroque sculptor was an Italian, Giovanni Lorenzo Bernini (1598-1680), who aimed at creating in metal and stone a sense of rapid, and sometimes violent, movement. His bust of Louis XIV as well as his *Apollo* and *Daphne* reflect a new approach. Bernini was also a first-class architect whose colonnade in St. Peter's Square provides a majestic setting for the great church.

Peter Paul Rubens (1577-1640) was one of the leading painters in the baroque style. Rubens was trained as a painter at Antwerp and Venice. He then worked for the Spanish court in Madrid and

This picture of Wolfgang Amadeus Mozart at the harpsichord was painted when he was seven. He was on tour giving concerts with his father and sister.

for Marie de' Medici in Paris. He was an international success and made frequent trips with his many assistants from court to court and from country to country. Among his best known works are the *Descent from the Cross* in the cathedral of Antwerp and a series of paintings depicting the marriage of Marie de' Medici to King Henry IV of France.

The Rococo Style

After the death of Louis XIV, the baroque developed in France into a new style called the rococo, which was more delicate and fanciful than the baroque. The new style spread quickly, and can be seen today in countless churches and palaces in France, Germany, and Austria.

Frederick the Great of Prussia erected the New Palace and Sans Souci Palace ("Carefree Palace") at Potsdam in the rococo style. The music room of the New Palace and Voltaire's bedroom at San Souci are fine examples of this international method of decoration. Rococo palaces were also built in Russia.

There were also rococo painters. One of the earliest and most famous was Antoine Watteau (1684-1721), who began the school known as *fêtes galantes* ("gallant festivals"). His *Embarkion for Cythera* shows a group of courtiers in a dreamy, park-like setting. Typical of this school of painting is its frivolous subject matter and fresh, sweet colors. François Boucher (1703-1770) and Jean Honoré Fragonard (1732-1806) continued Watteau's approach in works that depict elegant ladies and gentlemen in court costumes listening to musicians in a formal garden.

Music in the Age of the Baroque

Claudio Monteverdi (1567-1643) was for many years the choirmaster of St. Mark's Basilica in Venice. He was a successful composer of Masses and madrigals as well as a pioneer in developing operas. Italian-born composer Jean Baptiste Lully (1632-1687) came to France as a boy to work in the kitchen of a great family. Because of his skill in playing the violin and lute, he was made leader of Louis XIV's private band. Later he became the king's favorite composer, producing music for early French operas and incidental music for the comedies of Molière (see page 339).

Johann Sebastian Bach (1685-1750) brought church music in Europe to its high point. Born into a family of distinguished German musicians, he became head organist and violinist for the Duke of Weimar. Later he was made musical director at St. Thomas's Church in Leipzig. His sacred music included Easter and Christmas oratorios, and Masses such as the *Mass in B Minor.* Also he is famous for his *Passion According to St. Matthew,* which sets the words of St. Matthew to magnificent music.

In this period George Frederick Handel (1685–1759), a German-born composer, settled in England. He wrote *Water Music* for the king of England. His masterpiece is a famous oratorio, *The Messiah.* An *oratorio* is a musical composition for singers and instrumentalists, usually based on a religious theme.

About the middle of the 1700s, Vienna replaced Italy and Paris as Europe's most creative musical center. Austrian composer Franz Joseph Haydn (1732–1809) gained the admiration of music lovers everywhere with his many compositions. He wrote oratorios, such as *The Creation* and *The Seasons,* and more than a hundred symphonies. Because Haydn developed the symphonic form, he is sometimes called the "father of the symphony."

Haydn promoted the career of an Austrian composer far younger than himself, a child prodigy named Wolfgang Amadeus Mozart (1756–1791). In his all-too-short life Mozart gave the world some of its most delightful symphonic and operatic works. These include operas like *The Marriage of Figaro, Don Giovanni,* and *The Magic Flute;* forty-one symphonies; and many concertos. He also wrote beautiful *chamber music*—music for a small number of instruments, usually performed in a small concert hall.

French Writers of the Classical Age

During the seventeenth century a remarkable group of writers developed in France. Their aim was to represent life and human nature clearly, rationally, and nobly. These writers created what has been called the "classical age" of French writing. Louis XIV, his court, and the aristocrats of Paris were the public for which these people wrote.

The classical age was noted for its great dramatic writers. On the basis of Aristotle's teachings and the works of others, French literary critic Nicholas Boileau (1636–1711) defined the rule of the three unities. Unity of action required a single, clear plot. Unity of place limited that action to a single locality. Unity of time meant that the action had

to take place within a single day. Many of the characters and plots were inspired by the Greek or Roman tradition.

The first great classical dramatist was Pierre Corneille (1606–1684), whose masterpieces included *The Cid, Horace,* and *Cinna.* Corneille's best plays were presented first during the reign of Louis XIII. Jean Racine (1639–1699) wrote for the court of the young Louis XIV. Racine's tragedies like *Andromaque, Britannicus,* and *Phèdre* combine psychological understanding of human motives with beauty of poetic language. Working at the same time was one of the comic geniuses of all time, Molière (1622–1673). In immortal works like *The Miser, The Would-Be Gentleman,* and *The Imaginary Invalid,* he courageously attacked human pretensions and defended common sense.

Jean de La Fontaine (1621–1695) was a close friend of Boileau, Racine, and Molière. Inspired by the Greek fables of Aesop, La Fontaine composed his own *Fables* between 1668 and 1690. Giving to animals the characteristics and problems of human beings, the author described these poems as:

> . . . an ample comedy with a hundred different acts whose setting is the universe.

The seventeenth century also produced excellent prose writers. The *Thoughts* of Blaise Pascal (1623–1662) is a strong defense of Christian faith. Madame de Sévigné's (1626–1696) letters to her daughter give a remarkably vivid picture of the times. The *Memoirs* of the Duke de Saint-Simon (1675–1755) present unforgettable scenes of the court of Louis XIV.

Check on Your Reading

1. Name two characteristics of the baroque style in architecture, as shown by the Church of Santa Maria della Salute.
2. Who were Giovanni Lorenzo Bernini and Peter Paul Rubens? Describe some of their accomplishments.
3. What are some of the features of the rococo style in architecture and painting?
4. Discuss the music of Johann Sebastian Bach, George Frederick Handel, Franz Joseph Haydn, Wolfgang Amadeus Mozart.
5. What was the rule of the three unities of French classical drama? Name some of the writings of Corneille, Racine, Molière, and La Fontaine.

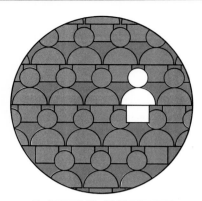

The Lady of Society

At seven o'clock the countess—a rich widow in her fifties—is politely awakened by her maid. The countess lives in a large red brick and slate mansion in Paris. After kneeling before a crucifix to say her prayers, she puts on a long silk gown. Then she breakfasts on rolls and hot milk while the maid arranges her hair into attractive curls.

The countess next goes over the household accounts with the housekeeper, an experienced woman who has been in charge of the mansion for many years. Instructions for the day's activities are given to the housekeeper, who will pass them on to the other servants.

Afterwards, the countess sits at her desk and writes a letter to her daughter in southern France who is married to an important official of the king. The countess also writes to her son, a young lieutenant serving with a cavalry regiment near the Rhine River. She offers many suggestions for her children's welfare, and urges them to visit her soon.

At noon, two ladies arrive. They have been invited to share dinner with the countess. This is the main meal of the day, and consists of lentil soup, bread, veal and chicken, salad, and white wine. Fruit and cheese are offered as well. Dinner is presented with great ceremony in the main dining room. Each guest is served by a valet in uniform. The ladies talk about their favorite charity—a convent school for girls who are either orphans or from noble but poor families. The countess and her friends not only support the school, but also often spend an afternoon with the students. At least one day in the week the countess enjoys teaching courses in Latin and Italian.

Now is the time for the countess to change into an elaborate gown of blue velvet adorned with blue and white ribbons. She makes a quick inspection of the two salons, or reception rooms, on the ground floor of the mansion. These are large elegant rooms decorated with blue and gold curtains and blue wallpaper. The armchairs and sofas are covered with embroidered cloth. Violins, a lute, and a fine spinet, an early form of the piano, are along the wall of one of the salons. Flowers in silver and glass vases fill the air with their perfume.

Between two and five each Thursday afternoon, the countess is at home to about thirty regular visitors. Her guests are either aristocrats or well-to-do members of the middle class. Included are men and women of letters, an architect, government officials, and a number of lawyers and their wives.

Moving easily among her guests, the countess encourages them to talk freely. They discuss an eloquent sermon recently delivered in a fashionable church by a famous orator. There is much interest in a new play by Racine. Some prefer the work of the older dramatist, Corneille. A colonel reports on the progress of the French armies in the Rhineland area of Germany. A courtier describes the magnificent festival given earlier that week in the gardens of Versailles. After a light refreshment the guests take formal leave of the countess and each other. The countess then retires to her bedroom, where she reads a book on religion. By ten o'clock she is fast asleep.

The sketch above is based primarily on *The Splendid Century: The France of Louis XIV,* by W. H. Lewis, Anchor Books, 1957; *Old Paris: Its Court and Literary Salons,* by Catherine Charlotte and Lady Jackson, L. C. Page & Company, 1895; and *France Under Richelieu and Mazarin,* by James Breck Perkins, G. P. Putnam's Sons, 1902.

CHAPTER REVIEW

Think and Discuss

1. Do you agree that Richelieu's goals were desirable for the France of his day: First, the majesty of the King; and second, the greatness of the realm? Why?
2. Do you think Cardinal Mazarin was as successful a leader as Cardinal Richelieu? Why?
3. How did mercantilism contribute to royal absolutism?
4. Was Louis XIV a wise or unwise ruler? Why?
5. How did the power struggles in Europe affect peoples in other parts of the world?
6. In the light of your study of this chapter, do you believe that "history makes great leaders" or that "great leaders make history"? or both? Why?
7. What changes in warfare of this period do you think had the greatest impact on people's lives? Why?
8. Peter the Great ruled "as czars were expected to rule—as autocrats." Why did many Russians expect their czars to be autocrats?

Past and Present

1. Compare the idea of the "Divine Right of Kings" with today's idea of Democracy.
2. The United States government helps to subsidize certain industries and businesses. Colbert did the same. Were his reasons the same as the reasons for government subsidies today?
3. Debate the following: Resolved, that the Soviet Union's present foreign policy is a continuation of Russia's historic foreign policy.

Activities

1. Debate the following: Resolved, that Louis XIV did more good than harm.
2. Imagine that you are Louis XIV. Write a paragraph entitled "Why I Should Be Called the 'Sun King.'"
3. Compile a list of rulers whom you have studied whose ambition led to disaster. What conclusions can you draw?
4. Write a short biography of a composer or artist about whom you have read in this chapter.
5. Display pictures on the bulletin board of the Baroque and Rococo styles.

6

Revolutionary Struggles in the West

Simple arithmetic can lead to amazing answers. Consider this question: How many revolutions have there been in the last twenty-five years? Five? Too low. Ten? Keep going. Twenty? Getting there.

Actually, there have been over fifty revolutions just in Europe, the Middle East, Africa, and Asia in the last twenty-five years. Begin at 1900, and there have been over ninety revolutions in Latin America since that date. Go back further, and you find that the idea of revolution is thousands of years old.

The importance of revolution in world history should therefore be clear. Fortunately, we can understand today's revolutionary movements better by studying the nature of revolutions of the past.

Representative Government Grows in England

KEYNOTE

Spurs and sword—golden bracelets—robe of cloth of gold—orb—sapphire and ruby ring—sceptre with cross—and finally the crown! These magnificent articles were presented to Elizabeth II at her coronation as Queen in London, England in 1953.

Even as the crowds shouted "God Save the Queen," they knew that the real governing power was in the hands of the people. Men and women hailed their new monarch and were proud to be citizens of their nation. At the same time, they were thankful that their Parliament had freed them from the absolute power of royalty.

The people took pride in both their nation and their representative government. It was a pride based on this important fact of history: As the English nation developed, so did the rights of the people.

A meeting of the House of Commons of Parliament in 1793.

1. Geography and History Are Closely Related

Harold Nicolson, a famous English writer, once said:

> I have sought to persuade my American friends that what they resent as our [the English] patronizing manner is due almost entirely to an adenoidal infection resulting from the dampness of our soil and climate.

Mr. Nicolson was joking. Even in jest, however, he was making the important point that a person cannot understand the people of a nation without understanding the geography of their country.

England and the United Kingdom

Great Britain is an island off the northwest coast of the European mainland. This island is separated from the mainland by the English Channel, the Straits of Dover, and the North Sea. Great Britain consists of England, Scotland, and Wales. England is the southern part of the island.

Farther to the west is Ireland, the second important island in the British Isles. It is separated from Great Britain by St. George's Channel, the Irish Sea, and the North Channel. This island today is divided politically into two areas—Northern Ireland and the Republic of Ireland. The term *United Kingdom* (of Great Britain and Northern Ireland) refers to England, Scotland, Wales, Northern Ireland, the Isle of Man, and the Channel Islands. (See the map on this page.)

An Island Nation

No part of Great Britain is more than seventy-five miles from the sea. Along the coast are many good bays and harbors. The island also has a number of rivers, including the Thames in southern England, which flows eastward through London to the North Sea.

No wonder many of the people of Britain have gone to sea. In fact, they had to if they wished to go very far in any direction.

The United Kingdom is quite small. It covers an area about the size of the state of Wyoming. Its people began going to sea long ago to secure fish for food. Also the small area of the country resulted in a lack of certain raw materials and markets for its products. This has been a major reason for the growth of Britain's overseas trade.

British Isles

The islands of Great Britain and Ireland are off the northwest coast of the mainland of Europe.

Check on Your Reading

1. What is the United Kingdom?
2. How has its island position affected the history of the United Kingdom?

---

2. Parliament Disputes the "Divine Right of Kings"

Two important developments took place in England from the seventeenth through the eighteenth century. 1. The growth of the power of Parliament, or representative government, greatly reduced the royal power. 2. The interests and power of England spread from one-half an island to a worldwide empire. This chapter concentrates on the growth of representative government, while the next traces the evolution of the British Empire.

After the death of Elizabeth, King James VI of Scotland became the King of England as James I (ruled from 1603-1625). Although James was a member of the *Stuart* royal family of Scotland, Scotland and England continued to have separate governing bodies. Except for brief intervals, the Stuarts ruled England for over one hundred years.

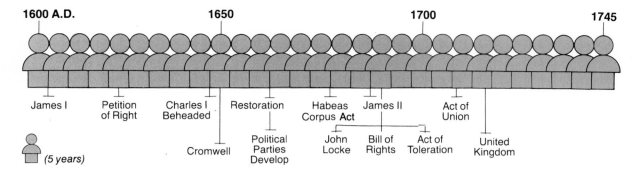

| 1600 A.D. | | 1650 | | 1700 | | 1745 |

James I — Petition of Right — Charles I Beheaded — Restoration — Habeas Corpus Act — James II — Act of Union

Cromwell — Political Parties Develop — John Locke — Bill of Rights — Act of Toleration — United Kingdom

(5 years)

King James versus Parliament

The reign of King James I was dominated by a struggle between the king and the Parliament for authority in government. The king believed that he ruled by divine right. He intended to govern without the interference of Parliament, and he told its members:

I conclude . . . That as to dispute what God may do is blasphemy, . . . so is it sedition in subjects to dispute what a king may do in the height of his power.

James argued with Parliament over his extravagance, his methods of taxation, and his plan for an alliance with England's traditional rival, Spain. He also did not please the *Puritans,* who continued to insist that formality and rituals should be eliminated from the Church of England. To anyone who criticized his actions, King James pointed out:

It is . . . high contempt in a subject to dispute what a king can do, or say that a king cannot do this or that.

Charles I Is Compelled to Accept the Petition of Right

Charles I, the son of James I, ruled from 1625 to 1649. Like his father, Charles quarreled with Parliament over taxation. He waged unsuccessful wars against Spain, the Netherlands, and France. He imprisoned people who would not lend him money for his activities.

Charles I greatly underestimated the ability and determination of the representatives who controlled Parliament, the men who sat in the House of Commons, one of the two branches of Parliament. R. J. White describes these leaders:

. . . self-government had become a habit in England, and the men who made it a reality

were the country gentlemen who sat in the House of Commons . . . . They were men who had done well on the land and who possessed money and real political ability, acquired through years of political experience. Men of business educated in the market place, on the bench [in the courts], or at the universities, they were accustomed to conducting government affairs on a daily basis.

The leaders of Parliament became determined to protect the rights of Parliament and of the people of England against the acts of the king. They used his great need for money to force King Charles I to accept the *Petition of Right.*

The Petition of Right (1628) was a landmark in the growth of democracy in England. These were three of its important provisions.

1. No taxes could be imposed without the consent of Parliament.

2. Free people could not be imprisoned without a proper trial.

3. Civilians were not to be tried in military courts in time of peace.

Two of these three provisions were not new. Nevertheless, the Petition of Right made these principles a more permanent part of English life.

"Scepter and Crown . . . Tumble Down!"

Charles I, however, continued to assert the "divine right of kings." He neglected the provisions of the Petition of Right. For eleven years (1629-1640) he ruled the country without any meeting of Parliament. He raised funds by illegal methods. He tried people in special courts. He permitted his officials to persecute the members of Protestant sects.

Then an uprising occurred in Scotland. Scots who insisted on following their Presbyterian faith rose against Charles. The king was desperate for funds to finance a campaign in Scotland. He was forced to call Parliament into session to ask for money. This Parliament, which lasted from 1640 to 1660, is known as the "Long Parliament."

A bitter struggle developed between the king's opponents (*Roundheads,* because they wore their hair short) and the king's supporters *(Cavaliers).* The Roundheads included middle-class business people and landowners, many members of Parliament, and many Puritans. One of their leaders was Oliver Cromwell, a dedicated Puritan. The Puritans could not accept the king's claims to special God-given privileges. The Cavaliers included wealthy landowners, aristocrats, and Catholics.

Civil war broke out between the Cavaliers and Roundheads in 1642, and the king's forces were defeated. Representatives who supported Cromwell were now in charge in Parliament. This "Rump" Parliament chose a special court to try Charles I.

It was a dramatic moment when the court made this decision:

> [The king] is a tyrant, traitor, murderer, and public enemy to the good people of this nation, [and he] shall be put to death. . . .

King Charles I was beheaded in 1649. The poet James Shirley wrote:

Death lays his icy hand on Kings,
   Scepter and crown
   Must tumble down
And in the dust be equal made,
With the poor crooked scythe and spade.

Check on Your Reading

1. Why did Parliament and King James I clash?
2. What rights were won in the Petition of Right?
3. Why did the Roundheads revolt?

King Charles I conferring with his officers before the Battle of Edgehill in 1642. This was one of the battles in the Civil War.

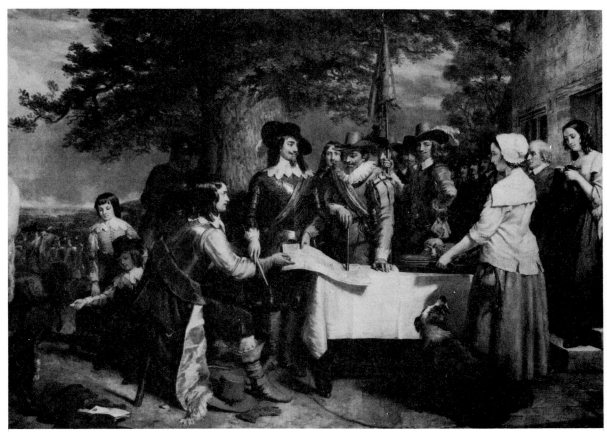

3. Oliver Cromwell Rules the Commonwealth

The execution of Charles I left the country without a king. The Rump Parliament proclaimed England a "Commonwealth," a term used to describe a republic. However, Oliver Cromwell was the actual ruler of the state. Supported by his army, he became "Lord Protector" and governed the country as a dictator.

Puritan Principles Influence Government

Oliver Cromwell was a devout Puritan and a strict ruler. As the great English poet John Milton described him, he was guided in all things "by faith and matchless fortitude." Like other Puritans, Oliver Cromwell believed in the following principles: 1. There was a close spiritual relationship between himself and God. 2. People who truly believed in God would have common interests to bind them together. 3. Sin was real and should be strongly resisted. 4. Self-reliance and hard work were highly desirable. When carried to the New World by other Puritans, these ideas influenced American history.

Cromwell tried earnestly to restore discipline. Clad in plain black clothes, he frowned on lace-trimmed clothing, dancing, and frivolity. He closed the theaters as unnecessary amusements. He also advocated religious toleration for all Puritan sects, including the Presbyterians and Independents, but he put down any attempt to restore Catholicism or Anglicanism.

Foreign Affairs under Cromwell

Cromwell faced difficult problems in foreign affairs. In Ireland, Catholics and influential noblemen declared that Charles II, son of the beheaded English monarch, was their new ruler. They also vowed to overthrow the Commonwealth. Cromwell and his troops, therefore, invaded Ireland and conquered the island. After much bloodshed, the English confiscated a considerable part of the land.

There had been a long history of antagonism between England and Ireland. In the sixteenth century, King Henry VIII had put English laws into effect in Ireland. Queen Mary had tried to colonize Ireland with English families. Queen Elizabeth I had ordered that the Roman Catholic religious services followed by most of the Irish people be stopped. In the seventeenth century, King James I had attempted to colonize north Ireland with Scottish settlers.

Cromwell also faced revolt in Scotland. A number of Scots announced in 1649 that Charles II had agreed to become the king of Scotland and to support Presbyterianism. Charles II landed in Scotland in June 1650. Cromwell crushed the Scots as he had the Irish rebels, and reaffirmed that he was "Lord Protector of the Commonwealth of England, Scotland, and Ireland." Then Charles II led an army into England. It was defeated and he fled to France.

England and Holland were both building overseas trade and colonies, as will be described in the next chapter. England was determined to drive Dutch merchants out of the trade between England and other countries. Parliament, therefore, passed the Navigation Act of 1651. This act provided that only English vessels could transport to England goods from Asia, Africa, and America. The only products that Dutch ships were permitted to carry to England were those made in Holland. War broke out between the two countries and the Dutch were forced to agree to the Navigation Act.

England also battled against Spain, and an English fleet seized Jamaica in the West Indies. The English fleet became, therefore, as successful and as important as the English army.

Check on Your Reading

1. What were Cromwell's religious beliefs and his code of behavior? How did these affect his approach to government?
2. What did Cromwell do about Ireland? Scotland?
3. What successes did the English navy achieve?

4. The "Restoration" and the "Glorious Revolution"

Shortly after the death of Oliver Cromwell, the Commonwealth came to an end. The exiled Charles II was brought back from France and made king in the so-called *Restoration*. He promised to pardon those who had rebelled against his father. He also swore to obey the Petition of Right and to respect the Magna Carta, and he accepted the authority of Parliament.

Merrier Times

Charles II (king from 1660-1685) realized that in a final test of strength between the ruler and Parliament, power was in the hands of Parliament. He exercised his royal rights so carefully that one of his nobles said in jest:

Here [is] a great and mighty king,
    Whose promise none rely'd on;
He never said a foolish thing,
    Nor ever did a wise one.

Gone were the solemn, puritanical days of Oliver Cromwell. Theaters were reopened. The drab clothing of the Commonwealth era was replaced by frills and ruffles. Women began to wear beauty patches. Men carried muffs to protect their hands. Young dandies covered their heads with elaborately curled wigs. The pace of life speeded up. Carriages—aided by new roads and methods of changing horses at posthouses—could travel at the unprecedented speed of fifty miles in one day!

The Church of England

Charles II personally preferred Roman Catholicism, but Parliament reinstated the Anglican Church as the official Church of England. There were many *Dissenters*—Presbyterians, Baptists, Puritans, and other Protestants who did not accept the doctrines of the Anglican faith. They were permitted to worship, but only under many restrictions.

The Clerk of the Crown reads the Bill of Rights to the Prince and Princess of Orange. After they accepted and signed this document, they were offered the crown of England and became King William and Queen Mary.

The Test Act of 1673 made it impossible for Catholics to take part in the government of the nation. By another act, neither Catholics nor Dissenters could participate in local government.

Political Parties and the Habeas Corpus Act

Under Charles II, political parties began to develop in Parliament. The growth of political parties helped individuals to unite to achieve their goals. It also strengthened the power of Parliament because in the long run rulers and their ministers had to agree to the wishes of the majority party in Parliament.

The *Tory* party supported the policies of the king and the Church of England. The *Whig* party wanted to reduce the king's powers and supported toleration for other Protestant groups.

In 1679 the Whig party helped to pass the famous Habeas Corpus Act. This law was designed for "the more speedy relief of all persons imprisoned for any . . . criminal or supposed criminal matters." It gave a judge authority to grant a *writ of habeas corpus,* an order protecting an arrested person's rights. 1. This meant that arrested persons had to be brought before a judge and told why they were arrested. 2. If the arrest were legal, the person had to be given a trial within a reasonable period of time. 3. If the arrest were illegal, the person had to be released. This law proved to be a safeguard against unfair and arbitrary arrest. Although little interest was taken in its passage at the time, the Habeas Corpus Act is a landmark in the history of democracy. The right to habeas corpus is one of our basic safeguards against illegal arrest in the United States.

Foreign Affairs and Mercantilism

England tried to strengthen itself economically during the seventeenth century. The English followed many of the practices of mercantilism. (See page 322.)

Mercantilism was a European-wide development that affected many areas in the world. It brought a number of significant results: 1. It stimulated the development of industries at home and the exploration of overseas areas. 2. It increased the competition for colonies and markets overseas. The Dutch, French, Prussians, Austrians, and Russians established trading companies to compete with the English and Spaniards for trade. 3. It intensified the rivalries between European countries and often led to war. 4. It often created dangerous tensions between colonies and home countries. The Navigation Acts passed by the English, for example, restricted the trade of the American colonies for the benefit of England. Opposition to these acts by the colonists was one of the factors that led to the American Revolution.

Economic rivalry led to a renewal of the overseas war between England and Holland. In America, the English gained some islands in the West Indies, and in 1664 they took New Amsterdam and renamed it after the Duke of York.

The Glorious Revolution

James II (ruled from 1685-1688), the brother of Charles II, became King of England upon the death of Charles. James was a Catholic, and he tried to restore the Catholic Church in his country. He also was determined to rule with a strong hand, and he dissolved a Parliament that criticized his activities. By 1688 he had become so unpopular that his opponents decided to oust him.

Parliament invited James' Protestant daughter, Mary, and her husband, William of Orange, to come from Holland and govern England. William and Mary accepted the offer and entered England with their Dutch soldiers. Realizing that he had lost the support of the leaders of England, James fled the country.

Parliament then offered the crown to William and Mary. They became the rulers of England in 1689, with the understanding that they were to rule with the advice and guidance of Parliament. This bloodless overthrow of James II and the crowning of William and Mary is known as the "Glorious Revolution." It was extremely important because it made clear that Parliament—not the king—was supreme in the government of England.

The Bill of Rights

To protect English rights in the future, Parliament made William and Mary sign a Bill of Rights. This Bill of Rights (1689) was one of the most significant landmarks in the growth of representative government. It had the following provisions: 1. The ruler could not suspend or carry out a law without the consent of Parliament. 2. The ruler

ENGLISH BILL OF RIGHTS

It is the right of the subjects to petition the king. . . .

The subjects which are Protestants may have arms for their defense. . . .

Excessive bail ought not to be required, nor excessive fines imposed, nor cruel and unusual punishments inflicted.

BILL OF RIGHTS IN THE U.S. CONSTITUTION

Congress shall make no law . . . abridging . . . the right of the people . . . to petition the government for a redress of grievances.

. . . the right of the people to keep and bear arms shall not be infringed.

Excessive bail shall not be required, nor excessive fines imposed, nor cruel and unusual punishments inflicted.

A new flag was created in 1707 to symbolize the United Kingdom. It became known as the Union Jack.

the philosophy, or basic ideas, behind it. These ideas were best expressed by the Englishman John Locke (1632-1704). Locke believed:

Governments are formed to protect people's lives, liberties, and property.

Government must be by the consent of those who are governed. Or, as Locke put it: "The liberty of man, in society, is to be under no other legislative power but that established by consent in the commonwealth. . . ."

If a government interferes with a person's life, liberty, or property—or rules without the consent of those who are governed—the people may take steps to change the government.

Locke rejected the idea of "divine right of kings." Locke insisted that government should be based on the consent of the governed. He believed that people were capable of judging whether or not a government protected their life, liberty, and property. He felt that people should change any government that denied them these rights.

Parliament Deals with Religious Problems

The Act of Toleration was passed in 1689. This act gave Dissenters freedom of public worship, but they were not allowed to hold government office.

Catholics were given permission to participate in private religious observances, but they were not allowed to hold government office. By a provision that was included in the Bill of Rights, no Catholic was to be permitted to become ruler.

Check on Your Reading

1. How did life change in the Restoration period?
2. How did Parliament deal with religion?
3. What was the Habeas Corpus Act?
4. How did mercantilism affect relations among the European nations?
5. What was the importance of the "Glorious Revolution"?
6. Why was the Bill of Rights so important?
7. Explain Locke's basic ideas.

could not levy taxes or keep an army without the consent of Parliament. 3. Freedom of speech and debate was guaranteed in Parliament.

This English Bill of Rights also protected other rights that later were included in the American Bill of Rights. (See the chart on page 351.)

The Philosophy of John Locke

The English Bill of Rights was to influence many people and nations. It is important to understand

5. The "United Kingdom of Great Britain" Is Formed

Queen Anne (ruled from 1702-1714) was the last of the Stuart monarchs to rule Great Britain. During her reign, an event of great importance occurred. Scotland was united with England to form the "United Kingdom of Great Britain."

The Act of Union

Since the time of James I (ruled from 1603-1625), Scotland had been under the jurisdiction of the English monarch, but the Scots had their own separate Parliament. By the Act of Union (1707), one Parliament was established for both England and Scotland. It also was agreed that there would be a sharing of "all . . . rights, privileges, and advantages, which do or may belong to the subjects of either kingdom."

The square red cross representing England was united with the diagonal white cross representing Scotland to form a single flag for both lands. That flag was the Union Jack—the symbol of the New United Kingdom. (See page 352.)

Leaders Become Responsible to the House of Commons.

Upon the death of Queen Anne, George, Elector of Hanover (in Germany), was the nearest Protestant relative.

Parliament named George to be king. George I (ruled from 1714-1727) knew little about England and could not understand English. The new king, therefore, turned over most of the affairs of government to his *Cabinet.* The Cabinet was a group of advisers tracing its origin back to the days of William and Mary. They were members of Parliament who were usually ministers in charge of government departments. At first the Cabinet included members of both political parties in Parliament. Then William and Mary discovered that the Cabinet ran the government more smoothly when all Cabinet ministers were chosen from the majority party.

During the reign of George I the most influential member of the Cabinet was Sir Robert Walpole, who became the leader of the Cabinet, or the first *Prime Minister.* Gradually a system developed by which the Prime Minister and his Cabinet directed the government (see the chart below).

This system is still in operation. It is a system of *ministerial responsibility.* This means that the Prime Minister and the Cabinet are responsible to the House of Commons for their actions. The development of ministerial responsibility was very important to the growth of representative government. British government leaders became fully responsible to the elected representatives, the House of Commons. Gradually the hereditary House of Lords lost almost all of its power. The Prime Minister, the Cabinet, and the House of Commons control the British government today.

Check on Your Reading
1. What was achieved by the Act of Union?
2. How did Cabinet government develop? How does it work?
3. Define: Prime Minister, Cabinet, ministerial responsibility, majority party.

The Cabinet System

PRIME MINISTER: The Prime Minister must be the person who is the leader of the majority party in the House of Commons or who has the support of the majority of the members of the House of Commons. The monarch invites this person to become Prime Minister; that is, to direct the government.

CABINET: The Cabinet is a group of advisors to the Prime Minister. The Prime Minister suggests the names of the persons to be in the Cabinet, and the monarch appoints them to their offices. Most of the Cabinet members are heads of departments, such as Defense, Foreign Affairs, and Labor.

PERIOD OF OFFICE: The Prime Minister and the entire Cabinet must resign or ask that the people be permitted to elect a new House of Commons if a majority of the House of Commons stops supporting their policies. If the majority elected to the new House of Commons supports the Prime Minister, he or she stays in office. If the majority opposes the Prime Minister, a new person is appointed Prime Minister. This person is, of course, the leader of the new majority party in Parliament.

The Owner of a Coffeehouse

Tobacco smoke filled the large room and rose toward the beamed ceiling of the English coffeehouse. The owner moved quickly about the sanded floor and past the baretopped tables. He was dressed in a white shirt and a waistcoat, plain breeches fastened below the knees, cotton stockings, and black leather shoes. And he seemed to be everywhere! Most of his customers agreed that he "is in continual motion, but it is only from the fire-side to the table; and his tongue goes . . . faster than his feet. . . ."

The owner had many tasks. First, he had to see to it that the coffee was brewed properly. Since the beverage was drunk without sugar or cream, the taste had to be acceptable. He also tried to convince his customers that coffee was good for their health:

> [Coffee] makes the heart lightsome. It is good for a cough. It is excellent to prevent and cure the dropsy, gout, and scurvy. . . . It will prevent drowsiness and make one fit for business. . . .

Most important of all, the owner had to be sure that the latest printed and spoken news was made available to his customers. He knew that many men who came into his coffeehouse hungered for political news.

"What news have you, Master?" a customer would ask him.

The owner would stop promptly. Then—in a whisper loud enough to be heard by almost all in the room:

> He [would relate] some mysterious intrigue of state, told him last night by one that is a barber to the tailor of the servant of a great man!

The owner kept himself well informed by thrusting his head into groups of debaters and listening with great attention "to the narratives that were made in those little circular audiences." He tried to keep his establishment a "university of information" for these men, for—above all—he wanted his customers to continue to say:

> So great a University
> I think there ne'er was any,
> In which you may a scholar be
> For spending of a penny.

The sketch above is based on: Edward P. Cheyney, *Readings in English History Drawn from the Original Sources,* Ginn and Company; Mary I. Curtis, *England of Song and Story,* copyright 1931 & 1945 by Allyn & Bacon, Inc.; G. M. Trevelyan, *Illustrated English Social History,* David McKay Co., Inc.; Percy H. Boynton, *London in English Literature,* The University of Chicago Press, copyright 1931 by The University of Chicago Press; D. Yarwood, *English Costume from the Second Century B.C. to 1950,* B. T. Batsford, Ltd.

CHAPTER REVIEW

Think and Discuss

1. John Milton, the English poet, spoke out boldly against people in any age who flee rather than fight for what they believe in. Which is better? Why?
2. Why were arguments about religion not separated from the political questions in seventeenth-century England?
3. Why was habeas corpus important?
4. "Competition is the life of trade," is an old saying. Did mercantilism illustrate its truth? How?
5. Can you find the theory of the "right to revolt" against tyranny in the philosophy of John Locke? In what American document was this theory adopted by a group of people?
6. Why didn't Parliament give complete religious freedom to all people in 1689?
7. Is the Cabinet system more or less democratic than our own presidential system?

Past and Present

1. Can you find any examples of mercantilism in the world today?
2. Can you cite examples of "divine right" rulers in the twentieth century?
3. What nations today are strongly democratic? Why?

Activities

1. Write a report to give to the class on how the King James Version of the *Bible* came into being.
2. Make a chart showing the steps taken toward the development of representative government in England.
3. On a map of the British Isles, locate Belfast, Dublin, Edinburgh, England, English Channel, Great Britain, Irish Sea, Isle of Man, London, North Sea, Northern Ireland, Republic of Ireland, Scotland, United Kingdom, and Wales.
4. Write a short essay on John Locke's philosophy and influence.

CHAPTER
20

England Wins an Empire and Loses Some American Colonies

KEYNOTE

An expert in international law once remarked:

> [Empire-building] resembles opening a window. When you do it, it's fresh air. When the other fellow does it, it's a draught.

This statement certainly applies to the activities of the English in the eighteenth century. It was in this period that they won an empire in India and America and felt a sense of pride in that achievement. Yet it was in this same century that some of the American colonies—resentful rather than pleased by England's control over them—revolted and established their own nation.

An English merchant ship in a foreign harbor.

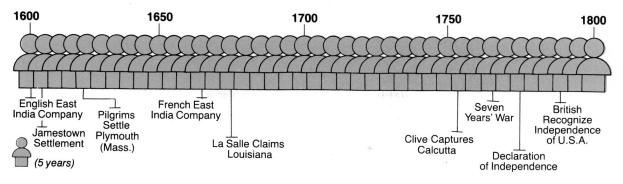

1600   1650   1700   1750   1800

English East India Company

Jamestown Settlement

Pilgrims Settle Plymouth (Mass.)

French East India Company

La Salle Claims Louisiana

Clive Captures Calcutta

Seven Years' War

Declaration of Independence

British Recognize Independence of U.S.A.

(5 years)

1. Portuguese, Dutch, and English Clash

At the same time that representative government was developing in England, the English were building an empire overseas. They were especially active in India and North America.

In the sixteenth century, Portugal and Spain were the leaders in establishing contacts with the Far East and with the Americas. The Portuguese set up trading posts on Ceylon; on Java, Sumatra, and the Moluccas or the Spice Islands (all of which are part of Indonesia today); and at Goa, on the west coast of India. Meanwhile the Spaniards took over some of the Philippine Islands and gained a considerable empire in America.

The Dutch Oppose the Portuguese

Portugal was annexed to Spain in 1580 and did not regain its independence until 1640. Under Spain's control, Portuguese merchants were handicapped by the acts of the Spanish king, Philip II. For example, Philip forbade his enemies—England, France, and the Netherlands—to trade with the chief ports of Portugal. He also weakened both Spain and Portugal by his unsuccessful struggle against England, climaxed by the defeat of the Spanish Armada in 1588.

Spain declined in power after the defeat of the Armada. Portugal faced serious problems, too. The United Netherlands had won its independence from Spain in 1581, and the Dutch became the rivals of the Portuguese for foreign trade. In 1602 the Dutch East India Company was organized to develop trade with the Far East. Aggressive Dutch officials and bold merchants moved into trading areas held by the Portuguese. So successful were the Dutch that by the beginning of the eighteenth century they had taken over most of the trading posts once controlled by the Portuguese.

The English Oppose the Dutch

Just as the Dutch had moved against the Portuguese in the Far East, so the English were determined to drive out the Dutch. English merchants were particularly eager to trade with ports on the coast of India and with the Molucca Islands. They hoped to exchange English cloth for spices, calico, dye woods, and precious stones.

In 1600 Queen Elizabeth I, therefore, chartered the English East India Company to trade with lands in the Indian and Pacific oceans. This company gained the right to administer the government of trading areas it controlled, protect itself against traders from other countries, and fight against local peoples who would not cooperate with the English traders.

The English established posts at Madras and other places in India and worked hard to take over Dutch trade in the Far East. They forced the Dutch to accept the Navigation Act. This was one of a series of acts designed to ensure English control over the trade of their colonies.

In the reign of Charles II (1660–1685), economic rivalry led to a renewal of the overseas war between England and the Netherlands. The Dutch forced the English out of the Moluccas, and the English took over Dutch islands in the West Indies. The English also attacked the Dutch colony of New Amsterdam in North America. In 1664 New Amsterdam (later renamed New York) surrendered to the English.

Check on Your Reading

1. How did the actions of Philip II weaken Portugal?
2. What did the Dutch gain from the Portuguese?
3. What did the English East India Company achieve in the Far East?
4. What did the English gain from the Dutch?

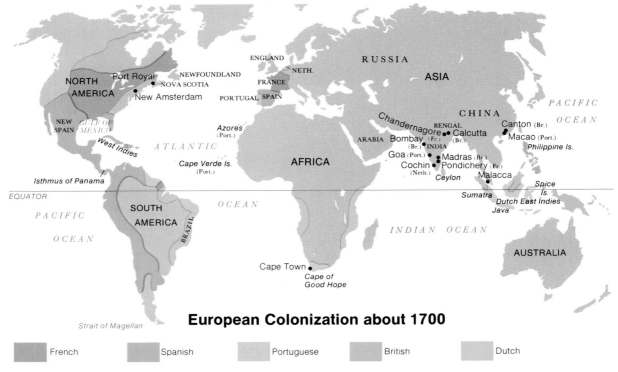

European Colonization about 1700

French		Spanish		Portuguese		British		Dutch	

By 1700 Portugal, Spain, the Netherlands, France, and England had established trade contacts and colonies on the coast of Africa, in the East, and in the Americas.

2. The English and French Clash

The setting for the struggles among the English, the French, and rulers of India had come into focus by the eighteenth century. (See the map above). The English East India Company had established trading stations or forts at Madras, the Bengal area, Calcutta, and Bombay.

The French East India Company had been chartered in 1664. It was given the authority to trade and, if necessary, to fight to establish its position in India. It had set up trading bases at Chandernagore in the northeast and Pondichéry in the southeast.

In India, the Mogul Empire had disintegrated. India had split into many provinces ruled by princes. It was not strong enough to drive out foreigners.

Clive Helps Win India for the English

France had brilliant colonial administrators, such as Joseph François Dupleix, who in 1742 became the commander of the French possessions in India. Dupleix made alliances with different princes in southern India, trained Indians to fight as

soldiers for the French, and led the French in their battles against the English. A series of disagreements with the French East India Company led to his recall to France in 1754.

The English were still more fortunate. They had the services of young Robert Clive. According to the legend, as a boy Clive had demonstrated his courage by sitting on the top of a church steeple. Clive started as a clerk and transferred to the military arm of the English East India Company. He built up a strong military force that included Indian soldiers or *sepoys*. Clive proved a brilliant, if moody, leader who loved action and who was most effective in times of danger.

The ruler of the region of Bengal, who favored the French, became very angry when the English began strengthening the defenses of their trading post in Calcutta. In 1757 he seized the town and locked up one hundred forty-six Englishmen in a small cell described by an eyewitness as "a room not twenty feet square, with only two small windows, and these obstructed by the veranda." All that night the terrified prisoners remained in this so-called "Black Hole of Calcutta." Some raved in delirium. Others prayed desperately. Still others scrambled over the heads of those who stood between them and the windows. The pressure of the bodies against one another, the terrible heat, and the lack of air suffocated most of them. In the morning, when the doors were finally opened, only twenty-three were still alive! Recent scholarship suggests that the number of people locked up in the "Black Hole" has been exaggerated, and that the event was later overdramatized.

Robert Clive determined that the ruler should be punished for this action and for challenging the rights of the English. He attacked and recaptured Calcutta. Then he crushed the ruler's army at the great Battle of Plassey (in Bengal) in 1757. Clive's victory was extremely important, since it made possible the control and use of Bengal as a center for further expansion in India by the English East India Company.

The Seven Years' War (1756-1763) was fought in India as well as in Europe and America. During the war Clive and other English leaders captured important French settlements in India. They allowed the French to return to their posts but took away their power by forbidding them to keep troops. The prestige of France had been seriously weakened. The supremacy of the English East India Company was firmly established.

The French in North America

About seventy years after Jacques Cartier discovered the St. Lawrence River (1535), France began to build a colonial empire in the Americas. In 1604, the French established a settlement at Port Royal, Acadia (Nova Scotia). A few years later, Samuel de Champlain founded a colony at Quebec (1608). The French also built a permanent settlement at Montreal (1642) which became an important center for trade.

Father Jacques Marquette, a Jesuit missionary, and Louis Joliet, a fur trader, followed the Mississippi from Wisconsin as far south as the Arkansas River in 1673. La Salle led an expedition down the Mississippi River to its mouth (1680-1682). He claimed for France a region which he named Louisiana in honor of King Louis XIV. Eventually the French claimed the land between the Gulf of Mexico and the Great Lakes, and their holdings extended far to the west and northeast.

The English in North America

The English settled in North America at a later date than the French. In 1607 the London Company founded the colony of Jamestown in Virginia. This was the first permanent English settlement in America. Despite the hardships, the Jamestown settlement survived.

In 1609 the river we call the Hudson was discovered by Henry Hudson, an English sea captain in the employ of the Dutch. In 1620, Pilgrims seeking a place where they could worship as they wished established the colony of Plymouth, Massachusetts. The Pilgrims believed in Calvinistic ideas. They were *Separatists;* that is, they wanted to break away from the Anglican Church rather than try to reform it from within.

This painting by Benjamin West shows the ruler of Bengal giving Robert Clive the right for the English East India Company to collect revenues in his kingdom.

During the reigns of James I and Charles I, Separatists and Puritans were discriminated against or persecuted in England. Also, many who dissented from the Anglican Church were without work because of agricultural and economic problems in England. About 70,000 people left England and came to the New World between 1620 and 1640. Most of them sought land, work, and religious freedom for themselves.

Additional English settlers arrived during the seventeenth century. The Puritans were active in Massachusetts. The Catholics, who sought a religious refuge, settled in Maryland. The Quakers (the Religious Society of Friends) migrated to Pennsylvania. According to church historian Williston Walker, they believed that "every [person] received from the Lord a measure of light, and . . . if this 'Inner Light' is followed, it leads surely . . . to spiritual truth." They also believed that a professional ministry is unnecessary.

In 1664 the English forced the Dutch to give up New Amsterdam. By 1733 the English controlled thirteen colonies along the Atlantic coast. (See the map on page 358.)

The English Settlers Come to Stay

The English settlers had come to stay. They were determined to settle permanently in America. While they continued to think of England as the "homeland," they soon developed pride in their American homes and ways of living.

The English settlers wanted considerable self-government in local affairs. In 1818 John Adams, who had served as the second President of the United States, wrote:

I have always laughed at the affectation of representing American independence . . . as a late invention. The idea of it . . . has been familiar to Americans from the first settlement of the country.

Check on Your Reading

1. Why were France and England able to establish trading stations in India?
2. Describe the work of Dupleix and Clive.
3. What were the results of the Seven Years' War in India?
4. Describe the French and English settlements in North America.

3. The English Take French Lands

The international wars occurring in the eighteenth century in Europe spread. In North America, they led to a struggle between the English and the French.

Queen Anne's War

Europe fought the War of the Spanish Succession in 1701-1713. The struggle became so widespread that it led to fighting between the French and English in America. In America it was known as Queen Anne's War.

Settlers in New England waged a successful campaign against France's Port Royal in Acadia. By the Treaties of Utrecht (1713), France gave Nova Scotia to England, and recognized England's claims to Newfoundland and the Hudson Bay region.

The French and Indian War

The Seven Years' War (1756-1763) involved most of the countries of Europe, and again England and France were on opposite sides. In America, the war was known as the French and Indian War.

English troops and American colonists fought successfully against the French. The climax came when the French stronghold of Quebec in Canada was captured by General Wolfe and his English forces. Then the English troops spread through Canada, capturing Montreal in 1760.

By the Peace of Paris (1763) that ended the war: 1. France gave Canada, Prince Edward Island, Cape Breton Island, and most of France's lands east of the Mississippi to England. France kept St. Pierre and Miquelon (two islands off the coast of Newfoundland) and its West Indian island possessions. 2. France gave New Orleans and Louisiana west of the Mississippi to Spain. 3. Spain gave the Floridas to England.

Check on Your Reading

1. What were the results of Queen Anne's War?
2. What were the provisions of the Peace of Paris (1763)?

4. The Thirteen Colonies Win Their Independence

England had struggled against France in the New World from 1689 to 1763. The English finally defeated the French and forced them to turn over most of their holdings in America. However, it was

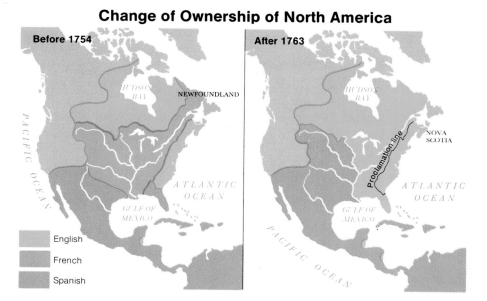

These two maps show the territory that France lost as a result of the Seven Years' War. What lands did England obtain? What territory did Spain gain?

Change of Ownership of North America

Before 1754

After 1763

- English
- French
- Spanish

not long before American colonists arose to spoil the English victory.

Complaints of the American Colonists

During the reign of King George III (1760-1820), the American colonists became increasingly displeased with the home government in Britain. They were angry for several reasons.

1. British officials placed oppressive economic restrictions on the colonies, such as prohibiting them from exporting articles that would compete with those produced in England.

2. They also interfered with the colonies' right to trade. For example, the Navigation Acts required American colonists selling goods to other countries to transport them in English ships and to have these vessels stop at England on their voyages. Colonists were allowed to sell their sugar and several other products only to the American colonies or to England, not to foreign markets. Other restrictions were also set up on colonial trade.

3. Britain taxed the colonies without permitting them to send representatives to the British Parliament. For example, the Stamp Act of 1765, passed by Parliament, required the American colonists to buy special government stamps and place them on newspapers, business documents, and other papers. This unpopular act aroused resistance and demonstrations. The Stamp Act Congress (1765) of representatives from nine colonies denied that Parliament could tax the colonies without their consent.

A boycott by the colonists of British products led to repeal of the Act.

4. British officials took away a number of political rights of colonial governments. They stationed British soldiers in the homes of colonists, and in other ways violated the privacy of the people.

The Viewpoint of the British Government

The British government took the position that Parliament had an obligation to pass laws to protect the well-being of Britain. The British believed that the prosperity of the home country would stimulate the prosperity of the colonies.

The British pointed out that the Navigation Acts were designed to help Britain, not to hinder the colonies. The British had given bounties and monopolies to the colonists to develop industries that did not compete with those of Britain.

The British government expected American colonists to pay taxes to help meet the costs of governing and defending the colonies. Britain needed money desperately. During the Seven Years' War the British had helped to protect the American colonists from French domination. Britain's debt at the end of the war was about seventy-two billion dollars (by our currency standards today). The British considered unreasonable the protest of the colonists against "taxation without representation." They argued that the British Parliament had free debate on matters involving the American colonies, and members of Parliament represented all the British.

They argued that members of Parliament expressed all viewpoints—including those of the colonists.

The "Tea Party" Leads to Reprisals

The famous "Boston Tea Party" showed that the colonists were willing to defy British authority. The Tea Act of 1773 had given the British East India Company a monopoly on the tea trade in America. No American could buy tea legally from anyone but this company. Many colonists were angered by this monopoly and by other regulations concerning the importation of tea. They boycotted the trade in tea.

On the night of December 16, 1773, about one hundred fifty colonists, disguised as Mohawks, boarded a tea ship in Boston Harbor and threw its cargo of tea overboard. This act led the British to close the port of Boston and to place more restrictions on the people of Massachusetts.

The Continental Congress Declares War

The advice of British statesmen like Edmund Burke, who opposed the British use of coercion in the colonies, was ignored. The British government continued to restrict the rights of the colonists. As a result, the First Continental Congress met in Philadelphia in 1774 to determine what to do.

Fifty-six representatives from twelve colonies attended the First Continental Congress. The Congress drew up plans to make the British change their policies, but it did not advocate that the colonies break away.

In 1775 violence replaced discussion. On April 19 British troops and Americans clashed at Concord and Lexington in Massachusetts. The *New-York Mercury* then observed: "All that is attended to, besides plowing and planting, is making ready for fighting." The Second Continental Congress officially declared war on Britain on July 6, 1775.

This painting shows the Second Continental Congress approving the Declaration of Independence. Benjamin Franklin is shown seated in the middle.

The Declaration of Independence

The American Revolution was led by moderates and members of the upper class. Many colonists joined the American forces directed by George Washington, the commander-in-chief. Sturdy farmers enlisted, dressed in "clothes [they were] accustomed to wear in the field." Excited fifteen-year-old boys volunteered, handling their muskets awkwardly but willing to learn. A brave woman dressed herself in a man's clothing, said that her name was Robert Shurtleff, and enlisted.

Most of these people at first were fighting to regain their rights, not to separate from Britain. However, the king branded them "rebels," and it was not long before they were playing this role. There were great disagreements over how far the colonists should go in defying England.

Then in January 1776 there appeared a pamphlet, *Common Sense,* by Thomas Paine. He pointed out that it was ridiculous for America, a great continent, to be ruled by a small island, Britain. America should move toward free trade, independence, and westward expansion. It should set up a republic, remain clear of European problems, and develop its rich resources. *Common Sense* was widely read and highly influential in moving public opinion toward seeking American independence.

Finally, as the British refused to make major concessions, a Declaration of Independence was drawn up. It was adopted July 4, 1776. The Declaration announced to the world:

> . . . these United Colonies are, and of Right ought to be, Free and Independent States; . . . they are Absolved from all Allegiance to the British Crown, and . . . all political connection between them and the State of Great Britain, is and ought to be totally dissolved. . . .

Thomas Jefferson, a key figure in the writing of the Declaration of Independence, declared that he "turned to neither book nor pamphlet" in working on this document. However, there were ideas in the Declaration that were very similar to those of John Locke. Jefferson and other educated men of the time were familiar with Locke's writing and admired his ideas.

An Evaluation of British and American Strength

The Declaration of Independence alone could not guarantee independence. If the United States (the thirteen former colonies) were to be free, the Revolutionary War would have to be won.

The British had the following advantages:

1. Their army was better trained then the American troops.

2. Their navy was far more powerful than the ships available to the Americans.

3. They had the money needed to hire mercenary troops (paid professional soldiers) to fight for them.

4. They retained the loyalty of many colonists who were known as *loyalists.* About one-third of the population in the colonies were loyalists.

On the other hand, the Americans had important advantages:

1. The war was being fought on their home grounds, while the British were many miles from Britain.

2. They had the effective leadership of Washington and others whose tactics often proved superior to those of British generals.

3. They had the eventual support of France and of the Netherlands and Spain.

4. Their cause stirred some Americans to deeds of unusual heroism.

Final Victory

There were bitter campaigns in New England, Canada, South Carolina, New York, Pennsylvania, and New Jersey. The Americans had to survive some serious setbacks. Then, in 1777, American troops won an important victory at Saratoga, New York, where they defeated the forces of the British General Burgoyne.

The victory at Saratoga convinced France that Americans were capable opponents of the British. France was eager to strike back at a Britain that had fought against French interests. In 1778 France made an alliance with the Americans. The French recognized the independence of the new American nation and provided it with vital financial and military assistance.

In 1778, the war moved to the Southern states where Americans won some important victories. Then, with the support of a French fleet, Washington forced General Cornwallis to surrender at Yorktown, Virginia (1781). Soon after this American victory, the Revolutionary War came to an end.

By the Treaty of Paris (1783): 1. The independence of the United States was recognized by Great

Britain. 2. The Mississippi River was recognized as the western boundary of the United States, and navigation on the Mississippi was opened to both the United States and Britain. 3. The fishing rights of Americans off Newfoundland were protected.

To the south, Spain held Florida, which it had reconquered from the British in 1783. To the west, Spain controlled land west of the Mississippi. And to the north, the British remained in Canada.

A New Nation

The successful American Revolution had a number of important results: 1. It brought into existence a new nation, the United States. 2. Written constitutions were devised for the newly freed states and later for the American nation. 3. Americans now could settle on the western lands that had been under the restrictive control of the British government. 4. It weakened the prestige of monarchical governments. 5. It influenced events in France, a country moving toward revolution.

Check on Your Reading

1. What were the colonists' grievances? What was the British government's attitude?
2. What incidents and events led to the outbreak of the American Revolution?
3. In your opinion, which side had the greater advantages in the war? Why?
4. What was France's role?
5. What did the Americans gain in 1783?

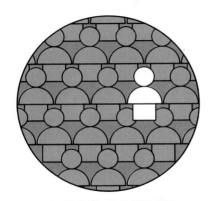

LET'S MEET THE PEOPLE

Prisoner of War

During the American Revolution, the British used anchored ships as prisons.

Fort Washington, the 16th day November, A.D. 1776. This day I, William Slade, was taken [by the British] with 2,800 more.

William Slade, a young soldier in the forces of the American revolutionists, wrote the above notation in his diary. Then he waited for his British captors to determine his destination.

On December 2, William Slade was moved to the North River and transported to the *Grosvenor,* a British prison ship. "There was . . . 500 men on board," he observed, "this made much confusion." In the days that followed, Slade struggled to survive in the dark and putrid hold of the prison ship. He conserved his small rations of wormy biscuits, watered broth, rice, and bits of rotting meat. He protected himself from the cold and the vermin as best he could. And he kept "hoping for good news."

On December 23, Sergeant Kieth and Job March "broke out with smallpox," and the dreaded disease spread rapidly. William Slade counted the number as the prisoners died about him. "One dies almost ever day," he wrote in his diary. Then the disease struck William Slade! A British sailor made two incisions in William's hand and let out "the impure blood." Still Slade grew weaker.

Finally, on December 28, Ensign Smith came for William Slade. The ensign's orders were to move the sick man ashore at once. When Slade heard the news, he wrote with feverish fingers: "I now feel glad." For, though his body was tormented by disease, he was leaving the prison ship at last. Leaving it—perhaps—forever.

The sketch above is based on William Slade's own account as it appears from: *The Spirit of 'Seventy-Six* by Henry Steele Commager and Richard B. Morris, copyright 1958 by The Bobbs-Merrill Company, Inc., reprinted by special permission of the publishers.

CHAPTER REVIEW

Think and Discuss

1. Is it better to remain within an organization of whose actions you do not approve or to resign and establish a new organization? Consider the Pilgrims and the American revolutionists.
2. On what grounds do you think John Adams based his opinion that the spirit of independence had existed in the English colonies since the first settlement?
3. If you were an English citizen in the seventeenth century, how would you have justified the control of colonial possessions and at the same time accepted John Locke's philosophy of liberty and self-government at home?
4. How do you explain the fact that the chief supporters of the American Revolution included business people, lawyers, and landowners?
5. What did France gain by aiding the American colonies in the Revolutionary War?
6. A historian has said that "something new and portentous was injected into world affairs by the successful revolt" of the American colonists. What was it?
7. The establishment of the United States convinced many liberals in Europe that the ideas of the "Enlightenment" were practical. What events might have convinced them?

Past and Present

1. Compare the American Revolution of 1776 with those of the African states after World War II. What differences and similarities are there?
2. What revolutions are occurring at the present time or have recently occurred? What were their causes?

Activities

1. Make up and question several generalizations from this chapter. Sample: When people have experienced many injustices, they will eventually rise in revolt. Questions: How many injustices? What is an injustice? Will the people always rise in revolt? Do you agree with the generalization?
2. On a map show British and French world possessions before the Peace of Paris in 1763.
3. Write a report on the question: "Was Britain able to give its attention to the war in the colonies?" What are your conclusions?
4. Write a summary contrasting a pro-British account of the Revolution with a pro-American account. What conclusions can you draw?
5. Write a report on the question: "Was England able to give its undivided attention to the war in the colonies?" What are your conclusions?

The French Revolution and Napoleon Shake Europe

KEYNOTE

"LIBERTY, EQUALITY AND FRATERNITY"

These words formed the slogan of the French revolutionists who overthrew the monarchy and established the first republic in France. One of the central facts of history is this: The French Revolution in the eighteenth century brought great changes, and these have continued to affect France and the world down to the present day.

When Napoleon Bonaparte took over the command of an army of the French Republic, he told his troops:

> Soldiers! You are naked, ill-fed . . . I [am going] to lead you into the most fertile plains of the world. Rich provinces, great cities, will be in your power; you will find honor, glory, and riches there.

Napoleon kept that promise. However, he did it by concentrating all power in his own hands and by leading France into bitter military campaigns throughout Europe. From 1799 to 1814 Napoleon obtained great power and used it to dominate France and Europe. The changes he brought about have also continued to affect France and much of Europe down to the present day.

The storming of the Bastille in Paris on July 14, 1789.

1. Louis XV Ascends the French Throne

In 1715 the Duke of Bouillon placed a black feather on his cap and walked out to the balcony of the great palace at Versailles. Then he solemnly announced: "The King is dead." The Duke returned to the palace, put on a white feather, and went out to the balcony again. This time he proclaimed: "Long live the King." The long reign of Louis XIV had ended, and the rule of Louis XV, his great-grandson, had begun.

Louis XV (1715-1774), the new king of France, was a boy when he came to the throne. Even after he reached manhood, he refused to face his responsibilities. Historian Albert Guérard points out:

> . . . untrained except to laziness, prejudiced and unprincipled, timid at heart while absurdly proud, superstitious and skeptical, he yawned his life away.

Yet there were times when Louis XV's observations proved to be uncannily right. This was the case when he declared: "Bah! the old machine will last out my time, at any rate!" He was equally correct when he agreed with his companion Madame de Pompadour that "After us [comes] the deluge!" The "old machine" is better known as the *Old Régime,* a term that refers to institutions and conditions of life in eighteenth-century Europe before the French Revolution.

Government

Louis XV could not provide strong leadership, and the government of France was extremely inefficient. Attempts to administer the many laws added to the confusion. French author-statesman Alexis de Tocqueville later observed: "New rules followed each other with such bewildering rapidity that its agents never knew which to obey."

The Estates-General, or assembly, had not met since 1614, and there was little development of representative government. The *parlements,* the high courts of justice, did assume the right to refuse to register some of the decrees of the king. However, the parlements themselves were hereditary courts of justice. Their magistrates were chiefly concerned with adding to their own power.

The Three Estates

There were three main classes or "Estates." The First Estate, the clergy, numbered about

A French cartoon shows the King and the First and Second Estates crushing the Third Estate—the majority of the French people. The First Estate was the clergy and the Second Estate was the nobility.

100,000. They were members of the powerful Roman Catholic Church, which had many privileges. The Second Estate, the nobility, numbered about 400,000. The Third Estate consisted of the great majority of the population of 26,000,000.

It is important to remember that there were great variations in income and social position within each of the three estates. Nevertheless, the three estates were recognized by the French legal system.

The first two estates were privileged. They helped to run the government and were exempt from the land tax and other burdens. The Third Estate bore the costs of government and was denied many rights.

The *bourgeoisie*—the business people, merchants, lawyers, and other members of the "middle class"— were becoming more powerful economically. They wanted freedom of competition in trade and industry and a reasonable system of taxation. As members of the Third Estate, they were denied many rights.

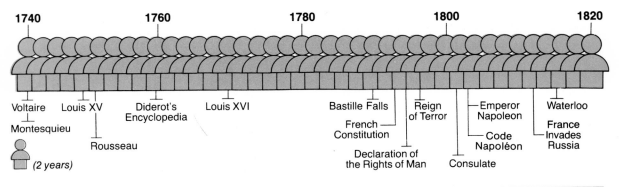

1740   1760   1780   1800   1820

Voltaire Louis XV   Diderot's   Louis XVI   Bastille Falls   Reign   Emperor   Waterloo
                      Encyclopedia   of Terror Napoleon
Montesquieu   French   France
                                                     Constitution   Code   Invades
               Rousseau   Napoléon   Russia
(2 years)   Declaration of   Consulate
                                                     the Rights of Man

The French Economy

Compared to other Europeans, the French were relatively well off. Commercial activities increased. Ports prospered. Useful public works were carried out throughout the country. Even the peasants, nine-tenths of the population, had a better standard of living than those elsewhere on the continent.

However, the government was close to bankruptcy, as a result of the extravagance of the king and court, the exemption of the upper classes from direct taxation, and the chaotic system of collecting taxes. Taxes were "farmed out" to private individuals or companies that collected them for the king. These collectors did not hesitate to line their own pockets with the people's money. Over 60 per cent of the gross revenue collected did not reach the government.

As a result of the Seven Years' War, the public debt increased and France lost an empire in America and India. The loss of the empire was later to deprive France of many economic resources. In addition, France's participation in the American Revolution drained a large sum from the French treasury.

Remnants of Feudalism

Remnants of feudalism—such as the payment of fees for the use of a lord's mill to grind grain into flour—still existed in some parts of the country. Such feudal restrictions greatly annoyed the peasants.

Several outdated feudal relationships continued to exist. For example, the nobles originally had been exempt from taxation in exchange for the protection that they provided for their lands. Since then, many nobles had left their estates to live at Versailles. They no longer had to defend their lands. Nevertheless, the nobles remained free from nearly all direct taxation.

Check on Your Reading

1. Under the Old Régime, what groups helped run the government?
2. Why was the government of France nearly bankrupt?
3. In what ways was the tax structure unfair to many people?

2. The Enlightenment Spreads throughout Europe

The Enlightenment was stimulated by the work of the scientists who applied reason to the study of natural phenomena to derive the laws of nature. It was not long before "enlightened people" determined also to use reason to find the natural laws of society and to solve the problems of society.

The term *natural law* meant a law according to which society would operate if there were no formal governmental law, just as the law of gravitation naturally operated in the universe. For example, it was said that one natural law of society was that each person tries to survive for as long as she or he can. Reason and Nature became the key ideas of the Enlightenment. The Enlightenment tried to use reason to study all fields: science, politics, law, and even religion. Thus religious beliefs were to be based on reason, not on revelation, dogma, or authority.

The Philosophes Stimulate People's Minds

During the Enlightenment, the sharpest critics of abuses in society and the most effective voices for reform in France were the *philosophes,* or the philosophers. Among the most important of the philosophes were Voltaire, Montesquieu, Rousseau, and Diderot. The ideas of these men stimulated people to think seriously about conditions in their country.

Voltaire's keen wit and intelligence are suggested in this statue by Houdon.

Voltaire and Freedom of Thought and Speech

François Marie Arouet, who was known as Voltaire (1694-1778), was a thin and sickly person who was one of the best representatives of the Enlightenment. Voltaire wrote a vast number of works—essays, histories, plays, long poems, and stories. He was the author of many letters, among them letters to rulers like Frederick the Great of Prussia and Catherine the Great of Russia. Among his best-known works are his satire *Candide* and his *Essay on the Manners and Spirit of Nations*.

Voltaire was a staunch and brilliant defender of the right of people to think and to say what they pleased, provided that they did not commit crimes against society. Voltaire made his position clear when he wrote:

> Do I propose, then, that every citizen shall be free to follow his own reason, and believe whatever this enlightened or deluded reason shall dictate to him? Certainly, provided that he does not disturb the public order.

Voltaire was particularly insistent that people be allowed to follow their own thoughts about religion and to worship as they wished. As he put it:

> The supposed right of intolerance [toward another's religion] is absurd and barbaric. It is the right of the tiger; nay, it is far worse, for tigers do but tear in order to have food, while we [rip] each other for paragraphs. . . .

Voltaire, like many other eighteeth-century philosophers, believed in what was called *deism*. Deists believed in God as the creator of the universe. They held, however, that God had merely started the universe going as a person starts a watch and never after interferes in events. This meant that God did not answer prayer or extend grace to anyone, though God judged human conduct. Deists usually attended no church, though they usually claimed that God was present everywhere in nature.

Montesquieu and Separation of Powers

Baron de Montesquieu (1689-1755), wrote a very important book—*The Spirit of Laws*. Montesquieu was a nobleman who was convinced that liberty could best be protected by placing checks on the unlimited power of government. He believed that no person or governing body should have all of the power in a country.

Montesquieu supported the idea of the *separation of powers*. The executive, legislative, and judiciary branches of government should be separate. Each one should have certain responsibilities and serve as a check on the power of the other two. Montesquieu issued a warning that anticipated the rise of future tyrants:

> There would be an end of everything were the same man or the same body . . . to exercise those three powers, that of enacting laws, that of

executing the public resolutions, and of trying the causes of individuals. . . .

Montesquieu's ideas influenced American leaders. The United States Constitution takes the separation of powers as one of its basic principles.

Rousseau and the Social Contract

Jean-Jacques Rousseau (1712-1778), who was born in Geneva, Switzerland, was an emotional and colorful person. He differed from most of the other French philosophes. 1. He believed that instinct was more important than reason. 2. He rejected the sophisticated society of the Parisian salons, or private drawing rooms where distinguished guests gathered to converse. 3. He preferred what he believed to be the natural goodness of primitive peoples to the artificial ways of civilization.

Above all, Rousseau loved nature and despised the corrupt ways of society. "Man is born free; and everywhere he is in chains," he declared. To Rousseau, the "chains" were those that the rulers of society had forged to deny people their freedom.

Rousseau expressed his ideas of government in a book called *The Social Contract*. Rousseau's ideas, expressed in *The Social Contract* and *Emile* (on education), had a considerable influence on the thinking of many future leaders of European and American nations. Rousseau urged love of one's nation. Thus he influenced the development of modern nationalism, which became an important factor in the world by the late eighteenth century.

Ideas of the Social Contract

In the beginning of history, people were free. Then people joined together in a common community for their mutual protection. Each person accepted an informal "contract" or agreement in which he placed himself and all of his power under "the supreme direction of the general will of all." Historians are not agreed on the exact meaning of the term "general will." In time, many people interpreted the term to mean that each person owed obedience to the will of the community even if his own personal will or desires differed from the community, or general, will.

No one—not even a king—had the right to go against the will of the community as a whole. If a ruler was tyrannical and ignored the will of the people, the Social Contract was broken and people had the right to demand their freedom.

Diderot and the Encyclopedia

Denis Diderot (1713-1784) was the editor of the famous twenty-eight volume *Encyclopedia*. Diderot published the *Encylopedia* in spite of government censorship. His goal was an aim of the Enlightenment as a whole:

> to assemble the knowledge scattered over the face of the earth; to explain its general plan to the men with whom we live, and to transmit it to those who will come after us . . . so that our descendants, by becoming better informed, may in consequence be happier and more virtuous. . . .

Voltaire, Rousseau, and other philosophes wrote articles for the *Encyclopedia*. They did not hesitate to criticize slyly the existing regime. For example, in the article on "Torture," Diderot quoted a seventeenth-century author: "[The use of torture is] a sure means of convicting an innocent man who is physically weak and of acquitting a guilty person born with great endurance." In this way—without directly attacking the methods of French justice—Diderot struck at a most undesirable feature, the use of torture.

François Quesnay and the Physiocrats

Some people also tried to find the natural laws that would keep the economy strong. For example, the natural law of "supply and demand" might determine price in this way: If the demand of people for a product exceeded its supply, prices would go up. If the supply of a product exceeded the demand for it, prices would go down.

One group, known as the *Physiocrats*, was led by a French physician, François Quesnay (1694-1774). The Physiocrats declared that government regulation of the economy was frequently contrary to natural law. They also claimed that land is the only source of wealth and that agriculture increases wealth. They suggested that a single tax on the net income from land be the sole tax of a country. They favored the protection of property but few restrictions on commerce or business.

The Physiocrats, like some other Europeans of the time, believed in *laissez-faire*. This policy included removing government restrictions on the economy and keeping to a minimum government interference in economic affairs.

The principles of *laissez-faire*, were an abandonment of mercantilism. They were best expressed by a Scottish economist, Adam Smith, in his book *The Wealth of Nations* (1776). The idea of *laissez-faire* also had much influence on the leaders of the American Revolution.

This was the situation in France under the Old Régime. 1. France was a country with an extravagant and inefficient government. 2. Society was divided into Three Estates, with the Third Estate deprived of political power. 3. The bourgeoisie was becoming economically powerful. 4. The government was nearly bankrupt. 5. Some remnants of feudalism existed. 6. The questions and answers of the philosophes stimulated the minds of people. This was the setting for one of the most important events in history—the French Revolution.

Check on Your Reading

1. What were the key ideas of the Enlightenment? Explain.
2. What were the principal ideas contributed by Voltaire, Montesquieu, Rousseau, and Diderot?
3. What were the economic principles of the Physiocrats?
4. Summarize the situation in France under the Old Régime.

3. The French Revolution

In 1789 the King of France was Louis XVI (1774-1792). He was quite incapable of providing France with the leadership needed. Madame Roland, who later joined the revolt, described his character: "He was neither [a] brutish blockhead . . . nor [an] honest, kind, and sensible creature." Rather, he was a man "without . . . energy of mind, or firmness of character."

Louis' wife, the beautiful Marie Antoinette, was the daughter of Empress Maria Theresa. Fond of luxury and extremely extravagant, Marie Antoinette was too superficial to aid her husband in affairs of state.

The Revolution Begins

In 1789, the king's chief concern was to obtain money for his empty treasury. This became such a serious problem that he had to call a meeting of the Estates-General to be held at Versailles. The Estates-General was the so-called "national assembly" of France, but it had not met since 1614.

In the past, the Estates-General had voted by separate Estates. This meant that the clergy as a group (the First Estate) had one vote. The nobles as a group (the Second Estate) had one vote. The Third Estate, which included about 96 per cent of the population, also had one vote. This meant the clergy and nobles were able to outvote the far more numerous Third Estate by two to one.

Most of the representatives of the Third Estate came from the middle class. They felt that the system of voting would have to be changed if any improvements were to be introduced into the country. They therefore proposed that the three Estates should meet together, that each person should have a single vote, and that the vote of the majority should be accepted.

King Louis XVI, supported by the clergy and nobles, rejected this proposal. When the king tried to prevent the Estates-General from meeting, the Third Estate defiantly gathered on an indoor tennis court. Here its members declared themselves to be the real National Assembly of France. They also took an oath, by which they promised "never to separate, and to reassemble wherever circumstances require, until the constitution of the kingdom shall be established and fixed upon firm foundations."

A number of the lower clergy and liberal nobles joined the newly formed Assembly. King Louis XVI then had to change his position. He instructed all three of the Estates to meet together and to vote as a single organization. The old Estates-General had developed into a body known as the National Assembly. The drama of the French Revolution had begun!

The Bastille Falls

The uprising of the Third Estate in 1789 was mainly the work of members of the bourgeoisie. As French historian André Maurois points out, these men "had a mind to repair the house, not to tear it down." However, the king had no intention of following their wishes. He did not realize the seriousness of the situation.

To King Louis XVI, July 14, 1789, was just another day. When it came time for him to jot down in his diary the important events of the day, he wrote a single word—"Nothing." Yet it was on July 14 that a crowd in Paris stormed the Bastille!

The Bastille was an old fortress that had been converted into a prison. The people believed that its dungeons held many innocent men and women whose only crime was opposition to the king. Equally important, the crowd desired the arms which were stored in the Bastille. The prison became a hated symbol of the king's oppression.

On July 14 a crowd of Parisians attacked the Bastille. They cut the chains to the drawbridge, withstood the fire of the guards in the courtyard, and forced the commanding officer to surrender. When they rushed through the prison to free the prisoners, they found only seven men. The date of the storming of the Bastille is celebrated as national independence day in France.

Many Flames Light the Revolutionary Fires

The storming of the Bastille at last made Louis XVI aware of the crisis in Paris. The attack was followed by uprisings of the peasants in the country, new demands on the monarchy, and a general speeding up of movements for reform. The French Revolution was on in earnest.

What had caused this momentous revolution? The revolution was a result of a combination of factors. 1. Louis XVI and his administrators were not performing their duties of keeping justice, order, and harmony in the land. 2. The national treasury of France was facing bankruptcy, and both the collection and distribution of national finances needed reorganization.

3. The bourgeoisie wanted greater political rights and better management of the state's economic affairs. They also desired social equality with the upper classes. 4. The bourgeoisie and peasants were angry because the nobles and higher clergy enjoyed special privileges, such as being exempt from paying heavy taxes.

5. A major economic depression from 1787 to 1789 added to France's economic troubles. Crops were damaged by frost, drought, and rain. City workers faced unemployment because peasants could not afford to buy manufactured goods. The peasants wanted to be free of all feudal restrictions which added to their economic hardship. Spain's tariff and England's competition interfered with the sale of French goods abroad and contributed further to the depression.

6. The ideas of the French philosophes stirred many persons to desire greater freedom. 7. The ideas of the American revolutionists, carried to France by Frenchmen who had supported the Americans, influenced the intellectuals. An English traveler wrote: "The American Revolution has laid the foundations of another in France. . . . "

The National Assembly Introduces Major Changes

It was the responsibility of the newly formed National Assembly to introduce the changes that the country desired. Peasants were setting manor houses on fire to destroy the records of their feudal obligations and refusing to pay their taxes. The National Assembly, therefore, first focused its attention on the peasant and on eliminating inequalities in society.

On August 4, 1789, the National Assembly issued a series of decrees. 1. They abolished feudalism in France completely. 2. They did away with the tax to support the Church. 3. All class privileges in taxation were wiped out. The Assembly provided that the "collection [of taxes] shall be made from all citizens and on all property, in the same manner and in the same form." 4. All citizens were given the right to hold any public office.

These decrees were not designed to overthrow the king. It concluded:

> The National Assembly solemnly proclaims King Louis XVI Restorer of French Liberty. . . . [and shall] bear him the homage of its most respectful gratitude. . . .

The Declaration of the Rights of Man

The National Assembly then issued a most famous document: the *Declaration of the Rights of Man* (August 26, 1789). It included the following:

> Men are born, and always continue, free and equal in respect of their rights.
> [The natural rights of Man are] liberty, property, security, and resistance of oppression.
> The Nation is essentially the source of all sovereignty; nor can any Individual, or Any Body of Men be entitled to any authority which is not expressly derived from it.

The Move to Paris

In October, several thousand poor women of Paris marched to Versailles and boldly demanded bread from the King. Then they made the "baker"—Louis XVI—and his family return with them to Paris. The National Assembly also moved from Versailles to Paris.

On October 5, 1789, a band of Parisians, consisting mainly of women, marched from Paris to Versailles to demand from the King bread for the hungry people of Paris.

The Civil Constitution of the Clergy

In November, 1789, the National Assembly confiscated Church property, and in December it issued *assignats*. Assignats were paper money based on the future sale of the confiscated property of the Church and the king.

In July, 1790, the National Assembly issued the *Civil Constitution of the Clergy*. This provided that bishops and parish priests were to be civil servants of the state. They were to be elected by all citizens—including Protestants, Jews, and non-believers. They were to be paid by the state and were to take an oath of allegiance to the Constitution.

This action by the National Assembly added to the troubles of France. The Pope denounced the Civil Constitution of the Clergy, and thousands of clergymen refused to take the oath. What is more, the measure angered many French Catholics.

The King Tries to Escape

Louis XVI had signed the *Civil Constitution of the Clergy* with misgivings. As a faithful Catholic, he was shocked and frightened by what he had been compelled to do. This was one reason why he decided to flee France and join the *émigrés* and his loyal troops. The *émigrés* were nobles who had left the country and who were plotting to invade France and drive out the revolutionists.

On the night of June 20-21, 1791, Louis XVI and Marie Antoinette fled from their palace in Paris. They had almost reached the border—and safety—when they were caught. The royal couple was brought back to Paris through jeering mobs. Louis XVI's flight discredited him in the eyes of many leaders of the National Assembly.

The First French Constitution

The National Assembly also made changes in the government. Most important of all, it drew up a constitution for France. Its provisions were put into effect piecemeal. The entire document was not completed until 1791 after two years of work. This constitution, which the king had to sign, established a constitutional monarchy. It provided the following:

1. A Legislative Assembly. This was a one-house body to make the laws. All the French over twenty-five were citizens, but only those who paid certain direct taxes could vote for the members of the Legislative Assembly.

2. The King. The monarch could block the passage of a law for four years, but he could not pre-

vent its final passage. The armed forces were no longer under the control of the king.

3. Départements. Eighty-three *départements*, or territorial divisions, were set up to replace the provinces. Each department was subdivided into districts (roughly comparable to our county).

The National Assembly had finished its task and prepared to disband. Unfortunately the National Assembly decided that none of its members were to be eligible for election to the Legislative Assembly. This meant that the new government would be in the hands of inexperienced people.

France Forms a Republic and Goes to War

The French Revolution then moved from a moderate to a radical stage. The new Legislative Assembly met in October 1791. This body soon faced threats from abroad.

Leopold II of Austria (brother of Marie Antoinette), some rulers of the German states, and other European monarchs were being stirred up by the

In 1792 many Frenchmen volunteered to fight for the Republic. This painting shows a review of some of these soldiers.

French *émigrés*. These rulers became fearful that the revolution would spread to their own countries. They decided to check the French Revolution, and prepared their armed forces for a possible war with France. In April 1792, the French Assembly took the initiative by declaring war on Austria. Prussia came to the aid of Austria, and France was involved in a major war.

At first, French troops were defeated and the enemy entered France. Disorder and panic swept the country. A mob smashed its way into the king's palace in Paris. Its leaders accused the royal family of plotting with foreign rulers to invade France and crush the revolution. They made the king and his family virtual prisoners, and Paris came under the control of the radical city government known as the *Paris Commune*.

Under pressure by the radicals of Paris, the Assembly called for the election of a National Convention to establish a republic. In the six weeks before the National Convention met, France was torn by great internal strife. Hundreds of citizens accused of opposing the revolution were killed. In September 1792, the National Convention met and proclaimed France a republic. This was the *First French Republic* (1792-1795).

French Patriotism Is Aroused

Louis XVI was beheaded on January 21, 1793. Marie Antoinette met a similar fate several months later.

The beheading of Louis XVI made the monarchs of Europe more fearful than ever that the ideas of the French Revolution would spread to their lands. A French army had stopped the allied forces and pursued them across the Rhine into the Austrian Netherlands. The French had stated that they intended to extend their borders to the Rhine. The National Convention had proclaimed "the Liberty and Sovereignty of all the peoples to whose Homeland [the French troops] have carried and are carrying their arms." In 1793 England, Spain, and the Netherlands decided to aid Austria and Prussia in the conflict with France. The French National Convention promptly declared war against all three powers.

The French people met the new threat to their country with heroism and patriotic fervor. The army was reorganized and strengthened. A decree of August 23, 1793, declared that "all Frenchmen are permanently requisitioned for service in the armies." This was the first national conscription in European history. Single men between the ages of 18 and 25 were drafted.

The *Marseillaise*, written in 1792, was heard throughout the land. Today it is the French national anthem. The welfare of *La Patrie* (the homeland) became the chief concern of the French. Despite the patriotism of the French, the Austrians succeeded in driving them out of the Netherlands.

The Reign of Terror Bleeds France

While French troops were fighting foreign enemies, the revolution at home reached a bloody stage. The National Convention created a Committee of Public Safety to deal with dangers abroad and at home. This small committee became dominated by the *Jacobins*, led by Robespierre and Danton. The Jacobins were a radical group that replaced the more moderate group as leaders of the National Convention. Under the direction of Robespierre, some of these extremists started a *Reign of Terror*.

From 1793 to 1794 thousands of people were charged with being traitors or potential traitors and were sent to their death. About twenty thousand people were beheaded by the *guillotine*, which consisted of a heavy blade that dropped between two upright grooves. Another twenty thousand were killed by other means or died in prison. The leaders of the Terror claimed that their aim was to save France by eliminating all those who supported foreign countries or opposed the revolution.

At the same time the Committee of Public Safety took measures to build up the army. As a result, France had over 800,000 well-trained, well-armed, and well-led troops—the most powerful army on the continent. This army drove back France's enemies and won additional victories. By July, 1794, France was no longer in danger of being conquered.

When the country was under attack, the people would accept the brutal Terror. Now that France was safe, the French leaders brought the blood bath to a close. Danton died on the guillotine. After Robespierre himself was executed in July, 1794, the Reign of Terror ended.

The Directory Is Established

The National Convention drew up a new constitution for the Republic. It provided for a government with a two-house legislature and five "directors" chosen by the legislature. Voting rights were limited to those who had certain property qualifications. This government is known as the *Directory* (1795-1799).

Results of the French Revolution

What were the important results of this revolution that shook France and the world from 1789 to 1799? They included the following: 1. The revolution overthrew the French monarchy and set up a republican government based on a written constitution. 2. It helped to complete the unification of France by unifying the financial and legal systems. 3. The revolution deprived the clergy of special privileges and supported the idea of freedom of worship. 4. It strengthened the idea of social equality by sweeping away the privileges of the classes. The last remnants of feudalism were removed. The peasants were able to acquire more land by buying property confiscated from the *émigrés* and the Church. France now became a country of independent farmers. 5. The revolution aided business activities. Guild restrictions were abolished. A code of commercial law was set up. A uniform system of weights and measures—the metric system—was introduced. 6. The revolution introduced a system of universal military service in France. 7. It stimulated discussion of ways to establish a national and secular system of education in France. 8. The revolution influenced the growth of democracy in many countries of the world. 9. It stimulated the development of nationalism in France and Europe. Nationalism soon encouraged the peoples of Germany, Italy, and other divided lands to fight for the right to have their own united nations.

Check on Your Reading

1. What were the causes of the French Revolution?
2. What reforms were put into effect by the National Assembly?
3. Why was a republic formed? How was patriotism aroused?
4. What caused the Reign of Terror? its end?
5. What economic effects did the revolution have?
6. How did the revolution change French government and administration? business? education?
7. What significant effects did the revolution have outside France?

---

4. Napoleon Makes Himself Emperor

Napoleon Bonaparte was born on the island of Corsica in 1769. France had recently purchased Corsica from the state of Genoa, and Napoleon's parents were of Italian ancestry. Napoleon attended a military academy in France, where his teachers noted that he was "ambitious [and] aspiring to everything." He became a second lieutenant in the French artillery and rose rapidly to the positon of brigadier-general.

Napoleon Becomes First Consul

The Directory, which involved France in wars against several countries, gave Napoleon command of the French army in Italy. Before starting on his new assignment, he married Josephine de Beauharnais from the island of Martinique.

When the ragged French soldiers in Italy first saw Napoleon, who was extremely short, they called him "Puss-in-Boots." He soon won their admiration by leading them to victories. "Soldiers," Napoleon was able to announce, "you have in two weeks won six victories [and] taken twenty-one battle flags." Indeed, the Austrians were defeated in less than a month!

Napoleon then arranged a treaty with Austria (1797). 1. A Cisalpine Republic, under the domination of France, was formed in Italy. Napoleon thus tried to show the people of Italy that he was "liberating" them from Austrian rule. 2. Austria gave the Austrian Netherlands and the Ionian Islands to France. 3. What remained of the republic of Venice was given to Austria.

Napoleon next directed a campaign against Egypt (1798). He captured Alexandria and crushed the Egyptian forces at the Pyramids. However, the French fleet was defeated by the British Admiral Nelson. Cut off from France, Napoleon suffered major setbacks in Syria.

In 1799 Napoleon learned that the Directory was having serious difficulties. He left his weary troops in Egypt and hurried to France. He found the Directory plagued by graft, inefficient administration, and the heavy expenses of war. France was ready for a "strong man," and Napoleon believed that the French would say, "This is the man!"

On November 9, 1799, he and a group of leaders overthrew the Directory. He helped establish a new government known as the *Consulate* (1799-1804). It consisted of a legislature and three

executives, or Consuls. Napoleon became First Consul for a ten-year term, and most of the power was placed in his hands. In 1802 he was made First Consul for life by a vote of about three and a half million to eight thousand.

Napoleon the Man

Napoleon was described by one of his contemporaries as a very short man, "his hair a dark brown crop . . . his complexion smooth, pale, and sallow . . . his mouth and nose, fine, sharp, defined, and expressive beyond description." Madame de Rémusat, a friend of Napoleon's wife, added, "the heart was left out [of him]" for "he was always too much engrossed by himself to be influenced by any sentiment of affection."

Napoleon was intelligent, alert, and extremely hard-working. He once said: "I am born and built for work. I have known the limitations of my legs. I have known the limitations of my eyes. I have never been able to know the limitations of my working capacity."

Napoleon believed that everyone should have an equal opportunity to advance. As a leader, he loved political power and had no intention of dividing it with the people. A friend explained:

> He would willingly have agreed that every man should be free, on the condition that he should voluntarily do only what [Napoleon] wished.

Or, as Napoleon himself said: "I must command, or be silent."

Napoleon Crowns Himself Emperor

Napoleon tried to satisfy many groups. He let the peasants keep the lands they had acquired. The clergy were restored to a position of respect. He pleased the liberals by granting all citizens equality before the law, and the bourgeoisie by protecting property and encouraging economic growth. The people of France were given a sense of security. Yet Napoleon's chief love remained the military. He was convinced that his future depended on the might of his armies.

In Europe Napoleon fought successfully against the Second Coalition, made up of Great Britain, Austria, and Russia. This group of countries had four main aims. It wanted to 1. regain lands in Italy for Austria; and 2. restore the independence of Switzerland, where Napoleon had set up a French-dominated republic. 3. It planned to release Holland from the domination of France, which had controlled it since 1795. 4. It hoped to add to the lands of Great Britain and Russia at the expense of the French.

In 1800 Napoleon's forces defeated the Austrians in Italy and in Germany. As a result, he forced most of his enemies to sign treaties that were very favorable to France (1801–1802). 1. France gained control of lands on the west bank of the Rhine held by the Holy Roman Emperor. 2. The French position in Italy was strengthened. 3. France regained the Austrian Netherlands (present-day Belgium). In 1802 even Great Britain signed a peace treaty with France.

The ambitions of Napoleon could no longer be contained. He decided to discard the position and

Jacques David did this sketch of Napoleon at his coronation. The artist explained that his sketch showed "he who has known how to win the crown will also know well how to defend it."

title of First Consul for something more powerful. The obedient French Senate promptly invited him to become "Emperor of the French." The people voted their overwhelming approval.

On December 2, 1804, a coronation service was held at the Cathedral of Notre Dame in the presence of the Pope. When it came time for the Pope to crown the new emperor, Napoleon motioned him aside. Then Napoleon took the crown and placed it on his head himself. He also crowned Josephine as Empress of France. It was a striking gesture that was not lost on the people—Napoleon was showing that he owed his position to no one but himself.

Check on Your Reading

1. What did Napoleon gain for France by the treaty with Austria in 1797?
2. How did Napoleon become First Consul? Emperor?
3. Describe the character of Napoleon.
4. What did Napoleon gain from the Second Coalition by 1802?

5. The Napoleonic Program in France

As First Consul and later emperor, Napoleon was responsible for major changes. These changes helped to shape modern France.

The Concordat of 1801

Napoleon lessened the tensions between the Roman Catholic Church and the state by the *Concordat* of 1801. It had these provisions: 1. People who had bought Church lands confiscated by the state could keep them. 2. Church buildings would be returned to the Church. 3. The state would pay the salaries of the clergy. 4. Bishops would be nominated by the state, but they would be installed in office by the Pope.

The Concordat of 1801 recognized that Catholicism was "the religion of the great majority of French citizens." However, the Catholic Church remained under the control of the government. By other agreements, Protestants and members of other faiths were permitted to worship as they wished.

The Code Napoléon

Napoleon chose a committee of legal experts to bring uniformity to the laws of France. It drew up the so-called *Code Napoléon* of 1804. Roman law formed the basis of French law. Geoffrey Bruun, an American historian, points out:

In four important particulars the new code preserved the social aims of the [French] Revolution, for it affirmed:

The equality of all citizens before the law.
The right of the individual to choose his profession.
The supremacy of the lay state.
The freedom of the individual conscience.

However, other laws placed restrictions on the liberty of the individual. For example, one of the first orders issued by Napoleon limited freedom of the press. Other codes placed heavy penalties on persons guilty of political offenses.

The principles of the *Code Napoléon* spread from France to Italy, the Netherlands, southern Germany, and other European countries. The Code also influenced the legal system of the state of Louisiana in the United States. (Louisiana once belonged to France. Napoleon sold the entire Louisiana region to the United States in 1803.)

Centralization of Government

Napoleon also centralized the government. The heads of the *départements*, and even lesser officials, were appointed by and responsible to Napoleon and his advisers. The legislature and the various assemblies had limited power. Napoleon and his central government made all major decisions.

Reorganization of Education

Napoleon helped to establish a system of public schools under the supervision of the central government. However, historian André Maurois states:

[Napoleon] organized education as though it were the training of an army. In all France's secondary schools, the same Latin passage was being translated at the same hour; the military drum would summon the pupils to recitations— and it was still rolling in 1900. . . .

By 1813 only one-eighth of school-age children were enrolled in primary schools.

Economic Activities

Napoleon wanted to strengthen agriculture, build up manufacturing, and stimulate commerce. His government therefore took an active part in economic affairs. It collected taxes efficiently. Animal-breeding stations were set up to improve the quality of stock. Exhibitions were held to encourage the exchange of information about industrial inventions. The government built commercial as well as military roads. Efforts were made to increase exports and to balance the national budget. Later Napoleon forced countries that he had conquered to pay France large sums of money.

Also, Napoleon encouraged the founding of the Bank of France (1800), which was based primarily on private investment. The Bank of France, Napoleon declared, "does not belong exclusively to the stockholders; it belongs also to the State, for the latter gives it the privilege of [issuing] money."

Check on Your Reading

1. How did the Concordat of 1801 change the position of the Catholic Church in France?
2. How did the *Code Napoléon* preserve the social aims of the French Revolution?
3. How did Napoleon organize education?
4. How was the French economic system affected by Napoleon?

6. Many Triumphs and Then Disaster

As Emperor of France, Napoleon faced many new challenges. In 1803 war again broke out between France and Great Britain. Two years later a Third Coalition of Great Britain, Russia, and Austria, assisted by Sweden, was formed to fight the French.

Napoleon's Armies Win an Empire

In 1805 Napoleon's Grand Army was in excellent condition. It had fine generals, experienced soldiers, and good equipment. It was directed by Napoleon, who dictated his orders "bending over and sometimes stretched at full length upon his map where the positions of the enemy were marked."

Napoleon forced an Austrian army to surrender at Ulm (Germany) in 1805. In the same year he defeated the armies of the Austrian and Russian emperors at Austerlitz. By a treaty signed in 1805, Austria then gave up Venetia and other areas in Italy. These became part of the Kingdom of Italy which Napoleon had created (1805) with himself as king.

In 1806 Napoleon set up a *Confederation of the Rhine* in Germany. This was a loose confederation of German states with Napoleon as "Protector." The establishment of the Confederation of the Rhine brought about the dissolution of the Holy Roman Empire.

In 1806 Francis II abdicated as Holy Roman Emperor, but he remained Emperor of Austria with the title Francis I. In the same year Napoleon placed his brother Joseph on the throne of Naples and made his brother Louis ruler of the Netherlands.

A Fourth Coalition was formed against France. Its principal members were Great Britain, Prussia, and Russia. Yet, despite the power of the new alliance, Napoleon continued to triumph. In 1806 the French defeated the Prussians in Germany and occupied Berlin. In 1807 they were victorious against the Russians in East Prussia. As a result Prussia lost considerable territory to France, and the Grand Duchy of Warsaw was set up to the east of Prussia. The Kingdom of Westphalia, with Napoleon's brother Jerome as its king, was carved out of Prussian and other land. Emperor Alexander I of Russia agreed to assist France to crush Great Britain by economic methods.

Napoleon Triumphant in Europe

The French forces next occupied Portugal (1807). Then Napoleon forced the Bourbon rulers to abdicate from the throne of Spain. He made his brother Joseph the new king of Spain (1808), and appointed his brother-in-law Joachim Murât to rule Naples in place of Joseph. In 1809 Napoleon again defeated the Austrians. By 1810 he held or controlled most of the lands in Europe. Napoleon had become the head of an empire that exceeded in size the territory once held by Charles V. After Napoleon had divorced Josephine, Emperor Francis I of Austria even permitted him to marry his daughter, the Archduchess Marie Louise (1810).

The Continental System and Its Effects

One nation still remained to defy Napoleon. That was Great Britain, a country which Napoleon had hoped to invade and conquer. In 1805 Lord Nelson and the British fleet had defeated the French fleet at the Battle of Trafalgar, off the coast of Spain. This setback had made it too difficult for France to invade Britain. Napoleon therefore had decided to try to subdue Britain by economic warfare.

In 1806, after Britain announced a blockade of the French coast, Napoleon put into effect the *Continental System*. This system was to include all of the European countries under the control of Napoleon. It forbade European countries to import any British products or to export goods to Britain. It also denied admittance to continental ports to any British ship or neutral ship that sailed from Britain or any of her colonies or stopped at a British port.

Great Britain replied by declaring that all ships that traded in European ports closed to British vessels were liable to capture by the British. (Some exceptions were made later.) A blockade was placed on all ports that excluded British vessels.

The French and British restrictions affected the trade of the United States and other neutral countries. However, British interference with American ships angered the United States even more than did France's Continental System.

Disputes over these and other matters and the desire of some Americans for land in Canada led to the War of 1812 between Great Britain and the United States. The war settled very little. Neither side could win a clear-cut victory, and the conflict ended in 1814.

This painting by Francisco Goya shows the execution of Spaniards in Madrid by French soldiers during the time when Napoleon ruled Spain by the force of his armies.

The Continental System Fails

The Continental System did not achieve its goal. There were several reasons for its failure.

The Continental System deprived France of some vital raw materials, such as cotton and sugar. In addition, it could not be completely enforced. Napoleon lacked the necessary sea power, and smuggling continued. The peoples dominated by the French needed British goods. They also were stirred by growing feelings of attachment to their countries (nationalism) and wanted to be free from French control. For example, the Spanish and Portuguese peoples revolted. Aided by the British, they fought heroically against the French in the Peninsular War (1808-1814).

Napoleon's Invasion of Russia Ends in Disaster

Unable to subdue Great Britain in the West, Napoleon turned toward the East. In 1812 he in- vaded Russia! In the beginning, Napoleon's army of about 600,000 men was successful. It defeated Russian forces in several engagements and pushed on toward Moscow. However, the Russian em- peror, Alexander I, refused to risk the outcome of the war on a single battle. His forces retreated deep into Russia.

Napoleon's army entered Moscow the middle of September and found—a deserted city! Napoleon waited for the Russian emperor to surrender. He waited while Russian peasants stole into Moscow at night and set fire to parts of the city. He waited while Russian Cossacks raided his supply routes and cut his lines of communication. He waited while the winds of Russia became colder and sharper.

With the approach of winter and his supplies running dangerously low, Napoleon finally decided to move his army out of Russia. On October 19 he left Moscow. Thus began a disastrous retreat. Sol- diers starved or froze to death. Horses, kept on the move for fourteen and fifteen hours a day, collapsed. The wounded fell off carts only to have the drivers of other vehicles ride over their bodies so as not to lose their place in line. The Cossacks waylaid stragglers and raided transport wagons.

Then on December 5, Napoleon abandoned his doomed army and hurried to Paris to strengthen his position in France. About 100,000 of Napoleon's troops completed the retreat.

Napoleon Is Forced to Abdicate

The crushing setback suffered by Napoleon in Russia encouraged the countries of Europe to rise against him. Equally important, many of the actions of Napoleon stimulated the growth of nationalism among the peoples of Europe.

Many of the people of the Netherlands, Belgium, and Italy—lands under Napoleon's domination—became increasingly nationalistic. In Germany, rebellions further threatened the French position. Prussia had developed into a major opponent of France. National feelings in Prussia grew stronger.

In 1813, Prussia, Russia, and Austria, aided by Great Britain and Sweden, defeated Napoleon in the great Battle of the Nations (near Leipzig, Germany). The armies of the allies converged on France itself. On March 31, 1814, the allies entered Paris. On April 11, the once invincible Napoleon abdicated.

Napoleon Takes One Last Gamble

Napoleon was sent into exile on the little island of Elba, off the coast of Italy, and the Bourbon monarchy was restored in France. Louis XVIII, the

By 1810 Napoleon controlled most of Europe except Great Britain and Russia. What territories were controlled directly by Napoleon? What countries were allied with him? Napoleon's attempts to conquer Russia and Great Britain ended in disaster.

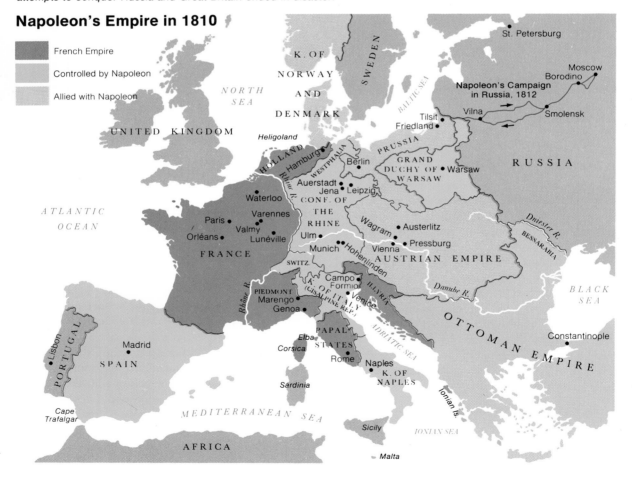

Napoleon's Empire in 1810

French Empire

Controlled by Napoleon

Allied with Napoleon

This watercolor shows the remnants of Napoleon's huge army retreating from Russia over hastily constructed bridges across an icy river.

brother of the executed Louis XVI, was made the French king. Even as the allies met in Vienna to discuss a peace settlement for Europe, Napoleon took one last gamble to win back his power. He escaped from Elba and returned to southern France.

The French government sent troops to capture him but the soldiers joined him. Napoleon reached Paris in March. He gathered an army of about 125,000 men. "The moment has come to conquer or perish," he told them.

The allies were equally determined to stop him, and they quickly regrouped their forces. At the Battle of Waterloo in Belgium (June 18, 1815), British, Prussian, Dutch, and Belgian soldiers crushed Napoleon's army for the last time.

Napoleon was exiled to the isolated island of St. Helena in the South Atlantic, where he died in 1821 at the age of 52. His last words were said to have been: "France, Chief of the Army . . . Josephine!"

Napoleon in Perspective

Napoleon left an important legacy. Significant effects of Napoleon's activities included these:

1. Napoleon consolidated some of the gains of the French Revolution—such as establishing the equality of all men before the law in his *Code Napoléon*. 2. His troops conquered other countries, and carried to other peoples many of the ideas of the French Revolution. These ideas later helped to undermine societies that granted special privileges to the few and discriminated against many.

3. Most of Napoleon's territorial changes would

be cancelled. Others, such as the erasure of the Holy Roman Empire, would remain. 4. His oppressive treatment of other countries stimulated the growth of nationalism.

5. Napoleon left to France the memories of his past "glories." A "Napoleonic legend" grew up. After his downfall, the history of France was marked by struggles among three groups. One group believed in "Bonapartism"—that is, that one "strong man" should govern France. Another group favored a return to some type of monarchy. The third group sought to establish a democratic republic.

Check on Your Reading

1. Why did Napoleon crown himself?
2. What areas had Napoleon conquered by 1810? What changes had he made in the governments of Italy, the Holy Roman Empire, Poland, and Prussia?
3. Describe the Continental System. Why did it fail?
4. How was Napoleon defeated in Russia?
5. Name five important effects of Napoleon's actions.

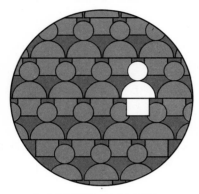

LET'S MEET THE PEOPLE

Citizeness Jullien

"The blindness of kings is the scourge of humanity!" declared Madame Jullien during the French Revolution. Citizeness Jullien, as she was called, could be recognized as a defender of the revolution by her appearance as well as by her opinions. She dressed in the white robes worn by women favorable to the revolution, and she displayed almost no jewelry. On her hat she wore the tricolor cockade of the revolution, a knot of ribbon of red, white, and blue colors. Let anyone disturb this national cockade—and she would deal with him!

Yet, although she was a loyal revolutionist, Citizeness Jullien sometimes saw events and heard stories that filled her with horror. How shocked she was to discover that innocent people were being slaughtered in prison by fanatical revolutionists!

"My pity makes me weep over the fate shared alike by the guilty and the innocent [she wrote]. My God! Have mercy on a people provoked to such horrible bloodshed!"

Her appeal to God was in keeping with her religious nature. Yet Citizeness Jullien's love of the nation and liberty almost became a new religion for her. One summer day she visited the lovely Church of St. Germain l'Auxerrois. There in the nave she saw a stone tablet, and on this tablet was engraved the Declaration of the Rights of Man. Citizeness Jullien was so moved by this democratic symbol in a house of God that she fell to her knees and offered up a special prayer.

When she finally left the church, Citizeness Jullien could embrace more fully than ever the idea expressed in these revolutionary words: "I believe in a Supreme Being, who has made men free and equal!"

Madame Jullien kept a diary and wrote numerous letters. The sketch above is based on these materials, and on passages from the book *Women of the French Revolution* by Winifred Stephens. Published by E.P. Dutton & Co., and reprinted with their permission.

CHAPTER REVIEW

Think and Discuss

1. Explain why you agree or disagree with the statement: If the "Enlightenment" had not taken place, there would have been no French Revolution in 1789.
2. Compare the American Declaration of Independence with the Declaration of the Rights of Man.
3. Explain why you agree or disagree with this statement: Hard work is a key to the success of great persons; it is also a key to the success of lesser people. How might Napoleon have reacted to this statement?
4. Napoleon tried to model much of his career after that of Julius Caesar. Compare their lives.
5. Military ambition has been a major factor in the downfall of several great leaders. Prove or disprove this statement.
6. What were the factors that contributed to Napoleon's downfall? Which were most important? Why?
7. Which type of government do you think would have been best for France after the downfall of Napoleon? Why?

Past and Present

1. Foreign affairs affected the course of the French Revolution. Have they also influenced the developments of revolutions in Asia, the Middle East, and Africa in the twentieth century? Support your answer with proof.
2. In the light of the world's experiences with Napoleon, what do you think is the best way for people to deal with ambitious military conquerors today?

Activities

1. Debate the statement: Resolved, that the French Revolution had more significance for other peoples of the world than it did for the leaders of the American Revolution.
2. Have a mock trial of Robespierre. Let class members serve as judge, prosecutor, defense attorney, witnesses, and jury.
3. Debate the following: Resolved, that freedom is a greater asset than security.
4. Write a short report on "Nationalism."
5. Debate the following: Resolved, that unification of Europe under Napoleon would have been very beneficial.

Latin American Colonies Revolt

Wendell Phillips, an American reformer, once declared: "Revolutions are not made; they come." He meant that revolutions are not manufactured artificially but are a natural outgrowth of certain historical conditions.

Such was the case in Latin America, where centuries of rule by Spain led to revolutions. In the first quarter of the nineteenth century many Latin Americans rose in revolt against foreign domination, and the roots of their revolution were embedded in the past.

José San Martín led the revolutionary army across the Andes from Argentina to surprise the Spanish forces in Chile.

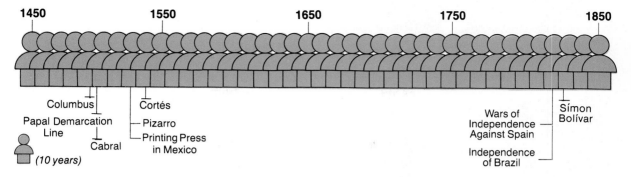

Columbus

Papal Demarcation
Line

Cabral

Cortés

Pizarro

Printing Press
in Mexico

Wars of
Independence
Against Spain

Independence
of Brazil

Símon
Bolívar

(10 years)

1. Latin America—Huge and Varied

Latin America is over twice the size of the United States. It is made up of over 25 independent countries as well as of areas that have special ties to countries in Europe and to the United States. Latin America includes the little Spanish-speaking country of Costa Rica and the very large Portuguese-speaking country of Brazil. It includes the inland countries of Bolivia and Paraguay and the island countries of Cuba and Jamaica. In five Latin American countries, the population is largely *Native American,* a far more precise term than the word *Indian.* In seven others, *mestizos* (mixtures of Native Americans and whites) are the largest single groups. In Haiti, blacks predominate; and in the Dominican Republic, *mulattoes* (mixtures of blacks and whites) are the most numerous.

Little flower girls in the cities—women driving their burros to market—farmers working in the fields—factory workers hurrying to their jobs—priests strolling quietly before their churches—medical students at the universities—all these are Latin Americans. The individuals of Latin America are as varied as people everywhere.

What Is a Latin American?

The people of Mexico speak Spanish and live on the continent of North America. The people of Guatemala speak Spanish and live in Central America. Brazilians live in South America and speak Portuguese. However, they all speak a language that is directly descended from Latin. In addition, features of their cultures can be traced back to Spain, Portugal, and France, and farther back to ancient Rome. They are therefore known as Latin Americans.

The countries of Latin America have shared some important experiences. The first people who lived in all of them were the Native Americans.

Over thousands of years these peoples created rich and varied cultures and civilizations. (See Chapter 12.) The lands of the Native Americans were then explored, conquered, and settled by people mainly from Spain and Portugal. For about three centuries these lands were colonies of countries thousands of miles away across the ocean.

The Giant Southeast of the United States

Latin America extends from the northern boundary of Mexico to the southern tip of South America—a distance of roughly 7,000 miles, or about 11,263 kilometers. (See the map on page 390.) This is about three times as long as the air route from Seattle, Washington, to New York City.

Latin America includes Mexico, Central America, islands in the West Indies, and South America. It is a huge territory. Brazil is over five and a half times the size of Alaska, and Argentina is four times larger than Texas. In the past, the tremendous size of Latin America made it difficult for the Latin American countries to work together. Modern means of transportation are helping to solve this problem.

Most of Latin America lies in tropical regions; only about one-third is in the temperate zone. The climate varies, depending on altitude and winds. Many Latin Americans who live in the tropics enjoy a pleasant climate because their homes are in the highlands. Most of the cities of the tropics are in the highlands. The lowlands are generally hot and sticky the year round. Some of the lands in the temperate zones have a pleasant and mild climate, while others have very cold winters.

Latin America has a variety of lands. Much of the region is mountainous. The lofty Andes Mountain chain runs through the western part of South America from the Strait of Magellan to Venezuela. It is a rugged chain of mountains subject to earth-

This Aztec drawing of the sixteenth century shows the Aztec ruler surrendering to Cortés.

quakes. The older Brazilian highlands are in the east. In Central America, other highlands have volcanic peaks that still occasionally erupt. In Mexico, two ranges—the Sierra Madre Occidental and the Sierra Madre Oriental—stand on the western and eastern sides of the central plateau.

In the past, the Andes, which run through the western part of South America, made it difficult for peoples on the west coast to have much contact with the eastern parts. This problem is being solved by modern transportation.

Latin America has broad lowland areas as well. The largest are in the central part of South America. There are many coastal plains. Those in Central America and on the western side of South America are much narrower than those in Mexico and along the east coast of South America. Four important river systems in Latin America are located in South America. These are the Magdalena-Cauca and Orinoco, which flow into the Caribbean; and the Paraná-Paraguay and the great Amazon, which empty into the Atlantic.

Then there are the jungle areas of Latin America. There are thick forests soaked by rains and steaming with heat, rotting trees with creepers that twist about them, and dangerous swamps coated with slime. These jungles contrast sharply with the deserts of South and Central America, where the sun beats down and rain seldom falls. The jungle regions have been major obstacles to the settlement of the interior of Latin America. In many countries, they also have interfered with efforts to unite the various peoples.

Check on Your Reading

1. What do Latin Americans have in common?
2. How do Latin Americans differ?
3. How has Latin America's history been affected by its size, mountains, and jungles?

2. Explorers and Conquerors

In 1493, shortly after the first voyage of Columbus to America, Pope Alexander VI drew on the map an imaginary line that ran through the New World. This was the so-called *Papal Line of Demarcation.* One of its purposes was to establish regions for Christian missionary work. Spain was to have all of the land that it discovered west of the line. This meant that Spain could claim nearly all of the Americas. Portugal was granted territory that Portuguese explorers found to the east of the line. By the Treaty of Tordesillas, Spain (1494), the line was moved farther westward. This change gave Portugal its later claim to Brazil.

The Spaniards soon established bases on the island of Hispaniola (today's Haiti and Dominican Republic) and Cuba. From there the Spanish *conquistadors* spread Spain's control over many areas.

Cortés in Mexico

In 1519 Hernando Cortés and about six hundred men sailed from Cuba and landed in Mexico. According to his private chaplain, Cortés was "very strong, high-spirited, and skilled in the use of arms." On his shield Cortés put the motto: "The judgment of the Lord overtook them; and his strength supported my arm."

When Cortés invaded the lands of the Aztecs, he was looking for riches, land, and trade. The Aztecs' golden bowls and silver dishes were tempting bait.

The Aztecs viewed Cortés and his men with mixed emotions. Many of them were impressed by the horses that the Spaniards rode, as the Aztecs had never seen a horse. Others considered Cortés

The Cathedral of Mexico City was built on the main square, or plaza, of the city. Mexico City was built on the site of the Aztec capital that had been destroyed by the Spaniards.

to be a great god who had been expected to return to the Aztecs some day. Still others treated him as a friend.

Cortés was a determined conqueror. He did not hesitate to use force and treachery to subdue this people who greatly outnumbered his soldiers. He had a great advantage in possessing steel swords and firearms, which the Aztecs had never seen before. Aided by reinforcements and by Native Americans who hated their Aztec rulers, he pushed on and finally took the Aztec capital of Tenochtitlán. By 1521 Spain controlled Mexico.

Pizarro in Peru

In January, 1531, Francisco Pizarro and about one hundred and eighty men sailed south along the Pacific coast from Panama. They landed on the coast of Ecuador. From here they marched into Peru. The people of what was to become Peru, the Incas, misunderstood many things about Pizarro. They thought that the Spaniards' horses were useless at night, that their swords were poor weapons, and that their guns could fire only twice. Pizarro

was quite willing to use deceit and military power to conquer the Incas.

The Spaniards arranged for a meeting with the Inca king, Atahualpa. When Atahualpa came with an estimated five thousand unarmed men, the Spanish soldiers remained in hiding. A friar tried to convince the Inca ruler to become a subject of the Spanish king and to accept Christianity. Atahualpa refused and is said to have replied:

> I will be no man's tributary. I am greater than any prince on earth. . . . For my faith, I will not change it.

Pizarro then raised a scarf as a signal. The Spanish soldiers rushed out and killed several thousand Incas. Using such methods and profiting from a civil war that had disrupted the country, Pizarro and his men were able to conquer the Inca people. By 1533 Spain controlled the lands of the Incas.

Native American resistance continued, however. The Spanish conquerors also quarrelled and fought among themselves. It was not until almost four decades later that peace and order were restored.

Other Explorers and Conquerors

Other explorers and conquerors were active in spreading Spain's power. These included Pedro de Alvarado in Central America and Pedro de Valdivia in Chile.

Portugal was more concerned with obtaining the spices and riches of the East than with searching for the wealth of the New World. Even so, Pedro Alvares Cabral from Portugal did land on the coast of Brazil in 1500.

By about 1580, as a result of the work of these and other men, many of the known regions of Latin America had been brought under Spanish and Portuguese control.

Evaluation of the Conquerors' Activities

The work of the sixteenth-century conquerors was extremely important. They opened the way for colonists to come to Latin America and to develop regions that later became nations. At the same time they often treated the Native Americans cruelly. They allowed them little self-government or opportunity to lead lives of dignity and comfort.

When the conquerors used cruel and undemocratic methods, they were not doing anything differently from many of the Native American rulers of kingdoms and empires. The Spanish conquerors and the Native American rulers whose power they seized both bore a responsibility for the checks on freedom.

Latin America in 1828

Independent countries by 1828

—— Bolívar's route

- - - San Martín's route

By 1828, almost all the Latin American countries had obtained their independence. In 1830 Venezuela and Ecuador broke away from Colombia and became separate states. After 1838 the United Provinces divided into the states of Guatemala, El Salvador, Honduras, Nicaragua, and Costa Rica. Haiti and the Dominican Republic remained united until 1844. Panama became independent of Colombia in 1903.

Check on Your Reading

1. How did Spain and Portugal obtain claims to Latin America?
2. How did Cortés conquer Mexico?
3. How did Pizarro conquer Peru?
4. What were some good and bad effects of the Spanish conquests?

3. The Colonial Period

The conquerors had fought their way to power. Colonists followed the conquerors and came to settle in Latin America.

Colonists Have Little Democratic Experience

What did the colonists from Spain bring with them? They brought the rich civilization of Spain. Did they come with experience in using tools of democracy? In general, they did not. In Spain they had few opportunities to take part in democratic government. Did they come seeking religious freedom? Again, in general, they did not. Did they come with the idea of working the land themselves? Not if they could help it! They came to find riches or to obtain lands that could be worked for them by the Native Americans.

Spain's System of Colonial Government

Spain's overall approach to its colonies was that of a master to a servant. The Spanish rulers intended to use the colonies as places from which to obtain gold, silver, and other raw materials. The colonies were markets for the products of Spain and areas in which to spread Christianity. They were a means of increasing Spanish prestige and power among other Europeans.

The government established in Spanish America reflected Spain's desire to dominate its colonies. The political institutions of government included the following:

1. The Council of the Indies. The Council members were chosen from leaders in Spain by the King of Spain and were responsible for the overall direction of the colonies.

2. Viceroy. The King of Spain divided Spanish lands in the New World into three main governmental units, called Viceroyalties. A Viceroyalty was governed by a Viceroy appointed by the King and the Council of the Indies. The Viceroys were the personal representatives of the King of Spain in Latin America.

3. Audiencias. These were law courts with administrative and legislative duties.

What about the people's role in this government? The people—whether they were the Spanish settlers, Native Americans, mestizos, black slaves, or mulattoes—had one principal duty. This was to obey the orders of their superiors.

In general, Spain's system of colonial government was a major obstacle to the growth of democracy. On the other hand, this system of government often aided the development of future Latin-American nations.

Catholicism Spreads throughout Latin America

The Catholic religion played an important role in the settlement of the colonies. Most Spanish colonists were Catholics. The Spanish king dominated the Church in Spanish America. He nominated Church officials, collected revenues, and approved the building of monasteries and churches.

Through the efforts of missionaries most of the Native Americans of Latin America were converted to Christianity. The Jesuits were particularly active. Sometimes the Jesuits challenged the authority of civil officials, landholders, and even the kings themselves. As a result, they were expelled from Spanish America in 1767.

A Small Group Holds Social and Economic Power

The people of the colonies were kept apart by their different social and economic positions. Most of the power in society was controlled by a small group. At the top were the *peninsulares,* people born in Spain of Spanish parents. Next came the *creoles,* people usually of Spanish descent born in the New World.

The mixed groups came next. These included mestizos, mulattoes, and *zambos*—mixtures of Native Americans and Africans. Below these groups were the Native Americans. At the bottom of the scale were the slaves, who were mainly African.

The land was concentrated in the hands of a few. Influential persons were awarded *encomiendas* by royal order. The owner of an encomienda was given control of both land and of Native Americans to work the land. The king tried to protect these

Native Americans and declared that they were to be cared for by their masters. However, the encomienda owners often exploited their workers.

Some changes were made in the system, but the encomiendas continued to exist until the end of the eighteenth century. The concentration of social and economic power in the hands of a small group proved a major block to the development of democracy.

Spanish and Portuguese Rule Compared

Similarities existed between Spain's rule of colonies and Portugal's government of Brazil. For example, Catholicism spread throughout Brazil and the Spanish colonies. Also great social and economic power was held by the large plantation owners. Both Brazil and the Spanish colonies had some degree of representative government in the cities, but autocracy was the rule.

On the other hand, differences existed. Although Portugal was under Spanish control for sixty years (1580-1640), Brazil succeeded in keeping clear of many Spanish restrictions. The government of Brazil was less stern. Relations among ethnic groups were better.

Cultural Progress in the Colonial Period

The first printing press was set up in Mexico about 1535. Despite censorship, reading material and ideas circulated among the intellectual groups.

Universities were established long before such institutions were started in the English colonies. Histories were written and considerable poetry was composed. Many handsome churches and other buildings adapted Spanish and Portuguese architecture to the environments of the New World.

Colonial Latin America was the setting for progress in several fields, including farming, ranching, and the arts. By 1800 some colonists believed that the colonies were strong enough to be able to govern themselves.

Check on Your Reading

1. How did Spain govern her colonies?
2. What role did the Church play?
3. Describe government and society in Spanish America.

4. The Wars of Independence

In 1808 Napoleon Bonaparte of France had gained control of Spain. The Spanish king was forced to turn over his power to the French. Napoleon placed his brother Joseph on the Spanish throne. Several city councils in the Spanish colonies refused to permit France to rule them. Then, realizing that this was an opportunity to rid themselves of Spain as well, the councils also rebelled against the Spanish authorities. In 1810, the Wars of Independence against Spain broke out in Spanish America.

Conditions in the Spanish Colonies

At the outbreak of the revolutionary wars, the population in the colonies was about seventeen million. About three and one-half million of this number were Europeans, most of whom were creoles. There were Native American, mestizo, mulatto, and black heroes among the revolutionists, but the creoles provided most of the leadership. The creoles had had the opportunity to have an education and to become well-to-do landowners and merchants. They were also very dissatisfied.

What were the factors that led the creole leaders and their followers to rise against Spain? Among the most important causes were these:

1. The creoles objected to the power of the Spanish officials and wanted to play a more important part themselves in the government.
2. The intellectuals were stimulated by the liberal ideas of authors in the United States, France, and Great Britain.
3. The American and French Revolutions encouraged some colonists to believe that a rebellion might succeed.
4. Many large landholders and Spanish officials had abused their workers. This made the workers eager to rebel against their masters.
5. Spain's restrictions on the trade of the colonies were considered unjust.
6. The heavy taxes imposed by Spain angered the colonists.

The Wars of Independence were not mass uprisings. About one-third of the population remained loyal to Spain. Neither were the revolts in different areas usually coordinated with one another.

Simón Bolívar and Other Liberators Lead the Way

There were many leaders of the independence movements. There was Miguel Hidalgo, the white-haired priest who led the Native American revolt in Mexico. There was Bernardo O'Higgins,

Toussaint L'Ouverture, born of African slave parents, led the fight for the independence of Haiti.

son of a Chilean mother and an Irish father, who fought heroically to free Chile. There was José de San Martín, who directed the fight in southern South America and yet said, "I do not want military renown—I have no ambition to be the conqueror . . . I want solely to liberate the country from oppression."

Above all, there was Simón Bolívar (1783-1830), known as the "Liberator." He was a daring leader who inspired others to trust and follow him. One could sense Bolívar's conviction that he was doing right. One could feel that he had energy and courage to support his ideas with action.

Some claim that Bolívar was chiefly interested in personal glory and power. Bolívar himself denied this and predicted that:

> History will say [that] Bolívar took the command in order to free his fellow-citizens, and, when they were free, he permitted them to govern themselves by laws, and not by his will.

Bolívar led the revolutionary forces in northern South America. He helped to liberate the lands of present-day Venezuela, Colombia, Peru, and Ecuador. San Martín headed the attack in southern South America. At the Battle of Ayacucho, Peru, in 1824, the revolutionists delivered the final defeat to Spain.

Latin America Divides into Many Nations

The Wars of Independence against Spain (1810-1824) led to the development of the future nations of Latin America. These wars resulted in independence for almost every Spanish colony in Latin America. (See the map on page 390.)

The colony of Brazil gained independence from Portugal without a major war. In 1807 when Napoleon had occupied Portugal, the Portuguese king fled to Brazil. In 1821, six years after Napoleon's defeat, the king returned to Portugal. His son Pedro was left behind to rule Brazil.

The people of Brazil were no longer willing to have their country remain a colony. They demanded their freedom. Pedro accepted their wishes. On September 7, 1822, he proclaimed the independence of Brazil from Portugal and became its king as Pedro I.

Check on Your Reading

1. What factors led to revolt in the colonies?
2. Describe the work of Bolívar.
3. How did Portugal become independent?

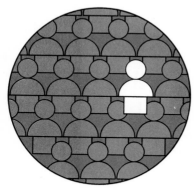

LET'S MEET THE PEOPLE

Juana Inés de la Cruz: Poet of Colonial Mexico

Juana de Asbaje was born in Mexico in November 1651, into a Spanish landowning family. When she was three years old, she tagged along to school with her older sister and soon learned to read. Before she was ten, on her own she mastered Latin so that she could read the books in her grandfather's library. Soon thereafter, she added Aztec to her store of languages.

At age thirteen Juana went to live with an aunt in Mexico City. There she became acquainted with both a world of music and literature, and a social life of banquets and outings.

She made many friends, but a life of idle pleasure did not appeal to Juana. She possessed wide-ranging curiosity and a desire for knowledge. She realized that marriage would deprive her of the freedom to study and express herself. So, when she was fifteen, she turned toward the convent. As a nun she became Juana Inés de la Cruz.

Juana Inés continued her studies, and she wrote poetry. Her poems honored the Viceroy, the highest Spanish authority in Mexico, and the Catholic Church. She wrote poems in praise of the love of God and nature. Also she created poem songs and short plays in verse.

Church officials, and men in general, remained suspicious of Juana Inés's intelligence and her talent. She had reached higher than a woman in that society was expected to do. In one of her poems she responded to male attitudes, rebuking men for their hypocrisy by beginning:

Ignorant men, who disclaim women with no reason [intelligence], you do not see you are the reason for what you blame.

Then, Juana Inés made a serious mistake. At the bishop's invitation, she published an analysis of a famous priest's sermon. Her analysis pointed out that he had made numerous errors in theology and in Catholic doctrine. The bishop then publicly criticized Juana Inés for daring to criticize the priest. She responded in turn with a defense, concluding:

Does being a woman make any difference? Am I not as free to dissent from his opinion as he is from mine? Is my understanding any less free than his?

This was her last piece of published writing. Plague swept Mexico City in 1695. Nursing the sick, Juana Inés de la Cruz caught the disease and died, at the age of forty-three. She left behind a rich treasury of poetry and a record of courage.

Sources: Judith Thurman, *I Became Alone: Five Women Poets.* Athenaeum, 1975. Poem from page 98. Other quote: page 94. Fanchon Royer, *Sor Juana Inés de la Cruz.* St. Anthony Guild Press, 1952.

CHAPTER REVIEW

Think and Discuss

1. How do you think that the geography of Latin America affected its history?
2. What differences might there be between a person who had never known freedom and one who had known it and then been deprived of it?
3. Simón Bolívar is often called "the George Washington of Latin America." In what ways does his career parallel George Washington's?
4. How do you explain the fact that Portugal did not strongly resist Brazil's desire for independence?
5. Explain whether you agree or disagree with this statement: A supply of food and mineral resources is necessary to the development of an advanced culture.
6. In what ways do you think that the achievements of Native American cultures helped the colony builders from Europe?

Past and Present

1. Panel discussion: The major problems of Latin America today as compared with those of the past.
2. What do the United States and Latin America have in common?
3. What historical events are responsible for the similarities and differences between the United States and Latin America?

Activities

1. On a map of Latin America, show the boundaries and important cities, rivers, and mountains of the Latin American countries.
2. Make an album including maps; pictures of scenery, people, rulers, buildings, and industries; cartoons; and flags of Latin America.
3. Inform yourself thoroughly on the history of one Latin American country, and report your findings to the class. Consult pamphlets and other material from the Organization of American States and other references.

Revolutions Challenge Autocratic Rule

KEYNOTE

There is a story told about Prince Metternich, the Austrian chancellor in the post-Napoleonic period:

> One day in the garden of his castle on the Rhine, Metternich watched an eclipse of the sun. A great sense of relief came over him when the moon finally completed its path across the sun and the temporary darkness was dispelled. There was *order* again in the world.

In a sense, this story illustrates a key feature of the years from 1815 to 1848: It was a period in which Metternich and other leaders worked hard to keep the old order unchanged in Europe, while liberals and nationalists struggled to change the existing political system.

Workers put up barricades in the streets during the rebellion of the Paris Commune in 1871.

1. The Congress of Vienna Rearranges the Map of Europe

If the problems of peace often end in war, war ends in peace bringing old and new problems. Napoleon had been defeated for the second time and had been exiled to the tiny island of St. Helena. Meanwhile the Congress of Vienna (1814-1815) gathered to work out a peace settlement after the Napoleonic Wars.

The Congress of Vienna was an exciting affair. Uniformed military leaders, famous statesmen, and visitors from all over Europe gathered and enjoyed the banquets, the dances, the music, and other social gatherings. It seemed like a holiday season in Vienna. Yet the representatives of the Congress of Vienna had come to try to solve a number of problems involving the boundaries, governments, and possessions of the countries of Europe.

The Goals of the Congress

The Congress was dominated by Austria, Russia, Britain, and Prussia. Later, a clever French diplomat, Prince Talleyrand, maneuvered defeated France into this select circle. Most of the representatives wanted to establish a *balance of power*. That is, they wished to prevent any one nation from becoming powerful enough to threaten the security and independence of the others. The leaders of the Congress also followed the principles of *legitimacy*—restoring rulers to the thrones they had held before the French Revolution and Napoleon. Finally, the leaders of the Congress gave territory to countries as *compensation* for the loss of the lands they held before 1789.

Achievements and Failures

The members of the Congress of Vienna failed to take two factors into consideration. One was the force of *nationalism*. Nationalism grew in strength during the early nineteenth century. As a result, some settlements made at Vienna were doomed to survive for only a brief period. Nor was the Congress of Vienna concerned with *liberalism,* or the aspirations of the people for greater political rights. Prince Metternich, Austrian Chancellor, was the dominant figure of the conference. He expressed the opinion of many of the representatives when he later wrote, "The first need of society is to be maintained by strong authority . . . and not to govern itself."

The Congress therefore restored to power those so-called legitimate monarchs who had lost their positions during the Napoleonic period. Louis XVIII, a Bourbon, became King of France. Other Bourbons were returned to the thrones of the Two

Congress Of Vienna

MEMBER Austria
LEADERS Chancellor Metternich, Emperor Francis I

TERRITORIAL CHANGES Gained Lombardy, Venetia, and the Duchy of Milan in Italy. Regained most of Galicia, principally inhabited by Poles.

MEMBER Britain
LEADERS Viscount Castlereagh, Duke of Wellington

TERRITORIAL CHANGES Received Ceylon and the Cape of Good Hope (South Africa) from Holland plus other overseas areas from France and Spain.

MEMBER Germanies

TERRITORIAL CHANGES A loose union of thirty-nine states, including Austria and Prussia, was set up as the German Confederation. Each state was ruled by its own sovereign, and Austria acted as head of the confederation.

MEMBER France
LEADER Talleyrand

TERRITORIAL CHANGES Returned to frontiers of 1790.

MEMBER Holland

TERRITORIAL CHANGES Belgium was joined to Holland to form the Kingdom of the Netherlands. This compensated Holland for losing several colonies to Britain and established a stronger state to check future French aggression.

MEMBER Italy

TERRITORIAL CHANGES Italy remained divided into many states, dominated by the Austrian Hapsburgs. The King of Sardinia regained some territory.

MEMBER Prussia
LEADERS King Frederick William III, Prince Hardenberg

TERRITORIAL CHANGES Gained Swedish Pomerania, about two-fifths of Saxony, and important lands on the Rhine.

MEMBER Russia
LEADERS Czar Alexander I, Count Nesselrode

TERRITORIAL CHANGES Received the Duchy of Warsaw and the part of Poland that Prussia had once taken from Poland.

MEMBER Sweden

TERRITORIAL CHANGES Norway was taken from Denmark and joined to Sweden.

MEMBER Switzerland

TERRITORIAL CHANGES Swiss Confederation was granted its independence, and its neutrality was guaranteed.

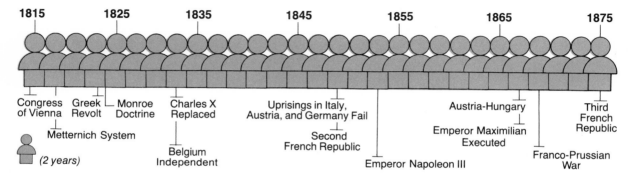

| 1815 | 1825 | 1835 | 1845 | 1855 | 1865 | 1875 |

Congress of Vienna

Greek Revolt

Monroe Doctrine

Charles X Replaced

Metternich System

(2 years)

Belgium Independent

Uprisings in Italy, Austria, and Germany Fail

Second French Republic

Emperor Napoleon III

Austria-Hungary

Emperor Maximilian Executed

Franco-Prussian War

Third French Republic

Sicilies and Spain. Hapsburg monarchs were re-established in Modena, Parma, and Tuscany—north Italian states.

The Congress of Vienna compensated the countries which had lost lands held before 1789 with other territory. (See the Chart on page 397.)

It is true that the Congress of Vienna made many settlements which were changed or undone in the decades between 1815 and 1871. Yet the Congress should not be dismissed as a failure. It inaugurated a period of *relative* peace in Europe despite numerous small wars and revolutions.

Check on Your Reading

1. Why did the Congress of Vienna meet? What countries dominated it?
2. How did the Congress change the map?
3. Which principles did the Congress follow?

2. The Metternich System Attempts to Control Europe

Under the leadership of Metternich, a *reactionary* period began. Rulers tried to erase all remnants of the revolutionary spirit. They wanted to restore political and social conditions as they were before the French Revolution to retain the *status quo*. From 1815 to 1848 this approach to affairs, the *Metternich System*, dominated Europe.

Metternich Fights Freedom

Metternich led the attack on freedom of the press, constitutional rights, and nationalism. In Austria and its possessions, he established censorship of books and newspapers. Also he set up an extensive spy system. In Germany, Metternich pressured the German Confederation to censor the press and suppress liberal activities. Everywhere Metternich fought those who "deny . . . the value of

the past and declare themselves the masters of the future."

To achieve their objectives, Metternich and the other leaders of Europe banded together. Russia, Austria, and Prussia joined the so-called *Holy Alliance*. Under this alliance the monarchs of these three countries agreed to be guided by rules of justice, Christian charity, and peace. Most of the other rulers of Europe eventually signed this resolution, but they rarely followed its principles.

A far more important agreement was the *Quadruple Alliance* between Great Britain, Russia, Austria, and Prussia. France joined in 1818 and the alliance became known as the *Concert of Europe*. The powers agreed to meet regularly:

> for the purpose of consulting upon their common interests, and for the consideration of measures . . . most salutary for the repose and prosperity of nations, and for the maintenance of the peace of Europe.

Liberals Rise against Oppression

The Concert of Europe worked hard to check liberalism. *Liberals* were people who did not accept the sacredness of the past and who did not fear change. They were reformers who demanded freedom of their countries from foreign control and who wanted governments more representative of the people. They wanted freedom of speech and press and the right to vote. The liberals were active in many countries.

In Naples the liberals forced the King to grant the country a constitution in 1820. Metternich, with the approval of Russia and Prussia, used Austrian troops to help the King cancel this constitution. There were also unsuccessful uprisings in other parts of Italy.

In Spain, in 1820, the liberals forced King Ferdinand VII to promise to restore the constitution of 1812, which he had annulled. French troops helped the King to put down this uprising.

In Greece the people revolted against the Turks in 1821. A year later they declared their independence (p. 478).

In Latin America the countries gained their independence from Spain and Portugal between 1810 and 1824 (see page 393). When members of the Concert of Europe discussed helping the Spanish king to regain these lands, Great Britain and the United States opposed the plan. The leaders of both countries knew that their nations would lose trading rights in Latin America if Spain regained its possessions. In addition, they recognized that most of the people of Great Britain and of the United States favored the independence of Latin America.

The Monroe Doctrine (1823)

George Canning, the British foreign minister, suggested that Great Britain and the United States issue a statement jointly opposing any attempt to crush the new Latin American republics. However, John Quincy Adams, the American Secretary of State, preferred that the United States make its own declaration. Why, he asked, should the United States always be a "[small boat] in the wake of the British man-of-war"? The United States could count on the support of the British fleet, so why not make a policy statement of its own? On December 2, 1823, President James Monroe sent a message to Congress, known as the *Monroe Doctrine*. The major points in the Doctrine were the following: 1. The Western Hemisphere was no longer to be an area for future colonization by European

The Congress of Vienna, under the leadership of Prince Metternich, restored a number of rulers to their thrones and also shifted about the territories of several countries. Use the chart on page 397 with this map to locate the major changes made by the Congress.

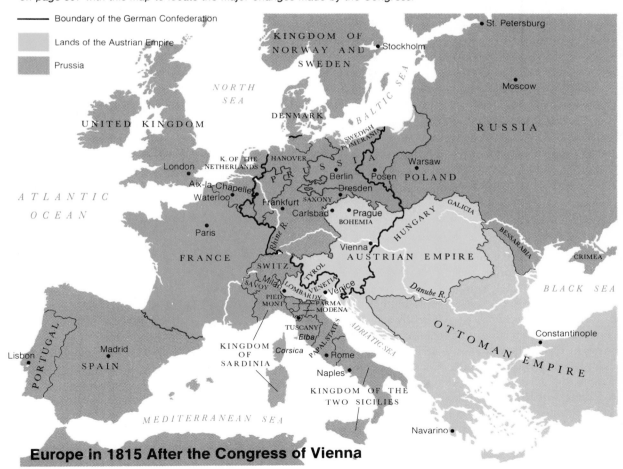

Europe in 1815 After the Congress of Vienna

Louis-Philippe, the so-called "Citizen King," is shown meeting with his ministers in 1842.

Check on Your Reading

1. Identify: reactionary, Metternich System, Holy Alliance, Quadruple Alliance, Concert of Europe, liberals, Monroe Doctrine.
2. How did Metternich and his allies try to maintain the status quo?

3. The Revolutionary Years in France

The Congress of Vienna in 1815 restored the so-called legitimate dynasty to the throne of France. Louis XVIII became the new king. He had enough common sense to avoid the mistakes that had led to the execution of his brother, Louis XVI. Louis XVIII followed a moderate course and governed within the terms of the Charter granted to the people in 1814. This Charter provided that the king was to cooperate with the legislature in making the laws. It also guaranteed religious freedom.

Rebellion under Charles X

Louis XVIII died in 1824, and his brother became the new king as Charles X. Charles X (1824-1830) was an autocrat who believed that "Louis XVI was lost through concessions. I have but one choice, to drive or be driven." He attempted to restore the absolute power of the monarchy. He curtailed religious freedom and strengthened the position of the Catholic Church. He gave the nobles money to compensate for their loss of property during the French Revolution, and interfered with the activities of business people. He also issued royal decrees that suspended freedom of the press, dissolved the national legislature, and gave the king powers to crush liberty.

As a result of these acts, a rebellion broke out in July 1830. Republicans, journalists, business people, dissatisfied legislators, university students, and workers joined the uprising. The rebels took control of Paris, and Charles X was forced to abdicate.

The monarchy was not abolished. The national legislature chose Louis-Philippe of the House of Orléans to be the new king. The white flag of the Bourbons was replaced with the tricolor of the French Revolution, and the Revolution of 1830 was deemed a success.

From Monarchy to Second Republic

Louis-Philippe (1830-1848) was a hard-working ruler. At first he played the role of a "Citizen-

countries. 2. The United States would consider any attempt by European countries to extend their system of government to the Western Hemisphere as "dangerous to our peace and safety." 3. It would be "unfriendly" to the United States for any European country to try to regain areas in the Western Hemisphere that had declared themselves independent. 4. The United States would not interfere with the way in which European countries ran their own affairs in Europe.

The Monroe Doctrine was designed to discourage European countries from helping Spain regain her former colonies. It also was aimed at preventing the Russians in Alaska from expanding southward.

King" whose powers were limited by the constitution. Representatives of the middle class dominated the government. Louis-Philippe's reign was so favorable to business people, merchants, and the middle class that it is known as the "Bourgeois Monarchy." Even the right to vote was limited to wealthy people who paid heavy taxes. "If you want a vote, get rich!" advised Louis-Philippe's chief minister.

It was a period of great cultural creativity, particularly in literature. It was also a time in which the drive for business gains led some people to ignore the importance of the arts. The novelist Honoré de Balzac compared that business world of France with "a basket of live crabs seeking to devour one another."

Some of the most serious problems resulted from the change from the domestic system of production to the factory system. Many people who had worked at home now labored long hours for low wages in factories that were not safe. Reforms in working and living conditions were badly needed. However, when socialists demanded such reforms, the government banned all writings and actions critical of the regime.

The "Bourgeois Monarchy" could not last. Its failures were too many. It refused to grant more people the right to vote and it censored the press. It was timid in foreign affairs and became involved in financial difficulties. In February 1848, street riots broke out. Louis-Philippe was overthrown and the monarchy was abolished. The Second French Republic was proclaimed on February 27, 1848.

Rebellion in the Second Republic

The first months of the Second Republic were a difficult period of transition. A provisional government was established which contained a number of middle-class leaders. The city workers, who had played a major part in the February revolution, demanded immediate reforms. The government reluctantly established *national workshops,* which were government work projects to provide jobs.

The workshop plan, whose chief supporter was the socialist Louis Blanc (1811-1882), was not administered properly and did not prove effective. Louis Blanc protested that he had wanted the workshops "to consist of workmen belonging to the same trade . . . [who] were to pursue their business, the

State lending them capital, to be repaid according to certain stipulations." Instead, the state had set up workshops that were "utterly unproductive and absurd" and did little more than feed "a rabble of paupers." The number of unemployed still continued to increase. They were supported by unemployment relief payments from the government.

A new National Assembly was elected that was dominated by the bourgeoisie. The new government abolished relief payments to the unemployed. This action led to bloodshed. In June 1848, there were fierce battles in Paris between government troops and the unemployed, who were directed by socialists. According to Alexis de Tocqueville, a French author and statesman of the time, "the insurgents fought . . . without leaders, without flags, and yet with a marvelous harmony." *Du pain ou du plomb*—bread or lead—was the cry! Many French people, frightened by the chaos, became convinced that only a strong leader could save the country. When elections were held in December 1848, Louis Napoleon, nephew of Napoleon Bonaparte, was elected President of the new republic.

From the Second Republic to Empire

Louis Napoleon believed in "Bonapartism." That is, he wanted all power to be placed in the hands of a strong ruler, himself. Then, as "strong man" of France, he would have the responsibility of ruling in the interests of the people. The "Napoleonic legend" and the Bonaparte name helped to elect Louis Napoleon.

When Louis Napoleon was campaigning for the presidency, he promised to protect the republic. A few years after he was elected, he tried to persuade the people to do away with the republic and make him emperor.

President Louis Napoleon failed to persuade the National Assembly to amend the 1848 Constitution to allow him a second term as president. Therefore, on December 2, 1851, he seized power. He reestablished universal male suffrage and called for a plebiscite, or popular vote, to "give me means to assure your prosperity, or choose another in my place." The people accepted his rule by a vote of 7,500,000 in favor to 640,000 opposed. This gave him the right to draw up a new constitution in place of that of 1848.

A year later, he made himself Emperor of France as Napoleon III. The Second French Republic had lasted only four years, from 1848 to 1852. The period of the Second Empire began, and Napoleon III remained emperor for nearly two decades.

Check on Your Reading

1. Why did the French accept the rule of Louis XVIII but revolt against Charles X?
2. Describe the "Bourgeois Monarchy." What problems were immediately faced by the Second Republic?
3. Trace Louis Napoleon's rise to power.

4. Revolutionary Fires Spread throughout Europe

Revolutionary forces were at work throughout Europe in the years 1830 to 1848. The liberals in many countries were inspired by the example of France. Uprisings broke out in Belgium, Poland, the Austrian Empire, Germany, and Italy. Most of these revolutions were unsuccessful.

Belgium Becomes a Nation

When the diplomats at the Congress of Vienna joined Belgium and Holland together in 1815, they ignored the differences between the two regions.

Belgium and Holland differed in religion and language. The Belgians were principally Roman Catholic. The Dutch were chiefly Protestants. The two peoples clashed over religious affairs. They also did not speak the same language. The Belgians spoke French and Flemish. They were therefore disturbed when Dutch was made the official language of government documents.

The Belgians were proud of their past. They recalled the fifteenth and sixteeth centuries, when Antwerp was a great center. They spoke with admiration of their brilliant artists and crafts workers. Similarly, the Dutch were proud of their own history, particularly of their "Golden Age" in the seventeenth century. Pride of each group in the superiority of its own history was sometimes a cause of tension.

The Belgians felt they did not receive equal treatment with the Dutch in government, education, military service, or economic well-being. Many Belgians wanted to have their own nation. The nationalistic feelings of the people of Belgium were too strong to be held in check. In 1830 the Belgians revolted. Their revolt was successful, and the new nation of Belgium was born.

The Polish Revolt Fails

In 1830, the Poles revolted against the Russian rulers who dominated them, but their revolt was crushed. The Poles were deprived of all constitutional privileges and placed under rigid military control.

One-tenth of the Polish land was seized by the Russians. Universities were closed. Thousands of Poles were killed or imprisoned. The Polish poet Krasinski described Poland after 1831 as:

> The land of graves and crosses. Thou mayest know it by the silence of its men and the melancholy of its children.

Although other rebellions took place, Poland did not win its independence until 1919. By then Poland had been out of existence as a nation for almost 125 years. Yet its people preserved their language, traditions, literature, and strong feeling of nationality. The history of Poland provides an outstanding example of the power of nationalism, a force overlooked by the Congress of Vienna.

The Austrian Empire

Meanwhile, dissension continued to plague the Austrian Empire. Many of the tensions resulted from the growing nationalism of various groups within the Empire. These included Germans; Magyars; Italians; and Slavs—Czechs, Poles, Slovenes, Slovaks, and Croats. The problem that faced the Hapsburgs in ruling these people has been described by historian Hans Kohn:

> In the 19th century—the age of nationalism—this multinational [Austrian] empire faced the problem of establishing an order which could give its various nationalities freedom of development and a feeling of equality.

Austria did not solve this problem, and a spirit of rebellion grew. In 1848 the Magyars and other peoples sympathetic to their cause revolted against the Austrian emperor. The Magyars had settled along the Danube River in the tenth century. Their land, known as Hungary, eventually had become a part of the Austrian Empire.

Louis Kossuth (1802–1894), the leader of the Magyars, first demanded constitutional government in Hungary—then independence. Many of the rebels stressed that they fought "to save ourselves

In einem Monat wird
Fürst Metternich
gestürzt sein
Es lebe das constitutionelle
Oesterreich!

A poster in Vienna demands the ouster of Prince Metternich and a constitutional government. The rebels did force Metternich to resign, but their revolution soon was crushed.

from being struck off the earth as a nation." Liberals in Bohemia, part of the Austrian Empire, also demanded that they be granted an independent constitution.

On March 13, 1848, the Liberal party in Vienna, excited by the February revolution in France, rose against the Austrian government. Prince Metternich was forced to resign. He went into exile in England, where he insisted that the things he had done were right. "My mind has never entertained error," he declared.

By the end of March, the Austrian emperor was compelled to grant both Hungary and Bohemia the right to have new constitutions and more freedom. However, tension between different ethnic groups prevented these lands from consolidating their gains. There was, for example, conflict between the Germans and Czechs in Bohemia, and tensions between the Magyars in Hungary and the minority groups whom they sought to dominate. As a result, by the end of August 1848, Austrian and Russian

troops had crushed the revolutionary movements. Bohemia and Hungary again fell under the control of Austria.

In 1867, after Austria was defeated in a war with Prussia, the Austrian Empire was changed into a "dual monarchy" known as Austria-Hungary. Under this organization, Austria and Hungary had a common ruler, defense organization, budget, and foreign policy. Still the problems of governing people belonging to different nationality groups had not been solved.

Italians Revolt against Austrian Control

A British magazine noted that the news of the February revolution in France (p. 401) acted "like an electric shock upon Italy." Then in March 1848, news of the fall of Metternich reached the Italians. The people of Milan boldly rose against their Austrian rulers. They built barricades in the streets out of pianos, sofas, and chicken coops. Women pulled up rows of paving stones from the streets to hinder the movement of the Austrian troops.

A part of Lombardy broke away from Austrian control, and the people of Venetia set up an independent republic. In Rome, Italian rebels forced the Pope to flee the city, and Giuseppe Mazzini and his followers established a Roman Republic. In Naples, Tuscany, and Piedmont, the rulers granted their people constitutions. The Kingdom of Sardinia went to war against Austria.

Despite their heroic efforts, the rebels were crushed. Austrian troops put down the revolt in Milan. French troops captured Rome and returned control of the city to the Pope. The Sardinians were defeated by the Austrians, and the Sardinian ruler Charles Albert abdicated. He was succeeded by his son, Victor Emmanuel II. By the end of 1849, Austria had regained its hold on Italy. Italian efforts to gain freedom had been checked.

German Liberals Revolt

News of the February revolution in France also stirred the liberals of Germany to action. In March 1848, they led a series of demonstrations throughout Germany. Events reached a climax with an insurrection in Berlin. The frightened King of Prussia, Frederick William IV (1840-1861), agreed to call for the meeting of an assembly to write a constitution satisfactory to the liberals. He also promised to work to free the German Confederation from Austrian control. This assembly met at Frankfurt in 1848. It consisted of representatives from all of the states in the German Confederation. Austria also attended the conference.

The Frankfurt Assembly did not achieve the objectives of the liberals. Its members did not cooperate well with each other. Also they were not strong enough to force Austria out of Germany. When a constitution was drawn up, King Frederick William IV of Prussia rejected the invitation to become emperor of the new government. He refused because he did not want to risk a war with Austria. Also he believed a crown came from God, not from an assembly of people. The Frankfurt Assembly was disbanded. German liberals had suffered a serious defeat. After the failure of 1848, many of them left Germany. These included a number of liberals who emigrated to the United States.

In 1850 the King of Prussia did grant his own country a constitution. However, it established a government whose leaders were responsible to the monarch—not to the people.

Results of the Revolutions

On the whole the revolutionary uprisings during the years 1830 to 1848 were failures. The revolutions in Poland, the Austrian Empire, Italy, and Germany were crushed. Only Belgium obtained its independence. Efforts to win constitutions failed, except in Prussia and Sardinia. The liberals learned that they would have to use other methods.

Why did the revolutions fail? The revolutionaries were united in their efforts to drive out the rulers, but they could not agree on the kind of government to be organized. They also failed to agree on the political privileges to be granted to different classes. Religious differences and national loyalties further divided them. The era of revolutionary activities seemed to be at an end.

Check on Your Reading

1. Why did the Belgians revolt against the Dutch in 1830? What was the result?
2. Describe the uprisings in Poland, the Austrian Empire, Italy, and Germany. What were the results?

5. From the Second Empire to the Third Republic in France

By 1852, Louis Napoleon had become Emperor of France as Napoleon III. He granted a constitution that provided for a Legislative Assembly to be elected by universal manhood suffrage. While maintaining the semblance of a democratic government, Napoleon III kept the real governing power in his hands. He imposed strict censorship and controlled the elections so that candidates who supported the government were elected. Newspapers critical of the government were suppressed, and the government's opponents were either jailed or exiled.

Domestic Affairs

As emperor, Napoleon III appealed to all groups. To Catholics, he pledged defense of the Church. To business people, he promised prosperity. To workers, he indicated that there would be public works projects.

At first, conditions favored him. It was a time of business prosperity. Napoleon III supported the

Emperor Napoleon III and Empress Eugenie. Her style of dressing influenced fashions throughout Europe and the Americas.

building of factories, banks, and railroads. A program of public works, under the direction of Baron Haussmann, created new jobs. Magnificent public buildings, monuments, and theaters were built throughout Paris. Long, broad avenues were constructed. The city again became the art and intellectual capital of Europe.

Napoleon III also tried to win the support of the Church. He allowed Church leaders to control a number of areas of education in the schools and universities. He also stationed French troops in Rome to protect the Pope.

Yet, despite his efforts to please all groups, the opposition to Napoleon III increased. Republicans were displeased because he had destroyed the Second French Republic and had taken away many of the people's rights. Catholics were angry because he had encouraged the unification of Italy.

Conservatives were opposed to many of his policies. To divert people from their opposition, Napoleon III focused attention on foreign affairs.

Foreign Policy Leads to Disaster

In 1854, France joined Britain against Russia in the Crimean War. A victory in this war helped France to regain some of its prestige. A few years later, Napoleon III supported the Italians against the Austrians.

In Mexico, Benito Juárez, a Native American, led a revolt against the Mexican dictator and overthrew the regime. He declared that his government could not repay the foreign debts of the previous dictatorship, including money borrowed from European bankers. As a result of Juárez's actions and for other reasons, France joined Great Britain and Spain in sending armed forces to Mexico in 1862. Their troops occupied Veracruz.

Spain and Britain soon reached an agreement with Juárez and withdrew their troops, but French troops remained. Napoleon III thought that he could establish a French colony in Mexico as a "grand design" of his reign. His troops overthrew Juárez, and Napoleon III persuaded Archduke Maximilian, brother of the Emperor of Austria, to become Emperor of Mexico.

The United States protested this violation of the Monroe Doctrine, but it could not take action because it was involved in the Civil War, which ended in 1865. Then the United States sent an army to the Mexican border to force Napoleon III to withdraw his troops. Juárez and his forces captured Maximilian and executed him in 1867. Napoleon III lost considerable money, troops, and prestige.

Meanwhile, conditions at home were becoming worse. Napoleon III had to grant concessions. Workers were again permitted to strike, and the press was allowed to criticize the government. The Assembly was permitted to initiate legislation, vote on the budget, and require ministers to be responsible to it. However, these concessions did not satisfy the opposition.

Meanwhile, Prussia had become a strong power in Europe. In 1870, France fought against Prussia in the Franco-Prussian War. In six weeks, the French armies were defeated, and Napoleon III and a large army surrendered at Sedan, near the Belgian border. When the news reached Paris, the Assembly deposed the emperor and proclaimed France a republic. Napoleon III had lost his empire on the battlefield.

6. The Third Republic

A provisional republic was set up. A difficult period followed, during which a National Assembly governed France (1871-1875). The government had to sign a peace treaty ending the Franco-Prussian War. By the Treaty of Frankfurt, France lost Alsace and a part of Lorraine and had to pay an indemnity of one billion dollars.

Another crisis followed. A revolutionary city government—known as the Paris Commune—was established. Its forces were crushed by the National Assembly, which tried to restore order to France. In 1872, a system of obligatory five-year military service was started.

In 1875, the National Assembly drew up laws that established a Third French Republic. This government consisted of a two-house legislature (a Chamber of Deputies and a Senate), a president chosen by both houses, and a premier responsible to the Chamber of Deputies. A number of small political parties developed.

About 1880 a national system of public education was established. Under this system, primary education was to be free, compulsory, and in the hands of lay teachers. Religious instruction was not permitted. In 1905 laws were passed separating the Church and the State. This meant that the clergy would not be paid by the government, and bishops would no longer be nominated by government officials.

Between 1871 and 1914 the French made conscientious efforts, both at home and abroad, to surpass the other countries of Europe. France expanded overseas in Tunis, parts of Indo-China, and Northwest Africa. National pride—and hostility to Germany—stimulated these efforts.

Check on Your Reading

1. How did Napoleon III maintain control and try to satisfy opposition groups?
2. Describe the Mexican intervention.
3. What was a major result of the Franco-Prussian War for France?
4. What problems did the Third French Republic face?
5. How was the Third French Republic governed?

An Incident during an Uprising

It was the evening of February 23, 1848, and Paris was filled with excitement. Around the Ministry of Foreign Affairs—official residence of Louis-Philippe's unpopular minister, Guizot—there was "a heavy force of . . . troops of the line, dragoons [mounted infantrymen], and municipal guard."

Lieutenant-Colonel Courant, commander of the Fourteenth Regiment, and his troops were stationed near Guizot's residence. It was his assignment to protect the building against demonstrators. Rifleman [Private] Henri was a soldier in the first squad of the regiment. It was his job to do as he was told.

Lieutenant-Colonel Courant ordered his first squad to block the boulevard. Rifleman Henri made the move with the others. They were not a moment too soon, for a mob of Parisians, including some national guardsmen, was rapidly approaching. The demonstrators shouted "Long live reform! Down with Guizot!"

Then, suddenly, someone fired a shot! It may have been an overly excited soldier, or perhaps one of the mob aiming at the lieutenant-colonel. Only one thing was certain: The bullet missed its intended target. It struck Rifleman Henri in the face. The rifleman fell to the ground dead. The mob was now out of hand, and it took great effort to restore order.

In March, a few weeks after this uprising, Lieutenant-Colonel Courant made an official report of what had happened:

> I believe that this event has been exaggerated [he declared, calmly] . . . only one man from my squad was killed.

The late Rifleman Henri was not in a position to argue whether the event was exaggerated or not.

The above account is based on primary materials in *The Quest for a Principle of Authority in Europe, 1715 to the Present,* by Thomas C. Mendenhall and others, 1948, Holt, Rinehart and Winston, Publishers.

CHAPTER REVIEW

Think and Discuss

1. Why did the Congress of Vienna fail to check the growth of nationalism?
2. What role was played by the Concert of Europe, 1820–1848?
3. How could Poland keep the spirit of nationalism alive?
4. Why did the revolutions in 1830 and in 1848 break out in France rather than in another country?
5. A historian has said that Metternich's policy in enforcing the decisions of the Congress of Vienna was like a fire department putting out the fires of liberty. What do you think? Why?

Past and Present

1. What groups, if any, today hold ideas comparable to those of Metternich?
2. Compare the views of "liberals" of the 1800s with those held by "liberals" today.

Activities

1. In parallel columns, list the actions of Louis Napoleon and Napoleon Bonaparte. To what extent did Louis Napoleon imitate his uncle?
2. On a map of Europe, indicate the boundaries and territorial changes of the European countries as a result of the Congress of Vienna.
3. Make a chart of the revolutions of 1830 with the causes and results of each.
4. Make a chart of the revolutions of 1848. List the countries, leaders, causes, and results.

7

The Industrial Revolution Changes the Western World

Twenty Questions is a game that cannot be played easily with major developments in history. The more answers we receive about the past, the more questions we have to ask in the present. Thus, a person living today may ask:

What has the Industrial Revolution to do with me? Why should I be interested in 200-year-old inventions? After all, I live in the 1980s, and life today is very different.

Such questions need answers. Yes, life is different, but it is different in large part because of the Industrial Revolution. Also, today there are more inventions than ever before, and a study of history can help us to understand how they affect our lives. What is more, some nations are just beginning to industrialize. They are encountering many of the same problems that faced nations which industrialized 200 years ago.

Most of the world's nations today share a serious problem: How can they cope with the changes brought by a continuing Industrial Revolution? We can divide this problem into three basic questions. 1. How can people adjust to new inventions? 2. How can countries protect the welfare of people affected by new inventions? 3. How can harmonious and productive relationships be established between the industrialized and non-industrialized peoples of the world?

Inventions Revolutionize
Industry and Ways of Living

KEYNOTE

From about 1750 to 1860, what has been called an "Industrial Revolution" changed and speeded up ways of doing things in England. Then this "revolution" began to spread to other countries, including the United States. Like all revolutions, however, this one grew out of the past.

Such inventions as the spinning machine, the steam engine, and the electric telegraph brought great changes. Yet the ideas on which such machines were based had been known for a long time to some people. Steam power was known to several of the early Greeks. Hundreds of years before Christ, East Indians used a simple machine to spin yarn. The idea of electricity was discussed in the days of Queen Elizabeth I. Thus, the past, present, and future continue to be linked.

A painting of blast furnaces in England in 1801.

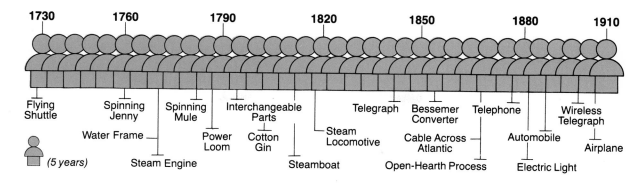

Timeline (5 years per figure):

1730 — Flying Shuttle
1760 — Spinning Jenny; Water Frame; Steam Engine
1790 — Spinning Mule; Power Loom; Cotton Gin
1820 — Interchangeable Parts; Steam Locomotive; Steamboat
1850 — Telegraph
1880 — Bessemer Converter; Cable Across Atlantic; Open-Hearth Process; Telephone; Automobile; Electric Light
1910 — Wireless Telegraph; Airplane

1. The Industrial Revolution Develops First in England

Between 1000 and 1750 A.D. few basic changes were made in the way people lived in England. Most of the people in 1750 worked the land in about the same way their ancestors had in 1000. Their crops, animals, and tools had not changed much either.

England's population was a little over six million. Its pace of living was said to be that of "a slowly-moving stream." There were some industries, but most of them were small. There was some manufacturing, but much of this work was done at home or in small shops. Besides their work in the fields, many women and children spun yarn, wove cloth, or made cheese, butter, and other products to sell at a nearby market town. Most families worked as a unit to grow their food and produce other needed items. There were some important business centers, but none of them had yet felt the frantic rush of modern industrial life.

Then, inventions, new techniques, and new sources of power helped to speed up tremendously the pace of life. By 1850 vast changes had taken place. The fairly self-sufficient English farm family had almost completely disappeared. Some small market centers had grown into large, smoky, industrial cities crowded with workers. Many people no longer lived by the slow pace of the seasons. Now they lived by the clock or the factory whistle. For many of England's people, life had changed sharply within a few generations. The many changes of this period from 1750 to 1860 make up what has been called the "Industrial Revolution."

The term "Industrial Revolution" is misleading, for it suggests that there was sudden overthrowing of the past. Such was not the case. Actually, changes of this so-called "revolution" grew out of the past and extended far into the future.

The Industrial Revolution developed first in England. There were numerous reasons why it occurred there.

England's Escape from Military Destruction

The European continent had been ravaged by the French Revolution and the Napoleonic Wars. England had escaped this military destruction. It also had gained valuable markets by selling to war-torn countries.

England's Wealth and Natural Resources

England had a number of people wealthy enough to invest money in industries. Many of them had made their money through England's trade with its colonies and other overseas areas. The demands of the overseas markets for goods also encouraged manufacturers to search for ways to increase their production.

Some of these wealthy people invested their money in ways to produce more goods. They backed the development of inventions and improvements in machinery.

England also had many of the natural resources necessary for industrial development. These included coal, iron ore, and water power. It was also important that these natural resources were located near each other. Shipping them over long distances would have been difficult and expensive.

Labor Supply

England had the supply of labor that was necessary to work in new industries. Part of this supply came from an increase in population. England's population increased by over 50 percent from 1750 to 1801. Other laborers came to England from Ireland and Scotland.

411

Changes in Agriculture

For many years English farmers had owned or worked as permanent tenants small strips of land around their villages. A farmer's holdings were scattered. There were also special areas that were set aside for the use of all the people of a village. These "common lands" could be used for grazing cattle, gathering firewood, and other purposes.

In the sixteenth, seventeenth, and the first half of the eighteenth century, this system of farming was gradually eliminated by what is called the *enclosure movement*. Farmers' scattered strips of land were combined and fenced in. Also the "common lands" were brought under the control of private individuals.

Many small farmers sold their strips to large landowners and became tenant-farmers or farm laborers. In the eighteenth century many of them left the farms and moved to the towns to find work. They provided many of the workers for the growing factories.

Many changes in agriculture after 1700 made it possible to grow more food. Important improvements came with better methods of planting seed, fertilizing the soil, rotating crops, and breeding cattle. The result was an increase in production of crops and meat animals. Machinery developed in the Industrial Revolution further increased agricultural production.

Creative Individuals, the Special Factor

A land free from war's destruction, plus wealth, natural resources, and labor supply—all helped England to become the center for the Industrial Revolution. But they were not enough. Something else was needed. That "something" was creative individuals who could invent machines, find new sources of power, and develop better ways to manufacture products and run businesses.

The inventors who sparked the Industrial Revolution came from many backgrounds. Most were practical people who were looking for solutions to a particular problem. Not every inventor was successful. Many worked for years to achieve results. The government helped inventors by passing laws to prevent the theft of new ideas. Private organizations gave prizes for inventions. Often one invention created the need for another and still another invention. Once started, the inventive process continued to grow.

The new machines needed people with new skills to make and run them. At every step, the process of work became more complex and more productive. The Industrial Revolution, once begun, moved at an ever-increasing pace.

Check on Your Reading

1. What is meant by the term "Industrial Revolution"?
2. What part did changes in farming play in the Industrial Revolution?
3. What factors made possible the Industrial Revolution in England?

---

2. Inventors Revolutionize the Textile Industry

By the early 1700s, Britain was trading with much of the world. British merchant ships, protected by a strong navy, carried goods between Great Britain, its colonies, and distant countries. For years the British had produced and exported woolen cloth. Now cotton cloth from India became very popular in Europe.

Most cotton cloth came from India and other parts of Asia where labor was cheap. Handmade British cloth was too expensive to compete. Britain needed a way to spin and weave with less labor. The solution came with the invention of machines to do the work once done by hand.

The "Flying Shuttle" and the "Spinning Jenny"

In the 1730s, John Kay invented the "flying shuttle." This device increased the speed at which yarn was threaded through the strands of a loom. Also the "flying shuttle" cut the number of workers needed on a loom by half. Until Kay's invention, cloth over thirty inches wide required a worker on each side of the loom. Now only one was needed. Thus the same number of weavers could now produce twice as much cloth.

Within thirty years, many English weavers could not get enough yarn to supply their looms. Spinning was still done by hand, one thread at a time. Often a weaver had to walk several miles to call on half a dozen spinners before collecting enough yarn for a day's work. The spinners, many of them women, were in great demand and received high wages for their work.

A method had to be found to make more yarn for

James Hargreaves' "spinning jenny." As the model shows, one wheel operated a number of spindles spinning yarn. Each spindle replaced one person spinning by hand.

the weavers. In the late 1760s, James Hargreaves invented the "spinning jenny." This machine made it possible for one wheel to operate eight spindles. The jenny was improved until, by 1784, eight threads of yarn could be spun by one person.

A number of textile workers were afraid of what we call *technological unemployment;* that is, unemployment that results from technical progress in the use of machinery. They feared that the "jenny" would deprive them of their work as spinners. A mob broke into James Hargreaves' house and drove him from town! In some places rioting workers destroyed the new machinery.

The Water Frame and the Rise of Factories

About 1769, Richard Arkwright put together ideas from several other inventors to improve spinning still more. He developed the water frame, a spinning machine run by water power. This machine used sets of revolving rollers to pull out and stretch the fibers of cotton yarn. The water frame produced stronger yarn than that produced by the "spinning jenny."

The "spinning jenny" was small enough to be used in a spinner's home. The water frame was a large machine which required a large building located near fast-moving water. Thus large factories were created. This brought an important change to the spinners' lives. Instead of working in their homes, spinners now had to travel to factories. Arkwright, who set up many mills in England, was one of the founders of the "factory system."

The "Spinning Mule"

In 1778, Samuel Crompton combined features of the "spinning jenny" and the water frame to create a new machine called the "spinning mule." The "mule" was easier to run than Arkwright's water frame. It could produce a thread 300,000 yards long from a single pound of cotton. With the "mule," English weavers were able to compete with India in making fine cotton.

The Power Loom Speeds up Weaving

In 1787 Edmund Cartwright completed a rather clumsy power loom to weave cloth from the thread

413

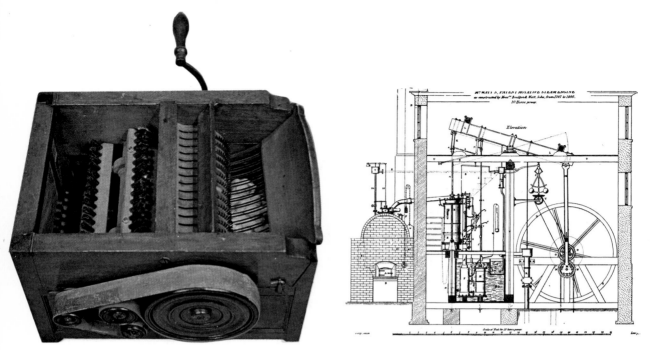

On this page are illustrated three key inventions of the early Industrial Revolution. Above left, Eli Whitney's cotton gin removed seed from cotton fibers as rapidly as fifty persons could do it by hand. At the right above, James Watt's steam engine, which was used to power factory machinery as well as to run railroads and ships. Below, a factory using power looms for weaving cloth.

produced by the spinning machines. In the 1820s a more efficient power loom was marketed. After 1830 machine-powered looms replaced more and more of the hand weavers.

The Cotton Gin and Interchangeable Parts

Meanwhile a problem was developing in providing cotton for the fast growing textile industry. It took a long time and many workers to remove the seeds from cotton. In 1793, Catherine Littlefield Greene, the alert owner of a cotton plantation in Georgia, asked Eli Whitney to develop a machine to remove the seeds from cotton. He invented the cotton gin. The cotton gin removed the seeds from the cotton fibers as rapidly as fifty persons could do it by hand. Whitney's invention spread rapidly throughout the southern United States. More and cheaper cotton could now be shipped to the textile factories.

Perhaps an even more important contribution to the Industrial Revolution was Eli Whitney's development of the technique of using uniform and interchangeable parts in the manufacture of rifles. This made it possible to assemble and turn out guns in large numbers. Today Eli Whitney is recognized as one of the founders of *mass production,* the basis of our modern factory system.

"Flying shuttle"—"spinning jenny"—"mule"— these and other early machines of the Industrial Revolution increased tremendously the export value of England's cotton manufactures. In 1835 England produced over 60 percent of the cotton cloth manufactured in the world.

A New Source of Power

Experiments with steam pressure had been made in the 1660s, but the first practical steam engine was not invented until the 1700s. In a curious way, one of the reasons the steam engine was developed was to solve a problem caused by the shortage of wood in Great Britain. Iron was removed from iron ore by a separation process known as smelting. For hundreds of years, charcoal, made by burning hardwoods, was used to smelt iron. As wood supplies began to grow short, iron smelters turned to coal. As the demand for coal increased, miners dug shafts deeper into the ground. They often struck water which flooded their mines. Someone had to design a way to pump out this water from coal mines and also from tin mines.

In the early part of the eighteenth century, Thomas Newcomen built a steam engine which could drive the pumps in the coal mines. Newcomen's engine was so large that it consumed vast amounts of coal fuel. It was not practical to move the engine very far from its fuel supply. It remained for James Watt of Scotland to develop by 1769 a really workable steam engine.

Watt had gone through moments of discouragement and despair. At one point he wrote: "Of all things in life, there is nothing more foolish than inventing." But the spark within him drove him. When his steam engine was marketed in 1776, its fourteen strokes per minute became the pulse beat for new industrial growth.

Watt's steam engine was important for several reasons: 1. It made it possible to establish mills anywhere. Previously mills had to be built near streams to obtain water power. 2. It helped industries to expand tremendously. 3. It contributed to development of new means of transportation. A monument was erected to Watt's memory in Westminster Abbey hailing him as one of the "real benefactors of the world."

Check on Your Reading

1. What changes did the new machines bring to the textile industry? to workers?
2. How did the new textile machines affect the economy of England?
3. Why was the steam engine important?

---

3. Iron—the Backbone of the Industrial Revolution

Before the 1700s, iron was removed from iron ore by smelting it using charcoal for fuel. In time the amount of wood near the iron ore deposits became scarce. Also Britain needed the scarce wood for building ships, houses, and furniture. You may remember that Britain imported forest products from the American colonies.

Coal Replaces Charcoal in Making Iron

Without charcoal, little iron could be made. Between 1709 and 1713, Alexander Darby found that *coke,* made by burning coal, could replace charcoal in smelting iron. Fortunately, most iron ore deposits and coal deposits were near each other.

Remember that Newcomen's steam engine was developed to pump water from coal mines and from tin mines. Using the steam engine, miners were able to produce enough coal to meet the demand for iron.

Henry Cort Improves Iron Production

Henry Cort was next to contribute to the growth of the iron industry. In 1784 Cort developed a method of using "puddling furnaces" to change pig iron into wrought iron. Pig iron was iron cast in molds as it first came from the ore. Wrought iron was iron that was ready to shape. Cort's process made it possible to produce more and better iron than before.

Sir Henry Bessemer Improves the Making of Steel

Puddled iron was used to make products such as railroad rails and bridge girders. However, such iron often broke apart under strain. Items like springs or wire cables needed a much tougher metal—steel. Unfortunately, steel was very expensive to produce.

What was to be done? Sir Henry Bessemer in England, William Kelly in America, and others set about answering this question. Bessemer was convinced that he could make steel from iron by using blasts of air to clear molten pig iron of most of its impurities. "The whole scheme [is] the dream of a wild enthusiast," wrote one newspaper. Many others refused to take Bessemer seriously.

Nevertheless, in 1856 Bessemer succeeded in his efforts. His "Bessemer converter" blew air through molten pig iron at a tremendous pressure. The oxygen in this air burned out most of the impurities from the iron. The "Bessemer converter" made

An iron and steel manufacturing plant in Sheffield, England. Sheffield became a center for the making of fine products from steel.

A print of the Liverpool and Manchester railroad in 1831. Notice how the passenger cars resemble the stagecoaches which they will replace.

steel from pig iron in twenty to thirty minutes. It also lowered the cost of producing steel from two hundred dollars to about four dollars a ton. Eight years later, another method of making steel was invented by Pierre Martin (French)—the Siemens-Martin "open-hearth process."

Check on Your Reading

1. Why was the substitution of coal for charcoal in smelting iron important?
2. In what ways is steel superior to iron? Explain the Bessemer process of making steel.

4. Improved Transportation and Communication

The growth of industry required that people and places be linked together. Unfortunately, the conditions of the roads during the early part of the eighteenth century blocked rather than encouraged the movement of people and goods.

Improvements in Road Building

English roads were narrow, poorly maintained, and often both impassable and impossible. According to the English writer Daniel Defoe, after a heavy rain the water remained on the roads "as in a dish," and horses sank in it "up to their bellies." Roads were so dangerous that people sometimes wrote their wills before starting on a journey.

In the seventeenth and eighteenth centuries England made some efforts to improve conditions. Individuals and private companies ("Turnpike Trusts") were encouraged by Parliament to construct and improve roads. As a reward for their efforts, they were permitted to charge tolls.

Even more important were the attempts made to improve the surface of the roads. Improvements included well-drained roadbeds and hard road surfaces. Thomas Telford built roads in two layers. John L. McAdam designed a crushed stone surface. His "macadamized" road was adopted in various parts of the world.

Improved roads brought safer and faster travel by horsedrawn coach. In 1692 an advertisement declared:

> There is an admirable [convenience] . . . to travel from London, the like of which has not been known in the world; and that is, by stage-coaches, . . . the stage-coaches called "Flying Coaches" make forty or fifty miles a day.

By 1775, "Flying Coaches" were covering the then amazing distance of one hundred miles a day.

Canals Move Heavy Loads

The new roads improved trade, but there was a limit to the weight a team of horses could pull. A horse-drawn wagon might haul about a ton of goods. Britain's new industries needed a way to ship hundreds and thousands of tons of material. How was this to be done?

Part of the answer was the canal. Canals could link centers of industry with many market areas. During the late 1700s many miles of canals were built in Great Britain. Canal barges were slow, but they could carry large amounts of goods. A horse-drawn barge could easily move fifty tons of material on a canal.

Railroads Solve Many Problems

Canals were expensive to construct and could not be built over rugged ground. A faster means of transportation which could link every part of Great Britain was needed. Inventor George Stephenson believed that the "locomotive" was the answer. He was called "mad" and out of his senses when he tried to construct one. Stephenson answered his critics with the words, "One locomotive is worth fifty horses"—and went on with his work.

In 1814 he built an engine that could pull thirty tons uphill at the speed of four miles an hour. Then, in a trial run in 1829, one of his steam locomotives reached the then extraordinary speed of twenty-nine miles an hour. Stephenson named this engine the *Rocket.*

By about 1850 Great Britain had over six thousand miles of railroad track. Goods could be shipped to and from industrial centers. People could move more rapidly throughout the country. Distant regions could be linked.

New coal mines and steel mills had to be built to provide the iron and steel needed for railroad tracks and equipment. Many new jobs were created, not only in the railroad industry but also in the factories whose products could now reach wider markets.

The Steamboat Links People by Water

Steam power could be used on water as well as on land. This fact had been demonstrated even before the coming of the railroad. A Frenchman, an Englishman, a Swiss, and a Russian all had done important work on the development of the steamboat. Then Robert Fulton, an American, proved that the steamboat could be of commercial value.

In 1807 Fulton's famous *Clermont* steamed up the Hudson River. An observer reported the amazement of the people who watched this steamboat from the banks or who heard about its journeys:

> Some imagined it to be a sea monster, whilst others did not hesitate to express their belief that it was a sign of the approaching judgment. . . . the whole country talked of nothing but the sea monster, belching forth fire and smoke.

The smoke and the fire heralded the coming of great days in water travel. In 1838 the *Great Western,* a steamship, crossed the Atlantic in a little over two weeks. After about 1860 steamboats gradually began to replace sailing ships in sea transportation.

The Telegraph and Cable Help People Communicate

As people came into closer touch by land and sea, they also were joined together by electricity. Carl Steinheil, Sir Charles Wheatstone, and Samuel F. B. Morse helped to develop the electric telegraph. This made it possible to send messages by making and breaking the current in an electric circuit. Morse's first telegraph line, between Washington and Baltimore, was opened in 1844. The first message on the line was: "What hath God wrought!"

In 1866 Cyrus W. Field arranged for the successful laying of a cable under the Atlantic Ocean. This permitted the sending of telegraphic messages across the ocean. A cable between Europe and the United States was of tremendous value. As one American President, James Buchanan, said:

> [Laying an Atlantic cable] is a triumph . . . far more useful to mankind than was ever won by a conqueror on the field of battle.

SETUP OF A CORPORATION

A corporation is owned by the stockholders. They choose directors.

Directors choose and direct officers who manage the corporation and its workers.

Directors

Officers

Workers

Part of the profits is paid as dividends to stockholders. The amount of dividends a stockholder receives depends on the amount of stock he or she holds.

The Stream of Invention Flows On

When would the stream of inventions and discoveries stop? In 1876 Alexander Graham Bell successfully demonstrated the telephone. Three years later, Thomas Edison developed the electric incandescent light. *The New York Herald* hailed it as:

> a light that produces no [harmful] gases, no smoke, no offensive odors—a light without flame, without danger, requiring no matches to ignite . . . free from all flickering . . . a little globe of sunshine, a veritable Aladdin's lamp.

Outside the United States, many similar discoveries were being made. In Russia, for example, Lodigin and others did pioneer work in developing the electric light.

Still the inventions kept coming! In 1887 Gottlieb Daimler in Germany built probably the first automobile in history. In 1901 Guglielmo Marconi in Italy perfected wireless telegraphy to a point where it could send trans-Atlantic messages. Then in 1903 the Wright brothers in the United States made a successful flight with the airplane.

When did the inventions and discoveries stop? The answer is: They never did! Neither did their effects on the Industrial Revolution as it spread to other parts of the world.

Check on Your Reading

1. How was road travel improved?
2. When did railroads become important? What economic effects did they have?
3. Explain the importance of the steamboat, the telegraph, the telephone, the transoceanic cable, the automobile, and the airplane in changing transportation and communication.

5. The Industrial Revolution and Business Organization

The Industrial Revolution created new problems in organizing and financing business. As a result, it produced important changes in the ways businesses were organized.

Earliest Forms of Business Organization

Private business was at first generally owned and operated by individuals or partners, who shared equally in the risks and rewards of an enterprise. After the fourteenth century, there was an increasing number of influential capitalists in Europe.

The explorations and overseas expansion of the fifteenth and sixteenth centuries brought a great increase in trade and business. Many expeditions were more costly than one or two persons could manage. Therefore, about 1600, joint-stock companies were organized. (See page 308.)

Part of a huge iron plant built in Germany in the nineteenth century. This plant included ovens for making coke. In front of the coking ovens molten iron is being poured into molds.

Corporations and Banks

Joint-stock companies provided one way of raising large amounts of capital. However, as business expanded during the Industrial Revolution, a better way of raising money was needed. The old joint-stock companies usually raised funds for one expedition. The industrial leaders of the 1800s needed a continuing source of large amounts of capital to build factories and machines. A new kind of business organization was needed in order to gather enough investors to raise millions of dollars. Thus, an organization known as the *corporation* became increasingly important.

In a modern corporation the public buys shares of *stock* in a company. "Buying shares of stock" means that a person is purchasing a part of the ownership of the company. The company is generally run for the stockholders by directors who receive payment for their services. If there are profits, they are divided among the stockholders according to the number of shares each holds. If there are debts, each stockholder generally is responsible only for his or her share of them—and not for all of the debts. This feature, called "limited liability," was introduced in England in 1844.

The development of *investment banks* about the middle of the nineteenth century supported the growth of corporations. These banks, particularly in France and Germany, helped to raise funds that could be invested in new enterprises.

The rise of corporations produced many significant results. Huge sums of money could be accumulated to support the growth of business. Also the corporation eventually separated the people who owned a company from those who operated it. Many stockholders of large-scale corporations never even saw the factories of their companies.

Combinations of Corporations

Beginning in the late nineteenth century, some corporations producing or selling the same or related products merged their interests. They formed organizations known as *trusts*. These organizations had several purposes: 1. They permitted several corporations to operate under one policy. 2. They could cut down costs by controlling the production or distribution of a product. 3. They could eliminate the competition from rival corporations. 4. They could regulate the price of the goods produced.

Cartels also developed in Europe. A cartel has been defined by John W. McConnell as "a relatively loose association of businessmen in similar industries in the same or different countries who agree to control the amount and method of production and sale of their product or services." Although the terms "cartel" and "trust" often were used interchangeably in Europe, they were not technically the same. One of the principal differences is that a cartel is an association of independent business firms, while a trust is an organization that brings a number of business firms under one management.

Trusts and cartels frequently disregarded the rights of smaller companies or took advantage of the public. Laws eventually were passed to regulate or break them up. On the other hand, many large-scale corporations dealt fairly with smaller organizations. They also provided the public with necessary goods at reasonable prices.

Check on Your Reading

1. What advantages were there in corporate organization?
2. Why did some corporations combine?

6. The Industrial Revolution Spreads

In time, the Industrial Revolution spread to other countries from England. The industrialization of countries developed at different times and at different rates of speed.

Europe Becomes Industrialized

Belgium was one of the first countries to use new machines and techniques to develop industry. It had natural resources, such as coal and iron, and skilled workers necessary for industrialization. Belgium had an excellent system of canals and waterways. Then in 1835, the Belgian government built one of the first railroads on the continent. Within a few years, Belgium built many miles of hard-surfaced roads and railroad tracks.

The other nations of western Europe needed to improve their transportation network in order to industrialize. Railroads provided the solution. Between 1850 and 1870 Europe tripled its railroad network. Germany led all other countries in building railroads. The independent German states had formed a customs union to do away with local taxes and other barriers to trade. This cooperation, plus the discovery of coal in the Ruhr region, encouraged the rapid building of railroads. In 1871 the German states united to form the country of Germany, and industrialization speeded up even more.

Germany's rapid rise to a leading industrial nation was encouraged by the government's help to industry. Also the government supported education in science and technology in the public schools. By 1890, Germany's output of steel had passed that of Great Britain. Only the United States produced more steel. Also German scientists had created a huge new chemical industry which made such products as dyes, drugs, and fertilizers.

The Industrial Revolution moved more slowly in France. A large industrial region grew up in the northeast near important coal and iron deposits. Also France's growing chemical industry produced the first synthetic fiber, rayon. French railroad engineers built tunnels through the Alps Mountains. The new railroad lines connected with northern Italy's growing industrial region.

Spain and Italy remained agricultural countries even though they did have some mineral resources to develop industry. Northern Italy developed some industries after Italy became a united nation in 1861.

Russia, a European and Asian country, had its principal development in industry after 1890. It had many mineral resources but it lacked capital, a supply of free labor, and the skills for early industrial growth.

United States: A Great Industrial Nation

Industry became important in the United States after 1860 as textile, steel, and shoe industries developed. Why did the United States become a great industrial nation? 1. It had a wealth of natural resources, including coal, oil, and iron. 2. Immigrants from many countries provided workers for the growing industries. 3. Some Americans had inventive skills and the ability to apply science to industry. For example, Charles Goodyear experimented with rubber, and Charles Hall discovered an inexpensive process for making aluminum from bauxite. 4. Some Americans had excellent business skills. Men like Andrew Carnegie and John D. Rockefeller built great empires in steel and oil.

5. In the twentieth century, methods of mass production were perfected. By these methods, parts of a product were turned out in large numbers in standard forms and quickly assembled into finished articles. Henry Ford was a pioneer in using mass production for automobile manufacturing. By 1918 the United States had become the leading industrial nation in the world, producing great quantities and varieties of goods.

Industry in Latin America, Asia, Africa, and the Middle East

Modern methods of industrialization were introduced to the Latin American countries in the nineteenth century. However, it required World War I and World War II to provide real stimulation to industrial growth.

As late as 1939 only one major nation in Asia was highly industrialized. That nation was Japan. Japan had adopted modern industrial methods in the latter part of the nineteenth century.

Countries in Africa and the Middle East did not seriously attempt to industrialize until comparatively recent times. One of the problems of many newly independent African states is how to modernize their economies.

Check on Your Reading

1. What countries experienced the Industrial Revolution before 1900?
2. What factors are necessary for a country to become industrialized?

LET'S MEET THE PEOPLE

A Busy Inventor

In 1827 Walter Hunt invented a gong to warn pedestrians of the approach of stagecoaches. In 1833 he invented a stove to give off heat equally in all directions. In 1847 he invented the fountain pen. In 1848 he invented suction shoes to enable people to walk upside down on ceilings. In 1849 he invented the safety pin. Yet, while other people benefited from his ideas, Hunt was forced to sell many of his inventions for small sums in order to pay off his debts. Those that he kept brought him little profit.

Finally, Hunt had one last chance. Between 1832 and 1834 he had invented the first workable model of a sewing machine that could sew a lock stitch. However, it had never been patented.

In 1846 Elias Howe patented a sewing machine similar in principle to that of Walter Hunt's machine. Isaac M. Singer also manufactured the same type of sewing machine and became involved in a lawsuit with Howe over patent rights. Hunt believed that when the suit came to trial, he himself would surely receive reward as the first inventor of the lock-stitch sewing machine. Hunt was wrong again. The judge ruled that he was not entitled to legal rights to the machine.

It seemed that Walter Hunt would never make a fortune. However, in 1858, Isaac M. Singer called him to his office and said: "We'll give you $50,000 [in installments] for all [of your] claims against our sewing machine." Hunt accepted the offer at once. At last he would be rich. Then— shortly before the first payment was to be made—Walter Hunt died!

The above sketch is based on primary source materials in an article, "The Man Who Invented Just About Everything" by David A. Weiss, reprinted from *Coronet*, August 1956, and on extracts from Howe v. Underwood, "12 Federal Cases," © 1956 by Esquire, Inc., as they appear in Roger Burlingame, *March of the Iron Men*, 1949, Charles Scribner's Sons.

CHAPTER REVIEW

Think and Discuss

1. Why did the first inventions occur in the textile industry?
2. Is the adage "Necessity is the mother of invention" true? Apply it to inventions mentioned in this chapter.
3. Often a single invention can change or affect an entire industry. How did the railroads affect the steel industry? How did the telegraph affect the railroads?
4. What problems face a country that does not have natural resources for industry?
5. Why is foreign trade necessary to most industrialized nations?

Past and Present

1. When the Industrial Revolution began, many people began moving from farms to find work in cities. Is the movement of people in our country today still from farming areas to urban areas? Why?
2. What is the chief difference between the Industrial Revolution in the 1700s and the 1800s and the great industrial changes occurring today?

Activities

1. Debate the statement: Living before the Industrial Revolution was more desirable than living in the period after the Industrial Revolution.
2. If you are interested in farming, make a report on stock-breeding in Britain in the 1700s. Many of our breeds of pigs, horses, cattle, and sheep were developed in that period.
3. Make a chart of inventions, inventors, and the countries in which important inventions were made for the period from 1750 to 1860. What are your conclusions?
4. Try to find an example of single ownership, a partnership, and a corporation in your community.

25

The Industrial Revolution Changes
Ways of Living, Thinking, and Creating

KEYNOTE

In 1754 a trip from Manchester, England, to London, England, took four and one-half days. Today a supersonic commercial plane can cross the Atlantic Ocean in three and a half hours!

However much twentieth-century machines startle our imagination, we must not underestimate the importance of the far simpler machines of centuries ago. Certainly, the Industrial Revolution in the period from about 1750 to 1860 left its mark on European culture. It affected conditions of life in the cities, contributed to the development of economic theories, and influenced the work of writers, artists, and composers.

This painting of a railroad was created by the famous English artist J.M.W. Turner.

Great Britain 1700-1911

Great Britain had the coal and iron deposits necessary for industrialization. Urbanization developed rapidly, as the two maps show.

1. Machines Change People's Lives

The Industrial Revolution created new jobs, new opportunities, and new problems. It also drastically changed the ways of life that grew out of old traditions. The lives we lead today have been greatly affected by the enormous changes brought about by the Industrial Revolution.

From Home to Factory

In 1750, most people in England grew their own food and made most of their own clothes and the other things that they needed. Most people lived in the country in small farming villages. Organized manufacturing took place on a small scale. Outside of the cities, cloth and other products were often produced in individual homes. Employers provided the raw materials to working families that, in turn, made the finished product. The employer paid each working family for its labor, collected the finished material, and sold it for profit.

Many families combined farming with some form of home industry. Wives worked with their husbands as partners. The family was an economic unit. Each member contributed her or his labor for the benefit of the family. Quite often the wages women earned from spinning or weaving carried the family through poor harvests. A writer of the time said a wife could "produce nearly as much money in the course of a year as her husband by all his labour during the same time." Also some women were in charge of profitable businesses, such as dairying, making cheese, and brewing. Other women were working partners in some of the small businesses and craft shops in towns and cities.

The new inventions and sources of power gradually brought an end to most of the small family industries. Older hand methods could not match the speed of machines run by water or steam power. Large power-driven machinery made it necessary to shift work from the home to the factory. Workers at home had usually finished the entire product from raw materials. Inside the factory, work began to be divided into many smaller tasks. Factory workers spent their days operating machines to make or assemble parts of the product.

The change, however, was not a sudden break with the past. In some countries, a simple factory system had existed in some industries for some time.

Workers went to a factory or a large workshop where a great many of them worked for the owner, each doing some work by hand or using a simple hand-operated machine. The silk industry of France, the Low Countries, and Prussia was operated this way. Cannon foundries and shipbuilding yards were also run under this system.

In time, the beginnings of the modern factory system replaced both work at home and the earlier factory system. Under the modern factory system, as it first developed, the factory, tools, and materials were generally owned by *capitalists,* who hired the workers. *Capital* is wealth used to produce additional wealth. People who used their factories, tools, and materials (or wealth) to turn out more goods are called *capitalists.*

After about 1780, an increasing number of men, women, and children left their homes to seek work in factories and mines. They came for many reasons: 1. Some had lost their farms by the enclosure movement and wanted jobs. 2. Some were part of the labor surplus that resulted from the rapid increase in population. 3. Others were immigrants from Ireland who sought jobs in industry. 4. Still others, particularly children, were paupers who were assembled by unfair tactics.

Population Changes and Urbanization

The shift to factory work was helped by the rapid growth of population in Western Europe. Im-

provements in medical care meant that more children survived and that people lived longer. In the past, many workers had delayed marriage until they had mastered the difficult skills of their trade and could earn a living. Machines reduced the need for highly skilled workers. People began to marry earlier and have larger families. During the early days of factories a large family was valuable. Children added to a family's income by working in the factories.

Western Europe's growing population swelled the size of towns and cities. Cities also drew immigrants who could not find work in their own countries. The shift from the farms to the towns and cities meant more and more people were available to work in the growing factories.

This shift also meant the gradual urbanization of the population of industrializing countries. By 1914, eighty percent of the population of Britain lived in urban areas. Sixty percent of all Germans, fifty percent of Americans, and forty-five percent of the French were urban.

Some cities grew so quickly that they could not provide adequate housing or sanitary conditions for the new working inhabitants. Cheap housing was hastily constructed. Overcrowding was so bad that entire families often shared single rooms. Many houses did not have running water. One worker, who had to get water a quarter of a mile away, said, "We can't use it for cooking . . . but only for drink-

The industrial city of Leeds in 1885.

ing and tea." Water for cooking and washing came from the river. The same worker said the river "is muddy and often stinks because all the filth is carried there." In "Frying Pan Alley" in London, houses were built over sewers. According to the government's *Report on the State of Large Towns and Populous Districts,* a tenant told an investigator:

> That hole [in the room] is over a common sewer and the rats come up, sometimes twenty at a time, and if we did not watch for them they would eat the baby up.

Large slum areas soon expanded outwards from factories and railroad centers. Garbage and sewage piled up faster than the means to remove them properly. As the sewage seeped into the water supply, disease increased sharply. It took some years before people recognized the connection between impure water and diseases like typhoid. Smokestacks of factories belched black smoke so thick that often the sun was only a dim disc at noon.

Slowly some cities began to work on these problems. Sewers were improved and water was purified. Laws were passed setting building standards. Zoning laws prevented factories from being built too close to areas where people lived. Work on these problems continues today.

The Factory System: Good or Evil?

When the workers moved to the factories and mines, their ways of living came to depend on the treatment they received in the new industrial centers. How were they treated in the factories and mines during the Industrial Revolution? At one time the answer generally given to this question was: "With unbelievable harshness!"

There was considerable evidence to support this view. Factory discipline was very strict, and a worker could even be fined for "leaving his oil can out of place." Wages were low for most workers, and some women and children labored for as little as two dollars a week—or less. Factories had few safety devices. Little attention was paid to preserving the health of workers. The work day was very long, even for children. Housing for workers was usually wretched.

Women and children worked in the coal mines from twelve to sixteen hours a day. If they fell asleep at their work, they could be beaten with the "billy roller," a heavy rod. Some of the children were only four and five years old.

On the other hand, recent scholarship indicates that conditions may not have been as bad in English factories and mines as once was believed. Certainly, only the worst abuses received publicity, and there were a number of laborers who had satisfactory working conditions. The factory system in England was accompanied by many abuses in factories and mines, but living and working conditions were not evil everywhere. They varied with the time, the place, and the employer. Some employers were genuinely concerned for the welfare of their workers.

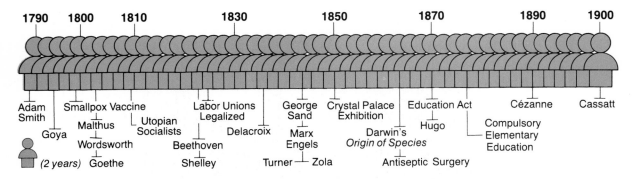

1790 1800 1810 1830 1850 1870 1890 1900

Adam Smith
Goya
(2 years)
Smallpox Vaccine
Malthus
Wordsworth
Goethe
Utopian Socialists
Labor Unions Legalized
Beethoven
Shelley
Delacroix
George Sand
Marx Engels
Turner
Zola
Crystal Palace Exhibition
Darwin's *Origin of Species*
Antiseptic Surgery
Education Act
Hugo
Cézanne
Compulsory Elementary Education
Cassatt

Check on Your Reading

1. How did many families work as an economic unit before the Industrial Revolution?
2. What were the features of the factory system?
3. Describe early working conditions.

2. The Industrial Revolution and Reform

The Industrial Revolution stimulated serious discussion of the attitudes that people should take toward their economic system. One of the most important questions raised was this: To what extent should a government regulate the economic activities of its people?

A Scottish scholar named Adam Smith proposed an answer even before the factory system had grown to any extent. Smith died before many of the great changes of the Industrial Revolution. Nevertheless, his writing influenced the thinking of every generation down to the present.

Adam Smith and "Laissez Faire"

Adam Smith (1723-1790) served as a professor at the University of Glasgow for a number of years. He presented many of his ideas in a book known as *The Wealth of Nations.* Adam Smith supported the idea of "laissez faire":

Every man, as long as he does not violate the laws of justice, [should be] left perfectly free to pursue his own interest his own way, and to bring both his industry and capital into competition with those of any other man, or order of men.

"Laissez faire," he believed, would promote the economic well-being of a nation by promoting the economic well-being of individuals through free competition.

Adam Smith also pointed out that "the man whose whole life is spent performing a few simple operations under division of labor, of which the effects are perhaps always the same, or very nearly the same . . . generally becomes as stupid and ignorant as it is possible for a human creature to become." Smith declared that this would occur unless the government "takes some pains to prevent it."

In other words, Adam Smith was not opposed to all government action. Rather, he wanted to keep government interference in private affairs to a minimum.

Thomas Malthus and David Ricardo Make Gloomy Predictions

Two other writers who lived after Adam Smith made some gloomy predictions about the future of poor working people. In 1798 Malthus wrote that the population was growing at a faster rate than the supply of food. This meant that every so often the population would be reduced by famine or disease. The poorest people would be hurt the most as they were the least able to pay for food and health care.

David Ricardo suggested that it was almost impossible for workers' wages to rise above the bare level of subsistence. Ricardo's theory was that when wages rose, workers had larger families. This meant more workers had to compete for jobs. This, in turn, would bring wages down and the number of workers would decline as people starved. When the number of workers became scarce, wages would rise again. Ricardo argued that no government laws or labor unions could prevent this from happening.

Reformers Work for Change

Despite these theories, many people wanted the government to take a more active part in economic activities. They were disturbed by evils in the factory system, and they wanted the government to correct many abuses.

These reformers tried various methods. Some sought to pass laws to help working people. Others tried to establish unions, organize co-operatives, introduce socialism, or uproot the economic system.

Legislation Improves Working Conditions

The British Parliament was not blind to the evils that accompanied the factory system. It established parliamentary committees to investigate conditions in factories. These committees interviewed workers, supervisors, and others. Their reports led some members of Parliament to work for reform. Other representatives were motivated by more practical political reasons. As more people obtained the right to vote, a politician who wished to be re-elected had to pay increasing attention to the voters!

For these reasons, laws were passed to improve living and working conditions. These laws were approved only after a hard fight. Many members of Parliament continued to resist change.

The Factory Act of 1833 was a landmark in labor legislation. It included the following: 1. It prohibited the employment of children under the age of nine in silk mills. 2. It limited children under

thirteen to nine hours of work a day. 3. It set maximum workday of twelve hours for those between the ages of thirteen and eighteen. Factory inspectors were to enforce its provisions.

Equally important, this act pointed the way to further reform. In 1847, a law was passed that limited women and children to ten hours of work a day in factories. Other significant labor laws were passed later.

In the twentieth century, legislation was approved that provided compensation to the injured worker, pensions to the old, and insurance to the unemployed and sick.

Reform of Education

The Industrial Revolution stimulated the education of adults in Scotland and England. For example, after 1823 industrial engineers and mechanics who wished to add to their education could attend Mechanics' Institutes.

Legislation was needed to strengthen education. Not until 1833 did Parliament make its first grant for public education. Even in the middle of the nineteenth century, one-half of English children received no regular school training!

The Education Act of 1870 was an important step forward. It provided for the establishment of

This print shows Elizabeth Fry visiting Newgate prison in 1818. She was a leader in the movement to improve conditions in prisons.

This print shows Florence Nightingale checking the wounded in a hospital in Turkey during the Crimean War. She returned to Britain after the war to spend the rest of her life improving the nursing profession. Women played a key role in improving conditions in hospitals.

secular schools where church schools were insufficient to educate all of the students. It permitted local school boards—if they wished—to establish compulsory school attendance for those between the ages of six and thirteen. In 1876, elementary education was made compulsory by law.

Labor Unions Are Organized

Some people in England believed that the establishment of labor *unions* was one of the best ways of improving the conditions of workers. Unions often strive for higher wages, shorter hours, and better working conditions for their members. They carry on much of their work by *collective bargaining*. This means that the members of the union, usually through their leaders, act as a group in bargaining with an employer. When unions do not gain their objectives by bargaining, they sometimes *strike*.

At the beginning of the 1800s labor unions were illegal in England. The wealthy tailor Francis Place, the physician Joseph Hume, and others led the fight to win recognition for unions. In 1824 Parliament made labor unions legal. However, there were so many labor disturbances that a law in 1825 practically prohibited unions from striking and from forming into permanent organizations.

Workers made some gains in the next half century, but labor unions often were checked in their efforts to organize properly and perform their functions. In 1871, the right of unions to exist was again declared by law.

In the first decade of the twentieth century, the position of labor unions finally became secure in England. The right of unions to strike peacefully also became firmly established. Today unions are of great importance in England and in many countries of the world.

Co-operatives Are Tried

Some reformers tried to improve living conditions by *co-operatives*. There were several types of co-operatives. A *producers' co-operative* was generally an organization of workers to control the production and sale of the goods they turned out. The members of producers' co-operatives hoped to produce and sell their goods more advantageously than they could separately.

Far more successful were *consumers' co-operatives*.

A consumers' co-operative was generally an organization of people who shared in the purchase of goods and the resale of such goods to members of the co-operative (and often nonmembers). The members of a consumers' co-operative hoped to obtain good merchandise at less expense than if they bought separately.

Efforts to establish co-operatives won the support of important leaders in Great Britain. Co-operatives also became quite successful among farmers' organizations in Denmark, Sweden, Norway, and Finland.

Check on Your Reading

1. Explain the ideas of Adam Smith.
2. What were the predictions of Thomas Malthus and David Ricardo?
3. Why were laws on work and on education enacted?
4. How did labor unions and co-operatives try to help workers and consumers?

3. Socialists and Communists Offer Different Solutions

Many of the reformers who sought change through laws, unions, and co-operatives still believed in the capitalist system. See page 426 for a description of this system. Other reformers felt that capitalism itself had caused many of society's problems.

Many of these people were *socialists*, and the system they favored is known as *socialism*. Although they differed, the socialists in general agreed on six basic ideas: 1. Excessive competition for private profit was not good and brought evils. 2. Private property caused many problems. 3. The public should own many of the means of production (such as factories and mines), and the means of distribution (such as railways and ships). 4. Consumer goods (such as homes and clothing) should continue to be owned privately. 5. Individuals should work according to their ability and receive according to their work. 6. Socialism should be achieved by peaceful, gradual, and legal means.

Utopian Socialists

Some of the more idealistic socialists are known as the *Utopian Socialists*. Utopia refers to a place or situation of ideal perfection, usually impossible to attain. There were many different groups of Utopian Socialists, and they did not agree on all of their aims. In general, they wanted to establish ide. and self-sufficient societies, or Utopias.

The Utopian Socialists of the nineteenth century wanted to eliminate poverty, unhappiness, and conflict. The members of Utopian societies were to

- use reason to free themselves from greed, selfishness, and desire for private gain.
- own or control together the means of producing and distributing goods.
- live and work together as a harmonious community.
- share together the fruits of their labor.

The Utopian Socialists believed that the success of such communities would encourage some capitalists to turn over their holdings to similar communal societies.

The dream of a perfect community was an ancient one. The Greek philosopher Plato had written about a Utopia. Between 1600 and 1700, there were nine important books about Utopias.

In the first half of the nineteenth century outstanding Utopian Socialists were the Frenchmen, Claude Henri de Saint-Simon (1760–1825) and François Fourier (1772–1837), and the British industrialist Robert Owen (1771–1858). However, the several Utopian communities that were set up in Europe and America were not permanently successful. They lasted for a time, and then broke up as the members disputed over various problems.

Despite the ultimate failure of their communities, the Utopian Socialists stirred up considerable debate over the need for changing society. They prepared the ground for the more revolutionary seeds.

Radicals Seek to Uproot the Capitalistic System

The word "radical" has meant different things to different people. Actually, it comes from the Latin "radix"—meaning "root." A radical, therefore, is a person who wishes to solve a problem by going to its roots. A radical wants immediate, fundamental, and extreme changes made in government and society. Two of the most important radicals of the 1800s were Karl Marx and Friedrich Engels.

Marx (1818–1883) and Engels (1820–1895) worked to form the basis for what is known today as *communism*. Engels was the son of a well-to-do textile manufacturer. He had managed a factory of his father's in Britain. Engels and Marx first met

's vividly described many of the
~~ons~~ of workers in the *Condition of the*
~~ss in England in 1844.~~

~~to~~gether Marx and Engels wrote the revolution-
~~a~~y *Communist Manifesto* (1848). They called for all
the world's workers to unite against the owners of
industry in a great revolution.

Marx became involved in an attempted revolution in Germany. When it failed, he fled to England, where he wrote *Capital* (1867), a book which
explained his theories. Engels edited and contributed to two more volumes of this work.

The Ideas of Karl Marx

The major ideas of Karl Marx and his disciples,
with the objections raised by scholarly critics, are
discussed below.

1. ECONOMIC INTERPRETATION OF
HISTORY. Marxists took the view that the events
and institutions of society and history are basically
determined by economic forces. Thus the method
by which people produce and exchange goods is
said to be the foundation for their political, social,
religious, and cultural activities.

Objections: The economic interpretation over-
simplifies history. There have been major events
that were not based primarily on economics. The
growth of the Christian Church is one example.

2. SURPLUS VALUE THEORY. The Marx-
ists believe that the value of the goods produced
rests on the "human labor" that goes into their production. They claim that despite the fact that
workers produce the goods, they receive only low
wages. Most of the profit that comes from the sale
of the goods is taken by the capitalists, the people
who own the factories and the other means of production. Thus, the capitalists grow richer and the
workers poorer.

Objections: Economists point out that there are
many people who give value to goods by providing
buildings, tools, materials, and ideas to help produce goods. "Capitalists," too, are entitled to reward.

Moreover, despite some areas of poverty, the poor
are not growing poorer in the United States or in
most industrialized countries of Europe. With the
growth of unions, collective bargaining, and labor
legislation, workers in these countries generally are
given a substantial part of the value of the goods
they produce.

It is true that there is still great poverty in Asia,
the Middle East, Africa, and in other places. But
these areas are mainly agricultural, not industrial.
Milovan Djilas has pointed out, "Marx's theories
about the increasing impoverishment of the working
class were not borne out by developments in those
countries [industrialized Europe] from which his
theories [were] derived." Djilas is a once prominent Communist leader who broke with the Communist party of Yugoslavia.

3. CLASS STRUGGLE. The Marxists took the
view that inevitably there is a continuous struggle
between the *proletariat* (the wage workers) and the
bourgeoisie (those who own or control the means of
production and exchange). This class struggle is a
bitter and hateful one.

Thus, Marx and Engels wrote in the *Communist
Manifesto*, "The history of all hitherto existing society is the history of class struggles. Freeman and
slave, patrician and plebeian, lord and serf . . . in a
word, oppressor and oppressed."

Objections: Marxists overlooked the rise of the
vast *middle class,* including industrial workers receiving good wages, salaried workers engaged in basically nonmanual jobs, professional people, and
many others. This middle class has served as a bal-
ancing factor to prevent great extremes which Marx
counted upon to bring about the class struggle.

4. USE OF FORCE. The Marxists took the
view that the proletariat have the right to use force
to overthrow the bourgeoisie and seize control of a
country. Karl Marx admitted that in certain countries the proletariat might attain their objectives
without violence. However, Marx believed in the
general necessity for the use of force.

Objections: Violence destroys people physically.
It degrades the role that reason can play in the
settlement of problems. It fails to see that major
changes can be made peacefully in democratic societies.

5. DICTATORSHIP OF THE PROLETAR-
IAT. The Marxists took the view that after the
proletariat overthrow the bourgeoisie by force there
will be a temporary period in which the proletariat
dictate to the bourgeoisie until all opposition is
wiped out. Class distinctions will be abolished and
a classless society will emerge.

Objections: What has resulted has been the dictatorship of a small group of people in the Communist party over the proletariat and over everyone

else in the country. Instead of being temporary, the dictatorship of the Soviet Union has already lasted over six decades. Indeed a "new class" of Communist bureaucrats has arisen. Such dictatorship has led to frantic efforts to escape on the part of many people.

6. THE ESTABLISHMENT OF COMMUNISM. Marxists took the view that during the period of dictatorship of the proletariat, the state "withers away" and communism eventually is established. Under communism, there would be only public ownership of the means of production, distribution, and consumption. This would eliminate competition among people for profit. Since there would be no classes, there would be no class struggle. Each person would work according to her or his ability and receive according to need, as directed by the people for the good of all.

Objections: Communism in practice has seen a constant strengthening of the power and size of governments rather than a withering away. The result has been more regulation and an increasing bureaucracy rather than less. It is ironical that the ideas of Marx, to whom the all-powerful state was abhorrent, should have contributed to statism.

Check on Your Reading

1. What are the basic ideas of socialism?
2. What did the various Utopian Socialists have in common?
3. What are the major ideas of Karl Marx and his followers? What were the objections raised by the people who were critical of Marx's ideas?

4. The Industrial Revolution and the Arts

The effects of the Industrial Revolution were not limited to economic affairs. Industrial changes also influenced—and were influenced by—literature, art and architecture, and music.

Romanticism in Literature

Authors, known as Romantic writers, sought escape from the dreariness of daily life. They saw the ugly side of industrial society and turned to nature and what they saw as the "romantic past." They gave freedom to their emotions and believed in self-expression—in expressing their personal feelings.

The last part of the eighteenth and the first half of the nineteenth century often is called the "Ro-

Charlotte Bronte's novel Jane Eyre was a great success in 1847. Her novels show a feeling for the problems of childhood and the darker side of human nature as well as a love of the beauties of nature.

mantic Period" of English literature. In England, William Blake (1757-1827), an artist and poet, wrote poetry that expressed his misty visions of a highly imaginative world. This was particularly true of his poems in *Songs of Innocence*. The famous Scottish poet and novelist Sir Walter Scott (1771-1832) filled his historical novels—*Ivanhoe, Kenilworth,* and others—with romantic adventures drawn from legend. Samuel Taylor Coleridge (1772-1834) wrote poems—such as the well-known *The Rime of the Ancient Mariner*—that were marked by a supernatural and eerie quality.

Other writers turned to nature. William Wordsworth (1770-1850), one of the most noted poets, and Samuel Taylor Coleridge wrote *Lyrical Ballads*. In this work, Wordsworth urged people to turn to "humble and rustic life" because "in that condition the essential passions of the heart find a better soil

an attain their maturity." Lord By-
_, in *Childe Harold, Don Juan,* and
_, not only described nature beautifully,
_ attacked the hypocrisy of society. John
_eats (1795-1821) lived only a short life, but he
produced romantic poetry of great beauty. His
command of language and his love of beauty dominate his famous "Ode on a Grecian Urn." In his
long poem *Endymion* he wrote the famous line: "A
thing of beauty is a joy forever. . . ."

In France, the poet-dramatist-novelist Victor
Hugo (1802-1885) was the leading figure of French
romantic literature. Hugo's ability to analyze human behavior and to depict a variety of characters
was outstanding. *Notre Dame de Paris (The Hunch-
back of Notre Dame)* and *Les Misérables* are two of his
famous novels. Alexandré Dumas, the Elder
(1802-1870), wrote historical novels of intrigue and
adventure. Two of his novels, *The Three Musketeers*
and *The Count of Monte Cristo,* are familiar to many
readers.

Amandine Lucie Aurore Dupin, who wrote under the pen name of George Sand (1804-1876), has
been called both romanticist and, to a degree, realist. She started by writing romantic novels, but
soon became deeply concerned with the realities of
social problems.

In Germany, poet-dramatist-novelist Johann
Wolfgang von Goethe (1749-1832) wrote several
outstanding works. One of his most famous is the
poetic drama *Faust.* "I am ever the new-born
child," Goethe said; and he wrote like a person who
discovers something fresh and fascinating in the
world each day.

Romanticism in American literature developed
later. Washington Irving (1783-1859), sometimes
called the "father of American literature," wrote
such popular romantic stories as "The Legend of
Sleepy Hollow" and "Rip Van Winkle." Nathaniel Hawthorne (1804-1864) wrote about the inner
conflicts of men and women in his novels *The Scarlet
Letter* and *The House of the Seven Gables.* Edgar Allan
Poe (1809-1849), who played a major role in the
development of the short story, is famous for his
tales and poetry of mystery and suspense. His
poem "The Raven" and his tales "The Purloined
Letter" and "The Pit and the Pendulum" are well
known.

A great American essayist and poet, Ralph
Waldo Emerson (1803-1882) was strongly influenced by European romantic writers and mystics.
Walt Whitman (1819-1892) was a product of
American democracy. He glorified the plain people and their work in his poetry. He is best known
for a volume of poetry, *Leaves of Grass.* In the pref-
ace he wrote:

> The United States themselves are essentially
> the greatest poem. . . . Here at last is
> something in the doings of man that corresponds
> with the broadest doings of the day and night.
> Here is action untied from strings. . . .

Romanticism in Art

Like many romantic writers, artists turned to nature and the emotions for their themes. In England
John Constable (1776-1837) painted lovely scenes
of the countryside. Placing paint on the canvas in

On page 434 is Dante Gabriel Rossetti's painting The Blessed Damozel. *Above is John Constable's* A View of Salisbury Cathedral. *Below, Delacroix's painting of a lion hunt.*

lots of color, he created works that ... ...on of light playing over a surface. ...urner (1775-1851) painted poetic land- ... in which objects seem to dissolve into light. ...urner demonstrated that there can also be beauty in the relationships of mechanical objects to nature.

Dante Gabriel Rossetti (1828-1882) and a group of friends in England reacted against the Industrial Revolution. They turned to painting the legends of the Middle Ages and the mysterious beauties of nature. They also worked to revive the crafts, the making of objects by hand rather than by machinery. Some of the members of this group were poets. Dante Gabriel Rossetti wrote and illustrated a long romantic poem, "The Blessed Damozel." He was the brother of Christina Georgina Rossetti, who also became known for her poetry.

The leader of the French Romantic movement in painting was Eugène Delacroix (c. 1798-1863). Delacroix chose his subjects from literature and history. Another French painter, Camille Corot (1796-1875), painted landscapes into which he infused an aura of mystery and romance. The famous paintings of animals by Rosa Bonheur (1822-1899) seemed to merge an inner romanticism with elements of realism.

Romanticism in Music

Several of the leading romantic composers were German. Ludwig van Beethoven (1770-1827) was a genius whose works cannot all be fitted into a single type of music. As music historian Helen L. Kaufmann states:

> In his improvements on the formal side, Beethoven belongs with the classical school. But his strides toward greater freedom and more individual expressiveness take him straight into the camp of the romantic composers of the nineteenth century. . . . It is best to think of Beethoven in large general terms.

Beethoven brought a strong note of Romanticism to music. He demonstrated that music could superbly express deep emotions and intense and idealistic feelings. He composed nine symphonies, many piano sonatas, several concertos, and other musical works. Among Beethoven's symphonies are the *Third*, or *Eroica*, and his magnificent *Ninth*, or *Choral*.

Felix Mendelssohn (1809-1847) created many

Ludwig van Beethoven was a genius whose music cannot be fitted into a single style.

musical works that expressed great romantic feeling. One of his best-known compositions is *Overture to a Midsummer Night's Dream*. Another important work on a religious theme is *Elijah*.

Richard Wagner (1813-1883) wrote many operas built around the legends of the past. Among his famous operas are *Tristan and Isolde, Tannhäuser,* and *Lohengrin*. Wagner stressed the dramatic qualities of opera, and skillfully fused words, music, and actions into a powerful whole that reflected philosophic ideas.

Johannes Brahms (1833-1897) continued the musical tradition of Beethoven. Music historian Helen L. Kaufmann declares "[Brahms] may be labelled neoclassic, but trailing scarlet robes of romanticism cling about him." Among the well-known works by Brahms are the *Lullaby, Hungarian Dances,* and *Symphony No. 4 in E Minor*.

Hector Berlioz (1803-1869), a French composer,

wrote considerable *program music;* that is, music that relates a story, depicts a character, or describes an event. His *Requiem* and *Fantastic Symphony* are well known.

Frederic Chopin (c. 1810-1849), a Polish-French composer, wrote many piano compositions. In his music he often used the rhythms of Polish peasant dances. The Hungarian Franz Liszt (1811-1886) was a superb pianist. He also composed the *Hungarian Rhapsodies.*

Voices of Protest in Britain

Some British writers used their pens as swords to fight for reforms. One of these was the romantic poet Percy Bysshe Shelley (1792-1822). He was concerned with the inequalities among people. He told the working people:

> The seed ye sow, another reaps;
> The wealth ye find, another keeps;
> The robes ye weave, another wears;
> The arms ye forge, another bears.

Shelley urged people to free themselves from selfish and tyrannical masters. He wrote:

> Shake your chains to earth, like dew!
> Ye are many, they are few!

Thomas Carlyle (1795-1881) pointed out the ugly aspects of industrialization. In his book *Sartor Resartus (The Tailor Retailored),* he attacked these evils:

> Call you that a Society [asks Professor Teufelsdröckh] where . . . each [person] . . . regardless of his neighbor, turns against his neighbor, clutches what he can get and cries, "Mine!" and calls it Peace, because in the cutpurse and cut-throat Scramble no steel knives . . . can be employed?

Charles Dickens (1812-1870) was the most famous realistic English novelist of his day. He personally had experienced the hardships of poverty. In his books, particularly *Hard Times, Oliver Twist,* and *David Copperfield,* he vividly pictured wretched living and working conditions. In *Oliver Twist,* he showed the ill treatment that children received in poorhouses and how slums bred crime and delinquency. Meanwhile, the activities of Elizabeth Gurney Fry (1780-1845) had called attention to the need for prison reform.

John Ruskin (1819-1900) was an art critic and writer as well as a reformer. He declared:

> Even a laborer serves his country with his spade and shovel as the statesman does with his pen, or the soldier with his sword.

Realistic Literature

Realistic writers of the nineteenth century, such as Charles Dickens, tried to describe the lives of people as honestly as possible. They were concerned with the actual activities of men and women and their problems.

French realistic literature was dominated for many years by Honoré de Balzac (1799-1850). In a series of ninety-four novels, novelettes, and short stories, called *The Human Comedy,* Balzac depicts contemporary French society. His characters show the effects of greed, misery, and self-satisfaction on their lives.

Emile Zola (1840-1902) attempted to be naturalistic and as objective as possible in depicting the life of his day. He showed the grim, sordid aspects of human life.

The American writer Mark Twain (1835-1910) often used humor to comment on what he considered to be evil in society. He disliked undemocratic distinctions between people. He believed that, like certain vegetables, the differences among people were often a result of their rearing. "Cauliflower," he declared, "is nothing but cabbage with a college education." Mark Twain is well known for his novels *The Adventures of Tom Sawyer* and *The Adventures of Huckleberry Finn.* Another American author, Stephen Crane (1871-1900), wrote realistic novels. His most famous novel is *The Red Badge of Courage.*

Henrik Ibsen (1828-1906), a Norwegian dramatist, wrote a number of realistic plays. He stirred up considerable controversy with his plays *A Doll's House* and *An Enemy of the People.* In them, he exposed the hypocrisy and false values and ideals in the society of his day.

Realism in Art

Many artists turned from Romanticism to Realism. One of the earliest painters to portray realistic themes in his art was Francisco Goya (1746-1828). As the official painter of the Spanish king, he did many portraits. Goya also showed the struggles of the Spaniards against Napoleon's army. The horror and suffering inflicted by war are pictured in many of his paintings, such as *The Third of May, 1808.*

In France, Jean François Millet (1814-1875) painted scenes showing the everyday life of farmers. For example, *The Gleaners* shows three women gleaning (gathering) grain. Gustave Courbet (1819-1877) also painted the life of the workers and farmers. Courbet's *The Stone Breakers* shows peasants removing stones from fields.

Honoré Daumier (1808-1879) kept his art close to the people. Daumier was a brilliant newspaper illustrator for many years. In his satirical drawings, he attacked dishonesty, hypocrisy, poverty, and social injustice. He showed the strength of character of ordinary men and women.

In the United States, Winslow Homer (1836-1910), a realistic artist, painted seascapes and fishermen at work. His paintings *The Maine Coast* and *The Herring Net* are two of his well-known works.

Impressionism in Art and Music

Impressionism in art began during the 1870s. According to art historian Sarah Newmeyer, impressionism is art in which the painters "attempted to record on canvas not what they knew was form but what they saw as light." The term "Impressionists" came from a reference to a painting by the French artist Claude Monet entitled *Impression, Rising Sun.* The French artist Édouard Manet (1832-1883) was the chief forerunner of Impressionism. The French painters—Claude Monet (1840-1926), Camille Pissarro (1830-1903), and Pierre Auguste Renoir (1841-1919) were leading Impressionists. Alfred Sisley (1839-1899) was another important Impressionist artist.

Impressionism developed in other countries, too. Mary Cassatt (1845-1926), an American, went to

"The Advocates" by Honoré Daumier. He used his genius to depict realistically the social injustice, dishonesty, and poverty in the world around him.

Above, "The Banks of the Seine" by Claude Monet. At the left below, a painting by
Mary Cassatt. At the right below, Pierre Auguste Renoir's painting of a couple at the theater.

At the left, a still life by Paul Cezánne. Below, "The Starry Night" by Vincent Van Gogh.

study in Paris when she was in her twenties. In time she became famous for her paintings of women and children in their everyday activities.

Impressionist art had these features: 1. It showed the momentary play of light on objects, particularly outdoor light. 2. More attention was given to primary colors than to line. 3. Impressionism tried to create an impression of an action that could be gone in a moment, such as that of a woman about to take off her gloves. 4. Spontaneity was stressed. 5. It viewed objects from unusual angles. 6. The artist used "undisguised" brush strokes.

Claude Monet captured the Impressionists' spirit when he said "he wished that he had been born blind and then had suddenly gained his sight so that he would have begun to paint without knowing what the objects were that he saw before him."

Some French artists used Impressionism to develop their own styles of painting. Edgar Degas (1834-1917) was famous for his paintings of ballet dancers. Toulouse-Lautrec (1864-1901) was well known for his impressions of café life.

Other artists, *post-Impressionists,* tried to correct what they considered to be deficiencies in Impressionist art. The post-Impressionists included the French artists Paul Cézanne (1839-1906) and Paul Gauguin (1848-1903), and the Dutch artist Vincent Van Gogh (1853-1890). Paul Gauguin spent the later years of his life in Tahiti. In his paintings he captured the bright colors of the tropics and obtained striking results with pure colors and design. Vincent Van Gogh poured his own feelings into his work. Flaming colors and twisting forms dominate his painting.

Paul Cézanne was to have an important effect on twentieth-century art. He is often called the "father of modern art," and he influenced the development of *Cubism, Expressionism,* and other styles. He gave the light in his paintings an appearance of permanence. He tried to show that nature could be reduced in art to certain basic forms, such as the cube, cone, and cylinder. Cézanne said:

> I wanted to make Impressionism into something as solid and durable as the art of the museums.

Impressionism also became a style of music. Such music *suggests* mood or emotion, rather than presents emotion boldly and dramatically. The French composer Claude Debussy (1862-1918) was stimulated by the paintings of Renoir and other Impressionist painters. His compositions include *Nocturnes for Orchestra* and *The Sea.* One of the best ways to understand what Impressionism is in music is to listen to one of his compositions.

The Arts Come within the Reach of Many People

Before the Industrial Revolution, painters, writers, and composers often worked for kings, queens, nobles, wealthy merchants and business people, or the Church. Most paintings were in churches or the private homes of the wealthy. Many composers, such as Franz Joseph Haydn, lived and worked in the household of a noble. Books were very expensive. Except for viewing some art in public buildings, most people seldom saw paintings or sculpture.

During the 1800s more and more people were able to enjoy the work of writers, painters, and composers. Managers, supervisors, clerks, and other members of the growing middle class had money to spend. Art dealers and publishers were eager to sell to this new market. Improvements in printing machinery lowered the cost of printing books, magazines, and newspapers.

In Britain three times as many books were published in the 1850s as in the 1820s. To lower prices, books were published in monthly installments. Many works of Charles Dickens were sold in this way. In France, newspaper owners cut their prices and accepted advertising. To increase the number of readers, newspapers published novels in serial form. Soon anyone who could afford a newspaper could read novels by Balzac and Dumas.

Literature in newspapers and monthly magazines brought the work of many authors to a wide range of people. Nobles and house servants could now read the same books. Ideas about political and social problems were available to all who could read.

Concert halls and opera houses were built for the general public. Public concerts became common. Anyone who could afford the price of a ticket could enjoy them.

Painters also enjoyed a growing audience. In France the government supported art schools and built or expanded art museums. Art dealers helped support artists while they worked. After the 1850s, special art galleries were started to buy and sell paintings. The work of many artists was engraved and sold as inexpensive prints.

Art, literature, and music were becoming available to more and more people. In 1851 a huge international exhibition was opened in London. It became known as the Crystal Palace Exhibition. Within the Crystal Palace, products, inventions, and art from all over the world were exhibited. Cheap railroad transportation made it possible for millions of people to attend. Similar exhibitions were held in France and the United States in the years that followed. To those who attended these exhibitions, there could be no doubt that the Industrial Revolution was bringing a new life to millions of people.

Check on Your Reading

1. What were the characteristics of Romanticism, Realism, and Impressionism?
2. Identify: Beethoven, Debussy, Constable, Daumier, Monet, Cassatt, Van Gogh, and Goya.
3. What contribution did Paul Cézanne make to modern art?
4. In what way did industrialization affect art?

The Crystal Palace in London was probably the world's first prefabricated building. It was built in about seven months and could easily be taken down and put up again. It was a creation of the Industrial Revolution.

5. Science Advances Rapidly

Throughout the late 1700s and in the 1800s scientists learned much about scientific processes in the world. Many inventors based their work on the new scientific theories and discoveries.

Rapid Progress in the Sciences

In the 1830s, Michael Faraday in England and Joseph Henry in the United States found that electricity could be generated from magnetism. Samuel Morse applied their discovery to his work on the telegraph. At the same time work was being done on developing an electric generator.

In 1870 one of the first practical dynamos was built. This dynamo could generate electric current on a continuous basis. This meant a new and efficient source of power was now available. Soon electric wires fanned out from power stations to run industrial machines, street lights, and home appliances.

Antoine Lavoisier (1743-1794) is often called the "father of modern chemistry." He proved that burning was a result of a chemical combination in which the burning substance unites with the gas oxygen. This process is called oxidation. He also presented evidence to prove the law of conservation of matter—this is, matter can neither be created nor destroyed but can only be changed from one form into another.

Medical Science

Science also contributed greatly to the protection and saving of human lives. For example, smallpox had spread terror, tragedy, and death. Then Edward Jenner (1749-1823), an English physician, developed a method of vaccination against smallpox. The disease at last could be checked.

About ten years later Ephraim McDowell (1771-1830) proved that surgery of the abdomen did not have to be fatal for the patient. Ether as a painkiller was demonstrated by William Morton (1819-1868) in 1846.

Louis Pasteur (1822-1895), a French bacteriologist, discovered that certain tiny living organisms, called bacteria, visible under a microscope, could cause disease. He developed a vaccination to prevent rabies (hydrophobia) in people and animals. His discoveries led the English surgeon Joseph Lister (1827-1912) to start the practice of antiseptic surgery. The German physician Robert Koch (1843-1910) discovered the germs that cause the diseases tuberculosis and Asiatic cholera. The British Florence Nightingale (1820-1910) made major contributions in the fields of nursing and sanitation.

Charles Darwin and the Theory of Evolution

Charles Darwin (1809-1882) was an English scientist who studied plants and animals in their natural settings. In 1859 Darwin startled scholars with his book *The Origin of Species.* In 1871 another of his major works, *The Descent of Man,* was published. The impact was widespread.

Darwin's theory stated that all forms of life are descended from earlier forms. Every living thing has ancestors that reach far back in time. Darwin said that each species produces more individuals than can possibly survive. The result is that each individual struggles against others to survive. Darwin called this *the struggle for existence.* Individuals of the same species vary somewhat from each other. An individual may have a variation that gives it a better chance to survive than others of the same species. If the favorable variation can be inherited, it may be passed on to the offspring. In this and other ways, all forms of life slowly and gradually evolve from earlier forms. Some species gradually change. Others die out because they cannot adapt. Human beings share these features. They, too, Darwin said, are descended from earlier forms of life.

Alfred Russel Wallace, an English naturalist, developed a similar theory independently about the same time. In addition, Darwin was influenced by the earlier work of Edward Blyth.

Some people accepted the theory of evolution. Others considered it basically correct but insisted that several points had not been proved. Still others rejected Darwin's theory because it contradicted certain aspects of the story of creation in the *Bible.*

The ideas of Charles Darwin had a great impact. They challenged the idea that life was fixed, rigid, and without change.

Check on Your Reading

1. Name several scientific developments discussed in this section.
2. What was the theory of evolution? Why were Darwin's ideas rejected by some?

William Morris

William Morris smiled as he looked at the meadow where his new home, Red House, would soon stand. It was close to the little village of Upton and not far from London. William Morris planned to build a house surrounded by apple and cherry trees and away from the ugliness of industrial life.

William Morris was a writer, painter, architect, printer, interior decorator, and social reformer. He was a short, muscular man who spoke in a loud voice and dressed carelessly. Despite his rugged appearance, he was sensitive. He expressed "a deep love of the earth and the life on it, and a passion for the history of the past. . . ." He read romantic poetry "rocking from one foot to the other like an elephant." And he loved to walk alone through the fields.

Above all, William Morris disliked what he called "the dull squalor of [industrial] civilization." So he launched "a crusade and holy war against the age"—and went to build a house in the green countryside where beauty could be found.

William Morris built his house carefully and well. He planned the garden with its fences covered with roses. Then, when the building was completed, William Morris and his friends set about to make the furniture and decorations to be placed in the house. "Have nothing in [the] home, which is not both beautiful and useful," William declared.

William and his friends designed and made a fine oak dining table, sturdy chairs, delicate copper candlesticks, and lovely table glass. They painted pictures of scenes from ancient Greek wars and from medieval romances. They painted on the walls designs that blended with the furniture of the house. They even arranged the window ledges so that apples would fall gently through the open windows in autumn.

Finally, the house and all of its furnishings were completed. In 1860 William Morris and his wife at last moved into Red House. How pleasant were the next five years! William and his friends smelled "the sweet air" of the apple and cherry orchards. They took "swinging rides" through the countryside in a carriage with leather curtains. They cast away from them the ugliness of the new industrialization and "laughed because we were happy."

In 1861, William Morris helped to found the firm of Morris, Marshall, Faulkner, and Co., Fine Art Workmen in Painting, Carving, Furniture and Metals, with an office in London. By 1865 the firm's business had grown so large that William decided that he had to return to the city. Thus, five years after Red House had been built, William Morris sold it and went back to live in the increasingly industrial city of London.

William never tried to see Red House again. As he himself said: "The sight of it would be more than I could bear!"

The sketch above about William Morris is based on primary source material in J. W. Mackail, *The Life of William Morris,* Vol. I, 1901; and Philip Henderson, *William Morris,* 1952 (*Writers and Their Work* Series No. 32, Longmans for the British Council).

CHAPTER REVIEW

Think and Discuss

1. The Industrial Revolution created many problems. How did each of the following attempt to solve some of these problems: unions, co-operatives, socialism, communism, increased voting rights?
2. It is often said that art and literature reflect the life of the people of the period. Do you think this statement is true of life during the Industrial Revolution? Why?
3. Do you agree with Daumier that people, rather than riches, are the chief possessions of society? Why?
4. What is the essential difference between revolution and evolution?

Past and Present

1. The Industrial Revolution stimulated many artists to create different forms of art. Has this reaction continued? Can you find some examples of artists today who are responding to the continued effects of the Industrial Revolution?

2. How has the Industrial Revolution affected your school and the education you receive?

Activities

1. Have each member of the class pick one person mentioned in this chapter who she or he thinks contributed most to change. Write a report on the person you selected and give reasons for your choice.
2. Have an art exhibit in your classroom illustrating the art movements discussed in this chapter.
3. Try to find an example of a co-operative in your community or a community nearby. How does it try to help its members?
4. One of the ideas that socialists favored was public ownership of the means of production and distribution. Does the United States government own any means of production or distribution? Have a panel discussion in which several students discuss whether it should or should not own them.
5. Visit a modern factory that has some form of assembly-line work. Observe the efforts being made to lessen boredom and to safeguard health.

8

Nations, Wars, and Imperialism

Thousands of major and minor wars have been recorded in historic times. No one can estimate the many thousands more that occurred throughout prehistory. The cost in terms of human lives and the destruction or disruption of cultures and their achievements is too great to be calculated.

Many of these wars were fought by antagonistic nations; others were a result of imperialist ambitions. The following unit focuses on the relationships between nations, imperialism, and war. By understanding these relationships, we may be better equipped to work for a future of peace and constructiveness.

Italy and Germany Form Nations

KEYNOTE

Many of us have become accustomed to thinking of Italy and Germany as old nations, and we look forward to the day when we can visit the "old country." Yet actually both Italy and Germany are comparatively young nations, younger than our own. One of the important facts of history is this: Italy and Germany did not become nations until the second half of the nineteenth century.

Garibaldi visits Victor Emmanuel II.

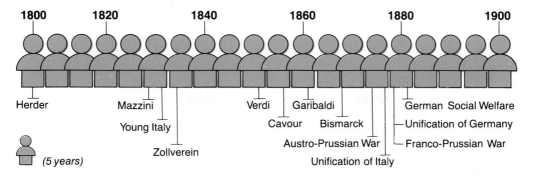

| 1800 | 1820 | 1840 | 1860 | 1880 | 1900 |

Herder
Mazzini
Young Italy
Zollverein
Verdi
Garibaldi
Cavour   Bismarck
Austro-Prussian War
Unification of Italy
German Social Welfare
Unification of Germany
Franco-Prussian War

(5 years)

1. Italy Is Unified

Italy as a nation is comparatively new. The word *Italy* had largely a geographic meaning until well after the 1850s. Before that time, Italy consisted of a number of separate states. (See the map on page 450.) These included the Kingdoms of Piedmont-Sardinia and the Two Sicilies; Lombardy-Venetia; the Papal States; and the Duchies of Parma, Modena, Lucca, and Tuscany. Most of these states were dominated by rulers from Austria and other foreign countries.

Giuseppe Mazzini, leader of "Risorgimento"

Napoleon's control of Italy had helped to spread the ideas of the French Revolution. It also had stimulated Italian nationalism and caused many people to demand freedom from their foreign masters. The *Carbonari* ("Charcoal Burners"), a secret society, began to work to rid the country of foreign rulers.

The awakening of Italian nationalism in the early 1800s became known as the "Risorgimento" (the "Revival" or "Reawakening"). Giuseppe Mazzini (1805–1872) was a leader of the "Risorgimento." A sensitive man, Mazzini often showed his sympathy for persecuted people by wearing black clothing as a sign of his mourning for them. In 1831, he founded the society known as *Young Italy.*

Members of Young Italy attempted to "educate" people to the need for rebellion against foreign rulers. Mazzini hoped that an Italian republic could then be established. Young Italy dedicated itself "to the great aim of reconstituting Italy as one independent sovereign nation of free men and equals. . . ."

The groundwork for rebellion was laid by Mazzini and other Italians. The revolution of 1848 against Austria failed, however.

Many Factors Unite Italians

Other factors helped to unite the Italian people.

1. Common customs, religion, and traditions existed in Italy.

2. Most people of Italy spoke a common language, though local dialects existed.

3. Members of the growing commercial and agricultural middle class believed that they would benefit by a united country. A united Italy could remove tariff barriers that existed between separate states and eliminate the confusion caused by the variety of coinage systems. It could build roads and railways to aid commerce, and stimulate foreign trade. It could eliminate Austria's interference in their business activities.

4. Music also served to unite the Italian people. Giuseppe Verdi (1813–1901) is famous for such operas as *Rigoletto*, *La Traviata*, and *Aïda*. Choruses from some of Verdi's operas often produced patriotic anti-Austrian demonstrations. An English music critic pointed out that: "Verdi's music became especially identified with the national cause."

5. Writers, such as Count Giacomo Leopardi and Alessandro Manzoni, helped create a national Italian literature. Manzoni (1785–1873) is famous for his novel *I Promessi Sposi (The Betrothed)*. It was written in the dialect of Tuscany. (See the map on page 450.) Its great success helped to establish a common language for Italian literature. The story dealt with a tyrant in seventeenth-century Lombardy and with the oppression of Italians by foreigners (the Spaniards). It thus indirectly preached anti-Austrian nationalism.

Cavour Strengthens the Position of Sardinia

In the 1850s many Italians were ready to make another attempt to expel foreign rulers. They needed energetic and imaginative leaders to direct their actions. Such leaders appeared in the Kingdom of Sardinia (Piedmont-Sardinia), which was ruled by the Italian House of Savoy.

King Charles Albert had led the Sardinians in an unsuccessful war against the Austrians. He had also granted his people a constitution. Many people looked to the new king of Sardinia, Victor Emmanuel II, for the same courageous leadership provided by his father.

In 1852 Victor Emmanuel appointed Count Camillo Cavour as his prime minister. Cavour was an excellent diplomat. He was prime minister of Piedmont-Sardinia from 1852 to 1859 and 1860 to 1861. Cavour was a liberal statesman who stood for "Independence, Union, Moderation, and Reform." He was determined to make the dream of a united Italy come true.

Cavour first worked to strengthen the economy of Sardinia. He supported public works, aided agri-culture, and encouraged the development of industry. Then he joined Sardinia with England, France, and Turkey in a war against Russia, the Crimean War of 1854-1856. Cavour used the peace conference after the war as a place to denounce Austria's domination of Italy.

Northern and Central Italy Are United

Cavour knew that he would need the help of other countries to achieve his goal of driving out the Austrians. He used shrewd diplomacy to obtain the aid of Emperor Napoleon III of France. Napoleon III promised to help Sardinia in a war against Austria if Austria could be made to attack the Kingdom of Sardinia first. This would justify France's entry into the war to defend Sardinia. In return for this aid France would receive Nice and Savoy.

Cavour maneuvered Austria into declaring war on Sardinia. In 1859 Sardinia and France allied

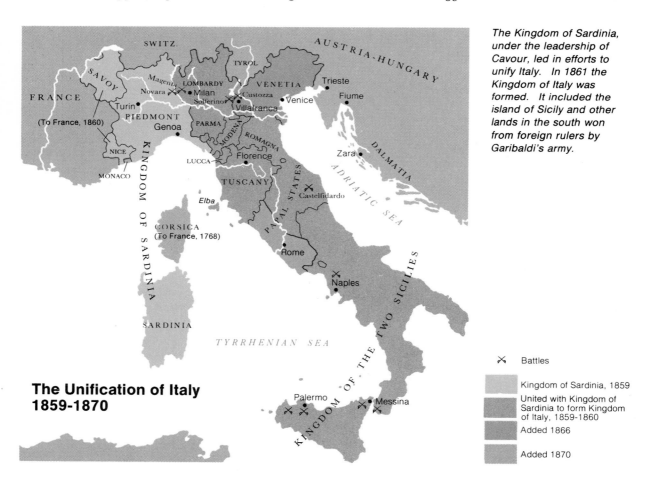

The Kingdom of Sardinia, under the leadership of Cavour, led in efforts to unify Italy. In 1861 the Kingdom of Italy was formed. It included the island of Sicily and other lands in the south won from foreign rulers by Garibaldi's army.

The Unification of Italy 1859–1870

✕ Battles

Kingdom of Sardinia, 1859

United with Kingdom of Sardinia to form Kingdom of Italy, 1859–1860

Added 1866

Added 1870

themselves in the war against Austria. Austrian armies were defeated in bloody battles. However, in a few months, Napoleon III made a separate peace with Austria without consulting Cavour. This peace agreement had the following provisions: 1. Lombardy was given to the Kingdom of Sardinia. 2. Venetia continued to be a province of Austria.

The war aided the unification of Italy in another way. Tuscany, Modena, Parma, and Romagna (a part of the Papal States) deposed their Austrian rulers. Then these states agreed to unite with the Kingdom of Sardinia. Northern and Central Italy at last were joined together.

Garibaldi Conquers the Kingdom of the Two Sicilies

The first parliament of Italy met in 1860 at Turin, capital of Sardinia. However, Sicily and the southern part of the Italian peninsula, known as the Kingdom of the Two Sicilies, still remained outside the nation. So did Savoy and Nice, which had been given to France.

Giuseppe Garibaldi (1807–1882) was the military hero who helped free Sicily and Southern Italy from foreign rulers. Garibaldi had gone to sea at sixteen and became a sea captain at twenty-four. Dressed in his famous red shirt, grey flannels, and old grey cloak, Garibaldi was a dramatic and colorful leader.

He assembled about a thousand volunteers and prepared to invade the island of Sicily, which was ruled by an autocratic Bourbon king. "Our war-cry will be Italy and Victor Emmanuel!" proclaimed Garibaldi. In 1860, when the people of Sicily revolted, Garibaldi saw his chance to attack.

Garibaldi's troops became known as the "Red Shirts" because of their red woolen shirts. They were small in number; but with Garibaldi as their leader, the "Thousand" took the island of Sicily. They then crossed over to the mainland and freed the rest of the Kingdom of the Two Sicilies.

The New Kingdom of Italy Is Proclaimed

Garibaldi turned over his conquests in Sicily and Southern Italy to Victor Emmanuel II. Italy's territory had been greatly extended, and the new Kingdom of Italy was proclaimed in 1861. Victor Emmanuel II became king and Cavour the prime minister.

In 1866 Italy joined Prussia in a war against Austria. As a result, Venetia was added to Italy. In 1870 the city of Rome was taken from the Pope when French troops who were defending it had to be withdrawn. Rome became the capital of Italy. The unification of Italy had been achieved.

Check on Your Reading

1. What factors inspired Italian nationalism in the 1850s?
2. What did each of these people contribute to Italian unification: Mazzini, Verdi, Cavour, Napoleon III, Victor Emmanuel II, Garibaldi?
3. Explain how Northern and Central Italy were united and how the Kingdom of the Two Sicilies was acquired.

---

2. Independent Italy from 1870 to 1914

The leaders of the newly unified Italy made a number of changes in the government of the country. A limited monarchy was established with a two-house parliament. The members of one house were elected and the members of the other were largely appointed by the king. A prime minister was responsible to the elected house of Parliament. Suffrage was limited to those who were property owners and who paid certain taxes.

The Pope's Position in a United Italy

The Pope had lost Rome as well as considerable land and civil power as a result of the unification of Italy. The Pope was very angry at the seizure of the lands he had ruled. Nevertheless, efforts were made to reconcile him.

The Law of Papal Guarantees, passed by the Italian government in 1871, provided the following: 1. The Pope was to be sovereign within the Vatican. 2. An annual payment of over $600,000 was to be made to the Pope by the Italian government to replace the income he had received from the Papal States. 3. The government was to give up its right to appoint bishops. 4. Many monasteries were to be closed. 5. Church courts were to cease to function.

Pope Pius IX and later Popes refused to accept either the money or the other terms of the Law of Papal Guarantees. To show their opposition, they refused to leave the Vatican. A settlement between Church and state was at last reached in 1929 under dictator Benito Mussolini.

Other Activities of the New Government

The government built railroads and canals, subsidized shipping, and helped the development of industries. Laws were passed to regulate child labor and to provide workers with compensation for industrial accident, sickness, and old age.

Italy was eager to equal the achievements of other nations in securing non-European territories. The temptations of imperialism caused Italy to seek colonies in North Africa and to attack Abyssinia, or Ethiopia, in 1896.

Italy Has Problems

A number of serious problems plagued Italy from 1870 to 1914. The Italians lacked experience in self-government. Tensions continued between the Italian government and the Papacy. Class distinctions separated group from group. The country was burdened by a large national debt and high taxes. The taxes were a heavy burden on the poor.

The people in many parts of the country had a low standard of living. In addition, many people of the industrialized north were hostile to those in the relatively underdeveloped south.

In 1860, between 70 and 75 per cent of the people were illiterate. A system of compulsory education was declared in 1877, but it was not enforced.

All these problems remained to be solved. As a result, more than eight million people emigrated between 1876 and 1905. About one-half went to the United States and South America, particularly Argentina. Others settled throughout Europe. This exodus relieved some of the economic pressures. It also made Italian leaders more aware that much had to be done to make Italy a politically stable and economically sound country.

Check on Your Reading

1. Describe the Italian government's relations with the Pope from 1871 to 1929.
2. What problems did the new government of Italy solve? Which remained unsolved?
3. Where did Italy wish to expand? Why?

---

3. Germany Is Unified

Germany, like Italy, did not exist as a nation until the second half of the nineteenth century. "Germany" in the 1840s was a loose confederation of thirty-nine states, the most important of which was Prussia. Each state had its own ruler, military forces, and diplomats for foreign affairs. The German Confederation did have a parliament. However, it was made up of representatives of the rulers of each state. Austria dominated this German Confederation. The revolutionary uprisings of 1848 (page 404) failed to drive the Austrians out of Germany.

Many Factors Unite the Germans

As in Italy, there were a number of factors that inspired the nationalism of many Germans. There was a common language, though there were local dialects. Common traditions and customs were shared by the people of the various German states. The people were proud of the great achievements of German writers and composers. Napoleon's domination of Germany had stimulated the growth of German nationalism. After Napoleon's defeat, Prussia had taken the lead in efforts to unify the country.

Prussia helped to establish the *Zollverein*, a customs union among certain states in the German Confederation. This made it possible for goods to pass more freely among its member states. By 1834, nearly all of the states in the German Confederation had joined, but Austria was excluded. The cooperation developed by the customs union was an important step toward future political union.

Influential German authors encouraged nationalism. Johann Gottfried von Herder (1744-1803) wrote that every nation had its own individual spirit, which can be felt in its literature. Germans became interested in the study of medieval German tales. The brothers Jakob and Wilhelm Grimm published their famous collection of *Fairy Tales,* stories going back to early German legends.

The failure of the Frankfurt Assembly of 1848 made German leaders realize that it would take far more than words to unite the German people. The man who saw this most clearly was Otto von Bismarck.

Otto von Bismarck

Otto von Bismarck (1815-1898) became chief minister of Prussia in 1862. He was a conservative who supported monarchy. He said, however, that "absolutism primarily demands impartiality, honesty, devotion to duty, energy, and inward humility in the ruler."

Bismarck believed in the importance of strength

and power in dealing with other countries. He declared:

> Not through fine speeches and majority votes are the great questions of the day decided . . . but by blood and iron.

Bismarck knew when it was necessary to use force and when it was wiser to act with moderation. He played the leading role in the building of the German nation.

Three Wars Lead to German Unification

As chief minister of Prussia, Bismarck determined to do everything possible to unite Germany. His plan of action had four main parts: 1. Prussia was to provide the necessary leadership to unite Germany. 2. German national loyalty was to be centered on the Prussian ruler. 3. Austria was to be isolated and driven out of Germany. 4. Military power was to be used to accomplish the objective of unifying Germany.

The War against Denmark

In 1864 both Prussia and Austria fought against Denmark over control of Schleswig and Holstein. Both these territories were the personal possessions of the King of Denmark. However, Holstein was in the German Confederation and there were many Germans in Holstein and in southern Schleswig. Denmark was defeated in the war. By the terms of the peace settlement, Prussia gained the right to govern Schleswig and to establish a naval base at Kiel. Austria gained the right to govern Holstein.

The Austro-Prussian War

Bismarck next worked carefully on Napoleon III to gain France's neutrality if Prussia went to war.

Prussia, under the leadership of Otto von Bismarck, led the movement for German unification that was completed by 1871.

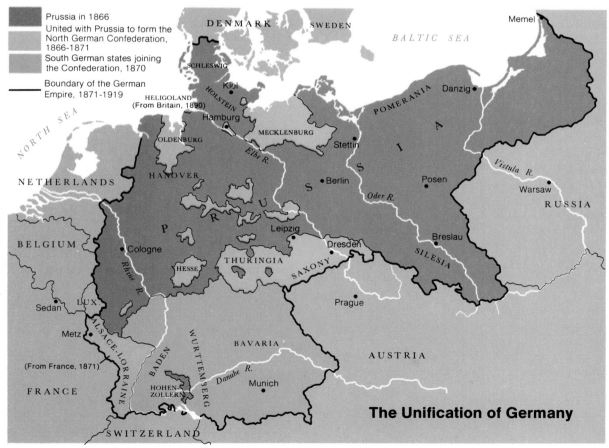

Prussia in 1866
United with Prussia to form the North German Confederation, 1866-1871
South German states joining the Confederation, 1870
Boundary of the German Empire, 1871-1919

The Unification of Germany

Otto von Bismarck, the chief minister of the King of Prussia, played the key role in the unification of Germany.

mans—the Catholic South Germans as well as the Protestant North Germans—would fight. He hoped that such a war would stir up the nationalism of the South German states, and make them want to join the North German Confederation in a united German nation.

Bismarck considered France to be the enemy. He used a dispute over who should inherit the throne of Spain to help cause a war between France and Prussia. The issue was whether a prince related to the king of Prussia should seek the Spanish throne. Under French pressure, King William I of Prussia had his candidate withdraw. It seemed as if the matter was settled, but Bismarck used the incident to incite a war with France. He deliberately left out some of the words in a diplomatic dispatch, the *Ems Dispatch,* describing William I's interview with the French ambassador. He made it appear that the French and German governments had insulted each other. This helped spread a war fever in both countries. Inept French diplomacy and emotional reporting by French newspapers led France to declare war on Prussia.

The war proved to be disastrous for France. Not only was France defeated, but Emperor Napoleon III was captured with his army. By the terms of the Treaty of Frankfurt (1871), France turned over to Germany all of the region of Alsace and the eastern part of Lorraine. Also France had to pay Germany a war indemnity of one billion dollars.

The Franco-Prussian War helped to complete the unification of Germany. The South German states had joined with the North German states in the fight against France. Now they agreed to form a single Germany. The new German Empire was proclaimed in a ceremony at Versailles in 1871. William I, King of Prussia, became Emperor of Germany. Bismarck was made the first Chancellor. Emperor William wrote to Bismarck: "The most distant generations will never forget that the elevation of the Fatherland to new power . . . [is] essentially due to your penetration, your energy, and skill."

He also obtained Italy's promise of aid if a conflict broke out between Prussia and Austria. He had made friends with Russia, partly by supporting Russia against the Poles when they revolted in 1863. Then Bismarck used arguments over the future of Schleswig-Holstein as one of several excuses for stirring up a war between Prussia and Austria. The Austro-Prussian War broke out in 1866.

Led by the astute General von Moltke, the Prussian army defeated Austria in seven weeks. The peace settlement provided that Austria give Holstein to Prussia and agree to the dissolution of the German Confederation. Austria also agreed to the formation of a new confederation of North German states under the leadership of Prussia. Austria was excluded from membership. This North German Confederation (1867) had a population of thirty million people, twenty-five million of whom were governed by Prussia. The South German states remained outside the confederation.

The Franco-Prussian War

Bismarck felt that one more war was necessary. He wanted to find an enemy against whom *all* Ger-

---

Check on Your Reading

1. What factors inspired German nationalism?
2. How did Bismarck plan to unite Germany?
3. Explain the step-by-step development of his plan.

A German painting shows the victorious German army and Count Moltke before Paris in 1871.

4. Independent Germany to 1914

The leaders of newly united Germany set about reorganizing the country. There were many important developments from 1871 to 1914.

The Government

The King of Prussia became the Emperor of Germany. The Emperor chose the Chancellor, controlled the military forces, and provided overall direction of foreign affairs. The Chancellor was the most powerful government official in the country.

The legislature consisted of two houses. The lower house (the Reichstag) was elected by universal manhood suffrage. The upper house (the Bundesrat) was chosen by the rulers of the various states in the Empire. Neither house had power to control the actions of the Chancellor. Bismarck was Chancellor from 1871 to 1890.

Religious Affairs

In the beginning, Bismarck directed a struggle against the Catholic Church and its political ally, the Catholic Center Party in Germany. This struggle is known as *Kulturkampf*. Bismarck tried to undermine the position of the Catholic Church because he felt that the Church's political influence weakened the power of the state. He believed that the Catholic Church would never cooperate fully with a Protestant government. Most of the Poles in Germany were Catholic and joined with the Center Party to oppose Bismarck.

Laws were passed requiring civil marriages. Catholic clergy were fined heavily for criticizing the government. Religious organizations were forbidden to instruct in the schools. The Jesuits were expelled.

Nevertheless, the Catholic Center Party remained strong. After 1880, when he needed Catholic support against the socialists, Bismarck stopped the government's anti-Catholic policies. Most laws restricting Catholics were repealed.

Economic Affairs

An outstanding development was the transformation of Germany from a largely agrarian country

The Prussian King William I is proclaimed German Emperor at Versailles in 1871. Bismarck is in the center.

to a highly industrialized one. Between 1871 and 1900 there was an Industrial Revolution. This revolution was given impetus by progress in science and technology, the unification of the country, and the annexation of Alsace and part of Lorraine. These areas had important textile factories and iron-ore deposits.

Germany built railroads, strengthened its merchant marine, and increased its armaments. It developed a great variety of manufacturing industries, including factories making chemical fertilizers to improve its farmlands. By 1913 Germany was the rival of Great Britain in many economic fields.

Social Welfare

The industrialization of Germany brought many problems, such as poor working conditions and the employment of children. In 1881 Chancellor Bismarck declared that "the state is not only an institution of necessity but also one of welfare."

Bismarck and the German government took action in this area for these reasons: 1. To prevent the socialist party from growing stronger, they passed some of the legislation it advocated. At the same time the government dissolved socialist organizations and suppressed their publications. 2. By providing for people's needs, they felt that they could strengthen the nation and keep the loyalty of its citizens. 3. They believed that better living and working conditions would raise the health and morale of the men recruited into the army. 4. They were influenced by the activities of the Conservative Party in Britain, a political party that helped bring about social reforms.

The German government, therefore, passed some important social legislation: 1. A Sickness Insurance Act (1883) provided insurance financed by employers and employees. 2. Also passed were an Accident Insurance Act (1884), financed by employers; and 3. An Old Age and Incapacity Act (1889), financed by employers, employees, and the German government. Other laws regulated working conditions in factories. Thus Germany became a pioneer in setting up government systems of social welfare.

Foreign Relations

Germany under Bismarck played a major role in European international relations. Bismarck had great skill in diplomacy and he used it to preserve the balance of power and prevent any alliance of great powers against Germany. He allied Germany with Austria-Hungary and Italy while working to maintain satisfactory relations with Russia and Britain. He prevented an alliance of France and Russia, which he felt was highly dangerous to German security.

Bismarck tried not to antagonize European nations. He wanted Germany to concentrate on building up its strength in Europe rather than seek a colonial empire.

Check on Your Reading

1. Describe the government of the new German nation.
2. In what ways did Germany change economically?
3. What social welfare acts were passed in Germany between 1871 and 1914?
4. What was Bismarck's foreign policy?

456

A Soldier in Garibaldi's Army

The soldier in Garibaldi's army was dressed in a long-sleeved woolen shirt, trousers tucked in below the knees, leggings, and old shoes. He wore a soft-brimmed felt hat, or a cap held to his head by a chin strap. He was armed with a rifle and a bayonet.

He rarely had enough to eat, and his pay was very low. Yet he learned not to complain. Had not Garibaldi himself said: "What do you want with pay? . . . when the affairs of the country are going well, what more can anyone want?"

Yet there were times when the soldier was shocked by the horrors of war. Certainly, he could never forget Palermo, Sicily, where he saw the ruins of shelled houses and where:

> you stumble over the remains of a human body, a leg sticking out here, an arm there. . . . You look around and see half a dozen gorged rats scampering off in all directions. . . .

Little wonder that there came a day when the soldier wanted to stop fighting. Later he told why he had not:

> I was in despair myself, and thought of giving up the whole thing. I was sitting on a hillock. . . . Garibaldi came by. . . . Well, he laid his hand on my shoulder and simply said . . . "Courage; courage! We are going to fight for our country." Do you think I could ever turn back after that?

The soldier did not turn back. Stirred by nationalistic feelings he continued to fight for himself, for Garibaldi, and for a free Italy!

The above sketch is based on materials in G. M. Trevelyan, *Garibaldi and the Making of Italy,* Longmans, Green, 1912; *Passages from the French and Italian Notebooks of Nathaniel Hawthorne; Readings in European History,* edited by Bernard and Hodges, Macmillan, 1958; and *Fifty Major Documents of the Nineteenth Century,* edited by L. L. Snyder, Van Nostrand, 1955.

CHAPTER REVIEW

Think and Discuss

1. Make a generalization supported by historical facts about the growth of national consciousness that would apply to Italy, Germany, and other countries that you have studied.
2. Since Austria had the same language as the other German states, why was it not included in the growth of German national consciousness?
3. Evaluate Bismarck's contributions to the unification of Germany.
4. In what ways does the growth of manufacturing industries increase the power of a country?
5. Compare the achievements of Cavour and of Bismarck.

Past and Present

1. How have "new nations" today won their independence? Compare them with the ways in which Italy and Germany became nations.
2. Compare the welfare legislation in Germany between 1871 and 1914 with that of the United States in the 1930s.

Activities

1. In two columns list the steps taken by Cavour and Bismarck in the unification of their respective countries. What are your conclusions?
2. Panel discussion: In building a nation, what means are justified to achieve worthwhile ends?
3. Draw a cartoon illustrating an important event in Bismarck's career or in Cavour's career.

27

Britain Strengthens Itself at Home and Expands Abroad

KEYNOTE

A philosopher once said: "History never begins a new chapter. Only historians do." This was particularly true of nineteenth-century Britain.

It was then that the British people strengthened their democracy at home and expanded their power abroad. In doing so, they were not starting new chapters in British history. They were continuing the pattern of domestic and foreign developments that reached back to the seventeenth century—and beyond.

A meeting of the House of Commons in the nineteenth century.

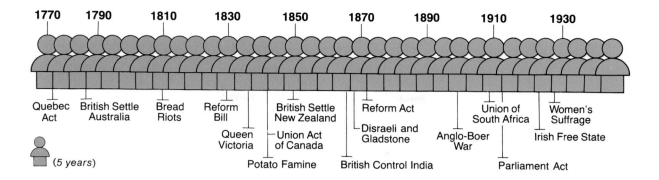

1770	1790	1810	1830	1850	1870	1890	1910	1930

Quebec Act

British Settle Australia

Bread Riots

Reform Bill

Queen Victoria

Union Act of Canada

British Settle New Zealand

Potato Famine

Reform Act

Disraeli and Gladstone

British Control India

Union of South Africa

Anglo-Boer War

Parliament Act

Women's Suffrage

Irish Free State

(5 years)

1. The Growth of Democracy in Britain

England at the beginning of the nineteenth century was governed primarily by Parliament. The power of the King was limited, and the press had considerable freedom to express its opinions. Also the wealth of England exceeded that of any European country.

Political Abuses in Britain

On the other hand, England was plagued by a number of evils, particularly in the area of political rights. For example, the right to vote for members of Parliament was limited to wealthy property owners. Some 96 per cent of the male adults in England and Ireland could not vote. Only one in every five hundred persons in Scotland had suffrage rights. No women could vote in Great Britain, or in most other countries. Only men who belonged to the Church of England were eligible for government offices. Roman Catholics and Dissenters could not hold office, but they had to contribute to the support of the Church of England.

Elections were often corrupt and costly. For example, Lord John Russell pointed out that in Liverpool "bribery [was] employed to the greatest extent . . . every voter receiving a number of guineas [coins] in a box, as the price of his corruption."

Certain old districts, called "rotten boroughs," continued to send representatives to Parliament even though their populations had declined to a point where they had few or no voters. Dunwich, a town that was sinking under the North Sea, still had representation in Parliament.

In some areas, called "pocket boroughs," the voters were controlled by landlords who practically named the representatives to be sent to Parliament. In 1831, the Duke of Buckingham appointed the representatives from Buckingham (population 13).

Lord Monson chose the representatives from Gatton—population 5.

New cities that had grown up as industrial centers, such as Manchester and Birmingham, had no representation in Parliament.

In 1831, Lord John Russell asked the members of the House of Commons to imagine what "a stranger from some distant country" would see if he visited England:

What then would be his surprise, if he were taken by his guide, . . . to see a green mound and told that this green mound sent two Members to Parliament—or, to be taken to a stone wall . . . and told that [three niches in it] sent two Members to Parliament. . . .

The visitor's astonishment would increase, Lord Russell went on:

if he were carried into the North of England, where he would see large flourishing towns, full of trade and activity, . . . and were told that these places had no representation in the Assembly which was said to represent the people.

The time was ripe for political reform. People like Lord Russell were ready to introduce the necessary changes or reforms.

Demands for Political Reform

The demand for political reform grew because the wealth of the nation was the possession of the few. A popular newspaper pointed out: "Elegant dresses, superb furniture, stately buildings, fine roads and canals, fleet horses and carriages, numerous and stout ships, warehouses teeming with goods—all these . . . are so many marks of national wealth and resources. But all these spring from la-bor." Thousands of laborers, declared the newspa-per, were living in poverty and misery. Indeed, in 1801 one out of every seven persons had to receive financial aid (poor relief) from the government.

Laborers in Britain worked long hours for low pay. They suffered from lack of permanent em-ployment, poor housing, high taxes, and depres-sions. They had to pay high prices for food, largely as a result of the *Corn Laws*. These laws protected British gentlemen farmers by putting duties on grain coming from other countries. British reform-ers became convinced that the best way to change such conditions was to give political power to more people.

The Pressure for Reform Grows Stronger

In 1812 there were "bread riots" in Sheffield, where mobs of women rushed through the markets emptying stalls of their wares. In 1819 there was a clash between agitators for reform and troops of the government in Manchester. In 1828 laws discrimi-nating against Dissenters were repealed. In 1829 the Catholic Emancipation Act finally granted Ro-man Catholics equal political rights.

In 1830 the Tory Party, which had blocked ef-forts for basic changes, lost some of its power in Par-liament to the Whig Party. The Whigs promptly presented a major reform bill to Parliament. This bill met with great opposition but, after a new elec-tion, it was finally passed by the House of Com-mons. The largely hereditary House of Lords still refused to pass the bill, and there were angry dem-onstrations and riots in the country. Finally, Prime Minister Charles Grey, the Whig leader, made it clear that, if necessary, the king would appoint new members to the House of Lords to assure the pas-sage of the bill. The Reform Bill was then passed in 1832.

The Reform Bill of 1832

The principal provisions of the Reform Bill were the following:

1. It lowered the property requirements for vot-ing, giving the right to vote to many members of the middle class—merchants, businessmen, industrial-ists, and others. 2. It eliminated many "rotten" and "pocket" boroughs and redistributed the seats of Parliament. Large towns and counties which formerly had no or little representation now had more representatives in Parliament. 3. It in-creased Scotland's representation in Parliament by eight new members and Ireland's representation by five. 4. It provided for the more careful registra-tion of voters.

The extension of suffrage was to have extremely important effects. The aristrocracy's control of the political system was broken. Now political power

A cartoon in favor of the Reform Bill of 1832. Earl Grey, a strong backer of the bill in Parliament, is shown sweeping out the rotten boroughs.

was divided between the landlords and some of the middle class.

The Reform Bill of 1832 did not give the ballot to workers in industry, farmers with little property, women, and many others. Twenty-one of every twenty-two adult males in Britain still could not vote. However, the Reform Bill opened the way to later legislation that established suffrage on a broad and democratic basis in Britain.

A Cluster of Reforms

The Reform Bill of 1832 was followed by other laws improving life in Britain. The Emancipation Act of 1833 freed "under certain conditions all slaves owned by British subjects or in British dominions." It also prohibited slavery on British soil in the future. The Factory Act of 1833 tried to improve working conditions in the factories.

The history of English justice had been filled with cases of unjust and inhumane treatment of offenders. In the early 1800s, the death penalty could be given for over two hundred crimes, including shoplifting or "injuring Westminster Bridge." Many juries refused to declare a person guilty—even when he or she had committed a crime—because they felt that it was unfair to sentence the person to death for a minor crime.

In 1835 a law was passed eliminating many cruel and inhumane ways of treating people in prison. As a result of reforms introduced during the next three decades, the use of the death penalty for petty offenses was discontinued. Capital punishment was reserved for only the more serious crimes.

The Liberal and Conservative Parties Develop

Changes also were made in the political parties. The Whig Party became the *Liberal Party,* and included manufacturers, merchants, some landlords, and some radicals. The Tory Party became the *Conservative Party* and included aristocrats, some shopkeepers, wealthy industrialists, and military officers.

Neither party could claim the support of all the members of a class. For example, some workers supported the Liberal Party and some supported the Conservative Party. In addition, neither party had a monopoly on reform legislation. Both the Liberals and Conservatives made contributions to the important changes introduced into the country.

Check on Your Reading

1. What conditions in Britain made political and economic reforms necessary?
2. What were the main provisions of the Reform Bill of 1832?
3. What other bills to improve conditions were passed?

2. The "Victorian Age" in Britain

In 1837 eighteen-year-old Victoria became Queen of the United Kingdom of Great Britain and Ireland. She was to reign for sixty-three years. This young and inexperienced queen became one of the most highly respected and popular monarchs in English history. During Queen Victoria's reign, Britain developed at home and expanded abroad. In tribute to her, this period is known as the "Victorian Age."

The Corn Laws Are Repealed

Shortly after Victoria became Queen, there was bitter agitation over the Corn Laws, which taxed grains imported from foreign countries. These laws were designed primarily to protect the sale of foodstuffs produced by the British themselves. However, opponents of the Corn Laws protested that they resulted in high prices for bread and other foods and caused many hardships.

More and more people demanded that the Corn Laws be abolished. Merchants and manufacturers joined in the Anti-Corn-Law League to fight for repeal of the Corn Laws. They wanted cheaper food for the growing numbers of industrial workers. They also wanted to encourage the exchange of their industrial products for the food of other countries. They thus had practical reasons for seeking freer trade. A crop failure in England and a potato famine in Ireland increased the cries for economic reform. In 1846 the Corn Laws were repealed.

During the next two decades, the protective tariffs on other imported articles were removed. This was done because it was believed that other countries could afford to buy British products if they could sell their own goods in Britain. In 1852 Parliament passed a resolution declaring that:

[Free trade] will best enable the industry of the country to bear its burdens, and will thereby most surely promote the welfare and contentment of the people.

Chartists demonstrating in London in 1848. They were demanding the reforms listed in their "People's Charter."

England became one of the leading exponents of the philosophy of free trade.

The Chartists Demand Reform

In the middle of the nineteenth century demands for reform grew stronger. Reformers known as the *Chartists* had organized in 1836. In 1848 they marched through London demanding the reforms listed in the "People's Charter." These were:

- universal manhood suffrage,
- secret ballot,
- annual election of members of the House of Commons,
- abolition of property qualifications for members of the House of Commons,
- salaries for members of the House of Commons,
- equal election districts

In this year revolutions were sweeping through Europe. The British government was afraid that the revolutionary fever might cross the Channel. The government took sharp measures against the Chartists, arresting several of their leaders. The leadership of the Chartists was not strong enough in this crisis, and the movement collapsed.

Even in failure the Chartists provided later reformers with many goals. By 1918 all of their program, except the annual election of members of the House of Commons, had been put into effect.

William Gladstone and Benjamin Disraeli

The two men who now dominated the political scene were Benjamin Disraeli of the Conservative Party and William Gladstone of the Liberal Party. Between 1868 and 1894, except for six years, these two statesmen alternated as prime minister.

William Gladstone was a leader of great physical vitality. Sir James Graham, a contemporary of his, believed that "Gladstone could do in four hours what it took any other man sixteen to do, and he worked sixteen hours a day."

Benjamin Disraeli was clever, witty, and often brilliant in his approach to problems. He was a worthy rival of Gladstone in Parliament.

Disraeli was fortunate in winning the friendship and support of Queen Victoria. As a realist, however, he knew that it was Parliament, not the

Queen, who held the governing power. He worked energetically to gain parliamentary support. Nevertheless, he continued to rely on his own judgment in making decisions.

Suffrage Rights Are Extended

Under the leadership of these two men, the British government continued to carry out gradual changes. New laws extended suffrage rights.

The Reform Act of 1867 was passed under a Conservative ministry. 1. It gave the vote to townsmen who paid taxes or rented lodgings at an annual rate of at least $50. 2. It granted voting rights to more people in rural areas by lowering the property and rental requirements necessary to vote. 3. It gave four industrial cities—Manchester, Birmingham, Liverpool, and Leeds—additional representatives in Parliament. This act gave the vote to urban workers and nearly doubled the electorate. Some legislators warned that this would lead to disaster. Instead, the Reform Act of 1867 stimulated additional reforms.

Other acts granted Jews the right to be elected to Parliament. Later atheists were also permitted to serve in the House of Commons. In 1872 the secret ballot (or the Australian ballot) was adopted for use in elections.

The Reform Act of 1884 was passed mainly by the efforts of Gladstone. It extended the vote to many farm laborers and other men living in rural areas. The electorate was increased by about two million new voters. The Redistribution of Seats Act of 1885 took steps to establish equal election districts throughout the country.

The suffrage laws of the nineteenth century were a landmark in the growth of democracy in Britain because they extended the right to vote to most men. It was not until 1928 that all men and women over the age of twenty-one could vote.

The House of Lords Is Stripped of Power

Despite the reforms passed by the House of Commons, the House of Lords still stood in the way of change. The House of Lords was a body of men who held their positions principally by inheritance.

In 1909 the Lords were challenged. The Liberals were in power and the Chancellor of the Exchequer (Treasury), David Lloyd George, submitted a budget that hit hard at the upper classes. This budget taxed large incomes and estates and lands whose value had increased without their owners contributing to their improvement. The House of Commons passed this budget, but the House of Lords refused to accept it. A bitter struggle followed. After a newly elected House of Commons exerted pressure, the House of Lords passed the budget.

The actions of the House of Lords had infuriated the Liberals. They were determined that the Lords should never again block important legislation. In 1911, the Parliament Act stripped the Lords of most of their power. 1. The House of Lords was not allowed to stop the passage of any money bill passed by the House of Commons. 2. Any other bill passed by the House of Commons in three successive sessions would become a law—even if the House of Lords did not accept it. Two years had to pass between the introduction of the bill and its final passage. 3. The House of Commons would be elected every five instead of every seven years.

Check on Your Reading

1. Why did people oppose the Corn Laws?
2. What were the political reforms of the Reform Act of 1867? the Reform Act of 1884?
3. What changes were made by the Parliament Act of 1911?

---

3. Britain and Ireland

The relatively peaceful growth of democracy in Britain contrasted with developments in Ireland. In Ireland it was a story of bitter—and often bloody—clashes between the English and the Irish.

The English Dominate Ireland

The history of Ireland was marked by the efforts of the Irish to win their freedom from their English rulers. By the Act of Union of 1801 the Irish Parliament at Dublin was abolished. Ireland was given some representation in the British Parliament. Great Britain and Ireland were to be governed by the British Parliament. The British Isles became a single state known as the United Kingdom of Great Britain and Ireland.

Reasons for Irish-English Tensions

Throughout history, English rulers had deprived Irish farmers of their land and had given it to English noblemen. As a result, most of the Irish did not own the land they worked. Much of the land was owned by absentee landlords who lived in England and rarely came to Ireland. The Irish had to pay heavy rent and taxes.

Most of the Irish were Roman Catholics. (The Scotch Presbyterians lived primarily in Northern Ireland.) Like everyone else, the Irish Catholics had to pay tithes to support the Anglican Church. The Irish showed their opposition to this situation by trying to prevent the collection of tithes.

The Irish felt that they were not sufficiently represented in the British Parliament. They also believed that the British government was not interested in the welfare of Ireland. Some Irish leaders wanted to build an Irish nation that would be free from foreign domination.

Gladstone Works for Reform

In the late 1840s a terrible potato crop failure in Ireland brought great famine. Thousands of Irish left their country and emigrated to the United States and other lands.

During the latter part of the nineteenth century Prime Minister Gladstone worked to improve conditions in Ireland. He helped to bring about the separation of Church and state in Ireland. This meant that the Irish people no longer had to pay taxes to support the Anglican Church. Gladstone also introduced land reforms in Ireland, which provided for the following: 1. The tenant's rent would be fair. 2. The tenant would have "fixity of tenure." This meant that a tenant could not suddenly be forced off the land by a landlord who demanded a rent he could not pay. 3. The tenant could sell his own property and receive compensation for the improvements that he made.

The Irish demands for home rule, or self-government, continued to grow. "Ireland stands at your bar expectant, hopeful, almost suppliant. Her words are the words of truth . . .," Gladstone told Parliament. His efforts to have Parliament pass a Home Rule Bill were not successful.

The Irish Free State Is Formed

The *Sinn Fein* ("We Ourselves") movement developed early in the twentieth century. The supporters of the *Sinn Fein* insisted that Ireland should be governed only by the Irish.

In 1916, while Britain was at war with Germany, the Irish revolted. This rebellion was crushed, but there was bitter fighting between the Irish and English from 1919 to 1921. In 1921 the self-governing *Irish Free State* was formed. It had a Parliament with the authority to make laws and an executive responsible to that Parliament.

Northern Ireland contained people of Scottish descent and was largely Protestant. It did not join the Irish Free State but remained a part of Great Britain. Today tensions continue in Ireland.

At a midnight meeting the Fenians protest against the Perpetual Coercian Act passed by Parliament in 1887. The Fenians were a secret society dedicated to overthrowing British rule in Ireland.

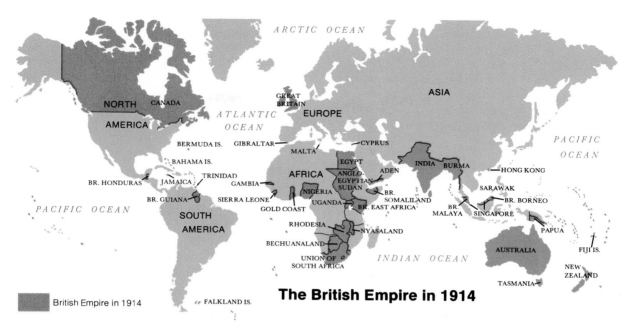

The British Empire in 1914

By 1914 Britain had built a vast empire including Australia, Canada, New Zealand, India, and South Africa.

Check on Your Reading

1. What were the basic reasons for tensions between the Irish and English?
2. What did Gladstone try to do for Ireland? What success did he have?

4. Britain and Canada

England had acquired Canada from France in 1763 as a result of the Seven Years' War. At that time there were about 70,000 people, mostly French, living in Canada. Then many English people migrated to Canada. Differences in language, customs, and education caused conflicts between the English and the French. Differences in religion also caused problems. Most of the English were Protestant and most of the French were Catholic.

The British Parliament Sets Up a Government for Canada

In 1774, Parliament passed the Quebec Act. This act granted to the French Canadians the right to have their own laws, language, customs, religion, and system of land ownership.

The English population in Canada continued to grow. It increased largely as a result of the immigration of *Loyalists* (American colonists who were loyal to Britain) who fled to Canada during the American Revolution.

In 1791, Parliament passed an act that divided Canada into two provinces. *Lower Canada* was inhabited principally by the French. *Upper Canada* was inhabited chiefly by the English. Each province was allowed its own assembly.

Lord Durham's Report

Basic political and religious problems still remained, and various publications fanned the fires of discontent. Some demanded that the language, religion, and culture of the British dominate Canada. Others, like *Le Canadién*, defended the interests of the French people. When the disagreements were not settled, rebellions broke out in both provinces (1837–1838) against the British government. These rebellions were put down.

In 1839, after carefully studying conditions in Canada, Lord Durham made a report to the British Parliament. He recommended that Lower and Upper Canada be reunited, and that the people of Canada be given self-government in their internal or domestic affairs. By the Union Act passed in 1840, these and other reforms were carried out.

Lord Durham's report proved to be very important. In his report he had declared that the strength of the government of Canada would come: "not by weakening, but strengthening the influence of the people [of Canada] on its government. . . ." Such comments helped to advance the idea that the colonies should be given self-government when they were ready for it.

The British North America Act

The British North America Act was passed in 1867. This act provided for the formation of a Canadian confederation to consist of Ontario (Upper Canada), Quebec (Lower Canada), Nova Scotia, and New Brunswick. Provision was made to admit additional provinces and the confederation was called the *Dominion of Canada*. The British North America Act also provided that each province was to have its own government to deal with provincial matters, such as education. The Canadian government would handle matters involving all of Canada, such as the defense of the country.

The idea of *Dominion status* within the British Empire was considered sound. This status was later extended to other areas, including Australia, India, and the Union of South Africa. They became self-governing countries with ties of economic interests, traditions, and loyalty holding them to Britain.

Check on Your Reading

1. What problems complicated Britain's government of Canada after 1763?
2. Summarize Lord Durham's report.
3. Why do you think the British North America Act was called "the most important single law in Canadian history"?

---

5. Britain and Australia

In the seventeenth century a Dutch sea captain, Abel Tasman, discovered lands which are known as Tasmania, New Zealand, and Australia. The Dutch never took possession of these lands. Captain James Cook of the British navy also explored the coasts of Australia and New Zealand during 1769-1770. The report of Cook's expedition encouraged British settlement of Australia.

Australia Is Settled

After 1776 the British began to use Australia as a penal colony. A number of the criminals sent to Australia were guilty of only petty offenses, such as poaching. Some parts, such as South and Western Australia, were first settled by free settlers. After 1840, prisoners were no longer sent to most of the regions of Australia.

In 1851 gold was discovered in New South Wales and Victoria. Thousands of adventurers and settlers came to Australia. However, sheep-raising and the production of wool proved to be far more important than the mining of gold. The raising of wheat also became a major occupation.

Self-Government Is Achieved

People now came to Australia "not in despair but in hope." In time, six colonies developed in Australia and the island of Tasmania. These colonies gradually gained rights of self-government from Great Britain.

Then in 1901, with the approval of the British Parliament, a constitution went into effect. It set up a federal union of all of the colonies, or states. Included in this Commonwealth of Australia were New South Wales, Victoria, South Australia including Northern Territory, Western Australia, Queensland, and Tasmania.

Check on Your Reading

1. How did Britain acquire Australia?
2. How was Australian self-government achieved?

---

6. Britain and New Zealand

In 1642 Abel Tasman discovered a group of islands southeast of Australia. The Maoris, who lived in these islands, called their land *Ao-tea-roa (Long White Cloud)*. The Dutch renamed it *Nieuw Zeeland (New Zealand)* after the province of Zeeland in Holland. In 1769 Captain James Cook of the British navy explored the coasts of New Zealand.

Britain Gains Control of New Zealand

In 1840 Great Britain signed the Treaty of Waitangi with the Maoris' chiefs, each of whom received a blanket and some tobacco as a special gift. This treaty had the following provisions: 1. The Maoris ceded to the British Crown the sovereignty of New Zealand. 2. The Queen guaranteed the Maoris exclusive and undisputed possession of their lands, except as the Crown might wish to purchase them. 3. The Queen gave to all Maoris the rights and privileges of British subjects.

This engraving from an English newspaper of 1852 shows emigrants panning for gold in Australia.

Settlers from England, Scotland, Wales, and Ireland began to move into the country. The Maoris became angry at the ways in which the settlers were acquiring land, and fighting broke out. These clashes eventually were ended.

As in Canada and Australia, the people of New Zealand were able to gain self-government. In 1852 a federation of settlements was formed, and the provinces of New Zealand were given self-government. Thirteen years later a central government for all of New Zealand was established.

New Zealand Introduces Advanced Legislation

New Zealand became known as a leader in political, economic, and social laws. For example, in the last decade of the nineteenth century the government did the following things: 1. Large estates were broken up to provide land that could be sold to small farmers. 2. Suffrage was extended to women in 1893, making New Zealand the first country to permit women to have the same voting rights as men. 3. Boards were established to settle labor disputes by arbitration. 4. A program of ac-

cident insurance was set up for workers. 5. A system of old-age pensions was developed so that "veterans of industry shall have pensions as well as veterans of war. . . ."

In 1904 an observer from the United States was so impressed with the accomplishments of New Zealand that he called its inhabitants: "an earnest, open-minded, common-sense, true-hearted people . . . [with] laws and institutions based on principles that accord with the public good." In 1907 New Zealand became a British Dominion.

Check on Your Reading

1. How did Britain gain control of New Zealand?
2. Why did clashes occur between the British settlers and the Maoris?
3. What form of government was gradually established there?
4. Give examples of New Zealand's advanced social laws.

7. Britain and South Africa

The British also were active in the region known today as South Africa, although they were not the first settlers there. In 1486 Bartholomeu Díaz, a Portuguese explorer, discovered the Cape of Good Hope. In 1652, the Dutch East India Company, which had taken control of Portuguese trading areas, established a "refreshment station" at Cape Town. It was used by the crews of ships as a place to take on fresh supplies of green vegetables, to care for the sick, and to leave mail to be carried back to Europe.

The original inhabitants of Cape Town were the Bushmen and Hottentots. Both of these groups were small in number.

The Dutch East India Company's station on the coast of South Africa gradually developed into a Dutch colony. In 1710 there were only seventeen hundred white settlers. About 50 per cent of these were Dutch; the rest were Germans or French Huguenots.

About 1775 these European settlers of South Africa came in contact with the Bantu, who are believed to have migrated southward from the central part of the continent. (See pages 209-211.) The Bantu were struck by the strange color of the Europeans and called them "[people] whose ears reflect the sunlight" and "[people] having the color of a yellowish clay pot." The Bantu groups made many contributions to the development of South Africa. They developed and worked on farms and in mines. They built roads and towns. However, the Europeans and Bantu fought fiercely on many occasions.

When the Dutch opposed Great Britain in the Napoleonic Wars, the British seized the colony at the Cape. After the Napoleonic Wars, a number of British settled in South Africa.

The "Great Trek"

When the British took control of the colony at the Cape, they came in close contact with the *Boers.* The Boers (Dutch word for farmers) were a hardy people primarily of Dutch descent who had settled in South Africa. The Boers disliked the British, for they felt that the British did not give them power in the government. They also were angered when the British freed the slaves in Cape Colony, because the Boers were using slaves to work their farms.

Beginning about 1836 many Boers therefore made a long journey northward, called the "Great Trek." The Boers established two new states in the interior, the Orange Free State and the Transvaal.

Here they hoped "to govern ourselves without [British] interference."

The British recognized the independence of the Orange Free State and the Transvaal in 1852. However, problems between the British and the Boers continued. They quarrelled over a section of land that both claimed. Then the British government annexed the Transvaal in 1877 and denied its people self-government for about four years.

The Anglo-Boer War

About 1885-1886 gold was discovered in the Transvaal. Attracted by the riches in the gold and diamond mines, many British and other peoples hurried into the Transvaal.

The Boers resented the coming of these *Uitlanders,* or "foreigners," most of whom were British. They taxed the Uitlanders heavily, made it difficult for them to become citizens, and refused to give them voting rights. These acts increased the hostility between the Boers and the Uitlanders. The actions of British Empire builders like Cecil Rhodes, the prime minister of Cape Colony, added to the tension. Rhodes is believed to have encouraged a conspiracy against the Boers.

Finally, the allied Boer states of the Transvaal Republic and the Orange Free State declared war on Great Britain (Anglo-Boer War, 1899-1902). After a determined struggle, the Boers were defeated. In 1902 the British annexed these Boer states.

Formation of the Union of South Africa

The victorious British did not deprive the Boer states of all governing powers. In 1906-1907 the right of self-government was returned to the Transvaal and the Orange Free State.

In 1910, the Union of South Africa was officially formed, and became a self-governing dominion of the British Empire. The new union consisted of Cape Colony, Natal, the Orange Free State, and the Transvaal. The English and Dutch languages were both established as official languages.

Check on Your Reading

1. Describe the principal African and European groups living in South Africa in the early 1800s. What tensions developed after 1852?
2. What events led to the Anglo-Boer War? What were the results of the war?

8. Britain and India

The building of the British Empire in India was started by the English East India Company. The Company was far more than an organization for trade. In many regions of India, it ruled the people, collected taxes, handled justice, and backed up its decisions with military force.

Soon there was evidence that some Company officials were accepting graft and administering their areas dishonestly. The English historian Thomas Macaulay reported that "Enormous fortunes were . . . rapidly accumulated at Calcutta, while thirty millions of human beings were reduced to the last extremity of wretchedness."

The British Parliament passed the Regulating Act in 1773 to supervise the actions of the East India Company. This act was designed to keep the Company's trading practices separate from its policies of government. Warren Hastings was appointed the first Governor-General to supervise the administration of the British lands in India.

The British Expand Their Control of India

In the nineteenth century British rule expanded throughout India. British forces defeated tribesmen in northern India and gained control of their land. In western and central India, they crushed a group of local princes, and annexed much of their territory. The British also took over the Sind, an important region in northwestern India, to their possessions.

The British forces fought two years against the Sikhs and took over the Punjab region in the northwest. They also pushed back Burmese invaders, taking control of Burma in 1884–1885. They kept Russia from controlling Afghanistan. In time, British control extended to the borders of Afghanistan, Nepal, China, and Indo-China.

A battle during the Sepoy Rebellion.

The Sepoy Mutiny

Differences between the practices of Europeans and the beliefs of the peoples of India caused serious tension. In 1857 a number of Indian troops (the *Sepoys*) became angry because they believed that the rifle cartridges given to them by British officers were coated with cow and pig grease. The Hindus considered the cow to be a holy animal, and the Moslems considered the pig to be too unclean to touch. This grievance combined with other factors to produce the *Sepoy Mutiny*. During this uprising many Sepoys mutinied and killed the British in Delhi and other cities. After a number of atrocities by both sides, the mutiny was brought under control.

After the Sepoy Mutiny, the British government took away the political power of the East India Company. By the Act for the Better Government of India (1858) the Crown took over direct control of India. Parliament appointed a viceroy as the chief administrative official in India.

On January 1, 1877, Victoria was proclaimed "Empress of India." This title remained with the British royal family until the middle of the twentieth century.

Check on Your Reading

1. How did the English East India Company govern India?
2. Describe the Act for the Better Government of India (1858).

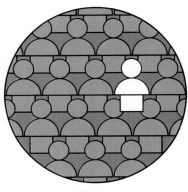

LET'S MEET THE PEOPLE

A Schoolmaster of Ireland

The schoolmaster was a tall, thin man with a brown beard and hair that tumbled over his eyes. He wore "[a coat] that hung limply from his sloping shoulders. There was a great square patch on one knee."

The pupils sat on backless benches. They were "nearly all barefoot, and their clothing was ragged and much patched." The schoolmaster declared: "Now, then, we will read!"

A red-headed boy stepped forward and opened the *First Book of Lessons*. The aim of the book was to make a child "recognize the differences between [words] that resembled each other closely," and many of its paragraphs were deliberately jumbled. The boy read:

> Can a worm walk? No, it has no feet; but it can creep. The child is sick; tell her not to cry; let her stay in bed and sleep. This cliff is steep, and I feel my head light as I look down. Did you meet Fred in the street? Weep no more. My boot is too tight; it hurts my foot.

The boy read slowly, stumbling over many words.

"Scoundrel, try that again!" declared the schoolmaster, angrily.

The boy started to read, only to be interrupted again.

"Say it out?!" shouted the schoolmaster. "Or . . . I'll throw you out of the door. . . ." He knocked the book out of the boy's hand.

"Now pick that up and give it to me!" was his next command.

The boy obeyed, tears trickling down his face. The schoolmaster looked at him for a moment; then he sent him back to his seat.

"I have been harsh with him again," thought the schoolmaster, "but he must learn. He must be educated so that he can raise himself above this poverty. He must do this—for he is my son."

The above sketch of a schoolmaster at the close of the nineteenth century is based on an eyewitness account in Clifton Johnson, *The Isle of the Shamrock*, 1901, the Macmillan Company.

CHAPTER REVIEW

Think and Discuss

1. Why was Britain one of the first nations to develop into a democracy?
2. How much of the success of nineteenth-century reforms in Britain was a result of freedom of the press?
3. Britain had religious toleration but not complete freedom of religion. What is the difference?
4. How might an increase in the political power given to the people help bring about economic reforms?
5. With what other political documents in English history would you rank the Reform Bill of 1832? Why?
6. How do you explain the support which the British Conservative Party gave to reform legislation?
7. Why would the payment of salaries to members of Parliament be important?

Past and Present

1. What independent nations were once a part of the British Empire? In which of these countries is English an important language?
2. The tensions that developed between the French and the English in Canada in the late 1700s are still a problem in Canada today. Look for articles on this subject in newspapers and magazines and report your findings.

Activities

1. Panel discussion: Is free trade or high tariffs the better policy for international trade?
2. On a map of the British Isles, locate England, Northern Ireland, the Republic of Ireland, Scotland, and Wales. Then designate the principal cities and bodies of water.
3. On a map of the world, show all the possessions of the British Empire in the nineteenth century.

CHAPTER

28

Autocratic Russia and Cultural Creativity

Leo Tolstoy, a great Russian novelist, once wrote:

> In every hurtful thing there is something useful. [When a house is burning down], we may sit and warm ourselves, and light our pipes with one of the firebrands; but should we therefore say that a conflagration is beneficial?

Tolstoy's question applies to nineteenth-century Russia. In this period the Russian people suffered severely under the harsh rule of autocratic czars. Yet in this same century the Russians created great literature, art, science, and music. A key feature of nineteenth-century Russia was the appearance of superb cultural achievements at the same time that the government acted autocratically at home and abroad.

Czar Alexander II in church.

1. Autocracy in Nineteenth-Century Russia

In 1837 two Russians were condemned to death for attempting to escape from Russia. Czar Nicholas I (1825-1855) commuted the death penalty and decreed: "The convicts are to [be clubbed by] a thousand men—twelve times." This brutal decree was in keeping with the character of Nicholas I. His character had been deeply affected by the events of Russian history.

Nicholas I, a Czar of Repression

Nicholas I had become Czar of Russia in 1825. Opposition to his rule arose immediately from Russian intellectuals and from others. On December 26, 1825, two thousand persons rose in rebellion. Among them were members of the Northern Society, an organization that wanted a constitutional monarchy for Russia; the Moscow Guards Regiment; some young nobles and officers; and some workers.

The rebels demanded a government by "Constantine [the brother of Nicholas I] and [a] Constitution." This revolt was crushed by Nicholas' troops. As historian Sidney Harcave points out: "Nicholas was convinced that he had crushed a revolution, not a mere revolt; and he lived under the shadow of the events of December 26 . . . for the rest of his life."

The Rule of Czar Nicholas I

Nicholas I attempted to develop an effective government for Russia. For example, he encouraged the codification of law. However, he was equally determined that the people should obey his orders without question. He ruled as an autocrat. People who dared to challenge his authority were punished by the political police. Publications were censored by government agencies. Education was controlled by the state, and all "dangerous ideas" were eliminated. Religious sects that refused to accept the principles of the Russian Orthodox Church were persecuted.

Equally important, non-Russian nationality groups under Russian control were forced to accept the almost complete domination of Russia. They were forced to undergo "Russification." "Russification" was a program to eliminate cultural differences in the Russian empire and to establish uniform language, institutions, and loyalty.

Alexander I had transformed the Grand Duchy of Warsaw into the Kingdom of Poland. He had granted Poland a liberal constitution and the right to exist as an autonomous state. In 1830 the Poles revolted and demanded independence. Then the revolt spread to the Russian-controlled province of Lithuania. Nicholas I crushed the revolt with great cruelty. The former "Kingdom of Poland" was made a province of Russia, and a program of "Russification" was imposed on the Polish people.

The Serfs Are Freed

Czar Alexander II (1855-1881), the successor of Nicholas I, was keenly aware that the conditions of the Russian people needed to be improved. Alexander II felt that it was better to introduce reform "from above" than to "have it happen from below." It was he who brought about the freeing of the serfs.

The Act on the Emancipation of the Peasants from Serfdom, March 1861, and later decrees had the following provisions: 1. About twenty-two million serfs were declared to be free. 2. These newly freed peasants were allowed to buy from their landlords some of the land they had worked as serfs. 3. Under certain circumstances the state agreed to pay the landlords for the lands that they sold to the former serfs. These peasants were to repay the state in installments spread over a number of years. A law of 1866 also made it possible for the almost twenty-five million peasants who worked for the state to obtain land. By 1881 about 85 per cent of the landlords had given up part of their lands.

The land was not sold outright to the peasants but was transferred to village communes. These communes—called *mirs*—supervised the redistribution of the land among the peasant families living in them and collected payments and taxes owed to the state. They also directed farming activities and kept order.

The emancipation of the serfs was an extremely important reform. The serfs of Russia not only were freed but also were assisted in buying land.

On the other hand, Alexander II's freeing of the serfs did not greatly improve the conditions of the peasants. There were too many weaknesses in the system of emancipation to make possible a strong and balanced economy. The peasants often could not buy enough good land to provide themselves with a decent living. The lands that the peasants bought on installment were usually overvalued.

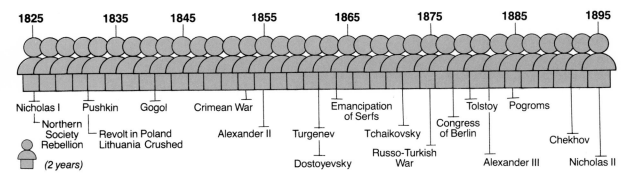

1825 1835 1845 1855 1865 1875 1885 1895

Nicholas I Pushkin Gogol Crimean War Emancipation of Serfs Tolstoy Pogroms

Northern Society Rebellion Revolt in Poland Lithuania Crushed Alexander II Turgenev Tchaikovsky Congress of Berlin Chekhov

(2 years) Dostoyevsky Russo-Turkish War Alexander III Nicholas II

This made their payments to the state a heavy burden. Most peasants were still not completely independent farmers, for the mirs regulated many of their activities. "What is decided by the mir must come to pass," became a popular Russian proverb. As the population of a mir grew, the land was continually redivided. This made for a smaller share of land for each family.

The life of the peasant remained a difficult one, and protests continued throughout Russia. From 1855 to 1861 there had been 474 cases listed where groups of serfs on private estates had challenged the authority of their lords. Within several months *after* the Emancipation Decree of 1861, there were over 300 peasant outbreaks that had to be put down!

Alexander II's reforms were not limited to the emancipation of the serfs. 1. He developed a system of local self-government. 2. He re-established town councils. 3. He reformed the court system and introduced trial by jury. 4. Alexander also established universal military conscription in place of a less democratic system of army service.

Despite these reforms, an attempt was made to assassinate Alexander II in 1866. This and other events caused him to draw back from reform and to become more autocratic. Despite increased activity by groups demanding reform, the government of Russia remained firmly in the hands of the czar and his officials. After several unsuccessful attempts were made on his life, Alexander II was assassinated in 1881 by members of a revolutionary group. His successors ruled Russia as autocrats.

Alexander III Suppresses Freedom

Alexander III (1881–1894) and his officials did everything that they could to wipe out liberal movements. In the last part of the reign of Alexander II, thousands of people had been exiled for their political views. Alexander III continued this policy.

The police of Alexander III were everywhere. They spied on the people, beat those who complained, and exiled to Siberia anyone listed as "dangerous" to the government. The czar's police did not need evidence before they acted.

The press also was censored. An American writer visiting Russia reported that one Russian newspaperman had been arrested, kept two days in prison without food, flogged, and sent home in weather that was thirty-five degrees below zero. His crime was "furnishing his paper with news."

Innocent men and women were attacked for their religious beliefs. The Jews were singled out. They were called "monsters" and subjected to *pogroms,* or organized massacres. In desperation, thousands of Jews left Russia to seek asylum in the United States and other countries.

At the close of the nineteenth century, autocracy was still dominant. When Nicholas II succeeded Alexander III in 1894, the new czar left no doubt that he would continue in the autocratic tradition. Nicholas II made this declaration:

> Let it be known by all that I shall devote my whole power to the best service of the people, but that the principle of autocracy will be maintained by me as firmly and unswervingly as by my lamented father.

Check on Your Reading

1. Why did a revolt occur in December 1825?
2. How did Nicholas I rule Russia? What did he do about non-Russian nationalities?
3. Describe the emancipation of the serfs. What problems remained?
4. How did Alexander III and Nicholas II rule?

2. Russians Create Great Literature

No country, however autocratic, has ever been without its defenders of freedom. No leader, however repressive, has ever been without his critics urging reform.

In Russia many who cried out for liberty, reform, and better lives for human beings were writers. They included Pushkin, Gogol, Turgenev, Dostoyevsky, Tolstoy, Chekhov, and others. They helped to create the so-called "Golden Age of Russian Literature."

Alexander Pushkin

Alexander Pushkin (1799-1837) is recognized as one of Russia's greatest poets. He wrote superb lyrics and contributed to the development of the Russian language. At times he also used literature to defend people against oppression. In his poem "Message to Siberia," he urged Russia's exiles to "keep your patience proud" and predicted:

> The heavy-hanging chains will fall,
> The walls will crumble at a word;
> And Freedom greet you in the light,
> And brothers give you back the sword.

It was Pushkin's belief that Russia would someday "rouse from her long sleep" and break the hold of autocracy.

Nikolai Gogol

Nikolai Gogol (1809-1852), a Ukrainian, is a very important writer in the development of Russian literature. Professor Ivar Spector declares: "In the history of Russian literature, 1842 should be hailed as a red-letter year. For the appearance of *Dead Souls* [by Gogol] in that year marked the birth of the genuinely realistic Russian novel, thereby inaugurating the age of prose in Russian literature. Gogol was the father of the Russian novel. . . ." *Dead Souls* is a satirical novel that dealt with the problems of serfdom and government bureaucracy.

Gogol is also famous for his short story "The Cloak" or "The Overcoat," in which he examines the pitiful condition of the poor Russian clerk. His play *The Inspector-General* ridicules corrupt and inefficient bureaucrats.

Gogol's humor and satire have delighted thousands of readers. Yet it must be remembered that his wit was directed against the tragic evils in Russian society. As he wrote in *An Author's Confession*:

> But if we must laugh, why not laugh at what really deserves to be laughed at by us all. In

my *The Inspector-General* I decided to bring together and to deride all that is bad in Russia. . . .

Ivan Turgenev

Ivan Turgenev (1818-1883) was a leading *Westernizer*. He urged Russians to study the ideas and methods of Western countries. He wanted Russia to discard its outmoded ways of doing things and to "modernize" itself. He believed that Russia could be reformed if people acted by their reason, rather than by their emotions.

In his famous novel *Fathers and Sons*, Turgenev popularized the word *nihilist*. Turgenev defined a nihilist in this way:

> [He] is a man who does not bow before any authority whatever, who does not accept a single principle on faith. . . .

Turgenev seemed to be saying: Unless Russia reforms itself, some people will become nihilists. They will challenge the authority of everyone, and the result will be destruction.

Fyodor Dostoyevsky

Fyodor Dostoyevsky (1821-1881) was a leading literary *Slavophile*. In contrast to the Westernizers, Slavophiles believed Russia should develop its own unique Slavic qualities and not try to imitate the West. Dostoyevsky urged Russians to find strength in the heritage of their country, rather than in the ways of Western nations. He believed that it was dangerous for people to be guided by reason alone. He was convinced that it was better for Russians to "listen to their hearts" than to their minds. He wanted people to follow their natural emotions.

Crime and Punishment is one of Dostoyevsky's and the world's great novels. Its plot revolves around a problem. A young student wishes to continue his education so that someday he can serve humankind. Yet he is too poor to go on with his studies or to help his family. Does he have the right to rob a useless and corrupt old pawnbroker to obtain money for his education and other worthwhile purposes? Dostoyevsky puts the question this way:

> [Should he] take her money and with the help of it devote [himself] to the service of humanity? Would not one tiny crime be wiped out by thousands of good deeds?

Dostoyevsky's great novels probe deeply into the minds and emotions of a great variety of nineteenth-century Russians.

sia." In his writings and life Tolstoy showed his hatred for war, his love for the peasants, and his understanding of human beings.

In *War and Peace,* which covered the Napoleonic period, Tolstoy denounced war:

> War is . . . the most horrible thing in life. . . . [Armies] kill and maim tens of thousands, and then have thanksgiving services for having killed so many people. . . . How does God above look at them and hear them?

In the same novel, Tolstoy demonstrated his understanding of human beings. For example, here is a scene in which a father has just said good-bye to his son who is leaving for war. The father is in the study. He loves his son deeply and finds it difficult to hold back his tears. Nevertheless, he does not want to admit his grief. Tolstoy captured both the sorrow and the strength of the father:

Leo Tolstoy recorded his social and moral views of life in Russia in a series of great novels.

Dostoyevsky's answer in this book is a resounding NO! The crime is committed, and it involves the murder of the pawnbroker by the student. Dostoyevsky then shows how the crime "drives the murderer through the tortuous blind alleys of attempted escape and suffering conscience to a confession of his crime and an expiation [atonement] of it in the frozen wastes of Siberia. From this . . . comes redemption for the man. . . . Seldom have the incalculable implications of a crime been explored with such meticulous detail."

In a sense, Dostoyevsky was the conscience of Russia, calling the Russian people back to the basic values of life. He was also concerned with the welfare of all people. In a famous speech he declared, "To become a true Russian is to become the brother of all men, a universal man."

Leo Tolstoy

Leo Tolstoy (1828–1910) is generally recognized as Russia's greatest writer of prose. His book *War and Peace* is considered "the national novel of Rus-

[The son] walked quickly out of the room. . . . From the study came, like pistol shots, the repeated angry sounds of the old [father] blowing his nose. Then suddenly the door of the study was flung open, and the old man in his white dressing-gown peeped out.

"Gone? Well, and a good thing too!" he said. . . . He shook his head and slammed the door.

Anton Chekhov

Anton Chekhov (1860-1904) is noted for his short stories and for such plays as *Uncle Vanya, Three Sisters,* and *The Cherry Orchard.*

The dominant theme in many of Chekhov's works is the inability of people to face reality or to check the disintegration of their lives. This theme he presented with a realism found in everyday life. As Chekhov said:

No literature can surpass actual life in its irony. . . . Artistic literature is called so just because it depicts life as it really is. Its aim is truth—unconditional and honest. . . .

Chekhov described life as truthfully and objectively as he could.

Check on Your Reading

1. How did Gogol criticize Russian government and society?
2. What did Turgenev try to teach?
3. Why is Dostoyevsky called a Slavophile and "the conscience of Russia"?
4. What were the points of view of Tolstoy and Chekhov?

---

3. Russian Art, Science, and Music

The creative activities of the Russians in the nineteenth century were not limited to literature. Great work was also achieved in art and architecture, science, and music.

Art and Architecture

Russian art and architecture from about the middle of the tenth to the eighteenth centuries had been marked by the influence of Byzantine art and the deep religious feelings of the Russians. It was also influenced by contact with the art of Persia, Italy, India, and other areas.

Peter the Great had stimulated secular art and had encouraged the study of the artistic styles of the West. In the nineteenth century several artists tried to depict events more realistically and to put more "Russian" feeling into art. The historical scenes painted by two of these artists, Vereshchagin and Repin, are still famous.

Mathematics, Science, Invention, and Medicine

In mathematics, science, invention, and medicine, the Russians accomplished many things. Some of their outstanding achievements included the following: 1. Lobachevsky developed principles of non-Euclidean geometry. 2. Mendeleyev aided modern chemistry by drawing up his Periodic Law for the elements. 3. Metchnikov described the action of the white corpuscles in the blood. 4. Pirogov advanced the methods of surgery used during war.

In addition, Lodigin may have developed an electric light before Edison. Also Popov sent radio signals before Marconi.

Music

In the field of music, Russian nationalism gained strength. More composers turned away from the influence of foreign countries and sought to write music that grew out of Russian life. These composers were inspired by Russian history, folklore and legend, folk songs, and patriotism.

Mikhail Glinka was one of the founders of "national Russian music." Other important composers belonged to a group known as "The Mighty Five." This was made up of Balakirev, César Cui, Borodin, Mussorgsky, and Rimsky-Korsakov.

"The Mighty Five" were interested in capturing in music the national flavor of Russia. Borodin composed a great opera, *Prince Igor,* that was based on a Russian epic. Mussorgsky went to the lives of the Russian people for many of his themes. Rimsky-Korsakov drew heavily on Russian folklore and folk songs.

Perhaps the most famous of all Russian composers was Peter Ilich Tchaikovsky (1840-1893). He wrote operas, symphonies, ballets, and other compositions. (Examples are: *Eugene Onegin, The Fourth Symphony, The Sixth Symphony, Swan Lake, The Sleeping Beauty, The Nutcracker,* and *Capriccio Italien.*) Although Tchaikovsky was an individualist, he too showed his nationalistic feeling in such works as his *1812 Overture* and *March Slav.*

1. What were some of the influences on Russian art and architecture?
2. Describe the chief Russian contributions to mathematics, science, medicine, and music.
3. What concerns did Dostoyevski express in his writings?

4. Russia and the Ottoman Empire in World Affairs

In the nineteenth century Russia also played a role in world affairs. It extended its empire by adding lands in the Caucasus, Central Asia, the Far East, and other regions. As Professor Warren Walsh points out: "The Russian counterpart of overseas expansion was overland expansion into adjacent territories. . . ." Equally important, Russia became involved in events in Turkey and in southeastern Europe.

Turkey Becomes "The Sick Man of Europe"

Modern-day Turkey is an important remnant of the old Ottoman Empire. The Ottoman (or Turkish) Empire had a very complicated history. We have already traced its history briefly to 1600 (pages 309 and 336).

The Turks early extended their control over the Balkans. In 1683 the Turks were defeated in their attempt to capture Vienna. After this setback, the Ottoman Empire continued to decline. In the eighteenth century, the Russians defeated the Turks and forced them to give up land near the Black Sea. Russia's determination to control Constantinople and the straits that linked the Black Sea with the Aegean and Mediterranean seas became stronger.

In the nineteenth century the Ottoman Empire was called "The Sick Man of Europe." Czar Nicholas I of Russia, assuming the attitude of a physician, declared: "I repeat to you that the sick man is dying; and we must never allow such an event to take us by surprise."

There were many factors that contributed to the "sickness" of the Ottoman Empire. These included the following: 1. The Turkish government and the governors (*pashas*) sent to rule its possessions were inefficient and frequently corrupt. 2. Some of the Muslim Turks clashed with the Christian subjects of the Ottoman Empire. 3. Jealousies and rivalries developed among the different peoples living under the control of the Turks. 4. Nationalism grew stronger among the various Balkan groups and led to demands for the establishment of new nations.

Russian leaders felt that they had a responsibility to protect their fellow-Slavs in the Ottoman Empire. Austria, France, Russia, and Great Britain had conflicting interests in Turkish territories. Great Britain was determined to check Russian expansion into the Mediterranean.

The Greeks Revolt

In 1804-1805 the Serbs in the Balkans had rebelled against the Turkish rulers. Then in 1821 the Greeks revolted. Nationalism played an important part in the Greek revolt. The Turks recognized Greece as an independent nation in 1829-1830.

The Great Powers Go to War

After Greece gained its independence, tensions continued in the Ottoman Empire. Great Britain was worried that Russia might seize the city of Constantinople and other Turkish areas. If that happened, Britain's interests in the Middle East might be threatened.

A religious dispute developed. The czar demanded that Russia be given a protectorate over all the Sultan's Orthodox Christian subjects in European Turkey and their holy places. Emperor Napoleon III claimed that the French already had the right to guard the Christian holy places on behalf of the Roman Catholics because of a French agreement with the Sultan. Great Britain was fearful that Russia would use the argument as an excuse to take over Turkish lands. Therefore, Great Britain supported France.

This religious dispute, the Russian army's occupation of certain Turkish lands, Britain's fear of Russian expansion, and other factors led to the outbreak of the Crimean War (1854-1856). Great Britain, France, Sardinia, and Turkey fought against Russia.

The Crimean War

The war was fought on the Crimean peninsula. It was marked by disastrous errors. One such error was "the charge of the Light Brigade," when about

The Breakup of the Ottoman Empire

| Areas ceded by the Ottoman Empire 1699-1913 | The Ottoman Empire in 1913 |

Beginning in the seventeenth century, the Ottoman Empire gradually declined. In the nineteenth century it became known as "the Sick Man of Europe" and by 1913 it had lost much of its territory.

six hundred British cavalrymen attacked and were slaughtered by a much larger Russian army. "I am an old man and I have seen many battles, but this is the worst of all!" declared one French general. A courageous Englishwoman, Florence Nightingale, and a small group of volunteers hurried to the Crimea. They established hospitals at Scutari and Balaclava. There they nursed the wounded and fought cholera.

After many soldiers on both sides lost their lives, Russia was defeated. Some important provisions of the peace treaty included the following: 1. All the signers agreed to guarantee the independence of the Ottoman Empire and promised not to interfere in Turkish internal affairs. The Sultan was to treat his subjects fairly. 2. The Black Sea was to be neutralized. That is, no ships of war were to enter the Black Sea, and the shores of the sea were not to be fortified. Ships of commerce were to be free to travel on the Black Sea. 3. Russia had to give up control of important territories.

The Congress of Berlin

The Crimean War did not put an end to the territorial ambitions of Russia. Nor did it change the national hopes of the peoples of the Balkans. In 1876 the Bulgarians revolted against Turkish rule. (See the map above.) Then the peoples of the regions of Serbia and Montenegro also went to war against the Turks. Finally, in 1877 Russia declared war on Turkey.

The Russo-Turkish War (1877–1878) ended in a victory for Russia and her Balkan allies. When the peace treaty gave Russia great control over the Balkans, Great Britain and Austria refused to accept it. These countries wanted to hold a general conference of major powers to decide the future of Turkish territories.

Russia finally agreed. The delegates met in Berlin. Some important results of the Congress of Berlin (1878) were the following: 1. Austria was granted the right to occupy and administer Bosnia and Herzegovina in the Balkans. 2. Great Britain received Cyprus, a large island in the Mediterranean. 3. Macedonia remained a part of Turkey. 4. Russia was given some territories near the Black Sea. 5. The Congress of Berlin recognized the independence of the nations of Serbia, Rumania, and Montenegro, and the right of Bulgaria to govern itself.

Check on Your Reading

1. How did Turkey become "The Sick Man of Europe"?
2. What were the results of the Congress of Berlin?

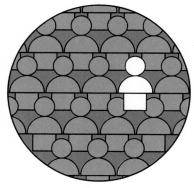

LET'S MEET THE PEOPLE

A Russian Landowner in 1860

Ivan Ivanovitch was a well-to-do Russian landowner of the nineteenth century. He was sitting in his comfortable armchair by the window. At nine A.M. he had tea. After tea Ivan Ivanovitch began his labors of the day "by resuming his seat at the open window and having his Turkish pipe filled and lighted by a boy whose special function [was] to keep his master's pipes in order." Here Ivan sat "till the sun [had] so far moved round that the veranda at the back of the house was completely in the shade." Then he ordered a servant to move his armchair to the veranda, and he sat there until dinner.

Ivan ate an excellent dinner at one o'clock. Then "a deathlike stillness [fell] upon the house." It was the time for the after-dinner nap. Ivan Ivanovitch retired to his room, from which the flies had been chased by a servant, and slept for two hours.

In the afternoon Ivan Ivanovitch rode about in the fields for an hour. He returned to the house long before it was time for supper and rested himself in his chair by the window.

That evening, after supper, a group of serfs came to see him.

"Well, children, what do you want?" Ivan demanded.

"Little father! Grant us [more grain for our families]. Please, little father, please," the serfs begged.

"Now enough—enough!" declared Ivan Ivanovitch. "You are blockheads! There's no use talking; it can't be done."

With these words Ivan Ivanovitch reentered the house. He had had a tiring day, and he did not intend to let his serfs keep him from a well-earned night of rest.

The above sketch is based on an eyewitness account in Donald M. Wallace, *Russia,* 1877, London; selections from this book can be found in *Reading in Russian History,* compiled and edited by Warren B. Walsh, 1959, Syracuse University Press.

CHAPTER REVIEW

Think and Discuss

1. What ideas were considered dangerous to the state under Nicholas I?
2. Why was there a long period of unsuccessful revolts against autocracy in Russia?
3. Some historians consider that serfdom in Russia and slavery in the United States came to an end at this time because they both were becoming unprofitable to the landowners. Evaluate this statement and compare the way in which the serfs in Russia and the slaves in the United States were freed.
4. Do the art, music, and literature of nineteenth-century Russia have anything in common? Justify your answer.
5. Some historians state that the intellectuals of Russia who believed in and wrote about liberal reforms did not reach the common people because they themselves did not belong to the lower groups or fully understand the people's problems. What evidence can you find to support or refute this statement?
6. Why didn't Russia undertake extensive overseas expansion as did England, France, Spain, Holland, and Portugal?
7. The term "Turbulent Balkans" has often been used to describe southeastern Europe. What does it mean? Is it true? Why?
8. What causes for future wars can you find in the results of the Congress of Berlin?

Past and Present

1. What similarities and differences are there between the mirs in the nineteenth century and the collective farms in the Soviet Union today?
2. How does the music of the Russian "Mighty Five" compare with the music of today?
3. Are there any leaders of today who prefer to "listen to their hearts"—as did the nineteenth century Slavophiles—in making decisions?

Activities

1. Have a concert in class. Play records of music by Tchaikovsky and other well-known Russian composers.
2. Tolstoy frequently used in his writings the very old idea that "happiness consists in living for others." Have a round-table discussion on the status of this idea today.
3. Make a chart of nineteenth-century scientists and mathematicians, indicating their countries of origin and their discoveries or works.

Imperialism and World Tensions

KEYNOTE

Western imperialism reached a peak in the last part of the nineteenth century, a time when Western nations expanded into Asia, Africa, and parts of Latin America. To these areas, this imperialism often brought modern means of communication and transportation, modern medicine, improved means of sanitation, and new methods of agriculture.

However, there was a price—the other side of the imperialism coin. Peoples dominated by foreigners often lost control of their own affairs. Their economies were organized to produce products that the imperialist nations wanted, and many of them became essentially one-product countries. Age-old cultures were disrupted. Subject peoples were treated as inferiors.

Materially, imperialism benefited the imperialists and some of the subject peoples. In other respects, however, many observers considered the experience as harmful to all concerned.

Admiral Perry and his officers are greeted by Japanese officials.

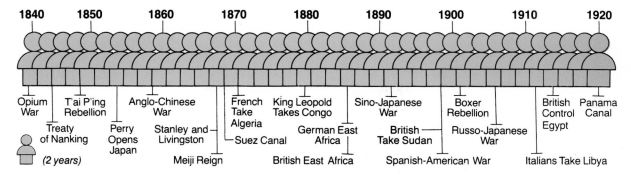

| 1840 | 1850 | 1860 | 1870 | 1880 | 1890 | 1900 | 1910 | 1920 |

Opium War
T'ai P'ing Rebellion
Anglo-Chinese War
French Take Algeria
King Leopold Takes Congo
Sino-Japanese War
Boxer Rebellion
British Control Egypt
Panama Canal

Treaty of Nanking
Perry Opens Japan
Stanley and Livingston
Suez Canal
German East Africa
British Take Sudan
Russo-Japanese War

(2 years)
Meiji Reign
British East Africa
Spanish-American War
Italians Take Libya

1. A Brief History of Imperialism

A specialist on international politics has defined imperialism as "the political domination of a state over an alien people, usually for an indefinite period of time but conceivably with a promise of eventual independence." Imperialism in the modern sense usually, but not always, means the establishment of colonies. However, a country may gain strong influence over a foreign land by economic, military, or cultural means as well.

Imperialism Has a Long History

In ancient times, imperialist governments built great empires. The Egyptian Empire, the Babylonian Empire, the Empire of Alexander the Great, and the Roman Empire are examples. Other thrusts of imperialism began in the fifteenth and sixteenth centuries, with European voyages of discovery. In time, Portugal, Spain, England, the Netherlands, and France built empires.

During the last part of the eighteenth and most of the nineteenth centuries, imperialism began to lose favor. There were several reasons why: 1. England lost its American colonies. 2. Spain and Portugal lost most of their Latin American colonies. 3. The idea of free international trade became popular.

Britain's Prime Minister Disraeli, who had helped to build the British Empire, said: "These wretched colonies . . . are a millstone around our necks!"

Then in the 1870s, efforts to gain colonial possessions increased tremendously. The competition for colonies and influence over other lands was intense during the next few decades.

Reasons for Nineteenth-Century Imperialism

There were many reasons for the revival of imperialism in the latter part of the nineteenth century.

These included the following: 1. The Industrial Revolution of the previous century had greatly improved means of transportation and communication. It also had increased the demand for raw materials and for markets where finished products could be sold. 2. Government leaders thought that by gaining colonies they could increase their nation's power abroad, add to its military security, and strengthen it in case of war.

3. The nationalistic feelings of people in various Western countries stirred them to want their nation to excel others in the size of its empire. People believed that an empire was a symbol of national success and glory. 4. Government leaders believed that colonies would become lands to which their country's surplus populations would migrate. 5. Ambitious business people, investors, banks, and companies were convinced that colonies would help them make great profits. Some ambitious statesmen believed that they could add to their popularity by imperialistic efforts. 6. Some people claimed that their countries had a duty to educate and "civilize" the inhabitants of other lands. 7. Others wished to bring Christianity to other peoples of the world.

Check on Your Reading

1. What is imperialism?
2. Why was there a revival of imperialism?
3. Discuss the motives behind imperialism.

2. Imperialism in Asia

European leaders worked hard to spread their nations' influence in Asia. China was one of the countries affected by imperialism. By the nineteenth century, the great and ancient Chinese Empire was no longer strong enough to resist foreign domination.

This painting by a Chinese artist shows the offices of foreign traders in Canton. Each office flies the flag of its country.

Contacts with the West in the Sixteenth and Early Seventeenth Centuries

The first Europeans to arrive in China by sea in the sixteenth century were the Portuguese. The rulers of the Ming dynasty soon learned to mistrust these adventurers who raided their coasts and seized their ships. However, the Chinese were willing to trade with these foreigners if the trade could be controlled. In 1557 a compromise was reached, and the Portuguese were allowed to live and trade at Macao, a peninsula near Canton. (See the map on page 486.) Later, the Portuguese and other Westerners were permitted to trade at Canton during certain times of the year.

When the Dutch and the English arrived by sea, they also plundered coastal towns and cities and seized Chinese ships. Shortly after their arrival, the Ming dynasty was overthrown.

China in the Eighteenth Century

The Manchus of Manchuria came to power in China as the Ch'ing dynasty in 1644. Under a series of able Ch'ing emperors, China enjoyed a century and a half of good government. At the same time these rulers increased the size of the Chinese empire by taking control of lands in Central Asia and of the island of Formosa (Taiwan).

The rule of K'ang-hsi (from 1662-1722) opened a period of achievement in the arts and literature as well as in agriculture. K'ang-hsi was thoroughly Chinese in cultural background. He wrote poetry and encouraged the writing of scholarly books, including a huge encyclopedia. He welcomed Jesuit missionaries and studied Latin and science with them. The imperial kiln developed new and beautiful types of porcelain.

During the eighteenth century, China grew in wealth and population. During this period, things in an ornate Chinese style, or *chinoiserie*, were greatly admired in Europe. Chinese silks, porcelains, and tea were in great demand in Europe and America. Ships from the United States joined European ships in the Canton trade.

However, by the end of the eighteenth century, serious problems developed in China. Later emperors were weak and their governments became corrupt. Also there was a growing economic crisis. Farmlands had been expanded by new techniques of growing rice and by the introduction of new crops such as peanuts, sweet potatoes, and corn. Now, however, almost all possible farmland had been occupied; and the population had grown from 100 million in 1650 to 300 million in 1800. The population pressure was beginning to cause poverty, hardship, and unrest. There was widespread suffering, and flood and famine took thousands of lives. Wars drained the treasury. There were numerous rebellions against the Ch'ing. None of them were successful, but all brought death and destruction.

In addition, China by the nineteenth century lagged far behind the West in military technology. The Industrial Revolution and science and invention provided Western armies and navies with weapons and equipment far superior to those of the Chinese. European nations were ready to take advantage of this.

China and the Opium War

By the end of the eighteenth century, Great Britain had become the leading country in the China trade. Early in the nineteenth century, tensions developed between China and Great Britain. These tensions had several causes. Britain wanted more trading rights in China and greater recognition of British diplomats there. Also Britain demanded better treatment for British citizens in China. Britain's initial interest in China was in developing trade, rather than in building an empire.

Finally, a bitter controversy arose over the opium trade. British merchants were making considerable profit supplying the people of China with opium, a narcotic drug which was grown in India. The Chinese government insisted that this undesirable trade be stopped. It demanded that the British give up all supplies of opium "by virtue of that reason which Heaven hath implanted in all of us." When the British refused, the so-called Opium War broke out.

China was defeated in the Opium War of 1839-1842, and a treaty of peace was signed at Nanking in 1842. These were the key provisions: 1. Canton, Shanghai, and three other ports were to be open to British trade. 2. The island of Hong Kong was ceded to Great Britain. 3. British trade with China was made easier in several ways.

The Treaty of Nanking was important because it gave Great Britain a commercial hold in China and excited the ambitions of other countries. In 1843 the British also gained the right of *extraterritoriality*. This meant, in part, that British citizens who committed crimes in China would be tried by British judges or British officials under British law, not by the Chinese.

Other Nations Move into China

Other countries were quick to follow the British in gaining rights and privileges in China. Several European nations and the United States won the right of extraterritoriality. As a result of the Anglo-Chinese War of 1856-1860, more ports and regions were opened to foreign trade. Great Britain, France, Russia, and the United States gained more commercial privileges. In 1858, China ceded territory to Russia, which was expanding eastward.

In addition, an internal conflict known as the T'ai P'ing Rebellion (c. 1850-1864) disrupted China. Its principal leader was Hung Hsiu-ch'üan, a village teacher influenced by Christianity and Western ideas. Hung tried to overthrow the Manchus and establish a new dynasty to be called "T'ai P'ing" or "Great Peace." The Chinese government, aided by an army organized and led by foreign officers, finally suppressed the rebellion.

Foreigners continued to take advantage of China's weaknesses. European countries established *spheres of influence* there. A sphere of influence was

In the nineteenth century Chinese porcelain was very popular in western countries.

485

an area in which a foreign nation claimed practically exclusive rights to develop economic enterprises, build railroads, and profit from trade. It differed from a *colony* (that belonged to and was completely subject to a foreign nation); and from a *protectorate* (an area that maintained its sovereignty but was controlled by another nation). By the twentieth century, Great Britain, France, Russia, and Germany all had established economic or political domination over sections of China.

The Sino-Japanese War

Japan, impressed by Western victories, had its own ambitions. In 1894, friction over Korea, which China had long controlled and Japan coveted, led to war between those two nations. This Sino-Japanese conflict (1894–1895) resulted in victory for the Japanese.

The treaty which ended the war deprived China of more territory. Under its terms, Japan received the Liaotung peninsula, Formosa, and other territories. China also recognized Korean independence, and in 1910 Japan annexed that country. Several European nations forced Japan to return the Liaotung peninsula to China. However, Japan had now successfully joined the Western imperialists in taking advantage of China's weaknesses.

The United States in Asia

The United States had traded with China as early as Revolutionary War times, and this trade continued throughout the nineteenth century. Then the United States interest in Asia increased after the Spanish-American War of 1898.

After winning the war, the United States took possession of the Philippine Islands, Puerto Rico, and other areas. A great controversy now arose in the United States over whether the Philippine Islands should be a colony under the control of the United States.

By 1910 European nations, Japan, and the United States had established economic or political control over much of Asia. The inset shows the results of the Russo-Japanese War.

Imperialism in Asia 1910

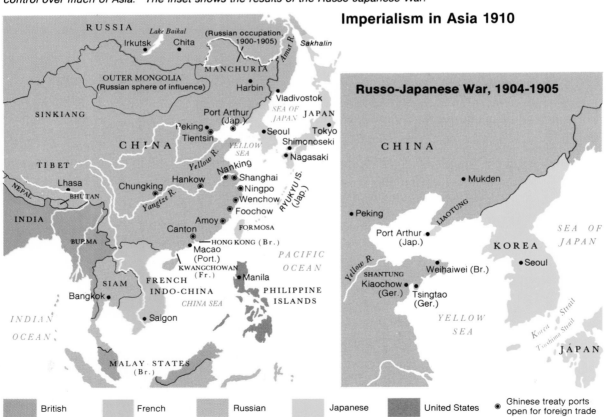

Many Americans did not believe that the United States should take the Philippines as a colony, especially since Filipinos had fought against Spain in order to win their independence. During the debate over the Philippines, Senator George F. Hoar of Massachusetts asked how the United States could "strut about in the cast-off clothing of pinchback emperors and pewter kings" by acquiring an overseas empire. William Jennings Bryan, who was the Democratic candidate for President in 1900, also opposed the annexation of the Philippines. He feared that it would contribute to militarism in the United States.

On the other hand, many other Americans believed that the Philippines should become a United States colony. They said that the United States had become a great naval power, and the country needed overseas bases. Also they felt that American trade would be helped by having the Philippines as a colony. Still others argued that just as it had been the destiny of the United States to expand across a continent, so too was its destiny to acquire an empire. Proclaimed United States Senator Albert J. Beveridge:

> We will not abandon our opportunity in the Orient. We will not renounce our part in the mission of our race, trustee, under God, of the civilization of the world.

The United States' early experiences in the Philippines showed that occupying land in Asia brought problems. William Howard Taft, the president of the commission appointed to govern the Philippines, called the Filipinos "our little brown brothers." However, Philippine patriots, who wanted their land independent, did not view Americans as brothers. They fought fiercely, and two years passed before the United States was able to "pacify" the Philippines.

The United States determined to end such hostility by carrying out a program of reform. It built schools, roads, and hospitals. It also gradually allowed the Filipinos to govern themselves. On July 4, 1946, with the approval of the United States, the Philippines became an independent nation.

The "Open Door" Policy

William McKinley, President of the United States from 1897 to 1901, described the official American policy toward China: "[Our policy] is to

. . . preserve Chinese territorial and administrative entity, protect all rights guaranteed to friendly powers by treaty and international law, and safeguard for the world the principle of equal and impartial trade with all parts of the Chinese Empire."

It appeared that several European nations did not feel that way. Evidence seemed to indicate that they planned to partition China among themselves. United States officials and business people feared that if this should happen, American commercial interests would be endangered. Therefore, the American Secretary of State, John Hay, sent notes to nations with interests in China, suggesting that an "Open Door" policy be established there.

Hay in 1899 proposed that the "Open Door" policy include these features: 1. The commercial rights of all nations should be respected in China, including spheres of influence. 2. The nations holding spheres of influence should not discriminate against the rights of other nations. Hay also pointed out that there would be "undoubted benefits" if there could be "perfect equality of treatment for . . . commerce and navigation [of all nations] within such 'spheres'. . . ."

This proposed "Open Door" policy did not greatly change the actions of most of the powers. Spheres of influence continued to exist. In 1898 the young Chinese emperor tried to reform the government and armed forces of China. He was blocked by the Empress Dowager, widow of a former emperor. She seized control of the government and abolished his reforms. China remained largely under the domination of foreign powers.

The Boxer Rebellion

Some Chinese, with their government's approval, rebelled against foreign control. During the summer of 1900, a Chinese organization known as the "Righteous Harmonious Fists" rose against foreigners in China. Westerners called its members "Boxers." The Boxers proclaimed: "Though these foreigners ride in sedans unbefitting their rank, China yet regards them as barbarians, of whom God disapproves and is sending down spirits and genii for their destruction!" The Boxers laid siege to the foreign legations in Peking and killed a number of Europeans.

A joint army that included troops from Japan, Britain, Russia, France, Germany, and the United States came to relieve the legations. They put down the Boxer Rebellion and captured Peking. The Chinese government was compelled to give up more rights to the foreigners and to pay an indemnity for damages that the Boxers had caused. The United States returned most of its share of the indemnity. The money was used to establish a scholarship fund to send Chinese students to American colleges.

Check on Your Reading

1. What were some of the achievements of the early Ch'ing emperors?
2. What problems did China face in 1800? How had these problems developed?
3. What was the importance of the Opium War and the Treaty of Nanking?
4. What did China lose in the war with Japan in 1894-1895?
5. What was the "Open Door" policy?
6. What was the outcome of the Boxer Rebellion?

---

3. Japan Becomes an Industrial Nation and an Empire Builder

Like China, Japan experienced the powerful influence of Western nations in the nineteenth century. However, by quickly adopting certain Western ways, Japan escaped foreign domination.

Hideyoshi and the Tokugawa Shogunate

Japan was not unified until the sixteenth century. Three leaders helped bring this about; the most important of them was Hideyoshi. Japanese tradition says that his predecessor, Nobunaga, found the stones on which to build the nation's unity. Hideyoshi (1536-1598) shaped them. And Ieyasu, Hideyoshi's successor, laid the stones in place.

Born into a peasant family, Hideyoshi was first a stable boy. Then he joined Nobunaga's army and rose in the ranks from a common soldier to leading general. His soldiers called him "Cotton" because he was a warrior whose talents could be put to many uses. His advisors called him "Taiko" ("Supreme Official"). And his biographers have called him the "Napoleon of Japan," for he was a great conqueror.

Nobunaga was assassinated in 1582. Hideyoshi took over. He completed the unification of Japan, spreading his control over the entire country. He failed, however, in his attempt to bring China under Japanese control.

Hideyoshi died a peaceful death in 1598. Ieyasu, who had also been one of Nobunaga's generals, fought his way to power. Ieyasu took the title of *Shogun,* or "Generalissimo." He centered his government around his castle at the small village of Yedo. In time Yedo became known as Tokyo.

Members of Ieyasu's family were the Tokugawa. Ieyasu established the Tokugawa Shogunate, which ruled Japan and kept the nation at relative peace from 1603 to 1867. During this period emperors came and went. Real power rested in the Shogun, who kept strict control over the emperor and his court.

Perry's Expedition to Japan

From about 1640 to the middle of the nineteenth century, Japan deliberately avoided contact with Europeans. Japanese were prohibited from traveling to other countries, and foreigners were told they were not wanted. The only European settlement allowed was the Dutch trading post at Nagasaki.

Japan's policy of exclusion of foreigners eventually became a source of concern among Western nations. Whaling and merchant ships from the United States and other countries frequently passed near Japan. Occasionally sailors were shipwrecked on the Japanese coast. Now and then a merchant ship put in at a Japanese port, seeking supplies. Japanese officials invariably ordered such ships to leave immediately. They refused to furnish supplies. Sometimes they even did not aid shipwrecked sailors. Seeking trade with Japan and its use as a supply station for ships in the China trade, Westerners wanted to "open" that country to the world. The United States attempted to perform that task.

On July 8, 1853, a squadron of United States ships appeared in what is now called Tokyo Bay. Commodore Matthew Perry commanded the fleet. He carried a letter from President Millard Fillmore to the Japanese government. It asked for an end to Japan's exclusion policy and the opening of trade with the United States.

After he had conferred with Japanese officials, Perry's ships sailed away. He promised to return the following year for the Japanese answer.

Perry's visit brought to a head a controversy that had been simmering in Japan for some time. Over the years, the country had not remained entirely isolated. The Dutch at Nagasaki exerted some Western influence. Japanese scholars had translated books the Dutch brought, and thus learned something about Western ways and technology. It soon became apparent that Japan, like China, had not developed technology as the West had done. Scholars and Japanese officials were also aware of what had happened to China. A number of Japanese consequently wished to modernize their nation, if for no other reason than to protect it from China's fate.

Also, Japanese merchants wished to open Japan to world trade to increase their wealth. They endorsed a favorable response to Perry's demands.

Moreover, the Tokugawa Shogunate was not the pillar of strength it had been. There had been peasant discontent and uprisings. Famine had driven thousands of peasants into cities, where for the most part they were unemployed. As the rural population declined, taxation became a greater burden on those who remained on the land.

The Japanese government split into two factions. One, the conservatives, insisted that Japan should resist the demands and continue its isolation. The other, recalling the large steam-powered ships and their guns, realized that Japan's outmoded armaments would be no match for those of a Western power. This side argued that Japan should give in.

The realist side won. When Perry returned in 1854 the Japanese government agreed to deal with him. It eventually made a treaty with the United States, opening two ports to American ships. The treaty also provided for better care for shipwrecked Americans, and permitted some trade.

Townsend Harris

Townsend Harris was the first American Consul to Japan. It was an important moment in history when Harris appeared before the Shogun on December 7, 1857, to present his credentials.

In his *Journal,* Harris wrote that the Shogun was seated in a chair placed on a platform raised about two feet from the floor. His clothing was made of silk, and his crown was a black lacquered cap shaped like an inverted bell. He wore neither rich jewels nor gold ornaments.

"My earnest wishes are to unite [our] two countries more closely in the ties of enduring friendship . . ." declared Consul Harris.

The Shogun answered: "I am pleased with [Consul Harris'] discourse. . . ."

The Japanese were fascinated by Perry's gift of a miniature railroad. Within fifteen years a railroad had been built from Tokyo to Yokohama.

Harris proved to be an excellent diplomat. In 1858, as a result of his activities, five more ports were opened to United States trade, and Americans were granted the right of extraterritoriality in Japan. Within a short time, several European nations also gained trade and extraterritorial rights in Japan.

Japan Changes Drastically

For the Japanese, this was not the end of controversy. "Honor the Emperor, expel the barbarians!" insisted groups opposed to the Tokugawa Shogunate. These people sought to remove the Shogun. They hoped to undo what they considered the damage and disgrace the Tokugawa had brought upon the country. In 1867 they succeeded in forcing the Shogunate from power. The Japanese government then was reorganized around the young emperor, known by his reign name as the Meiji (meaning "enlightened rule") Emperor.

The end of the Tokugawa Shogunate, however, did not mean an end to foreign presence in Japan. By 1868 Western powers were too firmly entrenched in Japan to be removed. Also the Japanese wanted to learn from them. The Japanese adapted Western ideas and technology to strengthen their nation.

During the Meiji reign (1867 to 1912), Japan went through changes that transformed the country. These changes were introduced from the top—that is, they came from the ruling groups, rather than from the people. A constitution was put into effect in 1889. Although there was an elected House of Representatives, great power was in the hands of the leaders of the armed forces and the wealthy merchants. A national army was organized, and a navy was built. Feudal divisions were eliminated.

Railroads were constructed. Modern industries were built. Foreign trade was encouraged. Education was improved, and Japanese students were permitted to do advanced study at universities in foreign countries.

At the same time, efforts were made to develop feelings of nationalism in the people. Love of country was linked to loyalty to the emperor.

Japan Wins Wars and Becomes a World Power

Pride of nation grew. The desire to increase national power led Japanese leaders to want to build an empire also. An already weakened China seemed a logical target for Japanese imperialism. In the Sino-Japanese War of 1894-1895 Japan won Formosa, and Korea was given its independence from China.

By the end of the nineteenth century, Japan had acquired sufficient prestige to call successfully for a revision of treaties with Western powers. Extraterritoriality, as well as other inequalities in trade treaties, eventually were removed.

The Japanese also began to prepare for a clash with Russia, which had taken control of Manchuria and was expanding into northern Korea. A historian who lived at that period pointed out that the goal of both Russia and Japan was "the immensely rich and yet undeveloped North China, of which Manchuria is a part, and to which Korea is an appendix."

In 1904, the Japanese attacked the Russians at Port Arthur, on the southern tip of Manchuria, without warning. Japanese troops soon occupied Port Arthur, and shortly thereafter Japanese warships dealt a Russian fleet a crushing blow in a battle in the Sea of Japan. By 1905 Japan had won the war.

By the Treaty of Portsmouth, New Hampshire, Japan was given a protectorate over Korea; and was permitted to lease the Liaotung peninsula, including Port Arthur. Japan also received control of the southern portion of Sakhalin Island, all of which had belonged to Russia; and valuable fishing rights in the Pacific Ocean. China was permitted to keep control of Manchuria. Westerners at the beginning of the twentieth century had to recognize Japan as the leading power in East Asia.

Check on Your Reading

1. What did Hideyoshi and Ieyasu accomplish?
2. What was gained by Perry's expedition to Japan and later by Townsend Harris?
3. What changes did Japan make in its government and economy during the Meiji period?
4. How did Japan achieve a position as a world power?

---

4. Imperialism in Africa

In Africa lay rich diamond deposits, gold and copper, and unlimited trading opportunities. There was also a variety of peoples who seemed easy prey for Europeans bent on rule and riches.

This lithograph shows a battle in the British campaign against the Zulus.

Prelude to Western Imperialism in Africa

Portuguese explorers established a trade in slaves and spices with Africa in the fifteenth century. Later, the Spaniards, Dutch, English, and French joined in the trade and set up trading stations along the coasts. From the middle of the sixteenth century to the early part of the nineteenth, some Europeans expanded their trade in Africa.

During the first half of the nineteenth century, British, French, and German explorers made journeys into the African interior. Europeans crossed the Sahara Desert, traced the courses of rivers, and explored the Sudan.

One dramatic event in the history of European exploration of Africa involved the finding of Dr. David Livingstone, a Scottish explorer and missionary, by Henry Morton Stanley, a newspaper reporter. In the 1850s, Livingstone made a remarkable east-to-west journey across Africa. He discovered Victoria Falls and Lake Nyasa. In 1866, he disappeared in East Africa. *The New York Herald* later sent Stanley to find Livingstone. The story of his success became famous.

But Dr. Livingstone refused to return home! He continued his explorations in Africa. Stanley never lost his own interest in Africa. He, too, made African journeys that were important, including one in which he followed the Congo River (now the Zaire River) from its source to the Atlantic Ocean.

Treaties and Land

Several factors combined to stimulate Europeans' interest in Africa in the second half of the nineteenth century. These included the fascinating reports by explorers of the continent; the geographic information that various expeditions accumulated; Stanley's account of his adventures; and the news of trading opportunities in Africa. Also Christian missionaries were increasingly determined to spread their faith there.

European powers competed with each other to seize portions of Africa. From the 1870s through the early years of the twentieth century, Africa was divided among European nations. This period was appropriately named "the time of the Great African Hunt."

There was no single method by which a foreign nation gained control of African territory. Methods varied according to the situation and the individuals involved. Sometimes a European nation backed one side in an African war and then set up a protectorate. Often the Europeans had to fight the Africans to occupy land, and they usually won in the long run because of their superior weapons and military techniques. A popular method was for a European nation to send an explorer to Africa. His job would be to persuade an African ruler to sign a "treaty" in return for gifts and help to strengthen the ruler's government. This document amounted to the ruler's surrender of control of his land to the Europeans.

European nations were successful in carving out colonies in Africa because of their overwhelming industrial and military strength. Also they were careful not to quarrel unnecessarily with each other in Africa, as one specialist in African history wrote:

> Except for the years between 1914 and 1918 [World War I], they were . . . able to control their rivalries in Africa within a general agreement among themselves. No matter how much they might quarrel elsewhere, they were usually careful not to quarrel in Africa. The broad limits of expansion for each of the interested powers—for Britain, France, Germany, Belgium . . . Italy, Portugal and Spain—were defined with little trouble at the Berlin colonial conference of 1884-5.

One observer at this conference wrote:

> The European governments have recently decided to take Africa from the Africans. This continent, in the latest maps, can be seen colored red, white, and blue according to the nation claiming the territory. The African kings, of course, were not consulted in these matters. They have had to submit.

King Leopold II and the Congo

Leopold II, King of Belgium, made one of the most important acquisitions. Using Henry Stanley as his representative in Africa, Leopold was able to gain control over a huge area in the Congo (now Zaire) (1879-1880). This territory, called the Congo Free State, was eighty times the size of Belgium. It became King Leopold's personal possession.

Leopold developed rubber and other natural resources in the Congo. Private companies were allowed to use African labor. They used a forced labor system with work camps, and African workers often were beaten and tortured. The local population was treated so harshly that an American observer who visited the Congo declared:

> . . . after my visit . . . I see the cruelty and fierceness of the white man's face. . . . For the first time I can appreciate fully the feelings of the natives. The white man's face is a dreadful prediction; where the white man goes, he devastates, destroys, depopulates.

In the early years of the twentieth century, several nations and various missionary groups became so disturbed by abuses in the Congo that they demanded that investigations and changes be made. Leopold finally was compelled to turn over his territory to the Belgian government in 1908. It was believed that the government would treat the people of the Belgian Congo, as the land was renamed, more fairly.

The French Expand in Africa

The French also built an African empire. In Algeria, the Arab ruler of Algiers in North Africa struck a French envoy in the face with a fan in 1827. Three years later, Charles X, the Bourbon King of France, and his government decided that the time was ripe to "avenge this insult." Charles' chief objective was to restore the prestige and power of the Bourbons by acquiring land abroad. In 1830 France sent troops to Algiers and captured the city. By 1871 the French finally were able to subdue most of the population and win control over the remainder of Algeria.

Tunis lay next to Algeria. It belonged to the Ottoman Empire, but was governed by the Muslim *Bey,* or governor. The Bey borrowed heavily from foreigners. When he could not repay the loan, he was compelled to give the French, British, and Italians financial concessions in Tunis. In 1881, after military incidents on the border between Algeria and Tunis, the French made Tunis a colony.

Africa in 1914

Legend:
- Belgium
- France
- Germany
- Great Britain
- Italy
- Portugal
- Spain

By the 1870s, Africa had become a major target for European imperialism. Over what areas did Belgium, France, Portugal, Spain, Italy, Germany, and Great Britain gain control?

France was allowed by other European nations to take control of a considerable part of Morocco in North Africa in return for allowing those European nations to expand elsewhere. France permitted Italy to try to take Tripolitania and Cyrenaïca, two Turkish provinces in North Africa. After a war with Turkey (1911–1912), Italy obtained these provinces, combined them, and renamed the area Libya. France allowed Great Britain to be the dominant power in Egypt.

In return for French support, Italy and Britain gave France a free hand in Morocco. In 1904 France and Spain secretly divided the area between them. Germany objected to France's actions in North Africa, and the French did not gain full control of Morocco until 1912.

In West Africa, France set up colonies along the coastal regions of Senegal, Dahomey, French Guinea, and the Ivory Coast. Then they moved into the Sahara area. Eventually they built a great empire in French West Africa.

The Germans and British Gain Colonies

Germany, which had not been unified until 1871, sought African lands later than did most European nations. Between 1884 and 1891, Germany acquired Togoland, German Southwest Africa, and the Cameroons.

Great Britain, which many Germans considered their greatest rival, established the colony of Nigeria, and smaller colonies on the west coast of Africa. The Germans and British competed for control of East Africa. In 1886, an arrangement was worked out. It had the following provisions: 1. The northern part of the region became British East Africa. 2. The southern part of the region became German East Africa. 3. The ruler of Zanzibar kept a strip of land along the Indian Ocean coast. 4. France became the dominant power on the island of Madagascar.

Italians Clash with Abyssinians

Italian leaders were eager to seize Abyssinia (now Ethiopia), which they called an escape from "[Italy's] imprisonment in the Mediterranean." In 1896 Italy invaded Abyssinia, but this time a European nation did not win a war in Africa. The Abyssinians, whose army had been trained by the French, crushed the Italians at Adowa.

By this time, only Abyssinia and Liberia remained free from European domination. Abyssinia itself finally fell under Italian control, following a war in 1935-1936.

The British Occupy Egypt

Meanwhile, the Frenchman Ferdinand de Lesseps and a French-organized company obtained permission from the *Pasha* (governor) of Egypt to build the Suez Canal to link the Mediterranean and Red seas. Egypt, although officially a part of the Turkish Empire, was virtually independent of Turkey's control. The Pasha considered himself to be the actual ruler of Egypt. He therefore felt he had the power to grant permission for the canal's construction.

French investors bought more than half of the shares of stock in the canal company. The Pasha also purchased shares. Construction began in 1859, and the canal was completed in 1869. The Suez Canal was extremely important because it provided a shorter route to India and beyond than the very long one around the southern tip of Africa.

When the Khedive of Egypt—a title later given to the Pasha—got into financial difficulties, he offered to sell his shares in the Suez Canal Company. The canal was vital to the British because it was part of the shortest water route to their possessions in India. Benjamin Disraeli, Prime Minister of Great Britain, therefore arranged for the purchase of the Khedive's shares in 1875. This gave Britain an important voice in the canal's management.

Even with the British stock purchase, the Egyptian government remained in financial trouble. Egypt was filled with tension. There was talk that the Egyptians might refuse to pay their debts to foreign bondholders. British and French creditors with investments in Egypt demanded that their countries protect their interests. British and French leaders insisted that the Suez Canal be kept safe from any internal disturbances in Egypt.

From about 1879 to 1882, Great Britain and France together dominated the financial affairs of Egypt and exercised considerable influence in other matters. This further strained relations between Egyptian nationalists and foreigners. In 1882, after several incidents, the British landed troops in Egypt and occupied it.

In 1888, Great Britain joined France, Turkey, and six other nations to sign the Constantinople Convention. This agreement stated that:

> The Suez Maritime Canal shall always be free and open, in time of war as in time of peace, to every vessel of commerce or of war, without distinction of flag. . . .

In 1914, Egypt became a British protectorate.

The French and British Compete for the Sudan

The British were also active in the Sudan. (See the map on page 493.) Near the close of the nineteenth century, a British general, Horatio Kitchener, marched his troops south from Egypt into the Sudan. He defeated a large army of *dervishes*. The dervishes were followers of a leader called the *Mahdi* (Guide), who claimed to have been divinely inspired to revive the Islamic faith and drive out the Europeans. General Kitchener also recaptured Khartoum, where dervishes had once destroyed a British military post. Then he continued south.

Meanwhile, France sent an expedition headed by Captain Marchand north from the French Congo into the Sudan. After a long and difficult journey, Marchand and his troops reached the village of Fashoda on the Nile on July 10, 1898. There he raised the French flag over an old fort.

A few months later, Kitchener and his troops arrived at Fashoda. Kitchener and Marchand each claimed the Sudan for his own nation! The historian Parker T. Moon described the meeting:

Kitchener congratulated Marchand on his remarkable journey and announced that he would hoist the British and Egyptian flags in token of Anglo-Egyptian sovereignty, whereat Marchand pointed out that the [French] tricolor was already floating over Fashoda. Kitchener courteously called attention to the numerical superiority of his own troops; Marchand retorted that he would be buried in the ruins of his fort rather than lower the tricolor without orders from Paris.

Kitchener then politely presented Marchand with a gift of wine; Marchand graciously presented Kitchener with a gift of fresh vegetables; and both prepared to fight if necessary.

War seemed inevitable. The French began to search for allies. The British government assured its people that "there are worse evils than war, and we shall not shrink from anything that may come."

The "Fashoda Incident" was finally settled peacefully. In 1899 it was agreed that Britain would govern the Egyptian Sudan. France's Congo Colony would be granted free commercial access through the Sudan to the Nile. Also France would be permitted to strengthen its position in the central and western Sudan. (See the map on page 493.)

Check on Your Reading

1. Why did Africa become a target of Western imperialism?
2. How did European powers acquire control in Africa?
3. Into what African areas did France, Germany, and Britain expand?

5. Imperialism in Latin America

While European powers were active in Asia and Africa, tension developed between the United States and Spain over Cuba. Cuba, the largest island in the Caribbean Sea, had long been a Spanish colony. (See the map on page 496.)

The Spanish-American War

Cubans revolted in the 1890s, seeking to throw off Spanish control. Tension between Spain and the United States was caused by Spain's harsh treatment of the Cuban people; by the desire of American business people to have their investments protected from disorder in Cuba; and by dramatic and often exaggerated stories in the American press about events in Cuba.

In February 1898, the United States battleship *Maine* was blown up in Havana harbor. People in the United States blamed the Spaniards, although no proof was ever found to show that Spain had been responsible for the explosion. Nevertheless, the Spanish-American War broke out.

The United States quickly defeated Spain. By the terms of the peace treaty, the Spaniards ceded the Philippine Islands, Guam, and Puerto Rico to the United States. As a result of the war, Spain also gave up its control of Cuba.

Cuba and the Platt Amendment

In 1898, the United States pledged that after Cuba's "pacification" the troops from the United States would "leave the government and control of the island to its people." With the guidance of the United States, Cuban representatives met in convention and wrote a constitution. However, the United States required Cuba to add the so-called Platt Amendment (1901) to the constitution. By this amendment, the United States reserved the right to buy or lease Cuban land for naval or coaling stations. Also the United States had the right to intervene:

. . . for the protection of Cuban independence, the maintenance of a government adequate for the protection of life, property and individual liberty, and for discharging [other] obligations.

Commercial agreements soon tied Cuba closely to the United States. The United States was able to exercise economic as well as political influence over Cuba.

Panama and the Canal

The government of the United States wanted to build a canal to link the Atlantic and Pacific oceans. The narrow Isthmus of Panama seemed a good place to build such a canal. A French company had tried and failed to construct a canal. The United States government now wished to take over the project. Since Panama then was under

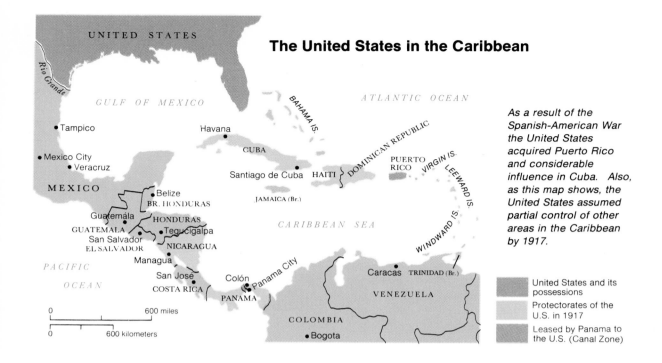

The United States in the Caribbean

As a result of the Spanish-American War the United States acquired Puerto Rico and considerable influence in Cuba. Also, as this map shows, the United States assumed partial control of other areas in the Caribbean by 1917.

United States and its possessions

Protectorates of the U.S. in 1917

Leased by Panama to the U.S. (Canal Zone)

the jurisdiction of Colombia, that country's consent was needed first. However, when the United States offered terms to Colombia, that government refused to accept them without changes. Essentially, Colombia wanted more financial compensation and additional rights before it would permit the United States to build the canal. The United States refused to offer more.

In 1903 a revolution broke out in Panama City. The rebels declared their independence from Colombia and set up the Republic of Panama. Three days after the revolution, the United States recognized the independence of the new republic. Less than two weeks later, the Republic of Panama—which now had possession of the canal area—signed a treaty permitting the United States to build the canal. In return, the Republic of Panama was to receive a sum of money that was less than the sum that had been asked for by Colombia.

It is generally accepted that President Theodore Roosevelt and others in the United States government aided the establishment of the Republic of Panama. For example, when Colombian troops were sent to put down the rebellion, United States ships prevented them from landing in Panama. Such acts prompted the Colombian government to protest:

[the] right of Colombia has been injured by the United States by an incredible transgression of the limits set by equity and justice. . . .

Several years later, Theodore Roosevelt admitted: "If I had followed conventional, conservative methods, I should have submitted a dignified state paper of approximately two hundred pages to the Congress and the debate would have been going on yet, but I took the canal zone and let Congress debate. . . ."

In April 1921, the United States Senate ratified a treaty giving Colombia an additional $25 million. It was hoped that this would result in "amity and commerce" between the two countries. Certainly the Panama Canal, which was opened officially on July 12, 1920, proved of great value to Latin America as well as to other parts of the world.

Check on Your Reading

1. What were the causes and results of the Spanish-American War?
2. Describe American relations with Cuba after 1900. What was the purpose of the Platt Amendment to the Cuban constitution?
3. Describe how the United States acquired rights to build the Panama Canal.

6. The Results of Imperialism

There were other cases of imperialist activities in the world. The Dutch were active in Indonesia. The French took over areas in Indochina. Other European nations set up spheres of influence in the Middle East. Our examination of imperialism in the Far East, Africa, and Latin America is sufficient to determine many of the effects of modern imperialism. The most important results of imperialism were:

1. European nations (including Russia), Japan, and the United States extended economic and often political control over many regions of the world.

2. In regions that became colonies, trade with foreign countries increased, and so did the development of natural resources. Foreign business people invested capital in colonial lands. Individuals and corporations of the foreign nations received most of the profit from these economic activities.

3. Some progress was made in improving the health and education of colonial peoples, depending on the foreign nation, the colonial region, the time, and the individuals involved.

4. Asia and Africa were brought into closer contact with, and were affected by, the cultures of foreign nations. For example, the lives of colonial peoples were influenced by systems of transportation and communication established by imperialist powers. Europeans, in turn, were affected by the rich cultures of African and Asian lands.

5. Eventually, domination by foreign powers helped to stimulate nationalism among colonial peoples. In time, they began to work for independence and the establishment of nations of their own.

Imperialism also created very serious problems. 1. The competition for colonies produced tensions among nations building empires. These tensions were one of the causes of future wars. 2. The imposition of Western cultures and technologies caused confusion and loss of identity among many peoples of ancient and rich cultures. These peoples were torn between their cultures and those of their foreign conquerors. 3. Also the experiences that some peoples had under Western imperialism developed feelings of mistrust, fear, and even hatred toward Westerners. Often these feelings were passed on to later generations.

Check on Your Reading

1. Which do you think are the most important results of imperialism?
2. Does imperialism exist in any areas of the world today? Explain.

During the struggle between the British and Chinese in 1856 the British burned houses in Canton.

LET'S MEET
THE PEOPLE

Lin Tse-hsu and the Letter That Was Never Sent

The emperor ordered that opium be prohibited from China, and he appointed Lin Tse-hsu to be commissioner to carry out that command.

Lin was a reasonable man, and he reasoned in this way: Opium was harmful. Victoria, Queen of England, must be a reasonable person too, and she would agree with him that trade in opium should be stopped. Since the trade continued, the Queen must not know about it. So Lin drafted a letter on the subject to inform her.

"The Way of Heaven is fairness to all; it does not suffer us to harm others in order to benefit ourselves," Lin began. He pointed out that since trade had been established with Britain it had "flourished with the blessing of the Heavenly Court, which treats all within the Four Seas as one great family."

However, Lin went on, "there is a class of evil foreigner that makes opium and brings it for sale, tempting fools to destroy themselves, merely in order to reap profit." He noted that the use of opium among the Chinese had once been very small, but now it was growing larger almost every day. This was ruining many of the people of his country, and the nation of China itself. Lin insisted, "our great, unified Manchu Empire regards itself as responsible for the habits and morals of its subjects and cannot rest content to see any of them become victims to a deadly poison."

Consequently, Lin wrote to the Queen, the Chinese government planned to take strong measures to halt the opium trade. "I now give my assurance that we mean to cut off this harmful drug forever." He concluded: "Do not say you have not been warned in time."

The letter apparently was never sent. Perhaps Lin concluded that there was insufficient time to wait for a response from the Queen, and that immediate action was necessary. Perhaps the letter would have made no difference anyway. In any event, Lin confiscated and burned the opium in the port of Canton, where most foreigners traded. To British merchants, who enjoyed high profits from the trade, this was one sufficient cause for war—and the Opium War of 1839-1842 began.

From John Gittings, ed., *A Chinese View of China.* New York: Pantheon Books, 1973, pp. 45-50. Translated by Arthur Waley in *The Opium War through Chinese Eyes.* Chester Springs, Pa.: Dufour Editions, Inc., 1966, pp. 66-72.

CHAPTER REVIEW

Think and Discuss

1. Do you think imperialism is ever justified? Why?
2. If you had lived in China in the 1800s, what would you have thought about the right of extraterritoriality? Why?
3. Do you think that the attitudes toward Western civilizations of such nations as China were influenced by Western imperialism? Why?
4. Do you think Commodore Perry's expedition to Japan was an interference in the internal affairs of that country? Why?
5. How did the changes made during the Meiji reign in Japan affect Japan's position in the world?
6. Evaluate the activities of the European powers in Africa at the end of the nineteenth century.
7. Compare United States imperialism of the period with that of European countries. In what ways were they alike? How were they different?
8. Evaluate the effects of imperialism in the nineteenth century.

Past and Present

1. The emotional writing of newspapers played a role in bringing about the Spanish-American War. Study newspapers today to see how emotional or objective they are in reporting foreign news.
2. Overpopulation became a serious problem in China in the 1800s. Is this a problem in some countries today? Explain your answer.
3. What may happen to people of a country when they come into contact with a culture more advanced in science and technology than their own?

Activities

1. On a map of Africa, show the colonial possessions of European nations in 1914.
2. On a map of the world, indicate the possessions of the United States in 1914.
3. Do research and write a paper in which you describe the actual construction of the Panama Canal. Give special attention to the solution of problems of engineering and sanitation.

9

Revolutions, Dictators, and Two World Wars

Courage, cruelty, anger, love, dedication, foolishness, and wisdom were all part of the events described in this unit. These events occurred in our own twentieth century. Tragic as they were, they have shaped our times, and there is much that we can learn from them in planning our future. In describing the events that led to World War I, a historian has said that "An age was about to end." Yet it was equally true that, after the war, an age was about to begin.

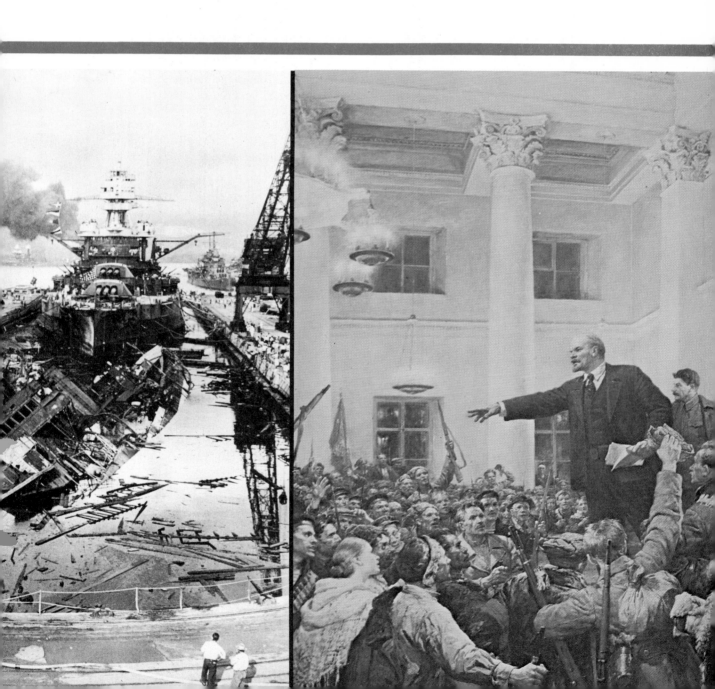

World War I and Its Legacy

Nine million soldiers died between 1914 and 1918 in World War I. Other millions were wounded or crippled for life. World War I was the war in which the airplane, the submarine, the machine gun, and the armored tank were widely used for the first time—with devastating results.

When the conflict ended, large parts of Europe were in ruins. Royal dynasties had collapsed and economies were shattered. Communists seized control of Russia during the war. Peace treaties changed national boundaries and created new nations. As new power structures developed, the effects of World War I became one of the key features of the following decades.

The burning of Ypres, Belgium. More than one million humans were killed or wounded in battles in and around this town.

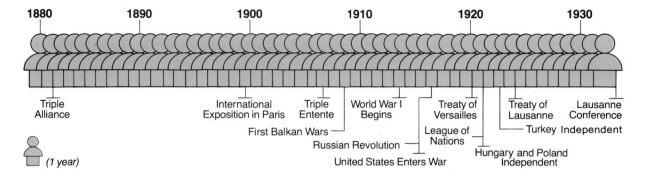

| 1880 | 1890 | 1900 | 1910 | 1920 | 1930 |

Triple Alliance

International Exposition in Paris

Triple Entente

First Balkan Wars

World War I Begins

Russian Revolution

United States Enters War

Treaty of Versailles

League of Nations

Hungary and Poland Independent

Treaty of Lausanne

Turkey Independent

Lausanne Conference

(1 year)

1. What Caused World War I?

Europe and a large part of the rest of the world were disrupted by World War I, and its results were far-reaching. Besides leaving in its wake millions of dead and crippled, and billions of dollars worth of property destroyed, the war also overthrew the rulers of Austria-Hungary, Russia, and Germany. European economies were devastated, and ways of living and thinking were changed.

So important was the war that people everywhere have asked: "What caused it?" Many scholars who have studied the matter agree that none of the powers in Europe wanted war in 1914. Yet it occurred. What factors were responsible?

Nationalism

Intense nationalism was a contributing factor. Nationalism had become a strong force in Europe in the 1800s. It had played an important role in the creation of the new nations of Germany and Italy. However, long-established nations did not want other nations to gain at their expense. For example, the national pride of the French had been given a sharp blow by their defeat in the Franco-Prussian War. The French grew increasingly hostile toward the Germans. The French were determined that Germany should not surpass France in war or peace.

During the nineteenth century, the British pride in their colonial possessions grew as they developed one of the world's great empires. In Austria-Hungary nationalism was a powerful and disruptive force. Austria-Hungary had become a dual monarchy in 1867. This arrangement gave rights to the Magyars, who dominated Hungary, and to the peoples of Germanic descent, who dominated Austria. However, it did not satisfy the demands of other national groups within the Austro-Hungarian Empire. These groups included Poles, Czechs, Serbs, Croats, and Slovenes.

The Turkish Empire had grown weak, but it still controlled part of the Balkans. People of that region, such as the Albanians and Macedonians, were becoming increasingly restive under Turkish rule.

Imperalism

European powers valued colonies as sources of raw materials and as markets for finished products. France, as well as Britain, had a number of colonies. Germany was a late starter in the colonial race, but it was no less eager for an overseas empire. For example, Germany wanted a share of Africa, a large part of which had already been carved up among Britain, France, Belgium, and Portugal.

France and Germany disputed bitterly over Morocco, in northern Africa. To avert war, a compromise was reached. France was given a free hand in Morocco. Germany received about 100,000 square miles of the French Congo.

Armaments

The increase of military forces and their weapons of war was another factor threatening peace. The increase of *armaments,* or military power, was closely connected with nationalism. Britain, the leading sea power, felt secure as long as it ruled the oceans of the world. Germany was ambitious also to become a naval power. By 1920 Germany had built nineteen new battleships and twenty-three cruisers. Alarmed, Britain began adding to its fleet.

New weapons were developed, and European nations eagerly acquired them. Publicly, each nation sought equality in weaponry. Actually, each wished for superiority.

France held an International Exposition in 1900 in Paris. It had displays of innovations in technology in many spheres. According to the historian Barbara Tuchman:

> In all the Exposition the two largest single exhibits were Schneider-Creusot's long-range cannon and Vickers-Maxim's collection of ferocious, quick-firing machine guns. Beholders gazed at them with solemn thoughts. An English correspondent in particular was moved to philosophize on the real meaning of the Exposition for the new era it introduced. Schneider's great guns seem to him to hold the world collected in Paris under its threat and to mark the passage of war from a realm of sport to a realm of science in which the making of weapons absorbed the ingenuity of mankind. If a lull ever came, he wrote, the arts of peace might revive, but meanwhile the Paris Exhibition has taught us that the triumph of the modern world is purely mechanical.

Alliances

Gradually, the major nations of Europe took steps that divided them roughly into two opposing groups. These were called the *Triple Alliance* and the *Triple Entente.*

The Triple Alliance was arranged by Bismarck, who tried to prevent other nations from overpowering Germany. He particularly wanted to protect Germany from any French attempt at revenge and recovery of the province of Alsace and part of Lorraine from Germany. In 1879 an alliance was formed between Austria-Hungary and Germany. Three years later Italy joined them to form the Triple Alliance. Each nation agreed to come to each other's assistance if any one or two of them were unjustifiably attacked by two or more of the other Great Powers.

Britain, France, and Russia then moved closer together. In 1894 France made a large loan to Russia, paving the way for a Franco-Russian alliance. In 1904 Great Britain settled numerous disputes with France over territory in North Africa. Three years later, Great Britain agreed with the Russians to divide Persia, now Iran, into two spheres of influence, with a buffer zone between the two. As a result of these settlements, the three nations—Great Britain, France, and Russia—were able to form the Triple Entente (1907).

The two alliances increased the possibility that a war in one part of Europe would spread. This is why Arthur Zimmermann, a German undersecretary of state in 1914, called this system of alliances "the curse of modern times."

Diplomatic Errors and Propaganda

The diplomats of the period before World War I varied in ability. Some were talented and level-headed and worked conscientiously for peace. Others were reckless and emotional persons whose errors of judgment produced dangerous results. On several occasions diplomatic errors increased tensions among nations.

Propaganda in speeches and the press helped to make citizens of one nation hate or fear those of other nations. When it seemed that war had finally come, most people did not protest. On the contrary! Russians cheered. Germans marched in the streets singing war ballads. The French wept with emotion when they were told by a Parisian mayor: "The hour of revenge for which we have prayed unceasingly for forty-four years has at last struck."

Balkan Crises

The outbreak of World War I was preceded by several crises in the Balkans, one of which triggered the war. The Balkans were a patchwork of states, some under Austro-Hungarian domination, others under Turkish rule, still others independent.

In 1908 Austria-Hungary annexed the provinces of Bosnia and Herzegovina. Many Serbian-speaking people who did not wish to join Austria-Hungary were in these territories. In theory Bosnia and Herzegovina had long been part of the Turkish Empire, although Austria-Hungary had administered them for about thirty years. Austria's action angered Serbia and Russia. Russia considered itself the protector of all Slavs.

Serbia allied itself with Bulgaria in March 1912, and Bulgaria joined Greece in an alliance. Bulgaria then demanded that Turkey give up Macedonia, north of Greece. Bulgaria, Greece, Montenegro, and Serbia declared war on Turkey. This First Balkan War ended with a treaty in 1913 under which Turkey agreed to give up territory in the Balkans.

Bulgaria then fell out with Greece and Serbia over territorial matters. Those nations, along with Rumania, Montenegro, and Turkey, fought Bul-

When World War I broke out in 1914, most of the nations of Europe divided into two armed camps. Italy, a member of the Triple Alliance, chose to remain neutral. In May 1915, Italy joined the Allied Powers.

Europe in 1914

Central Powers

Allied Powers

Neutral countries

garia in the Second Balkan War, which lasted about a month.

Animosities in the Balkans threatened the peace of Europe. Yet during the beautiful summer of 1914 few people worried about a widespread war.

In June 1914, Sarajevo, the capital of Bosnia, played host to Archduke Francis Ferdinand, heir to the Austro-Hungarian throne. On June 28, a young Bosnian-born Serb waited along a Sarajevo street. He was a member of a secret, nationalistic, and anti-Austrian society. His name was Gavrilo Princip. This obscure individual became known to history as the person who fired the opening shot of World War I. Princip assassinated Francis Ferdinand and his wife.

The Austrian government decided that the assassination was a plot planned with Serbian approval. Evidence later indicated that Serbia had heard about a plot, but the complicity of the Serbian government in the assassination is still uncertain. Austria decided to take drastic steps against Serbia to crush Serbian national ambitions.

Germany promised to back Austria-Hungary in this crisis. Germany did not expect a world war to result. Austria-Hungary sent an ultimatum to Serbia. It included demands that Serbia suppress the anti-Austrian movement and all publications hostile to the empire, cooperate with Austrian officials

investigating the assassination, and make apologies. Serbia suggested that the dispute be turned over to international arbitration. Not satisfied with Serbia's response, Austria-Hungary declared war on Serbia on July 28, 1914.

The system of alliances helped to spread the war. Russia, afraid that the Austrians would annex Serbia, mobilized. Russian mobilization stirred Germany to declare war on Russia. France as an ally of Russia was drawn in. After the Germans had invaded Belgium to attack France, Great Britain entered the conflict on the side of France and Russia. One nation pulled another into the war. Those on the side of Germany were called the "Central Powers," because they occupied Central Europe. Britain, France, Russia, and the other countries joining them were known as the "Allies."

Check on Your Reading

1. What factors helped bring on World War I?
2. Explain how the Triple Alliance and the Triple Entente were formed.
3. How did nationalism in Austria-Hungary and the Balkans lead to the outbreak of World War I?

2. A New Kind of War

Germany probably had more thorough war plans than other nations. Realizing that France and

Above, a German submarine has sunk a cargo vessel.   The first submarine was used in combat as early as the latter part of the eighteenth century.   The submarine was developed further as an offensive weapon during World War I.   Below, a long range field gun developed by the United States during World War I.

Russia were potential enemies on two fronts, the German General Staff had laid careful plans. First, in the west a concentrated and lightning blow at France was planned while a screen of forces held off Russia in the east. Then, after France was defeated, full power would be turned on Russia.

The War on the Western Front

Quick victory over France lay through Belgium, a small country whose neutrality Germany and other countries had guaranteed in the nineteenth century. Germany sent its armies through Belgium into France in August 1914.

Germany nearly won the war in the west that summer. Its armies reached the Marne River, fifteen miles from Paris, in September. British troops now joined those of France along the Marne, and together they withstood the German attack. After thousands of casualties on both sides, the French and British drove the Germans back to the Aisne River. Paris was saved, and a type of warfare new to the world began.

Most previous conflicts had been wars of movement and decisive battles. However, along the Western Front, neither the German nor the French-British side could muster an advantage. So both settled into positions, protecting themselves with a network of trenches and barbed wire. These trenches stretched hundreds of miles across Belgium and France. For much of the war, the conflict along the Western Front was largely a stalemate. Following an artillery barrage, soldiers on one side would stream from the trenches to attack the enemy. Territorial gains—if any—were usually in yards, seldom in miles. Later the defenders became attackers and the episode was repeated. Trench warfare meant mud and filth, rats and other vermin, and death from artillery and machine-gun fire and poisonous gas. Hundreds of thousands of men died from battle wounds and disease. Many thousands of others were made invalids for life.

On the Eastern Front

In the east, Russia faced many serious difficulties. Dissension within the government hampered the Russian war effort. Troops were poorly trained, equipped, and supplied. Nevertheless, in the first year of the war, Russian armies were able to invade both Germany and Austria-Hungary.

Then in East Prussia, German forces defeated the Russian armies at the Battle of Tannenberg. Russian casualties soared to more than 300,000. By the close of 1915, Russian forces had been driven back along the Eastern Front.

In October 1914 Turkey entered the war on the side of the Central Powers, closing the Dardanelles, which separated the Black Sea from the Mediterranean, to the Allies. This cut off a major supply route between Russia and its western Allies. Britain then declared Egypt to be independent of Turkey and under British protection.

Allied forces tried to reopen the Dardanelles with an invasion of the Gallipoli Peninsula later in 1915. The effort was unsuccessful, and helped influence Bulgaria to join the Central Powers. However, British and other Allied forces did turn back Turkish thrusts toward the Suez Canal, and persuaded Arabs of the Middle East to revolt against Turkish rule. Also Britain was able to occupy Palestine.

In May 1915, eager to obtain land in Europe and Africa, Italy joined the Allied side. Italian forces helped maintain Allied control of the Mediterranean.

In 1917, revolution in Russia led to the overthrow of the czarist government and eventually to the withdrawal of Russia from the war. Russia signed a peace treaty with Germany. This released German armies for action on the Western Front.

The War at Sea

In the spring of 1916 British and German fleets fought the Battle of Jutland off the coast of Denmark. Germany destroyed many British vessels, but suffered serious losses. The remaining German warships were confined to their bases for most of the rest of the war.

British ships blockaded Germany, attempting to cut it off by sea from food and other supplies. Germany, in turn, tried to break the blockade and used submarines to try to cut Britain off from outside aid.

German submarines torpedoed Allied military and merchant vessels without warning. Germany declared the waters around Britain a "war zone." On February 1, 1917, Germany began unrestricted submarine warfare. This meant that all enemy and neutral ships found in "war zones" would be subject to submarine attack. As a result some neutral vessels were torpedoed and sunk.

On land World War I was fought on two main fronts. The inset map shows the details of the Western Front.

The United States Enters the War

There were a number of reasons why the United States was drawn into the war against Germany.

As a neutral nation the United States insisted on *freedom of the seas*, on its right to trade with whatever country it chose. American trade with the Allies aided their war effort considerably. Since Britain dominated most of the surface waters, the submarine remained the principal naval weapon available to Germany.

Germany's submarine warfare cost a number of American lives as submarines sank merchant ships steaming for Allied ports. In 1915 American lives and the lives of many others were also lost when a submarine torpedoed the British liner *Lusitania*, which carried military supplies as well as passengers. Bowing to United States protests, Germany halted unrestricted submarine warfare for a time.

The United States had other grievances against Germany. A secret German document was discovered soon after the war began. It revealed that Germany had tried to win Mexico's support by promising to return to it the Mexican territories lost to the United States in 1848.

Anti-German articles and news stories helped turn Americans against Germany. Many Americans felt strong ties to Britain, and they tended to grow more pro-British as the war progressed. Many Americans came to view the war as a struggle between democracy and autocracy. They were determined to help make the world "safe for democracy" by defeating what they considered to be the undemocratic Central Powers.

After a lull, Germany resumed submarine warfare. On April 6, 1917 the United States declared war on Germany. The United States quickly mobilized and expanded its armed forces, and began shipping troops to Europe. American industry, which had been producing supplies for the Allies throughout the war, stepped up its efforts. American financial interests lent more money then ever before to Allied governments.

The War Ends

In 1918 the Germans faced a critical situation. The Allied blockade of Germany threatened the Germans with starvation. The increasing number of American troops arriving in Europe continued to strengthen the Allied forces. The German General Staff and General Ludendorff therefore decided to gamble everything on a major offensive.

In March 1918 German troops launched a tremendous attack on British, French, and American positions. They smashed through Allied lines and moved forward rapidly. The Allies responded by placing their separate armies under the command of Marshal Ferdinand Foch of France. A desperate struggle followed. Finally, the German offensive was stopped at the Second Battle of the Marne in the summer of 1918. Then the Allies took the offensive and broke through German positions known as the Hindenburg Line.

On other fronts, the Central Powers suffered serious setbacks. Also an Austrian offensive against the Italians ended in failure. Crushed by military defeat and disrupted by dissension within their countries, the Central Powers surrendered one after the other.

Tanks were introduced in warfare by the British in 1916.

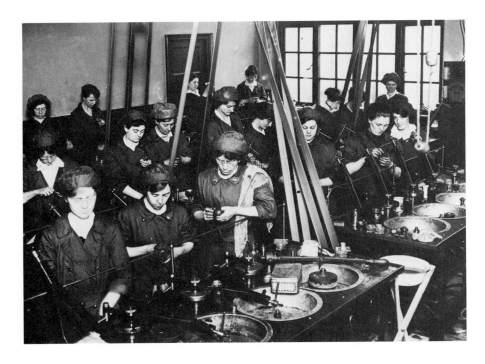

Many women contributed to the war effort by working in factories.

On November 11, 1918, an armistice agreement was signed between Germany and the Allies. Quiet came at last to the Western Front. The terrible war was over. The Allies were victorious.

Check on Your Reading

1. How would you describe the war on the Western Front?
2. What happened on the Eastern Front?
3. Why did the United States enter the war?
4. What was the effect of the entrance of the United States into the war?

3. The Treaty of Versailles

Before the war ended, President Woodrow Wilson of the United States drew up a statement of "War Aims and Peace Terms of the United States" that he hoped would provide for lasting peace in the world. His statement was known as the "Fourteen Points."

President Wilson's Hopes for Peace

The "Fourteen Points" included: conducting open, not secret, relations among nations; freedom of the seas; removal of economic barriers; reduction of national armaments; fair settlement of colonial claims; and restoration of land to several nations. Wilson's last point stressed the need to establish a *League of Nations,* an international body to guarantee political independence and to settle disputes among nations. President Wilson supported the idea of *self-determination of peoples.* This meant that the desires and interests of national groups should be taken into consideration when territorial and other changes were made.

Wilson's "Fourteen Points" favorably impressed the German people and helped influence them to accept defeat, but Wilson spoke only for the United States. Still, although with some reluctance, Allied leaders seemed to accept most of the "Fourteen Points."

The Peace Treaty

Germany was forbidden to send delegates to the peace conference that was held in Paris in 1919. Three leaders dominated the meetings. They were Georges Clemenceau, Premier of France; David Lloyd George, British Prime Minister; and President Woodrow Wilson. With Premier Vittorio Orlando of Italy, these men became known as the "Big Four."

The delegates completed a peace treaty, which was signed by Germany in June 1919. The provisions of this Treaty of Versailles vitally affected the history of the century: 1. Germany was to give up a considerable part of its land and its overseas colonies. A number of these colonies became *mandates* of the League of Nations. That is, they were placed under the administrative "tutelage" of various nations. 2. The size of Germany's army and navy was limited. The German air force was to cease to exist. 3. The Saar Basin, an important coal and industrial area, was placed under the jurisdiction of the League of Nations for fifteen years. During that time, France could mine the coal of the region. 4. The Rhineland area was to be demilitarized. 5. Germany was to give back the provinces of Alsace and Lorraine to France. 6. Germany was to recognize the independence of Czechoslovakia and Poland. 7. Japan was to receive Germany's rights in a valuable territory in China. 8. Article 231 of the treaty declared that Germany and its allies were responsible for causing the war. Therefore, a commission was to be set up to decide the amount of *reparations* that Germany was to pay. Reparations were payments in money and material that defeated nations made to victors for war damages. 9. A League of Nations was to be established.

Other peace treaties later were completed with the other defeated nations.

The Treaty of Versailles did respond to the desire of some peoples for self-determination. Some new nations were established and independence was returned to others. Also the treaty did set up the League of Nations, raising hopes generally that the world might achieve lasting peace.

However, many of the treaty-makers' decisions were not based on the "Fourteen Points." Some peoples were not permitted full self-determination. The heavy reparations demanded of Germany also were to cause many problems.

The United States Rejects the Treaty

By January 1920 the Treaty of Versailles had been ratified by nearly all the Allied powers. The United States had not yet accepted it. On January 10, 1920 the League of Nations began its existence with 24 members. The United States was not

among them. The treaty had not been ratified yet by the United States Senate.

The Senate, which in the United States is responsible for the ratification of treaties, voted against the Treaty of Versailles. Many of the objections of the senators revolved around the fact that in agreeing to the treaty they would agree to the United States joining the League of Nations. Some senators were afraid that the League would drag the United States into foreign entanglements and wars. Some felt that they would be giving up American sovereignty to a foreign organization. Other senators believed that the United States should concentrate on domestic problems.

In 1921 the United States finally made separate peace treaties with Germany, Austria, and Hungary. The United States never became a member of the League of Nations.

The League of Nations

The Covenant (or compact) of the League of Nations was written in Part I of the Treaty of Versailles. It provided that the activities of the League were to be carried on by an Assembly, a Council, and a Secretariat. Headquarters of the League was in Geneva, Switzerland.

The *Assembly* was made up of representatives from all the member nations of the League. It could deal with any matter affecting the peace of the world. However, its decisions on important matters required a unanimous vote of the members. The *Council* was to consist of representatives of the principal powers and representatives of four other member nations. It, too, could deal with any matter involving world peace, and its decisions on important matters required a unanimous vote.

The permanent *Secretariat* of the League was to handle all secretarial duties, gather information, register treaties, and carry out the everyday work of the League. At the head of the Secretariat was a *Secretary-General*.

Plans were to be drawn up to establish a *Permanent Court of International Justice*. This World Court was to "hear and determine any dispute of an international character which the parties thereto submit to it."

If a serious dispute arose between nations, the case was to be submitted to arbitration, to the Court, or to the Council. If a nation ignored the League Covenant and went to war, the League members could stop their trade and other economic relations with the offender. That is, they could apply *economic sanctions*. The Council also could recommend that the members of the League contribute to "the armed forces to be used to protect the covenants of the League."

The League was to supervise mandates. It was also to be concerned with the improvement of working conditions and with raising living standards throughout the world.

Peace Settlements after World War I

Territory lost by:

- Russia
- Germany
- Bulgaria
- Austria-Hungary
- Turkish Empire

1926 political boundaries shown

The peace treaties that ended World War I changed many boundaries in Europe and created a number of independent countries. What territories did Germany, Austria-Hungary, Russia, and Turkey lose? What countries gained their independence?

It is important to know what the League of Nations could and could not do. It *could* discuss any matter affecting the world's peace and make recommendations. It could warn an aggressor to stop its military activities, and serve as a forum where nations could exchange ideas. It *could not* take action on important matters without the unanimous consent of the Council or Assembly. It could not pass laws that were compulsory for all member nations. It could not back up its decisions with military force unless the member nations were willing to supply troops and weapons.

Check on Your Reading

1. Summarize Woodrow Wilson's Fourteen Points.
2. What were the provisions of the Treaty of Versailles?
3. What were the main bodies of the League of Nations? What could they do?

4. The Legacy of World War I: Nations in Transition

A troubled world emerged from the war. The Middle East was unsettled. The Austro-Hungarian and

An example of the destruction caused by World War I. This photo was taken in Austria.

Turkish empires had fallen apart. Germany had lost its empire. The Russian monarchy had been overthrown. Old nations of western Europe and newly organized nations of eastern Europe faced serious problems. A number of countries, created or re-created by the Treaty of Versailles, went through difficult periods of transition.

Eastern Europe

After World War I Poland became an independent nation. It was created out of Polish areas taken from Germany and Austria. The Poles were dissatisfied at their failure to regain territory to the east and fought against the Russians. They did gain some territory under terms of the Treaty of Riga (1921), but not all they wanted. Poland itself continued to be troubled by tensions between Poles and such minority groups as Ukrainians, Germans, Lithuanians, and Jews. More and more power was turned over to General Josef Pilsudski. By 1926 he became virtual dictator of Poland.

Minority and economic problems troubled Rumania. Little was done to quiet minority complaints. The Rumanian government did take land from large landowners to sell to peasants. However, the worldwide depression of 1929 brought economic misery, and Rumania seemed threatened by dictatorship.

Hungary, now separated from Austria, became a republic in 1918. The following year, a revolution led to the establishment of a Communist regime under Béla Kun. After five months the Communist government, weakened by internal strife and conflict with Rumania, was overthrown. A monarchy was proclaimed, but the throne remained vacant. Hungary was actually governed by a regent, Nicholas Horthy. By the Treaty of Trianon, signed with the Allies in 1920, Hungary lost much of its land and was left without seaports.

Yugoslavia—which consisted of Serbia, Montenegro, Croatia, and other areas—was proclaimed a kingdom in 1918. Religious and minority problems plagued the new country. Roman Catholic Croats argued bitterly with Greek Orthodox Serbs. Several minority groups demanded more rights of self-government.

The new Baltic states of Finland, Estonia, Latvia, and Lithuania had formerly been part of the Russian Empire. They made progress in solving their domestic problems but faced the threat of Russian expansion.

Greece and Turkey

Greece fought Turkey from 1919 to 1922 for control of the Turkish city of Smyrna. In 1923 the Greeks gave up their claims to Turkish territory.

After World War I the Turks fought against an Allied plan to divide their country. In 1923 Turkey signed the Treaty of Lausanne with the Allies. This saved Turkey from partition, and provided that the Dardanelles (the strait between the Aegean Sea and the Sea of Marmara) would remain under Turkish control but be open to ships of all nations. Also Italy would keep the Dodecanese Islands and Britain would keep the island of Cyprus. The former Turkish territories of Syria and Palestine and Mesopotamia would be mandates of France and Great Britain.

In 1923 Turkey became a republic. Mustapha Kemal—Kemal Atatürk or "Chief Turk"—served as President of Turkey from 1923 until 1938.

Under the often dictatorial leadership of Mustapha Kemal, the Turks tried to modernize their country. They developed industries, started a system of compulsory education, and extended more rights to women. Ernest Jackh, a professor of international relations, once said to Mustapha Kemal: "Your dictatorship frees an enslaved people while Hitler's tyranny enslaves a free people."

France Occupies the Ruhr

In Western Europe, much attention centered on German reparations payments. They amounted to around thirty-five billion dollars, and were to be distributed as 52 percent to France, 22 percent to Britain, 10 percent to Italy, and 8 percent to Belgium. The remaining 8 percent was to go to various European countries.

Germany made an effort to meet its reparations obligations. However, an unfavorable trade balance, rising inflation, a decline in credit, and other economic troubles made it increasingly difficult for Germany to continue to meet its payments. By 1922 it was unable to deliver wood and coal promised to France. France thereupon decided to collect them itself. In January 1923, the French, aided by Belgian troops, occupied the Ruhr.

The Ruhr was Germany's industrial heartland, source of more than 80 percent of its coal and steel. Its loss struck Germany's economy a crippling blow. Inflation also disrupted Germany. By 1923 it required 2,500,000,000,000 marks to equal one American dollar. Many Germans existed for a time on a barter economy.

Reparations and War Debts

Germany's difficulty in meeting obligations resulted in Allied revisions of their reparations programs. In 1924 the Dawes Plan went into effect. Germany was to make yearly payments on a sliding scale from 1924 to 1929. Despite a large loan to help Germany, this plan failed. It left the country under too many foreign controls and was vague about the overall reparations to be paid.

World War I made the United States a creditor nation. At the close of the war, the Allies owed the United States about eleven billion dollars in war debts. The Allies claimed that these war debts to the United States should be cancelled because the Allies had used the money to fight a war defending American interests as well as their own. Also, they pointed out that the Allies planned to use the money they received in reparations to pay their war debts. Therefore, if the Germans did not pay their reparations, the Allies were not responsible for paying their war debts.

The United States disagreed. Nevertheless, the Hoover Moratorium of 1931 permitted a one-year postponement of payment on both war debts and reparations.

In 1932 the Lausanne Conference, held in Switzerland, proposed to cut Germany's total remaining reparations to about three-quarters of a billion dollars. It also suggested that the United States cancel all war debts.

The United States refused to do so; but, with the deepening depression of the 1930s, Germany stopped the reparations payments. Except for Finland, the Allies then stopped all but token payments on war debts.

Check on Your Reading

1. What nations evolved in Eastern Europe as a result of World War I?
2. Describe some of the problems Eastern European nations faced.
3. What were some changes that Mustapha Kemal made in Turkey?
4. Why did Germany have to pay reparations? How were war debts and reparations linked?

LET'S MEET
THE PEOPLE

A German Soldier on the Western Front

Right after graduation from high school in 1914, Paul and his entire class enlisted in the German army. Seven of them became comrades in the same unit, spending the war in the trenches on the Western Front. Survival became uppermost in their minds.

Paul had once thought about the past. He recalled that many of his classmates, when they went to enlist, had proudly shaved for the first time. They were eighteen then, but now, he knew, they were young no longer.

All of them had aged rapidly under enemy bombardment, the clatter of machine guns, the attacks by fearsome tanks, the sickening smell of poison gas, and the sight of comrades blown to bits. It seemed to Paul that now there was no past. Nor was there a future. There was only war. It was hard to be concerned about the issues involved, to realize what the war was all about, or why it had begun.

As the conflict wore on, the ranks of comrades thinned. Then, one day in 1918, Paul's best friend, Kat, was hit. Hoping to save him, Paul carried Kat to an aid station, only to discover upon arriving there that he had been transporting a dead body. Numbly, too stricken for tears, he laid Kat down. Paul moved his own legs, and found himself walking in a circle. All is as usual, he thought. Only Private Stanislaus Katczinsky had died.

By autumn only a few of the old hands remained. Paul was the last of the seven from his class. Would there be an armistice? There had been rumors, but there also had been false rumors before. Paul hoped, but he felt so alone. Then:

> He fell in October 1918, on a day that was so quiet and still on the whole front, that the army report confined itself to the single sentence: All quiet on the Western Front.
> He had fallen forward and lay on the earth as though sleeping. Turning him over one saw that he could not have suffered long; his face had an expression of calm, as though almost glad the end had come.

From Erich Maria Remarque, *All Quiet on the Western Front.* Fawcett Crest ed. Quotation from p. 175.

CHAPTER REVIEW

Think and Discuss

1. Which of the contributing factors do you think were most important in causing World War I? Why?
2. Why was World War I called "a new kind of war"?
3. What circumstances and events do you think contributed to Germany's defeat?
4. Would full acceptance of Wilson's "Fourteen Points" have helped to remove the causes of war? Why?
5. Do you think the Treaty of Versailles was a treaty of justice, of compromise, or of vengeance? Why?
6. How was the principle of self-determination put into practice in the nations that emerged after World War I?
7. Why did the system of paying reparations and war debts fail?

Past and Present

1. In the present world situation, can you find any situations similar to those that caused World War I?
2. How is the principle of the self-determination of peoples influencing events in the world today?

Activities

1. Debate this statement: Resolved, that a balance of power does more to provoke war than to keep the peace.
2. Draw a chart showing the crises leading to the outbreak of World War I. Why was the war averted in each case? Why was war not averted in the last crisis?
3. Read newspapers and news magazines for several weeks to learn if any problems today are caused by imperialism. Report your findings.
4. Do research to learn how the use of submarines and airplanes influenced the course of World War I.
5. Do research to learn the part that women played in World War I.
6. Make a collection of the songs of World War I. Show how the lyrics reflected people's feelings.

Russia Becomes the Soviet Union

KEYNOTE

For many years the imperial eagle was a symbol of the authority of the Russian monarchy. Then, on March 16, 1917, Russians in the city of Petrograd destroyed every sign, decoration, or statue with an imperial eagle on it. The destruction of the imperial eagle symbolized the great changes that were taking place in Russia. The Czar had been forced to abdicate, ending the Russian monarchy. A new era was about to begin.

In the years that followed, democracy did not become a permanent part of Russian life. The imperial eagle had been destroyed; but the hammer and sickle—symbol of the new Soviet authority—took its place. The Communists rose to power in Russia.

A demonstration against the Czar during the Revolution of 1905.

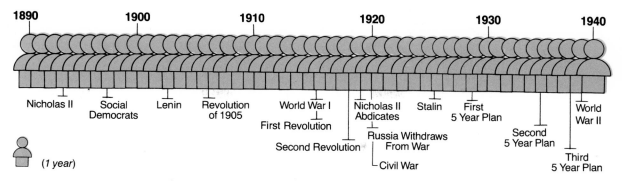

1890   1900   1910   1920   1930   1940

Nicholas II | Social Democrats | Lenin | Revolution of 1905 | World War I | Nicholas II Abdicates | Stalin | First 5 Year Plan | World War II

First Revolution

Second Revolution

Russia Withdraws From War

Second 5 Year Plan

Civil War

Third 5 Year Plan

(1 year)

1. The Russian Monarchy Is Threatened

As the twentieth century opened, few absolute rulers remained in Europe. In Russia, Czar Nicholas II, a member of the Romanov line, ruled as an autocrat.

The Russian Condition

Nicholas II had become Czar in 1894. He spoke English, French, and German well, but most of the rest of his knowledge consisted of loose odds and ends of information. He lacked self-confidence, but nevertheless he felt that he had the right to rule Russia as he wished. He was dedicated to the principle of autocracy.

Nicholas II was a kind, considerate, and gentle man to his family and friends. He was a loving husband to the German princess Alix, who became Alexandra, and a good father to four daughters and a son.

The Czarovitch Alexei, heir to the throne, particularly concerned his parents. He suffered from hemophilia, a hereditary disease that prevents the blood from clotting. As a consequence Alexei lived constantly with the danger that even a slight cut might bring a fatal hemorrhage.

Twice when it seemed that the boy was about to bleed to death, a pseudo-religious charlatan called Rasputin was said to have saved his life. Rasputin posed as a holy man; but he was illiterate, drunken, coarse, and cunning. The grateful Alexandra permitted Rasputin to influence her and her family in many decisions. Rasputin became a member of the imperial household, and soon he gained considerable power in the Russian government.

Rasputin actually cared little about government, but he did relish power. He contributed to the corruption and weakness of the Russian government until a group of Russian nobles succeeded in assassinating him in 1916.

Opposition to the Czar Grows

Individual rights were not respected in Russia. Criticism or disagreement with the government brought imprisonment, exile, or death. "In the pages [of Russia's history] we find only floggings, beatings, hangings, and the systematic exploitation of the people on behalf of the czar's treasury!" declared the Russian George Plekhanov late in the nineteenth century. Despite despotism, however, opposition to the government developed.

In December 1825, for example, army officers, soldiers, and other protestors gathered in St. Petersburg to demand a written constitution and the abolition, or at least the easing, of serfdom. At that time the first Nicholas Romanov was Czar. He ordered artillery turned on the people packed into Senate Square. The *Decembrists,* named after the month in which they had protested, were crushed.

This did not end protest. It continued throughout the nineteenth century in spite of efforts by the Czar's secret police to stamp out revolutionary groups. For example, the *Narodniki,* who advocated a peasant revolution and the establishment of an agrarian form of socialism, had supported a "movement to the people" in the 1870s and later. Then George Plekhanov in 1883 founded the "Liberation of Labor," the first Russian organization to advocate the ideas of Karl Marx (see page 432). Later, in 1898, Russian Marxists formed the Russian Social Democratic Workers' Party, known as the *Social Democrats.*

In 1903 the Russian Social Democrats held a crucial conference in Brussels and London. A split occurred within the group between Mensheviks and Bolsheviks. Both groups accepted the ideas of Karl Marx and both wanted to overthrow the Czar. They differed on how to reach this goal.

Mensheviks wanted the Party to be open to as many people as possible. The *Bolsheviks* wanted to

519

A Russian painting of Lenin addressing his supporters.

limit it to a small core of professional revolutionaries. As the historian Ivar Spector has made clear, the Mensheviks believed that a revolution could succeed only after "a careful and intensive preparatory campaign of education had trained the masses for a democratic regime." The Bolsheviks did not want to wait. They favored "an abrupt overthrow of the existing social and political order by a resort to force."

Lenin: Leader of the Bolsheviks

The Bolsheviks, led by Lenin (1870-1924), finally won out, although by a narrow margin. Lenin's real name was Vladimir Ilyich Ulyanov. He continued to work with the Bolsheviks for the revolutionary cause.

Lenin was an intelligent, shrewd, and, when he thought it was necessary, ruthless leader who had dedicated his life to the cause of revolution. Flexible as to tactics, he was still convinced that the bourgeoisie could be overthrown only by force. Lenin had a strong personal reason to hate czarism.

In 1887 his older brother, Alexander, had been arrested, tried, and executed for plotting against the Czar's life.

Since Lenin was to play such an important role in Russia, it is important that we understand his ideas. Here are some of his key statements:

> There is no middle way [between capitalism and communism].
> [We are dedicated to] overthrowing the Czar, overthrowing the capitalists, destroying the capitalist class. . . . We subordinate our Communist morality to this task.
> We must [if necessary] . . . resort to all sorts of stratagems, manoeuvres, illegal methods, evasions and subterfuges. . . .

To Lenin it was a fight to the finish between capitalism and communism!

Revolution in 1905

Internal unrest finally exploded in the midst of the Russo-Japanese War. The defeats suffered by

Russian troops in this war, the hunger of the people, and the inefficiency of the government contributed to the discontent. On Sunday, January 22, 1905, thousands of working men and women, accompanied by children, marched to the Czar's Winter Palace in St. Petersburg (today Leningrad). A Russian Orthodox priest, Father Gapon, who apparently was in the service of the Russian secret police, led the procession. The purpose of the demonstration was to present a petition to Nicholas II, requesting improvements in labor conditions and a more liberal government.

The Czar was not at the palace. When the people approached, the Czar's soldiers opened fire. Many people were killed or wounded that day. Even a seasoned reporter for the French press was shocked at the "streams of blood on the snow." The day became known as "Bloody Sunday."

The horror of "Bloody Sunday" set off uprisings of peasants and strikes of workers throughout the country. A *Soviet* (Council) *of Workers' Deputies* also was organized. This Soviet consisted of representatives of many socialist groups. It declared that it would protect the rights of the people.

The Czar's government decided to grant concessions. In October 1905, it issued a manifesto that promised reforms. These included freedom of speech, the right to vote, and the calling of a *Duma*, a representative assembly.

When the war with Japan ended, however, the Czar used loyal Russian troops now at his disposal to help him reestablish his authority. The Czar's government also issued new laws that it hoped would lessen peasant hostility. This legislation was designed to end the evils of land distribution that followed the freeing of the serfs. Under these reforms many peasant families acquired land between 1907 and 1915. Order gradually returned to Russia.

Four Dumas were called into session between 1906 and 1917, and they did try to bring about change. However, they did not have sufficient power to alter the basic character of the Czar's regime. Nicholas II had regained most of his power in Russia.

Life Between 1905 and 1914

Between the Revolutions of 1905 and 1914, crops were generally good. Some improvements were made in methods of agriculture, increasing

A Bolshevik poster hails the coming of a world-wide revolution. The flag of revolution is shown spreading throughout the world.

production. Steps were taken to abolish peasant communes (or *mirs*) and to set up more ownership of land by individuals. A number of peasant farms came into existence.

There was expansion in industry. The buying power of miners and factory workers was increased. The length of the working day was reduced.

Other developments were less encouraging. Taxes were high and living standards remained low. There were many strikes. The government was unstable, inefficient, autocratic, and often corrupt.

Check on Your Reading

1. How did Czar Nicholas II rule?
2. Describe the development of dissent in Russia during the nineteenth century.
3. State Lenin's ideas about capitalism.
4. How did Mensheviks and Bolsheviks differ? How were they similar?
5. What changes were brought about by the 1905 uprising?

2. The First and Second Russian Revolutions

The Russian people at first responded enthusiastically to their country's entry into World War I in 1914. Patriotism ran high. However, this situation changed. This was the result of many factors. Russia suffered great losses in the war. Discouragement spread among the troops who lacked adequate ammunition and equipment. The corruption within the government hindered the war effort, and food shortages developed in the cities. At the same time there were serious arguments between the fourth Duma and the Czar and Czarina.

In 1917 there were strikes and hunger marches. In March of that year (February by the old Russian calendar), crowds marched through Petrograd (formerly known as St. Petersburg). People denounced Czarina Alexandra and demanded food and reforms.

The Duma asked Nicholas II to remove the unpopular and inefficient persons in his government. The Czar refused and ordered the Duma dissolved. The Duma in turn refused to obey the Czar's order. Instead, on March 14, it helped establish a *Provisional Government.* This was more than a gesture of protest—it was an act of defiance.

The Provisional Government

The Provisional Government and a number of generals demanded that the Czar abdicate. Lacking popular support and the loyal troops needed to maintain his authority, Nicholas II gave up his throne on March 15. It is probably nearer the truth to say that the regime had collapsed rather than that it had been overthrown.

Those people who accomplished the first Russian Revolution were for the most part liberals, middle-class reformers, and agrarian socialists. They wanted a more democratic government for Russia. They advocated freedom of speech, trial by jury, equal rights for women, self-government for local areas, and universal suffrage. The Provisional Government tried to achieve these objectives.

Alexander Kerensky became head of the Provisional Government in August 1917. He worked hard to reestablish order. His government, however, gradually lost the support of many Russians for the following reasons: 1. Its authority was weakened by the opposition tactics of the Petrograd Soviet, a group that demanded quick and more radical changes in Russia. 2. It lost prestige as the result of an incident in which the troops of a Russian general attacked the Provisional Government. 3. It could not keep order in the provinces, where peasants were killing landlords and seizing land. 4. It insisted on continuing an increasingly unpopular war.

It was particularly in its conduct of foreign affairs that the Kerensky government lost favor. Despite turbulent conditions in Russia, the Provisional Government decided to fulfill its obligations to its allies and remain in World War I. This decision alienated many Russians, particularly when the Bolsheviks had come out for "Peace! Land! Bread!"

The Second Revolution Brings the Bolsheviks to Power

The first Russian Revolution was followed by a second. A Soviet of Workers' and Soldiers' Deputies was organized in Petrograd at about the same time that the Provisional Government was established. This Soviet demanded more radical changes than those promised by the Provisional Government. Thus, there were two competing governments.

At the time there were few Bolshevik leaders in Russia. Lenin was in exile in Switzerland. Another leader, Leon Trotsky, was in New York.

In and out of Russia over the years, Lenin in 1917 faced the problem of returning to his native land as quickly as possible. The Germans helped him because they hoped he would stir up further revolution and thus weaken Russia's war effort. They provided Lenin safe conduct through Germany, Sweden, and Finland to Petrograd, where he arrived on April 16, 1917.

Leon Trotsky came from New York City to become the organizer of the Bolsheviks' military forces. Joseph Stalin came out of exile in Siberia.

Bolsheviks did everything possible to strengthen their own position. Although they did not originally form a majority of the Petrograd Soviet, they gained control of it. Lenin concluded that the time for the use of force had come. "Everything now hangs by a thread . . .," he wrote. "We must not wait!"

On November 7, 1917 (October 25 by the old Russian calendar), the Bolsheviks overthrew the Provisional Government by force. When Kerensky failed to rally enough troops to his support, the Provisional Government lost all authority. The Bolsheviks controlled the government. Posters now proclaimed: "Long Live the Revolution of the Workers, the Soldiers, and the Peasants!"

Before the Provisional Government was overthrown, it had set November 25 as the date of elections to a Constituent Assembly, which was to draw up "the fundamental laws, guaranteeing to the country the inalienable rights of justice, equality, and liberty." Thus, elections were held about two weeks after the Bolsheviks had seized power. Bolshevik candidates received only about one-fourth of the 36 million votes cast. This mattered little, for Bolsheviks held the governmental power, election or no election. They arrested leaders of opposition parties and dissolved the Assembly. According to Kerensky: "Lenin [succeeded] in torpedoing the democracy and fighting his way to a dictatorship."

Check on Your Reading

1. What difficulties did the Provisional Government face?
2. What role did the Petrograd Soviet play?
3. In what manner did Communists seize power?

---

3. The Soviet Union under Lenin

After the Bolsheviks gained control, they changed their name to the *Communist Party* and moved the capital to Moscow. Under Lenin's leadership, the Communist government faced the serious problem of reorganizing the economic system, wiping out opposition, and establishing satisfactory relations with minority groups.

To remove some of the pressures on Russia, it withdrew from World War I by signing the Treaty of Brest-Litovsk with Germany in March 1918. This document provided that Russia recognize the independence of Georgia and the Ukraine, provinces in southern Russia; accept the independence of Finland; and permit Germany and Austria-Hungary to decide the future of Poland, Lithuania, Latvia, and Estonia. The Communist government abrogated this treaty following the defeat of the Central Powers.

Civil War and Allied Intervention

The new government went to work to consolidate power and to alter the economic and political systems. 1. It declared that title to all land belonged to the state, and that use of property and livestock would be transferred to the peasants. 2. It gave workers considerable responsibility for managing factories. 3. It nationalized railroads, banks, and church property. 4. It deprived the Orthodox Church of its privileges, and forbade religious instruction in schools. 5. It set up a new court system. 6. It developed a system of local councils (Soviets), while keeping power in the hands of a small group of Communist leaders. 7. It proclaimed equality of all nationalities in Russia, but tried to discourage them from seceding from the country. 8. It formed a special police (later known as the *Cheka*), whose principal job was to combat counter-revolution and sabotage.

These and other actions angered a number of people. These included Russian generals still loyal to the Czar, aristocrats deprived of their estates, liberals who hoped for a democratic government, church leaders, and many devout peasants. Early in 1918 civil war broke out in Russia between the *Reds* (Bolsheviks) and the *Whites* (Russians opposed to the Bolsheviks).

The Whites got help from abroad—France, Great Britain, Japan, Italy, and the United States sent military units to help the Whites in 1918 and 1919. The Bolsheviks angrily denounced these "Anglo-French, American and Japanese imperialist robbers."

Historians have advanced the following reasons for Allied intervention: 1. The Allies wanted to aid Czechoslovakian troops in Russia who were defying the Red Army. 2. The Allies hoped to protect economic investments and loans that citizens of the Allied nations had made in Russia. 3. They wanted to punish Russia for having made a separate peace with Germany, and 4. to weaken the position of the Bolshevik government in Russia. 5. They wanted to check the spread of Bolshevik power, which seemed a threat to Western governments.

Under the leadership of Leon Trotsky, the Soviet Commissar of War, an efficient Red Army was organized. The army, helped by the failure of the Whites to coordinate their attacks, withstood both internal and foreign challenge. The Whites also no longer had a symbol to rally around. As the civil war began, the Bolsheviks kept the Czar and his family in close confinement.

Then, when it appeared that White forces might

This photograph of Lenin and Stalin was taken in 1922. It was one of the last photos taken of Lenin before his stroke. Later, during Stalin's rule, this photograph was widely circulated to try to prove the close ties between Stalin and Lenin.

free the royal family, orders went out to execute all members of the family. The Czar, the Czarina, the Czarovich, and his four sisters were all shot in 1918. By 1920 most of the White forces had been defeated and Allied troops were withdrawn.

The Comintern

Allied intervention in the civil war had important results. The Bolsheviks had always intended that communism should spread throughout Europe. Now, however, as an authority on Russian history pointed out, "The action of the allies confirmed and intensified the ideological aspect of Soviet foreign policy and made international revolution once more its principal plank. . . ."

In March 1919 representatives of the Russian Communist Party and of nineteen foreign parties and groups met in Moscow to form the *Third Communist International*, or *Comintern*. The First International had been founded in 1864, the Second in 1889.

The Comintern called for the support of "the working masses of all countries." Its leaders declared: "The task of the International Communist

Party is now to overthrow this order [the bourgeois world order] and to erect in its place the structure of the Socialist world order." National interests were to be subordinated to "the interests of the international revolution." The Comintern was controlled by the Russian government.

It would prove difficult to expand Communist influence. In Hungary, for example, a Soviet Republic quickly collapsed. In 1920 the Poles and Ukrainians fought against the Red Army. Under terms of the Treaty of Riga in 1921, Russia had agreed to turn over territory to Poland.

The New Economic Policy

Lenin soon realized that it would be difficult and dangerous to establish complete public ownership of production and distribution at once in a country economically exhausted as a result of war and revolution. In 1921, therefore, Lenin introduced the *New Economic Policy, (NEP)*.

The NEP, which lasted seven years, temporarily restored some degree of capitalism to the Soviet Union. It permitted people some private enterprise and brought freedom of trade to various areas.

The NEP also encouraged some foreign capital to come into Russia.

Then, in 1924, in the middle of the NEP period, Lenin died. This touched off a power struggle. The chief opponents were Leon Trotsky, important theoretician and successful civil war army leader, and Joseph Stalin.

Check on Your Reading

1. What policies did the Communists introduce?
2. Why did the Allies intervene in the Russian civil war?
3. What were the chief purposes of the Comintern?
4. What was the New Economic Policy?

4. The Soviet Union under Stalin

Joseph Stalin (1879-1953) emerged as the new dictator. His real name was Joseph Vissarionovich Dzhugashvili. He took the name Stalin, which means "steel." In many respects Joseph Stalin was a "man of steel."

Stalin's Rise to Power

A short man with bushy hair and a mustache, Stalin had a habit of puffing calmly on his pipe and remaining silent. Such mannerisms might lead one to the conclusion that he was a man with little drive. As late as 1917 one of his contemporaries, Sukhanov, observed that "Stalin . . . produced—and not on me alone—the impression of a grey blur, floating dimly across the scene and leaving no trace." As a characterization, nothing could have been wider of the mark. As shrewd and ruthless as he was crafty, Stalin would leave a lasting mark on Russia. By 1922 he had risen to the highest post in the Communist Party, that of General Secretary.

Soon thereafter Stalin faced a crisis in his career. He lost Lenin's support. Disturbed by Stalin's "rude" character and his ambitions, Lenin recommended that Stalin be dropped from his position as General Secretary. Warned Lenin:

> Comrade Stalin . . . has concentrated enormous power in his hands, and I am not sure that he always knows how to use that power with sufficient caution.

Nevertheless, Stalin clung to his power. He knew how to manipulate those around him. Stalin not only survived, but, after the death of Lenin, he also emerged as the leader of the Soviet Union.

The Stalin-Trotsky Split

Leon Trotsky had played a key role in the Bolshevik Revolution of November 1917. He had served as the first Soviet Commissar of Foreign Affairs and as Commissar of War. He had written with insight on theories of Marxism. He had been close to Lenin. Many Communists had expected Trotsky to succeed Lenin, but Stalin had cleverly maneuvered himself to the top post.

Trotsky and his supporters thought that the Communist revolution should be carried throughout the world at once. They advocated "world revolution." Stalin wanted to build "socialism in one country [Russia]" first. He wanted to reconstruct Russia first before concerning himself with other countries. Once the Soviet Union was strong enough, Stalin was willing to help spread communism through the world. He later supported Communist revolutionary action in many countries.

After a bitter struggle for power within the Communist Party, Trotsky was expelled from the Party in 1927. Soon thereafter he went into exile. In 1940, while living in Mexico, Trotsky was brutally assassinated.

Under Stalin's rule, all of his rivals eventually were either removed from power, imprisoned, exiled, or killed. Some of these men had once been Stalin's friends. Others had been key figures in the Party long before Stalin had any influence. Nearly all had devoted their lives to the Communist cause.

During the "Great Purges" of the 1930s thousands of people who were considered dangerous to Stalin's regime were wiped out. With his opponents out of the way, Stalin ruled as virtual dictator until his death in 1953. From his rise to power until the outbreak of World War II (1939), Stalin helped to develop a number of important policies and programs.

Five-Year Plans

In 1928 Stalin launched the first of the extremely important *Five-Year Plans*. It had several main objectives: 1. The "capitalist elements" that existed during the NEP were to be eliminated, and the nationalization of industry was to be expanded. 2. Industrialization and agricultural production were to be increased. 3. The "socialization" of agriculture was to be advanced by increasing the number of peasants working on collective farms.

The First Five-Year Plan stimulated industrial growth and increased the production of machinery and electrical power. It also extended state control of industry and agriculture.

Ruthless and brutal techniques were often used to achieve these objectives. Dictatorial methods violated human rights. Freedom was trampled on in the race to reach statistical goals.

The Second Five-Year Plan (1933-1937) was followed by the Third Five-Year Plan (1938-1941). They also concentrated on increasing industrial production and putting farmland under collectives. By 1938 about 93 percent of peasant families lived on collective farms. Also transportation facilities had been improved and natural resources were developed.

Foreign Affairs

In foreign affairs the Soviet Union signed nonaggression pacts with a number of nations. Many of these agreements it later broke. These included the Turkish-Soviet Nonaggression Pact of 1925 (the Soviet Union denounced this pact in 1945); the Afghanistan-Soviet Nonaggression Pact of 1926 (the Soviet Union forced Afghanistan to cede frontier areas to the Russians in 1940); and the Lithuanian-Soviet Nonaggression Pact of 1926 (the Soviet Union annexed Lithuania in 1940).

In 1928 the Soviet Union signed the Kellogg-Briand Pact. In 1929, it violated the pact by invading Manchuria to regain possession of the Chinese Eastern Railway.

A major concern of the Soviet Union in the late 1930s was an expanding Germany. In August 1939 the Soviet Union signed a nonaggression pact with Germany. Scarcely a week after that, Germany invaded Poland to begin World War II. About a month later, the Poles defeated, the Soviet Union divided that country with Germany.

Check on Your Reading

1. Analyze Joseph Stalin's method of ruling.
2. What role did Leon Trotsky have in the Communist Party? How did his ideas differ from those of Stalin?
3. What were the results of the three Five-Year Plans?

5. A Picture of the Soviet Union in 1939

At the outbreak of World War II (1939), the Communists had been in control for about twenty years.

This is a picture of the society that they had helped to create.

The Political Scene

The Constitution of the Soviet Union was approved in 1936. It provided for a two-house legislature, the *Supreme Soviet,* which represented both the people and the various "republics" that made up the Soviet Union. These republics were regional areas with their own languages and cultures. Together they made up the *Union of Soviet Socialist Republics,* or *U.S.S.R.,* (generally known as the Soviet Union).

Elections for the Supreme Soviet were meaningless because opposition political parties had been abolished. Only one party—the Communist—remained, and it was far more than a political party. The name of only one candidate appeared on the ballot for each position in the Supreme Soviet—the candidate approved by the Communist Party. Also, those elected to the Supreme Soviet had no real power. The chief job of the Supreme Soviet seemed to be "to approve unanimously what [had] already been decided." It is important to understand that only about 5 percent of the population belonged to the Communist Party.

Real power was in the hands of the leaders of the Communist Party, particularly Stalin. Stalin was both the chairman of the powerful government body called the *Council of Ministers* and the *Secretary of the Communist Party.* As he himself said: "Here in the Soviet Union . . . not a single important political or organizational question is decided by our Soviet and other mass organizations without directions from the Party." The government of the Soviet Union in 1939 was actually a Party dictatorship headed by Joseph Stalin.

The Economic Scene

Nearly all land in the Soviet Union was owned by the state. However, most agricultural property was held by *kolkhozy,* or collective farms. Peasants on collective farms did not own the land, but they cultivated it together. Farm machinery was obtained from state-owned *Machine and Tractor Stations.*

After the crops were marketed, each person on a collective farm received a share of the return. Workers were rewarded according to the amount of work they had done. The hard-working and efficient farmer obtained greater rewards than the slow and inefficient one.

People on collective farms were permitted to own the small cottages in which they lived and household goods. Each family also might have a few animals and a small garden. The family could cultivate its garden for private gain.

In addition, there were *sovkhozy*, or state farms. Economist Harry Schwartz defined a sovkhoz as "entirely the property of the Soviet government, which operates it with hired labor directed by managers responsible to the government ministry having control of the particular farm."

Soviet agriculture encountered many serious problems. In the beginning there were shortages of farm machinery. In addition, many peasants preferred to spend their time working their private garden plots rather than the collective lands. In 1929-1930, persecuted *kulaks* killed their cattle and

destroyed farm implements rather than turn them over to collectives. Kulaks were peasants with more land, cattle, or wealth than their neighbors or simply those charged with not cooperating with the government. In the early 1930s there were crop failures. Peasants who deliberately violated Soviet regulations on collective farms were treated harshly, and thousands of kulaks were wiped out. Millions of Russians died of starvation or were killed by government troops.

In time acreage under cultivation was increased. More farm machinery was produced and food shortages gradually declined. However, progress was far from uniform and constant.

Practically all Soviet industries were owned by the state. Workers in factories were assigned quotas of work and were expected to meet them. Workers usually received wages and were permitted to own the consumer goods they bought.

This photo shows the arrival of the first tractor to a sovkhoz. Equipment was leased from government agencies known as Machine and Tractor Stations.

Everyone in industry did not receive the same reward. Workers who exceeded their quotas were given bonuses and granted better housing. *Stakhanovites*—the name given to workers with outstanding production records—received special rewards. Workers who fell below quotas or were late to work or careless in their jobs were punished.

Thus, there developed differences in the economic status of Russians. For example, there was a considerable difference between the wages of factory managers or top workers and those of ordinary workers. Similarly, the planners and agricultural experts for collective farms received higher rewards and lived far better than most peasants. In a country where classes were supposed to disappear, a new class system was developing!

A Party Dictatorship with a Socialist Economy

The Soviet Union's economy in 1939 could be described as socialistic, not communistic. It had not moved past the so-called "stage" of socialism, for people still received rewards according to their work and not, as under the theory of communism, according to their need. Economic differences and a class system continued to exist. The 1936 constitution of the Soviet Union itself declared that the principle applied in the U.S.S.R. was that of socialism: "From each according to his ability, to each according to his work."

The Soviet state—in reality, the Communist Party—dominated every aspect of the economy. It interfered continually with the freedom of the individual. For example, a state decree of 1932 ordered that "workers absent for one day without an acceptable excuse be fired and deprived of their housing." Also the state herded its opponents into brutal slave labor camps. Its secret police violated basic human rights and used terror to achieve the state's objectives.

In brief, the Soviet Union in 1939 was a hybrid nation. It was a Party dictatorship with a socialist economy.

Social and Cultural Scene

Stalin and the Communist Party dominated social and cultural affairs. It is important to understand their attitude toward religion and education.

The Communist Party opposed religion. Most of its members believed with Karl Marx that reli-

A parade in Red Square in Moscow celebrating the October Revolution.

gion was "the opiate of the people." In 1925 the *League of Militant Atheists,* or the *Godless League,* was formed. It tried to drive out religion. Some of its more extreme members burned churches. A tactical shift occurred in 1936 when the new Soviet constitution promised the Russian people religious freedom as well as freedom of anti-religious propaganda. The Party itself remained anti-religious.

Nevertheless, there were people—particularly the older generation—who continued to believe in their religions. Despite the fact that many young people turned from religious faith, the Russian Orthodox Church and other faiths managed to survive.

The Communist Party also devoted much energy to educating the people. Many schools were built and more people were trained as teachers. The number of children receiving some formal education increased greatly.

In addition to educating students, the Soviet school had the job of *indoctrinating* them—instructing them in the doctrines and beliefs of communism. Lenin had said that the principal purpose of the school was "the cultivation of communist morality in the pupils." All educational media—teachers, textbooks, newspapers, and others—were expected to be propagandists for the Communist cause.

Russian adults and children were indoctrinated with certain ideas. One of these was that Stalin was a great man. Another idea was that the Soviet Union was progressive and "capitalist" nations were not. A first-grade reader used in the middle 1930s included the following:

There goes the lunch bell. . . . How good the hot soup smells! . . . We get hot lunches every day. All children in America do not get hot lunches. All children in England do not get hot lunches. Only the children in the Soviet Union get hot lunches in school every day.

A third idea that was stressed was that there was great waste in "capitalist" nations. A textbook explaining the First Five-Year Plan (1928–1932) declared:

We have a plan.
In America they work without a plan. . . .
We make what is essential.

In America hundreds of factories consume raw materials and energy in order to make what is altogether unnecessary.

Similarly, the ideas of patriotism, national pride, and the need for hard work and sacrifice were instilled in the people.

Even music, literature, and art were to be propaganda vehicles for the Soviet government. Composers were expected to write music that would inspire the people with love of the Soviet Union and communism. Authors were expected to write books in praise of Communist ideas. Artists were expected to paint pictures favorable to the Communist cause. Thus propaganda influenced and molded the ideas and lives of the Russians.

Check on Your Reading

1. How was the Soviet Union governed under Stalin?
2. Describe conditions on a collective farm.
3. What problems did the Soviets encounter in agriculture?
4. What were the functions of Soviet schools, art, music, and literature?

LET'S MEET THE PEOPLE

Comrade Dukhovtsev and the Purge Trial

The three-man Purge Commission, headed by Comrade Galembo, sat behind a table on a platform decorated with portraits of Communist leaders. They called Comrade Dukhovtsev before them.

"Comrade Dukhovtsev, are you married?" they asked.

"Yes, I am."

"Tell me," continued Comrade Galembo, "did you register your marriage or not? In other words, how was your marriage consecrated?" The Communist Party believed that registering with the state was all that was necessary for marriage. It was violently opposed to church marriages.

Dukhovtsev fidgeted. Then, in a low voice, he told the truth: "I was married in church!" The audience in the hall laughed.

"I know, comrades, that it sounds funny," Dukhovtsev continued quickly. "It's ridiculous and I admit it. A church ceremony means nothing to me, believe me. But I was in love with my wife and her parents just wouldn't let her marry me unless I agreed to a church comedy. They're backward people."

The laughter of the audience became louder.

"We are not believers, I can assure you," shouted Dukhovtsev. ". . . I beg you, comrades, to forgive my mistake. I confess that I'm guilty for having hidden this crime from the Party."

Dukhovtsev's words of defense were useless now. Comrade Galembo rose stiffly and solemnly proclaimed, "Comrade Dukhovtsev, you are expelled from the Communist Party!"

Dukhovtsev looked about him in bewilderment. Then he left the hall. It would be of little comfort to him to remember that the suicide of an expelled Party member was never unexpected.

The account above is based on information in *I Chose Freedom* by Victor Kravchenko, 1969, Scribner.

CHAPTER REVIEW

Think and Discuss

1. What underlying problems were there in pre-revolutionary Russia that help explain the First and Second Revolutions?
2. Can you find any evidence in this chapter to support this statement: A militant minority can gain control of a country in which the people are not trained to govern themselves democratically? Explain your answer.
3. Evaluate the logic of Stalin's policy of establishing communism first in Russia before attempting to spread it throughout the world.
4. How valuable is the practice of establishing a set of goals to be achieved within a specified time, such as the Five-Year Plans?
5. Why do you think the membership of the Communist Party was limited to a small number?
6. What was the purpose of having an elected Supreme Soviet with little power?
7. Why do you think that the Communists opposed religion in the Soviet Union?

Past and Present

1. Compare the careers of Stalin and Brezhnev.
2. In what other countries today have leaders maneuvered their way to leadership as Stalin did; that is, without benefit of election?

Activities

1. Consult references to find an account of the Soviet constitution of 1936. Can you find any provisions guaranteeing the rights of individuals, such as the first ten Amendments to the United States Constitution? Why were such provisions placed in the Soviet Constitution?
2. Panel discussion: Choose one of these topics: agriculture, conditions of the working person, foreign policy, music, sports, or theater. Compare the features of each of these in the Soviet Union with its features in czarist Russia.
3. Draw a diagram showing the government of Russia in 1939. What conclusions can you reach?

Tensions and Problems Lead to World War II

KEYNOTE

At the town of Dachau, fifteen miles from Munich, Germany, there stood a gas chamber where certain Germans called *Nazis* killed thousands of innocent people. Scratched into one of the chamber's walls were these words about the Nazis: FORGIVE THEM.   Just below, someone had written: NEVER.

These words on the wall of the death house are sharp reminders of the not-too-distant past.   They recall the days when the brutal and inhumane actions of the Nazis shocked the world.   It was a time that saw the rise to power in Italy, Germany, and Japan of leaders who preferred violence to reason, and tyranny to justice.   It ended in a terrible conflict, World War II.

War's destruction in a Belgium village.

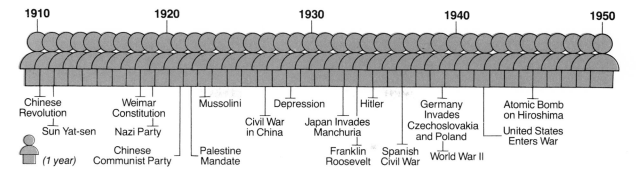

1910	1920	1930	1940	1950

Chinese Revolution

Sun Yat-sen

(1 year)

Weimar Constitution

Nazi Party

Chinese Communist Party

Mussolini

Palestine Mandate

Depression

Civil War in China

Japan Invades Manchuria

Franklin Roosevelt

Hitler

Spanish Civil War

Germany Invades Czechoslovakia and Poland

World War II

Atomic Bomb on Hiroshima

United States Enters War

1. Dictatorship in Italy and Germany

Italy after World War I was a troubled land. Although Italy had fought on the victorious Allied side, the war had cost that country about twelve billion dollars and the lives of more than 600,000 soldiers. Economic conditions were bad. Many people looked in vain for jobs. The value of Italian currency dropped, and prices rose to many times their prewar levels. Food supplies were inadequate. Strikes plagued the country. Farmers protested high rents for land. Conditions were ripe for violence and change.

Italy was a constitutional monarchy, but neither king nor government officials displayed leadership. Dangerous tensions resulted from a widespread fear of communism.

The Rise of Fascism

A number of groups demanded that reforms or radical changes be made in the Italian government and economy. Among the more violent agitators were the *Fascists*. A Fascist group known as the *Fasci di Combattimento* had been organized in March 1919. It was led by Benito Mussolini (1883-1945), a journalist. The Fascists did not then have a clear political program. However, 1. They fought against those who advocated communism; and used the fear of communism to gain support. 2. They tried to weaken the Socialist Party, which had adopted a radical program. 3. They demanded that Italy be developed into a world power.

In 1921 the Fascists made up only a small part of the Italian population of forty-five million. Nevertheless, their influence and power were growing. In October 1922, the Fascists made their move.

While Mussolini remained in Milan, four hundred miles to the north, poorly coordinated groups of his followers "marched" on Rome. According to an Italian historian, they were armed with "a few machine guns, rifles, revolvers and a small amount of ammunition, bludgeons, table legs and branches of trees." The Fascist marchers probably could have been dispersed. Instead, they met no military resistance. King Victor Emmanuel III was persuaded to appoint Mussolini Premier, an office he soon turned into a dictatorship.

Why did the Fascist "March" on Rome succeed? Many factors helped Mussolini to power. These included the weakness of the Italian government and the support given to the Fascists by certain military chiefs, industrialists and even the king's cousin. Also important were unsettled economic conditions, low morale among the people, and the fear of communism.

The phrase "Il Duce ha sempre ragione" ("The Leader is always right"), referring to Mussolini, appeared on billboards all over Italy in 1928. Mussolini won admiration from people abroad as well as at home. Said Richard Washburn Child, a former American ambassador to Italy: "The Duce is now the greatest figure of this . . . time."

Other foreigners seemed particularly impressed with Mussolini because he accomplished such things as making Italian trains run on time.

Benito Mussolini was a barrel-chested, rugged man who frequently posed with his fists pressed against his hips, his head tilted back, and his jaw jutting forward. He was willing to use any means to achieve his ends. As he once said: "Sometimes I must act like a surgeon, because operations are at times indispensable, but when the patient recovers he clasps the surgeon's hand and kisses the instruments that have restored him to health." Italians did have more political stability under Mussolini, and parts of the Italian economy improved. For the Italian people, the price was loss of freedom.

Mussolini denounces League of Nations sanctions against Italy. These sanctions were voted in the League of Nations when Mussolini's army invaded Ethiopia in 1935.

What is *Fascism?* Many scholars doubt that the word can be exactly defined. Nevertheless, in time Italian Fascism came to be based on these ideas:

1. The state was all-important. The Italian Fascists believed that people must serve the state and sacrifice their own well-being for the good of the state.

2. According to Fascism, the majority of the people were not fit to rule. Under Fascism a small group of people, directed by Mussolini, was to govern the country. The rest of the people were to take orders.

This does not mean that the Fascists did not seek the support of the masses. On the contrary, Fascism depended on mass support; but it repudiated the democratic principle of majority rule.

3. The Italian Fascists believed in using force to achieve their goals. They were convinced that war was good, not evil.

4. The Italian Fascists opposed freedom of speech, freedom of the press, freedom of elections, the existence of anti-Fascist parties, and other features of democracy.

5. The Italian Fascists believed that the economy should be dominated by the state—and in reality the "state" was the Fascist government.

In addition, the Italian Fascists advocated intense nationalism, imperialism, and *totalitarianism*— that is, they believed that the Fascists should have unlimited power to control every aspect of life.

Fascist Italy under Mussolini

Italy remained a monarchy in name under Mussolini. However, between 1925 and 1928, Mussolini obtained full dictatorial powers. His decrees were law, and all political parties except his Fascists were outlawed. Freedom of speech was suppressed. The words "Mussolini is always right" appeared under the dictator's picture in all classrooms!

The Italian economy was reorganized to form a *corporate state.* According to political scientist William Ebenstein, ". . . the Fascist government established corporations, which were administrative agencies in a given industry designed to unite and control the associations of workers and employers in that industry." The corporations controlled the Italian economy. They, in turn, obeyed Mussolini's decrees on economic matters. Strikes and lockouts were forbidden.

In religious affairs, Mussolini tried to lessen tensions between his government and the Papacy by settling the "Roman Question." The "Roman

Question" referred to problems that had existed between the Italian government and the Papacy since the final territorial unification of Italy in 1870. The Popes had refused to accept this loss.

In February 1929, the *Lateran Treaty* and an accompanying Concordat were concluded between Mussolini and a representative of the Papacy. This agreement had the following provisions: 1. The Pope was recognized as sovereign with "exclusive and absolute dominion" over the Vatican City. 2. The Papacy recognized Rome as the capital of Italy. 3. The Roman Catholic Apostolic religion was recognized as "the only religion of the State," and the marriage sacrament was recognized as "legal for civil purposes, when administered according to Canon Law." 4. Catholic religious education was to continue in public elementary schools and be extended to secondary schools. 5. Italy agreed to pay the Papacy compensation for territorial and other losses.

The Lateran Treaty was popular with many Italians. It increased Mussolini's prestige at home and abroad.

Conditions in Germany

After the defeat of the Germans in World War I, a republic with many democratic features was established under the Weimar Constitution (1919). Despite the Weimar Constitution there was great unrest. Germany was suffering from heavy losses of men and material in the war. Many Germans felt humiliated by defeat. There was dissatisfaction, both real and manufactured, with the Treaty of Versailles. Many Germans believed that the treaty was harsh and unfair.

Economic conditions in Germany were bad from 1919 to 1923. There was much unemployment, and demobilized troops looked in vain for work. The value of German money dropped and inflation spread throughout the country. The food supply was not adequate to meet the needs of the nation. Huge reparations provided an additional burden. The German economy recovered greatly between 1923 and 1929. However, after 1929 the worldwide depression and other factors seriously weakened German economic life.

Dangerous tensions resulted from a widespread fear of communism. Immediately after World War I there were a series of uprisings in Europe. Not only did Russian Communists take over Russia, but Hungarian Communists established a government in Hungary. In 1918 and 1919 there were two Communist revolts in Germany itself. As in Italy, groups in Germany used the almost hysterical fear of communism among the middle class and business leaders to promote Fascism.

The Nazis Rise to Power

One anti-Communist group was the *National Socialists* or *Nazis,* organized in 1919-1920. Adolf Hitler, a former corporal in the German army, became the leader of the Nazis.

Nazis and some army leaders tried to take over in Germany in 1923 with the so-called Beer-Hall *Putsch* in Munich. They bungled the attempt and Adolf Hitler was put in jail. There he wrote his *Mein Kampf (My Struggle),* a rambling book in which he outlined his plans for Germany. Few people at the time took the book seriously.

The growth of the Nazi movement was very slow before the postwar depression in Germany. The severe depression contributed heavily to the rise of the Nazis, who promised the people food and work for all. Eventually, the Nazi ranks included many different people: veterans; ardent nationalists; workers; small shopkeepers; intellectuals; people who hated Jews, democrats, and Communists; industrialists; and dissatisfied young people.

Adolf Hitler was a highly persuasive orator who knew how to play on Germans' fear of communism and on their desire for greatness. In 1934 a German writer, Konrad Heiden, declared: "As a mob-leader Hitler is certainly unrivalled today and almost unequalled in history. . . . Nothing like him has been seen in modern Europe."

When he spoke, there was an emotional fire in his voice, a dramatic forcefulness, at times almost a hysteria that swept his audience along with him. "His words were like a scourge," wrote one of his listeners. "When he spoke of the disgrace of Germany, I felt ready to spring on any enemy . . . glancing round, I saw that his magnetism was holding these thousands as one. . . ."

In addition, Hitler had drive, cunning, ability to glamorize his program, understanding of the methods of propaganda, and, of course, strong-armed men to convince the doubters. Finally, conditions in Germany and the world made some people believe that only a man like Hitler could "save" the German people.

Hitler gives the Nazi salute as he leaves a rally.

In April 1932, Hitler received 36.8 percent of the votes cast in the election for President of the German Republic. Paul von Hindenburg, a general and World War I hero, was the winner. Early the following year, after a complicated series of political maneuvers, von Hindenburg was persuaded to appoint Hitler Chancellor.

During the next few months, by using the emergency article of the constitution and an enabling act that the Reichstag (the principal body of the legislature) passed, Hitler took over most governmental powers. Within a short time he had abolished all parties except his National Socialists, and had become dictator of Germany.

All of Germany fell under the control of Hitler's central government. All political groups except the Nazis were banned. Hitler established the *Gestapo*, a secret police. Hitler used the Gestapo and the *Storm Troopers* to eliminate all opposition.

Basic Ideas of German Nazism

1. The Nazis believed that they belonged to a so-called "pure Aryan race," that was superior to all other people. They were convinced that they were destined to rule the world. These Nazi ideas were completely unscientific.

2. The Nazis were anti-Semitic—that is, they were bitterly opposed to the Jews. They believed that people of the Jewish religion or those descended from Jews should be denied all rights, driven from Germany, or killed.

3. Nazi leaders opposed the principles of Christianity. They tried to substitute devotion to Germany for devotion to God.

4. The state was all-important and was to have supreme power over individuals.

5. A dictator, Hitler, would rule with the aid of a Nazi "elite," or chosen few.

6. The economy would be based on a system of private ownership of the means of production, distribution, and consumption under strict state control.

In addition, the Nazis approved of the use of force and war, rejected democratic rights, and supported the principles of intense nationalism, imperialism, and totalitarianism. Many Nazi ideas resembled those of the Italian Fascists. Indeed, Nazism was a German form of Fascism.

Nazi Germany and the Holocaust

Adolf Hitler ruled as dictator. Every region and local area had to obey the orders of the central government. The Gestapo viciously eliminated any opposition to the Nazi regime.

The German economy was dominated by the state. Strikes were prohibited and unions were abolished. The interests of the state came first. In 1935 Hitler increased the number of German troops in violation of the Treaty of Versailles, and Germany concentrated on massive rearmament.

Hitler believed that the masses "more easily fall a victim to a big lie than to a small one." Schools indoctrinated students with bitter Nazi propaganda. Orators screamed Hitler's name at mass meetings. Censors, directed by Joseph Paul Goebbels, burned books considered dangerous.

Under the Nazis, religious groups were ridiculed, persecuted, and attacked. The brutal and deliberate mass murder by the Nazis of the Jews and their associates is known as the *Holocaust*, for—like a wildfire out of control—it carried death everywhere.

First, books by Jews and others were burned. Next, the Nuremberg Laws of 1935 launched a direct attack on individual Jews: "Marriages between Jews and subjects of German . . . blood are forbidden"; "Jews are forbidden to fly the . . . national flag"; "A Jew cannot be a [German] citizen." Then anti-Semitic riots broke out in Germany, synagogues were vandalized, and Jewish children were expelled from German schools. Finally, thousands of Jews were herded into Auschwitz, Buchenwald, Treblinka, and other concentration camps, where they were slaughtered by gas chambers, beatings, injections of deadly diseases, and other horrible methods. By 1945 the Nazis had killed six million Jews.

Hitler reviews troops at the great Nuremberg Nazi Party Rally in 1934. This dramatic spectacle was held every year for a week. Parades, music, and pageantry were used to win and hold the loyalty of the people to the Nazi Party's program.

Jews are herded into a concentration camp.

Among the victims were thousands of children. Elie Wiesel, who was deported to Auschwitz and then to Buchenwald, where his parents and a sister died, still remembers the sight of the children marching to their death: "Children for me evoke war, thunder and hate, shouts, screams, dogs howling, children in the street hunted, beaten, humiliated. . . . You watch them marching, marching, and you know they will never come back; and yet you go on seeing them, but they no longer see you."

Check on Your Reading

1. What problems faced Italy after World War I?
2. How did the Italian Fascists rise to power?
3. What were the basic ideas of Italian Fascism?
4. What were problems facing postwar Germany?
5. How did Adolf Hitler become dictator?
6. Describe life in Germany under Hitler.

2. Militarism in Japan, and Revolution in China

As a reward for joining the Allied side in World War I, Japan won rights to Shantung province in China as a sphere of influence, replacing Germany there. The war had benefited Japan, but it also ushered in a period of political instability.

Business-Military Conflicts

Japan had changed much since the 1860s, under the guidance of strong leaders. This change had been orderly; but by the time of World War I, most of the old leaders were dead. There was not a forceful and prestigious group to succeed them. Fighting for political control developed within the government, and governments changed frequently.

During the 1920s steps were taken toward a more representative democracy. Efforts were made to increase the powers of the lower house of the *Diet* (the Parliament). Suffrage was extended to include all adult men. This meant that out of a population of about 55 million, some 14 million could vote. At the same time, however, problems arose involving the military, business people, and the farmers that threatened the liberal trend and the effectiveness of the government itself.

The members of the military group were deeply conservative. They had risen high in the public esteem as a result of the Sino-Japanese and the Russo-Japanese wars; but they were feared by some business leaders and were losing prestige. The military leaders wished to continue to enjoy their former power and glory, and to continue Japanese expansion, by force if necessary.

Business interests also wished for Japanese expansion, but through the peaceful means of trade. War disrupted commerce and drained the public treasury. Many business leaders wanted reduced spending on the military, and under their influence the government cut the size of the Japanese army by fifty thousand men after World War I. The military resented this, and army and navy officers chafed under the general lack of sympathy for their cause.

Japan's farmers were also highly conservative, and they too developed grievances against the government. As the price of rice soared during the war, they enjoyed a measure of prosperity. However, prices dropped just as quickly once the war ended. At the same time, farmers were unable to produce enough to feed a constantly growing population, but increasing imports from abroad held the price of rice down. Worst of all, from the peasants' point of view, the government did little to relieve their distress.

Grievances against the government brought the farmers and the military together in opposition to business domination. Also, many farmers' sons, unable to make a living off the land, joined the army. This served further to link the farmers and the military.

Customarily, the army and the navy chose generals and admirals to head military departments in the government. By refusing to select persons to fill these positions, the military could hamstring the government. This occurred on more than one occasion during the 1920s, and it enabled the military to produce unrest and confusion.

In 1930, a severe, worldwide economic depression struck. As nations raised tariffs to protect their own industries, world trade diminished. Japan, which depended heavily on international commerce, was especially hard hit. The government could find no permanent solutions to Japanese economic problems. Popular discontent increased.

The Army Strikes

Japan had a sphere of influence in Kwantung province in Manchuria. Stationed there to protect Japanese interests was what was known as the Kwantung army. In September 1931, according to Chinese sources, leaders of that army manufactured an incident involving the blowing up of a section of railroad track. They then blamed the action on Chinese troops stationed in Kwantung. Fighting broke out, and by early 1932 the Kwantung army had subdued all opposition. Japan then set up the so-called "independent" state of Manchukuo in Manchuria. Actually Manchukuo was under the domination of Japan.

The Kwantung army had acted on orders from high officers in Japan and without the government's consent. Faced with army occupation of Manchuria, the government went along. The army regained lost prestige, and popular support for the Manchurian adventure became widespread. As the 1930s progressed, the military gained more and more control of the government.

Business people had little choice but to throw in with the military. They supported a program of increased armament—which provided jobs—to strengthen Japan's position and prestige as a great power. They came to favor overseas expansion by force to advance Japanese trade and to obtain raw materials and develop markets. They also joined the military in advocating expansion into areas of Asia where Japan's surplus population could be settled.

Revolution in China

In 1911, revolutionists overthrew the weak and corrupt Manchu government and established the Republic of China. The leader of these revolutionaries was Dr. Sun Yat-sen.

Dr. Sun Yat-sen (1866-1925) was born into a peasant family. When he was fourteen he left China for Hawaii to live there for three years with a brother. Returning home, he later studied in Hong Kong, receiving a medical degree in 1892. After practicing for two years, Dr. Sun Yat-sen began to devote his full attention to bringing down the Ch'ing dynasty, the ruling family line of the Manchus, and he traveled throughout the world to build support for the revolutionary cause. He was abroad when the revolution occurred, and hurried home to take charge of the government.

On January 1, 1912, Dr. Sun Yat-sen was inaugurated as Provisional President of the Republic. The Chinese had no real experience in running a republican form of government. As a result, the years following the republic's establishment were filled with confusion. In February 1912, in an effort to avoid civil war, Dr. Sun Yat-sen resigned as

This photo of Mao Tse-tung (right) was taken in 1938. It shows him with the "President of the Frontier Government" in the courtyard of Communist headquarters.

President in favor of Yüan Shi-k'ai. Yüan Shi-k'ai was a powerful general whose army might have challenged the infant republic had he not been made president.

Later in 1912 a number of people who had supported the revolt against the Manchus organized the *Kuomintang,* or *National People's Party,* which became the most important group in the national parliament. Yüan Shi-k'ai, the new President, was an ambitious man. In 1913 he dismissed the Kuomintang from the national parliament. He also tried to make himself emperor. Although Yüan Shi-k'ai failed in his attempt and died in 1916, China remained a divided and disrupted nation. Despite a supposed central government at Peking, China was disunited.

Dr. Sun Yat-sen: National Hero

Members of the Kuomintang refused to be discouraged. They had established a government at Canton, and in 1921 they elected Dr. Sun Yat-sen to head it. Thus, there was one government in Canton, another at Peking, and several lesser ones in regions run by *warlords,* or heads of local armies. Dr. Sun Yat-sen and the Kuomintang resolved to eliminate the rival governments in order to unite China.

As leader of the government at Canton, Dr. Sun Yat-sen did not prove to be an efficient administrator, but he inspired his associates with his patriot-

ism, sincerity, and hard work. He became one of China's national heroes.

An important part of Dr. Sun Yat-sen's philosophy can be found in his *Three Principles,* which he proposed as guides by which to organize China. The Three Principles were: 1. *nationalism,* the idea of freedom from the control of foreigners; 2. *democracy,* a limited democratic government; and 3. *livelihood,* a decent standard of living and economic justice for all.

Dr. Sun Yat-sen hoped that the Chinese could build a strong, united nation. He was willing to accept outside help to achieve this goal. In 1923 he accepted advice and assistance of Communists from Russia. However, Dr. Sun Yat-sen was not a Communist. On the other hand, a number of individuals within the Kuomintang were Communists or favorable to communism. Some of these people were to play important roles in the history of China. One was Mao Tse-tung (1893–1976).

Like Dr. Sun Yat-sen, Mao Tse-tung was born into a peasant family. He received a good education, and at age thirteen left school to aid his father on the family farm. Later he continued school in Changsha. Some scholars believe that the fact that Western nations refused to take steps to diminish foreign control of China after World War I helped turn Mao Tse-tung toward communism. In 1921 he and others founded the Chinese Communist Party.

Mao Tse-tung and other Communists within the Kuomintang shared certain goals with Dr. Sun Yat-sen. They too wanted a China free from foreign control, and a strong and united country. But they wanted the revolution to go further and abolish all private ownership of property.

Conflicts within the Kuomintang

After Dr. Sun Yat-sen died in 1925, the Kuomintang continued his work. Party leadership now fell to Chiang Kai-shek (1886-1975).

Chiang Kai-shek was born into a fairly well-to-do peasant family. After his elementary education, he attended a military school. He received more military training during three years in Japan, returning to China to join the revolution. He also spent several months in the Soviet Union and served as the first head of the Whampoa Military Academy in Canton. Chiang Kai-shek originally cooperated with the Chinese Communists and accepted Russian advice and assistance. However, he later became anti-Communist.

In 1926, under Chiang Kai-shek's command, Kuomintang armies moved northward from Canton. They were determined to unite the country. Town after town fell to the advancing Kuomintang forces, or welcomed them as people who could restore order. Then in 1927, a struggle for power occurred *within* the Kuomintang, pitting Chiang Kai-shek against Communist leaders.

Chiang Kai-shek set up his headquarters in Nanking while the Communists and their supporters established themselves at Hankow. By the end of 1927 the Communist government in Hankow lost public support and fell.

Chiang Kai-shek's armies continued to march northward. In 1928 they took Peking. By 1931 the Kuomintang controlled considerable territory in China, although the Communists and warlords still dominated some regions.

The Kuomintang government outlawed the Communist Party, and Chiang Kai-shek spent several years trying to eliminate Communists from China entirely. In 1934, his army surrounded Communist forces in the mountainous Hunan and Kiangsi provinces, but an estimated one hundred thousand escaped the trap. Led by Mao Tse-tung and others, in October 1934 this group of Communists began *The Long March*, a six-thousand-mile trek lasting many months to the Shensi province in north central China. There Mao Tse-tung set up his own government. Disillusioned with the city workers as a base for revolution, he determined to organize the peasantry as his foundation for revolution in China.

Chiang Kai-shek did not establish a democratic government. Even if he had seriously tried to do so, it would have been difficult to introduce democracy. The state of the country, the lack of democratic experience of the people, the weaknesses within the Kuomintang, and the invasion of the Japanese all interfered with democratic growth. Chiang Kai-shek became the "strong man" of China rather than head of a democratic government.

China Struggles between the Old and New

In addition to the upheavals in political affairs, there were significant occurrences and changes in other fields. In education modern methods were introduced. Many Chinese went to Japan, the United States, and other countries to study. Educational changes helped Chinese women and girls obtain more rights in everyday life.

In literature, some authors began to write in the vernacular of the Chinese, rather than in the classical style. In religion Confucianism declined in importance, although it continued to be a significant factor in the lives of many Chinese. In foreign affairs China was freed from a number of foreign controls and concessions.

Despite the changes that occurred during this period, many of the old ways of living continued. Most family ties remained strong. Numerous ancient customs were followed. Thus, the Chinese struggled between old and new ways of life. Before the Chinese could readjust themselves, Japanese invaders disrupted their country again.

Check on Your Reading

1. What conflicts arose between the military and business interests, and what grievances did the military and the farmers have?
2. How did militarists increase their power in Japan?
3. Why did Dr. Sun Yat-sen fail to unite China?
4. Describe the backgrounds of Dr. Sun Yat-sen and Chiang Kai-shek.
5. What conflicts developed within the Kuomintang and how were they resolved?
6. What changes in Chinese life occurred during this period?

3. The Democracies and Efforts to Ensure Peace

During the 1920s and 1930s democracies—such as Britain, France, and the United States—occupied themselves with serious domestic problems. They also devoted considerable energy to international efforts to strengthen their security and protect the peace.

France Rebuilds

France had suffered much from World War I. As the economic historian Shepard B. Clough notes: "In the devastated regions . . . 900,000 buildings, 200 coal mines, and 34 iron mines had been damaged or destroyed, 85 percent of the arable land had been devastated, and 94 percent of the cattle had disappeared. . . . French foreign commerce had shrunk to the point where exports were only 25 percent and imports 87 percent of the weight of those in 1913. . . . The franc had lost about 72 percent of its purchasing power." Between 1911 and 1921, France's population declined from about 39 million to 37 million. By the latter year, as a result of the war, there were 11 percent fewer males between ages 15 and 50 than in 1911.

During the 1920s, a coalition of parties worked to rebuild France and tried to force Germany to meet its treaty obligations. By the end of the decade, the country had improved economically. Industrial production in 1926 reached twice the level of 1919. The value of the franc increased and the tax system was improved.

France was strong enough not to feel most of the effects of the worldwide depression in 1930 until several months after it had begun. However, by 1931 France's foreign trade began to drop sharply, and industrial production fell by one-fourth between 1931 and 1935. Agricultural prices went down and unemployment rose.

In elections in 1936, the *Popular Front*—a coalition of Radical Socialists, Socialists, Communists, and others—gained control of the French government. Under the leadership of Premier Léon Blum, the Popular Front tried to check the growth of Fascist groups in France and to pull the country out of the depression. The government established a forty-hour work week, and took steps to raise farm prices. It also raised taxes, and it devalued the franc in an effort to improve France's position in international trade.

As Germany under Adolf Hitler began to rearm, France responded by building the *Maginot Line,* a 350-mile line of concrete and underground fortifications along the frontiers of Germany and Luxembourg. This, the French believed, would protect them in case of a German attack. For further protection, France signed treaties of alliance with Czechoslovakia, Yugoslavia, and Rumania.

Events in Britain

Great Britain also had its share of problems during the 1920s. Its foreign trade declined, partly as a result of stiff competition from the United States and Japan. A huge national debt resulting from the war rested heavily on the government. After a brief economic boom, unemployment increased, and in 1926 Britain suffered from a general labor strike. This began in the coal industry as a protest against long hours and low pay, and the strike quickly spread throughout the country.

The depression struck Britain hard. A *National Coalition* government was formed under Ramsay MacDonald in 1931 and it faced the task of grappling with depression problems. The government limited the payment of Britain's war debt, passed an Import Duties Bill designed to protect British goods, and increased unemployment benefits. The British economy began to improve, although during the 1930s it did not reach pre-depression levels.

Britain also made some changes with respect to its dominions: Canada, Australia, New Zealand, Union of South Africa, Ireland, and India. The *Statute of Westminster* of 1931 provided that even if the parliament of a dominion passed a law that conflicted with British law, Britain could not declare it void. The document also prohibited the British parliament from passing laws that applied to a dominion without that dominion's consent.

Great Britain in the Middle East

The relationships between Britain and lands in the Middle East were different from its associations with the dominions. For example, Egypt was made a British protectorate at the outbreak of World War I. In 1922, Britain recognized Egyptian independence, but the British kept special military and administrative rights in Egypt, particularly in the Suez Canal Zone.

Palestine and Iraq also were separated from the Ottoman Empire. Palestine became a mandate of

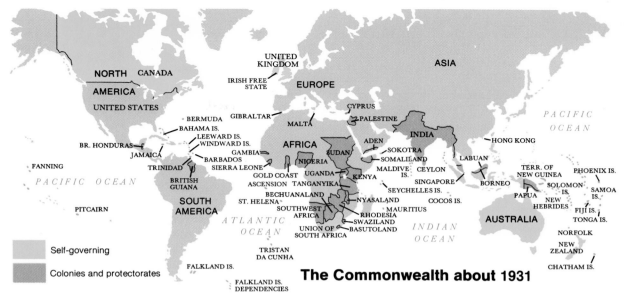

The Commonwealth about 1931

The term Commonwealth of Nations referred originally to self-governing countries.   Later the term was applied not only to dominions but to federated countries and areas directly governed by Britain.

Britain under the League of Nations in 1922. Jews and Muslims continued to clash over the desire of Zionists to establish an independent state in Palestine. British power remained an important factor in the country. Iraq became another British mandate. In 1932 it was recognized as an independent nation, but the British continued to exert considerable influence in Iraq.

British diplomats and administrators in Egypt, Palestine, and Iraq faced many problems. These included rising nationalism of local populations, demands for independence, agitation for economic reforms, and religious conflicts.

The United States in the Postwar Period

The immediate postwar years in the United States were marked by domestic disorders stemming from readjustment problems left by World War I. In 1919 there were strikes of harbor workers, dress and waist makers, cigar makers, subway workers, and steel workers for higher wages, better working conditions, or recognition of unions.

In 1919 and 1920, prices continued to rise. Shoes, for example, which before the war cost $3 a pair, now sold for $10 or higher. The *Buffalo News* declared ironically: "How cheerful it is to see a $4 pair of shoes marked down from $20 to $17.98." Prices went down during a brief depression in 1921-1922.

There were other signs of dissatisfaction and unrest: race riots, bomb scares, the attack on anyone labelled "radical," and the efforts of isolationists to "keep foreigners out" of the United States by means of immigration quotas. It was, as social historian Mark Sullivan pointed out, "a time of extraordinary public irritation."

The man who had responsibility for guiding the United States through the early 1920s was President Warren G. Harding. Harding described his task: "America's present need is not heroics, but healing; not nostrums, but normalcy . . . not surgery but serenity." However, President Harding's administration was marked by scandals involving high officials.

Harding died in 1923, and the Vice-President, Calvin Coolidge, succeeded him. Coolidge was returned to office in the election of 1924. At this point, the United States moved into a period of rising prosperity.

"How the money rolls in!" was a cheerful line of one popular song of the time. More and more the pace of American living quickened, while the jingle of "smart money" and the blast of jazz bands covered the less pleasant side of life. However, beneath the glittering surface were indications that America was moving toward economic disaster. The farmers had never recovered from the postwar collapse of agricultural prices, while installment buying and rash stock speculation had reached fantastic volumes.

Crash and Depression

The stock market crashed in October 1929, during the administration of President Herbert Hoover. Within a year, the United States was deep in a depression that spread throughout the world, with the following repercussions at home and abroad:

1. A sharp drop occurred in the incomes of American families. As a result, Americans had far less money to spend on foreign or American goods.

2. The depression decreased American trade with foreign countries and thus seriously weakened world commerce. The decline in the value of American imports and exports contributed to the closing of factories and rising unemployment abroad.

3. Foreign investments by Americans declined, and American long-term loans to foreign countries practically ended.

In 1932, American voters turned from Hoover to elect Franklin D. Roosevelt, a Democrat, to the presidency. Roosevelt proved to be one of the more dynamic and controversial leaders in American history.

President Roosevelt in his first inaugural address introduced the policies and programs known as the "New Deal." Under the "New Deal," the Federal government became more deeply involved in the lives of most people. It carried out many programs to help restore economic health to the country. The government also supported the Reciprocal Trade Agreements Program. Its objectives were to reduce tariffs, revive trade, and lessen international frictions by providing for a freer movement of goods among countries.

Gradually, as Roosevelt continued what he called his "persistent experimentation," the United States recovered somewhat from the depression. A recession between August 1937 and June 1938 spurred the government to renewed efforts. The outbreak of World War II in September 1939 ended the depression as war and defense production created new jobs.

Efforts to Maintain Peace

The horrors of World War I remained fresh in the minds of Americans and Europeans during the 1920s, and a number of efforts were made to maintain international peace and security. Unfortunately, as historian Raymond P. Stearns makes clear, "national views as to what constituted security differed so sharply as to jeopardize peace." To France, security meant a weak Germany. To Great Britain, security meant a revival of British overseas trade and power. To the United States, security meant insulating the country from situations that might drag it into foreign wars. To many nations, security meant protection from Communist expansion.

The League of Nations worked to maintain peace. Operating with an extremely small budget, the League helped settle a number of disputes that might have led to conflict. It was aided in its peacekeeping efforts by the *Permanent Court of International Justice,* known as the *World Court,* which handed down judgments on cases within its jurisdiction. However, nations were free to accept or reject those decisions.

Between 1920 and 1928 the League of Nations sponsored numerous international conferences dealing with a variety of important matters, such as the stabilization of international finance and the suppression of the growing trade in narcotics. It also assisted in the financial reconstruction of Austria and Hungary.

Representatives of nine nations met in the United States in 1921-1922 at the Washington Conference. At this conference the nations agreed to limit naval shipbuilding. For example, one of the principal items of agreement was that for every five warships of a certain class the United States and Great Britain could build, the Japanese could build three. Japan agreed to this only with great reluctance.

In 1925, representatives of Great Britain, France, Germany, Italy, Poland, Belgium, and Czechoslovakia met in the Swiss city of Locarno to work out security pacts. Germany, Belgium, France, Great Britain, and Italy agreed to respect and guarantee the frontiers between Germany and Belgium and between Germany and France. The signers also agreed to settle all future disputes by arbitration and not by war. After the Locarno Treaties were signed, Germany joined the League of Nations (1926).

A broader declaration in favor of world peace resulted from meetings in 1928 of representatives of fifteen nations, including the United States, France, Great Britain, Germany, Italy, and Japan. Out of this came the Briand-Kellogg Treaty. It declared that its signers "condemn recourse to war for the solution of international controversies, and renounce it as an instrument of national policy in their relations with one another." Eventually, more than sixty nations accepted the treaty.

Nations returned their attention to naval affairs in 1930 at the London Naval Conference, where Japan renewed its efforts to achieve equality among nations in naval construction. The conference members agreed to limit the tonnage of cruisers, destroyers, and submarines. However, an "escalator clause" permitted the United States, Great Britain, and Japan to exceed their limits if their national security were threatened.

Check on Your Reading

1. What postwar problems did France have?
2. What steps did France take to combat the depression?
3. Describe Britain's postwar problems?
4. How did Britain deal with the depression?
5. What change did Britain make in relation to its dominions?
6. Describe several major events in the United States during the 1920s.
7. What effects did the depression have in the United States?
8. What contributions did the League of Nations make to world peace?
9. What pacts and agreements did nations make from 1920 to 1930?

---

4. World War II

Some people believed that lasting peace was possible. Others had little interest in international affairs. They were preoccupied with their personal interests and with the problems of their own countries. Despite international peace agreements, nations were inclined to place what they perceived as their best interests above those of others.

Prelude to General War

In September of 1931, Japanese forces attacked and took control of Manchuria. The League of Nations protested this move, but the League proved only as strong as its members wished it to be. The League recommended that the Japanese control of Manchuria should not continue. Japan responded by withdrawing from the League in 1933.

Japan's successful defiance of the League of Nations greatly weakened the prestige of that organization. It made dictators in other nations feel that they too could break international rules and get away with it.

In Italy, dictator Benito Mussolini dreamed of restoring the Roman Empire and all its glory. As a first step, he focused his attention on Ethiopia, which had defeated Italian forces in 1896. In 1935 Mussolini launched an attack on Ethiopia.

Haile Selassie, the emperor of Ethiopia, called on the League of Nations to check the Italian aggressor. Several important member nations of the League hesitated to stop Italy. Some feared that strong action against the Fascists would lead to a major war. Others were more concerned with their own welfare than with the future of Ethiopia. The League of Nations eventually placed some economic sanctions against Italy. However, all of the members of the League did not apply these sanctions. Italian forces soon conquered Ethiopia.

Having solved many of Germany's unemployment problems with a rearmament program, Adolf Hitler was prepared to move. In 1936 he reoccupied the Rhineland, on the French border. This was an area that the Treaty of Versailles had declared demilitarized for fifteen years. Although this posed a threat to France, that nation did nothing significant about Hitler's action, and neither did Great Britain.

It soon became clear that the principal aggressor nations were banding into a bloc. In 1936 Germany and Italy reached an agreement to support each other in international affairs. Mussolini called this alliance an *Axis* between Rome and Berlin. In the same year Germany and Japan signed the Anti-Comintern Pact, agreeing to cooperate to check the international activities of the Communist Parties. In 1937 Italy joined the pact. The Italian-German-Japanese bloc eventually came to be called the *Rome-Berlin-Tokyo Axis*. Its members were referred to as the "Axis Powers."

In 1936, civil war broke out in Spain. That country had become a republic in 1931 with the ousting of King Alfonso XIII, but the new government had not been able to solve the country's many problems. There was still great poverty, injustice in land ownership, and lack of stable government. In July 1936 army officers rebelled against the Spanish Republic. The *Rebels* eventually were led by General Francisco Franco, who was a Fascist. Those who opposed the Rebels were known as *Loyalists*. In time, Spain became an international battleground. Italy and Germany supplied Franco with men and material. The Soviet Union later aided the Loyalists. Supported by most of the army, Franco finally defeated the Loyalists. He then proceeded to establish a Fascist dictatorship in Spain.

Some Japanese leaders, in the meantime, were planning to make Japan the dominant power to replace Western influence in Asia. Chiang Kai-shek's generals persuaded him to come to an agreement with Mao-Tse-tung's Communists and unite against the outside enemy. In July 1937, fighting between Chinese and Japanese troops broke out. The fighting quickly spread into a general but undeclared war between Japan and China. Japan took numerous Chinese coastal cities and began to move inland. The Nationalist Chinese government under Chiang Kai-shek retreated west, finally establishing itself at Chungking, in China's interior. The Japanese now planned the establishment of a "Co-prosperity Sphere," with Japan as its leader, in which they would integrate the economic life of Japan, Manchukuo, and areas of China which they controlled.

German Power Spreads through Europe

The following year, in 1938, Adolf Hitler once again drew worldwide attention to himself. After using local Fascist groups to stir up trouble in Austria, Hitler sent troops into that country and Germany annexed it.

In 1938 Hitler demanded that the Sudetenland be ceded to Germany. This was an area in Czechoslovakia occupied by about three and a half million Sudeten Germans. The Czechs, who were the allies of France, the Soviet Union, and other nations, refused to submit to the Nazi demands. The threat of a major European war was serious.

The Expansion of Japan

- Japanese Empire in 1930
- Japanese expansion 1930 - Dec. 7, 1941
- "Long March" of the Chinese Communists 1934-35

Between 1931 and 1941 Japan built an empire through armed conquest. What territories did Japan gain? The map also shows the route of the Chinese Communists' Long March of 6,000 miles.

German and Italian Aggression 1935-1939

Lands seized by Germany

Lands seized by Italy

The map shows the acts of German and Italian aggression that led to the outbreak of World War II in Europe in 1939. Italy conquered (1) Ethiopia in 1935 and occupied (7) Albania in 1939. Germany seized (2) the Rhineland in 1936, (3) Austria in 1938, (4) the Sudetenland in 1938, (5) the rest of Czechoslovakia in 1939, (6) Memel and Danzig in 1939, and (8) Poland in 1939.

In this time of crisis an important meeting was held in Munich, Germany, to decide the fate of Czechoslovakia. Great Britain, France, Germany, and Italy attended the meeting. The Soviet Union and Czechoslovakia were not even invited. As a result of the pact drawn up at Munich (1938), the four powers agreed to cede the Sudentenland to Germany. (See the map above.) War was temporarily avoided by *appeasement*—that is, by giving in to Hitler.

Before the Munich conference, Hitler had promised that the Sudetenland was "the last territorial demand I have to make in Europe." He soon broke that pledge. On March 15, 1939, Germany took possession of the rest of Czechoslovakia!

World War II Begins

Two other important developments occurred in 1939. The Spanish civil war ended with victory for General Franco and his Fascist followers. Then on August 23, 1939, Germany and the Soviet Union, bitter enemies for years, signed a nonaggression pact. They agreed "to refrain from any act of force, any aggressive action and any attack on one another. . . ."

There was also a secret protocol. It included a provision that Germany and the Soviet Union would each obtain control of territory in Poland "in the event of a territorial and political rearrangement of the areas belonging to the Polish state. . . ."

Nazi tanks supported by soldiers on motorcycles drive into Poland in 1939.

To Adolf Hitler, the Russo-German Nonaggression Pact was a green light for Nazi aggression. On September 1, 1939, German troops invaded Poland. Great Britain and France had promised to support Poland in case of attack. This time they did not back down. On September 3, 1939, both nations declared war on Germany. World War II had come to Europe!

The powerful German war machine struck quickly at Poland. German tanks cut through the Polish forces like scissors through paper. German planes dropped deadly loads of bombs on soldiers and on civilians alike.

About two weeks after Germany attacked the Poles, the Soviet Union invaded Poland from the east. Sandwiched between the advancing steel of two strong armies, the Polish defense collapsed. Poland was conquered in one month, and Germany and the Soviet Union divided the country. This was indeed a *blitzkrieg*, a conquest of lightning speed.

In November 1939, the Soviet Union invaded Finland. After meeting surprisingly fierce resistance, the Russians finally defeated the Finns.

By November 1940, through force or the threat of force, the Soviet Union had gained more territory. This included Estonia, Latvia, Lithuania, and Bessarabia.

Events in the West

Meanwhile there was a period of calm on the western front. The French remained stationed in their defensive positions in the Maginot Line. Many of their generals still were thinking in terms of the trench warfare of World War I and of armies slowly inching forward. They did not understand the nature of blitzkrieg war.

In April 1940, the Germans invaded Norway and Denmark. King Christian X of Denmark protested bitterly. However, to prevent the useless loss of lives, he accepted Nazi occupation of his country. In Norway there was difficult fighting. German military strength and use of air power, plus subversive activities of a group of pro-Nazi Norwegians, forced the Norwegian armies to surrender on June 9, 1940. King Haakon VII of Norway and his government leaders set up a government-in-exile in London. The conquest of Denmark and Norway was important because it provided Germany with harbors for its ships, bases for submarines and planes, and food supplies.

Meanwhile in May, without warning, German troops had invaded the Netherlands, Belgium, and Luxembourg. The lightning movements of German motorized infantry, planes, and paratroopers quickly defeated the Netherlands.

In Belgium, King Leopold III called for the aid of the Allies, and French and British armies moved into the country to meet the German offensive. The Germans could not be stopped. They attacked powerfully, and, by clever strategy, split the Allied armies. To the anger and dismay of many Belgians, King Leopold III surrendered to the Germans on May 28, 1940.

The fall of Belgium left the Allied forces unprotected on one side. A large part of the Allied troops were driven back to the city of Dunkirk, along the English Channel. With the sea in front of them and the Germans pressing in on all sides, it seemed that they were doomed.

The thousands of Allied troops who were on the beaches at Dunkirk were fiercely attacked. They were bombed by hostile aircraft, which came over with one hundred planes in each formation. They were machine-gunned in the sand dunes where they lay. Yet the British navy and hundreds of small private craft, aided by the Royal Air Force, were able to evacuate over 335,000 troops across the Channel to Britain.

The voice of Prime Minister Winston Churchill took on new determination as he told the world of the events at Dunkirk and concluded, ". . . we shall defend our Island . . . we shall never surrender. . . ."

In June 1940, a new German blitzkrieg cut around the Maginot Line. At the same time Italy, eager to be in on the prizes of victory, entered the war on the side of Germany. Then, on June 22, 1940, a defeated France signed an armistice with Germany.

France then was divided into two zones. One zone was occupied and governed by the Germans. The other zone was not occupied by the victors. It was in southern France with its government at Vichy. This Vichy government, headed by a Frenchman, Marshal Pétain, collaborated with the Germans.

Some French people refused to surrender or to live under Vichy rule. They escaped from France

Buildings damaged in London by German air raids are pulled down. All the metal collected was used in the war effort.

and continued to work against the Germans. General Charles de Gaulle became leader of these people. His resistance group was known as "Free France."

German forces controlled a considerable part of Europe. Great Britain was the only major Allied power that stood between Germany and complete victory.

The Germans sent their bombers over Britain day after day. Then night after night. Bombs destroyed buildings that had stood for centuries. Men, women, and children died with mounds of rubble as their only monuments. Everywhere the wail of the air-raid siren turned busy cities into ghost towns as people hurried for underground shelters.

Nearly all food and munitions supplies from Europe were cut off from Britain. Supplies had to be imported from across the Atlantic. German submarines patrolled the seas, attacked merchant ships, and seriously interfered with the shipment of goods. The British faced the threat of starvation, but they would not give in. Instead they used their ships and planes and improved their antisubmarine mines and other devices to cope with the threat.

In June 1940, Winston Churchill had declared:

> Let us therefore brace ourselves to our duties, and so bear ourselves that . . . men will say, "This was their finest hour."

In the terrible months of bombing that started in July 1940 and continued in 1941 the British people held firm. Hitler, who overestimated the actual military strength of the British defenses, decided to postpone the invasion of England!

The War Spreads

Meanwhile the war spread in eastern Europe. Italy had invaded Albania and occupied that nation. Mussolini next sent his forces into Greece, where they ran into deep trouble in the face of determined Greek resistance.

Adolf Hitler meanwhile moved another step forward in his grand plan for Germany's domination of Europe. He attacked Yugoslavia, where German armies met with considerable resistance but achieved success. Hitler then moved his forces into Greece to help Mussolini's beleaguered army. Greece was soon occupied by German armies.

In Africa, German armored units attacked the British in Libya and made their way into Egypt. The British, however, were able to prevent the Germans from reaching Cairo.

Then in June 1941, Hitler invaded the Soviet Union! The conquest of the Soviet Union had long been a dream of Hitler. However, he had misjudged the strength, courage, and determination of the Russians. His armies killed many Soviet soldiers. They captured considerable Soviet territory. They came close to Moscow itself. Yet they could not force the Russians to surrender.

Russian armies and civilians continued to defend their country through months of merciless bombings and shell fire and through periods of near starvation. Losses were terrible but still the Russians would not surrender. By 1943, after heroic defenses at Stalingrad and other cities, the Russian armies were preparing counter-offensives to force the Germans back out of Russia.

The United States Enters the War

Many Americans sympathized with the Allied cause, and the fall of France shocked them deeply. They admired Britain's heroic stand against German bombardment, and gradually the United States took steps to aid Great Britain.

Most of the American Pacific Fleet was damaged or destroyed by the Japanese surprise attack on Pearl Harbor, Hawaii on December 7, 1941.

The War in Europe and North Africa

Trondheim
NORWAY
Oslo
FINLAND
Surr. 1944
Leningrad
SWEDEN
ESTONIA
Moscow
IRELAND
GREAT
BRITAIN
DENMARK
LATVIA
LITHUANIA
1944
UNION OF SOVIET
SOCIALIST REPUBLICS
London
NORTH
SEA
Polish
Corridor
E.
PRUSSIA
Berlin
1945
NETH.
Cologne
GERMANY
Surr. 1945
Dunkirk
Cherbourg
NORMANDY
BELG.
English Channel
Warsaw
1944
Stalingrad
ATLANTIC
OCEAN
Caen
Reims
LUX.
1945
POLAND
Kiev
Paris
1944
Maginot
Line
SLOVAKIA
FRANCE
Vienna
HUNGARY
Surr. 1945
Vichy
SWITZ.
BESSARABIA
1944
CRIMEA
Odessa
Yalta
1944-45
RUMANIA
Surr. 1944
BLACK SEA
Marseilles
Toulon
ITALY
Surr. 1943
YUGOSLAVIA
1945
Ploesti
Corsica
Rome
Anzio
1943
BULGARIA
Surr. 1944
Sardinia
Naples
Salerno
ALBANIA
(It.)
Belgrade
TURKEY
Taranto
GREECE
Palermo
AEGEAN SEA
Tunis
1943
Sicily
SYRIA
ALGERIA
Malta
MEDITERRANEAN SEA
Crete
Cyprus
1942
Gibraltar
TUNISIA
PALESTINE
Tangier
SP.
MOROCCO
Oran
Algiers
Tripoli
Rommel's
Drive
Tobruk
Alexandria
El Alamein
Suez
Canal
TRANS-
JORDAN
Casablanca
El Aghelia
1942
Cairo
MOROCCO
LIBYA
(It.)
1943
EGYPT
SAUDI ARABIA

PORTUGAL
SPAIN

| Axis territory, Sept. 1, 1939 | Axis satellites | Greatest extent of Axis expansion | Allied Powers | Neutral states | Main Allied advances |

What lands did the Axis nations control at the height of their conquests? The Allies first launched an invasion of North Africa and then of Sicily and southern Italy. Then Allied forces invaded France and moved into Germany while the armies of the Soviet Union moved westward.

The United States had declared neutrality when World War II began. President Roosevelt and his advisers decided, however, that German domination of Europe would be dangerous to United States interests. The United States government was willing to risk war with Germany to keep Britain from defeat. Thus, in March of 1941, Congress passed the Lend-Lease Act. This made it possible for the President to lend or lease military and other supplies to anti-Axis powers.

It took a sudden Japanese attack to bring the United States into the war. This attack came at the end of a decade of tension between the governments of the United States and Japan. The Japanese were angered by the United States opposition to Japanese expansion in Asia and the Pacific. The United States criticized Japanese aggression in China, particularly the bombings of civilians. The United States also permitted aid to be sent to Chiang Kai-shek's government; and also eventually

Allied soldiers wade ashore from landing craft during the first assault on the Normandy beaches on June 6, 1944.

restricted the export to Japan of war materials, such as steel scrap and oil.

On the morning of December 7, 1941, over 250 Japanese planes took off from their aircraft carriers and attacked Pearl Harbor, the American naval base in the Hawaiian Islands. This sudden attack came before Japan had formally declared war on the United States. As a result of the attack at Pearl Harbor and nearby areas, most of the American Pacific Fleet was destroyed or damaged.

On December 8, 1941, President Roosevelt asked Congress to declare that "a state of war [now exists] between the United States and the Japanese Empire." The next evening, in a special radio address, he told the nation:

[The attack on Pearl Harbor] was a thoroughly dishonorable deed, but we must face the fact that modern warfare as conducted in the Nazi manner is a dirty business. We don't like it—we didn't want to get in it—but we are in it, and we're going to fight it with everything we've got.

On December 8, the United States and Great Britain declared war on Japan. Shortly after, Germany and Italy declared war on the United States, and the United States issued its own declaration of war against these two nations. The war soon became global.

Japan went on to take control of the Dutch East Indies, Indochina, Malaya, Singapore, and Burma. Japan also invaded the Philippines. After defeating United States forces there, Japan occupied the Philippines.

The Course of the War

The United States decided to help drive back the Axis in Europe before embarking on widespread operations against Japan. North Africa was chosen for an Allied attack.

The invasion of North Africa was considered important for several reasons: 1. This attack might relieve some of the pressure on the Russians by drawing German troops into Africa. 2. The Suez Canal needed additional protection. 3. African bases could be used for future attacks on the Axis in Europe.

Thus, in November 1942, after the British Eighth Army had driven the Germans out of Egypt, Allied forces invaded North Africa. This invasion army included Americans and British and was under the command of General Dwight D. Eisenhower. The fighting soon became bitter as Eisenhower's troops met determined German opposition. By May 1943, Eisenhower's forces controlled all of North Africa.

From North Africa Allied troops invaded Sicily and southern Italy. Mussolini was denounced by a number of Italian leaders. He was stripped of all power, his Fascist régime fell, and a new Italian government was established. Mussolini was later killed by members of the Italian underground.

The fall of Mussolini did not bring an end to fighting in Italy as German troops invaded the country from the north. The Allied forces took

Two days after the first landing, Allied troops were digging in on this beach. From their beachheads, Allied troops fought their way across France.

heavy losses as they slowly fought their way up the Italian peninsula.

D-Day!

During 1943, Allied plans for an invasion of northern Europe progressed. Then on June 6, 1944 ("D-Day"), after weeks of Allied bombardment of German positions, the invasion began. Allied forces under the supreme command of General Eisenhower sailed from the British Isles and landed on the French beaches at Normandy. American troops were directed by General Omar Bradley. British and Canadian troops were led by General Bernard Montgomery.

The invasion was a bloody one, but the Allied troops held on. Then they slowly pushed inland. Behind them, on the beaches, the soldiers left vivid evidence of the world they once had known. War correspondent Ernie Pyle reported: "[Strewn on the beach] there were socks and shoe polish, sewing kits, diaries, *Bibles* . . . the latest letters from home . . . toothbrushes and razors, and snapshots of families back home . . . [and] a tennis racket that some soldier had brought along. It lay lonesomely on the sand, clamped in its press, not a string broken." Behind them, too, the Allies left the troops who had given up their lives to clear a way for those who were to follow.

The fighting broadened out. Eisenhower's troops smashed through the German lines and moved eastward. Another Allied army successfully invaded southern France on August 15, 1944. Paris was liberated on August 25, and General de Gaulle was hailed for his wartime leadership. Then a desperate German counter-offensive in the Ardennes region in winter was checked at the so-called "Battle of the Bulge." Meanwhile the Russians pushed back the Germans in the east.

The Allied forces rolled forward rapidly. Eisenhower's troops crossed the Rhine. General Mark Clark, the American commander of all Allied forces in Italy, accepted the surrender of a million German and Italian soldiers. The Russians, under Marshal Zhukov, pushed on toward Berlin.

In April 1945, Eisenhower's forces from the west and the Russians from the east drew ever closer to each other. On April 30 Hitler committed suicide. Germany surrendered unconditionally on May 7–8, 1945. The war in Europe was ended!

Allied Progress in the Pacific

As the war in Europe raged, the conflict in the Pacific increased in tempo. There were great sea and air battles. A Japanese drive toward Australia was stopped at the Battle of the Coral Sea in May 1942. A Japanese invasion fleet attempted to take

Midway Island as a stepping stone to Hawaii the following month and failed. During the Battle for Midway, American planes sank four Japanese aircraft carriers and seriously weakened Japanese naval air power. Some military historians consider the Battle for Midway to be a turning point in the Pacific war.

American, Australian, and other Allied troops began an "island hopping" campaign to bypass Japanese garrisons and recapture strategic islands from the Japanese. These islands then were used as bases for new Allied attacks. One of the most dramatic events was the liberation of the Philippines in October 1944.

In 1945, the Japanese stronghold at Okinawa was taken by the Allied forces. This island gave the Allies air bases close to Japan. Thus the Allies defeated or bypassed Japanese military units. Allied leaders now faced the task of carrying out a final offensive against Japan.

The War in China

With Japan at war with the United States and Great Britain, China became one of the Allies. Chiang Kai-shek depended heavily on supplies from the outside, and for a time these were sent over the 800-mile Burma Road. The Japanese conquest of Burma in 1942 closed off this motor highway. The Allies then turned to air transport, flying supplies from India over the Himalayan Mountains—known as the "Hump." Work was also started on building and defending a new road west of the Burma Road. It was known as the Ledo Road.

At the same time that Chiang Kai-shek and his troops were fighting the Japanese, Chiang Kai-shek continued to work to strengthen his position against the Chinese Communists. There were indications that both Chiang Kai-shek's Chinese Nationalists and the Chinese Communists often were more concerned with building up their power against each

How far did the Japanese advance before they were stopped? Trace the route of the main Allied advances against Japan.

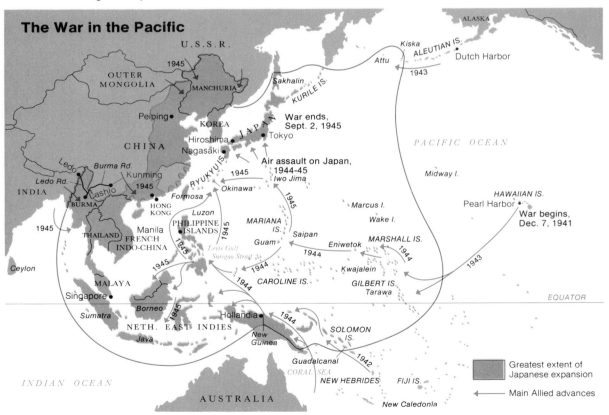

Women made an important contribution to the Allied victories by their work at home and in the armed forces. The photo shows a contingent of WAACS being welcomed as they landed in Britain.

other than in working as a team against the Japanese forces.

At the end of January 1945, the Allies stopped a Japanese drive to India and regained control of Burma. The Ledo Road was joined with the Burma Road, and the Japanese position in China was greatly weakened.

In February 1945, President Roosevelt, Prime Minister Churchill, and Joseph Stalin of the Soviet Union held an important conference at Yalta in the Crimea. One of the results of this meeting was that the Soviet Union agreed to enter the war against Japan. In return, Russia was to be given: 1. the southern part of Sakhalin and the islands adjacent to it, and the Kurile Islands, 2. certain rights in Manchuria, and 3. other territorial privileges in the Far East. In keeping with the Yalta Agreements, the Soviet Union later entered the war against Japan.

The War Ends

In the summer of 1945 the Japanese faced almost certain defeat. Nevertheless, they refused to stop fighting. The Allied leaders decided to take drastic action. In July 1945, at the Potsdam Conference, the United States, Great Britain, and the Soviet Union agreed to send an ultimatum to the Japanese government. This ultimatum demanded that the Japanese surrender unconditionally or face terrible destruction to their country. And still Japan would not surrender!

The United States had begun the development of a new and powerful weapon, an atomic bomb, the results of experimentation with nuclear fission. The device was tested in 1945 on the desert of New Mexico, and it proved successful.

President Franklin D. Roosevelt had died in April 1945, and Vice-President Harry S. Truman assumed the presidency. It fell to him to decide whether the atomic bomb should be used against Japan. President Truman later explained that two considerations were uppermost in his decision to unleash the bomb. They were Japan's refusal to surrender until its land itself had been conquered, and the many lives that would be lost if an invasion of Japan could not be avoided.

On August 6, 1945, one atomic bomb was dropped on the city of Hiroshima. The bomb equalled in energy 20,000 tons of TNT. A single, blinding explosion destroyed much of the city, and approximately 80,000 Japanese died from the blast or later from radiation sickness.

Events moved rapidly. A few days after the bomb was dropped on Hiroshima, the Soviet Union entered the war against Japan and invaded Manchuria. President Harry S. Truman again demanded that Japan surrender. When it did not, a second atomic bomb was dropped, this time on the city of Nagasaki. Five days later, Japan surrendered.

In September 1945, the Japanese representative signed the document of formal surrender. Then he stopped, checked the wristwatch of another Japanese delegate, and carefully wrote down the time. It was 9:04 A.M., September 2, 1945, almost exactly six years from the Nazi attack on Poland in September 1939.

Check on Your Reading

1. How did Japan's action in Manchuria affect the League of Nations?
2. Why did nations not try to stop Italy's invasion of Ethiopia?
3. What was the result of the civil war in Spain?
4. How did Germany increase its territory? What areas did it occupy?
5. Describe German strategy and tactics during the early years of World War II.
6. Describe the German invasion of the Soviet Union and its outcome.
7. What factors caused hostility between Japan and the United States? What happened at Pearl Harbor on December 7, 1941?
8. How did the Allies defeat Germany?
9. What was the Allies' strategy in the Pacific? To what extent was it successful?
10. Describe the end of the war in the Pacific.

LET'S MEET
THE PEOPLE

Sergeant Frank "Buck" Eversole

Sergeant Frank "Buck" Eversole of Idaho was a platoon sergeant in a line company of the 34th Infantry Division. As such, he was a non-commissioned officer in charge of about forty combat soldiers.

"Buck" did a good job as platoon sergeant. Several times he almost lost his life. Once a shell hit the room in which he was sitting—but did not go off. Another time he advanced through a mine field that killed everyone in his squad—but no mine exploded beneath him.

For more than a year "Buck" did everything that he could to see that the new men, and the handful of veterans, survived. Then one day it was his turn to leave the platoon and go to the rear for a five-day rest. "Buck" should have been pleased, but he wasn't. He knew that his outfit was going to attack that night and he wanted to be with it. "Buck" therefore hurried over to Lieutenant Sheehy, his commanding officer.

"Lieutenant," he said. "I'll stay if you need me."

"Of course I need you, 'Buck,' " answered his lieutenant, "I always need you. But it's your turn and I want you to go. In fact, you're ordered to go."

That evening, against his will, "Buck" left his platoon for a few days of rest. He kept his eyes down as he slowly walked towards the truck that was to take him away. Then he quietly said: "This is the first battle I've ever missed that this battalion has been in. . . . *I feel like a deserter.*"

Sergeant Frank "Buck" Eversole—the man who felt like a "deserter"—already had been awarded one Purple Heart and two Silver Star medals for bravery in action!

The sketch above is adapted from *Brave Men* by Ernie Pyle; copyright 1943-1944 by Scripps-Howard Newspaper Alliance; copyright 1944 by Holt, Rinehart, and Winston, Inc.

CHAPTER REVIEW

Think and Discuss

1. Do you agree or disagree with this statement: "No dictator who wants to stay in power can shrink from violence."? Why?
2. What similarities are there between Fascism and Communism? What differences?
3. Why did China fail to develop into a democracy?
4. What evidence can you find of an increase in technological progress during a war?
5. International security meant different things to different countries after World War I. Do you think it could have been achieved at that time? Why?
6. Compare the immediate causes of World War II with the immediate causes of World War I.
7. Why did many of the British people speak of the Battle of Britain in 1940 as their "finest hour"?
8. What questions of moral judgment and expediency were involved in the decision to drop the atomic bomb on Japan?
9. Compare and contrast Hitler, Mussolini, and Franco as dictators. What generalizations can you make?

Past and Present

1. How can you explain the *Holocaust* after many hundreds of years of civilization?
2. Are the major obstacles to world peace today the same as they were in the 1930s? Explain your answer.
3. Compare the efforts to keep peace before World War II with efforts to keep peace today.

Activities

1. Write an essay on "The Use of Propaganda by Dictators." Consult the *Encyclopedia of the Social Sciences, Syntopicon of Great Books,* and other references.
2. Debate this statement: Resolved, that disarmament is necessary to world peace.
3. Draw a chart of the underlying causes of World War II as compared with the underlying causes of World War I.
4. Write a report on the rise of Adolf Hitler to power in Germany. Try to find the reasons why he was able to become dictator.
5. If possible, discuss the brutality of Hitler's methods by speaking with someone whose relatives had been in a Nazi concentration camp.

10

Our Contemporary World: Rapid Changes and a Boundless Future

The world in which we live is one of impressive progress in many fields and of equally great problems in human relations. We will discuss both in this last unit of this book. In doing so, we may be able to:

1. increase our understanding of desirable and undesirable conditions in the contemporary world;
2. prepare ourselves to make the world a better place in which to live.

A reader may ask, "Can I—one individual—really contribute to the improvement of conditions in the world?" Albert Schweitzer, philosopher, physician, musician, and humanitarian, provided one answer to that question. He wrote: ". . . however much concerned I was at the problem of the misery in the world, I never let myself get lost in broodings over it; I always held firmly to the thought that each one of us can do a little to bring some portion of it to an end."

Power Struggles and a Search for Peace

KEYNOTE

In 1947, eighteen Communist leaders, deliberately using unsavory terms for those who opposed them, drew up the following statement: ". . . two camps [have formed]—the camp of imperialism and anti-democratic forces [headed by the United States] . . . and an anti-imperialistic democratic camp [headed by the Soviet Union]. . . . The battle of the two opposite camps . . . is waged."

The Commmunist leaders were referring to the existence of what Americans called the "Cold War," a struggle between the United States and its allies on one side, and the Soviet Union and its supporters on the other. It did not involve armed clashes between the antagonists. Rather, the Cold War was a contest between the two most powerful nations to strengthen their positions and to promote their ideologies throughout the world. This struggle was one of the key features of European life in the postwar period.

The wall set up by the Soviet Union between East and West Berlin.

1. The United Nations Organization and Its Activities

The idea of an international organization dedicated to world peace did not die with the League of Nations. As a consequence of a worldwide hope for international peace, there is a tiny piece of land along the East River in New York City that has been called "the world's most unusual independent territory." This area of only eighteen acres is the site of the permanent headquarters of the United Nations Organization.

United Nations headquarters is a fascinating and busy place. Here scholars from many lands prepare detailed statistical studies. Secretaries turn out reports on typewriters whose keyboards are arranged in many different languages. Telephone operators of many nationalities manage the UN switchboard and provide service 24 hours a day, 365 days a year. Language specialists examine and route the thousands of letters received by the UN each day.

As Eleanor Roosevelt, who served as a representative to the United Nations, pointed out: "[The United Nations] is the only place in history where the whole world has hung its hat and gone to work on the common problems of mankind."

The Establishment of the United Nations

The United Nations was founded as a result of a series of conferences. In August 1941, President Franklin D. Roosevelt of the United States and Prime Minister Winston Churchill of Britain held a conference on the U.S. cruiser *Augusta* off the coast of Newfoundland. Out of that meeting, among other things, came the *Atlantic Charter,* a joint declaration of principles that the leaders of both countries wished to see followed in the peace settlement after the war. One principle had to do with "the establishment of a wider and permanent system of general security," and served as the nucleus of the United Nations. On January 1-2, 1942, twenty-six nations signed their agreement to the purposes and principles of the Atlantic Charter.

Additional progress was made at a conference held at the Dumbarton Oaks estate in Washington, D.C., in 1944. Here the United States, the United Kingdom, the Soviet Union, and China drew up proposals to serve as the foundation of the future Charter of the United Nations. Next, Roosevelt, Churchill, and Joseph Stalin met at Yalta, in the Crimea, in 1945. There, among other things, they worked out a system of voting to be used in the Security Council of the planned organization.

In the spring of 1945, delegates from fifty nations met at San Francisco to draw up the Charter of the United Nations. After national legislatures had approved it, the document went into effect October 24, 1945.

The United Nations is neither a world government nor a super-state. It is an association of countries based on the principle of "the sovereign equality of all its members." Its major purposes are: 1. to maintain international peace and security, 2. to develop friendly relations among nations based on the principle of equal rights and self-determination of peoples, and 3. to achieve international cooperation in solving international problems.

The General Assembly

The General Assembly is one of six principal bodies within the United Nations. It includes representatives of 150 nations, and other countries may soon be admitted. Although each member nation can appoint five delegates, it has only one vote. Decisions in the General Assembly are made either by a majority or two-thirds of those members present and voting.

The General Assembly serves as a forum where the delegates of all member nations can express their countries' position on many issues and make recommendations. Also, the General Assembly can consider the general principles of cooperation in the maintenance of international peace and security. It can initiate studies and make recommendations to promote international peace and cooperation in political, economic, social, cultural, educational, and health fields.

The Security Council

The Security Council, another principal organ, consists of fifteen member nations. Five of these—the United States, the Soviet Union, the United Kingdom, France, and China—are permanent members. The remaining ten are elected by the General Assembly to two-year terms.

The Security Council has the following functions and powers:

- primary responsibility for keeping international

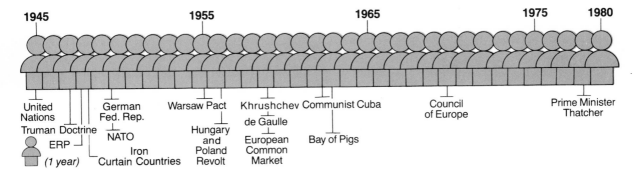

United Nations

Truman Doctrine

ERP

(1 year)

German Fed. Rep.

NATO

Iron Curtain Countries

Warsaw Pact

Hungary and Poland Revolt

Khrushchev

de Gaulle

European Common Market

Communist Cuba

Bay of Pigs

Council of Europe

Prime Minister Thatcher

peace and security and for drawing up plans for the regulation of armaments;

- encouraging countries to settle their disputes by peaceful means;

- taking action against aggressor nations by calling on UN member nations to halt economic relations with the aggressors or to "take such action by air, sea, or land forces as may be necessary to maintain or restore international peace and security."

Because the United Nations has no permanent armed forces of its own, it must depend on the willingness of member nations to supply troops.

Although the Security Council was given "primary responsibility" for peacekeeping, the General Assembly has gradually taken over aspects of this important UN function. This was done because many actions in the Security Council were blocked by the so-called *veto.* Article 27 of the Charter makes it possible for a veto to operate in the Security Council by providing that, on procedural matters or issues, decisions by that body shall be made by an affirmative vote of any nine of its fifteen members. On all other matters—that is, on substantive (or important) matters—decisions shall be made by the affirmative vote of nine members of the Council, including the permanent members. If any one of the five permanent members votes "No" on an important matter, its vote becomes a veto, because it prevents the Security Council from taking action on the issue. To help differentiate between the two kinds of issues, the General Assembly has drawn up a long list of procedural matters. Also, as a result of the *Uniting for Peace Resolution* adopted by the General Assembly in 1950, if a veto prevents the Security Council from acting during a time of crisis, the General Assembly can meet in emergency session and make recommendations to remedy the situation.

Within the first twenty years of the UN's existence, 111 vetoes had been cast. The Soviet Union used the veto 103 times, France 4, the United Kingdom 3, and Nationalist China once.

Economic and Social Council

A third important organ of the United Nations is the Economic and Social Council. It consists of 54 member nations, elected by the General Assembly to three-year terms. Decisions in the Economic and Social Council are made by a majority of members present and voting.

An important function of the Economic and Social Council is to make or initiate studies and reports on international economic, social, cultural, educational, health, and related matters. Also, it is expected to make recommendations to the General Assembly, to member nations, and to the Specialized Agencies concerned.

The Specialized Agencies

These agencies are established by intergovernmental agreements and are not an integral part of the United Nations. However, they are brought into a close relationship with the United Nations through the work of the Economic and Social Council, which coordinates their activities, and the General Assembly.

The *Food and Agriculture Organization (FAO)* is a Specialized Agency that tries to help countries raise their standards of living and to improve the nutrition of peoples everywhere.

The *World Health Organization (WHO)* works for "the attainment by all peoples of the highest possible level of health."

The *United Nations Educational, Scientific and Cultural Organization (UNESCO)* is another important Specialized Agency. It attempts "to contribute to peace and security by promoting collaboration among the nations through education, science, and culture." For example, UNESCO advised Turkey on ways to establish educational radio stations. It set up the first public library in India; and it helped train teachers in Afghanistan, Bolivia, Cambodia, Laos, Libya, and other countries.

Other Specialized Agencies include the *International Labor Organization (ILO),* the *International Atomic Energy Agency (IAEA),* the *International Monetary Fund (IMF),* and others.

Trusteeship Council

The Trusteeship Council, a fourth principal organ of the United Nations, supervises territories known as *trusts* and tries to help them develop toward self-government or independence. Trusts can be former League of Nation mandates, areas detached from the powers defeated in World War II, or territories voluntarily placed under the trusteeship system by countries responsible for their administration. The only remaining trust territory, which is administered by the United States, is the group of Pacific islands known as *Micronesia.* They include the Caroline Islands, the Marshall Islands, and the Mariana Islands except Guam.

International Court of Justice

The International Court of Justice is a fifth principal body of the United Nations. It consists of fifteen judges elected to nine-year terms by the Security Council and the General Assembly. The Court, which meets at The Hague in the Netherlands, is the principal judicial organ of the United Nations. It hears legal disputes between countries and gives advisory opinions on legal matters that might be referred to it by various organs of the United Nations. For example, the Court helped settle a dispute between the United Kingdom and Albania over the damage done to British destroyers and crews by mines in the channels between Albania and the island of Corfu. In 1979 the Court was asked to render a decision on the case involving the holding of United States hostages in Iran.

However, by 1980 there was little doubt that the International Court of Justice was not as effective as the founders of the United Nations had hoped it would be. Most of the member nations of the United Nations had not taken their disputes to the Court, and less than ten nations had agreed to accept the jurisdiction of the Court without reservations.

Secretariat

The Secretariat, the sixth principal organ, consists of about 10,000 employees appointed by the *Secretary-General,* the head of the Secretariat, under regulations established by the General Assembly. It performs day-to-day administrative functions.

The Secretary-General

The head of the Secretariat is the Secretary-General, who is appointed by the General Assembly upon the recommendation of the Security Council. The first Secretary-General of the United Nations was Trygve Lie, a Norwegian statesman, who held the post for seven years. Dag Hammarskjöld, a former Swedish professor and statesman, succeeded Lie. He remained in office until his death in an airplane accident in 1961. U Thant of Burma then became Secretary-General. On January 1, 1972, Kurt Waldheim of Austria succeeded him.

United Nations: an Evaluation

Major changes have developed in the functioning of the United Nations since the Charter went into effect in 1945. One authority, Jacob Robinson, has found that more than twenty articles of the Charter have been modified, become obsolete, or remained inactive since the United Nations' formation. There have been three significant results of these changes: The General Assembly has become more important; the duties and responsibilities of the Secretary-General have increased; and a tendency has developed on the part of many countries in the United Nations to vote by *blocs.* This means that a nation often votes the same way as the members of a group of nations with common interests. Many new African and Asian nations have been admitted to the United Nations. Because every nation has one vote in the General Assembly, these new nations have as much voting power as the larger ones. They have tried to get the United Nations to concentrate on African and Asian problems. Today more and more attention is being given to the developing and recently independent countries. Many of these are referred to as members of the "Third World."

The United Nations has experienced both failures and successes. It has succeeded in helping stop some wars—such as one between India and Pakistan over Kashmir—and prevented other conflicts from spreading. It has provided a forum where the United States and the Soviet Union, and other nations as well, can release tensions peacefully by debating before a world audience. It has helped settle several dangerous disputes—such as the clash between the Indonesians and the Dutch after World War II. It has tried to handle international crises, such as the one resulting from the seizure of United States hostages in Iran. The United Nations has provided facilities for useful discussion on disarmament and control of nuclear weapons. Important gains in economic, social, and educational fields have been made by the United Nations. For example, it has helped inoculate more than 20 million people against tuberculosis and has provided food for millions of needy children. Also it has established many centers to teach illiterates to read and write.

However, the United Nations has failed to prevent wars from breaking out. It has not brought about a permanent settlement of a number of disputes. It has been unable to achieve disarmament. Also, it has not been able to eliminate many disagreements between the industrial countries in the world (the so-called "North") and the developing countries (the so-called "South").

A major change occurred in UN membership in 1971. In that year, the General Assembly voted to admit the People's Republic of China to the United Nations and expel the Chinese Nationalist government (Taiwan). The People's Republic of China replaced the Republic of China on the Security Council.

Check on Your Reading

1. Describe the six principal bodies of the United Nations.
2. What major changes have developed in the functioning of the UN since 1945?
3. Assess UN successes and failures. What do you think is its most important success?

2. International Conflicts and Cooperation

With the United Nations in its infancy, during the second half of the 1940s serious rifts developed between the Soviet Union and Western nations, particularly the United States. Some of the roots of those differences lay in events that occurred as World War II drew to an end.

Postwar Arrangements

In 1945, as World War II drew to a close, Allied leaders met at Yalta in the Crimea and at Potsdam, Germany to make plans for postwar settlements. Agreement was reached on several territorial changes: 1. The U.S.S.R. was to be given part of eastern Poland and part of East Prussia. 2. The remainder of East Prussia and German land east of the Oder and Neisse rivers was to go to Poland.

Later, in 1947, the Allies drew up peace treaties for Italy, Hungary, Rumania, Bulgaria, and Finland, all of which, voluntarily or by force, had joined the war on the side of Germany. Some important results of the peace treaties were the following: 1. The Soviet Union received northern Bukovina and Bessarabia from Rumania; Ruthenia from Hungary; and a lease on the Porkkala Peninsula in Finland. 2. Italy was deprived of its colonial lands in Africa and lost islands in the Aegean and Adriatic seas. Territory in northwestern and northeastern Italy was ceded to France and Yugoslavia. 3. Certain African lands, such as Libya, were placed under the United Nations Trusteeship Council, and Trieste on the Adriatic Sea was made a Free City under the administrative control of the United Nations. 4. The defeated nations had to pay reparations that were not excessively heavy.

Problems in Poland

It was at Yalta in February 1945 that the Soviet Union agreed to enter the war against Japan, which it did in August 1945. In exchange, the Soviet Union was to gain the southern part of Sakhalin Island and islands adjacent to it, the Kurile Islands, certain rights in Manchuria, and other territorial privileges in Asia.

Equally important, at Yalta President Franklin D. Roosevelt, British Prime Minister Winston Churchill, and the Soviet leader Joseph Stalin discussed the troublesome Polish question.

After Germany conquered Poland in 1939, strongly anti-Communist Polish leaders had established a government-in-exile first in Paris and then in London. While the United States and the United Kingdom supported that government, Roosevelt and Churchill insisted that free and open elections be held in Poland when the war was over.

However, the course of the war gave Russian armies control of Poland. When they first entered that country, a Polish Committee of National Liberation was formed, in which Communists and some Socialists were influential. Also the Soviets supported the establishment of a government for Poland known as the *Lublin* government. Communist-controlled elections were held, and by 1947 Poland was under a Communist government.

A number of Western leaders felt that by the Yalta Agreement, the Russians had agreed to free elections and to permit non-Communist representation in the goverment. They were angered by the actions of the Soviet Union. Since the release of the Yalta Papers in 1955, there has been continued controversy over whether Stalin had agreed to free elections in Poland and later broke his word; whether he did not agree at all; or whether he had agreed only in a vague and meaningless way.

Poland had long been an enemy of Russia, and twice Russia had been invaded through Poland. From the Soviet point of view, Russia's security required a friendly Communist nation on its western border. From the Western point of view, the Soviet Union had committed a deliberate act of aggression by bringing Poland under its control. The United States and some western European nations were concerned that this was perhaps a step in a Soviet plan to dominate Europe.

Conflict in Greece

Events in another part of Europe were equally disturbing to the United States. The war had left Greece in an extremely dangerous condition. President Harry S. Truman reported that: "More than a thousand villages had been burned. Eighty-five percent of the children were tubercular.... Inflation had wiped out practically all savings."

As a result, a minority of Greeks became favorable to Communism, and civil war broke out. The British, who had helped to drive the Germans out of Greece, felt that they could no longer supply the men and funds needed to keep order. The United States therefore decided to step in.

On March 12, 1947, after the Greek government had sent the United States an appeal for economic aid, President Truman proposed the so-called *Truman Doctrine*. It stressed that "it must be the policy of the United States to support free peoples who are resisting attempted subjugation by armed minorities or by outside pressures." Congress approved his plan and voted the $400,000,000 that he asked

to assist the rehabilitation of both Greece and Turkey and to check the expansion of communism into the Middle East. The money voted to Turkey was to help that nation to modernize its economy and to resist Soviet pressure for concessions, particularly with respect to control of the Dardanelles Strait.

The Truman Doctrine helped the Greeks to stave off the Communist-led rebels. Equally important, the Truman Doctrine marked the inauguration of a

As a result of the peace treaties, Italy (1) ceded Alpine areas to France; lost Trieste, which became a free territory; and (2) ceded most of Venezia Giulia to Yugoslavia and (3) Dodecanesia to Greece. Rumania confirmed the cession of (4) southern Dobruja to Bulgaria and (5) northern Bukovina and Bessarabia to the Soviet Union. Hungary gave up (6) parts of Slovakia to Czechoslovakia, (7) Ruthenia to the Soviet Union and returned (8) northern Transylvania to Rumania. Finland (9) ceded Petsamo and (10) leased the Porkkala Peninsula to the Soviet Union.

Territorial Changes in Europe after World War II

Axis countries that signed peace treaties

Areas ceded as a result of treaties

Europe in the 1950's

Marshall Plan countries

East European satellites fo the Soviet Union

After World War II, Communists gained control of most of eastern Europe. The Marshall Plan aided recovery in western Europe. Name the countries that became satellites of the Soviet Union and the countries that joined the Marshall Plan.

FINLAND

NORWAY

SWEDEN

IRELAND

UNITED KINGDOM

DENMARK

SOVIET UNION

BENELUX

E. GERMANY

W. GERMANY

POLAND

CZECH.

ATLANTIC OCEAN

FRANCE

SWITZ.

AUSTRIA

HUNGARY

RUMANIA

YUGOSLAVIA (Independent Communist state)

BULGARIA

PORTUGAL

SPAIN

ITALY

ALB.

GREECE

TURKEY

MEDITERRANEAN SEA

United States policy known as "containment of Communism." It established a basis on which the United States signed treaties promising to help defend many nations.

Soviet Power Extends over Eastern Europe

From 1946 to 1949 Communists took over the government of the following: Albania and Bulgaria (1946), Poland and Rumania (1947), Czechoslovakia (1948), and Hungary and East Germany (1949).

The Soviet Union did not directly govern these countries. However, aided by the Russian forces and advisors that occupied eastern Europe during the war, Communists in these nations came into power. These countries became *satellites* of the Soviet Union. That is, they became dominated by the Soviet Union and dependent on that nation.

The satellite states had little freedom. Their governments were designed to further the interests of the Soviet Union. Soviet troops could be stationed in satellite countries. Soviet officers could hold important posts in satellite armies.

The Soviet Union drained the satellites of economic goods and made them manufacture arms for

Russian troops. The *Council for Mutual Economic Aid* (1949) linked the economies of these eastern European countries so that the Soviet Union could control their agricultural and industrial activities.

The Soviet Union led the satellites into an organization known as the *Cominform,* the *Communist Information Bureau* (1947). This Bureau consisted of representatives from the Communist parties of the Soviet Union, Yugoslavia, Bulgaria, Rumania, Hungary, Poland, Czechoslovakia, Italy, and France. It declared that its tasks consisted of "the organization of an exchange of experience between [Communist] parties, and, in case of necessity, [of] coordination of their activity on the basis of mutual agreement." Yet the Cominform really was designed principally to further the interests of the Soviet Union.

The Soviet Union then covered the satellite countries with a cloak of secrecy. The remark of the British statesman Winston Churchill seemed to describe the situation perfectly: "From Stettin in the Baltic to Trieste in the Adriatic, an iron curtain has descended across the Continent."

Yugoslavia was under the control of Communist leader Joseph Broz, known as Marshal Tito

(1892-1980). It managed to remain independent of the control of the Soviet Union. Tito had led one Yugoslav faction that waged guerrilla warfare against the Germans during World War II. After the war, Tito defeated rival guerrilla factions and won control of Yugoslavia. For a time, Tito cooperated with the Soviet Union. However, it soon became apparent that Tito upheld Yugoslavian national interests over those of the Soviet Union. Then Tito denounced attempts of the Soviet Union to dominate his country, and Yugoslavia went its own way.

European Recovery Program

World War II left western Europe with many serious problems of reconstruction. Cities had been smashed into rubble. Factories had been burned to the ground or stood as gutted ghosts of the past. Farmlands had been ripped apart by shells. The means of trade and transportation had largely been destroyed. The economy of western Europe was falling apart.

In June 1947, the United States Secretary of State, General George C. Marshall, presented the so-called *Marshall Plan* in an address delivered at Harvard University. The Marshall Plan proposed that the United States give extensive financial assistance to the nations of Europe, provided that "there . . . be some agreement among the countries as to the requirements of the situation and the part these countries themselves will take." Funds were to be used to help the European nations to help themselves to rebuild their economies.

All European countries were invited to join the Marshall Plan, but the Soviet Union and its satellites refused. Sixteen other nations met in Paris and formed a committee to draw up plans to participate in the Marshall Plan. In April 1948, the United States Congress supported the Marshall Plan by adopting the Foreign Assistance Act. This act made available a fund of several billion dollars and set up an administration for what was called the *European Recovery Program (ERP)*.

ERP, which extended from April 1948, through December 1951, was a cooperative program between the United States and countries accepting the Marshall Plan. The participating European nations formed the *Organization for European Economic Cooperation (OEEC)* to carry out their responsibilities under ERP and to continue their efforts to es-

tablish a sound economy for Europe. The 270,000,000 people of these nations were to provide the funds to match the dollars credited to their governments by the United States. The financial contribution of the United States proved to be about 25 percent of the total cost of European recovery. About 75 percent of the burden was carried by the European taxpayers themselves.

ERP contributed greatly to the recovery of western Europe. During the first two years of cooperative efforts under ERP, western Europe doubled its production of electric power. Agricultural yields increased considerably. Industrial production in Marshall Plan countries as a whole rose to 20 percent above prewar levels.

In addition, the Marshall Plan stimulated the activity known as *Technical Assistance (TA)*. The Technical Assistance program made it possible for American and European experts in industry, agriculture, and other fields to visit each other's countries, study each other's methods, and exchange creative ideas on the best ways to work.

The Soviet Union viewed the Marshall Plan as a form of United States imperialism. It responded with the *Council for Mutual Economic Aid (COMECON)* in 1949. This linked the economies of most eastern European nations and brought them closer under Soviet control.

Other Cooperative Measures in Europe

Besides participating in the European Recovery Program, European nations established other means of cooperation among themselves. Among the first postwar regional agreements was the *Benelux Customs Union*, which went into effect on January 1, 1948. Under this arrangement, Belgium, the Netherlands, and Luxembourg—the Benelux nations—were able to cooperate in determining customs duties and in other economic matters of importance.

On March 17, 1948, the Benelux nations, Britain, and France signed the *Brussels Treaty*, agreeing to organize a collective defense and to cooperate in economic, social, and cultural affairs. Italy and West Germany later became members of this *Western European Union*.

Events in Germany

At international wartime meetings, Roosevelt, Churchill, and Stalin had also discussed the future of Germany. Great Britain, the United States, and the Soviet Union eventually agreed that this nation would be divided among them and the French into four occupation zones. Berlin, Germany's capital, would also be so divided.

Conflicts over movement between the Soviet and other zones, and disputes over the issuance of a new German currency and over other matters soon arose. Viewing the Soviets as uncooperative, France, Great Britain, and the United States merged their zones of occupation in Germany. The single area thus formed was known as *West Germany* to distinguish it from the Soviet-controlled *East Germany*. The United States, Great Britain, and France also fused their sectors of West Berlin into one, and a new common currency was issued for all of West Germany.

Berlin lay entirely within the Soviet zone of occupation. The Soviet Union angrily retaliated for these acts of the Allies by blockading all land traffic to West Berlin. That is, it prevented food and other supplies from passing through the Soviet zone and reaching the people of West Berlin. The United States, Great Britain, and France refused to be forced out of Berlin by this blockade. They

loaded airplanes with provisions, flew as many as 8,000 tons of materials a day over the Russian zone, and supplied West Berlin by air. After nearly eleven months of this Berlin "airlift" (1948-1949), the Russians ended their blockade.

Conflicts between the Soviet Union and the United States, Great Britain, and France sealed Germany's immediate future. Before the war's end, the Allies, including the Soviet Union, had agreed to German unification. Now, however, there seemed no way to reconcile Soviet-Western differences and bring about unification. Consequently, in 1949, with the approval of the United States, Great Britain, and France, the people of West Germany proclaimed a new German constitution (called the Basic Law), which established the *German Federal Republic* for West Germany. In 1955, after the Allies ended their occupation of West Germany, the German Federal Republic became a sovereign state, with its capital at Bonn.

The Soviet Union, in the meantime, experienced difficulty in its zone of occupation. Conditions there became so unbearable that between December 1, 1949, and May 31, 1950, more than 117,000 persons fled from East Germany to West Germany.

After World War II, Austria and Germany were both divided into four occupation zones. Berlin was also divided, as the inset map shows.

Occupation Zones in Germany and Austria

- United States
- British
- French
- Russian

Children in Berlin wave to a United States plane bringing them food during the Russian blockade of Berlin in 1948.

This flood of refugees continued until 1961, when the East German government closed the border between East and West Berlin. In June 1953, a serious uprising broke out in East Berlin, and Soviet troops and tanks crushed it.

In 1954, the Soviet Union made East Germany an "independent" state. The following year the Russians recognized it as a "sovereign state." However, the so-called *German Democratic Republic* continued to be dominated by the Soviet Union.

Under the direction of Chancellor Konrad Adenauer and other leaders, the German Federal Republic grew into a strong and respected nation. At the same time, the German Democratic Republic, under the leadership of German Communists like Walter Ulbricht, also developed its strength.

In a dramatic action on August 13, 1961, the Communist East German government closed the border between East and West Berlin. The Communists then constructed a concrete and barbed-wire wall between the two areas. Escape from East to West Berlin became very difficult. President John F. Kennedy responded by reinforcing the United States garrison in Berlin.

In 1969 Willy Brandt, long the mayor of West Berlin, became Chancellor of the German Federal Republic in a coalition government. He began to seek an understanding with East Germany and the Soviet bloc as a basic aim of his foreign policy.

As the 1980s began, the German Federal Republic and the German Democratic Republic both played major roles in European and world affairs.

North Atlantic Treaty Organization

In April 1949, after the Communists had shown their aggressiveness, twelve nations met in Washington, D.C., and signed a treaty to establish the *North Atlantic Treaty Organization (NATO)*. The original signers were Belgium, Canada, Denmark, France, Iceland, Italy, Luxembourg, the Netherlands, Norway, Portugal, the United Kingdom, and the United States. Greece, Turkey, and West Germany later came into the organization.

NATO was a military alliance in which the member nations agreed to organize a common defense and to take collective action against possible Communist or other aggression in the North Atlantic area. The members of NATO declared that an attack on one would be considered an attack on all.

When the United States joined NATO, it marked the first time that this country had entered a peacetime agreement to aid the defense of countries outside of the Western Hemisphere. By 1960 the United States had signed treaties to help defend over forty countries in the world!

In 1966 President Charles de Gaulle announced that France would withdraw all its military forces from the unified command of the North Atlantic Treaty Organization. France, however, would continue to support programs for the mutual defense of Europe. De Gaulle asked that the military headquarters and installations of NATO be removed from France. The military headquarters was transferred to Belgium.

President Simone Veil of France listens to a debate at the meeting of the European Parliament in Strasbourg in 1979. Madame Veil is the first President of the European Parliament.

President de Gaulle made clear that his actions were partly motivated by a desire to free France from "subordination" to United States foreign policies. ". . . As a result of the internal and external evolution of the countries of the East," declared de Gaulle, "the Western world is no longer threatened as it was at the time when the American protectorate was organized in Europe under the cover of NATO."

The Soviet Union responded to the North Atlantic Treaty Organization by forming the Warsaw Pact in 1955. By its terms, the Soviet Union set up a 20-year military defense agreement with Albania, Bulgaria, Czechoslovakia, East Germany, Hungary, Poland, and Rumania. Article 4 of the pact declared that "in case of armed aggression in Europe against one or several States party to the pact," the other members would send aid—including "the use of armed force"—to those under at-

tack. Article 5 provided for setting up a "joint command of [the] armed forces" of the pact members. Albania withdrew in 1968.

Additional Cooperation in the West

In 1949 the *Council of Europe* was established, with headquarters at Strasbourg, France. The original members were Belgium, Denmark, France, Ireland, Italy, Luxembourg, the Netherlands, Norway, Sweden, and the United Kingdom. Later, Turkey, Greece, Iceland, West Germany, and Austria joined the Council.

In the beginning, members of the Council's Consultative Assembly represented the parliaments of the participating members. In 1979, general elections were held in the various countries to directly elect 410 representatives to the Assembly. They, in turn, elected a president, the majority casting ballots for Simone Veil, a Jewish Frenchwoman who had survived the Nazi death camp at Auschwitz during World War II. This "parliament of Europe" remains an advisory group only. Its chief function is "to provide for the development of cooperation between governments."

In 1950, Robert Schuman, a prominent French statesman, suggested that the coal and steel resources of France, West Germany, and other European countries be pooled. This led to the establishment in 1952 of the *European Coal and Steel Community,* which included France, West Germany, the Benelux nations, and Italy. The organization broke monopolies that were interfering with the production of coal and steel, helped create a free European market in coal and steel, and within five years increased coal and steel trade among the six Community nations by 93 percent.

The success of the European Coal and Steel Community led to the development of the *European Common Market,* formally known as the *European Economic Community (EEC).* The original members of EEC were the same six that had formed the Coal and Steel Community. The six nations agreed that over a period of twelve to fifteen years they would: 1. lower and gradually do away with import quotas and customs duties among them; 2. form a common market area and establish a single tariff on goods coming into this area; and 3. set up a bank whose funds could be used to help all six members.

The EEC produced many results. The lowering of customs duties helped increase the trade among the six nations by more than 40 percent in three years. It also led to new business agreements, such as those between Italian, German, and French automobile companies. Other economic activities stimulated economic growth and added to the wealth of countries belonging to the Common Market. The Common Market created many new industrial jobs and encouraged the freer movement of workers from one member nation to another one. Also, consumers were benefiting from lower prices. Administrators of the Common Market claimed that between 1958 and 1962 the prices of many goods fell an average of 40 percent as a result of tariff reductions among the six nations.

In 1973 Great Britain, Denmark, and Ireland joined EEC. In 1977 Portugal and Spain applied for membership.

A number of Americans thought that the Common Market posed a threat to United States trade with Europe. Congress, therefore, authorized the President of the United States to negotiate tariff reduction with Common Market countries and other nations as well. At a meeting in Geneva, Switzerland in May 1967, representatives of fifty-three nations, including the United States, agreed to reduce tariffs on a wide range of products.

In the latter part of the 1970s, inflation threatened the economies of the countries of Europe. The average annual rate of inflation in the Netherlands was 8.5 percent, in Belgium 9.0 percent, in France 9.6 percent. Inflation was even worse in other parts of the world. In Chile, for example, it was 234.2 percent. Many economists felt that the 1980s would require additional economic cooperation among nations to help solve the serious economic problems.

Check on Your Reading

1. What problems were there in Poland after World War II?
2. Describe how events in Greece led to the United States containment policy.
3. How was Yugoslavia different from other eastern European Communist countries?
4. What was the European Recovery Program? What were its objectives?
5. How were differences between the Soviet Union and the other Allies concerning Germany resolved?
6. Describe the various organizations in which Western European nations cooperated.

3. The Soviet Union after Stalin

On March 5, 1953, at 9:50 P.M., Joseph Stalin died. The era of his personal domination of the Soviet Union was at an end.

Khrushchev Emerges as the Leader

The leadership of the Soviet Union now passed to three men. Collective leadership did not last. A power struggle quickly developed, and one after another the three leaders lost their power. Finally, on March 28, 1958, Nikita Khrushchev (1894–1971), who had become First Secretary of the Communist Party, was named the Chairman of the Council of Ministers. Thus, he was both head of the Communist Party and of the government of the Soviet Union.

Nikita Sergeyevich Khrushchev was born in 1894 in a village in southern Russia near the Ukrainian border. As a boy, he received little formal education. Instead, he went to work and became a shepherd. Then he labored for a time as an apprentice to a pipe-fitter and later as a mechanic in the coal mines of the Ukraine.

In 1918 Khrushchev joined the Communist Party and was sent to a workers' school. There he received training in Communist ideas. Starting as an official in the Ukraine, Khrushchev rose until he reached the top of the Party and the government.

As head of the powerful Soviet Union, Khrushchev became a familiar figure in world affairs. He could be blunt, boastful, earthy, humorous, belligerent, shrewd, evasive—on the same occasion and at different times.

De-Stalinization Affects Soviet Life

Crafty, ruthless Joseph Stalin had for years been feared and hated by many, both outside of and within the government. He had been directly or indirectly responsible for the ruination or deaths of several million people throughout his career, and for the banishment of many thousands to what were known as slave-labor camps, many of them in Siberia. Three years after Stalin's death, Khrushchev played the chief role in an attack on the former Soviet leader. The denunciation of Stalin and the changes that resulted from it came to be known as *de-Stalinization.*

The climax to de-Stalinization came with a speech Khrushchev made before a secret meeting of the Twentieth Congress of the Communist Party in

February 1956. Khrushchev attacked the "cult of the individual," the idolization of Stalin as the ever-wise leader who was always right. Khrushchev called for the cult's abolition and for a return to "the main principle of collective leadership." He also denounced Stalin for his suspicious character, inefficiency as a military leader, unwise conduct toward Yugoslavia, and dictatorial methods by which he permitted "mass arrests and deportations of many thousands of people, and execution without trial and without normal investigation."

In 1961, the Twenty-second Congress of the Communist Party voted to remove Stalin's embalmed body from the mausoleum in Red Square where it had rested in a place of honor next to Lenin's. Stalin's remains were transferred to a simple grave under a short inscription: "J. V. Stalin, 1879–1953."

De-Stalinization affected life in the Soviet Union in many ways. Thousands of prisoners were released from slave-labor camps. Workers were permitted to change their jobs under certain circumstances. The length of the work day was reduced in various regions. Writers and artists were given greater freedom to express themselves. Awards for cultural achievements known as Stalin prizes became Lenin prizes. Textbook statements praising Stalin were altered.

What were the reasons for de-Stalinization? The new leaders of the Soviet Union wanted to disassociate themselves from the mistakes and the hated features of Stalin's regime. They also wished to stimulate further the industrial and agricultural productivity of the Soviet people. They believed it necessary "to restore the quality of initiative that had withered in Stalin's iron grip."

Rebellion in Poland

From the Soviet point of view, de-Stalinization had adverse effects in some satellite nations in eastern Europe. The creation of a more open society in the Soviet Union encouraged some of those nations to try to loosen their bonds.

In June 1956 a Polish revolt began with demonstrations by auto workers in Poznan, who were soon joined by other workers and students. The peaceful demonstrations quickly turned into bloody rioting. People were killed as the demonstrators fought the Polish secret police and security troops, who finally restored order.

As a result of the Poznan riots and negotiations conducted during the summer of 1956, the Polish Communist Party declared that workers would receive a wage increase. The Party went through a major shakeup and pro-Stalinist members were forced out of office. The Polish Communist leaders, under Wladislaw Gomulka, exerted pressure on the Soviet Union for greater Polish independence. By October 1956, high Soviet officers were withdrawn from Poland, and the Soviet Union promised greater "noninterference in [Poland's] internal affairs." Poland continued to accept Soviet leadership in foreign affairs while obtaining the right to its own national existence.

The Hungarian Revolution

Four months after the Poznan riots in Poland, Hungary also was rocked by a revolutionary storm. On October 23, 1956, students demonstrated in Budapest, demanding that Hungary be given greater independence from Soviet control. Their demands included the removal of Soviet troops from Hungarian soil, withdrawal of Hungary from the Warsaw Pact of 1955, and free elections in Hungary.

Workers and other demonstrators soon joined the students. A clash between students and the Hungarian security police ended in bloodshed. As the rebels armed themselves with guns and ammunition supplied by workers in munitions plants, the Communist government of Hungary declared martial law and issued a call for help from the Soviet Union.

On October 23 and 24 there was fighting between Soviet troops and Hungarians. Then, with the appointment of Imre Nagy as prime minister of Hungary, the Soviet Union seemed to be giving in to Hungarian demands. Nagy was a "national Communist"—that is, a Communist with deeper concern for his own country than for the Soviet Union.

On October 29, Nagy succeeded in obtaining the withdrawal of Soviet troops from Budapest. On October 30, Cardinal Mindszenty, a Roman Catholic leader whose imprisonment by the Communists had angered people throughout the world, was freed. On the same day, Prime Minister Nagy declared that the one-party system whereby the Communist Party had dominated Hungary would be abolished. Then, on November 1, Nagy announced Hungary's withdrawal from the Warsaw

Pact and asked the United Nations to consider the entire Hungarian situation.

The rebels had made it clear that they intended to go beyond the scope of the Polish revolt and end the power of the Soviet Union in Hungary. This caused Nagy's downfall. On November 4, Soviet troops and tanks attacked Budapest in force and crushed the Hungarian Freedom Fighters.

A new government, headed by János Kadar and supported by the Soviet Union, was established in Hungary. The Freedom Fighters continued to hold out for as long as they could, but the Russian troops finally brought the rebellion to a close. Many of the rebels fled to the West. Imre Nagy was later taken prisoner and executed. Russian military intervention in Hungary brought worldwide condemnation upon the Soviet Union, and many countries provided refuge for those who escaped from Hungary.

Czechoslovakia, 1968

Czechoslovakia, while making no move to overturn its Communist regime, also sought freedom from close Soviet control. The government under Communist leader Alexander Dubcek instituted numerous reforms, loosening its tight control over the people and increasing economic and political freedom. This trend worried the Soviet Union, for it greatly resembled the Hungarian situation of several years before.

On August 19, 1968, Soviet forces, along with those of Poland and other Warsaw Pact nations, invaded Czechoslovakia. There was fighting in Prague, that nation's capital, and Dubcek finally agreed to back off from reforms. This did not entirely settle the issue, however, for an anti-Soviet spirit remained in Czechoslovakia. Pro-Soviet forces within the government forced the resignation of Dubcek in April 1969. Gustav Husak, a man on whom the Soviets could depend, became head of the Czech government. Efforts toward reform and less Soviet control of Czechoslovakia ended. However, in 1977 more than 700 Czechoslovakian intellectuals and former Party leaders signed a human rights manifesto.

Soviet—United States Relations

Until 1949, the United States enjoyed a monopoly on nuclear weapons, but in that year the Soviet Union exploded its own nuclear device. The Soviet Union and the United States then developed an even more powerful weapon, the hydrogen bomb. Later France, China, and India joined the "nuclear club."

The Soviet Union and the United States were soon engaged in an arms race, each developing ever more sophisticated weapons, including missiles capable of carrying nuclear warheads for many hundreds of miles. At the same time, relations between the two countries were deeply influenced by mutual suspicion.

As part of his de-Stalinization program, however, Nikita Khrushchev stated that he did not believe that war between communism and capitalism was inevitable. This appeared to offer some hope of avoiding armed conflict that might result in mutual destruction.

But then the two countries confronted each other over Cuba. In 1959, Cuban rebels had overthrown the dictator who had ruled that nation for many years. The rebels then set up a Communist-oriented regime under Fidel Castro, and the Soviet Union soon began supplying Castro with arms and other aid. Castro refused to compensate United States citizens for their property in Cuba seized by his government. He accused the United States of economic aggression. He also denied the right of the United States to maintain a naval base at Guantánamo. On January 3, 1961, the United States broke diplomatic relations with Cuba.

On April 17, 1961, a force of about 1,300 armed anti-Castro Cubans, mostly Cuban exiles, landed at the Bay of Pigs on the south coast of Cuba. Unofficially aided by the United States with arms and training, the anti-Castro invaders fought to overthrow the Castro government. They were easily defeated after a short battle.

In October 1962 United States photo-reconnaissance planes flying over Cuba returned with disturbing pictures. They showed the construction of missile bases in Cuba and Soviet ships heading for that island with missiles lashed to their decks. President John F. Kennedy concluded that the installation in Cuba of Soviet missiles capable of carrying nuclear warheads posed a serious threat to the security of the United States. He therefore ordered an air and naval blockade of the island to prevent Soviet ships from reaching Cuba, and demanded that the missile bases be dismantled.

For a few days in October, the United States and the Soviet Union seemed poised on the brink of nuclear war. However, the crisis was finally settled. The Soviet ships turned back and the Soviet Union agreed to dismantle the bases. The United States, in turn, promised not to invade Cuba.

The Cuban missile crisis had been a sobering experience for both the Soviet Union and the United States. It demonstrated how quickly a dangerous crisis could develop, and served to stimulate efforts toward peaceful co-existence.

As for Nikita Khrushchev, the crisis may have helped bring about his downfall. In addition, his agricultural and industrial programs had not worked well. In October 1964 he was forced to retire from his positions of power. Leonid Brezhnev became First Secretary (Chief) of the Communist Party, and Alexei Kosygin replaced Khrushchev as Chairman of the Council of Ministers.

The Soviet Union after Khrushchev

As the years passed, several satellite nations became more independent. For example, Albania supported Communist China in its quarrels with the Soviet Union. Also, Rumania on its own played host for a visit by the United States President Richard M. Nixon.

The idea of peaceful co-existence seemed for the most part to persist into the 1970s. Leaders spoke of *détente,* which refers to a situation or atmosphere in which tensions are reduced, and countries of differing political, economic, and social systems live together without conflict. President Richard Nixon visited the Soviet Union in May 1972 for talks with Soviet leaders. Shortly thereafter, the United States and the Soviet Union signed the first *Strategic Arms Limitation Treaty (SALT),* aimed at placing ceilings on the number of nuclear weapons each country would possess. Further talks over a long period produced a second *Strategic Arms Limitation Treaty*

(SALT II) in 1979 for consideration by both nations.

The cold war had not been completely stopped. The Soviet Union, along with Cuba, gave aid to and sought to gain influence in countries undergoing revolution, such as Angola and Ethiopia in Africa. At the same time the United States, whenever possible, tried to counteract that influence.

At the opening of the 1980s, relations between the United States and the Soviet Union were complicated by relations with the People's Republic of China, the Russians' attitudes toward dissidents, the policies of Cuba, and the Soviet invasion of Afghanistan.

Check on Your Reading

1. How did de-Stalinization affect the Soviet government and people?
2. Compare the uprisings in Poland, Hungary, and Czechoslovakia and their outcomes.
3. Describe the course of Soviet-United States relations.

4. Events in Other European Countries

Assisted by the Marshall Plan and other United States aid, European countries experienced economic recovery. At the same time, each had its own particular problems to attack in its own way.

Great Britain Nationalizes Key Industries

In the first postwar general elections in July 1945, the British people voted the Labor Party into power. For the first time, a Labor government, headed by Prime Minister Clement Attlee, was organized with a majority in the House of Commons.

The Labor party had campaigned on the proposition that only a measure of *nationalization* of key industries—that is, placing them under the ownership and control of the national government—could adequately solve Britain's postwar problems. Immediately upon assuming power, the Labor government went ahead with plans to nationalize such industries. It nationalized the Bank of England, coal mining, transportation, civil aviation, international telecommunications, electricity, gas, and iron and steel. Eventually, about 20 percent of the national assets were brought under government ownership. The Conservative Party, still led by Winston Churchill, accepted many features of nationalization, but was opposed to the nationalization of iron and steel.

Prime Minister Margaret Thatcher receives an ovation at the end of a conference of the Conservative Party. She is the leader of this party.

Under the Labor government, Parliament also enacted important social legislation, much of it with Conservative support. Five acts of Parliament established a system of *National Insurance and Assistance* and a *National Health Service*. As a result of these laws, every citizen received protection against economic and health disasters, and was provided with insured medical, dental, and hospital care.

Both employees and employers contributed to the National Insurance and Assistance program. Benefits covered situations involving sickness, unemployment, injury, maternity, widowhood, guardian's allowance, retirement pensions, and death. The National Health Service was financed primarily by taxes, and cost the people of Britain in taxes around 5½ percent of their national income.

In the elections of 1951 for Parliament, the Conservative Party once more gained power. Although the Conservatives denationalized the steel industry, returning it to private hands, they kept many of the changes that the Labor government had introduced.

On February 6, 1952, King George VI died. The traditional coronation of the new ruler, Elizabeth II, took place on June 2, 1953.

Another Labor government held office from 1964 to 1970. In 1970 the Conservatives won a majority in Parliament, and formed a government. In 1979 the Conservatives once again gained victory in Britain, and for the first time in British history a woman, Margaret Thatcher, became Prime Minister. She began a program to stimulate British industrial production, reduce taxes, and cut down unjustified expenditures on some programs.

France Survives Many Crises

While postwar problems in Britain were being handled by a stable and orderly government, France went through one crisis after another. Under the postwar Fourth French Republic, proclaimed officially in 1946, the National Assembly became the most important organ of government. The members of the National Assembly were elected by *proportional representation,* a system in which various parties received representation in the National Assembly in proportion to the number of votes each polled. One result of this was that the French legislature was filled with representatives of many parties. Rarely did a single party have a majority.

The large number of conflicting parties made it difficult for the Premier of France to direct the government—or even to remain in office long. The Premier, appointed by the President of France, needed the support of a majority of the members of the National Assembly to obtain the appointment and to stay in power. Because no single party had a majority in the National Assembly, the Premier had to depend on a coalition of several parties to make up his majority. If he lost any support, he often also lost his majority and had to resign from office.

In addition, France faced serious economic problems. These included a need for greater industrialization, a shortage of housing, inflation, and an inefficient system of taxation. There was also a low rate of increase in agricultural production.

France attacked these problems. It increased coal production and rebuilt many war-damaged buildings. France also added to the tractors and other machinery on farms, strengthened the system of social security, and raised the standard of living.

The Fifth French Republic Is Established

France was faced also with rebellions and crises in its empire in North Africa and Indochina. Military defeat in Indochina finally forced France to give up that area. Then, an uprising in Algeria, North Africa, set off a chain of events that led to the fall of the Fourth Republic.

In May 1958, reports circulated that the government intended to give up Algeria. These reports infuriated the *colons*—people primarily of French extraction in Algeria. On May 13, 1958, thirty thousand *colons* rioted in the streets and stormed government offices in Algiers in protest. French army leaders in Algeria, who supported the *colons,* issued a call for General Charles de Gaulle to take charge of the French government. Only he, they said, could "save" France. On May 15 de Gaulle came out of retirement to meet the crisis and announced that he was "ready to assume the powers of the Republic."

After the fall of France in World War II, de Gaulle had escaped that country, and become a leader of the Free French movement. On August 25, 1944, he rode triumphantly atop a tank when the French army returned to Paris. Although he became a national hero and a world figure, General de Gaulle was disliked and distrusted by some French people and by some leaders of other countries. Nevertheless, few of them would have disagreed with the *Time* correspondent who wrote: "De Gaulle is a dedicated man whose entire strength, passion and intelligence have been devoted to his conception of France as a nation that 'is not really herself unless in the front rank.' " In May 1958, many French people were convinced that de Gaulle was the person who could restore order.

De Gaulle demanded and was granted special emergency powers to meet the crisis. Next he directed that a new constitution be drawn up. This constitution, approved in September 1958 by a referendum held in France and its territories, set up the Fifth French Republic.

The new constitution introduced changes to provide a stable two-house legislature and a more powerful French presidency. The changes included a system of voting for National Assembly members that provided one representative for each electoral district.

Charles de Gaulle was elected the first President of the Fifth French Republic. He demonstrated his ardent nationalism in many ways. He blocked British entrance into the Common Market, made a treaty of friendship with Germany, and withdrew French military forces from the unified command of

King Juan Carlos and his wife drive through the streets of Madrid.

NATO. Georges Pompidou, a de Gaulle supporter, became President in 1969. He was succeeded in 1974 by Valéry Giscard d'Estaing.

At the beginning of the 1980s, France was working diligently on problems of inflation, the development of new sources of energy, and the protection of the environment. President Giscard d'Estaing urged "reasonable coexistence" among political parties and declared "our country has suffered too much from political instability."

Events in Italy

In 1943 Italy had joined the Allies in the war against Germany. Many Italians therefore felt that the treaty of peace that Italy signed with the Allies in 1947 was unnecessarily harsh. Italy was required to give up Libya; Ethiopia; other overseas possessions; and the city of Trieste and the Istrian peninsula, which were constituted as the Free Territory of Trieste. The administration of the northern part of the Territory of Trieste was transferred to Italy in 1954. The remainder was placed under the administration of Yugoslavia.

In June 1946, the Italian people rejected a monarchy and voted to establish a republic. Alcide de Gasperi, leader of the Christian Democratic Party, served as Prime Minister for most of the period between 1946 and 1953. Aided financially by the Marshall Plan, de Gasperi and his associates worked to solve Italy's economic problems of overpopulation and unemployment.

Italian governments tended to change frequently, for the Christian Democrats, the major party, had difficulty mustering and maintaining a majority party in the parliament. The Communist Party enjoyed considerable strength in Italy, and from time to time the possibility existed that the Communists might establish a majority themselves. This did not occur, however, but during the late 1970s Communist ministers served in the Italian cabinet.

Austria Regains Its Independence

The Moscow Declaration of 1943, issued by the Soviet Union, the United States, and Great Britain, stated that Austria was to be reestablished as an independent state. At the end of the war, Austria was therefore treated as a "liberated" country. Like Germany, postwar Austria was divided into four occupation zones. Vienna was also occupied.

In 1945, while the country was under Allied occupation, the Second Austrian Republic was established. Ten years later, that republic regained its full independence. Bordered on three sides by Communist-dominated nations, Austria worked to build a democratic government.

Portugal and Spain Shed Dictatorships

In 1932, a government headed by Premier Antonio de Oliveira Salazar gained power in Portugal. Salazar eventually established a dictatorship and continued in power until illness forced his retirement in September 1968.

Portugal was the last European nation to hold a large colonial empire in Africa. For many years it battled independence movements, particularly in Angola and Mozambique. Partly with a view toward ending involvement in Africa, a military junta seized power in Portugal in 1974. Portugal then reached an agreement providing independence for Guinea-Bissau, Mozambique, Cape

Verde Islands, Angola, and São Tomé and Príncipe.

Within Portugal, banks, insurance companies, transportation, and other industries were nationalized. Then in 1976 free elections were held, and the Socialist Party gained the most seats in Parliament.

After the war Spain remained under the dictatorship of Francisco Franco. Officially, Spain was neutral in World War II, but Franco sympathized with the Nazi cause and sent some troops to fight the Soviet army on the eastern front.

In 1969 Franco designated Prince Juan Carlos as the future king of Spain and chief of state. Franco died in November 1975 and Juan Carlos became king. Spain then moved in the direction of democracy under a constitutional monarchy. However, the desire of ethnic groups, such as the Basques, for self-rule continued to plague the government in 1980.

Check on Your Reading
1. Describe Britain's nationalization program and the social legislation that the British government enacted.
2. Why was the Fourth French Republic an unstable government?
3. What changes did Charles de Gaulle make?
4. Describe postwar events in Italy and Austria.
5. What happened in Portugal and Spain after World War II?

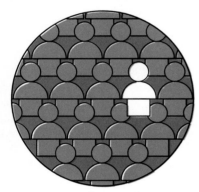

LET'S MEET THE PEOPLE

Agatha: Hungarian Patriot

Russian troops were stationed in Budapest. A strict curfew was in effect: "No one was permitted outside except the military. Civilians were shot on sight. For one hour a day people were permitted to move around and draw food from the rapidly dwindling supply. . . ."

One afternoon a truck loaded with 1,600 loaves of bread drove into the square. It arrived after the hour for obtaining food, and the Russian soldiers fired around the truck to keep the Hungarians inside their houses. Agatha, a very old, bent, white-haired woman, stood in her doorway, watching the truckload of bread.

Slowly, old Agatha walked across to the truck. She lifted two of the five-pound loaves, turned, and carried them back to the Hungarians in the houses. Then she started back to the truck again. A Russian soldier fired a warning shot at her, but Agatha kept walking. She lifted two more loaves and returned with the bread to the houses.

Shots were fired over Agatha's head, and a Russian officer hurried over to her. "You must stop defying the curfew!" he ordered.

Agatha answered: ". . . pray to God for forgiveness for your sins."

Then Agatha went back to distributing the bread. What was it that kept the Russians from shooting her: shame, admiration, or fear of arousing the Hungarians to new fury? All through the afternoon and evening Agatha distributed the bread. Finally at about 9 P.M., when there were only a few hundred loaves still on the truck, she collapsed. "From a nearby Soviet tank a soldier ran toward Agatha . . . the Russian gently lifted the frail old woman into his arms."

The soldier carried Agatha to the doorway from which she had started. He banged on the door and handed the old woman to the people within. Then he raced back to his tank—and prepared to fire on anyone foolish enough to break the curfew!

The above sketch is based on information in Leslie B. Bain's *The Reluctant Satellites,* 1960, Macmillan.

CHAPTER REVIEW

Past and Present

1. Compare the structure and functioning of the League of Nations and the United Nations.
2. Do the policies of the Soviet Union toward neighboring countries of eastern Europe today differ from the earlier policies of the Czars? Justify your answer.
3. In light of the divisions of Berlin and Germany, what do you think should have been decided at the Potsdam Conference in 1945?

Think and Discuss

1. Do you think any country should ever be ousted from the UN? What advantages and disadvantages are there to such action?
2. Can you find any similarities or differences between regional organizations such as NATO and the Warsaw Pact and the balance-of-power system of the nineteenth and early twentieth centuries? Explain your answer.
3. Do regional organizations preserve peace or promote war? Support your answer.
4. How do you explain the fact that a defeated country was aided to achieve prosperity by one of the victors? Do you think it would have been better to let the defeated country try to struggle back to prosperity by its own efforts alone? Why?
5. Why was Austrian reunification achieved by the four occupying powers without all the difficulties that arose over German reunification?

Activities

1. Panel discussion: "The European Common Market will eventually change the political structure of western Europe."
2. Write a 750-word biography of the person whom you think has contributed most to international peace in the twentieth century.
3. Make a chart showing health conditions in various countries of the world by using information and statistics obtained by writing to the World Health Organization.
4. Try to obtain a textbook used today in the Soviet Union or France or the Federal Republic of Germany and, with the aid of someone who reads Russian, French, or German, find out how it described events in this chapter.

Asia Undergoes Great Changes

In the summer of 1958 a popular song in the People's Republic of China was a number entitled "Catch Up with Britain." It contained the lines:

Leap forward, leap forward,
Outstrip Britain in fifteen years.
Gallop onward, gallop onward,
China fears not sweat nor tears!

This song and others like it—such as the tune "East Wind Prevails Over West Wind"—symbolized the fact that the peoples of Asia were on the march. Many Asian lands, long dominated by Western powers, were determined to "leap forward" into the present and in time surpass the West.

One of the key features of the period after World War II was the emergence of new nations in Asia and the rise of Asia to a position of great importance in world affairs.

This Chinese Communist peasant painting is titled "Happy Harvest of Cotton."

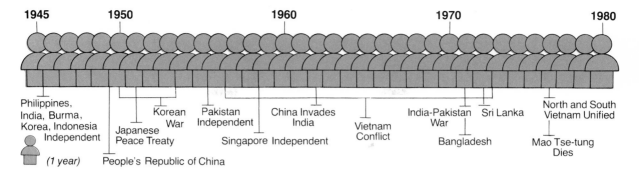

Philippines,
India, Burma,
Korea, Indonesia
Independent
(1 year)

Japanese
Peace Treaty

People's Republic of China

Korean
War

Pakistan
Independent

Singapore Independent

China Invades
India

Vietnam
Conflict

India-Pakistan
War

Bangladesh

Sri Lanka

Mao Tse-tung
Dies

North and South
Vietnam Unified

1. Democracy Develops in Japan

During the postwar years, most of Asia was in turmoil. Colonial territories sought to throw off European rule. There were revolutions and civil wars.
Communists made gains in some countries; democratic forces triumphed in others. There were
many differences in the postwar developments in
the countries of Asia. However, most Asians as-
pired to these things:

- the right to form their own nations;
- a higher standard of living and economic security;
- better education and medical care;
- an end to the colonial empires of the European
powers.

After the Japanese surrender in World War II,
American troops occupied Japan. General Douglas MacArthur was appointed Supreme Commander of Allied Occupation Forces. The United
States and its allies tried to help develop democracy
in Japan.

A New Constitution

A most important event was the introduction of
a constitution for Japan in 1947. This democratic
constitution included the following provisions:
1. The Emperor was no longer recognized as a descendant of the gods. 2. Legislative power was
placed in a two-house body (the Diet). The Prime
Minister and his Cabinet were responsible to the
Diet. 3. Freedom of speech and the press was
guaranteed. 4. Women were given the right to
vote. The United States also insisted that Article 9
be included in the new constitution. It stated:

> . . . the Japanese people forever renounce war
> as a sovereign right of the nation . . . land, sea,
> and air forces, as well as other war potential,
> will never be maintained.

As a further step toward democracy, the Japanese educational system was reorganized. Under
the old system, obedience to the Emperor and the
state was considered the chief duty of the citizen.
Under the new system, respect for the individual
was stressed.

A Peace Treaty Is Signed

Assisted by United States financial aid, Japan's
economy quickly revived. The Japanese increased
their foreign trade, strengthened their textile industries, and expanded their iron and steel and shipbuilding industries. Politically, Japan became more
stable.

In September 1951, the United States and forty-
seven other nations signed a treaty of peace with
Japan. Its terms were these: 1. Japan agreed to
conform to the principles of the United Nations
Charter; and to give up Korea, Formosa, the Pes-
cadores, the Kurile Islands, and southern Sakhalin.
Also Japan renounced all special rights in China.
2. Arrangements were to be made for Japan to
pay reasonable reparations. 3. Allied Occupation
Forces were to be withdrawn within ninety days
after the treaty went into effect. "Stationing and
retention" of foreign troops in Japan was to be allowed if foreign nations and Japan negotiated an
agreement.

Japan permitted United States military bases,
and Japan and the United States signed a Mutual
Defense Assistance Treaty in 1954. Faced with the
danger of aggressive Soviet and Chinese Communist action, the United States encouraged Japan to
become a strong ally.

Japan Seeks to Find Its Own Way

In time, a number of Japanese leaders responded to the "Cold War" by emphasizing Japanese nationalism. Several groups demanded that

Examples of the old and the new in Japan. At the left above is a scene from the Kabuki Theater, an old tradition in Japan. At the right, the subway in Tokyo, the largest city in the world.

Japan be independent from all foreign domination. Ichiro Hatoyama, who served as Prime Minister in 1955, spoke for them when he said: "I would like to awaken the people to a deeper . . . sense of their independence."

Near the close of President Eisenhower's administration, riots erupted in Japan to prevent the ratification of a new Japanese-American defense treaty. However, a treaty was ratified. Then in 1969 the United States agreed to return Okinawa and other Ryukyu Islands to Japanese control.

Economically, Japan was called the "miracle nation" of the postwar world. Its industries boomed and the nation prospered. Japan became known throughout the world for its radios, televisions, transistors, automobiles, and recording equipment. It also became a serious rival to Switzerland in the manufacture of watches, made inroads into the motorcycle industry in Britain and the United States, and came to rival United States manufacturers in the production of fine pianos, flutes, and other musical instruments. Japanese foreign trade continued to expand, and during some years it ran a trade surplus of upward to $75 billion. By 1980 an in-

creasing number of economic leaders of other nations were studying Japanese organizations and methods in an effort to strengthen their own countries' economies.

Check on Your Reading

1. In what ways did Japan try to become a democratic nation?
2. Describe United States-Japanese relations after 1954.
3. In what ways did Japan progress economically?

---

2. China Becomes a Communist Power

"Historical experience is written in blood and iron!" declared Mao Tse-tung, leader of the Chinese Communists. In the immediate post-World War II period, Mao Tse-tung and the Communist armies fought the Chinese Nationalists under Chiang Kai-shek. China was torn by civil war.

The Civil War Continues

The Chinese Communists differed sharply from the Nationalists in their principles and policies. The Chinese Communists wanted the Communist Party to have absolute rule, demanded seizure of private property of persons labelled as "landlords" and redistribution of their lands, and were favorable to the Soviet Union. The Nationalists wanted a period of "tutelage"—training of the people to govern themselves. Chiang Kai-shek and his associates would dominate the government until they thought the people were ready for self-government. The Nationalists also demanded the protection of private property and were favorable to the United States.

For years there were charges of corruption, dictatorial behavior, and inefficiency leveled against the Nationalists. At the same time there were reports that the Chinese Communists were holding mass trials and executing those who opposed them. In the midst of accusations and counter-accusations, the struggle for control of China continued.

The Communists Win Control

Long-time enemies, Mao Tse-tung and Chiang Kai-shek turned on each other as soon as the Pacific war ended in 1945. General George C. Marshall of the United States was sent to China to try to end the civil conflict. A truce was signed in 1946. It set up a government that included Communist and Nationalist representatives. However, neither Chiang Kai-shek nor Mao Tse-tung was satisfied with this, and peace did not last. Communist troops took Manchuria, and Mao Tse-tung started a major drive in 1947. Aided by arms sent by the Russians, the Chinese Communists eventually conquered the entire Chinese mainland.

Why were the Chinese Communists successful? Some of the reasons are these: 1. Russian military aid strengthened the Chinese Communist armies. 2. The government of Chiang Kai-shek was unpopular with millions of Chinese. There were charges that his government was favorable to landlords and business people, but not to peasants, who made up most of the population of China. 3. The Chinese Communists' promise of food, land, and justice appealed to many.

In 1949 the Communists drove the Nationalists to Formosa (Taiwan). On October 1, 1949, the Communists proclaimed the establishment of the People's Republic of China with Mao Tse-tung (1893-1976) as Chairman of the government and Chou En-lai as Premier. Thus, there were two Chinas and two Chinese governments, one on the Chinese mainland and the other on Taiwan.

Two Chinas

The Soviet Union promptly recognized the People's Republic of China as China's sole legitimate government. The two countries signed a treaty of alliance and mutual assistance in 1950. Great Britain, France, and many other nations of the world also recognized Mao Tse-tung's government. The United States, however, refused to do so. It continued to recognize only Chiang Kai-shek's government on Taiwan, and it continued to support him with military and economic aid.

Toward the end of the 1960s, United States policy slowly began to change. There were some exchanges with Mao Tse-tung's government. Then, in 1971, the United States dropped its official opposition to the People's Republic of China's entry into the United Nations. On October 25, 1971, the General Assembly voted to admit the People's Republic of China and to expel the Chinese Nationalist government on Taiwan.

Relations between China and the United States further improved when President Richard M. Nixon visited China for talks with Chairman Mao Tse-tung and Premier Chou En-lai in 1972. There followed more cultural exchanges between the two countries and trade began to develop. Then, on December 15, 1978, the United States government announced that it would extend formal recognition to the People's Republic of China. In March 1979, there was an exchange of ambassadors. Vice-Premier Teng Hsiao-p'ing also visited the United States in that year for talks with government officials.

China Transformed

Within China, the Communist regime worked to rebuild and reorganize the country's political, economic, social, and cultural structure. Under the Agrarian Reform Act of 1950, the government seized much land from wealthy landlords, redistributed it, but at first permitted some private ownership. Then, starting with its first Five-Year Plan in 1953, the government gradually brought almost all of the land under the control of communes. This was done by a program of forced "communalization." On these communes, peasants worked the land together in return for food, housing, and other necessities. At the same time, in some areas peasant families were allowed to cultivate small plots of land for their own use.

The Chinese today are proud of the creative achievements of their past and are protecting and restoring buildings such as these in Peking. They date from the fifteenth century.

A major goal of the Chinese Communists was to build their country into a strong industrial power. Intensive efforts were launched to build up industry as well as agriculture. For a while the Soviet Union helped by providing funds and technical advisors. The Chinese Communists allowed no opposition to their program. Anyone who opposed them was imprisoned, killed, or sent to labor camps. By 1957 the government controlled most industries as well as agriculture.

Meanwhile the Communist police, who were controlled by the Chinese Communist Party, watched every facet of life in China. Censorship and terror were employed to weaken or destroy anyone who dared to challenge the Communists. The press and schools were rigidly controlled. Literature and art were filled with propaganda.

By 1970 China's production of steel had increased more than 4,000 percent over production in 1950. Railroad lines destroyed during the war were rebuilt, and some new railroads were started. However, by the end of the 1970s, China was still far from being a major industrial nation.

At the same time tensions developed between the People's Republic of China and the Soviet Union.

Many Chinese leaders did not agree with Khrushchev's de-Stalinization program. Different interpretations of communism in the two countries led to serious disagreements. In the early 1960s, the Soviet Union supported India in clashes with China during a boundary dispute. The Soviet Union stopped, all military and economic aid to China. Mao Tse-tung's government ordered Soviet advisors home; and the People's Republic of China soon was openly competing with the Soviet Union for leadership of world communism.

Mao Tse-tung's Struggle for Control, and the Cultural Revolution

In 1958 Mao Tse-tung launched a second Five-Year Plan, which he called the "Great Leap Forward." China would increase industrial production and at the same time boost agricultural output. Peasants were urged to work harder and for longer hours. Thousands of small furnaces for producing iron were set up in villages. Factories were expected to produce ever greater quantities of goods. New factories were built.

Much was accomplished in building electrial power plants and railroads during the "Great Leap

Forward," but on the whole the program did not achieve its objectives. It had proved much too ambitious, and did not succeed in part from the sheer exhaustion of the people.

Some officials of the Communist Party had been trying to reduce Mao Tse-tung's control of the Party. Now they blamed him for the failure of the "Great Leap Forward" and for the growing tensions with the Soviet Union. A power struggle developed within the Party.

As a consequence, Mao Tse-tung launched the "Great Proletarian Cultural Revolution" as an effort to purge China of his enemies. He urged the Chinese to continue to develop a radical society. He denounced anti-Maoists for deviation from revolutionary Communist doctrine. In 1966 Mao Tse-tung sent groups of armed students across China to campaign against his enemies, and fighting broke out.

The struggle, which lasted during 1966 and 1967, disrupted nearly every aspect of Chinese life. Yet, when he considered the Cultural Revolution ended in 1967, Mao Tse-tung claimed that he was satisfied that the "Four Olds" had been eliminated. These were old thoughts, old culture, old customs, and old habits.

Mao Tse-tung and Chou En-lai died in 1976. Hua Kuo-feng became Premier and Party Chairman. Hua Kuo-feng and the new leaders of China seemed more interested in material results than in rigid Communist philosophy. They laid plans to make China a modern industrial nation by the year 2000, using, whenever necessary, technology from other countries.

Reversing some of the policies of Mao Tse-tung, they permitted schools to use books from foreign countries, made it possible for promising students to study abroad, were willing to examine useful ideas from Western nations, and sought to develop foreign trade.

By the opening of the 1980s, there were reductions in some tensions between the United States and the People's Republic of China. There were exchanges of educators, more tourism was permitted, and President Jimmy Carter and other government leaders of the United States planned to visit China.

Meanwhile there was no consistent pattern in the relationships between the People's Republic of China and the Soviet Union. Fearful of each other on

A worker in a factory making motors. Chinese Communist leaders are committed to industrializing China.

numerous occasions in the past and often differing in their approach to communism, the Russians and the Chinese continued to seek their own futures.

Check on Your Reading

1. How did Chinese Communists and Nationalists differ in their principles and policies? What were some reasons for Nationalist defeat?
2. Describe the changes in United States policy toward the People's Republic of China.
3. In what ways did the Chinese Communist Party change China?
4. What changes occurred following Mao Tse-tung's death?

3. Korea Becomes a Divided Nation

Korea has a long history and a rich civilization. In 1910 Korea was annexed by Japan, which held it until the end of World War II. At the Potsdam Conference in 1945, Allied leaders agreed that Korea would be given its independence after the war. At the conclusion of the conflict, Russian troops occupied Korea north of the 38th parallel and supervised the surrender of Japanese troops in that area. United States forces occupied Korea south of the 38th parallel.

The Russians helped establish a Communist government in their region of Korea and blocked every effort to unite North and South Korea. The Soviet Union also furnished arms and technical aid to North Korea. Meanwhile, elections were held in South Korea, and the Republic of Korea was established for this region in 1948.

The Korean War

On June 25, 1950, North Korean troops invaded South Korea. The United Nations Security Council immediately met in emergency session. (The Soviet Union was not present, because the Russian delegate had "walked out" earlier as a protest against the Security Council's refusal to permit Communist China to join the United Nations.) The Security Council condemned North Korea as an aggressor, called for the "immediate cessation of hostilities," and demanded that North Korean troops withdraw from South Korea.

The North Koreans refused to obey. The Security Council therefore called upon all members of the United Nations to take collective action. President Truman immediately ordered United States air, naval, and land forces to aid the South Koreans. Eventually over fifty nations sent troops, ships, or equipment for the United Nations forces. In July 1950, General Douglas MacArthur was made commander of the United Nations troops in Korea. North Korea had penetrated deeply into South Korea; but MacArthur's army soon recaptured Seoul, capital of South Korea, and began driving the North Korean forces back. On October 7 United Nations soldiers crossed the 38th parallel. North Korean troops were forced to retreat to the Yalu River on the border of Manchuria.

On November 26, some 200,000 Chinese Communist troops—calling themselves "volunteers"— crossed the Yalu to join the North Koreans in the fight against the United Nations troops. On February 1, 1951, the General Assembly declared the Chinese Communists to be the aggressors.

General MacArthur wanted to strike at Chinese bases in Manchuria. Many government leaders were afraid that this would lead to a world war. When General MacArthur continued to oppose the decision to limit military action to Korea, President Truman dismissed him from his command in Korea (April 1951).

In July 1951, negotiations between Chinese, North Korean, and U.N. representatives began. They dragged on for two years with periodic outbreaks of fighting. Finally, on July 27, 1953, the delegates agreed to an armistice, ending a war that had cost the United Nations 400,000 casualties. Korea remained divided into two parts: the Democratic People's Republic in North Korea under the domination of the Communists, and the Republic of Korea in South Korea supported by the United States and other nations.

South Korean Internal Politics

Dr. Syngman Rhee became President of South Korea. As President, Rhee was criticized for undemocratic acts, such as prohibiting freedom of speech, allowing corruption in the government, and introducing police-state measures. Moreover, after massive foreign aid, the South Korean economy still was not recovering.

Rhee was reelected in 1960, but many observers charged that he won by fraud. Student riots forced President Rhee's resignation when he was unable to keep the support of the armed forces. In 1961 a new administration under Park Chung-Hee took over. Some critics said that Park was no less autocratic than Rhee had been. In 1979 Park was assassinated. Choi Kyu Hah became President, and a struggle for power developed involving military and civilian leaders.

The United States kept troops in South Korea, and continued to supply that country with economic aid. The economy recovered and seemed to be flourishing by the late 1970s.

In the summer of 1972, North and South Korea announced that they would work for peaceful reunification by "transcending differences." Little came of that, however, and Korea remained a divided nation.

1. How did Korea become a divided nation?
2. Why did the United Nations send troops to Korea? Describe the course of the war and its outcome.
3. Describe political developments in South Korea.

4. British-controlled Lands Win Their Independence

In Asia after World War II a number of countries still remained under British control. Independence movements which had developed over the years soon led to independence for a number of these countries.

India Struggles for Independence

India's struggle to gain independence from Great Britain was a long one, dating back at least to World War I. Many obstacles blocked the way to a united and independent India. They included the following: 1. Some Indian states were ruled by princes who did not wish to surrender their power to a national government. 2. Hindus and Muslims clashed over religion and other matters. 3. There was a variety of languages and dialects on the subcontinent. 4. The Indian people lacked experience in governing themselves. 5. Many people lived in great poverty. 6. The caste system set up barriers among the people. 7. A number of British leaders wanted to continue Britain's control over India.

In 1919 the British Parliament passed the Government of India Act. According to this act, the British would continue to control the military forces, the system of justice, and several key areas of government. Indian provincial councils would have authority over a number of local matters, such as farming. Indian nationalists continued to demand more self-government. The struggle for independence increased in intensity during the period between the two world wars.

Mahatma Gandhi: Leader of Indian Nationalists

One of the most important leaders of the Indian nationalists was Mahatma (or Great Soul) Gandhi (1869-1948). Gandhi studied law in London. Then he lived in South Africa for twenty years, working to eliminate discrimination against Indians who lived there. He returned to India in 1914, and soon became the leader of millions of Indians seeking independence from Britain.

Gandhi was a gentle, compassionate person who dressed simply in a loincloth and sandals. He preferred spiritual meditation over material wealth. Gandhi advocated an independent and united India. He believed in using non-violent resistance to gain India's independence. Gandhi wanted peace

Many people consider Mahatma Gandhi to have been one of the greatest leaders of modern times. He is shown here with Jawaharlal Nehru, who became the first Prime Minister of the Republic of India.

and goodwill between people of all races and religions. Although Gandhi was a Hindu, he said: "All religions are almost as dear to me as my Hinduism. My veneration for other faiths is the same as for my own faith." He also advocated the abolition of untouchability.

India Becomes a Republic

As a result of the efforts of Gandhi and other Indian leaders, the Government of India Act of 1935 was enacted. It organized India as a federation of governors' provinces and Indian states governed by their own princes. The Indian people in the governors' provinces were allowed to help elect the members of provincial legislatures. A two-house federal legislature was established, representing both the governors' provinces and the Indian states. The act also provided that a viceroy, appointed by the British monarch, would serve as head of the country.

Hostility between the Hindus and Muslims continued during World War II. Mohammed Ali Jinnah, a Muslim leader, demanded that the Muslims be permitted to establish a separate state in India. Most of the Hindus opposed this plan.

On August 15, 1947, the Indian Independence Act ended Britain's control of India. Two dominions within the British Commonwealth were established: India, dominated by the Hindus; and Pakistan, dominated by the Muslims. (See the map on page 593.)

On January 26, 1950, India was proclaimed a sovereign democratic republic, but it remained in the Commonwealth of Nations. Pandit Jawaharlal Nehru became the first Prime Minister.

Pakistan Emerges as a Nation

Pakistan had been set up to include the largest possible number of Muslims. As a result, the country consisted of two areas—East and West Pakistan—separated by a thousand miles of territory lying in India. Millions of Muslims fled from India to Pakistan, while millions of Hindus moved from Pakistan to India.

Bitter clashes broke out between the two groups. Thousands of people were killed. Even Gandhi's call for peace did not succeed. On January 30, 1948, a Hindu fanatic assassinated him. This had a sobering effect on both Hindus and Muslims.

A new constitution changed Pakistan's status from that of dominion to a republic in March 1956. Like India, Pakistan remained a member of the Commonwealth. In 1958, General Ayub Khan took control of Pakistan and assumed most powers of government. He became President, and elections in 1960 and in 1965 confirmed his authority.

Kashmir Is a Source of Tension

The state of Kashmir continued to be a focal point for clashes between India and Pakistan. Its ruling Hindu maharaja wanted to turn Kashmir over to India in 1947. However, Pakistan claimed the right to possess the state on the ground that 85 percent of the people there were Muslims. Forces from both India and Pakistan invaded Kashmir and occupied parts of it.

In April 1948, the Security Council proposed a *plebiscite* for the region—that is, a vote to permit the people of Kashmir to decide which country they wished to join. The plebiscite was never held. In 1957, India formally took possession of the part of Kashmir that Indian forces had occupied. Inasmuch as this constituted two-thirds of Kashmir, tension between India and Pakistan remained high.

The Nehru Government

Meanwhile, the government of India under Prime Minister Jawaharlal Nehru attacked its numerous political, economic, and social problems. It needed to raise living standards among millions of people in India. Acute poverty and hunger were widespread. In the early 1950s, the average amount that nonagricultural workers earned was about $4 a week. Newspapers reported that more than 150,000 people were sleeping at night on Bombay sidewalks. The rapid increase of India's population made it extremely difficult to provide the people with sufficient food, decent housing, and other needs.

Under Nehru and other leaders, the Indian government established a socialistic economy in areas where it might help raise living standards, and took steps to develop industry and modern technology. The government also strengthened the system of education.

In the fall of 1962, following border clashes, Communist China invaded northern India. In November, China ordered a cease-fire, with no settlement on the territory involved.

Former Prime Minister Indira Gandhi campaigning in 1979. In 1980 she was again elected the Prime Minister of India.

Nehru died of a heart attack in May 1964, and Lal Bahadur Shastri succeeded him in office. Following Shastri's death in 1966, Nehru's daughter, Indira Gandhi, became head of the powerful Congress Party and India's first woman Prime Minister. The widow of a lawyer, she was no relation to Mahatma Gandhi.

The Indira Gandhi Regime

Economic discontent, food shortages, labor strikes, and rioting marked India of the early 1970s. In an effort to maintain order, Prime Minister Indira Gandhi took stern action, having strikers arrested, dismissed from their jobs, and evicted from company-owned houses in which they lived. She also tried to control prices. In addition, she curtailed freedom of the press and postponed elections scheduled for the spring of 1976 for one year. The Prime Minister also had political opponents thrown in jail. Her critics charged that by her actions she had dealt Indian democracy a crippling blow. She contended that such actions were necessary.

Indira Gandhi's measures did bring a degree of stability to India, and some groups in India cheered her for it. The state of emergency she had declared lasted until early 1977, when political prisoners were released and press censorship ended. The Prime Minister then scheduled elections.

Resentment and opposition toward Indira Gandhi had grown widespread and intense. The elections held in March 1977 toppled her and her party from power. She lost not only the prime ministership, but her seat in parliament as well.

A coalition of opposition parties organized a majority in the parliament, and Morarji Desai became Prime Minister. In the summer of 1979, a parliamentary vote of "no confidence" removed him from office. A new coalition was formed under Prime Minister Charan Singh. Then in 1980 Indira Gandhi was elected again as Prime Minister.

Bangladesh

In March 1971, dissatisfaction with the policies of the Pakistani government, located in West Pakistan, led to rebellion in East Pakistan. Inhabitants there raised the new flag of Bangladesh and showed their determination to obtain self-rule. A few days later, civil war broke out in East Pakistan as troops from Pakistan's central government tried to crush the people's attempt to gain independence. India sympathized with East Pakistani efforts and border fighting soon broke out between India and the central government of Pakistan.

In a two-week, full-scale war in December 1971, India defeated the Pakistani forces decisively with the aid of Bangladesh guerrillas. Bangladesh became a new and independent nation.

Pakistan's failure to hold the east section of the country toppled President Yahya Khan, who succeeded Ayub Khan in 1969. Zulfikar Ali Bhutto, head of the Pakistan People's Party, became President of Pakistan. His chief prewar rival, Sheik Mujibur Rahman, became Bangladesh's first President. Rahman was assassinated in August 1975, and Major General Ziaur Rahman, army chief of staff, took control of the government. He became President of Bangladesh in April 1977.

Bhutto also ran into trouble. During his regime the Pakistani government took control of a number of industries, introduced a land reform program, and nationalized a number of banks. However, Bhutto accumulated enemies, and his opponents charged that he had rigged the elections which returned him and his party to power in 1977. Bhutto finally agreed to hold new elections, but before this occurred the army stepped in to restore order to strife-torn Pakistan and remove Bhutto from office. He later was arrested for complicity in a murder. Found guilty, Bhutto was executed in 1979.

Burma

Burma, which had once been a powerful kingdom, borders on India, Thailand, and China. The British made Burma a part of their colony of India in 1886. In 1937 Burma was separated from British India and given some powers of self-government. On January 4, 1948, Burma became a fully independent country. The new republic was governed by a Prime Minister and a two-house legislature. U Nu became Burma's first Prime Minister and held this position until 1958.

During his long period in office, U Nu worked to establish peace and stability. He put down revolts by the Karens, a minority group seeking to set up a separate state, and he introduced a reform program by which land was given to poor farmers. He also tried to check the influence of Burmese Communists and supported the development of Burma as a partly socialist state.

In 1958, a political dispute and other problems caused serious tension and instability. The growing power of the Communists worried many Burmese. They feared that the Communists might try to seize control of the government. To block such a move, General Ne Win, with the approval of U Nu, formed a new military government to restore order. He checked inflation, lowered living costs, and crushed groups challenging the government. Then he returned the government to civilian control. New elections in 1960 returned U Nu and his asso-

ciates to office, but two years later General Ne Win once again returned to power. In 1970 the government began to write a constitution that made Burma a socialist republic. It went into effect in 1974, and Ne Win became President.

Sri Lanka

Sri Lanka, an island off the southeastern tip of India, had, as Ceylon, been a colonial possession of Britain. It was the world's principal exporter of cinnamon and fourth largest exporter of rubber. On February 4, 1948, Ceylon became a dominion.

The island's government faced many difficult domestic problems from 1950 on. There were clashes between the Sinhalese and the Tamils, two ethnic-religious groups. In September 1959, internal turmoil resulted in the assassination of Prime Minister S. W. R. D. Bandaranaike, who had taken office in 1956. In new elections, the Freedom Party, led by Bandaranaike's widow, Sirimavo, was victorious. She became the world's first woman Prime Minister.

The government expropriated oil companies and nationalized other industries. In 1965 the government agreed to compensate British and United States companies for their property.

On May 22, 1972, what had until then been known as Ceylon became the independent socialist Republic of Sri Lanka. In the 1977 election Junius Richard Jayewardene defeated Sirimavo Bandaranaike. He became President in 1978, and his position increased in power.

Federation of Malaysia and Singapore

On August 31, 1957, the Federation of Malaysia, another former British colony, became a dominion. This strategically important country faced many domestic and foreign problems. Among the domestic problems was the hostility between the Malays and the Chinese. The latter suffered much discrimination.

Singapore, the island off the tip of the Malaysian peninsula and also a British colony, became independent in 1959. In 1963 it joined the new Federation of Malaysia, which consisted of the states of Malaya, Singapore, and Sarawak and Sabah on the island of Borneo. President Sukarno of Indonesia considered Malaysia a threat to his nation, and Britain had to defend Malaysia against guerrilla attacks.

Singapore was compelled to withdraw from the Federation and became an independent nation in 1965. After Sukarno's removal from the presidency of Indonesia in 1967, relations between that nation and Malaysia improved. In the 1970s Malaysia tried to lessen the frictions between ethnic groups.

Check on Your Reading

1. What obstacles blocked the road to India's independence?
2. How and why was India divided?
3. How and why did Bangladesh come into being?
4. Describe developments in Burma, Sri Lanka, and the Federation of Malaysia.

---

5. Other Asian Nations Obtain Independence

Independence movements in Asia were widespread. They affected the Philippines, Indonesia, and what had been known as French Indochina.

The Republic of the Philippines

Under the Tydings-McDuffie Act of 1934, the United States had promised the Philippines independence. On July 4, 1946, the Republic of the Philippines was established. Manuel Roxas became the first President. Ramón Magsaysay was President from 1953 to 1957.

The Philippines included many islands and a population of more than 42 million, with a large Muslim minority. The redistribution of land to the small farmer was a vital need, but the new government did not move quickly enough on this issue. As a consequence, a Communist-led group called the Hukbalahaps seized estates of wealthy absentee landlords and distributed them among the poor farmers. The Huks also conducted guerrilla warfare against the government, and their efforts received support from some of the population.

Using force, and promising land reform, the government put down the Huk rebellion in the 1950s. However, insufficient reform was carried out, which sparked another rebellion. Guerrilla fighting continued sporadically for a number of years.

Charges of fraud and corruption marked elections during the early years of nationhood. Despite this, the presidency changed hands every four years. Ferdinand E. Marcos won the presidency in 1965. He was reelected in 1969 and faced a Muslim rebellion aimed at gaining Muslim autonomy in the southern Philippine provinces. Marcos declared martial law in 1972. In 1973 he proclaimed the ratification of a new constitution that gave him great power for an unlimited period of time. He soon was accused of imprisoning his opponents and violating political and civil rights.

In 1977, Marcos relaxed his authoritarian rule somewhat. He allowed elections for a legislature, but kept the right to override its decisions. His opponents called Marcos dictatorial, but as the 1970s ended he remained in power, aided by his chief deputy, his wife Imelda.

Indonesia Wins Independence

During World War II, Japan had occupied the Dutch East Indies, which had been ruled by the Netherlands for four and one-half centuries. After the war, the people of Indonesia demanded freedom from Dutch rule. Although the Dutch government promised eventual self-government, Indonesian patriots such as Sukarno, who had worked against Dutch rule for many years, insisted on immediate independence. Fighting broke out, and the United Nations intervened.

In 1949, the Dutch and the Indonesians agreed to form a Netherlands-Indonesian Union. The Republic of the United States of Indonesia came into existence with Sukarno (1901-1970) as its first President.

On August 15, 1950, the new republic merged with other Indonesian territory, and the country took the name of the Republic of Indonesia. On August 11, 1954, Dutch and Indonesian representatives agreed to dissolve the Netherlands-Indonesian Union.

The Course of Events in the New Republic

Indonesia had a population of nearly 100 million people, mostly Muslims. It was rich in such resources as oil, bauxite ores, copra, rubber, and tin. The new Indonesian government declared that it would be guided by the *Pantjasila,* or five principles. These were belief in God, humanitarianism, nationalism, democracy, and social justice. However, the new nation faced severe problems in producing and distributing its raw materials and in uniting a country that consisted of 3,000 islands scattered between Asia and Australia.

Farmers could not produce sufficient food. Many parts of the country lacked basic industries. When Indonesia achieved its independence, less than 5 percent of the people could read and write. There was only one doctor for every 65,000 persons.

In 1957 Sukarno introduced what he called "guided democracy." This was a policy by which majority rule was set aside and a coalition government of Communist and non-Communist representatives was formed. Sukarno and a national advisory council made all decisions.

In January 1965 Indonesia withdrew from the UN in protest against the election of Malaysia to the Security Council. Malaysia and Indonesia had had numerous disputes. Nineteen months later, Indonesia rejoined the United Nations. The country also established closer relations with Communist China, and seized American-owned private business property and United States Information Service libraries in Indonesia.

In September 1965, Indonesia was disrupted by a revolt influenced by Communists. Powerful Indonesian leaders charged that Sukarno had approved of this uprising as a means of eliminating military officers who opposed Communist influence and programs. When the military suppressed the rebellion, most of Sukarno's authority was taken from him. Thousands of Communists were killed in the following months.

All governmental powers were withdrawn from Sukarno in 1967, and General Suharto, an anti-Communist leader, was elected President for a five-year term the next year. He was reelected in 1973 and 1978.

The Struggle for Independence in Indochina

In Indochina the French gained control in the nineteenth century of lands that today make up most of Vietnam, Cambodia, and Laos. The Japanese drove the French from Indochina during World War II, and Vietnam and Cambodia declared themselves independent from France. When the war ended, the French sought to reestablish control there. A number of local groups, one led by Ho Chi Minh, a Communist, strongly opposed this.

In 1946, the French resorted to armed force to regain control of Indochina. They were unable to do so. Communist and nationalist armies finally

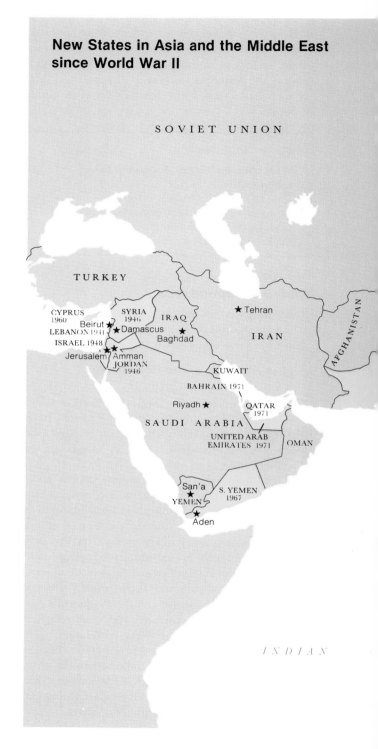

New States in Asia and the Middle East since World War II

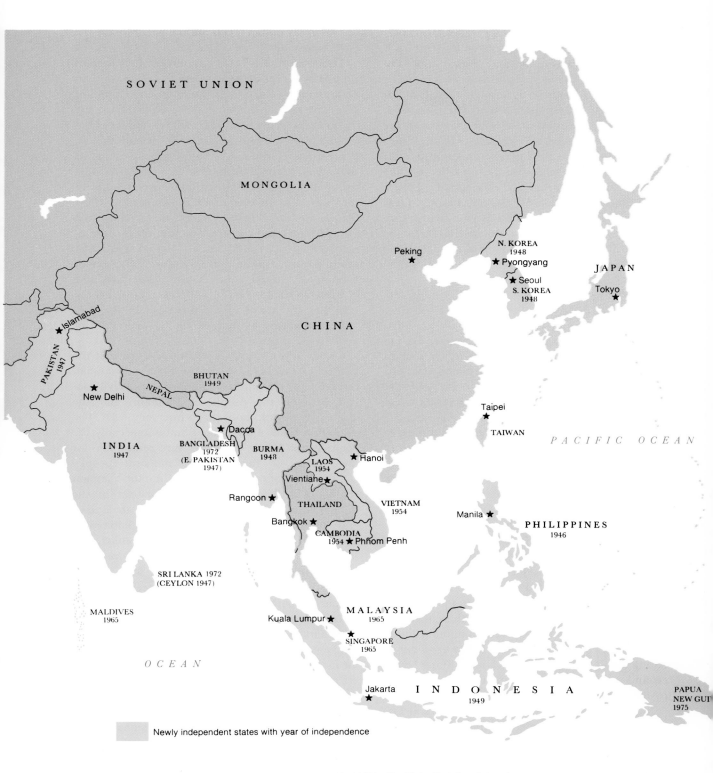

SOVIET UNION

MONGOLIA

Peking ★

N. KOREA
1948
★ Pyongyang

JAPAN

★ Seoul
S. KOREA
1948

Tokyo ★

CHINA

Islamabad ★

PAKISTAN
1947

New Delhi ★

NEPAL

BHUTAN
1949

Dacca ★

INDIA
1947

BANGLADESH
1972
(E. PAKISTAN
1947)

BURMA
1948

LAOS
1954

Vientiane ★

★ Hanoi

Rangoon ★

THAILAND

VIETNAM
1954

Bangkok ★

CAMBODIA
1954 ★ Phnom Penh

Taipei ★

TAIWAN

PACIFIC OCEAN

Manila ★

PHILIPPINES
1946

SRI LANKA 1972
(CEYLON 1947)

MALDIVES
1965

OCEAN

MALAYSIA
1965

Kuala Lumpur ★

★
SINGAPORE
1965

Jakarta ★

INDONESIA

1949

PAPUA
NEW GUI
1975

Newly independent states with year of independence

*Many nations in Asia won their independence after World War II. Note that the date when a
state gained its independence is given on the map.*

593

won the war, and the French fortress of Dien Bien Phu was captured in May 1954.

A conference in Geneva made several important arrangements. Vietnam was divided temporarily, and two governments were formed. North of the 17th parallel, Communists under Ho Chi Minh controlled the government of what they called the Democratic Republic of Vietnam, or North Vietnam. South of the 17th parallel, non-Communist groups established what was later to become the Republic of Vietnam, or South Vietnam. France also granted independence to Cambodia and Laos.

Following the overthrow of French power, it had been agreed that Vietnam would eventually be united. But the key question was: Under which government?

An Undeclared War

Beginning in 1957, a Communist-led rebellion developed in South Vietnam. The South Vietnamese Communist rebels became known as the *Vietcong*, and North Vietnam lent them aid, including troops. China and the Soviet Union also supported the Vietcong. Thirty-two other countries provided the opponents of the rebels with technical and economic aid.

The United States government interpreted events in South Vietnam as another example of Communist conspiracy and attempts at world domination. The United States furnished the South Vietnamese government with military advisors, economic aid, and weapons; and gradually the United States became deeply involved in the war.

By the mid-1960s the conflict in Vietnam had become an undeclared war involving the United States, South Vietnam, North Vietnam, and other countries. The United States sent additional troops to Vietnam until more than 450,000 were involved there. United States bombers regularly raided North Vietnamese cities and military installations. The war eventually spilled over to neighboring Laos and Cambodia, as United States bombers and troops sought out Communist troops taking refuge there.

Many of the people of the United States at first supported their government's efforts in Vietnam. However, as the war dragged on and as United States casualties increased, more people began to question the wisdom and justice of United States involvement. The war in Vietnam became a sub-

ject of great debate both within and outside the government.

Those who supported continued involvement presented the following reasons: 1. The war was an attempt by Communist forces to seize control of Vietnam, and the United States was justified in trying to check them. 2. The military actions of the United States were necessary to defend the independence of South Vietnam. 3. The entry of the United States into the Vietnam conflict was legal on the basis of United States defensive agreements with South Vietnam and membership in the Southeast Asia Treaty Organization, which the United States had promoted as part of its containment policy. 4. The Vietnam War was part of an international struggle. If Vietnam came under Communist control, other countries like Laos and Cambodia would too. 5. Peace should be the goal, but any act of appeasement toward the enemy, comparable to that of the Munich Pact of 1938, was dangerous.

On the other hand, those who believed that the United States should withdraw from the war had the following reasons: 1. The war was a civil conflict between the people of Vietnam, and the United States had no right to intervene. 2. The military actions of the United States, especially the bombings of North Vietnam, were responsible for the deaths of thousands of innocent people. 3. The entry of the United States into the Vietnam conflict was illegal because the Charter of the United Nations barred its members from the unilateral use of force without UN authorization. 4. The Vietnam War was a national conflict, and should not be viewed as part of an international conspiracy. The United States was supporting a regime in Saigon that did not truly represent the people of South Vietnam. 5. The United States should withdraw so peace could be established by compromise and negotiation.

Eventually, the war became extremely unpopular in the United States. Events such as the massacre of civilians at Mylai, South Vietnam; reports of thousands of homeless children wandering hopelessly about the countryside; and sights of starving old men and women clawing wildly for a handful of rice shocked many people. A number of students and others in the United States and throughout the world demonstrated, protested, and demanded an end to the war.

Vietnamese refugees arrive in Hong Kong on board a freighter in December 1979.

In 1969 President Richard M. Nixon began a new Vietnam policy. He started the withdrawal of American troops and what he called the "Vietnamization" of the war. This meant turning more and more of the fighting over to the South Vietnamese. By the summer of 1972 the number of United States troops in Vietnam had been substantially reduced.

Meanwhile, the leaders of the Vietcong and North Vietnam introduced economic and social changes in the areas they controlled. In South Vietnam, men and women from South Vietnam, the United States, and their allies carried out programs to immunize millions of Vietnamese against cholera and smallpox, to spray buildings against malaria-bearing mosquitoes, to build new schools, to irrigate land, and to construct dams.

Finally, on January 27, 1973, South Vietnam, North Vietnam, the United States, and the Vietcong accepted an agreement to end the fighting. The United States soon removed its last combat troops. The future of South Vietnam was to be decided by the Vietnamese themselves.

The fighting continued between North and South Vietnamese forces, however, with the North Vietnamese steadily building military pressure. In the spring of 1975 they captured Saigon, and the South Vietnamese government surrendered.

In 1976, North and South Vietnam were unified as the Socialist Republic of Vietnam, with the capital at Hanoi, in the north. Saigon was renamed Ho Chi Minh City.

Continuing Struggles in Southeast Asia

China had aided North Vietnam, but after the war relations between Vietnam and China became less friendly. There were many Chinese living in Vietnam whose families had lived there for several generations. The Vietnamese, who had been enemies of China in the past, now began driving these Chinese from Vietnam. In 1978 China staged a successful but short-lived invasion of Vietnam "to teach a lesson" to that nation's government.

In addition, thousands of Vietnamese in the southern part of the country fled or were driven out. These refugees became "boat people," putting to sea in whatever vessels they could find. Many of them drifted aimlessly for weeks trying to find a country that would take them. The United States and other countries took in some of them.

Laos and Cambodia also came under Communist control as a result of successful Communist-led rebellions in those countries. Then Vietnamese forces ousted the Chinese-backed Pol Pot regime; and, in 1979, installed the Heng Samrin government in Cambodia. As a result of conflict between opposing forces within the country, death by starvation faced many Cambodians. Each side tried to weaken the other by depriving its enemy's people of food. As one military observer said, "If you can't eat, you can't fight." "We have in the making . . . another 'Holocaust,' " said Reverend Theodore N. Hesburgh, President of Notre Dame University. Efforts were made by the United States and others to help wartorn Cambodia.

Thailand

Thailand, an ancient kingdom of Southeast Asia, had long been ruled by a monarch. Its kings managed to play European powers off against each other and avoid becoming a European colony. In 1941, Japan invaded Thailand, and the Thais signed a Treaty of Alliance with Japan.

In the field of government, in 1968 a new constitution limited the king's power and brought a measure of popular participation in government. In November 1971 a military-civilian group led by General Thanom Kittikachorn took over the government. Protesting oppressive government measures, civilians led by students rioted in 1973 and forced the Kittikachorn government out. Free elections were held in January 1975 and a coalition gained control. In 1980 political and social tensions continued to trouble the government.

Check on Your Reading

1. Describe the course of events in the Philippines following independence.
2. What problems did Indonesia face after World War II?
3. What were the opposing positions in the great debate over United States involvement in Vietnam?

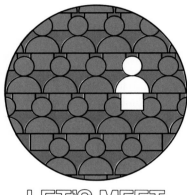

LET'S MEET THE PEOPLE

Yu-lan and Chang

"In looking for a marriage prospect, true feelings should be built on mutual labor." These words were told to Yu-lan when she came from the city to work on a co-operative farm in Communist China.

Yu-lan remembered those words whenever she looked at the peasant Chang. He was good-natured, frank, outspoken, and a member of the Young Communist League. Most important of all, Chang loved to work hard. Yu-lan believed that this was the reason why she was "drawn by some unknown emotional force closer and closer to Chang." Her dictatorial rulers had led her to believe this.

Later, when Yu-lan "appeared lost in handling harvesting work," Chang showed her how to do her farm work properly. He also helped her to do the heavy manual labor that was expected of all women on the co-operative farm. They labored together on the land.

Yu-lan now thought more and more about her feelings for Chang. "These feelings have been built up through mutual labor," she told herself. Then one night Chang said to Yu-lan:

"Do you have any opinions about me, Yu-lan?"

"I'm very much satisfied with you. I have made up my mind," answered Yu-lan.

"Since you have no bad opinion, let us get married," said Chang.

Yu-lan smiled and nodded her head. Thus it was that in early December Yu-lan and Chang were married. Immediately after the wedding, a friend of Yu-lan approached her and asked: "Why did you fall in love with Chang?"

"I am in love with *the land*," answered Yu-lan, blushing.

Her friend laughed for a moment; then she said:

"You have not said it fully. Not only have you been in love with the village land—but also with *a man* in the village!"

The above sketch is based on information in an article in the *Shansi Jih Pao (Shansi Daily News),* excerpts of which appeared in *The New York Times Magazine,* June 8, 1958.

CHAPTER REVIEW

Think and Discuss

1. What problems did most of the nations of Asia have in common after World War II?
2. Do you think a country has to "modernize" in order to achieve stability and survive as a nation in today's world? Explain your answer.
3. What are the advantages and the disadvantages of a "Five-Year Plan"?
4. What areas of life in a country do dictatorships concentrate on controlling? Why?
5. What problems might be encountered in trying to impose democracy suddenly upon a country without considerable democratic experience?
6. What factors can you find that favored the spread of Communist power in Asia? What factors can you find that opposed the spread of Communist power in Asia?

Past and Present

1. Contrast the world of the eighteenth century, in which the United States gained independence, with the world in which a number of Asian nations have recently gained their independence.
2. Compare the United States participation in Asian affairs after World War I with its participation after World War II.
3. Compare the principles of communism as developed by Karl Marx with communism as it is practiced today in one country in Asia with a Communist government.
4. In 1979 foreign language publications from the People's Republic of China began using a new system of putting Chinese words into the Roman alphabet. This system is called *Pinyn*. It is to take the place of the old system which is used in this Text and in many other books. Here are three examples of the differences between the two systems:

Old System	Pinyin
Mao Tse-tung	Mao Zedong
Peking	Beijing
Chou En-lai	Zhou Enlai

A number of newspapers and magazines in the United States may soon be using Pinyin. What other examples can you think of that indicate the constantly changing nature of languages?

Activities

1. Debate: Resolved, that a new country unprepared for independence has to have a period of autocratic rule before it can become a true democracy.
2. Write a 750-word biography of an individual who was an important leader in Asia after World War II. Be prepared to explain why you chose that person.
3. Read newspapers and magazines for two weeks to learn what is happening today in a country in Southeast Asia, such as Cambodia, Vietnam, Laos, or Thailand. Write a report on your findings. Give special attention to how events in one country affect events in another country.

Dynamic Changes in the Middle East and Africa

KEYNOTE

Political scientist Don Peretz wrote: "The Middle East is a Western or European concept, rather than one that the people of the region apply to themselves. Middle Easterners do not consider themselves either 'middle' or 'eastern.' . . . The Middle East is not a static concept, but an expanding one."

Similarly, the term "Africa" is often oversimplified by many non-Africans, particularly when they think of Africa as a single land mass. Actually, the peoples of Africa live in a world of diversity and constant movement.

The great changes that occurred in the Middle East and Africa in the twentieth century made clear the dynamic qualities of both areas. They were changes that affected every part of the world.

Nairobi, Kenya, one of the large modern cities of Africa.

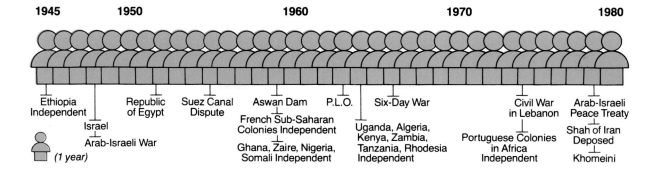

Ethiopia Independent

Israel

Arab-Israeli War

(1 year)

Republic of Egypt

Suez Canal Dispute

Aswan Dam

French Sub-Saharan Colonies Independent

Ghana, Zaire, Nigeria, Somali Independent

P.L.O.

Uganda, Algeria, Kenya, Zambia, Tanzania, Rhodesia Independent

Six-Day War

Civil War in Lebanon

Portuguese Colonies in Africa Independent

Arab-Israeli Peace Treaty

Shah of Iran Deposed

Khomeini

1. Israel Is Established as a Republic

The region known as the Middle East is generally said to consist of Egypt, Iran, Iraq, Israel, Jordan, Kuwait, Lebanon, Saudi Arabia, Syria, Turkey, United Arab Emirates, Yemen (Aden), Yemen (Sana), Oman, Qatar, Bahrain, and Cyprus. There is great diversity in peoples, geography, cultures, ethnic groups, and languages.

Over 180 million people live in the Middle East, roughly 80 percent of them in rural areas. Most of the people practice the religion of Islam. Other religions include Christianity and Judaism.

The Middle East in the twentieth century was an area of many problems. Some of these were: low standards of living for rising populations; hostility between Arab states and Israel, nationalistic tensions between countries; inadequate water supply in some regions; and lack of industrialization.

The Middle East also was an area of great potentialities. Its oil became a vital necessity to other lands, its geographic position was strategically important, and the creativeness of its cultures continued to affect the ways of life of millions of people throughout the world.

The Dream of Rebuilding the Jewish Homeland

After their dispersal centuries ago, many Jews continued to believe that one day their people would reestablish a homeland in Palestine. They declared that they had a right to such a homeland because their ancestors had inhabited Palestine in ancient times, and because there was a need for a land where Jews could assemble, live without persecution, and preserve their culture. The Jews in the Middle East were supported in their demands by Zionists throughout the world. *Zionists* were people of Jewish and other faiths who, according to the first Zionist Congress, "strive to create for the Jewish people a home in Palestine secured by public law." The Zionist movement began as early as 1897, and it was spearheaded by a Viennese journalist, Theodor Herzl.

On the other hand, the Arabs bitterly opposed Zionism and protested that Palestine had been artificially separated from Syria. They pointed out that Arabs had occupied Palestine for hundreds of years and made up the overwhelming majority of its population. They claimed that the establishment of a Jewish state would deprive Arabs of their land and interfere with the geographic and cultural unity of the Arab world.

The Balfour Declaration

Palestine had been part of the Ottoman Empire from the 1600s until World War I. During that war, British forces captured Jerusalem from the Turks. On November 2, 1917, the British government issued the *Balfour Declaration,* which stated:

His Majesty's Government view with favour the establishment in Palestine of a national home for the Jewish people, and will use their best endeavors to facilitate the achievement of this object, it being clearly understood that nothing shall be done which may prejudice the civil and religious rights of existing non-Jewish communities in Palestine. . . .

Many Jews considered that the Balfour Declaration was a British promise that Palestine would become a national homeland for the Jews. Arabs, however, claimed that Palestine had been theirs for centuries, and they vowed that the area would never come under Jewish control.

In 1923, Palestine became a British mandate under the League of Nations.

599

The State of Israel Is Created

Jewish migration to Palestine increased greatly, particularly during the period when Nazi Germany was persecuting the Jews. Between 1919 and 1948, over 450,000 Jews emigrated to Palestine. The Arabs protested that the newcomers were gradually taking over their country.

After World War II, the British turned over the problem of Palestine to the United Nations. In November 1947, the General Assembly recommended that Palestine be partitioned into an Arab state and a Jewish state, which were to be politically independent but were to work together in economic matters. The city of Jerusalem was to be internationalized.

Jewish leaders accepted this recommendation. In May 1948, the British ended their mandate and the Jews proclaimed the establishment of the state of Israel. Chaim Weizmann became the first President of Israel. David Ben-Gurion (1886–1973), a stocky, dynamic leader, was chosen Prime Minister of the new state.

Arab-Israeli War

The existence of the state of Israel was not recognized by the Arabs. Arab forces from Egypt, Iraq, Lebanon, Syria, and what is now Jordan attacked the Israelis.

The invading Arab troops were defeated in the Arab-Israeli War, and the United Nations worked to bring about a truce. A final cease-fire went into effect on January 7, 1949.

As a result of the Arab-Israeli War and various agreements, the following changes took place in Palestine: 1. Israel increased its territory by about 50 percent. 2. A new state of Jordan was formed out of Transjordan (the part of Palestine lying east of the Jordan River) and the Judean hills territories that were occupied by the Arab Legion during the war. Hussein, a relative of the King of Iraq, became King of the state of Jordan. 3. Jerusalem remained divided into two parts: the New City was in Israel and the Old City was in Jordan. 4. The United Nations turned over the Gaza Strip, an area 25 miles long and five miles wide along the Mediterranean Sea, to the Egyptian army to administer.

Arab Refugees and a Serious Problem

Many problems remained to mar the relations between Israel and the Arab states. One of the most serious involved the future of the 900,000 Arab refugees who had fled from Palestine. These refugees were living in temporary quarters in the Gaza Strip, Jordan, Lebanon, Syria, and Iraq.

Arab leaders claimed that the Arab refugees had the right to return to their homes in Palestine. The Israelis disagreed and declared that the Arab refugees should be resettled in Iraq and Syria.

The United Nations Relief and Works Agency for Palestine Refugees (UNRWA) attempted to provide housing and food for the Arab refugees. Meanwhile, there continued what novelist Martha Gellhorn called the "non-peace, non-war exercise" between Arabs and Israelis.

Check on Your Reading

1. Why did the Jews want to establish a homeland in Palestine? Why did the Arabs oppose this plan?
2. What were the results of the Arab-Israeli War?
3. What were the positions taken by the Arabs and by the Israelis concerning the Arab refugees?

---

2. Egypt Becomes a Republic

Egypt in the post-World War II period was a troubled land. An increasing number of Egyptians became dissatisfied with the corruption and inefficiency of King Farouk's government. They were disturbed by the social and economic inequalities in the country, and by the influence of the British in Egypt's affairs. As one Egyptian reformer, Gamal Abdel Nasser, said, "The problem was to restore human dignity in Egypt."

In the summer of 1952, Major General Mohammed Naguib and a group of army officers revolted against King Farouk and forced him to abdicate. On June 18, 1953, Egypt was proclaimed a republic. Lieutenant Colonel Gamal Abdel Nasser, one of the rebel leaders, soon became the spokesperson for the Egyptian nationalists. On April 18, 1954, he replaced Naguib as Prime Minister of Egypt. Later Nasser was also chosen President.

Egypt and the Suez Canal

After Farouk had been overthrown, British troops still remained in Egypt in control of the Suez Canal. Nasser was determined to force them out, and in October 1954 Great Britain agreed to remove its troops from the Suez Canal Zone. The last British troops withdrew in June 1956. Great Britain reserved the right to reoccupy the base at

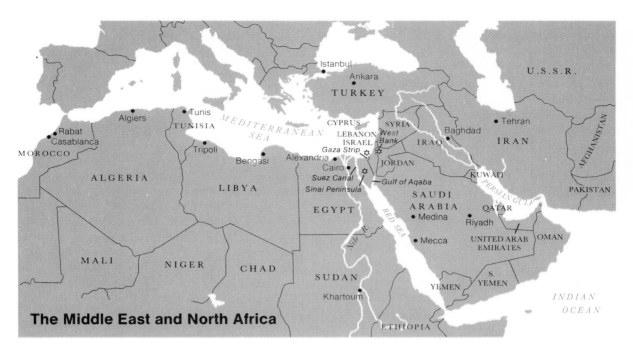

The Middle East and North Africa

✿ Areas of Arab-Isi

In the Middle East and North Africa are many Muslim states and the Jewish state of Israel. This strategic region is troubled with many problems and tensions that will vitally affect world affairs in the 1980s.

Suez if Egypt, Turkey, or any of the Arab states were attacked. Egypt, however, was free at last from foreign control.

Meanwhile, Nasser tried to build up Egypt's military and economic strength. In 1955, when Western nations did not agree to provide Egypt with arms, Nasser made a deal with Czechoslovakia. Czechoslovakia agreed to provide planes, tanks, and artillery in exchange for cotton.

Earlier, the United States and Great Britain had offered to provide $200 million in financial assistance to help Egypt build the High Dam at Aswan. It was hoped that the project would increase Egypt's agricultural production 50 percent by supplying irrigation water and reclaiming two million acres of land. It also was to furnish electricity for industries. The Czechoslovakian arms deal disturbed the United States and Great Britain. Therefore, they withdrew their offer to help finance the Aswan Dam. On July 26, 1956, Nasser retaliated by proclaiming the Egyptian seizure and nationalization of the Suez Canal.

The Suez Canal had been under the control of the Suez Canal Company, most of whose stockhold-ers were British and French. Nasser declared that the Canal was now Egypt's property. He said that the toll revenues from the Canal would help finance the Aswan project. Egypt's action led to an international crisis.

Egypt promptly barred Israeli ships from the Canal and interfered with other vessels bound to and from Israel. At the same time, the British and French grew concerned that Nasser might cut off oil coming through the Canal from such sources as Saudi Arabia and Iran.

On October 29, 1956, three months after Egypt nationalized the Suez Canal, Israeli troops invaded Egypt's Sinai Desert. One reason for the attack may have been Israel's determination to destroy Egypt's bases that it claimed were being used as "jumping off" places for attacks against Israel. Great Britain and France issued an ultimatum ordering Egypt and Israel to cease fighting. Israel indicated a willingness to do so, but Egypt ignored the ultimatum. Two days after Israel invaded Egypt, British and French forces based on Cyprus also attacked Egypt. The Egyptians sank ships in the Suez Canal to block passage of vessels.

The United Nations met in emergency session. The United States, the Soviet Union, and other countries voted to demand that Great Britain, France, and Israel withdraw from Egypt. The three nations withdrew, and a United Nations Emergency Force was sent to patrol the borders between Israel and Egypt.

The Aswan Dam project was then financed and engineered by the Soviet Union. Construction was begun in 1960. The dam was completed in 1970. Gains made by the dam have been threatened, however, by increases in population.

Check on Your Reading

1. How did Egypt become a republic?
2. Why did Egypt seize the Suez Canal? What events followed from that?

---

3. Tensions and Changes Elsewhere in the Middle East

Other countries in the Middle East were faced with serious problems. Tensions and changes affected Iran, Lebanon, Iraq, and Jordan.

Iran Nationalizes Its Oil Fields

Iran, once known as Persia, is a country where most of the people are Muslims but not Arabs. It is important in international affairs in large part because it is a major producer of oil and because its lands border on the Soviet Union.

In 1925, General Reza Pahlavi became hereditary *Shah*, or ruler. He tried to modernize and strengthen the country by introducing modern codes of law, establishing a system of compulsory education, building roads, and abolishing the extraterritorial rights of foreigners.

During World War II, the Allies needed use of the Trans-Iranian Railway. When the Shah refused to permit them to use it, British and Russian troops invaded Iran in 1941. They forced the abdication of the Shah. His twenty-one-year-old son, Mohammed Reza Pahlavi, replaced him as Shah.

Nationalism became an increasingly powerful factor in Iran after World War II. In 1951 nationalist and some Communist workers started strikes in important oil fields of the Anglo-Iranian Oil Company. The largest stockholder in the company was the British government. Strikers claimed that foreigners were making great profits from oil that really belonged to Iranians.

In 1951 the Prime Minister was shot. Dr. Mohammed Mossadegh, a nationalist leader, became the new Prime Minister. His government seized and nationalized the Anglo-Iranian Oil Company's properties. British administrators were ordered to leave the country.

After nationalization, Iran had difficulty selling its oil, and political conditions were very unsettled. In August 1954, British, Dutch, French, and American-owned oil companies signed new contracts with the Iranian government. For twenty-five years plus fifteen optional years, the companies could work the oil fields that formerly were operated by the Anglo-Iranian Oil Company. In return, they would pay Iran royalties equal to 50 percent of their earnings. The Anglo-Iranian Oil Company was to receive $70 million as compensation for its past investment.

Tensions Increase in Lebanon, Iraq, and Jordan

The League of Nations made Lebanon a mandate of France after World War I. In 1941 Lebanon gained its independence. It soon became a crossroads for Middle East trade.

In May 1958, President Chamoun of the Republic of Lebanon proposed a change in the constitution that would enable him to run for a second term. This sparked a revolt. Most of Chamoun's supporters were Christians. Christians made up about 54 percent of the Lebanese population. Most of the rebels were Muslims. Muslims made up about 44 percent of the population. Chamoun claimed that the rebels were receiving arms from the United Arab Republic (Egypt and Syria).

Events in Iraq complicated the situation. In July 1958, an army *coup d'état* placed Abdul Karim Kassem in power, and he established a military regime that was both nationalistic and anti-Western. Communists in Iraq threw their support behind Kassem's government.

President Chamoun considered Kassem's *coup d'état* and other events in Iraq as evidence of a general plan by nationalists to overthrow pro-Western governments in the Middle East. He asked for aid from the United States. On July 14, 1958, American Marines landed in Beirut, Lebanon's capital. President Eisenhower declared that the troops were sent "to encourage the Lebanese Government in defense of Lebanese sovereignty and integrity."

King Hussein of Jordan also requested assistance, and British troops were sent.

The United Nations intervened to restore order in the Middle East. Elections were held in Lebanon in August 1958, and the newly-elected President was able to gain the support of most people. American troops withdrew from Lebanon, and British troops left Jordan.

Middle East Security Measures

In 1955 the *Baghdad Pact* was signed by Great Britain, Iran, Iraq, Turkey, and Pakistan. The Pact was for "mutual security and defense." Iraq withdrew from the Pact four years later. Today the Baghdad Pact is known as the *Central Treaty Organization (CENTO)*. Without being a full member, the United States supports its purposes.

The concern of the United States with Middle East security was stated by President Dwight D. Eisenhower in January 1957. This so-called *Eisenhower Doctrine,* approved by the United States Senate, permitted the use of United States armed forces "to secure and protect the territorial integrity and political independence [of Middle East nations] requesting such aid against overt armed aggression from any nation controlled by international Communism. . . ." The Eisenhower Doctrine was a factor in the decision to send American troops into Lebanon in 1958.

Check on Your Reading

1. Why did the government of Iran nationalize the oil fields? What events followed?
2. What caused the revolt in Lebanon? What were the consequences?
3. What security arrangements involved Middle East nations?

---

4. The Middle East in the 1960s and 1970s

During the 1960s and 1970s, turmoil continued in the Middle East. During this period tensions between Israel and the Arab states increased.

The Six-Day War and Other Conflicts

In May 1967, Gamal Abdel Nasser of Egypt demanded that the United Nations withdraw "the UN Emergency Force in Egypt and the Gaza Strip." United Nations troops had been stationed in the Gaza Strip, where they acted as a buffer between Israelis and Egyptians. They were also in Sharm el Sheikh, where they saw to it that the Gulf of Aqaba was kept open for all ships, including those carrying oil and other vital supplies to the Israeli port of Elath.

United Nations Secretary-General U Thant, accepting the point that UN forces had entered Egyptian territory with the consent of Egypt, complied with Nasser's demand. Then, on May 23, the Egyptians announced a blockade of the Gulf of Aqaba "to vessels flying the Israeli flag and to the ships of any other country carrying strategic goods to Elath." (See map on p. 601.)

War broke out in June 1967, each side charging the other with responsibility for starting hostilities. Egypt, Jordan, Syria, Iraq, Kuwait, Sudan, Tunisia, Morocco, Lebanon, Saudi Arabia, Algeria, and Yemen joined the conflict against Israel. Arab radio stations spoke of a "Holy War," and Israel's 2.7 million people faced over 100 million hostile Arabs surrounding them.

It was a short war, lasting but a few days, but filled with much of the drama and tragedy of longer conflicts. "On to Tel Aviv!" the Arabs shouted in the streets of Cairo. "Soldiers of the Israel Defense Forces, on this day our hopes and security are with you!" answered the Israeli Defense Minister, Moshe Dayan.

Israeli forces could not be stopped. By sudden, coordinated attacks Israel's well-trained air force destroyed a major part of the air power of the Arab states. One military authority declared: "Israel would seem to have won the most outstanding air battle in history." In six days the "blitz" of Israeli planes, tanks, and infantry crushed their opponents and won the war.

As a consequence of this Six-Day War, Israel stopped the Egyptian blockade of the Gulf of Aqaba and occupied the Gaza Strip, much of the Sinai Peninsula, and the West Bank of the Jordan River. The Arabs demanded that Israel give up the land it had occupied in the war. The Israelis insisted that the Arabs recognize the right of Israel to exist as a nation.

Golda Meir, one of Israel's founders, became Prime Minister of Israel in 1969. The following year, upon Nasser's death, Egypt too underwent a change in the head of government. Anwar el-Sadat was elected to succeed Nasser as President.

Prime Minister Begin and President Sadat during Sadat's visit to Israel in 1978.

Following the Six-Day War, the Egyptians, Syrians, and Israelis rebuilt their armed forces. Then, on October 6, 1973, on the Jewish High Holy Day of Yom Kippur, Egypt launched a surprise attack against Israel in the Sinai. At the same time, Syrian forces also invaded Israel.

During the first days of the war the Israelis suffered heavy casualties. However, Israeli forces then went on the offensive in both the north and south and practically cut off the Egyptian Sinai army from its home base. The United Nations was able to arrange a cease-fire to end the war on November 11, 1973. The Israelis still refused to give up any territory they had occupied since 1967 unless agreements could be reached on other important matters.

The Oil Crisis

The relations of the Middle East countries with the rest of the world became crucial in the 1970s. In October 1973, during the war between Arabs and Israelis, Arab oil-producing nations banned oil exports to the United States and to other countries they claimed were supporting Israel. This ban was later lifted.

The brief boycott dramatically revealed Arab economic power. As the nations of the Organiza-

tion of Petroleum Exporting Countries (OPEC)—which included Iran, Iraq, Kuwait, and Saudi Arabia—began oil shipments again, they quadrupled the price of petroleum. The OPEC price increase pushed the cost of gasoline up in Western Europe, the United States, Japan, and elsewhere. Modern industrial nations, which depended on oil for much of the energy used for factories, transportation, and homes, faced crises.

The 1974 OPEC price increase was only the first. Representatives of OPEC met periodically after that to consider further boosts. By the fall of 1979, a barrel of imported oil in the United States cost from $18.50 to $30. This, plus periodic shortages, further raised the price of gasoline and other petroleum products.

Peace between Egypt and Israel?

Arab nations continued to refuse to recognize Israel or to negotiate with that state. Egypt's President Anwar el-Sadat, however, beset by serious domestic problems, sought a permanent peace with Israel. In 1977, in a dramatic gesture, he proposed direct talks between Egypt and Israel to try to work out peace terms. Sadat journeyed to Israel for conferences with Prime Minister Menachem Begin and to address the Israeli legislature, the *Knesset*. Begin later returned the visit by going to Cairo, Egypt.

In September 1978, United States President Jimmy Carter invited Begin and Sadat to meet with him at the presidential retreat at Camp David, in Maryland. The leaders remained there nearly two weeks, with Carter frequently acting as go-between, and negotiated tentative terms of a peace settlement. They discussed arrangements for the withdrawal of Israel from the Sinai, the Gaza Strip, and the West Bank of the Jordan River. It was hoped that this could be done in about five years. Out of the Camp David summit meeting came the promise of a peace treaty between Egypt and Israel.

Negotiating difficulties arose, and President Carter once again stepped in. He met with Begin in Washington, D. C., for several days in March 1979 to discuss peace treaty terms. Carter then personally took Begin's proposals to Sadat, and again moved back and forth between the two leaders as they sought to iron out differences. On March 26, 1979, Israel and Egypt signed a peace treaty in Washington, D. C. Nevertheless, many Arabs refused to accept it or to recognize the right of Israel to exist as a nation.

The Palestinian Issue

Under the treaty terms, Israel agreed to relinquish gradually control of the Sinai Peninsula and the Gaza Strip. The question of Israel's control of the West Bank of the Jordan River remained a vital issue to Palestinian Arabs who wished to have their own homeland. Many of them had become refugees during the wars with Israel. They had been living for years in refugee camps established by the International Red Cross and United Nations agencies.

About a million Palestinians lived in Jordan, while an equal number had sought refuge in countries on the Arabian Peninsula, in Lebanon and Syria, and on the Gaza Strip. Over 700,000 lived on the West Bank, which came under Israeli control during the 1967 war. Arab nations blamed the refugees' plight on Israel.

As the years passed, Palestinian demands for a homeland grew more urgent. They argued that their people had occupied what had become Israel for centuries, and that they had a right to a land of their own. On the other hand, Israelis feared that the establishment of an independent state of Palestinian Arabs next to their borders would threaten their security.

Several Palestinian organizations formed, but most of them accepted the general leadership of the Palestine Liberation Organization (PLO). Established in 1964, it took the position that it represented the Palestinian Arabs. Some members of the PLO engaged in terrorism—assassination, bombing crowded Israeli marketplaces, hijacking airliners, and shooting up airports. Often Israeli groups retaliated.

Israel took the position that it would deal with the Palestinian people, particularly the 700,000 on the Israeli-occupied West Bank, but not with the PLO. Meanwhile the PLO insisted on the establishment of a Palestinian state for these Arabs. The Palestinian issue has remained an obstacle to general peace in the Middle East.

Civil War in Lebanon

The Palestinian issue spilled over into Lebanon, which borders Israel and where about 400,000 Palestinians had taken refuge. Lebanon was unable to control Palestinian guerrilla activity, and there were clashes between Palestinian commandos and Israeli forces. The PLO sometimes used southern Lebanon as a base from which to launch attacks against Israel.

The Palestinian guerrilla actions frightened and angered some Christian groups in Lebanon. In addition, Muslims and other non-Christians wanted more political and economic power in Lebanon. In 1975 civil war broke out in Lebanon between Lebanese Christians and their supporters and Lebanese Muslims and their supporters.

In 1976, in an effort to end the fighting, a Syrian army moved into Lebanon. Most of the fighting was brought to an end, but periodic clashes still occurred. As the 1980s began, Lebanon continued to be a country of unrest.

Events in Iran

In Iran, the Shah continued his father's program of modernization, and a land reform program distributed more land to the people. After 1973 the Shah increased the money spent on schools, hospitals, roads, and factories as a result of additional income from oil. The Shah remained pro-Western.

To many people, however, the Shah ruled with an iron hand. He controlled the press and restricted freedom of speech, assembly, and political activity. His secret police were greatly feared by

Ayatollah Khomeini addresses a crowd of his followers after the overthrow of the Shah of Iran.

his opponents, who charged that the government did not hesitate to kill those who challenged the Shah's power. Iranian prisons held many political prisoners. In addition, the Shah continued to reduce the influence of Islam in Iranian public life. All this stimulated opposition from various groups.

Liberal, religious, and landowning groups joined in opposition to the Shah in 1978. Bloody rioting swept Teheran and other Iranian cities. Much of the activity against the Shah was directed by Ruhollah Khomeini, a powerful *ayatollah,* or religious leader, who had been living in exile in France since 1963. Khomeini encouraged his followers in Iran to stage strikes, especially in oil fields and refineries, and to demonstrate against the high rate of inflation in Iran. On January 17, 1979, the Shah and his family left Iran to live in exile. Khomeini returned to Iran in triumph.

Iranian oil production was low and the economy generally was in shambles. Officially, a civilian government was in charge in Iran; but the Ayatollah Khomeini seemed to hold the real power. In reality, there appeared to be two governments. Courts under Khomeini's control tried, condemned, and executed hundreds of people accused of wrongdoing under the Shah and for more recent offenses. Khomeini declared that his intent was to establish an Islamic republic, one based on Islamic law and adhering to Islamic ideals and faith.

Internationally, the Iranian revolution posed a serious threat to the world's oil supply. Although production gradually began to increase, for a number of months little oil flowed from Iran to other countries.

In November 1979 militant Iranian students seized the U.S. Embassy in Teheran and took over 60 hostages. In return for releasing the hostages, they demanded that the Shah, who was in the United States for medical treatment, be returned to Iran to stand trial for alleged crimes. The Iranian government approved of the students' action.

As the days went by and most of the hostages were not released, anti-American feelings continued to be expressed in Iran and in some other areas in the Middle East. Some of the hostages were accused of espionage, and the United States was said to have interfered in the internal affairs of Iran.

The United Nations Security Council unanimously adopted a resolution urgently demanding that Iran immediately release the hostages. The International Court of Justice ruled unanimously that Iran should release the hostages and return the U.S. Embassy in Teheran to American control.

Even after the Shah moved to Panama, however, the hostages continued to be held. Meanwhile, Iran was disrupted by groups in some parts of the country who demanded self-government.

Events in Turkey

Following the death of Kemal Atatürk in 1938, his Republican People's Party remained in control in Turkey. However, the rival Democratic Party gradually made gains; and in the election of 1950, that party swept to power.

Gradually, the government placed restrictions on freedom of speech. Also, it could not solve economic problems. Dissatisfaction grew. Following rioting early in 1960, the army overthrew the government. In 1961 a new Turkish constitution went into effect. It contained provisions to guard against one-person rule.

In foreign affairs, Turkey became involved in a dispute with Greece over the rights of the Turkish minority on the Greek-dominated independent island of Cyprus. In 1974, after the government of Cyprus had been taken over by Greek officers who hoped for a union of the island with Greece, Tur-

key invaded Cyprus. Turkey, Greece, Great Britain, and Greek and Turkish leaders of Cyprus sought a solution to the problem.

Check on Your Reading

1. What progress was made in achieving peace between Egypt and Israel?
2. What was the Palestinian Issue? How did it affect Lebanon?
3. What were the major events in Iran in 1978-1980?

In the post-World War II period many African countries gained their independence. Which ones were independent before 1945?

Independent States of Africa

Independent before 1945

Independent after 1945

5. The Struggle for Freedom in Africa

"Independence" was the key word in post-World War II Africa. A desire for freedom from foreign rule had simmered on that continent, and the independence movement grew in intensity as World War II ended. By 1961, four-fifths of the peoples of Africa were free of foreign control. Others gained their independence in the 1960s and 1970s.

Ghana and Kenya

The British Gold Coast in West Africa was one of the first areas to achieve independence, becoming the nation of Ghana. The struggle for the independence of Ghana was led by Kwame Nkrumah.

Nkrumah was educated in Catholic mission schools, attended a British colonial college, and later went to a college in the United States. During the last year of World War II, he studied law in London. Returning to his homeland, Nkrumah organized the Convention People's Party to work for independence from Great Britain. His political activity landed him in jail for a time; but then his party won a majority in the colony's legislative council and he was released. The British now cooperated to bring about independence, and that occurred in 1957. Ghana became a republic in 1960, and Nkrumah was elected President. Nkrumah led the country with a strong hand and established closer contact with Communist countries. He was ousted in 1966. In the years that followed there were many struggles for power between military and civilian leaders.

The struggle for independence in the British colony of Kenya was more difficult than in Ghana. British *colonials*, or settlers, had acquired extensive land in Kenya from the Kikuyu people, whose numbers had been greatly reduced by an epidemic. The number of Kikuyu eventually began to increase once more, and population pressure on remaining Kikuyu land grew intense. The Kikuyu demanded the return of land which, from their point of view, they had simply allowed Europeans to use. Europeans, who from their viewpoint had purchased the land, resisted. The result was conflict between some of the Kikuyu people and British colonials.

Despite the objections of most colonials, the British government came to favor independence for Kenya. This was achieved in 1963. Jomo Kenyatta, who had long fought for Kenyan independence and had spent time in British jails, became Kenya's first Prime Minister. In 1964 Kenya became a republic, and Kenyatta became President. He died in 1978.

The Belgian Congo Becomes the Democratic Republic of Zaire

The Belgian Congo's road to independence was also a difficult one. Under great pressure from such leaders as Patrice Lumumba, Belgium granted independence to its colony in 1960. The Belgian Congo then became the Independent Congo Republic, and Patrice Lumumba became its first Prime Minister.

Discord flared almost immediately among those who wanted a centralized government, those who wanted considerable self-government for the provinces, and those who wanted to protect Belgian economic interests. Congolese troops rebelled against the Belgian officers who still commanded the Congo army. Eleven days after independence, the copper-rich Katanga Province in the south, a stronghold of Belgian influence, seceded and formed its own government. Belgium sent troops to protect Katanga, the Kasai Province, and Belgian citizens. United Nations troops became involved in an effort to restore order. The Katanga secession movement was finally ended by 1964, and that province rejoined the Congo. United Nations forces at last left the reunited Congo.

The Congo gradually began to enjoy a period of relative peace under President Joseph Mobutu. The King of Belgium visited the country in 1970, and the two nations signed a treaty of friendship. The following year Mobutu had the name of the former colony changed to the Democratic Republic of Zaire. He also changed his own name to Mobutu Sese Seko, and ordered that all Africans take African names. In addition, a number of place names underwent changes. Mobutu won a seven-year term in office in 1970.

Nigeria, Tanzania, and Uganda

In 1960 the Federal Republic of Nigeria, with 63 million people became free from Britain. Its rich natural resources included oil, coal, limestone, natural gas, and iron.

Nigeria's early years of nationhood were troubled ones. Two military coups occurred; there were political assassinations; and tensions and conflicts existed between Yoruba, Fulani, Hausa, and Ibo peoples. In 1967 Ibos in the Eastern Region of Nigeria attempted to set up their own Republic of Biafra. The civil war that followed was won by the central government in January 1970, and Biafra surrendered.

The military who ran the Nigerian government promised eventually to return control to civilian hands. A new constitution was drafted in 1978, providing for a president, a judiciary, and a house of representatives and a senate. In 1979 free elections returned power to a civilian government.

The former British colony of Tanganyika joined with the nearby island of Zanzibar in 1964 to form the United Republic of Tanzania, under the presidency of Julius Nyerere. The government passed a number of socialist measures, including the nationalization of banks and numerous industries.

Uganda, a former British protectorate, became independent in 1962. Milton Obote became Prime Minister. The country soon became a republic. In 1971 Major General Idi Amin Dada, a former heavyweight boxer, gained control of the government.

Idi Amin soon achieved a worldwide reputation as a capricious and sadistic dictator. No one knows how many thousands of people he had killed, or just how many he had imprisoned. He wiped out a large portion of the middle class in Uganda when he forced between 47,000 and 95,000 Asians—Indians and Pakistanis—to leave the country. Amin allowed the Ugandan economy to go steadily downhill. He warred off and on with neighboring Tanzania, and in the spring of 1979 an invading Tanzanian army forced Amin to leave the country. A provisional government was then set up.

The French Sub-Saharan Areas

Many of the areas ruled by the French south of the Sahara achieved independence with relatively little struggle. The French, however, did try to influence sub-Saharan African peoples to stop short of complete independence.

Following World War II, France offered Africans either independence or representation in the French National Assembly and a greater voice in their colonial governments. If the Africans chose the latter, the French would assume responsibility for finance, defense, and foreign affairs.

Guinea was the first French colony to consider this offer, and it chose independence in 1958. When France then cut off all aid, Guinea turned to the Soviet Union for economic and other aid.

Other French colonies followed Guinea's example of choosing independence. Senegal, Mauritania, Mali, Ivory Coast, Niger, Upper Volta, Dahomey (today Benin), Gabon, Congo, Central African Republic (for a short time the Central African Empire), and Chad became independent nations in 1960.

Algeria

The French North African area of Algeria had a much more difficult struggle to achieve independence. In 1947 the French government granted citizenship to Algeria's eight million Muslims and assigned thirty seats in the French National Assembly to elected deputies representing Algeria's French and Muslim populations. Still, Muslims continued to be dominated and discriminated against by French officials in Algeria and by *colons*—people of primarily French extraction who settled in Algeria. The French possessed about a third of Algeria's arable land, although they accounted for scarcely 12 percent of the population of nearly 10 million.

A nationalist movement had been building in Algeria during and since World War II. Muslims wanted more political, economic, and social rights, and eventually independence. The *colons* resisted these demands fiercely, and called on the French government to protect what they considered their rights as French citizens.

Muslim Algerian nationalists rebelled against French authority in 1954, and eventually the rebel National Liberation Front (FLN) assumed direction of the struggle. By 1958 reports were circulating that the French government planned to "abandon" Algeria to the Muslims. This sparked rioting by 30,000 *colons*. French military leaders in Algeria who also opposed Algerian independence took over the control and the direction of the uprising.

General Charles de Gaulle came out of retirement to meet the crisis. (See page 576.) General de Gaulle took the position that the people of Algeria had the right to choose their own form of government, provided that peace was first established. He

added that there should be safeguards for the rights of both the Muslim majority and the French minority. Some French military leaders in Algeria, however, formed the Secret Army Organization (OAS) and engaged in violence and terrorism against the Muslims, who often retaliated. Between October 1958 and November 1961, there were two rebellions among French army units in Algeria, both of which the French government put down. Meanwhile, Algerian Muslims continued to demand independence.

Charles de Gaulle eventually had his way. In March 1962, a cease-fire ended the Algerian War. In a referendum held on July 1, 1962, Algerians voted overwhelmingly for independence from France. In a proclamation two days later, General de Gaulle declared: "France recognizes solemnly the independence of Algeria."

Following independence, Algeria experienced a brief civil war. Ahmed Ben Bella eventually became Premier of the government. His government took over many French-owned factories, and nu-

merous businesses. In 1965 a military revolt overthrew the government and placed Houari Boumedienne in power. Boumedienne remained President of Algeria until illness forced his retirement in 1978.

The Portuguese Areas

As the 1970s began, Portugal remained the only European country with extensive holdings in Africa—the areas of Mozambique, Angola, and Portuguese Guinea. Despite armed rebellion, Portugal resisted the idea of independence. The Portuguese spent millions of dollars and many lives fighting the rebels.

Then in 1974 the army took over the Portuguese government. Army leaders realized that Portugal could no longer afford to fight to keep its African holdings. Portuguese Guinea became independent in September 1974 and became Guinea-Bissau. Mozambique achieved independence in 1975. Civil war broke out in Angola during the transition to independence. Three groups sought to control

the new government. Following independence in November 1975, the MPLA, the faction that received aid from the Soviet Union and Cuba, won control.

Ethiopia and the Horn of Africa

Ethiopia regained its independence when Italy was defeated in World War II. Then Haile Selassie, said to be the 225th in a line of kings traced back to biblical times, returned to the throne. In time, the army, students, and others joined to oppose the emperor, who was deposed in September 1974.

Eritrea, a predominantly Muslim area along the Red Sea that had become an Italian colony in 1890, was administered by Great Britain just after World War II. Federated with Ethiopia in 1952, it became a province of Ethiopia in 1962.

Somalia, which stretches along the Indian Ocean on the Horn of Africa, had been an Italian protectorate. After World War II, the United Nations made it a trust territory under the British, whose colony of Somaliland was nearby. In July 1960, the two areas joined to become the Somali Democratic Republic.

In the 1970s, Muslim rebels in Eritrea fought for independence from Ethiopia, and Somalia joined the fighting. By the end of the 1970s, with the aid of Cuban troops and Russian military advisers and arms, Ethiopia had put down the rebellion and repelled Somali invaders.

South Africa and Rhodesia-Zimbabwe

As African independence movements swirled about them, South Africa and Rhodesia, both with large black majorities, remained under minority white rule. Both had at one time been British colonies. Rhodesia as a colony had been known as Southern Rhodesia. Northern Rhodesia had become the independent nation of Zambia in 1964.

The Republic of South Africa classified its people into four groups: blacks or Africans (over 70 percent of the population); whites (17 percent); colored—mixtures of blacks, whites, and Asians (9 percent); and Asians (3 percent). South Africa was controlled by its European-white minority that practiced the policy of *apartheid*—separateness—of the four groups. This system of segregating and controlling non-whites—politically, economically, and socially—originated with the early Dutch settlers. Africans were considered second-class citizens whose economic opportunities, housing, land ownership, and political activities were severely restricted. Africans had limited self-government only in what the South African government called "reserves," areas of all-black populations also known as "self-governing homelands." As the 1970s closed, there were strong demands in the United Nations and throughout the world that apartheid be ended because it was unjust and violated human rights.

Rhodesia declared its independence from Great Britain late in 1965. The basic issue that led to the

Rhodesian declaration of independence was the desire of the white minority to control the country and prevent the non-white majority from gaining power. Thus, the countries of the world did not recognize the existence of Rhodesia as a new nation. In Rhodesia about 220,000 whites were vastly outnumbered by five million Native Africans. This white minority governed and controlled the country. The black majority was denied its rights, and in 1966 the United Nations called for economic sanctions against Rhodesia.

In the 1970s black guerrilla groups in Rhodesia intensified their activities against the government, in some cases receiving aid from neighboring nations. The white government under Prime Minister Ian Smith, in the face of guerrilla activity and much criticism from other countries, gradually allowed Africans to have a share in Rhodesian affairs. In 1979, Prime Minister Smith stepped down in favor of Abel Muzorewa, a Methodist minister and moderate black leader. Many people now called the country *Zimbabwe*.

Some black leaders were not satisfied with the new government. They considered Prime Minister Muzorewa to be under white domination in a government in which whites exercised real control despite the facade of black participation. Guerrilla groups continued their activities.

In December 1979 the parliament of Rhodesia rescinded the 1965 Unilateral Declaration of Independence. British officials were to supervise the country until elections were held in the spring of 1980. At that time, power would be handed over to the new leaders of an independent Rhodesia.

Efforts at Black African Cooperation

As the countries of Africa struggled toward independence, some of them looked forward to creating a Pan-African Union on the continent. Twenty-nine Asian and African nations sent representatives to an Asian-African Conference at Bandung, Indonesia, in 1955. The report of the conference urged the promotion of economic progress and the self-determination of peoples.

In January 1961, the heads of five African states met at Casablanca, Morocco, and adopted an "African Charter." It proposed an "identity of views" in policymaking, neutrality in the "Cold War," and backing for liberation of African territories still under foreign domination. Plans were laid to establish an African Consultative Assembly and an African High Command.

Five months later, in May 1961, representatives of nineteen African countries met at Monrovia, Liberia. At the end of the conference their declaration called for: 1. equal sovereignty of African states, regardless of size or population; 2. respect for each state's right to exist and a prohibition on the annexation of one state by another; 3. freedom of African states to unite with one another; 4. nonintervention in the affairs of other nations; and 5. respect for the territorial integrity of all.

The Organization of African Unity (OAU) was founded at Addis Ababa, Ethiopia, in May 1963, by the leaders of thirty-two African governments. The OAU charter called for: 1. the promotion of unity and solidarity among African states; 2. the coordination of cooperative efforts to achieve a better life for the peoples of Africa; 3. the defense of their sovereignty, territorial integrity, and independence; 4. the elimination of all forms of colonialism from Africa; and 5. the promotion of international cooperation, with due regard for the Charter of the United Nations and the Universal Declaration of Human Rights. By the end of the 1970s, 49 African states were members of the Organization of African Unity.

Check on Your Reading

1. How was independence achieved by former British colonies?
2. What was the course of the independence movement in the Belgian Congo?
3. How did Algeria gain its independence from France?
4. What was the independence experience of Portuguese possessions?
5. What has been the black experience in South Africa and Rhodesia since World War II?
6. What efforts have been made toward cooperation among the nations in Africa?

---

6. African Arts and Literature

In the second half of the twentieth century, the creative past and the bright promise of Africa were "rediscovered" twice: once by the outside world, and once by the African peoples themselves.

After reading Basil Davidson's book, *African Kingdoms*, an editorial writer of a small-town American newspaper wrote:

Above, an exhibit of contemporary African art in Nigeria. Below left, a bronze statue of a Nigerian god stands before a skyscraper in Lagos. Below right, a sculpture in wood that was also created in Nigeria.

This painting by Ousmane Faye is titled "Spectators." The artist was born in Senegal, West Africa, and is also famous as a tapestry designer.

Among the surprises that Davidson springs are his avowals that prehistoric Africans: . . .

—Created what is called "the world's greatest gallery of prehistoric art"—15,000 rock paintings in the central plateaus of the Sahara which reflect Africa's cultural beginnings thousands of years ago. . . .

—Were superb sculptors. . . .

—Developed medieval cities such as Timbuktu into centers of learning and gracious living. . . .

Other people have been fascinated by their discovery or rediscovery of African arts, music, and literature. At the First World Festival of Negro Arts, held at Dakar in 1966, more than 10,000 visitors were stimulated by African plays, dances, and poetry.

Africans also were rediscovering their culture during the decades following World War II. Joseph Palmer, United States Assistant Secretary of State for Foreign Affairs, declared: "One of the most striking elements of the new Africa . . . is the rediscovery by Africans of themselves . . . the African has found a new dignity in his freedom, in his history, and in his color." Literacy, which increased threefold between 1951 and 1966, helped more Africans to appreciate their many cultural achievements.

African Poetry

There were important African writers of the short story, sketch, and novel in the twentieth century. However, poetry was the principal means of expression in many parts of Africa.

Senegal's Léopold Sédar-Senghor, widely acclaimed poet of French-speaking Africa, captured the moods of African life with lines like these:

The tall palms swinging in the night
    wind
Hardly rustle. Not even cradle songs.
The rhythmic silence rocks us.
Listen to its song, listen to the beating of our
    dark blood, listen
To the beating of the dark pulse of Africa in
    the midst of lost villages.

Gabriel Okara, an important Nigerian poet, depicted an African drawn by two appeals—and perhaps by two worlds—in his famous poem *Piano and Drums*. Okara wrote that his "blood ripples"

When at break of day at a riverside
I hear jungle drums telegraphing
the mystic rhythm, urgent, raw
like bleeding flesh, speaking of
primal youth and the beginning

Almost at the same time he hears

. . . a wailing piano
solo speaking of complex ways
in a tear-furrowed concerto;
of faraway lands
and new horizons. . . .

Moved by both the power of the first and the intricacies of the second, he concludes:

And I . . .
[keep] wandering in the mystic rhythm
of jungle drums and the concerto.

These and other creative writers presented striking images, ideas, and patterns as they viewed the changing world of Africa.

African Music

While drums play a very important part in African music, other instruments also are significant. These include: flutes, flageolets, zithers, lutes, lyres, and harps. The essential points to remember about African music are these:

1. There is a variety of musical styles in Africa. To the north of the Sahara, the music is affected by an Islamic background. To the south, the music reflects a variety of tribal cultures.

2. There is considerable public participation in African music and dance. As Professor Alan Merriam explains: "The distinctions between 'the artist' and his 'audience,' which are so sharply drawn in our society, do not seem to be of particular importance in Africa. Almost everyone sings, handclaps, and participates in group performance. . . ."

3. African music can express with great effectiveness the various moods expressed by music of the West—excitement, melancholy, joy, fantasy, beauty, and many more.

4. African music is integrated into the daily lives of the people. In political, economic, and social activities, music provides the emotional tone, expresses the spectrum of feelings, and reflects both the memories and aspirations of the Africans.

In Africa, music is more than "the food of love." It is a food of life!

African Art

Art continues to be a significant part of African culture. Features of artistic activity and expression in Africa today are:

There is a deep interest in African art of the past, and a determination to increase the people's appreciation of their artistic heritage.

A variety of tribal styles exists. However, some elements, such as a fondness for sculpturing in wood, are found in art throughout most of Africa.

There is impressive evidence of the skill and imagination of African artists; for example, in their cylindrical statuary and in the creation of dance masks.

Western influences are having an impact on African artists. The opposite is also true. As early as the beginning of the twentieth century, painters in the West such as Matisse and Derain had been influenced by African sculpture.

African art continues to be linked with the activities of the people themselves, such as religious ceremonial observances.

Check on Your Reading

1. What is an outstanding characteristic of African poetry?
2. What are the characteristics of African music? of African art?

A Young Ibo

The young man of the Ibo tribe lived in Nigeria in Iboland, "south of Lokoja to the Cross River in the east and from the swamps of Ikwerre Land to the grasslands fringing Ogoja in the north."

He was shorter than many other Nigerians, but strong. He developed his strength through wrestling. When he won a match, he was "carried about the streets and the spectators sang merrily while girls wiped his face and gave him presents." The value of manual work he learned from his parents, for it was said "an Ibo prefers to die than to be idle."

Sometimes the young Ibo fished in the rivers—the Imo, the Oji, and the Qua. On other occasions, he hunted the small antelopes called duikers. Most of the time he spent cultivating yams or tending to the mangoes, plantains, and other fruits.

Yet the most exciting times for him were often the market days. He welcomed them, not because they brought the new but because they displayed the familiar. Let others talk of machine-made products from Europe. As for him, he agreed with the writer who said:

> Before I came to know the principles of good feeling I thought that those who ate more tinned food and drink, more European imported wines and ales, had the best in life. But now, I come to know that our local foodstuffs, more or less regarded as bushman's foods, are the best nature provides in the whole planet. Our forefathers were well nourished with the same bushman's foods. Why should we replace them with imported articles . . .?

It was clear that the young Ibo was proud of his tribe. When he married and had children, efforts would be made to make them as proud of Nigeria as they were of their tribe. For the state now required that all schoolchildren recite the following pledge:

OUR PLEDGE

I pledge to Nigeria my country
to be faithful, loyal and honest
To serve Nigeria with all my strength
To defend her unity and uphold her honor
and glory, so help me God.

The above sketch is based on information in "Ibos as They Are" by Onyenaekeya Udeagu, in *An African Treasury,* selected by Langston Hughes. New York: A Jove/HBJ Book (Harcourt Brace Jovanovich), 1977, pp. 26-29; and from *Teaching Social Studies in Other Lands,* edited by Howard D. Mehlinger and Jan L. Tucker, Washington, D.C.: National Council for the Social Studies, 1979, p. 66.

CHAPTER REVIEW

Think and Discuss

1. What major problems do the peoples and governments of the Middle East face?
2. Read the Balfour Declaration. Might the wording of this document have been responsible for misunderstandings between Arabs and Israelis? Explain.
3. Do you think that if the Palestinian refugee problem were solved, other problems between Israel and the Arab countries also would be solved? Support your answer with as much evidence as possible.
4. Why do you think that many place names in Africa were changed after 1940?
5. What facts of population composition helped cause racial problems in the Republic of South Africa and Zimbabwe?
6. Why do you think many Europeans and Americans have known little about the achievements of the different peoples of Africa?

Past and Present

1. Compare the relations among the religions of Islam, Christianity, and Judaism in ancient and medieval times with the relations among these three religions today.
2. In what ways are the peoples of Africa today rediscovering their past?

Activities

1. Draw a pictorial chart showing oil resources in the Middle East and throughout the world. Present two conclusions that you can support on the basis of the data in your chart.
2. Compare the written languages of Hebrew, Arabic, and English as to the size, shape, and style of the words. Try your hand at writing a few words in Arabic and Hebrew.
3. Organize a week-long program on African culture. Plan lectures, illustrated talks, art exhibits, and musical programs on African cultural achievements.

Contemporary Changes and Future Challenges

KEYNOTE

An airlines executive fascinated by numbers once figured out that his life had become entangled in a mass of computerized statistics. For example, he was a *number* to the following: the Marines, the Social Security Administration, the Internal Revenue Bureau, the Department of State, the telephone company, a life insurance company, a real estate company, a magazine subscription department, an airline, a bank, an automobile bureau, and six stores. Indeed, his number with a national book club had 20 digits!

It was not surprising that he and many other people living today wondered whether their lives had become so dehumanized by machines that they were little more than numbers.

Yet the fact remained that, at the same time that technology was making extraordinary advances, there were other impressive achievements in such fields as literature, art and architecture, and music.

As a result, many people throughout the world declared that the solution of present and future problems depended on cooperation, not conflict, between the arts and sciences.

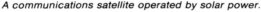

A communications satellite operated by solar power.

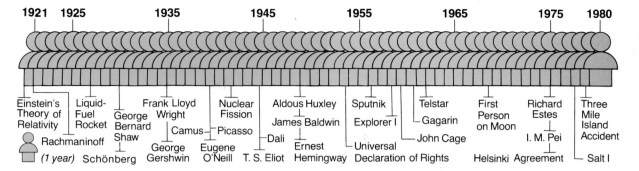

1921 1925   1935   1945   1955   1965   1975 1980

Einstein's Theory of Relativity
Rachmaninoff (1 year)
Liquid-Fuel Rocket
George Bernard Shaw
Schönberg
Frank Lloyd Wright
Camus—Picasso
George Gershwin
Eugene O'Neill
Nuclear Fission
Dali
T. S. Eliot
Aldous Huxley
James Baldwin
Ernest Hemingway
Sputnik
Explorer I
Universal Declaration of Rights
Telstar
Gagarin
John Cage
First Person on Moon
Helsinki Agreement
Richard Estes
I. M. Pei
Salt I
Three Mile Island Accident

1. Science: A Dominant Feature of Our Times

We live in wondrous times. A surgeon has re-attached a hand severed from a boy's arm. A computer has done a financial statement in two hours that would require a staff of accountants 320 hours to complete. A machine has translated Russian into English at a rate exceeding 2,400 words a minute. A laser light has been used to align bridges and dams. The "genetic code" has been deciphered, and molecules of DNA are revealing new secrets about life itself.

Indeed, advances in *pure* science (concerned with discovering the reasons for events in the natural world) and *applied* science (concerned with putting the findings of pure science to practical use) in the twentieth century have been so extraordinary that it is impossible for even trained scientists to understand them all. The Wizard of Science in fact has far exceeded the Wizard of Oz in fantasy.

Electronics: Radio, Television, Computers, and Beyond

Electronics is the science that studies the movements and actions of electrons as they flow through tubes filled with gasses, vacuum tubes, and other forms. Electrons are negative charges of electricity. The discovery of X-rays by the German physicist Wilhelm Konrad Roentgen in 1895 was one of the earliest findings related to the field of electronics. Two years later, Sir Joseph Thomson, a British physicist, revealed that electrons carry electrical current. Then, in the twentieth century, electronics helped to make possible the development of radio, television, radar, high fidelity phonographs, tape recorders, and electronic computers.

It was not long before an electronic computer was produced that could "remember enough information to fill a 1,836-page Manhattan telephone book—any figure, word, chemical, or mathematical symbol—and work the information at the rate of 7,200 unerringly logical operations per second."

Other scientific developments were equally impressive. For example, *transistors,* electronic devices, are used to operate television, an important point when we remember that 97 percent of all homes in the United States have television sets. Today *one integrated circuit* can do the work of thousands of such transistors—and this integrated circuit is no larger than the head of a pin!

Nuclear Energy Opens New Possibilities

Albert Einstein (1879-1955) was born in Germany and later became an American citizen. He was one of the scientists chiefly responsible for ushering in the Atomic Age. In 1905, when he was only 26 years old, Einstein published a paper which set forth his Special Theory of Relativity. Twelve years later, he presented his General Theory of Relativity.

Two of Einstein's findings were among the most important in the history of science: (1) There is an equivalence of mass and energy. This means that matter and energy are exchangeable and not separate. (2) $E = MC^2$. According to this equation, energy equals mass times the velocity of light squared.

These findings of Einstein and the investigations of scientists from several countries provided the foundation for the splitting of the atom. The United States achieved nuclear fission in 1942, and the development of the atomic bomb in 1945. As a result of the work of Igor Kurchatov and his associates, the Russians also produced an atomic bomb in 1949.

Work with nuclear *fission* (breakdown or division of the nucleus of the atom) and nuclear *fusion* (rearranging and uniting of elements to form heavier nuclei) opened the way to *nuclear power.* Nuclear

A hydrogen bomb explosion at Eniwetok Atoll in November 1952.

power can be used for many purposes. For example, in 1952 the United States started work on its first atomic-powered submarine, the *Nautilus*.

Radioisotopes, unstable forms of the ordinary atoms, also have become extremely useful. Radioisotopes are used by industry to measure thickness, density, and moisture content. In high concentration, they give off intense radiation that can help destroy cancerous tissues and kill bacteria. Tracer radioiodine can help control tumors.

In addition, with serious oil shortages today in the United States and in other countries of the world, nuclear power is being developed to supply energy for both industry and home. The use of nuclear energy led to many controversies, however,

particularly at the end of the 1970s. A dangerous accident at the nuclear power plant at Three Mile Island in Middletown, Pennsylvania, in 1979 raised serious questions about radiation's threats to life. Some newspapers referred to the event as a "Nuclear Nightmare," and one woman faced with the possibility of a nuclear explosion wrote in her diary: "We go to bed with one ear [alert] for sirens and with dreams filled with hydrogen bubbles. . . ."

Some people demanded that the building of nuclear energy plants be discontinued at once and those that already existed be dismantled. Others felt that the dangers of nuclear plants could be eliminated and that nuclear power could be used safely.

Chemical Technology Spreads Widely

Chemical technology had a major impact on society. For example, synthetic gasolines were produced for use in the high-compression engines of modern cars. Nylon also was developed. Nylon clothing, pleasant to wear and inexpensive to purchase, consists of two chemical compounds: hexamethylenediamine and adipic acid.

About 1828 French chemists discovered the first heat-softening plastics. By 1960 plastics had a range of physical properties that made them competitive with metals, woods, and glass.

Synthetic resins and fibers were used. Synthetic rubber was manufactured. In addition, nylon soon was challenged by Dacron and other synthetic fibers used in clothing and home furnishings.

Indeed, in the 1970s and early 1980s it was possible for a person to be surrounded by chemicals at home. One could sit in foam rubber chairs, gaze at resin paints on the walls, walk on vinyl tile flooring, and dine on a colorful assortment of plastic dishes!

Medicine: New Discoveries and New Procedures

If he were alive today, Hippocrates, the Greek "founder of medical science," would probably be confused by the important advances that were made in medicine. These included production of vitamin and hormone concentrates from natural and synthetic sources. Also, there was the discovery and use of *antibiotics* (such as sulfa drugs; and penicillin, which was discovered by British bacteriologist Alexander Fleming) for specific diseases.

Successful anti-polio vaccines were developed, first by Jonas E. Salk and later by Albert E. Sabin. Dorothy C. Hodgkin, a British scientist who won a Nobel Prize, did outstanding X-ray studies and helped combat pernicious anemia. New techniques in surgery included "open-heart" operations and transplanting vital organs such as the kidney. Use of tranquilizers was helpful in the treatment of mental illness.

One of the most significant developments in the 1970s and the early 1980s was the recognition that the *environment* could be a major factor in contributing to certain diseases. Automobile fumes, factory smoke, polluted rivers, careless use of pesticides, and other environmental factors became the serious concern of physicians and community members working in the field of preventive medicine.

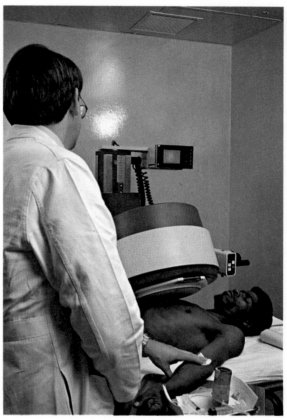

Nuclear medicine is being used in treating a variety of illnesses.

Transportation: "Faster Than the Speed of Sound . . ."

Revolutionary changes were made in transportation. Henry Ford's assembly line and other mass-production techniques were adopted by automobile manufacturers. By 1977 there were over 143 million registered automobiles, buses, and trucks in the United States alone.

Meanwhile, diesel-powered locomotives were introduced to the railroad systems of several nations. Ocean-going ships were constructed that could cross the Atlantic Ocean in less than a week. Commercial aircraft began to be used by an increasing number of people.

In 1939 Ernst Heinkel of Germany proved that jet-propelled planes could fly. In 1951 the *Skyrocket* flew faster than the speed of sound (above 738 miles per hour). By the 1960s jet planes were being used for a high percentage of commercial flights, and in the latter part of the 1970s a number of people flew from Washington, D.C., to Paris, France, in supersonic airliners in a little over three and a half hours. It is interesting to recall that it took Columbus over two months to make the first voyage to America!

The Sea Reveals Rich Resources

"I must go down to the seas again . . ." became more than just a poetic line in the twentieth century. Some 70 percent of our planet lies beneath the sea, and the depths of the sea held a strange and fascinating world for contemporary human beings. Explorations revealed the following important facts:

The sea holds rich sources of mineral wealth: petroleum, phosphates, nickel, copper, cobalt, and "grapefruit-sized nuggets" of nearly pure manganese. Bromine and even a minute amount of gold have been extracted from seawater.

Plankton, tiny sea animals, may be able to supply human beings with an additional source of food. There were predictions that the day would come when fish farms in the ocean depths would supply most of the world's food.

The force of ocean tides, currents, and waves could be converted into electricity in underwater power plants. Seawater could be converted into fresh water and used to transform desert regions into fertile lands. In the early 1980s there was also increasing interest in studying electrical generating platforms that float beneath the ocean floor as one method of tapping the sun's energy stored in the sea.

2. Space Explorations Probe New Worlds

July 20, 1979 marked the tenth anniversary of the landing of the first human being on the moon. "That's one small step for a man," Astronaut Neil Armstrong had said, as his boot touched the moon's surface, "one giant leap for mankind." It was a step that could not have been taken without years of careful preparation.

For centuries human beings had been fascinated by the sun, moon, stars, and the world of space that lay beyond. In 1687 Sir Isaac Newton's laws of motion were published. When a modern rocket engine shoots a jet of gas out of its tail cone, it operates in accordance with Newton's third law: For every action there is an equal and opposite re-

action. The gas shooting downward produces a powerful force acting in the opposite direction. This force lifts the rocket into the air.

In the nineteenth century, Konstantin Tsiolkovsky, a Russian, pointed out the importance of using liquid fuel to propel rockets. In 1926 Robert Hutchings Goddard, an American professor, made flight tests of the world's first liquid-fueled rocket. The German Hermann Oberth, "the father of practical *astronautics*" (the field of designing, building, and operating space vehicles), also did pioneer work in space rocketry.

Satellites, Artificial "Planet," and Space "Reporters"

On October 4, 1957, the Soviet Union launched the first human-made earth satellite. Named *Sputnik I*, this 184-pound sphere attained a maximum altitude of 560 miles and orbited Earth every 96.2 minutes. The United States launched its first Earth satellite, *Explorer I*, on January 31, 1958.

On January 2, 1959, the Russians launched a multi-stage rocket, *Lunik*, toward the moon. *Lunik* went into orbit around the sun and became the first artificial "planet."

Space vehicles now became "reporters," relaying to Earth scientific news from millions of miles away. *Mariner II*, launched in 1962, passed close to Venus and sent back more data about that planet than human beings had learned in 5,000 years. Other spacecraft and human-made satellites reported on the composition of space, radiation belts, and magnetic fields. *Tiros* satellites analyzed the weather.

Space Communications and Space Travelers

Achievements in space communications were equally impressive and significant. In July 1962, *Telstar*, a communications satellite, sent live television across the Atlantic Ocean for the first time. *Syncom II* traveled at the same relative speed as Earth to transmit radio and voice. In 1964 the United States and ten other countries agreed to establish the first international commercial communications satellite system.

Human beings themselves were traveling into space! On April 12, 1961, the Russian Yuri Gagarin became the first person in space by orbiting Earth in a capsule. Later, the United States launched *Project Apollo*, and on July 20, 1969, "Buzz" Aldrin, Neil Armstrong, and Michael Collins reached the moon. Additional successful moon landings followed. It no longer seemed a fantasy when two major airlines were said to be accepting reservations from people who wanted to be on the first commercial flights to the moon. In 1975, the *Apollo-Soyuz* mission resulted in the first international linkup in space between Americans and Russians. Then, in 1979 two Soviet astronauts orbited the earth in a space station for 175 days!

Unmanned spacecraft—unpeopled would be more exact, for the Russians had sent a woman into space, and women in the United States and the Soviet Union were training for space missions—traveled to and investigated the planets Jupiter, Mercury, and Venus. In 1976 two robots called *Vikings* landed on Mars and found—no life. Far more important, they sampled the soil, took pictures, and discovered significant facts about Mars. *Voyager 2's* color cameras focused on Jupiter and its moons in 1979. Later electronic eyes were turned on Saturn. Other plans called for an investigation of the planet Uranus in 1986.

Meanwhile, *Landsat* satellites moving around our own Earth in north-south orbits provided excellent photographs of the earth's environment. Landsat maps brought a new dimension to the teaching and learning of geography.

Next Stop: Space Shuttle!

The fall of pieces of *Skylab* in 1979 caught the temporary attention of the world, but greater interest was shown in the project for a space shuttle. It was designed to make repeated journeys between Earth and space. The *Columbia* was to be the United States' first space shuttle. It was to be launched like a rocket and land like an airplane!

3. Literature Analyzes Twentieth-Century Values

Literary historian J. Isaacs has said: "What is so remarkable about the twentieth century, and what marked it off from previous centuries, is . . . its innumerable attempts to describe what is happening while it is still happening."

Many authors of the twentieth century would have agreed. Despite a variety of writing styles, ideas, and approaches, they had one point in common: *they were deeply concerned with analyzing what was happening to twentieth-century society.*

This was true in Europe, where George Bernard Shaw (born in Ireland, 1856-1950), witty playwright, dissected the foibles of his time in such plays as *Man and Superman* and *Major Barbara.* It was true in Japan, where Toson Shimazaki (1872-1943), "father of modern Japanese poetry," examined the changing character of Japanese youth. It was true in the United States, where Eugene O'Neill (1888-1953) explored the problems of individuals in relation to society in *Long Day's Journey into Night,* and where Edith Wharton (1862-1937) described the effects of society's rules on sensitive people. It was true in Africa, where Léopold-Sédar Senghor (1906-) stressed in his poetry the importance of being aware of one's heritage and values. It was true in Latin America, where the Nicaraguan poet Rubén Darío (1867-1916) urged the spirit of Don Quixote to protect our earth from "detractors, malefactors, smooth and bland and evil actors." It was true in India, where Rabindranath Tagore (1861-1941), poet, dramatist, philosopher, and artist, observed the restlessness of human beings.

Some of the key ideas expressed in twentieth-century literature were (1) anxiety, (2) importance of time, and (3) need to live with dignity and courage.

Anxiety

Much of the literature expressed anxiety about the present and the future of human beings. Thus, the poet T. S. Eliot (1888-1965), an American who became a British citizen, reflected the chaos of many aspects of life in his famous work *The Waste Land.* In his poem *The Hollow Men,* he pointed out the emptiness he found in the modern world and declared:

We are the hollow men
We are the stuffed men
Leaning together
Headpiece filled with straw. Alas!

W. H. Auden (1907-1973), a distinguished poet born in England, even entitled one of his works of poetry *The Age of Anxiety.*

Importance of Time

In a period when the dangers of war and destruction threatened human beings, it was not surprising that some authors should become concerned about time and how people used it. The English novelist Aldous Huxley (1894-1963), who wrote

Brave New World, an imaginary picture of the world of the future, was interested in the nature of time. So was the French philosopher Henri Bergson (1859-1941). He pointed out that the *quality* of time can be more significant than its *quantity*—that is, one hour filled with rich experience is worth more than one week of monotony. Above all, Marcel Proust (1871-1922), the brilliant French novelist and author of *Remembrance of Things Past,* was fascinated by time. He demonstrated "the inseparableness" of people from their pasts. The American Willa Cather (1874-1947), author of *Death Comes for the Archbishop,* was also deeply concerned with the past and with the ways in which people remembered past triumphs and tragedies.

Human Beings Should Live with Dignity and Courage

A number of writers in the twentieth century refused to be overwhelmed by the problems of the contemporary world. For example, the French writer François Mauriac (1885-1970), author of *The Desert of Love* and *Thérèse,* showed the significant role that religion and faith could play in contemporary life. Others, such as Albert Camus (1913-1960), French novelist, essayist, and playwright who wrote *The Stranger, The Plague,* and other novels, took a different approach. Camus stressed that the lives of human beings may be "absurd," but they must live those lives with dignity and courage. He declared: "The problem is to serve human dignity by means which remain honorable in the midst of a history which is not honorable."

In *The Myth of Sisyphus,* Camus compared the lives of people to that of a Greek mythical hero Sisyphus, whom the gods condemned to roll a boulder to the top of a hill. Each time that Sisyphus reached the top of the hill, the boulder would roll down again. Camus urged human beings to recognize that they faced the same ultimate frustration as Sisyphus—and yet to go right on living with dignity and courage.

Other Developments in Twentieth-Century Literature

In addition to the ferment produced by the discussion of controversial ideas, there were other important developments in twentieth-century literature. These included:

1. *Rise of the novel to the dominant position in literature.*

There were some excellent dramatists, and some great poets, including William Butler Yeats (Irish, 1865-1939), one of the finest lyricists, and Carl Sandburg (American, 1878-1967), who described everyday people and events. There were talented writers of short stories, such as Isaac Bashevis Singer (born in Poland, 1904-). However, the novel dominated the literary scene.

Major novelists appeared in many lands. To give just a few examples: The United States—Ernest Hemingway (1898-1961), author of *The Old Man and the Sea;* William Faulkner (1897-1962), *The Sound and the Fury;* and John Steinbeck (1902-1968), *The Grapes of Wrath.* Great Britain—Virginia Woolf (1882-1941), *Mrs. Dalloway.* The Soviet Union—Mikhail Sholokov (1905-), *And Quiet Flows the Don.* Germany—Thomas Mann (1875-1955), *The Magic Mountain.* Austria—Franz Kafka (1883-1924), *The Trial.* Sweden—Pär Lagerkvist (1891-1974), *Barabbas.* There were other distinguished novelists in other countries of the world.

2. *Experimentation with "stream of consciousness" techniques.* These techniques presented the free-flowing thoughts of a character without an author inhibiting them or rearranging them into an artificial pattern. Katherine Mansfield (New Zealand-British, 1888-1923) wrote parts of her short stories in this way. James Joyce (Irish, 1882-1941) made even more advanced use of "stream of consciousness." For example, here is how he applied this technique to describe the actions and thoughts of one of his characters:

He crossed to the bright side, avoiding the loose cellarflap of number seventy-five. The sun was nearing the steeple of George's church. Be a warm day I fancy. Specially in these black clothes feel it more. Black conducts (refracts is it?) the heat. But I couldn't go in that light suit. Make a picnic of it. His eyelids sank quietly often as he walked in happy warmth.

3. *Increasing attention to the views of minorities.* In the 1960s and 1970s long-overdue recognition was given to gifted black writers, such as the poet Gwendolyn Brooks (1917-), who wrote *Annie Allen;* the novelist-essayist-playwright James Baldwin (1924-), author of *The Fire Next Time;* and the historian John Hope Franklin (1915-), who produced such scholarly works as *From Slavery to Freedom.* The writings of Tomás Rivera and the plays of Luis Valdez,

both Mexican Americans, also were given considerable attention. Books by Vine Deloria, Jr., aroused concern for the treatment of Native Americans by whites.

4. *Growing interest in oral history.* Partly as a result of the work of Alex Haley (1921-), author of *Roots: The Saga of an American Family,* and other writers, wide interest developed in tracing family roots and in studying the history of the family. Several books, as well as numerous publications based on student research—such as *Foxfire*—used interviews, informal conversations, field trips, and other means of oral history as the bases for their material.

4. Art and Architecture Are Expressed in Exciting Ways

One of the chief features of twentieth-century art was that it became universal. It was increasingly difficult to speak of *national* art. One referred to the Cubists, the Surrealists, the Expressionists, the New Realists, and other terms that included artists from many lands. Although in listing artists, the name of each artist's country was placed next to the name of the artist, the different approaches to art were worldwide.

Painting and Beyond

Fauves: In 1906 a group known as the *Fauves* (or "wild beasts") became active. The Fauves concentrated on using color as a means of building form.

Prominent French Fauve artists included Henri Matisse (1869-1954), Raoul Dufy (1877-1953), Maurice de Vlaminck (1876-1958), and André Derain (1880-1954). The Fauve artists never formed a distinct "school," and many of them developed their own unique styles.

Cubism: The painters Pablo Picasso (born in Spain, 1881-1973) and Georges Braque (French, 1882-1963) are credited with founding *Cubism.* Juan Gris (Spanish, 1887-1927) was another Cubist artist. According to art dealer D. H. Kahnweiler, Cubist painters wanted to show the essence, and not the appearance, of an object. (a) They mentally broke down an object into its elements or parts; (b) selected those parts that they wished to use in their paintings; and (c) re-created the object in a way that they hoped would capture its *essence.* They wanted their paintings to give a "truer" sense of the fundamental nature of an object than the original object.

"Head of a Woman" by Pablo Picasso.

Picasso experimented with many forms and styles of art and became one of the great artists of the twentieth century.

Surrealism: Surrealist art, which attracted attention after 1924, was marked by fantasy, symbolism, dreamlike qualities, and presentation of objects that did not exist in the real world. Sigmund Freud (1856-1939), the Austrian physician who founded psychoanalysis, took the position that human beings' minds were affected by the subconscious—that is, by experiences and instinctual drives of which people were not aware. Freudian concepts influenced the development of surrealist art. Artists who did important surrealist paintings, although they also did other types, were Salvador Dali (born in Spain, 1904-), Giorgio de Chirico (Italian, 1888-), Joan Miró (Spanish, 1893-), and Max Ernst (German, 1891-1976).

Above, a painting by Surrealist Giorgio de Chirico.   Below, a painting by Abstract Expressionist Jackson Pollock.

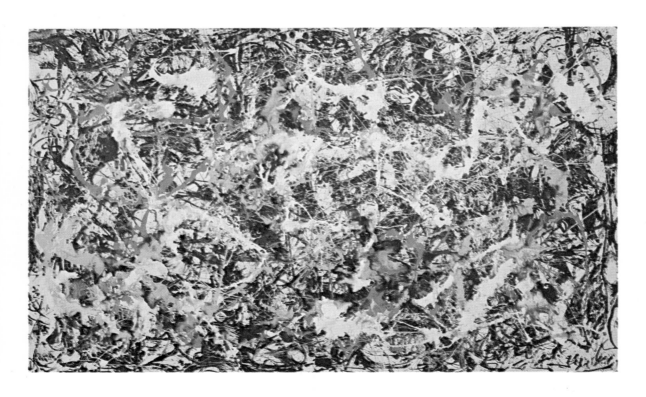

Georgia O'Keefe has become famous for paintings highlighting the beauty of abstract design in the world around her.

Expressionism: Expressionism refers to art that expresses emotion as intensely, poetically, and spiritually as the artist wishes. Expressionist artists did not hesitate to express emotions by distorting figures or substituting abstract forms for the figures found in nature. Expressionists included Oskar Kokoschka (born in Austria, 1886–) and Wassily Kandinsky (Russian, 1866–1944).

Abstract Expressionists went even further in stressing spontaneity and intensity of feeling. Of their paintings it was said: "The observer must learn to look at the picture as a graphic representation of a *mood* and not as a representation of *objects.*" Jackson Pollock (American, 1912–1956) and Franz Kline (American, 1910–1962) were major abstract expressionists.

Pop Art: Pop Art focused on commonplace objects and, as William Fleming points out, "[reveled] in nonsense for its own sake and [laughed] with the world, not at it." It dealt with such objects as Coca Cola bottles, heroes and heroines of comic strips, and soup cans. A number of people found such art to be fun and considered it an effective way to comment on the mass media. Robert Rauschenberg (American, 1925–) and Marisol (American, 1930–) were important pop artists. Marisol, who painted facial features on carved wooden blocks, combined her skills in drawing and in sculpturing with unusual effectiveness.

New Realism: The *New Realists,* who became increasingly important in the 1970s, were artists whose art seemed to be almost like a photograph. New Realists such as Richard Estes (American, 1941–) and Janet Fish (American, 1938–) chose popular subjects and depicted them with a cool objectivity and precision. The style of the New Realists was opposite to that of the Abstract Expressionists. Fortunately, in the 1980s, people were able to enjoy the art of both in a variety of public and private museums.

It is important to remember that twentieth-century art was not exclusively of European derivation. For example, one of the greatest painters of murals in the twentieth century was a Mexican, José Clemente Orozco (1883–1949).

Sculpture

After the end of World War II, there was considerable activity in the field of sculpture. One of the major developments was the artists' use of metals *directly,* instead of molding figures in clay and then sending them to a foundry to be cast. New or unusual materials were used. These included fiberglass, acrylic, wire coils, rope, steel, and even foam rubber.

Henry Moore (British, 1898–) used hollows, holes, and curves to create powerful figures. Alexander Calder (American, 1898–1976) devised

627

Sculptor Louise Nevelson is best known for her assemblages.

delicate and imaginative mobiles, abstract sculpture that was moved by air currents. Louise Nevelson (American, 1900-) made unusual assemblages of wood that was left in its natural state or painted gold or black. David Smith (American, 1906-1965) constructed distinctive works using stainless steel.

Architecture

Architecture, particularly in the industrialized countries of the world, was marked by changes and innovations. The first skyscraper was designed by William Le Baron Jenney and built in Chicago in 1894. Skyscrapers soon became familiar sights in the cities of the United States.

Philosophies of architecture became increasingly challenging. The Swiss-born Le Corbusier (1887-1965) declared that houses should be built on scientific principles and be fitted to human needs. He coined the phrase "The house is a machine for living in." Frank Lloyd Wright (1869-1959), an American architect, urged that designs of buildings fit naturally into their surroundings. He described his architecture as "organic."

Other architects also wrestled with a variety of building problems and devised exciting solutions. For example, in 1978 the new East Wing of the National Gallery of Art in Washington, D.C. opened. It was created by I. M. Pei and his associates, and its airiness, triangular designs, and architectural innovations delighted many people. Individuals from Finland, Germany, Italy, and other countries made other significant contributions in the field of architecture. This was reflected in the work of Eliel and Eero Saarinen; Walter Gropius and Ludwig Miës van der Rohe; Pier Luigi Nervi; and others.

5. Twentieth-Century Music Takes Many Forms

Much music in the twentieth century sought to be original in approach. In the 1970s and early 1980s experimental composers using computers stressed the importance of chance and spontaneity in their music. What was often forgotten, however, was that even in medieval times there were musicians who liked to do the same thing with Gregorian music—although without the use of machines. That is, few things in the present are complete breaks with the past, and twentieth-century music was not cut off from the past.

Thus, some composers were influenced by the earlier impressionist works of Claude Debussy. They included Paul Dukas (French, 1865-1935); Frederick Delius (British, 1862-1934); and Ottorino Respighi (Italian, 1879-1936).

Styles of Music

Neo-romanticism: In the twentieth century a style of music known as *Neo-romanticism* developed. Neo-romantic composers tried to recapture the spirit of romanticism that had dominated music in the preceding century. Neo-romanticists included Sergei Rachmaninoff (Russian, 1873-1943), and Richard Strauss (German, 1864-1949). Strauss' tone poems (such as *Till Eulenspiegel's Merry Pranks*) and operas (such as *Der Rosenkavalier*) were marked by exciting rhythms, powerful melodies, and romantic fervor.

Neo-classicism: Neo-classicism was a twentieth-century movement which reacted against the emotionalism of Romanticism. Neo-classicist composers tried to write music that had order, objectivity, and detachment. They sought guidance from the works of eighteenth-century classical composers.

Composers of the twentieth century who were affected by Neo-classicism were Sergei Prokofiev (Russian, 1891-1953) in his *Classical Symphony;* Igor Stravinsky (born in Russia, 1882-1971) in his *Octet for Wind Instruments;* Béla Bartók (Hungarian, 1881-1945); Paul Hindemith (born in Germany, 1895-1963); Walter Piston (American, 1894-1976), who studied with the stimulating teacher Nadia Boulanger in France; and others. Stravinsky expressed some of the ideas of the Neo-classicists when he said: "I evoke neither human joy nor human sadness. I move towards a greater abstraction." And "[Music] is given to us with the sole purpose of establishing an order among things."

Atonal Music: Professors Willi Apel and Ralph T. Daniel define *atonality* or *atonal music* as "terms used frequently to denote certain practices in twentieth-century music in which a definite tonal center or 'key' is purposely avoided. . . . The discarding of tonal centers or other references of a traditional character . . . means that some principles recognizable in tonal music are abandoned, and are replaced by others of a much more intangible nature."

Arnold Schönberg (Austrian, 1874-1951) was one of the leading composers of atonal music. He developed what is known as "12-tone technique." Schönberg's *Three Piano Pieces* (op. 11) is a good example of an atonal composition.

Use of Folk Songs, Dances, Legends, and Natural Rhythms: Some composers of the twentieth century continued to use native folk songs, dances, legends, and natural rhythms in their work. These composers included Heitor Villa-Lobos (Brazilian, c. 1881-1959), who incorporated Brazilian folk melodies into his fourteen *Chôros* (Serenades). Manuel de Falla (Spanish, 1876-1946), famous for his orchestral works; Aram Khachaturian (Armenian-Soviet, 1903-1978), who was inspired by the folklore of Armenia; and Aaron Copland (American, 1900-   ), composer of *Appalachian Spring.*

Symphonic jazz developed. Examples were *The Creation of the World* by Darius Milhaud (French, 1892-1974), and *Rhapsody in Blue,* by George Gershwin (American, 1898-1937). George Gershwin called jazz "an American folk-music." Afro-rhythms influenced a variety of jazz and other compositions.

Nadia Boulanger, orchestra conductor and teacher of musicians and composers.

New Approaches to Music

Transcribed music was widely used. The magnetic tape as a medium for recording was developed in 1947. The long-playing record appeared in 1948. Then came "high fidelity" and stereophonic sound. By the early 1960s the annual sale of records in the United States alone was over $400 million, and by 1980 the enjoyment of records had become a part of the lives of millions of people.

Experimentation with *electronic music* began in the 1950s. Sounds that existed in nature and sounds that were produced by electronic means were recorded on magnetic tape and used by the composer in his or her music. For example, the composer might smash a bottle on a stone, record the sound, and change it to a new sound by playing the tape backwards. The German Karlheinz Stockhausen (1928–) did interesting work with such music.

John Cage (1912–) of the United States helped to develop *aleatory* music. Such music depends primarily upon live musical performance. However, all of the pitches and rhythms of the music are not fixed, and the performer may add other elements. Each performance of a work of this music will be different from another performance of the same work.

Rock Music and Beyond

By the late 1950s, rock music, enthusiastically supported by young people, had become tremendously popular and successful. It stressed a strong beat with unusual accents, and provided additional musical impact by repetition of harmonic patterns. Electric bass, drums, and particularly the electric guitar were some of the instruments used by rock groups.

Elvis Presley, Chuck Berry, Bob Dylan, the Beatles, the Rolling Stones, and others presented a variety of exciting forms of rock. "Folk-rock" gained following among people of all ages when it combined music with words of social criticism. "How does it feel," asked Bob Dylan, "to be . . . like a rolling stone?"

In the 1970s and early 1980s new rhythms were being danced to in discos; new symphonies were being developed in composers' studios; and new concerts, both classical and popular, were being planned throughout the world. Music continued to be an international language.

6. The Challenge of Contemporary Problems

In the early 1980s the peoples of the world faced serious problems. These included the following:

Population Pressures

By 1979 the world's population had grown to over four billion, quadrupling in the last 150 years. World population was growing at a rate of 190,000 people per day, or almost 70 million more people each year. It was estimated that it would be possible for the world population to double in a little over 40 years.

New and promising projects were overwhelmed by numbers. For example, the huge Aswan Dam was built to irrigate enough additional farmland to feed four million Egyptians. Then, while the dam was being constructed, the population of Egypt rose by ten million!

Many nations tried to do something about the problems caused by large populations. China, for example, committed itself to achieving zero population growth between 1985 and 2000.

The Gap between Developed and Developing Countries

Many of the basic goods of the world were not shared by all. In the developing countries of Africa, Latin America, and Asia lived over 75 percent of the world's population. Yet these people had less than 20 percent of the world's income and only about 12 percent of its industrial output. The people of thirty-two countries around the world needed food desperately.

According to Estefania Aldaba-Lim, a *United Nations Report on Children* estimated that out of 100 children born every minute in developing countries, 20 would die within the year. Of the 80 who survived, 60 would have no access to modern medical care during childhood. During this period, their chances of dying would be ten to twenty times higher than if they lived in Europe or North America. The efforts of Mother Teresa, a nun who devoted her life to the care of the destitute in Calcutta, India and who was awarded the Nobel Peace Prize in 1979, underlined the seriousness of the situation.

The situation for education was no better. In the second half of the 1970s it was estimated that some 120 million children between the ages of six and eleven were out of school in the developing countries of the world. In some of the poorer countries of Africa and Asia, only about thirty-three percent of the children attended primary school. In some farming areas, the figure was as low as ten percent.

Energy Shortages

In the latter part of the 1970s, the developed countries, which had 20 percent of the total population, used 85 percent of the world's annual energy production. The United States and other countries became seriously concerned about energy shortages, particularly by a diminished supply of oil. These shortages were said to be a result of a variety of factors, including: 1. the excessive and often wasteful use of the earth's natural resources, 2. the cutting down of oil supplies from the Middle East, and 3. insufficient long-range planning. It was predicted that, at the present rates of consumption, the world's supply of oil and gas would be seriously depleted in another 30–35 years. Coal could last a while longer, but obtaining it and using it raised ecological problems.

Increasing attention was therefore given to new sources of energy: nuclear power, solar power, wind power, and others. Each type of energy had its supporters. One group pointed out that the solar energy reaching the continental United States was between 600 and 700 times the nation's total energy requirements. It estimated that if even a small percentage of that energy could be harnessed, all of the nation's energy needs could be met.

Environmental Pollution

Books such as Rachel Carson's *Silent Spring* warned against the abuse of the natural environment. The facts of life spoke for themselves.

Some rivers and lakes had become so polluted with industrial waste that fish could no longer live in them. Some foods had become dangerous to eat because of the indiscriminate use of lethal chemicals. The air had become filled with poisonous fumes from automobiles, and smoke covered some cities like a grey shroud. It often seemed a war was going on between humans and nature. Increasing numbers of people realized that—in the end—they would not be the victors.

Inflation

Inflation threatened the economic security of nations throughout the world. From 1971 to 1977, the average rate of change, or inflation, in Chile was 234.2 percent; in Argentina, 126.2 percent; in Saudi Arabia, 19.5 percent; in Japan, 11.5 percent; in France, 9.6 percent; in the United States, 7.0 percent; in Germany, 5.6 percent; and in Tunisia, 5.4 percent. By 1979 the rate of inflation in the United States was about 9.0 percent.

Prices rose feverishly and the cost of living reached dangerous levels. Living became especially difficult for the poor, the aged, and those with fixed incomes. Above everyone there hung the threat of a recession, a depression, and widespread unemployment.

Armaments

The danger of war still persisted all over the world. As a result, many nations continued to pour large sums into armaments. More than 400 billion dollars were spent each year on armaments. This was more than $750,000 a minute. For every living person there existed the equivalent of 15 tons of explosives.

The relationships between the United States and the Soviet Union were crucial. The nuclear bombs of these two powers were enough to destroy every city in the world—seven times! Thus, the SALT I and SALT II agreements were efforts to set limits on the strategic arms race between these countries.

SALT I focused on limiting deployment of missiles. Secretary of State Cyrus Vance called it "a vital beginning." SALT II was concerned with working out more extensive arrangements between the United States and the Soviet Union.

Extending Human Rights

The General Assembly of the United Nations adopted the *Universal Declaration of Human Rights* in 1948. This document declared that people should have such rights as liberty, freedom of speech, and opportunity for employment.

In 1975 the *Helsinki Agreement* was signed by the United States, Canada, the Soviet Union, and 32 other nations of Western and Eastern Europe. In one part of it, the signers agreed to support the idea of freer movement of people and ideas. However, there were disagreements between the Soviet Union and the United States and among other countries over the meaning of the terms of the Helsinki Agreement. There continued to be difficult obstacles to human freedom.

In the late 1970s and early 1980s, concerted efforts were made throughout the world to gain respect for the rights of all human beings regardless of race, religion, sex, language, national or ethnic background, or political, economic, social, and cultural ideas. Racism was combated throughout the world. The movement to extend the rights of women grew. In the past, many women had received lower pay than men for doing the same work, had been limited in their choices of careers, and had not been given opportunities to develop their potentialities. By 1980 considerable progress had been made in some countries to improve the rights of women.

However, serious problems remained. It soon became clear that words, in themselves, were insufficient guarantees of human rights. The attitudes and actions of people and nations were the keys to change.

A Not-So-Final Note

So we come to the beginning of our world history. The beginning, not the end, because history is always in the process of beginning. There are always new people, new ideas, and new events. Our history book is not a fixed, unchanging, closed body of knowledge. Rather, it is a beginning in an uninterrupted flow of beginnings in the history of humankind.

What, then, can we learn from our book? One of the principal points is this: The *basic* needs of most people are the same regardless of the period in which they live. They seek food, shelter, work, leisure, health, love, peace, and meaning to their lives.

No generation has ever achieved all of these things. Yet, with sufficient intelligence, compassion, and determination, some generation might. Will it be yours?

LET'S MEET THE PEOPLE

The Heart of Humankind: A Fable

Five centuries had passed since history's first heart transplant operation, but the facts in the case had all been carefully recorded. The heart had belonged to a young woman who had died of injuries incurred in a traffic accident. Specialists had transplanted the organ into the body of a middle-aged man believed to be dying, and the patient had survived the operation.

A UPI clipping, preserved through the ages, related the event:

The chief surgeon set up five teams.

The first team connected heart and lung machines to the man and to the body of the woman.

The second team removed the woman's heart and connected it to a pump to keep blood circulating in it.

The third team removed the man's heart.

The fourth team placed the woman's heart into the man's chest cavity. The medical team connected it to veins and arteries.

The fifth team placed electrodes against the transplanted heart and applied a short burst of electricity.

The heart began to beat on its own.

All this was five centuries ago, when medical techniques were in their infancy. Now, in 2480 A.D., surgeons had it in their power to place into a human body a heart that would beat not just for the individual but for all humankind. And scholars and sages from throughout the galaxy had gathered to decide the question: Whose heart should be selected?

"Let it be the heart of the poet," urged some, and spoke of lovely poems about tufts of flowers, the look of heather, and the sound of wind in the fields. Yet, even as they spoke, they remembered the biting poetry of T. S. Eliot and others. Why choose the heart of those individuals who thought of human beings as "hollow men"?

"Let it be the heart of the scientist," suggested others, pointing to Marie Curie, who rewarded humankind with the radium that destroyed her. Yet they could not deny a task force report that showed the dangerous effects of applying scientific knowledge: "A nuclear attack of 10,000 megatons in ground bursts could, in the course of sixty days, destroy 80 percent of the population of the United States."

"Let it be the heart of the philosopher," insisted others. Who can surpass Socrates, who preferred to drink a full cup of poison to an empty cup of life?

Yet what was one to do with the pessimism of the philosopher Schopenhauer, who said: "The young hydra which grows like a bud out of the old one, and afterwards separates itself from it, fights while it is still joined to the old one for the prey that offers itself, so that one snatches it out of the mouth of the other . . . the human race reveals in itself the most terrible destructiveness in this same conflict"?

"Let it be the heart of the statesman and stateswoman, the leaders of human beings," proclaimed others. Yet Catherine the Great had rejoiced in the slaughter of peasants; Napoleon had abandoned his doomed army to the Russians; and Adolf Hitler had gassed human beings at Buchenwald.

"Let it be the heart of the composer," declared others, as they filled the conference room with the music of Beethoven's *Ninth Symphony* and Debussy's *La Mer*. Yet it was recalled that in the Marseillaise-Deutschland über Alles-Yankee Doodle Dandy world of music, millions of human beings had hummed, whistled, and sung their way to war and death.

In this manner, in the year 2480 A.D., the sages of the galaxy considered, analyzed, discussed, debated, and argued concerning the selection of the heart to be chosen for all humankind. Then, suddenly, a child appeared.

In her cupped hands, whose cushioning fingers were stained red, she carried something soft, something feathery, something lifeless.

"I did not see it," the child said softly. "I was walking in the grass and I did not see it."

"I did not see it," the child repeated. "It was in the grass but I did not see it. And I crushed it under my shoe."

"I did not see it," the child said again. "Until I killed it."

Then she wept for life and death and life.

And suddenly all the sages assembled knew where they could find the only heart in the galaxy that beat not just for the individual but for all humans.

An original tale written by Daniel Roselle.

CHAPTER REVIEW
Think and Discuss

1. Discoveries in one field of knowledge can lead to accomplishments in other fields. Find examples to prove this statement. What are they?
2. Some scientific discoveries can be used for both constructive and destructive purposes. Give some examples of such discoveries in recent times.
3. Which of the following do you think is most difficult to write today: a poem, a short story, or a play? Why?
4. Do you have a favorite contemporary writer? Why do you like her or his writing?
5. What styles or style of painting do you find most enjoyable? Who are some of your favorite artists?
6. Which do you prefer: to listen to a record of modern music at home, or to go to a concert where it is performed? Why?
7. List five ways in which you think contemporary problems are going to affect your life.
8. What do you think is meant by the statement: "Our history book . . . is a beginning of an uninterrupted flow of beginnings in the history of humankind"?

Past and Present

1. Why do many artists, writers, and composers of this century refuse to follow the styles, techniques, and ideas of earlier generations?
2. Compare the present exploration of space with the exploration of the Western Hemisphere in the fifteenth and sixteenth centuries.

Activities

1. Have an art exhibit in your classroom illustrating the artistic movements mentioned in this chapter.
2. List some of the great scientific achievements of the past thirty years. Prepare a picture display to accompany your list.

INDEX

211; language of, 211; migrations of, 209-210
Barak, General, 133
Barbarians, 29-30
Barbarossa, Frederick, Holy Roman emperor, 253, 259, 261
Baroque art and architecture, 336, 338; *illus.* 337
Baroque music, 338-339
Bartók, Béla, 629
Basques, 578
Bastille, 371-372
Battles: of Ayachucho, 393; of Blenheim, 324; of the Bulge, 553; of Châllons, 127; of the Coral Sea, 553; of Dunkirk, 549; of Hastings, 268, of Jutland, 507; of Lepanto, 311; of Marathon, 90; of the Marne, 507; second of the Marne, 509; for Midway Island, 554; of Mohacs, 326; of the Nations, 382; of Pavia, 287; of Plassey, 359; of Poltava, 334; of Saratoga, 363; of Stalingrad, 550; of Tannenberg, 507; of Thermopylae, 91; of Tours, 156; of Zama, 109
Bay of Pigs, 574
Beatles, the, 630
Bedouins, 149-150
Beer-Hall Putsch, 535
Beethoven, Ludwig van, 436
Begin, Menachem, 604-605
Belgian Congo (Zaire), 492, 608, 609
Belguim: in Africa, 492, 608; in the Common Market, 570-571; founding of, 312; independence for, 402; industrial revolution in, 421; and Napoleon, 378; in NATO, 569; in World War I, 507; in World War II, 549
Bell, Alexander Graham, 419
Bella Coola tribe (Native American), 218
Ben Bella, Ahmed, 610
Ben-Gurion, David, 600
Benedictine monks, 238, 239
Benelux countries, 567
Benelux Customs Union, 567
Bengal, 358
Benin (Dahomey), 209, 609
Berber kingdoms, 204
Berbera, 212
Berbers, 201, 204-205, 207
Bergson, Henri, 624
Bering Strait, 217
Berlin, 568-569
Berlioz, Hector, 436-437
Bernini, Giovanni Lorenzo, 338
Berry, Chuck, 630
Bessarabia, 548
Bessemer converter, 416
Bessemer, Henry, 416
Beveridge, Albert J., 487
Bhagavad-Gita, 60, 61
Bhartrihari, 165

Bhasa, 164
Bhutto, Zulfikar Ali, 589-590
Biafra, Republic of, 609
Bible, The, early Jewish history in, 131, 132, 133, 134; epistles of, 140; gospels of, 136-137, 138; life of Jesus in, 136-138; testaments of, 138.   See also *New Testament, Old Testament*
Bill of Rights (England), 351-352; *Chart* of, 351
Bill of Rights (United States), 352
Bishop, 237
Bismark, Otto von: as Chancellor of Germany, 455, 456; unites Germany, 452-454; and the Triple Alliance, 504
Black Hole of Calcutta, 358-359
Black Sea, 249
Blake, William, 433
Blanc, Louis, 401
Blenheim, battle of, 324
Blitzkrieg, 548
Bloody Sunday (in Russia), 521
Blum, Leon, 542
Boat people, 595; *illus.,* 595
Boccaccio, Giovanni, 282
Bodhisattvas (Buddhist), 189
Boers, 468
Bohemia, 403
Boileau, Nicholas, 339
Bolívar, Simón, 392-393
Bologna, University of, 266
Bolsheviks, 519-520, 523, 524
Bonparte, Joseph, king of Naples and Spain, 380, 392
Bonparte, Louis, king of Netherlands, 380
Bonaparte, Napoleon.   See *Napoleon Bonaparte*
Bonapartism, 384, 401
Bonheur, Rosa, 436
The Book of the Dead, 47, *illus.,* 49
The Book of the Three Virtues (Christine of Pisan), 276
Book of the Travels of Marco Polo, 182
Borodin, Aleksandr, 477
Bosnia, 480, 504, 505
Boston Tea Party, 362
Botticelli, Sandro, 284
Boucher, François, 338
Boulanger, Nadia, 629
Boumedienne, Houari, 610
Bourbon, Henri de.   See *Henry IV, king of France*
Bourbon family, 397, 400
Bourgeois Monarchy, 401
Bourgeoisie: defined, 256; in Marxist theory, 432; origin of word, 259
Boxer Rebellion, 487-488
Brahe, Tycho, 292
Brahmagupta, 166
Brahman, 60
Brahms, Johannes, 436
Brandenburg, 328
Brandenburg-Prussia, 328

Brandt, Willy, 569
Braque, Georges, 625
Brazil: independence for, 393; Portuguese in, 305, 390, 392; size of, 387; slavery in, 308
Brest-Litovsk, treaty of, 523
Breughel, Pieter, 290
Brezhnev, Leonid, 574
Briand-Kellogg Treaty, 544-545
Britain.   See *England, Great Britain*
British East Africa, 494
British East India Company, 307-308, 313, 469, 470
British Gold Coast (Ghana), 608
British North America Act (1867), 466
Brooks, Gwendolyn, 624
Bruges, Belgium, 258
Brunelleschi, Filippo, 283
Brussels Treaty, 567
Bryan, William Jennings, 487
Buchenwald, 537
Buddha, Gautama, 62-63, 189
Buddhism: beliefs of Mahayana, 189; in China, 174, 175; in India, 62-63, 163-164, 167, 168; in Japan, 189, 190; of Mongols in China, 183
Bulgaria: in Balkan wars, 504-505; independence of, 480; revolts against Turkey, 479; Soviet control of, 566; in Warsaw Pact, 570; in World War I, 507; in World War II treaties, 564
Bulge, battle of the, 553
Bundesrat, 455
Burgundy, duke of, 272
Burial: of Mound Builders, 222; Neanderthal, 8-9; of Pharaohs, 47; prehistoric, 13
Burin, 10
Burke, Edmund, 362
Burma, 469, 590
Burma Road, 554
Bushmen, 201, 210, 468
Bushido, 193
Byron, Lord, 434
Byzantine Empire, 249-254; art of, 250; crusades and, 251-254; demise of, 253, 309; *map,* 252; religion of, 154; trade in, 251; warfare of, 331
Byzantium, 249

Cabinet (Britain), 353
Cable, trans-Atlantic, 418
Cabot, John, 305
Cabral, Pedro Alvarez, 303, 305, 390
Caesar, Julius, 112-114
Cage, John, 630
Calcutta, India, 358-359
Calder, Alexander, 627-628
Calendar: Chinese, 69, 175; Egyptian, 41-42; Julian, 123
Caliph, the, 154
Callicrates, 93
Calvin, John, 295-297

Crusades, 251-254, 271
Crystal Palace Exhibition, 442
Cuba, 495, 574; *map,* 496; in Africa, 611
Cubism, 441, 625
Cui, César, 477
Cuneiform, 25-26
Culture, defined, 3
Cuzco, 230, 231
Cyprus, 599; British in, 480, 515; Turkish-Greek war over, 607
Cyrus, king of Persia, 33
Czar (source of word), 332
Czechoslovakia: and Egypt, 601; Hitler's Germany in, 547; Soviet Union in, 566, 573-574; in Treaty of Versailles, 511; in Warsaw Pact, 570

D-Day, 553
da Feltre, Vittorino, 286
da Palestrina, Giovanni, 286
da Vinci, Leonardo, 278, 282, 284-285, 287
Dachau, 532
Dahomey (Benin), 493, 609
Daimler, Gottlieb, 419
Dali, Salvador, 625
Danelaw, the (Viking), 242
Dante, 275
Darby, Alexander, 415
Dardanelles, the, 507, 515, 565
Darío, Rubén, 623
Darius, king of Persian Empire, 33, 90
Darwin, Charles, 443
Daumier, Honoré, 438
David, king of Israel, 134
Dawes Plan, 515
Dayan, Moshe, 603
de Falla, Manuel, 629
de Gaulle, Charles: in Algeria, 609-610; forms Fifth Republic, 516; in World War II, 549, 553; and NATO, 569-570
de' Medici, Catherine, 314
de' Medici, Cosimo, 280, 281
de' Medici family, as bankers, 259
de' Medici, Lorenzo (the Magnificent), 280-281; portrait of, 280
de' Medici, Marie, queen of France, 319
de Montaigne, Michel, 288
de Ronsard, Pierre, 288
de Soto, Hernando, 305
Dead Sea, 131
Deborah, 133
Debussy, Claude, 441, 628
Decembrists, 519
Declaration of Independence, 363
Declaration of the Rights of Man (France), 372
Degas, Edgar, 441
Deism, 369
Dekanawidah, 220
del Verrocchio, Andrea, 284

Delacroix, Eugene, 436
Delaware tribe (Native Americans), 220
Delhi Sultanate (India), 168
Delian League, 97
Delius, Frederick, 628
Deloria, Vine, Jr., 625
Delphi, 89
Demeter, 83, 89
Democracy: in America, 362, 363; Bill of Rights and, 351-352; in Britain, 268, 346-347, 349, 350, 351-352, 353, 462-463; British regressive acts in, 459; after Congress of Vienna, 397, 398; in France, 374-406; French Declaration of the Rights of Man, 372; as a goal in World War I, 509; in Greece, 85-87; Habeas Corpus Act and, 350; Magna Carta and, 269; source of term, 80
Democritus, 97
Demosthenes, 98
Denmark: in the Common Market, 571; in NATO, 569; war with Prussia and Austria, 453-454; in World War II, 548-549
Depression of 1930, 542, 544
Derain, André, 615, 625
Dervishes, 494
Desai, Morarji, 589
Descartes, Rene, 293
d'Este, Isabella, 282, 286; *portrait* of, 282
Détente, 574
Developing countries (defined), 630
Devolution, war of, 324
Diaz, Bartholomew, 303, 468
Dickens, Charles, 437
Diderot, Denis, 368, 370
Dido, queen of Carthage, 35
Dien Bien Phu, 594
Diet, the (Japan), 538, 581
Diocese, the (Catholic), 237
Diocletian, emperor of Rome, 125
Dionysus, theater of, 95
Directory, French, 375-376
Disarmament, 544, 545, 631
Disraeli, Benjamin, 462, 483, 494
The Divine Comedy (Dante), 275
Divine right of kings, 322, 346; rejected, 352
Djilas, Milovan, 432
Dogma, religious, 293
Dominican Republic, 387
Dominions, British, 466, 467, 542
Don Quixote de la Mancha (Cervantes), 289
Donjon, 246
Dostoyevsky, Fyodor, 475-476; *portrait* of, 476
Drake, Francis, 313
Dravidians, 60, 61
Dubcek, Alexander, 573
Dufy, Raoul, 625
Dukas, Paul, 628

Duma, the (Russia), 521, 522
Dumas, Alexandre, (the Elder), 434
Dumbarton Oaks conference, 561
Dunkirk, battle of, 549
Dupliex, Joseph François, 358
Dürer, Albrecht, 290
Durham, Lord, 465-466
Dutch East India Company, 307, 357, 468
Dutch East Indies, 591
Dutch Netherlands, the, 316
Dutch Rebellion, 311-312
Dylan, Bob, 630

East Frankland, 241
East Germany, 566, 568, 570
Eastern Europe: Soviet Union in, 566-570. See also names of countries
Eastern Orthodox Church, 251
Eastern Roman Empire. See *Byzantine Empire*
Economic sanctions, 512, 545
Economics: Capitalism, 260, 306, 419-421; and colonial trade, 308; cooperatives and, 430-431; Fascist corporate state and, 534; in the Industrial Revolution, 419-421; laissez-faire, 370-371; of Malthus, Thomas, 428; mercantilism, 322, 351; Physiocrats on, 370-371; post-World War II, 567; reform efforts in, 428-429; of Ricardo, David, 428; of Smith, Adam, 428; Socialist, 431, 528; of Soviet Union, 525-526, 528; United Nations and, 562
Edict of Clarendon, 268
Edict of Milan, 143
Edict of Nantes, 314, 322
Edison, Thomas, 419
Education: Aztec, 228; compulsory, 430; in developing countries, 630; Education Act of 1870, 429-430; French, 379, 406; Greek, 87, 89; in India, 163, 167; in Islamic Empire, 159, 160; Italian, 286, 452; Japanese, 581; in Mali empire, 207; in medieval Europe, 266; in Roman Republic, 117; in Soviet Union, 529-530; Sumerian, 26, 36
Edward I, king of England, 269-270
Edward III, king of England, 272
Edward VI, king of England, 312
Egypt, 38-52, 599; architecture of, 48, 51; art of, 48-51; British in, 494, 507, 542; calendar of, 41-42; conquered by Alexander the Great, 99; conquered by Muslims, 155; and Czechoslovakia, 601; earliest people in, 201; empire of, 43, 45; farming in, 39; France in, 494; government of, 40-41, 42-43;

Byzantine Empire, 331; as cause of World War I, 503-504; eighteenth century progress in the, 331; French, 324, 375; Greek, 88; Japanese, 538-539; Muslim, 156; of Ottoman Empire, 309; Prussian, 329-330; of Roman Empire, 108, 111; Russian, 334; Samurai of Japan, 193; Spanish, 331; Sumerian, 28

Millet, Jean François, 438

Miltiades, 90

Minamoto clan (Japan), 193

Minaret, 154

Mindszenty, cardinal, 572

Ming dynasty (China), 183, 484

Ming Huang, emperor of China, 176

Minnesingers, 274

Minoan civilization, 81-82

Minorities, in literature, 624-625

Miracle plays, 274

Miró, Joan, 625

Mirs, 473, 521

Missionaries: in Africa, 491; apostles, 138-140; Buddhist, 163-164; Jesuit, 297; in Latin America, 391; in North America, 359

Moabites, 133

Moat, 246

Mobutu, Sese Seko (Joseph), 608

Mogul dynasty (India), 162, 168-169, 170

Mohacs, battle of, 326

Mohammed, 150-153

Mohawk tribe (Native American), 220

Mohenjo-daro, 56

Molière, 339

Moltke, general von, 454

Monasteries, 238, 258

Monet, Claude, 438, 441

Mongol Empire (China), 181-183, 184; map of, 180

Mongols (Tatars): defeated by Japan, 194; invade China, 179, 181; in Russia, 331-332

Monks: of Cluny, 248; original communities of, 238-239; in the Reformation, 295

Monotheism, defined, 131

Monroe Doctrine, 399-400, 406

Monroe, James, 399

Monsoon, 56

Monte Cassino (monastery), 238

Montenegro: independence of, 480; as part of Yugoslavia, 515; in Second Balkan War, 504; war with Turkey, 479

Montesquieu, baron de, 368, 369-370

Monteverdi, Claudio, 338

Moon landing, 622-623

Moore, Henry, 627

Moors, 273

Morality plays, 274

More, Thomas, 290

Morocco: Berbers in, 204; France in, 492; Franco-German dispute over, 503; war with Israel, 603

Morris, William, 444

Morse, Samuel F.B., 418, 443

Morton, William, 443

Mosaics, 250

Moscow, 332, 523

Moscow Declaration, of 1943, 577

Moses, 132, 134

Mosque, 154, 159

Mossadegh, Mohammed, 602

Mound Builders (Native Americans), 222-223

Mozambique, 306, 577-578, 610

Mozart, Wolfgang Amadeus, 339

Mu'awiyah, caliph of Islam, 156

Muezzen, 154

Mulattoes, 387, 392

Munich conference of 1938, 547

Munich, Germany, 258

Muqtadir, caliph of Islam, 158

Murât, Joachim, 380

Musa, Mansa Kankan, emperor of Mali, 208, 214

Muscovy, state of, 332

Music: of Africa, 615; aleatory, 630; atonal, 629; Baroque, 338-339; Egyptian, 51; electronic, 629-630; impressionistic, 441; Italian, 286, 449; neo-classical, 628-629; neo-romantic, 628; recording of, 629-630; rock, 630; romantic, 436-437; Russian, 477, 530; twentieth century, 628-630

Muslims: in Algeria, 609-610; in Byzantine empire, 251; in conflict with Jews, 543; Crusades against, 252-254; definition of, 152; in Ethiopia, 611; and European explorers, 302; in India, 168, 588; influence on Europe of, 266, 281; in Iran, 602; in Lebanon, 602; in Mali empire, 207; in medieval Europe, 240, 241; Ottoman Empire of the, 309; in Pakistan, 588; in the Philippines, 591.   See also *Islam*

Mussolini, Benito: and the Catholic church, 451; described, 533; in Ethiopia, 545; fall of, 552; and Fascist Italy, 533, 534-535; in World War II, 550

Mussorgsky, Modest , 477

Mutual Defense Assistance Treaty (Japan-United States), 581

Muzorewa, Abel, 612

Mycenae, 82, 83

Mycenaean Age (Greece), 82

Mylai, 594

Mystery plays, 274

NATO, 569-570

Nagasaki, 556

Naguib, Mohammed, 600

Nagy, Imre, 572-573

Nalanda, University of, 167

Nanking, treaty of, 485

Napata, 201

Napoleon I (Bonaparte), 366; abdication and exile of, 382-383, 397; Catholic church under, 379; crowned emperor, 378; described; 377-378; *portrait* of, 377; economy under, 379; education under, 379; law under, 379; legacy of, 383-384; *map* of empire of, 382; in Spain, 392; in Russia, 381-382; youth of, 376

Napoleon III (Louis), emperor of France: in Austro-Prussian war, 453; in Franco-Prussian war, 454; government under, 404-406; in Italian politics, 450, 451; as president, then emperor, 401-402; *portrait* of, 405

Nara, Japan, 191

Narodniki, the, 519

Nasser, Gamal Abdel, 600, 603

National Assembly (France): First, 371, 372, 374; of Fourth Republic, 576; of Second Republic, 401

National Coalition government (Britain), 542

National Health Service (Britain), 575

National Insurance and Assistance (Britain), 575

National Liberation Front (Algeria), 609

National People's Party (China), 540

National Socialists (Nazis), 535-537

National workshops (France), 401

Nationalism: in Austrian empire, 402; as cause for World War I, 503; European, 397; German, 452; in India, 587; in Iran, 602; in Italy, 449; in Japan, 490, 581-582; Napoleon and, 382; in Pakistan, 590; in Poland, 402; and the Reformation, 294; as a result of imperialism, 497; Rousseau on, 370; stimulated by French Revolution, 376

Nationalization: in Iran, 602; in Portugal, 578; in Tanzania, 609

Nations, the origin of, 267

Nations, battle, of the, 382

Native Africans: Almoravids, 207; Axumites, 203-204; Bantu, 209-210, 212-213; Berbers, 201, 204-205; Bushmen, 201; in early Africa, 201; Fulani tribe, 609; Hausa, 609; Ghanans, 206-207; Karimojong, 210; in Kenya, 608; Kikuiyu, 608; Kushites, 201-203; Lunda, 211; Malawi, 210; Pygmies, 201, 210; in Rhodesia, 612; Shona, 210, 213-214; Sossos, 207; Sotho, 210; in South Africa,

empire of, 306-307; exploration by, 301-303, 389-390; in the Far East, 306-307; founding of, 274; in NATO, 569; in Peninsular War, 381; science in, 302; slave trade of, 308-309; and Spain, 301, 311, 357; trade of, 301, 357; since World War II, 577-578

Portuguese Guinea, 610

Potsdam Conference, 555, 564, 586

Pottery: Bantu, 211; Chinese, 177; Kushite, 203; prehistoric, 11, 17

Poverty, world, 630

Power loom, 413, 415

Poznan riots, 572

Pragmatic Sanction, the, 326

Prehistoric humans, 2-18; agriculture of, 14-18; art of, 11-13; copperwork of, 17-18; Cro-Magnon, 10-13; culture of, 4-5, 6-9; earliest sites of, 2-3; farming by, 14-17; at Jarmo, 15-16; at Jericho, 16; in Israel, 16; *map* of, 4; migrations of, 3-4; Neanderthal, 6-9; tools of, 5-6, 10-11, 16

Presbyterian Church, 297, 349

Presley, Elvis, 630

Prime Minister (Britain), 353

Prince, The (Machiavelli), 283, 311

Princip, Gavrilo, 505

Príncipe, 578

Printing: in China, 177; early, 290; invention of, 279

Prokofiev, Sergei, 629

Proletariat, 432

Prophets, in Judaism, 134

Proportional representation, 576

Protagoras, 94

Protectorate, defined, 486

Protestant Reformation, the, 290, 293-297, 310

Protestants, 295, 349

Proust, Marcel, 624

Provisional Government (Russia), 522-523

Prussia: in Austro-Prussian War, 453-454; background of state of, 328; Bismark and, 452-454; and the Congress of Vienna, 397; constitution of 1850 in, 404; in the eighteenth century, 328, 329-330; in Franco-Prussian war, 454; and French Revolution, 375; geography of, 328; military of, 328-329; Napoleon defeats, 380; in Seven Years' War, 326; unification of, 330; war with Denmark, 453

Ptolmey, 267, 292

Ptolmey group, 99

Pueblos, 218

Pugachev, 335

Punic wars, 108-110

Purges, Great (Soviet Union), 530

Puritans: in America, 360; in England, 297, 312, 347; ideas of,

348; and King James I, 346

Pushkin, Alexander, 475

Pygmies, 201, 210

Pyramids: of Aztecs, 228; Egyptian, 42, 48, 50, *illus.,* 38, 42; of Kush, 202; Maya, 225, *illus.,* 225; of Mound Builders, 222; of Olmecs, 224; of Teotihuacán, 227

Pyrenees, treaty of, 321

Pythagoras, 97

Qatar, 599

Quadruple Alliance, 398

Quakers, 360

Quebec Act, 465

Queen Anne's War, 324, 360

Quesnay, François, 370

Quetzalcoatl, temple of, 227

Quipu (Incan form of communication), 231

Quito, Ecuador, 230

Quraysh tribe (Arab), 152

Rabelais, François, 288

Rachmaninoff, Sergei, 628

Racine, Jean, 339

Radical, defined, 431

Radio-carbon dating, 15

Radioisotopes, 620

Rahman, Mujibur, 590

Rahman, Ziaur, 590

Railroads, 418, 421

Rain forest, 210, 225

Ramadan, 154

Ramayana, the, 60

Ramayana of Tulsi Das, 169

Raphael, 285

Rasputin, 519

Rauschenberg, Robert, 627

Realism (in the arts), 437-438

Rebels (Spanish Civil War), 546

Rebellions. See *Revolutions*

Reciprocal Trade Agreements Program (United States), 544

Reconquista (Spain), 273

Red Sea, 149

Red Shirts (Italy), 451

Reform Act of 1867 (Britain), 463

Reform Bill of 1832 (Britain), 460-461

Reformation. See *Protestant Reformation*

Refugees: East German, 568-569; Palestinian, 600, 605; Vietnamese, 595

Regulatory Act (Britain), 469

Reichstag (Germany), 455, 536

Relativity, theories of, 619

Religion: African, 207; American colonies and, 360; in Austria, 327, 328; Babylonian, 30; Bantu, 209; Buddhist in India, 62-63, 163-164; Buddhist in Japan, 189; Catholic-Protestant conflicts and, 322; and Catholic Reformation, 297-298; in China,

175, 541; communities for, 238-239; Confucian, 71-73; Deist, 369; in East Africa, 212; Egyptian, 39, 47-48, 131; in German empire, 455; Greek, 83, 89; Hindu, 60-61; Inca, 230; in India, 60, 62-63, 163-164, 167, 168; Indo-Aryan, 60; Irish conflict over, 464; Jesuits and, 297; Kushite, 202-203; in Latin America, 391; *map* of, in 1560, 312; of Middle East, 599; of Northern Native Americans, 223-224; Maya, 225; medieval Christian, 237-239; in Nazi Germany, 536; Neanderthal, 9; persecution and colonization and, 360; of Persian Empire, 33-34; Phoenician, 35; prehistoric, 13; Protestant Reformation and, 293-297, 310; as a reason for exploration, 306; in Restoration England, 349-350; in Roman Empire, 117-118; in Russia, 332, 473, 523, 528; Shinto, 188; Spanish Inquisition and, 274; Sumerian, 24-25; Taoist, 73; tolerance of, in England, 352, 463; tolerance for, in France, 314, 315-316; wars of, 310-311, 314-316, 346-347, 349. See also *Catholic Church* and names of religions

Renaissance, the, 278-298; architecture of, 283, 285; art of, 282, 284-285, 288-290; education in, 286; in England, 290-291; effect of, on Europe, 281; in France, 287-288; ideal gentleman of, 298; in Italy, 279-286; literature of, 281, 282-283; medieval transition to, 279; music of, 286; origin of word, 278; at the Papal Court, 285; philosophical ideas of, 293; science of, 292-293; in Spain, 288-289; women of, 286

Renoir, Pierre Auguste, 438

Reparations, war, 511, 515-516

Repin, 477

Republic, The (Plato), 94

Republic of China (Taiwan), 564

Respighi, Ottorino, 628

Restoration, the (England), 349-350

Revolution of 1830 (France), 400

Revolutionary War (American), 360-364

Revolutions: American, 360-364; in Austria, 402-403; Bangladesh, 589-590; Belgian (1830), 402; in Bohemia, 403; Boxer Rebellion, 487-488; Bulgarian, 479; in Canada, 465; in China, 485, 539, 541; in the Congo (Zaire), 608; Cuban, 574; Eastern European, 572-574; in Egypt, 600; in

in, 266; Napoleon in, 380, 392; in Americas, 307; in Peninsular War, 381; under Philip II, 311; and Portugal, 301, 311, 357; Renaissance in, 288-289; in the Spanish-American War, 495; and Thirty Years' War, 321; unification of, 273-274; Vikings in, 242; Visigoths in, 273; wars with Elizabethan England, 313; war with France, 316; in World War II, 578; since World War II, 578

Spanish-American War, 486, 495
Spanish Armada, 313
Spanish Civil War, 547
Spanish March, the, 240
Spanish Netherlands (Belgium), 311, 326
Spanish Succession, War of the, 324
Sparta, 88, 97
Special Theory of Relativity, 619
Spheres of influence, defined, 485-486
Spinning jenny, 413
Spinning mule, 413
Spirit of Laws, The (Montesquieu), 369
Squire, (medieval), 246-247
Sri Lanka (Ceylon), 590
Ssu-ma Ch'ien, 174
Stakhanovites, 528
Stalin, Joseph, 567; death of, 571; denunciation of, 571-572; photo of, 524; returns from exile, 522; Soviet Union under, 525-530; and United Nations, 561; at Yalta, 555, 564, 565
Stalingrad, battle of, 550
Stamp Act of 1765 (Britain), 361
Stampa, Gaspara, 286
Stanley, Henry Morton, 491, 492
Statute of Westminster (Britain), 542
Steam engine, 415
Steamboat, 418
Steinbeck, John, 624
Steel industry, 416-417
Steinheil, Charles, 418
Stelae, 203, 224
Stephenson, George, 418
Stock Market crash of 1929, 544
Stockhausen, Karlheinz, 630
Stoicism, 124
Stola, 119
Storm Troopers, 536
Strait of Magellan, 303
Straits of Gibraltar, 258
Strategic Arms Limitation Treaty (SALT), I and II, 574-575, 631
Strauss, Richard, 628
Stravinsky, Igor, 629
Strikes, labor: in ancient Egypt, 46-47; in India, 589
Stuart family, 345, 352
Stupas, 164
Sudan, 201, 494-495, 603; map, 493

Sudetenland, 546, 547
Suez Canal, the: Britain and, 542; construction of, 494; crisis over, 600-601
Suffrage: British, 459, 460-461, 463; Japanese, 538, 581; for women, 467
Suharto, president of Indonesia, 592
Sui dynasty (China), 175
Sukarno, 590-592
Suleiman, sultan of Ottoman empire, 309
Sulla, 111
Sumerians, 24-29; culture of, 26, 28; kings of, 28-29; government of, 28; military of, 28; religion of, 24-25; writing of, 25-26
Summa Theologica (Aquinas), 267
Sun Yat-sen, 539-541
Sundiata, king of Mali, 207
Sung dynasty (China), 179-181; map, 177
Sunni Ali, emperor of Songhay, 208
Supreme Soviet, the, 526
Surrealism, 625
Swahili, 211
Swahili culture, 212-213
Sweden, 397
Switzerland, 295, 316, 397
Synagogue, 134
Syria, 599; conquered by Alexander the Great, 99; conquered by Arab Muslims, 154-155; in Lebanon, 605; as a mandate, 515; Seljuk Turks in, 252; and war with Israel, 600, 603, 604

Tables of the Law (Israeli), 134
Tablinum, 117
Tacitus, 121
Taft, William Howard, 487
Tagore, Rabindranath, 623
T'ai P'ing Rebellion (China), 485
T'ai Tsung, emperor of China, 175
Taiwan (Formosa), 484, 486, 490, 583
Taj Mahal, 169
Tale of Genji, The (Lady Murasaki Shikibu), 191
Talleyrand, prince, 397
Tamerlane, 168
Tang dynasty (China), 172, 175-179; in Japan, 192; map of, 177
Tanganyika, 609
Tannenberg, battle of, 507
Tanzania, United Republic of, 609
Taoism, 73
Tapestries, 246
Taro root, 210
Tasman, Abel, 466
Tasmania, 466
Tatars, 332
Taxation: early European, 254; in Ireland, 464; Sumerian, 29
Tchaikovsky, Peter Ilich, 477

Tea Act of 1773 (Britain), 362
Technical Assistance plan (TA), 567
Technology: Assyrian, 32; Chinese ancient, 70, 167; in India, 166; in Mesopotamia, 24, 31; of Middle Ages, 245-246, 266-267; from 1000 to 1750 A.D., 411; prehistoric, 5-6, 10-11; transmitted during Crusades, 253. See also Science
Telegraph, 418, 419
Telephone, invention of, 419
Telford, Thomas, 417
Temples: Aztec, 228; Greek, 93; Inca, 230-231; Japanese Buddhist, 192; in Jerusalem, 134, 135, 136; of Kush, 202; of Mound Builders, 222 illus. 222; Sumerian, 25; of Teotihuacán, 227
Ten Commandments, 132
Teng Hsiao-p'ing, 583
Tenochititlán, 228, 388
Teotihuacán, 217, 226-228; illus, 227
Teresa, Mother, 630
Test Act of 1673 (England), 350
Teutonic Knights, 328
Texococo, Lake, 228
Textile industry, 258, 412-415
Thailand, 596
Thales, 97
Thant, U, 563, 603
Thatcher, Margaret, 576
Theater: French classical, 339; in ancient Greece, 95-96; medieval, 274
Thebes, 97
Themistocles, 91
Theocritus, 101
Theodoric the Ostrogoth, 126
Theodosius, emperor of Rome, 143
Thermopylae, battle of, 91
Third Coalition, 380
Third Communist International, 524
Third French Republic, 406
Third World, the, 563
Thirty Years' War, 314-316, 320-321
Three Estates (France), 367
Three Mile Island accident, 620
Three Principles (Sun Yat-sen), 540
Thucydides, 96
Thutmose I, 43
Thutmose III, 43, 45; map of Egypt under, 45
Tiara clan (Japan), 193
Tiber River, 106
Tigris River, 15, 23, 24, 32, 157
Tikal, 225
Timbuktu, Mali, 207
Tipis, 223
Titicaca, Lake, 230
Tito, Marshal (Joseph Broz), 566-567

warfare at sea in 507; on the Western Front, 507, 516

World War II, 545-556; D-Day in 553; declaration of, 548; end of, 553, 555-556; fighting of, 548-556; *map* of changes after, 565; *map* of, in Europe and Africa, 551; *map* of in Pacific, 554; in North Africa, 552-553; in the Pacific, 551-552, 553-555; recovery efforts after, 567; Soviet Union in, 550; treaties after, 564; United States in, 550-552; on the Western Front, 549-550; world prior to, 545-547

Wright Brothers, 419

Wright, Frank Lloyd, 628

Writing: Assyrian, 32; Aztec, 228; Chinese, 68, 69; cuneiform of Sumerians, 25-26; Egyptian, 41; Greek, 82, 83; ideograms in, 26; Inca quipu, 231; in India, 56; in Japan, 188, 191; Kushite, 203; Maya, 226; of Olmecs, 224; Phoenician, 36; pictograms in, 25. See also *Alphabet*

Wu, empress of China, 176

Wu Tao-tzu, 177

Wu Ti, emperor of China, 173-174

Wycliffe, John, 294, 301

X-rays, 619

Xerxes, king of Persian empire, 90-92

Yakima tribe (Native American), 223

Yalta Conference, 555, 561, 564, 565

Yamato, prince-chiefs of, 188

Yangtze River, 67

Yazid, caliph of Islam, 156

Yeats, William Butler, 624

Yellow River, 67

Yemen, 599, 603

Yoritomo, shogun of Japan, 193; *portrait* of, 193

York, House of, 271

Yorktown, Virginia, 363

Yoruba tribe (Native African), 609

Young Italy, society of, 449

Yuan Shi-k'ai, 540

Yucatán, 225

Yugoslavia: under Tito, 566-567; after World War I, 515; in World War II, 550

Zaire, 210, 492

Zaire, Democratic Republic of, 608

Zaire (Congo) River, 200, 210

Zama, battle of, 109

Zambia, 611

Zambesi River, 200, 210

Zambos, 391

Zanzibar, 494, 609

Zeila, 212

Zemsky Sobor, 333, 334

Zeno, 101-102

Zeus, 83, 89

Zhukov, Marshal, 553

Ziggurats, 25, 30, 32

Zimbabwe, 213-214, 612

Zionists, 599

Zola, Émile, 437

Zollverein, 452

Zoroastroanism, 33-34, 154

Zwingli, Ulrich, 295

SOURCES

Sources are keyed to the left (l) or right (r) column on a page. Top, middle (mid.), or bottom (bot.) location in a column may also be indicated.

Prologue

Page

8(r)   Ralph S. Solecki, "Shanidar IV, A Neanderthal Flower Burial in Northern Iraq," *Science*, November 28, 1975, p. 880.

16(r,mid.)   Kathleen M. Kenyon, *Archaeology in the Holy Land*, 3rd ed. (New York: Praeger Publishers, 1970), p. 50.

17(r)   Ibid., p. 72.

Unit 1

29(l)   Chester G. Starr, *A History of the Ancient World* (New York: Oxford University Press, 1965), p. 45.

29(r)   Ibid., p. 47.

30(l)   Philip K. Hitti, *The Near East in History: A 5000 Year Story* (New York: D. Van Nostrand Co., 1961), p. 41.

30(r,top)   James B. Pritchard, ed., *Ancient Near Eastern Texts Relating to the Old Testament* (Princeton: Princeton University Press, 1955), p. 175.

Page

30(r,mid.)   James Wellard, *Babylon* (New York: Saturday Review Press, 1962), p. 123.

32(l,bot.)   Starr, *History of the Ancient World*, p. 133.

34(r)   *The New English Bible* (Cambridge, England: Oxford University Press, 1970), Ezek., 27:3-7.

37(r)   Samuel Noah Kramer, *The Sumerians: Their History, Culture, and Character* (Chicago: University of Chicago Press, 1963), pp. 244-45.

39(r)   Pearl M. Steinhaus, "The Nile Valley," *United Nations World*, March 1951.

47(l,top)   Paul Jordan, *Egypt the Black Land* (New York: E. P. Dutton & Co., 1976), p. 133.

48(l,bot.)   Ibid., p. 147.

60(l)   Will Durant, *Our Oriental Heritage*, The Story of Civilization: Part I (New York: Simon & Schuster, 1963), p. 566.

62(l)   Ibid., p. 493.

66   James Legge, *The Chinese Classics Translated into English*, vol. 1 (Seattle: University of Washington Press, 1960).

69(l)   Charles O. Hucker, *China's Imperial Past* (Stanford: Stanford University Press, 1975), pp. 29-30.

Unit 2

Page

94(l) Bertrand Russell, *A History of Western Philosophy* (New York: Simon & Schuster, 1945), p. 76.

94(r) Robert F. Davidson, *Philosophies Men Live By* (New York: Holt, Rinehart and Winston, 1952), p. 23.

103(r) John M. Good, *The Shaping of Western Society: An Inquiry Approach,* 2nd ed. (New York: Holt, Rinehart and Winston, 1974).

117(l) William Warde Fowler, *Social Life at Rome in the Age of Cicero* (New York: Macmillan Co., 1959), p. 185.

117(r) Ibid., p. 203.

122(r,mid.) Charles Theophilus Murphy, Kevin Guinagh, and Whitney Jennings Oates, *Greek and Roman Classics in Translation* (New York: Longmans, Green & Co., 1947), pp. 1002-1003.

131(l&r) *The New English Bible* (Cambridge, England: Oxford University Press, 1970), Gen. 11:31-12:2.

132(l) Ibid., Exod. 20:3-17.

133(l) Ibid., Judg. 5:2-3.

134(r,bot.) Abram Leon Sachar, *A History of the Jews* (New York: Alfred A. Knopf, 1964), p. 61.

136(r) Will Durant, *Caesar and Christ,* The Story of Civilization: Part III (New York, Simon & Schuster, 1944), p. 554.

137(l) *New English Bible,* Matt. 6:19-21.

138(r) Ibid., Acts, 9:3-9.

139(l) Ibid., Acts, 16:11-15.

Unit 3

148 Arthur Jeffery, trans., *The Koran: Selected Suras* (New York: Heritage Press, 1958), p. 23.

152(l) Philip K. Hitti, *Makers of Arab History* (New York: St. Martin's Press, 1968), p. 7.

153(l) Ibid., p. 18.

154(r) Ibid., p. 30.

156(l) Reynold A. Nicholson, *A Literary History of the Arabs* (Cambridge, England: Cambridge University Press, 1969), p. 195.

156(r) Ibid., p. 418.

157(l) Philip K. Hitti, *History of the Arabs* (New York: St. Martin's Press, 1967), p. 4.

163(r,bot.) Jawaharlal Nehru, *The Discovery of India* (New York: John Day Co., 1946), p. 125.

165(l) Mark Van Doren, ed., *An Anthology of World Poetry,* rev. and enl. ed. (New York: Harcourt, Brace & World, 1964), p. 61.

Page

168(r,bot.) H. G. Rawlinson, *India: A Short Cultural History,* ed. C. G. Seligman (New York: D. Appleton-Century Co., 1938), p. 319.

174(l) Yong Yap and Arthur Cotterell, *The Early Civilization of China,* p. 81.

176(r) Arthur Waley, *The Poetry and Career of Li Po* (New York: Macmillan Co., 1950).

177(l) Arthur Waley, *Translations from the Chinese* (New York: Alfred A. Knopf, 1941), pp. 848-49.

180(r) Lin Yutang, *My Country and My People* (New York: Halcyon House, 1935), p. 307.

182(l) Manuel Komroff, ed., *The Travels of Marco Polo* (New York: Liveright Publishing Corp., 1958), p. 104.

191(r) Arthur Waley, trans., *An Anthology of Japanese Literature* (London: George Allen & Unwin).

Unit 4

203(r) Robert W. July, *A History of the African People* (New York: Charles Scribner's Sons, 1970), p. 38.

206(l) Alvin M. Josephy, Jr., ed., *The Horizon History of Africa* (New York: American Heritage Publishing Co., 1971), p. 184.

206(r) Ibid., p. 182.

207(r,top) Geoffrey Pardrinder, *African Mythology* (London: Paul Hamlyn, 1967), p. 15.

207(r,bot.) Josephy, *Horizon History of Africa,* p. 186.

208(l) Ibid., p. 179.

211(l) Ibid., p. 273.

213(l) Basil Davidson, *Discovering Our African Heritage* (Lexington, Mass.: Ginn & Co., 1971), p. 11.

217(r) William W. Canfield, *The Legends of the Iroquois* (New York: A. Wessels Co., 1902), pp. 52-53.

218(r) Alvin M. Josephy, Jr., *The Indian Heritage of America* (New York: Alfred A. Knopf, 1968), p. 23.

224(l) Ruth M. Underhill, *Red Man's Religion* (Chicago: University of Chicago Press, 1965), p. 116.

228(r) Josephy, *Indian Heritage of America,* p. 189.

229(l) Miguel Léon-Portilla, *Pre-Columbian Literatures of Mexico* (Norman: University of Oklahoma Press, 1969), p. 79.

230(r) William H. Prescott, *History of the Conquest of Peru,* vol. 1 (Boston: Phillips, Sampson and Company, 1855), pp. 96-97.

231(l) Ibid., pp. 118-119.

Unit 5

Page

252(l)   Frederick A. Ogg, ed., *A Source Book of Medieval History* (New York: American Book Co., 1935), p. 287.

259(l)   Roy C. Cave and Herbert H. Coulson, *A Source Book for Medieval Economic History* (Milwaukee: Bruce Publishing Co., 1936), pp. 120–24.

261(r)   Harry J. Carroll, Jr., and others, *The Development of Civilization*, rev. ed., vol. I (Glencoe, Ill.: Scott, Foresman & Co., 1969), p. 274.

267(l)   Ibid., p. 334.

272(r)   Victoria Sackville-West, *Saint Joan of Arc* (New York: Doubleday, Doran & Co., 1938), p. 185.

283(l)   Henry S. Lucas, *The Renaissance and the Reformation* (New York: Harper & Brothers, 1934), ch. 18.

285(r)   Will Durant, *The Renaissance* (New York: Simon & Schuster, 1953), pp. 202–203.

292(l)   Stillman Drake, trans., *Discoveries and Opinions of Galileo* (New York: Doubleday & Co., 1957).

293(l)   S. F. Mason, *Main Currents of Scientific Thought* (New York: Henry Schuman, 1953), p. 174.

293(r,mid.)   Sarah K. Bolton, *Famous Men of Science* (New York: Thomas Y. Crowell Co., 1960), p. 47.

303(r)   M. Lincoln Schuster, ed., *A Treasury of The World's Great Letters* (New York: Simon & Schuster, 1940), pp. 65–66.

304(l)   Samuel Eliot Morison, *The European Discovery of America* (New York: Oxford University Press, 1974), pp. 430–431.

304(r)   John N. L. Baker, *A History of Geographical Discovery and Explanation* (New York: Cooper Square Publishers, 1967), p. 107.

315(l)   Hugh Trevor-Roper, ed., *The Age of Expansion* (New York: McGraw-Hill Book Co., 1968), p. 144.

322(l,top)   Raymond Phineas Stearns, *Pageant of Europe: Sources and Selections from the Renaissance to the Present Day,* rev. ed. (New York: Harcourt, Brace & World, 1961), pp. 245–46.

322(l,bot.)   Ibid., p. 250.

327(r)   Constance Lily Morris, *Maria Theresa: The Last Conservative* (New York: Alfred A. Knopf, 1937), p. 259.

334(r)   Warren B. Walsh, ed., *Readings in Russian History* (Syracuse, N.Y.: Syracuse University Press, 1950).

Unit 6

Page

345(l)   Crerar Harris, "Britons: A Self Portrait," *The New York Times Magazine,* Sept. 16, 1951.

346(l,top)   Edward Cheyney, *Readings in English History Drawn from the Original Sources,* new ed. (Lexington, Mass.: Ginn & Co., 1922), p. 426.

346(l,bot.)   R. J. White, *The Horizon Concise History of England* (New York: American Heritage Publishing Co., 1971), pp. 92, 94.

347(r,mid.)   W. H. Auden and Norman Holmes Pearson, eds., *Poets of the English Language,* vol. II (New York: Viking Press, 1950), p. 427.

349(r)   Cheyney, *Readings in English History,* p. 539.

360(l)   Bliss Perry, *The American Spirit in Literature* (New Haven: Yale University Press, 1918), pp. 11–12.

366   Albert Guérard, *France: A Modern History* (Ann Arbor: University of Michigan Press, 1959), p. 263.

367(l)   Ibid., p. 193.

369(r,mid.)   Irwin Edman, *Fountainheads of Freedom* (New York: Reynal & Hitchcock, 1941), p. 382.

370(r)   Seligman and Johnson, *Encyclopedia of the Social Sciences* (New York: Macmillan Publishing Co., 1959), pp. 528–29.

379(l)   Geoffrey Bruun, *Europe and the French Imperium, 1799-1914* (New York: Harper & Row, 1938), p. 27.

379(r)   André Maurois, *A History of France,* trans. Henry L. Binsse (New York: Grove Press, 1960), p. 338.

396   Koppel S. Pinson, *Modern Germany: Its History and Civilization,* 2nd ed. (New York: Macmillan Publishing Co., 1966), p. 56.

402(r,top)   Frederick B. Artz, *Reaction and Revolution: 1814-1832* (New York: Harper & Row, 1934), p. 284.

402(r,bot.)   Hans Kohn, "The Future of Austria," *Headline Series,* July–August 1955, p. 5.

Unit 7

418(l)   Sherwood Taylor, *A Short History of Science and Scientific Thought* (New York: W. W. Norton, 1949), p. 268.

418(r,top)   Frank P. Bachman, *Great Inventors and Their Inventions* (New York: American Book Co., 1946), p. 253.

427(l)   Taylor, *Short History,* p. 271.

Page	
434(r)	Walt Whitman, *Leaves of Grass* (New York: Doubleday & Co., 1855).
436(l)	Helen L. Kaufmann, *How Music Grew* (New York: Grosset & Dunlap, 1960), p. 157.
437(l,bot.)	Thomas Carlyle, *Sartar Resartus* (New York: Macmillan Publishing Co., 1927), p. 189.

Unit 8

Page	
453(l)	James Robinson and Charles Beard, *Readings in Modern European History,* vol. II (Lexington, Mass.: Ginn & Co., 1909), p. 143.
459(r)	James E. Gillespie, *Europe in Perspective, 1815 to the Present* (New York: Harcourt, Brace & World, 1945).
472	Donald O. Wagner, *Social Reformers: Adam Smith to John Dewey* (New York: Macmillan Co., 1934), p. 682.
474(r)	Raymond Phineas Stearns, *Pageant of Europe,* rev. ed. (New York: Harcourt, Brace & World, 1961), p. 675.
475(l,top)	Babette Deutsch and Avrahm Yarmolinsky, trans., *Russian Poetry* (New York: International Publishers Co., 1927), p. 33.
475(l,bot.)	Janko Lavrin, *Russian Writers: Their Lives and Literature* (New York: D. Van Nostrand Co., 1954), p. 66.
475(r,mid.)	Ivar Spector, *The Golden Age of Russian Literature,* rev. ed. (Caldwell, Idaho: Caxton Printers, 1939) p. 92.
475(r,bot.)	Fyodor Dostoyevsky, *Crime and Punishment* (New York: New American Library, 1949), p. 30.
476(r)	Jon Cournos, *A Treasury of Russian Life and Humor* (New York: Coward- McCann, 1943), p. 442.
477(l,top)	Leo Tolstoy, *War and Peace,* trans. Manuel Komroff, 1956, pp. 82–83.
477(l,mid.)	Vincent Wall and James P. McCormick, eds., *Seven Plays of the Modern Theater* (New York: American Book Co., 1950), p. 97.
492(l,mid.)	Basil Davidson, *Africa in History,* new rev. ed. (New York: Macmillan Publishing Co., 1974), p. 242.

Page	
492(l,bot.)	James I. Clark, *Africa* (Evanston, Ill.: McDougal, Littell & Co., 1976), p. 41.
492(r)	Robinson and Beard, *Readings in Modern European History,* p. 440.
495(l)	Parker Thomas Moon, *Imperialism and World Politics* (New York: Macmillan Co., 1926), p. 152.

Unit 9

Page	
504(l)	Barbara W. Tuchman, *The Proud Tower* (New York: Macmillan Co., 1966), p. 270.
520(r)	David Shub, *Lenin: A Biography* (New York: Doubleday & Co., 1948), pp. 196, 391.
525(l)	Ibid., p. 381.
529(r,bot.)	M. Ilin, *New Russia's Primer: The Story of the Five-Year Plan,* George S. Counts, trans. (Boston: Houghton Mifflin Co., 1931), pp. 13–14.
538(l,top)	Elie Wiesel, "Then and Now: The Experiences of a Teacher," *Social Education,* April 1978, p. 271.
552(l)	Robert E. Sherwood, *Roosevelt and Hopkins: An Intimate History* (New York: Harper & Brothers, 1948), p. 437.
553(l,bot.)	Ernie Pyle, *Brave Men,* (New York: Henry Holt & Co., 1944), p. 367.

Unit 10

Page	
559	Robert F. Davidson, ed., *The Humanities in Contemporary Life* (New York: Holt, Rinehart and Winston, 1960), p. 627.
598	Don Peretz, "Ten Keys to the Middle East," *Social Education,* October 1978, p. 448.
615(l,top)	Langston Hughes, ed., *Poems from Black Africa* (Bloomington: Indiana University Press, 1963), p. 138.
615(l,mid.)	Ibid., pp. 82–83.
623(r)	T. S. Eliot, *Collected Poems 1909-1962* (New York: Harcourt, Brace & World, 1963), p. 79.
624(r)	James Joyce, *Ulysses* (New York: Modern Library, 1946), p. 57.

ACKNOWLEDGEMENTS

Design: Richard Bartlett
Production: Kirchoff/Wohlberg, Inc.
Photo Research: Ginn Staff and Judy Greene
Cover Design: Kirchoff/Wohlberg, Inc.

Cover Illustration: Michael Hampshire
Illustrations: Michael Hampshire
Cartography: Dick Sanderson

The photographs and illustrations on the pages below are reproduced by courtesy of the sources listed. The following abbreviations are used:

Bettmann — The Bettmann Archive, Inc.
EPA — Editorial Photocolor Archives, Inc.
FPG — Free Lance Photographers Guild

HPS — Historical Pictures Service, Chicago
LC — Library of Congress
PR — Photo Researchers, Inc.

Page
i EPA
ii left to right: Frank Siteman; Paolo Koch/PR; Shostal Associates; Peter Larsen/PR; British Museum
iii left to right: Michael Philip Manheim; Bettmann; J. M. W. Turner, *Rain, Steam, and Speed* (detail)/National Gallery of Art, London: Bettmann; NASA
v Iraq Museum, courtesy Ministry of Culture and Arts, State Antiquities Organization; Museum of Fine Arts, Boston
vi China Pictorial; Museum of the American Indian, New York; LC
vii Bibliothèque Nationale, Paris; Smithsonian Institution; LC
viii Bettmann; NASA
2 The American Museum of Natural History
12 Tom McHugh/PR
13 H. Breuil, Musée de l'Homme
15 The Institute of Archaeology, Academia Sinica, Peking
16 The Oriental Institute, University of Chicago/Rosenthal Art Slides
20 top left—Frank Siteman; top right—George Holton/PR; bottom—George Holton/PR
21 EPA
22 Trustees of the British Museum
26 EPA
27 top left—The University Museum, University of Pennsylvania; top right—Ciccione-Bulloz/PR; bottom left—Louvre, Paris/Photo. Giraudon; bottom right—EPA

Page
28 Iraq Museum, courtesy Ministry of Culture and Arts, State Antiquities Organization
31 Louvre, Paris/Photo. Giraudon
33 Staatliche Museen zu Berlin, DDR
35 Brooklyn Museum
38 Shostal Associates
40 George Holton/PR
41 Trustees of the British Museum
43 Thames & Hudson Ltd.
44 top—The Metropolitan Museum of Art, Museum Excavations, 1926-1928, Rogers Fund; bottom left—George Holton/PR; bottom right—© 1974 George Holton/PR
46 The Oriental Institute, University of Chicago/Rosenthal Art Slides
47 © George Holton/PR
48 Brian Brake/PR
49 top left—Egyptian Museum, Cairo/© Lehnert & Landrock; top right—Brian Brake/PR; bottom—Trustees of the British Museum
50 John G. Ross/PR
51 Trustees of the British Museum
54 Shostal Associates
57 top—Museum of New Delhi/Photo. Giraudon; middle—Larry Burrows Life Magazine © Time Inc.; bottom—Museum of Fine Arts, Boston
58-59 *The Siege of Lanka*, Ross-Coomaraswamy Collection, Museum of Fine Arts, Boston
62 © 1978 Susan McCartney/PR
63 Shostal Associates

Page
66 The Metropolitan Museum of Art. Anon. Gift, 1942
69 Smithsonian Institution, Freer Gallery of Art, Washington, D. C.
71 Smithsonian Institution, Freer Gallery of Art, Washington, D. C.
72 Collection of the National Palace Museum, Taiwan, Republic of China
73 George Holton/PR
74 Howard Nelson
76 The Art Institute of Chicago
77 People's Republic of China Permanent Mission to the U. N.
78 left—Neil Leifer for *Sports Illustrated;* right—Frank J. Miller/PR
79 left—Paolo Koch/PR; Fred Maroon/PR
80 The Granger Collection
83 © Leonard von Matt/PR
84 Museum of Fine Arts, Boston. Wm. Amory Gardner Fund
86 Royal Ontario Museum, Toronto, Canada
87 Museum of Fine Arts, Boston. Seth Kettell Sweetser Fund
89 Hirmer Fotoarchiv
90 Museo delle Terme. Alinari/EPA
96 Farrell Grehan/PR
99 EPA
101 Louvre, Paris/Photo. Giraudon
104 Teresa Zabala/PR
105 © Leonard von Matt/PR
107 Museo Archaeologico, Florence. Scala/EPA
109 Alinari

BCDEFGHIJ 086543210
Printed in the United States of America